Dictionary of Classical Mythology

Dictionary of Classical Mythology

SYMBOLS
ATTRIBUTES
& ASSOCIATIONS

by Robert E. Bell

Illustrations by John Schlesinger

ABC
CLIO

Oxford, England
Santa Barbara, California

Library of Congress Cataloging in Publication Data

Bell, Robert E.
Dictionary of classical mythology symbols, attributes, and associations.

Includes index.
1. Mythology, Classical—Dictionaries. I. Title.
BL715.B44 292'.13'0321 81-19141
ISBN 0-87436-305-5 AACR2
ISBN 0-87436-023-4 pbk.

ABC-Clio, Inc.
Riviera Campus
2040 Alameda Padre Serra, Box 4397
Santa Barbara, California 93103

Clio Press Ltd.
Woodside House, Hinksey Hill
Oxford, OX1 5BE, England

Manufactured in the United States of America

Contents

List of Illustrations

Introduction

Until recently there has been no exclusively topical dictionary of classical mythology. While this work was nearing completion, a small volume appeared with a similar purpose, but its inadequacies caused it to be overlooked by most libraries and individual collectors as a useful acquisition. Until now it has been necessary to turn for topical uses to two principal sources. The first, Jobes' *Dictionary of Mythology, Folklore and Symbols,* is devoted to world mythology, including Biblical folklore, and it is as general in treatment as it is broad in scope. The other is the monumental Pauly-Wissowa *Realencyclopädie der Altertumswissenschaft,* but it covers all classical literature and is not confined to mythology or a topical approach alone. Moreover, with a complicated system of supplements, it is extremely difficult to use, even if one is fluent in German and an expert in classical scholarship. Also, most libraries, except for large academic ones, cannot afford to own this huge and erudite work. The scope of the *Dictionary of Classical Mythology: Symbols, Attributes, and Associations,* on the other hand, is limited to Greek and Roman mythology, with only occasional references from Assyrian, Phoenician, Etruscan, or Egyptian mythologies if there is some special relationship with a classical subject. There are approximately one thousand subject headings, with entries ranging in number from one to one hundred. Four appendices are devoted to special topics which deserve separate treatment.

The value of such a dictionary can best be appreciated by those who have ever needed the kind of information which this volume provides. There is a definite use for historical writing, when examples are needed to illustrate an idea, such as references to wine in Greek and Roman myth. Poets and novelists might find this dictionary useful for supplying images and allusions. Librarians will find a variety of uses for it, since formerly one either would just happen to know an answer or take a chance on finding the information after lengthy searching. There are more subtle uses, such as evidence of the persistence of surnames of deities after ancient migrations took place; availability of these names in an organized manner might provide clues useful to archaeological or anthropological research. Identification of figures on vases or coins might be possible by tracing a pictured symbol or action to its original story.

The compiler makes no claims for having put together a scholarly work, but rather for having provided a convenient means of locating information in a multitude of standard classical dictionaries which are accessed by proper names. Moreover, a substantial number of the entries include citations to original sources, and these are in the standard bibliographical format used in classical scholarship. For convenience, these sources are confined to works included in the *Loeb Classical Library* series, which most libraries own or have access to. The entries give enough information to qualify the inclusion of the mythical being under such and such a heading. Cross references are to persons listed under the same topic by an alternate or better-known name.

Subject headings represent a wide range from general to specific, from concrete to abstract. There is some overlapping, as will be noted in such headings as the ones concerning livestock; for one will find *cattle, bull, ox, heifer, calf,* and *cow.* On the other hand, the multitude of small bodies of water, such as fountains, pools, ponds, and springs will be found under the general heading *well.* There may be a question as to the difference between a *rock* and a *stone,* and the general rule is that a rock usually stays in one place, while a stone may be rolled or thrown or be descriptive of a physical property, as in the case of Medusa's head turning beholders into stone. Abstract terms may be a little confusing, since in some cases they are meant to reflect such and such a quality through patron divinities, and in other cases actual expressions of the quality are listed. There may be both, as in the case of *hospitality.*

Citations under headings may lead to a few questions. Under *incest,* for example, one will not find any of the Titans or Olympian gods. Incest was the province of the gods, and misfortune befell the mortals who ignored or accidentally transgressed this divine law. One might ask why there are twice as many names under *homosexuality* as there are under *friendship.* The answer is simple. Except in a few cases, friendship was nothing exceptional; everyone had a friend or two, but very few stories used the fact of a friendship as their basis. In this connection, one might wonder why the greatest friendship of all, that of Damon and Pythias (more correctly, Phintias), is not included. But legend though this might have been, it is associated with a definite historical period and a real person, Dionysius I, tyrant of Syracuse (431?-367 B.C.). Other instances of near history excluded some tempting stories, such as the geese which saved Rome. The determining factor in every case was whether or not the principals were generally accepted as mythological beings. Even so, there are certain to be a few instances which will be challenged.

One of the most troublesome problems in compiling this work was the matter of transliteration of classical spellings, and, although a valiant effort at consistency was attempted, there will be examples of two ways of spelling related names (e.g., *Iphigeneia* and *Medea*) and, worse, the same name. In every place possible an attempt was made to observe the most commonly accepted spellings (e.g., *Helen* instead of *Helena*).

Almost everyone is going to be able to find omissions. These are inevitable. The only advice for dealing with the frustration of not finding a name where it should be is a resort to marginalia, in the classically accepted tradition of the scholiasts. The compiler, with a view to a revision some day, will certainly keep a copy of the dictionary handy for this purpose.

I am grateful to my associate, Dr. Gail Schlachter, who shared my belief that this dictionary would fill a serious need and who gave me a great deal of encouragement in hastening its completion and bringing it to the attention of a receptive publisher.

Guide to Citation Abbreviations

Sources cited in the text are confined to those included in the *Loeb Classical Library* series. Only those works listed below are used in the citations. Thus, for example, all references to Augustine (August.) are to *De Civitate Dei* only, and not to any of his many other works.

Aelianus (Aelian.)
De Natura Animalium (De Nat. Anim.)
Aeschylus (Aeschyl.)
Agamemnon (Agam.)
Choephori (Choeph.)
Eumenides (Eum.)
Persae (Pers.)
Prometheus Vinctus (Prom.)
Septem Contra Thebas (Sept.)
Supplices (Suppl.)
Alciphron (Alciph.)
Ammianus Marcellinus (Amm. Marc.)
Anacreon (Anacr.)
Apollodorus (Apollod.)
Apollonius Rhodius (Apollon. Rhod.)
Apuleius (Apul.)
Aratus (Arat.)
Aristophanes (Aristoph.)
Acharnenses (Acharn.)
Aves (Av.)
Ecclesiazusae (Eccles.)
Lysistrata (Lys.)
Nubes (Nub.)
Pax (Pax)
Plutus (Plut.)
Ranae (Ran.)
Thesmophoriazusae (Thes.)
Aristotle (Aristot.)
Historia Animalium (H. A.)
Rhetorica (Rhet.)
Arrian (Arrian)
Athenaeus (Athen.)
Augustine (August.)
De Civitate Dei
Caesar (Caes.)
Bellum Gallicum
Callimachus (Callim.)
Epigrammata (Epigr.)
Hymnus in Apollinem (Hymn. in Apoll.)
Hymnus in Delum (Hymn. in Del.)
Hymnus in Dianam (Hymn. in Dian.)
Hymnus in Jovem (Hymn. in Jov.)
Hymnus in Selenem (Hymn. in Sel.)
Lavacrum Palladis (Lav. Pall.)
Cato (Cato)
Catullus (Catull.)
Cicero (Cic.)
Academicae Quaestiones (Acad.)
Brutus (Brut.)
De Divinatione (De Div.)
De Haruspicum Responso (De Harusp. Resp.)
De Legibus (De Leg.)
De Natura Deorum (De Nat. Deor.)
De Officiis (De Off.)
Epistulae ad Atticum (Ep. ad Att.)
Epistulae ad Quintum Fratem (Ep. ad Q. Frat.)
In Catilinam (Cat.)
In Verrem (In Verr.)
Tusculanae Disputationes (Tusc.)
Claudian (Claud.)
De Consulatu Honorii (De Consul. Hon.)
De Consulatu Stilichonis (De Consul. Stil.)
Epithalamium de Nuptiis Honorii Augusti et Maria (De Nupt. Mar.)

Gigantomachia (Gigantom.)
De Raptu Proserpinae (Rapt. Proserp.)
In Rufinum (In Rufin.)
Clemens Alexandrinus (Clem. Alex.)
Protrepticus (Protrept.)
Stromateis (Strom.)
Columella (Columell.)
De Re Rustica
Dio Cassius (Dio Cass.)
Dio Chrysostomus (Dio Chrys.)
Diodorus Siculus (Diod.)
Dionysius Harlicarnassensis (Dionys.)
Euripides (Eurip.)
Alcestis (Alcest.)
Andromache (Androm.)
Bacchae (Bacch.)
Cyclops (Cycl.)
Electra (Elect.)
Hecuba (Hec.)
Helena (Hel.)
Hercules Furens (Herc. Fur.)
Hippolytus (Hippol.)
Ion (Ion)
Iphigenia Aulidensis (Iphig. Aul.)
Iphigenia Taurica (Iphig. Taur.)
Medea (Med.)
Orestes (Orest.)
Phoenissae (Phoen.)
Rhesus (Rhes.)
Supplices (Suppl.)
Troades (Troad.)
Gellius (Gell.)
Herodotus (Herod.)
Hesiod (Hes.)
Opera et Dies (Op. et D.)
Scutum Herculis (Scut. Herc.)
Theogonia (Theog.)
Homer (Hom.)
Hymnus in Apollinem (Hymn. in Apoll.)
Hymnus in Cererem (Hymn. in Cer.)
Hymnus in Mercurium (Hymn. in Mer.)
Hymnus in Minervam (Hymn. in Min.)
Hymnus in Solem (Hymn. in Sol.)
Hymnus in Venerem (Hymn. in Ven.)
Hymnus in Vulcanum (Hymn. in Vulc.)
Iliad (Il.)
Odyssey (Od.)
Horace (Hor.)
Ars Poetica (Ars Poet.)
Carmina (Carm.)
Carmen Saeculare (Carm. Saec.)
Epistulae (Epist.)
Epodi (Epod.)
Satirae (Sat.)
Juvenal (Juv.)
Livy (Liv.)
Lucan (Lucan)
Lucian (Lucian)
Charidemus (Charid.)
De Morte Peregrini (De Mort. Per.)
Dei Marini (Dei Marin.)
Dialogi Deorum (Dial. Deor.)
Dialogi Meretricii (Dial. Meret.)
Dialogi Mortuorum (Dial. Mort.)
Gallus (Gall.)
Piscator (Pisc.)
Timon (Tim.)
Lucretius (Lucret.)
Lycophron (Lycoph.)
Martial (Mart.)
Moschus (Mosch.)
Nonnon (Nonn.)
Ovid (Ov.)
Amores (Amor.)
Ars Amatoria (Ars Am.)
Epistulae ex Ponto (Ep. ex Pont.)
Fasti (Fast.)
Heroides (Her.)
Ibis (Ib.)
Metamorphoses (Met.)
Remedia Amoris (Rem. Am.)
Tristia (Trist.)
Pausanias (Paus.)
Petronius (Petron.)
Philostratus (Philostr.)
Imagines (Imag.)
Vita Apollonii (Vit. Apoll.)
Pindar (Pind.)
Fragmenta (Fragm.)
Isthmian Odes (Isth.)
Nemean Odes (Nem.)
Olympian Odes (Ol.)
Pythian Odes (Pyth.)
Plato (Plat.)
Cratylus (Cratyl.)
De Re Publica (De Re Pub.)
Ion (Ion)
Phaedrus (Phaedr.)
Symposium (Sympos.)
Timaeus (Tim.)
Plautus (Plaut.)
Amphitruo (Amphitr.)
Asinaria (Asin.)
Cistellaria (Cistell.)
Curculio (Curcul.)
Menaechmi (Men.)
Mercator (Merc.)
Truculentus (Truc.)

Pliny (the Elder) (Plin.)
Historia Naturalis (H. N.)
Plutarch (Plut.)
Moralia: Amatoriae Narrationes (Amat. Narr.)
De Curiositate (De Curios.)
De Defectu Oraculorum (De Def. Orac.)
De E apud Delphos (De E ap. Delph.)
De Fraterno Amore (De Frat. Am.)
De Ira Cohibenda (De Ir. Cohib.)
De Musica (De Mus.)
De Placitis Philosophorum (De Plac. Philos.)
De Sera Numinis Vindicta (De Ser. Num. Vind.)
De Superstitione (De Superst.)
Parallela Graeca et Romana (Paral. Gr. et Rom.)
Quaestiones Graecae (Quaest. Gr.)
Quaestiones Romanae (Quaest. Rom.)
Quaestionum Convivalium (Quaest. Conviv.)
Quomodo Adolescens Poetas Audire Debeat (De Aud. Poet.)
Vitae Parallelae: Agesilaus (Ages.)
Agis (Agis)
Aristides (Aristid.)
Camillus (Camil.)
Numa (Num.)
Pelopidas (Pelop.)
Pyrrhus (Pyrr.)
Romulus (Romul.)
Sertorius (Sertor.)
Themistocles (Them.)
Theseus (Thes.)
Polybius (Polyb.)
Propertius (Propert.)
Quintus Smyrnaeus (Q. Smyrn.)
Seneca (the Younger) (Senec.)
De Beneficiis (De Benef.)
Epistulae (Epist.)
Quaestiones Naturales (Quaest. Nat.)
Silius Italicus (Sil. Ital.)
Sophocles (Soph.)
Ajax (Ajax)
Antigone (Antig.)
Electra (Elect.)
Oedipus Coloneus (Oed. Col.)
Oedipus Tyrannus (Oed. Tyr.)
Philoctetes (Phil.)
Statius (Stat.)
Silvae (Silv.)
Thebias (Theb.)
Strabo (Strab.)
Suetonius (Suet.)
Divus Augustus (Div. Aug.)
Domitianus (Domit.)
Gaius Caligula (Calig.)
Nero (Ner.)
Tiberius (Tib.)
Tacitus (Tacit.)
Annales (Ann.)
Historiae (Hist.)
Tertullian (Tertull.)
Apologeticum (Apol.)
De Spectaculis (De Spect.)
Theocritus (Theocrit.)
Theophrastus (Theophrast.)
Thucydides (Thuc.)
Tibullus (Tibull.)
Valerius Flaccus (Val. Flacc.)
Varro (Varr.)
De Lingua Latina (De Ling. Lat.)
De Re Rustica (De Re Rus.)
Virgil (Virg.)
Aeneid (Aen.)
Eclogues (Ecl.)
Georgics (Georg.)
Vitruvius (Vitruv.)
Xenophon (Xenoph.)
Anabasis (Anab.)
Hellenica (Hellen.)
Symposium (Sympos.)

Symbols, Attributes, and Associations

Abandonment

ARIADNE, daughter of Minos, was abandoned on the island of Naxos by Theseus during their voyage to Athens after Theseus had, with her assistance, overcome the Minotaur in Crete.

DIDO, queen of Carthage, having been abandoned by Aeneas, with whom she was in love, raised a funeral pyre ostensibly to sacrifice animals, and then on the pyre she stabbed herself with a sword and was burned.

OENONE, daughter of the river god Cebron, married Paris, but he abandoned her in order to sail for Sparta and fulfill his destiny of carrying away Helen. When he was mortally wounded in the Trojan War, he returned to Mt. Ida to ask Oenone to heal him, but she refused. She repented her decision too late to save him and hanged herself (Apollod. 3. 12.6).

See also: INFANT EXPOSURE

Abduction

AEGINA was the daughter of Asopus. When Zeus carried her off, Sisyphus betrayed the matter to Asopus and was rewarded with a well on Acrocorinthus, but Zeus punished Sisyphus in the lower world (Apollod. 1. 9.3, 3. 12.6).

AETHRA, the mother of Theseus, was carried off when the Dioscuri invaded Attica to recover their sister, Helen, who had been carried there by Theseus and placed under the care of his mother (Plut. *Thes.* 34).

ANAXO was a daughter of Alcaeus. Theseus abducted her, slew her sons and raped her daughters (Plut. *Thes.* 27).

ANTIOPE (1), daughter of Nycteus, was carried off by Epopeus, king of Aegialia. Nycteus took revenge by invading with a Theban army the territory of Sicyon but was defeated.

ANTIOPE (2) was queen of the Amazons. In one of his most renowned adventures, Theseus led an expedition against the Amazons. He is said to have assailed them before they had recovered from an earlier attack by Heracles and to have carried off Antiope.

ASTYNOME (See CHRYSEIS)

BRISEIS, daughter of Briseus of Lyrnessus, was captured by Achilles but was later seized by Agamemnon. Thus arose the dire feud between the two heroes. Commonly called Briseis from her father, her proper name was Hippodameia.

CASSANDRA was the daughter of Priam and Hecuba. According to some accounts, upon the fall of Troy, Agamemnon took her to Mycenae, where she was killed by Clytemnestra.

CEPHALUS, son of Hermes and Herse, was carried off by Eos, goddess of the dawn, because of his extraordinary beauty.

CHLORIS was the wife of Zephyrus, the west wind, who carried her away by force and by whom she had a son, Carpus (Ov. *Fast.* 5. 197–204).

CHRYSEIS, daughter of Chryses, a priest of Apollo, was taken prisoner by Achilles at the capture of Lyrnessus. In the distribution of the booty, she was given to Agamemnon. Her father came to the camp of the Greeks to solicit her ransom, but he was repulsed by Agamemnon. Apollo, however, sent a plague into the Greek camp, and Agamemnon was obliged to restore her to her father. Her proper name was Astynome.

CHRYSIPPUS, a son of Pelops, was carried off while still a boy by Laius of Thebes, who instructed him in driving the chariot and made him his charioteer (Apollod. 3. 5.5).

CLEITUS, son of Mantius, was carried away by Eos, goddess of the dawn, because of his extraordinary beauty.

CLYMENE was a relative of Menelaus and a companion of Helen, together with whom she was carried off by Paris (Hom. *Il.* 3. 144).

CORONIS was a bacchant in the train of Dionysus. When Butes, son of Boreas, colonized Strongyle (later called Naxos), he had no women, so he and his men made a predatory excursion to Thessaly, where Butes carried off Coronis. She invoked Dionysus, who struck Butes with madness so that he threw himself into a well and was drowned (Diod. 5. 50).

DIDO was queen of Carthage. Fleeing Tyre to escape her brother, Pygmalion, she was accompanied by a number of noble Tyrians. They landed at Cyprus, where they abducted eighty maidens to provide wives for the emigrants.

DIOMEDE, daughter of Phorbas of Lesbos, was carried off by Achilles (Hom. *Il.* 9. 665).

DRYOPE, daughter of Dryops, was befriended by Hamadryads, who eventually carried her off and concealed her in a forest, and in her stead a well and a poplar were left in the temple of Apollo in Oeta (Ov. *Met.* 9. 325).

EUMAEUS, son of Ctesius, had been carried away from his father's house by a Phoenician slave, and Phoenician sailors sold him to Laertes, the father of Odysseus, by whom he was retained as a swineherd (Hom. *Od.* 15. 403).

EUROPA, daughter of Agenor and sister of Cadmus, was carried off from Phoenicia by Zeus, who had metamorphosed himself into a bull. In this form he carried her to Crete, where she became by him the mother of Minos, Rhadamanthys, and Sarpedon (Apollod. 3. 1.1; Ov. *Met.* 2. 839).

GANYMEDE, son of Tros and the most beautiful of mortals, was carried away by the gods to fill the cup of Zeus. Later writers stated that Zeus himself carried him off, either in his natural shape or in the form of an eagle, or that he sent his eagle to fetch Ganymede into heaven (Apollod. 3. 12.2; Virg. *Aen.* 5. 253; Ov. *Met.* 10. 255; Lucian *Dial.Deor.* 4). Some statements of later times have him carried off by Tantalus or Minos. One tradition has him carried off by Eos.

HARMONIA. Cadmus, on his voyage to Samothrace, after being initiated in the mysteries, saw Harmonia and carried her off with the assistance of Athena.

HELEN, daughter of Zeus and Leda, was in her youth carried off by Theseus, assisted by Peirithous, to Attica. According to others, Theseus had promised Idas and Lynceus, who had carried her off, to guard her at Aphidna. Her brothers, the Dioscuri, went after her and ravaged the country round the city. They retrieved her and also carried off Aethra, the mother of Theseus. Later, Paris carried off Helen from Sparta. According to some, she followed her seducer willingly, owing to the influence of Aphrodite (Hom. *Il.* 3. 174); some say that the goddess deceived Helen by giving to Paris the appearance of Menelaus, her husband; according to others, Helen was carried off by Paris by force, either during a festival or during the chase (Lycoph. 106). According to one story, Hermes brought Helen to Proteus, king of Egypt, after her abduction by Paris (Eurip. *Hel.* 46), or, according to others, Proteus himself took her from Paris, gave Paris a phantom, and restored the true Helen to Menelaus after his return from Troy (Herod. 2. 112, 118).

HERMIONE, daughter of Menelaus and Helen, was carried away by Orestes, to whom she had been promised before Menelaus offered her to Neoptolemus. She still loved Orestes, so she was willingly abducted.

HILAIRA (ILAEIRA), one of the daughters of Leucippus of Messenia, was carried off with her sister, Phoebe, by the Dioscuri (Apollod. 3. 10.3; Ov. *Fast.* 5.700).

HIPPODAMEIA (See BRISEIS)

HYRNETHO was carried away by force by her two brothers, Ceisus and Cerynes, who were trying to persuade her to leave her husband, Deiphones.

LEUCE, a nymph, daughter of Oceanus, was carried off by Pluto. After her death, she was changed into a white poplar in Elysium.

MARPESSA, wife of Idas, was carried off by Apollo, and she wept for her husband, just as Alcyone wept for Ceyx. Consequently, she called her daughter Alcyone (Hom. *Il.* 9. 561; Paus. 4. 2.5).

MELIA, daughter of Poseidon and sister of Caanthus, was carried off by Apollo. By him she became the mother of Ismenius and of the seer, Tenerus. She was worshipped in the Apollonian sanctuary, the Ismenium, near Thebes (Paus. 9. 10.5).

OENOTROPAE were the daughters of Anius of Delos. Because of their power to change water into wine and anything else into grain and olives, Agamemnon wanted to carry them off by force so that they might provide for the army of the Greeks at Troy; but they implored Dionysus for assistance and were accordingly metamorphosed into doves (Ov. *Met.* 13. 640).

OREITHYIA was a daughter of Erechtheus and Praxithea. When she strayed beyond the river Ilissus, in Attica, she was carried off by Boreas, the north wind (Apollod. 3. 15.1).

ORION, son of Hyrieus, was carried away by Eos, goddess of the dawn, because of his extraordinary beauty.

PANCRATIS, daughter of Aloeus and Iphimedia, was carried off along with her mother and other women from Mt. Drius, where they were celebrating a festival of Dionysus, by Thracian pirates under Butes. The women were carried to Naxos (or Strongyle), but they were delivered by the Aloidae, sons of Iphimedia (Diod. 5. 50).

PANDAREUS. The Harpies carried off the daughters of King Pandareus and gave them as servants to the Erinyes (Hom. *Od.* 20. 78).

PERSEPHONE was the daughter of Zeus and Demeter. The story of her being carried off by Hades, or Pluto, is not mentioned by Homer, who simply describes her as the wife and queen of Hades. Her abduction is first mentioned by Hesiod. According to the story, Zeus, without the knowledge of Demeter, had promised Persephone to Hades; and while the unsuspecting maiden was gathering flowers in the Nysian plain in Asia, the earth suddenly opened, and she was carried off by the god of the underworld. Demeter sought her and eventually found her, only to discover that because Persephone had swallowed six pomegranate seeds she would have to spend six months of the year in Hades. On one occasion, the hero Peirithous attempted to carry her off from the lower world and was assisted by Theseus.

PHAETHON, a son of Cephalus and Eos, was carried off by Aphrodite, who appointed him guardian of her temple (Hes. *Theog.* 986).

PHINEUS. Some accounts state that he was carried off by the Harpies into the country of the Bistones or Milchessians (Strab. 7. 302).

PHOEBE, a daughter of Leucippus and sister of Hilaira, was a priestess of Athena. Carried off with her sister by the Dioscuri, she became by Polydeuces the mother of Mnesileos (Apollod. 3. 10.3).

PROTOGENEIA, a daughter of Deucalion and Pyrrha, was carried off by Zeus, who became by her, on Mt. Maenalus in Arcadia, the father of Opus.

ROMULUS. Unable to acquire women for the male population of newly founded Rome, he proclaimed to his neighbors, the Latins and Sabines, that games were to be celebrated in honor of the god Consus and invited them to the festival. Suspecting no treachery, they came in numbers with their wives and children, but the Roman youths rushed upon their guests and carried off the virgins.

SEGESTA was one of the daughters of Phoenodamas. When her father tricked Laomedon of Troy by causing him to offer his own daughter, Hesione, as a sacrifice to a sea monster instead of one of Phoenodamas' daughters, Laomedon took vengeance by sending some sailors to take Phoenodamas' three daughters to a desert part of the coast of Sicily.

SINOPE, a daughter of Asopus or of Ares, was carried off by Apollo from Boeotia to Paphlagonia, where she gave birth to Syrus.

SYME, a daughter of Ialysus and Dotis, was carried off by Glaucus to an island near Rhodes, off the coast of Caria, which received its name from her (Athen. 7. 296).

TECMESSA was the daughter of the Phrygian king, Teleutas, whose territory was ravaged by the Greeks during a predatory excursion from Troy. Tecmessa was made prisoner and was given to the Telamonian Ajax, who lived with her as his wife and had a son, Eurysaces, by her (Soph. *Ajax* 333).

THEOPHANE, a daughter of Bisaltes, was carried off by Poseidon because of her exceptional beauty.

TITHONUS, son of Laomedon, was carried away by Eos, goddess of the dawn, because of his great beauty. She bore him Memnon and Emathion.

Abundance

ACHELOUS was god of the river which divides Acarnania from Aetolia. The Achelous, like the Nile, was a bestower of nourishment, water, and plenty (Virg. *Georg.* 1. 9).

AMALTHEA. The broken horn from the goat, Amalthea, which suckled Zeus, is used as the symbol of plenty and called cornucopia (Strab. 10. 458; Diod. 4. 35).

ANNA PERENNA was the Roman goddess of plenty.

COPIA was a Roman goddess of plenty and was represented by the cornucopia.

OENOTROPAE (Oeno, Spermo, and Elais) were the daughters of Anius. Dionysus gave them the power of producing at will any quantity of wine, grain, and oil.

OPS was a female Roman divinity of plenty and fertility.

TYCHE was the personification of chance or luck. With Plutus or the horn of Amalthea she was the symbol of the plentiful gifts of fortune.

See also: WEALTH

Acanthus

ACANTHA was a nymph loved by Apollo, who changed her into the acanthus flower.

Accident, see Luck

Aconite

CERBERUS. When Heracles brought him to the upper world from Hades, the multiheaded dog could not stand the light and spat forth the poisonous plant called aconitum.

Aegis, see Shield

Afterthought

EPIMETHEUS was a son of Iapetus and Clymene and the brother of Prometheus. His name signifies afterthought.

Agriculture

ANDROGEUS, son of Minos of Crete, originally might have been worshipped as the introducer of agriculture into Attica.

ARISTAEUS, son of Apollo, was worshipped as the divinity who averted the burning heat of the sun and other causes of destruction to crops from the fields of men.

ATHENA was the protectress of agriculture.

CABEIRI were mystic divinities, probably Phrygian in orgin, who protected crops.

DEMETER was the Olympian goddess of the earth, the producer of fruit and, consequently, of agriculture. Human food, or bread, is called by Homer (*Il.* 13. 322) the gift of Demeter.

DIONYSUS SABAZIUS was a surname identifying the god with Sabazius, a Phrygian agricultural divinity and a son of Rhea or Cybele (Aristoph. *Av.* 873).

FAUNUS, son of Picus and king of the Laurentes, promoted agriculture and the breeding of cattle among his subjects and also distinguished himself as a hunter (Plin. *H.N.* 9. 6; Propert. 4. 2.34).

LACTANS, LACTURNUS, and LACTURCIA were Roman divinities who were believed to protect the young crops of the field (August. 4. 3).

MARS. Originally, sacrifices were offered to him for the prosperity of fields and flocks, usually under the name of Mars Silvanus.

OPS, a female Roman divinity, wife of Saturnus, was protectress of everything connected with agriculture.

PELASGUS, son of Triopas, founded the city of Argos. He received Demeter in her wanderings and taught the people agriculture (Paus. 1. 14.2, 2. 22.2).

PERSEPHONE AUXESIA was a surname describing Persephone as one who grants growth and prosperity to fields.

PRIAPUS, son of Dionysus and Aphrodite, was regarded as the promoter of fertility both of the vegetation and of all animals connected with an agricultural life. He was also the protector of all garden produce.

PYGMIES were conceived as an agricultural people. In many ancient histories they are reported to wage war each spring against the cranes which arrive near the sources of the Nile to devour the crops (Aristot. *H.A.* 8. 12; Strab. 1. 42, 17. 821).

RUSOR, a Roman divinity, was worshipped as one of the companions of Tellus, though the name was probably nothing but an attribute of Tellus which personified the power of the earth to bring forth seeds buried in the ground.

SABAZIUS, a Phrygian agricultural divinity and a son of Rhea or Cybele, was represented with horns because he was said to be the first to yoke oxen to the plow for agriculture (Diod. 4. 4).

SATURN was a mythical king of Italy, to whom was ascribed the introduction of agriculture and the habits of civilized life in general.

SILVANUS was a Latin divinity of the fields and forests. He is described as a god watching over the fields and husbandmen, and is also called the protector of the boundaries of fields (Hor. *Epod.* 2. 22).

TELCHINES were a family, a class of people, or a tribe, said to have been descended from Thalassa or Poseidon (Diod. 5. 55; Nonn. 14. 40). They appear sometimes as cultivators of the soil and ministers of the gods.

TELLUS (TERRA) was the Roman goddess of the earth, comparable to the Greek Gaea. She was connected with agricultural pursuits. (See also RUSOR)

THALLO was one of the Attic Horae (or Seasons) who was believed to grant prosperity to the young shoots of plants.

TRIPTOLEMUS was a son of Celeus and Metaneira, a favorite of Demeter, and inventor of agriculture. When Demeter accidentally killed his brother, Demophon, she gave Triptolemus a chariot with winged dragons and seeds of grain. In works of art he is represented on a chariot drawn by dragons. After receiving the dragon chariot, he rode it all over the earth, acquainting man with the blessings of agriculture. He first sowed barley in the Rharian plain and from there the cultivation of grain spread all over the earth.

TUTELINA was an agricultural divinity among

the Romans, or perhaps an attribute of Ops. She is described as the goddess protecting the crops brought in at harvest time from the fields.

VERTUMNUS was an Etruscan deity whose worship was connected with the transformation of plants from blossom to fruit (Propert. 4. 2.10).

ZEUS SABAZIUS was a surname from the god's identification with Sabazius, the Phrygian agricultural divinity, a son of Rhea or Cybele (Aristoph. *Av.* 873).

Alcyone, see Halcyon

Almond

AGDISTIS was a Phrygian divinity, both male and female, feared by the gods. When the divinity was emasculated, an almond tree grew from its severed genitals.

ATYS was born when the daughter of the Phrygian river god, Sangarius, put almonds from the tree of Agdistis in her bosom.

PHYLLIS, a daughter of king Sithon in Thrace, hanged herself when Demophon was prevented from keeping his promise to marry her by the agreed-on time. She was metamorphosed into an almond tree just at the moment when Demophon returned and in vain embraced the tree (Ov. *Her.* 2).

Alphabet

CADMUS was said to have been the inventor of the Greek letters by bringing the Phoenician alphabet from Asia Minor.

CARMENTA was one of the Camenae, or Roman Muses, who changed fifteen characters of the Greek alphabet into Roman ones when Evander introduced the alphabet into Latium.

EVANDER, a son of Hermes, migrated from Arcadia to Italy, where he taught the natives the arts of peace and social life, especially the art of writing which he himself had been taught by Heracles (Plut. *Quaest. Rom.* 56).

HERMES was said to have been the inventor of the alphabet.

PALAMEDES, son of Nauplius, was described as the inventor of the alphabet.

PHOENIX, son of Amyntor, is one of the mythical beings to whom the ancients ascribed the invention of the alphabet.

Altar

HESTIA was the Olympian goddess of the hearth, or rather of the fire burning on the hearth. She was also regarded as the goddess of the sacred fire of the sacrificial altar.

PIETAS, a personification of faithful attachments, love, and veneration among the Romans, is seen represented on Roman coins as a matron throwing incense upon an altar.

Ambassador

AJAX, son of Telamon, was one of the warriors sent by Agamemnon to attempt to conciliate Achilles.

ANTENOR, a Trojan elder, received Menelaus and Odysseus into his house when they came to Troy as ambassadors to negotiate for Helen's return (Hom. *Il.* 3. 146, 203).

ANTIMACHUS. When Menelaus and Odysseus came to Troy to ask for the surrender of Helen, he wanted to have them put to death (Hom. *Il.* 11. 122, 138).

ODYSSEUS. Before the Greeks set out against Troy, he, in conjunction with Menelaus, went to Troy, where he was hospitably received, for the purpose of inducing the Trojans by peaceful means to restore Helen and her treasures (Hom. *Il.* 3. 205).

Amber

ERIDANUS was a river god, on the banks of whose river amber was found (Virg. *Georg.* 1. 482; Ov. *Met.* 2. 324). Writers have disagreed on the location of this river, some identifying it with the Po and others with a tiny tributary of the Athenian river Ilissus. Herodotus (3. 115) doubted its existence.

HELIADES. When Phaethon was struck down by Zeus after attempting to drive the chariot of the sun across heaven, his sisters the Heliades (who had yoked the horses to the chariot) were metamorphosed into poplars and their tears into amber (Ov. *Met.* 2. 338).

Ambisexuality, see Hermaphroditism, Transexualism

Ambrosia

APOLLO. After his birth, his mother, Leto, was not able to nurse him, so Themis gave him nectar and ambrosia.

HECTOR. In order to protect his body from decay and from being devoured by dogs after he was killed by Achilles, Aphrodite embalmed it with ambrosia, and Apollo protected it by a cloud (Hom. *Il.* 23. 185).

TANTALUS. Some say that his severe punishment in the lower world resulted from his stealing nectar and ambrosia from the table of the gods and giving them to his friends (Pind. *Ol.* 1. 98).

Ambush

ARES GYNAECOTHOENAS, "the god feasted by women," was a surname of the god at Tegea, where the women singlehandedly won a battle by surprising the enemy from ambush.

BELLEROPHON was a son of Glaucus. Upon his return from a battle with the Amazons, he was set upon by the bravest Lydians, whom Iobates had placed in ambush, but Bellerophon slew them all.

LYNCEUS was son of Aphareus and brother of Idas. He was one of the Argonauts and famous for his sharpsightedness. His vision was so keen that in the battle with the Dioscuri he could see through the trunk of an oak tree where Castor and Polydeuces were lying in ambush. He pointed them out to Idas, who slew Castor. Polydeuces pursued them and slew Lynceus with a spear thrust (Apollod. 3. 11.2; Ov. *Fast.* 5. 700).

Anchor

TENES (TENNES). Exiled by his father, Cycnus, and left for dead, he came to Tenedos, where he became king. When his repentant father came seeking him, he did not allow him to land, but instead cut off the anchor from the ship (Paus. 10. 14.2).

Anemone

ADONIS, the son of Cinyras by Myrrha, was beloved by Aphrodite. He was killed by a boar and metamorphosed by Aphrodite into an anemone.

Anger

CYBELE BRIMO was a surname describing Cybele as angry or terrifying.

DEMETER BRIMO was a surname describing Demeter as the angry or terrifying goddess.

HECATE BRIMO described Hecate as angry or terrifying. Some derive the name from *bromos,* so that it would refer to the cracking of fire, as Hecate was pictured bearing a torch.

PERSEPHONE BRIMO was a surname describing Persephone as the angry or terrifying goddess.

Anguish

ANGERONA (ANGERONIA) was the Roman goddess of anguish and fear. She not only produced this state of mind but also relieved men from it.

Ant

AEACUS was a son of Zeus and Aegina. A pestilence having destroyed his subjects, he entreated Zeus to repeople his kingdom. Zeus changed the ants in an old oak tree into people and called them Myrmidons.

DAEDALUS was the famous inventor of the labyrinth in Crete. When he fled the island after assisting Theseus in his escape from the labyrinth, King Minos pursued him. Minos gave a spiral seashell to rulers in all the countries he touched, asking them to thread it. No one could do so, until Minos reached Sicily. There, King Cocalus was able to have this accomplished, and Minos knew that his search was over, that Daedalus was the only one who was ingenious enough to do it. Daedalus managed the feat by tying a thread to an ant, which crawled through the labyrinthine shell.

EURYMEDUSA. Zeus deceived Eurymedusa in the disguise of an ant and fathered Myrmidon, ancestor of the Myrmidons in Thessaly (Apollod. 1. 7.3; Apollon. Rhod. 1. 56).

MIDAS was a wealthy king of Phrygia. When he was a child, ants carried grains of wheat into his mouth to indicate that one day he would be the richest of all mortals.

MYRMEX was an Athenian maiden who was beloved by Athena. When the goddess invented the plow, Myrmex boastfully pretended to have made the discovery herself, whereupon she was metamorphosed into an ant.

PELEUS came in exile to Thessaly without companions. He prayed to Zeus for an army, and the god, to please Peleus, metamorphosed the ants into men, called Myrmidons.

Anvil

ACMON, one of the obscure spirits called Dactyli, presided over the anvil.

HEPHAESTUS was the god of fire. In his Olympian palace he had a workshop, which contained an anvil and twenty bellows, all of which worked spontaneously at his bidding (Hom. *Il.* 18. 370).

HERA. Once when she tried to put Zeus in chains, he hung her up in the clouds with her hands chained and with two anvils suspended from her feet (Hom. *Il.* 8. 400, 477, 15. 17).

Anxiety

BACCHUS LYAEUS, the god who frees men from care and anxiety, was a surname of Bacchus (Virg. *Georg.* 2. 229).

Apotheosis

ARISTAEUS, son of Apollo, was once a mortal, but he ascended to the rank of a god through the benefits he had conferred upon mankind.

BONA DEA (See FAUNA)

BRITOMARTIS, a huntress and daughter of Aeus and Carme, was rescued from fishermen's nets by Artemis, who then made her a goddess.

DAPHNIS. After he became blind, he prayed to his father, Hermes, and the god raised him up to heaven and caused a well to gush forth on the spot where it had happened.

FAUNA (FAULA) was an ancient and obscure Roman goddess, wife of, or otherwise related to, Faunus. Before she became a goddess, she became intoxicated and for that reason was killed by Faunus. After that, he raised her to the rank of a goddess, and she was often referred to as Bona Dea, "the Good Goddess."

HERACLES. While his funeral pyre was burning, a cloud came down from heaven and amid peals of thunder carried him to Olympus, where he was honored with immortality (Hes. *Theog.* 949; Apollod. 2. 7.7; Diod. 4. 38).

INO was a daughter of Cadmus. When she threw herself and her son, Melicertes, into the sea to escape the murderous insanity of her husband, Athamas, she was raised to the rank of a divinity and was called Leucothea.

IPHIGENEIA was the daughter of Agamemnon and Clytemnestra. Some traditions state that she was not sacrificed at Aulis but was endowed by Artemis with immortality and eternal youth, and under the name of Oreilochia she became the wife of Achilles on the island of Leuce.

JUPITER LATIARIS (See LATINUS)

LATINUS was the king of Latium. After his battle with Mezentius, the Tyrrhenian king, he suddenly disappeared and was changed into Jupiter Latiaris.

LEDA, queen of Sparta, was the mother of the Dioscuri, Helen, and Clytemnestra. After her death, she was raised to the rank of a divinity under the name of Nemesis.

LEUCOTHEA (See INO)

MELICERTES. When Ino, his mother, was driven mad, she threw herself with her son from the Molurian rocks on the Isthmus of Corinth into the sea, and both were changed into marine deities. Ino became Leucothea, and Melicertes became Palaemon (Apollod. 3. 4.3; Ov. *Met.* 4. 520, 13. 919).

NEMESIS (See LEDA)

OREILOCHIA (See IPHIGENEIA)

PALAEMON (See MELICERTES)

ROMULUS, son of Mars, was the founder of Rome. One day, as he was reviewing his people in the Campus Martius, the sun was suddenly eclipsed, darkness spread over the earth, and a dreadful storm dispersed the people. When daylight returned, Romulus had disappeared, for his father had carried him up to heaven in a fiery chariot (Hor. *Carm.* 3. 3; Ov. *Fast.* 2. 496).

SEMELE THYONE. Under this name, Semele was brought by her son, Dionysus, from Hades and introduced among the immortals (Apollod. 3. 5.3; Cic. *De Nat.Deor.* 3. 23; Pind. *Pyth.* 3. 99).

SILVIA was the mother of Romulus and Remus by Mars. Because she was a vestal virgin, she was condemned with her babies to die. Mother and infants were set adrift in a river. Silvia was changed into a goddess and became the wife of the river god, Anio.

Apple

ACONTIUS wrote on an apple a vow of marriage to him by Cydippe, who read aloud the vow while sacrificing at the altar of Artemis at Delos. She was thus forced to marry him (Ov. *Her.* 20, 21).

APHRODITE. The apple was sacred to her.

ATALANTA (ATALANTE) was a virgin huntress. One of her suitors, Meilanion (or Hippomenes), raced with her in order to gain her hand in marriage and dropped, one after another, three golden apples, which Atalanta stopped to pick up. This delay caused her to lose the race, and she was forced to take the winner as her husband.

ATLAS was represented in certain sculptural works as holding in his hands the golden apples of the Hesperides.

ERIS was the goddess of discord, who threw the apple into the assembly of the gods. Inscribed "for the fairest," it was claimed by Hera, Athena, and Aphrodite. The judgment of Paris in favor of Aphrodite led indirectly to the Trojan War.

HERA. On her marriage to Zeus, Gaea gave her a tree with golden apples, which was watched by the Hesperides in the garden of Hera at the foot of Mt. Atlas (Apollod. 2. 5.11).

HERACLES. The eleventh labor of Heracles was bringing back the apples of the Hesperides. These apples had been received by Hera at her wedding, and she had entrusted them to the keeping of the Hesperides and the dragon Ladon in a garden at the foot of Mt. Atlas in the country of the Hyperboreans. When Heracles brought the apples back, Eurystheus made him a present of them, but Heracles dedicated them to Athena, who later restored them to their former place.

LADON was the dragon which helped guard the apples of the Hesperides.

MELUS, son of Cinyras and companion of Adonis, hanged himself when Adonis died. He was metamorphosed by Aphrodite into an apple.

NEMESIS. The Rhamnusian statue of Nemesis, goddess of retribution, bore in its left hand a branch of an apple tree.

PARIS. In works of art he is represented with an apple in his hand. The fatal apple thrown by Eris was given to him to judge which of the goddesses—Athena, Hera, or Aphrodite—was the fairest.

April

APHRODITE. This spring month was sacred to her (Cic. *De Nat.Deor.* 3. 20; Ov. *Fast.* 4. 90).

VENUS. Solemnities were celebrated to Venus in April, because that month, being the beginning of spring, was thought to be particularly sacred to the Roman goddess of love.

Archer

ALCON was a skillful archer, who, when a serpent entwined his son, shot the serpent without hurting the child (Val.Flacc. 1. 399).

CROTUS asked the Muses, with whom he had been brought up, to place him among the stars as Sagittarius, as he had been a skillful shooter.

EURYTUS, son of Melaneus and Stratonice, was king of Oechalia in Thessaly and a skillful archer who instructed Heracles in the use of the bow (Theocrit. 24. 105; Apollod. 2. 4.9). He offered his daughter, Iole, as the prize to whoever could conquer him and his sons in shooting with the bow. Heracles won the prize, but Eurytus and his sons refused to give up Iole (Apollod. 2. 6.1), so Heracles marched against Oechalia with an army and killed Eurytus and his sons (Apollod. 2. 7.7). According to Homeric poems, Eurytus was killed by Apollo, whom he presumed to rival in using the bow (*Od.* 8. 226).

MELANEUS, son of Apollo and king of the Dryopes, was the father of the renowned archer, Eurytus, and a famous archer himself.

PANDARUS, son of Lycaon, was distinguished in the Trojan War as an archer.

PHILOCTETES, son of Poeas and Demonassa, was the most celebrated archer in the Trojan War (Hom. *Od.* 3. 190, 8. 219).

TEUCER, a son of Telamon and Hesione of Crete and a step-brother of Ajax, was the best archer among the Greeks at Troy (Hom. *Il.* 8. 281, 13. 170).

Architecture

AGAMEDES and his brother Trophonius were distinguished in architecture, especially for their temples and palaces.

CYCLOPES were regarded in later accounts as skillful architects.

DAEDALUS was a famous inventor in Crete. He was celebrated by the Greeks as the earliest developer of the art of architecture.

OTRERA, a daughter or wife of Ares, was said to have built the temple of Artemis at Ephesus.

PROMETHEUS acquainted men with the art of architecture.

PTERAS of Delphi was a mythical artist who was said to have built the second temple of Apollo at Delphi.

Arm

ENCELADUS, son of Tartarus and Gaea, was a giant who had one hundred arms and made war with fellow giants on the gods (Virg. *Aen.* 4. 179; Ov. *Ep.ex Pont.* 2. 2.12; Ov. *Amor.* 3. 12.27).

GYGES, another hundred-armed giant, was sometimes called Gyas or Gyes (Apollod. 1. 1.1; Hes. *Theog.* 149).

Armor

ACHILLES. After Patroclus was slain, Hephaestus fashioned new armor for Achilles. Thetis promised this armor, after her son's death, to the bravest among the Greeks. (See also PATROCLUS)

ACRON, king of the Caeninenses, was slain by Romulus. His arms were dedicated to Jupiter Feretrius.

Philoctetes

ACTOR was a companion of Aeneas. Of his conquered lance Turnus made a boast which probably gave rise to the proverbial saying: "Actoris spolium" (Juv. 2. 100), referring to any poor spoil in general.

AJAX. When he and Hector were separated in their contest, they exchanged arms as a token of mutual esteem. After the death of Achilles, Ajax and Odysseus engaged in combat over the fallen hero's armor. Odysseus was victorious.

APHRODITE AREIA, the warlike, was a name by which the goddess was called when she was represented in armor like Ares (Paus. 3. 17.5).

APOLLO CHRYSAOR was a surname referring to the god with the golden sword or arms (Hom. *Il.* 15. 256).

AREITHOUS was king of Arne in Boeotia. He had been slain by Lycurgus, king of Arcadia, who took his armor and later bequeathed it to Erythalion, who wore it in the Trojan War (Hom. *Il.* 7. 138).

ARTEMIS CHRYSAOR was a surname referring to the goddess with the golden sword or arms (Herod. 8. 77).

ATHENA. Many accounts of her birth say that she sprang fully-armed from the head of Zeus (Philostr. *Imag.* 2. 27). As goddess of war and protectress of heroes, she usually is depicted in armor.

CYCLOPES. As assistants to Hephaestus they helped forge the armor of the gods and heroes.

DEMETER CHRYSAOR was a surname signifying the goddess with the golden sword or arms (Hom. *Hymn. in Cer.* 4).

DEMOLEUS was a Greek who had been slain by Aeneas and whose coat of mail was offered by Aeneas as a prize in the games which he celebrated in Sicily (Virg. *Aen.* 5. 258).

EIRENE (IRENE), goddess of peace, is represented as burning a pile of arms.

HEPHAESTUS in his workshops on Olympus and elsewhere forged armor for gods and heroes, notably the famous armor worn by Achilles and Patroclus in the Trojan War.

HERACLES was instructed by Castor in fighting in heavy armor. For his battle against the forces of King Erginus of Orchomenus, Athena presented him with a suit of armor. Hephaestus also gave him a golden coat of mail.

HONOR (HONOS), the personification of honor, is represented as a male figure in armor.

LUA was an early Italian deity. When arms were taken from the defeated enemy, they were dedicated to her and burnt with a view to averting punishment or any other calamity (Liv. 8. 1, 14. 33; Gell. 42. 22; Varr. *De Ling. Lat.* 8. 36).

MEMNON. His armor was said to have been made for him by Hephaestus at the request of his mother, Eos.

MINERVA was represented with a helmet, shield, and coat of mail.

ODYSSEUS. After the death of Achilles, he contended for the hero's armor with the Telamonian Ajax, and gained the prize (Hom. *Od.* 11. 545; Ov. *Met.* 13).

PATROCLUS. Along with Achilles he withdrew from battle at Troy, but when the Greeks were hard-pressed, he begged to put on Achilles' armor and with his men to hasten to the assistance of the Greeks (Hom. *Il.* 16. 20). Achilles granted the request. In the armor, Patroclus succeeded in driving back the Trojans and extinguishing the fires raging among the ships (16. 293). But he was struck unconscious by Apollo, Euphorbus ran him through with a lance from behind, and Hector gave him a last fatal blow (16. 791). Hector also took possession of his armor (17. 102).

PELEUS. Upon his marriage to Thetis, he was presented with arms by the Olympian gods (Apollod. 3. 13.5; Hom. *Il.* 16. 381, 17. 433, 18. 84).

ZEUS CHRYSAOREUS, "the god with the golden sword or arms," was a name under which Zeus had a temple in Caria (Strab. 14. 660).

Armor-Bearer

ABDERUS, armor-bearer of Heracles, was torn to pieces by the mares of Diomedes.

PHILOCTETES, son of Poeas, was said by some to have been the disciple, friend, and armor-bearer of Heracles.

Arrow

ABARIS was a quasi-mythical Hyperborean priest, who traveled about giving prophecies. He carried an arrow as the symbol of Apollo and was reported to ride on the arrow through the air.

ACHILLES was slain by the arrow of Paris. He had been made immortal by his mother, Thetis, except for the heel by which she held him when she immersed him in the river Styx. It was in this vulnerable heel that he received the fatal arrow wound.

APHRODITE. The arrow was sometimes mentioned as one of her attributes (Pind. *Pyth.* 4. 380).

APOLLO. One of his symbols was an arrow, and one of his priests, Abaris, was reputed to have ridden on an arrow in the air. Sudden deaths were thought to be the effect of Apollo's arrows.

ARISTODEMUS, a descendant of Heracles, was killed by an arrow of Apollo, just as he was setting out on an expedition to Peloponnesus, because he had failed to consult the Delphic oracle (Paus. 3. 1.5).

ARTEMIS was represented as carrying arrows. Sudden death was explained as the effect of her arrows.

BELLEROPHON killed the Chimaera with an arrow shot from above while riding Pegasus, the winged horse.

CAANTHUS, a son of Oceanus, was sent out by his father in search of his sister, Melia, whom Apollo had abducted. Unable to rescue her, he threw fire into a grove sacred to Apollo and was slain by one of his arrows.

CHEIRON. During his struggle with the Erymanthian boar, Heracles became involved in a fight with the centaurs, who fled to Cheiron. Heracles shot at them with poisoned arrows, and one of them struck Cheiron, who, although immortal, preferred to die. He gave his immortality to Prometheus.

EROS. The arrows with which Eros wounded people had different powers: some were golden and kindled love in the heart they wounded; others were blunt and heavy with lead and produced aversion to a lover (Ov. *Met.* 1. 468; Eurip. *Iphig.Aul.* 548).

HERACLES. During his labors, he succeeded in catching the Ceryneian stag by wounding it with an arrow. With burning arrows and with club and sickle he cut off the heads of the Hydra. He dipped his arrows in the poison which came from the wounds, and thereafter the arrows had no antidote when one was struck. He startled the Stymphalian birds with a brazen rattle and then killed them with arrows (Apollod. 2. 5.6). On one of his journeys he became annoyed with the heat of the sun and shot arrows at the sun, and Helios so much admired his boldness that he presented him with a golden cup (or bowl). When Nessus, the centaur, tried to rape Deianeira, Heracles shot him with an arrow. (See also CHEIRON)

ILIONEUS was a son of Niobe whom Apollo would have liked to save, because he was praying, but the god had already shot the fatal arrow and it was no longer under his control (Ov. *Met.* 6. 261).

ISMENUS, son of Niobe and Amphion, when struck by an arrow of Apollo leaped into a river near Thebes, which was called Ismenus after him.

NEOPTOLEMUS. Helenus prophesied that Neoptolemus and Philoctetes, armed with the arrows of Heracles, were necessary for the taking of Troy (Soph. *Phil.* 115).

NIOBE, daughter of Tantalus and wife of Amphion, bragged that she had twelve children while Leto had only two. Apollo and Artemis, outraged at such presumption, slew all her children with arrows (Apollod. 3. 5.6).

ODYSSEUS went to the Thesprotian Ephyra to fetch from Ilus poison for his arrows, but, as he could not get it there, he obtained it from Anchialus of Taphus (Hom. *Od.* 1. 259). When he returned to Ithaca and found his house overrun by rapacious suitors for Penelope's hand, disguised as a beggar, he entered a test with them of stringing a bow and shooting through twelve ax heads. After winning the contest, he turned the arrows on the suitors, and with the help of his son, Telemachus, he slaughtered all of them.

ORION. According to some, he was carried off by Eos, goddess of the dawn, to Ortygia, and Artemis in anger killed him with an arrow (Hom. *Od.* 5. 121). According to others, he was beloved by Artemis, and Apollo, indignant at his sister's affection for him, contrived to have her do target practice on an object far out in the sea. One of her arrows struck the target, which was the head of Orion, who had been swimming in the sea (Ov. *Fast.* 5. 537). Still another account says that he violated Upis, for which Artemis shot him.

PARIS. When Troy was taken, he was wounded by Philoctetes with one of Heracles' famous poisoned arrows (Soph. *Phil.* 1426) and then returned to his long-abandoned first wife, Oenone. She either refused to or could not heal the wound, as it had been inflicted by an arrow tipped with poison for which there was no antidote.

PHILOCTETES was a son of Poeas and friend of Heracles, who instructed him in the use of the bow and bequeathed to him his bow with the never-erring poisoned arrows. According to some, the wound which so long tormented and incapacitated him was not from a snakebite but from one of his own poisoned arrows. He lay ill from the wound for years on the island of Lemnos. Finally, Odysseus and Diomedes came to him as ambassadors to inform him that an oracle had declared that without the arrows of Heracles, Troy could not be taken. He proceeded to Troy to decide the victory by his arrows (Q.Smyrn. 9. 325, 460).

PHLEGYAS was a king of the Lapithae, son of Ares and Chryse. By his own mother he became the father of Coronis, who became by Apollo the mother of Asclepius. Enraged at this, Phlegyas set fire to Apollo's temple, and Apollo killed him with arrows and condemned him to severe punishment in the lower world.

POEAS, a son of Phylacus or Thaumacus, is said to have killed Talos in Crete with an arrow during the expedition of the Argonauts (Apollod. 1. 9.26). This was probably one of the famous arrows of Heracles, which the hero had bestowed on him for kindling the pyre on which the hero burnt himself (Apollod. 2. 7.7).

PORPHYRION, one of the giants, was a son of Uranus and Gaea. When he intended to rape Hera during the war between the giants and the gods, or tried to throw the island of Delos against the gods, Zeus hurled a thunderbolt at him, and Heracles completed his destruction with arrows (Apollod. 1. 6.1; Pind. *Pyth.* 8. 12; Hor. *Carm.* 3. 4.54; Claud. *Gigantom.* 114).

RHOECUS was a centaur who, together with Hylaeus, pursued Atalanta in Arcadia but was killed by her with an arrow (Apollod. 3. 9.2; Callim. *Hymn.in Dian.* 221).

SARPEDON, son of Zeus and Laodameia, became prince of Lycia when his uncles were quarreling over the government and it was proposed that they should shoot through a ring placed on the breast of a child. Laodameia, their sister, gave up her own son, Sarpedon, for this purpose. He was thereupon honored by his uncles with the kingdom to show their gratitude to their sister.

STYMPHALIDES, the rapacious birds near the Stymphalian lake in Arcadia, were armed with brazen wings from which they could shoot out their feathers like arrows (Apollod. 2. 5.6; Paus. 8. 22.4). Heracles eventually killed these monsters with arrows.

TALOS, the wonderful brass creature made by Hephaestus, was, according to some stories, killed by Poeas, the Argonaut, who wounded him in the ankle with an arrow (Apollod. 1. 9.26).

TITYS, a son of Gaea, was a giant in Euboea. Instigated by Hera he made an assault upon

Leto or Artemis, when she passed through Panopaeus to Pytho, but was killed by the arrows of Artemis or Apollo; or, according to others, Zeus killed him with a flash of lightning (Paus. 3. 18.9; Pind. *Pyth.* 4. 160; Hor. *Carm.* 4. 6.2).

VEIOVIS was an Etruscan divinity of a destructive nature, whose fearful lightnings produced deafness in those who were struck by them (Amm. Marc. 17. 10). He was represented in art as a youthful god armed with arrows (Gell. 5. 12; Vitruv. 4. 8).

Art

ATHENA ERGANE was a surname designating Athena as the worker, who presided over and instructed men in all kinds of arts (Paus. 1. 24.3, 5. 14.5).

CHARITES. The most perfect works of art are called the works of the Charites, or Graces, and the greatest artists are their favorites.

HEPHAESTUS, like Athena, gave skill to mortal artists and, together with her, was believed to have taught men the arts which embellish and adorn life.

MINERVA was worshipped by the Romans as patroness of all the arts and trades, and was particularly invoked by those who wished to distinguish themselves in any art or craft, such as painting, poetry, the art of teaching, medicine, dyeing, spinning, or weaving (Ov. *Fast.* 3. 809; August 7. 16).

MUSES were the divinities who presided over the arts.

Artist

EPEIUS, son of Panopeus and an artist, built the Wooden Horse of Troy (Hom. *Od.* 8. 492, 11. 523; Hom. *Il.* 23. 664, 840; Paus. 2. 29.4). He was also said to have carved images of Hermes and Aphrodite (Paus. 2. 19.6). Plato (*Ion* 533) mentioned him as a sculptor.

EUCHEIR was a relation of Daedalus and the inventor of painting in Greece.

HEPHAESTUS appears to have been originally the god of fire alone; but as fire is indispensable in working metals, he was afterwards regarded as an artist. His palace on Olympus contained the workshop where he made all his beautiful and marvelous works, both for gods and men. He built all the palaces on Olympus, made the armor of Achilles, the fatal necklace of Harmonia, and the fire-breathing bulls of Aeetes.

HYPERBIUS, a mythical artist of Corinth, was said to have invented brick walls and the potter's wheel.

Ash

NEMESIS was the goddess of retribution. Sometimes she appears in a pensive mood, holding in her left hand a bridle or a branch of an ash tree and in her right hand a wheel, with a sword or a scourge.

Ashes

APOLLO SPODIUS was a surname of Apollo at Thebes, derived from *spodos,* ashes, because his altar consisted of the ashes of the victims sacrificed to him (Paus. 9. 11.5).

ORESTES pretended to be a messenger of Strophius to Argos to announce the death of Orestes, and brought what were supposed to be the ashes of the deceased (Soph. *Elect.* 1110).

Asphodel

DIONYSUS. Asphodel was sacred to him.

Ass

CLEINIS of Babylon tried to institute the sacrifice of asses to Apollo, but Apollo objected and demanded that only sheep, goats, and heifers should be sacrificed to him. When the sons of Cleinis persisted, Apollo caused the animals to attack the family; but the other gods took pity and changed the family into various birds.

DIONYSUS. On his way to the oracle of Dodona, his passage was cut off by a lake. One of two asses he met there carried him across the water, and the grateful god placed both animals among the stars; asses from that time remained sacred to him.

EMPUSA was a monster sent by Hecate to frighten strangers. It was believed usually to appear with one leg of brass and the other of an ass (Aristoph. *Ran.* 294; Aristoph. *Eccles.* 1094).

MIDAS was king of the Mygdonians in Phrygia. When he decided in favor of Pan over Apollo in a musical contest, Apollo punished him by changing his ears into those of an ass. Midas concealed them under his Phrygian cap, but the servant who cut his hair discovered them. The secret so much obsessed this man that, as he could not betray it to a human being, he dug a hole in the earth and whispered into it: "King Midas has ass's ears." He then filled up the hole, but on the same spot a reed grew up, which in its whispers betrayed the secret to the world (Ov. *Met.* 11. 146; Aristoph. *Plut.* 287).

ODYSSEUS did not want to join the Greeks against Troy (Hom. *Od.* 24. 116). When Palamedes came to persuade him, Odysseus pretended to be mad. He yoked an ass and an ox to a plow and began to sow salt. Palamedes, to try him, placed the infant Telemachus before the plow, so that the father could not continue his deception.

PRIAPUS was son of Dionysus and Aprodite and god of the fructifying powers and manifestations of nature. Sacrifices to him included asses.

SILENUS (SEILENUS) was one of the satyrs, the son of Hermes or Pan by a nymph. He took part in the contest of the giants and gods and slew Enceladus, putting the other giants to flight by the braying of his ass (Eurip. *Cycl.* 5). He generally rode an ass, since he was usually intoxicated and could not stand on his own legs.

Assembly

ATHENA AGORAEA was a surname designating Athena as protectress of assemblies of the people (Paus. 3. 11.8).

ZEUS AGORAEUS was a surname of Zeus as protector of assemblies of the people in the agora (Paus. 3. 11.8).

ZEUS HETAEREIUS, "the protector of companies or associations of friends," was a surname of Zeus. Jason was believed to have offered the first sacrifices to him when the Argonauts were assembled for their expedition (Athen. 13. 572).

ZEUS HOMAGYRIUS was a surname as the god of the assembly or league. Under this name Zeus was worshipped at Aegium on the northwestern coast of the Peloponnesus, where Agamemnon was believed to have assembled the Greek chiefs to deliberate on the war against Troy. Under this name Zeus was also worshipped as the protector of the Achaean League (Paus. 7. 24.1).

Astronomy

HERMES was said to have invented astronomy.

HESPERUS, according to Diodorus (3. 60), was the son of Atlas and was fond of astronomy. Once, after having ascended Mt. Atlas to observe the stars, he disappeared.

PROMETHEUS brought the knowledge of astronomy to men.

URANIA, the Muse of astronomy, appears with a staff, pointing to a globe.

Asylum

JUNO EMPANDA was a surname of Juno in Rome. Her temple was always open for asylum. The name Juno Panda is equivalent.

Atmosphere

HERA. Some regarded her as the personification of the atmosphere.

Atonement

ATHENA AREIA was a surname of Athena. Her worship under this name was instituted by Orestes after he had been acquitted by the Areiopagus for matricide (Paus. 1. 28.5). Athena cast a deciding vote in case of a tie. The surname could therefore refer to propitiation or atonement.

CEPHALUS built a temple to Apollo on Cape Leucas in order to atone for the accidental murder of his wife, Procris (Strab. 10. 452).

DIONYSUS MEILICHIUS was a surname designating the god as one who could be propitiated, or as the gracious, at Naxos (Athen. 3. 78).

HECATE was a goddess of expiation.

LITAE, daughter of Zeus and the personification of prayers offered up in repentance, followed closely behind crime and endeavored to make amends for what had been done. Whoever disdained to receive them had himself to atone for the crime that had been committed (Hom. *Il.* 9. 502).

PELOPS. In order to atone for the murder of Myrtilus, Pelops founded the first temple of Hermes in the Peloponnesus (Paus. 5. 15.5), and also erected a monument to the unsuccessful suitors of Hippodameia, at which an annual sacrifice was offered to them (Paus. 6. 21.7).

ZEUS AREIUS was a name describing Zeus as a propitiating or atoning god.

ZEUS CATHARSIUS was a surname meaning the purifier or atoner. Under this name he, in conjunction with Nike, had a temple at Olympia (Paus. 5. 14.6).

See also: PURIFICATION

Auger (or Gimlet)

DAEDALUS was the reputed inventor of the auger.

Augury, see Prophecy

Autoerotism

NARCISSUS was an exceptionally beautiful young man. When he spurned the love of all those who tried to approach him, he was punished by falling in love with his own image in the water.

Ax

DAEDALUS was the reputed inventor of the ax.

ERYSICHTHON, a son of Triopas, once cut down an oak tree in a grove sacred to Demeter, ignoring the groans of the Dryad who lived in the tree and whose blood ran out from the wounds made with the ax. He was punished by Demeter by being afflicted with insatiable hunger, so that he eventually devoured his own flesh and died.

HEPHAESTUS. When Athena was about to be born from the head of Zeus, he was seized with a fierce headache, and Hephaestus split open the god's head with his ax so that the goddess could be delivered (Pind. *Ol.* 7. 35).

PYGMIES, the fabulous race of diminutive individuals, were reported to have cut down separate wheat ears with axes.

TEREUS. When he learned that his wives, the sisters, Procne and Philomela, had killed his son Itys and served his flesh to him, he pursued them with an ax, and all three were changed into birds.

ZEUS POLIEUS, "the protector of the city," was a name under which Zeus had an altar on the acropolis at Athens. Upon this altar, barley and wheat were strewn, which were consumed by the bull about to be sacrificed to the god. The priest who killed the victim threw away the ax as soon as he had struck the fatal blow, and the ax was then brought before a court of justice (Paus. 1. 24.4, 21.11).

Bag

ASCUS was a giant who threw the chained Dionysus into a river. For this act he was flayed and a bag made of his skin.

ICARIUS. For his hospitality to Dionysus, he was taught by the god the cultivation of the vine. Once he killed a ram for having injured his vines, made a bag of its skin and then performed a dance on it.

ODYSSEUS. After spending a month on the island of Aeolus, he departed with a bag of winds, a gift of Aeolus, which were to carry him home; but his companions, without his knowing it, opened the bag, and the winds escaped (Hom. *Od.* 10. 1).

PERSEUS. For his mission to fetch Medusa's head, the nymphs provided him with a bag in which to carry the severed head after he had accomplished the feat (Hes. *Scut.Herc.* 220, 222).

Baking, see Bread

Ball

EETION. The iron ball that Eetion, the father of Andromache, hurled in battle became the property of Achilles, who proposed it as a prize at the funeral games of Patroclus (Hom. *Il.* 23. 826).

GLAUCUS, young son of Minos and Pasiphae fell into a cask of honey while playing ball, and died in it. He was later restored to life by the seer Polyidus.

NAUSICAA, daughter of Alcinous, while playing ball with her handmaidens, discovered the exhausted Odysseus where he had been cast ashore at the mouth of a river.

POLYPOETES, a son of Peirithous and Hippodameia, at the funeral games of Patroclus gained the victory throwing the iron ball (Hom. *Il.* 23. 836).

TYCHE was the personification of chance or luck. Holding in her hand a ball, she represented the varying unsteadiness of fortune.

Barbiton, see Lyre

Bard

DEMODOCUS was a minstrel at the court of King Alcinous who entertained Odysseus and his hosts with songs of the fall of Troy.

EUMOLPUS was regarded as an ancient priestly bard, and poems and writings on the mysteries were fabricated and circulated at a later date under his name.

ORPHEUS. Pindar enumerates him among the Argonauts as the celebrated harp player and composer of songs, sent forth by Apollo (*Pyth.* 4. 315).

PHEMIUS, the famous minstrel, was a son of Terpius and entertained the suitors in the house of Odysseus in Ithaca (Hom. *Od.* 1. 154, 17. 263, 22. 330).

THAMYRIS, an ancient Thracian bard, was the son of Philammon and the nymph Argiope. He went so far in his conceit as to think he could surpass the Muses in song, and so was deprived of his sight and of the power of singing (Hom. *Il.* 2. 595; Apollod. 1. 3.3; Paus. 4. 33.4, 10. 7.2; Eurip. *Rhes.* 925). He was represented with a broken lyre in his hand (Paus. 9. 30.2).

Barley, see Grain

Basket

DEMETER. In artistic representations, she often carried a basket.

Bat

ALCATHOE (ALCITHOE) was a daughter of Minyas. When she and her sisters, Leucippe and Arsippe (Aristippa) or Arsinoe (Plut. *Quaest.Gr.* 38), refused to participate in the Bacchic revels introduced into Boeotia, Dionysus changed them into bats.

Bath

ACTAEON, a hunter on Mt. Cithaeron, was changed into a stag and torn to pieces by his dogs when he observed Artemis bathing with her nymphs in a stream.

AGAMEMNON, upon his return to Troy, was slain by Aegisthus and/or Clytemnestra while taking a bath.

ERYMANTHUS, son of Apollo, was blinded by Aphrodite because he had seen her bathing.

TIRESIAS (TEIRESIAS), a son of Everes (or Phorbas) and Chariclo, was one of the most celebrated soothsayers in all antiquity. He was blind from an early age, and some accounts attribute his blindness to having seen Athena in her bath.

Battle Cry

APOLLO BOEDROMIUS was a surname of Apollo at Athens, which arose, according to some, because in the war of Erechtheus and Ion against Eumolpus, Apollo had advised the Athenians to rush upon the enemy with a war shout (*boe*) if they wanted to conquer (Callim. *Hymn.in Apoll.* 69).

Battlefield

CER was the personification of the necessity of death. Usually referred to in the plural, the Ceres were the daughters of Nyx and sisters of the Moirae and were responsible for punishing men for their crimes. During a battle, the Ceres wandered about with Eris and Cydoimos in bloody garments, quarreling about the wounded and the dead, and dragging them away by the feet (Hom. *Il.* 18. 535).

Bean

CARNA (CARNEA) was a Roman divinity regarded as the protector of the physical well-being of man. Sacrifices of bacon and beans were offered to her on the festival called *fabrariae calendae.*

CYAMITES, the hero of beans, was a mysterious being who had a small sanctuary on the road from Athens to Eleusis (Paus. 1. 37.3).

LEMURES were the spectres of the dead who tormented the living. During Roman purification ceremonies each year on the nights of May 9th, 11th, and 13th, the *pater familias* rose at midnight and went outside, making certain signs with his hand to keep the spectres at a distance. He then washed his hands three times in spring water, turned around, and took into his mouth black beans, which he afterwards threw behind him. The spectres were believed to collect these beans. After he had spoken certain words without looking around, he again washed his hands, made a noise with brass basins, and called out to the spectres nine times: "Begone, you spectres of the house!" This done, he was allowed to look around, for the spectres were rendered harmless (Ov. *Fast.* 5. 419).

Bear

ARCEISIUS was a son of Cephalus and a she-bear.

ARTEMIS. The she-bear was the symbol of the Arcadian Artemis. (See also CALLISTO and IPHIGENEIA)

ATALANTA (ATALANTE). In her infancy, after being exposed, she was suckled in the wilderness by a she-bear, the symbol of Artemis.

CALLISTO was metamorphosed by Zeus into a she-bear to prevent his relationship with her from being found out by Hera. But Hera learned of this device and caused her to be slain by Artemis during the chase (Apollod. 3. 8.2). After her death, Zeus placed her among the stars. Arcas, her son by Zeus, was also placed among the stars.

CRIMISSUS the river god, in the shape of a bear or dog, begot by Segesta (Egesta), daughter of Phoenodamas, Aegestus (Egestus or Acestes), by whom Egesta in Sicily was built (Dionys. 1. 52).

HELICE, a daughter of Lycaon, because she was beloved by Zeus, was metamorphosed by Hera into a she-bear, whereupon Zeus placed her among the stars under the name of the Great Northern Bear.

IPHIGENEIA. When she was on the point of being sacrificed by the Greeks at Aulis, Artemis carried her away and substituted, according to some, a she-bear for the sacrifice.

PARIS. When Priam had the infant Paris exposed, the task was left to the shepherd Agelaus, who left the child on Mt. Ida but returned five days later to find the child alive and suckled by a she-bear. He took the child and raised it as his own (Eurip. *Troad.* 921).

ZALMOXIS (ZAMOLXIS) was a Getan who had been a slave to Pythagoras in Samos. He was regarded by some as a deity, introducing doctrines regarding the immortality of the soul. He was called Zalmoxis from the bear's skin in which he was clothed as soon as he was born.

Beard

DIONYSUS PSILAS was a surname meaning, perhaps, the unbearded, under which Dionysus was worshipped at Amyclae (Paus. 3. 19.6).

PAN, the great god of flocks and shepherds, had horns, beard, pug nose, tail, and goat's feet and was covered with hair.

VENUS BARBATA, "the bearded," was a surname of Venus among the Romans. Some also mention a statue of Venus in Cyprus, representing the goddess with a beard in female attire, but resembling in her whole figure a man.

Beauty (Female)

ALCESTIS. Homer calls her the fairest among the daughters of Pelias.

ALOPE, daughter of Cercyon, was beloved by Poseidon because of her great beauty.

ANDROMEDA. Her mother, Cassiopeia, boasted of Andromeda's beauty as surpassing that of the Nereids. As a consequence, Andromeda was chained to a rock to be devoured by a sea monster but was rescued by Perseus (Apollod. 2. 4.3; Ov. *Met.* 4. 663).

APHRODITE was the Olympian goddess of beauty. (See also CHARITES and HELEN)

CASSIOPEIA (CASSIEPEIA) extolled the beauty of her daughter, Andromeda above that of the Nereids. According to others, it was her own beauty she boasted about (Arat. 187).

CENTAURS. The female centaurs were said to be of great beauty (Philostr. *Imag.* 2. 3).

CHARITES were the personification of grace and beauty. It was related that Aphrodite and the three Charites disputed about their beauty with one another. Tiresias awarded the prize to Cale, and was changed by Aphrodite into an old woman; but Cale rewarded him with a beautiful head of hair and took him to Crete.

CHIONE, daughter of Daedalion, was beloved by Apollo and Hermes on account of her beauty. She was killed by Artemis for having found fault with the beauty of the goddess.

FAUNA (FAULA) was identified by some of the ancients with the Greek Aphrodite.

GERANA, a Pygmean woman, was highly esteemed and praised for her beauty. Her vanity incurred the wrath of Artemis and Hera, who metamorphosed her into a crane (Ov. *Met.* 6. 90).

HELEN, daughter of Zeus and Leda, was of surpassing beauty. She was the prize Paris received for his selection of Aphrodite as the fairest of the goddesses. Helen's beauty became an indirect cause of the Trojan War.

HERA. Proetus' daughters, Iphinoe, Lysippe, and Iphianassa, were seized with madness because they boasted of equalling Hera in beauty. They were cured by Melampus the soothsayer. (See also GERANA and SIDA)

HIERA, wife of Telephus and commander of the Mysian women on horseback in the Trojan War, was described as being more beautiful than Helen herself.

HORA was a Roman deity who presided over beauty.

Helen of Troy

LAMIA was a female phantom by which children were frightened. According to tradition, she was originally a Libyan queen of great beauty and a daughter of Belus.

LETHAEA was the wife of Olenus on Mt. Ida. Olenus wanted to take upon himself the punishment which his wife had incurred by pride in her own beauty and so was metamorphosed, along with her, into stone (Ov. *Met.* 10. 68).

PENTHESILEIA, queen of the Amazons, was killed in the Trojan War by Achilles, who then lamented his deed because of her beauty, youth, and valor (Paus. 5. 11.2; Q.Smyrn. 1. 40).

PERO, a daughter of Neleus and Chloris, was married to Bias and celebrated for her great beauty (Hom. *Od.* 11. 286; Apollod. 1. 9.9; Paus. 10. 31.2).

PSYCHE, a daughter of a king, by her beauty excited the jealousy and envy of Venus. In order to avenge herself, the goddess ordered Amor (Cupid) to inspire Psyche with a love for the most comtemptible of all men, but Amor was so stricken with her beauty that he himself fell in love with her.

SCYLLA. One tradition relates that she was originally a beautiful maiden who was beloved by the marine god, Glaucus. He asked Circe for means to make Scylla return his love; but Circe, jealous of the fair maiden, threw magic herbs into the well where Scylla bathed, and by these herbs she was metamorphosed in such a manner that the upper part of her body remained that of a woman, while the lower part was changed into the tail of a fish or serpent surrounded by dogs (Ov. *Met.* 13. 732, 905, 14. 40).

SIDA, wife of Orion, was sent by Hera into Hades because she pretended to be more beautiful than the goddess (Apollod. 1. 4.3).

THEOPHANE was a daughter of Bisaltes, who, because of her extraordinary beauty, was beleaguered by lovers. She was carried off by Poseidon to the isle of Crinissa. As the lovers followed her even there, Poseidon metamorphosed the maiden into a sheep and himself into a ram, and all the inhabitants into animals. As the lovers began to slaughter these animals, Poseidon changed them into wolves.

TISIPHONE was the daughter of Alcmaon, who gave her to Creon, king of Corinth, to educate. Creon's wife was jealous of the girl's beauty and sold her as a slave. Alcmaon unwittingly purchased his own daughter.

VENUS was the Roman goddess of beauty. (See also PSYCHE)

Beauty (Male)

ACHILLES was the most beautiful among the Greeks at Troy.

AJAX, next to Achilles, was the most beautiful among the Greeks at Troy.

ANCHISES was the son of Capys and Themiste. His beauty matched that of the immortal gods, and he was beloved by Aphrodite, by whom he became the father of Aeneas (Hom. *Il.* 2. 820; Hes. *Theog.* 1008).

ANTILOCHUS was said to be one of the youngest, bravest, and handsomest of the Greeks in the Trojan War. Achilles was especially devoted to him (Hom. *Od.* 3. 112; Hom. *Il.* 18. 16, 23. 556, 607).

APOLLO was the divine representation of youthful manliness and beauty.

ATYMNIUS, son of Zeus and Cassiopeia, was a beautiful boy beloved by Sarpedon (Apollod. 3. 1.2).

ATYS, son of Nana, was a shepherd in Phrygia beloved by Cybele. He was of such extraordinary beauty that Agdistis, the hermaphroditic deity, also fell in love with him and caused his death.

BORMUS, son of Upius, was a youth distinguished for his beauty. While drawing water for the reapers he was pulled into the well by nymphs and never appeared again. (Cf. HYLAS)

BRANCHUS, son of Apollo, was renowned for his great beauty.

CANDAON (See ORION)

CEPHALUS. Because of his handsomeness he was beloved by Eos, goddess of the dawn, who carried him off.

CLEITUS, son of Mantius, was carried off by Eos, goddess of the dawn, on account of his great beauty (Hom. *Od.* 15. 250).

CYCNUS, son of Apollo and Thyria, was an extremely handsome hunter living in the district between Pleuron and Calydon.

CYLLARUS was a beautiful centaur, who was married to Hylonome and killed at the wedding feast of Peirithous (Ov. *Met.* 12. 393).

ENDYMION, son of Aethlius and Calyce and distinguished for his beauty, was beloved by the moon goddess, who caused him to fall into eternal sleep so that she could visit him forever.

EROS, son of Aphrodite, was represented as a handsome youth by erotic poets up to the time of Alexander the Great.

GANYMEDE was the son of Tros. Being the most beautiful of all mortals, he was carried off by the gods to fill the cup of Zeus and live among the eternal gods (Hom *Il.* 20. 231; Apollod. 3. 12.2).

HYACINTHUS, son of Amyclas (or Pierus or Oebalus), was a youth of extraordinary beauty and beloved by Thamyris and Apollo.

HYLAS. When the Argonauts landed on the coast of Mysia, Hylas went out to fetch water for Heracles, but when he came to the well, his beauty so excited the love of the Naiads that they drew him down into the water, and he was never seen again (Val.Flacc. 3. 545; Theocrit. 13. 45).

HYMEN (HYMENAEUS), the god of marriage, was a youth of such delicate beauty that he might be taken for a girl.

IDOMENEUS, son of Deucalion, was a man of remarkable beauty.

LINUS, son of Apollo, was a handsome and lovely youth and a favorite of the gods.

NARCISSUS was a son of Cephissus and the nymph, Liriope, of Thespiae. He was a very handsome youth, but because he spurned the advances of those who admired him, he was caused to fall in love with his own image in a pool and to pine away from the unrequited love.

NIREUS, son of Charopus and Aglaia, was considered, next to Achilles, the handsomest among the Greeks at Troy. His beauty became proverbial (Lucian *Dial.Mort.* 9).

ORION, son of Hyrieus of Hyria, was a very handsome giant and hunter and was said to have been called Candaon by the Boeotians (Hom. *Od.* 11. 309; Strab. 9. 404). According to some legends, he was carried away by Eos, goddess of the dawn, because of his surpassing beauty.

PANTHOUS was one of the elders of Troy. Originally, he was a Delphian but had been carried to Troy by Antenor on account of his beauty (Lucian *Gall.* 17).

PARIS, son of Priam, was renowned for his beauty.

PELOPS was so beautiful as a boy that Poseidon carried him off, and he, like Ganymede, stayed with the gods for a time (Pind. *Ol.* 1. 46).

PHAENON was a beautiful youth created by Prometheus. Knowing Zeus' fondness for handsome boys, Prometheus did not present the youth, as was his custom, to the king of the gods. When Zeus learned of this, he sent Hermes to fetch the boy with promises of immortality. He was carried off to heaven, where he became the planet Phaenon, later called Jupiter.

PHAON, a boatman of Mitylene, was already of an advanced age and ugly appearance; but on one occasion he very willingly and without accepting payment carried Aphrodite across the sea. For this service, the goddess gave him youth and beauty. After this, Sappho is said to have fallen in love with him (Lucian *Dial. Mort.* 9).

SELEMNUS was beloved by Argyra, a nymph, who, when his exceptional youthful beauty vanished, left him, causing him to pine away with grief (Paus. 7. 23.2).

TITHONUS was carried away by Eos, goddess of the dawn, because of his very great beauty. She prayed to the gods to grant him immortality, which they did, but she forgot to ask for eternal youth.

Bed

DAMASTES (See PROCRUSTES)

HELIOS. Some writers represented the sun god as making his nightly voyage from west to east while slumbering in a golden bed (Athen. 11. 470).

POLYPEMON (See PROCRUSTES)

PROCRUSTES, "the stretcher," was an epithet of the famous robber, Polypemon or Damastes. He forced all the strangers who fell into his hands into a bed which was either too small or too large, in which he had their limbs stretched or cut down to the proper length (Plut. *Thes.* 11; Paus. 1. 38.5; Ov. *Met.* 7. 438).

Bee

ARISTAEUS, son of Apollo and Cyrene, was worshipped as the deity who taught men to keep bees. When his own bees began to die he sought the advice of Proteus, the prophetic sea god. Proteus told him that he had been responsible for the death of the nymph, Eurydice, and that he must sacrifice bulls and hang their carcasses in a sacred grove. Having done this, Aristaeus returned to the grove after nine days and found a swarm of bees had made a hive in one of the rotting carcasses.

ARTEMIS. The symbol of the Ephesian Artemis was a bee.

LAIUS, a Cretan, together with Aegolis, Celeus, and Cerberus, entered the sacred cave of bees in Crete in order to steal honey. They succeeded in their crime but perceived the cradle of the infant Zeus, and that instant their brazen armor broke into pieces. Zeus thundered and wanted to kill them by a flash of lightning, but the Moirae and Themis prevented him, as no one was allowed to be killed on the sacred spot. Instead, the thieves were metamorphosed into birds (Plin. *H.N.* 10. 60, 79).

MELISSA was the nymph who discovered and taught the use of honey and from whom bees were believed to have received their name. Bees seem to have been the symbol of nymphs, who themselves are sometimes said to have been metamorphosed into bees (Columell. 9. 2). Also, nymphs in the form of bees are said to have guided the colonists who went to Ephesus (Philostr. *Imag.* 2. 8). According to the scholiasts of Pindar and Euripides, priestesses of Demeter received their name (Melissae) from the purity of the bee.

MELITEUS, son of Zeus and an Othreian nymph, was exposed by his mother in a wood, so that Hera would not discover the affair. Zeus took care that his son was reared by bees, and thus the boy grew to manhood.

NYMPHS (See MELISSA)

PAN. As god of flocks, Pan was also considered a protector of bees.

POLYIDUS, the soothsayer from Argos, was by his prophetic powers and by guidance from an owl and bees able to find Minos' missing son, Glaucus, who had drowned in a vat of honey (Aelian. *De Nat. Anim.* 5. 2).

PRIAPUS, son of Dionysus and Aphrodite, was worshipped as the protector of bees.

PTERAS of Delphi, a mythical artist, was said to have built the second temple of Apollo at Delphi. The tradition said that the first temple was made of branches of the wild laurel from Tempe and that the second was made of wax and bees' wings.

ZEUS. The nymphs of Crete reared him, and fed him the milk of the goat, Amalthea. The bees of the mountain provided him with honey (Apollod. 1. 1.6).

Beetle

CERAMBUS (TERAMBUS), a son of Euseirus and Eidothea, a shepherd and a musician, lived on Mt. Othrys. He was warned by Pan that a severe winter was coming on and to leave the mountain, but did not follow the advice and even mocked Pan and the nymphs. When the predicted cold weather destroyed his flocks, he was metamorphosed by the nymphs into a beetle.

Beggar

IRUS, the well-known beggar of Ithaca, was celebrated for his voracity. The suitors of Penelope arranged a boxing match between him and Odysseus, who was disguised as an elderly beggar. Irus was felled with one blow and disgraced (Hom. *Od.* 18. 1–116).

ODYSSEUS. When he finally returned to his kingdom, Athena disguised him as an elderly and unsightly beggar so that he would not be recognized.

Beginning

ARCHE, Muse of beginning, was one of the four Muses mentioned as a daughter of Zeus and Plusia.

JANUS was the Roman god of the beginning of everything.

JANUS CONSIVIUS was a surname of Janus as protector of the beginning of all occupations and actions, as well as of human life.

Bellows

HEPHAESTUS was the god of fire. His workshop in his Olympian palace contained an anvil and twenty bellows, which worked spontaneously at his bidding (Hom. *Il.* 18. 370).

Belt, see Girdle

Benefactor

ARISTAEUS, one of the most beneficent divinities in ancient mythology, was worshipped as the protector of flocks and shepherds and vine or olive plantations. He taught men to hunt and keep bees, and averted from the fields the various causes of destruction to the crops.

HERMES ACACESIUS was a surname of Hermes (Callim. *Hymn.in Dian.* 143). Some derive the name from *kakos* and assign to it the meaning: the god who cannot be hurt or who does not hurt. By extension it may have the meaning of benefactor or deliverer from evil.

PROMETHEUS ACACESIUS was a surname which meant the god who cannot be hurt or who does not hurt. Hesiod (*Theog.* 614) assigns this name to Prometheus, and it may be inferred to mean benefactor or deliverer from evil.

Bird

AESACUS was changed into a bird while lamenting the death of his wife Asterope. Ovid, though, relates that while he was pursuing Hesperia, she was stung by a viper and died. Aesacus threw himself into the sea and was changed into an aquatic bird.

ALCATHOE (ALCITHOE). Reluctantly converted to extreme Dionysiac worship, she and her sisters, Leucippe and Arsippe (Aristippa or Arsinoe), became mad and were changed by Hermes into birds.

ALCYONE. She and her husband, Ceyx, were metamorphosed into birds (Apollod. 1. 7.3).

ANTHUS was torn to pieces by horses and metamorphosed into a bird which imitated the neighing of a horse but always fled from the sight of a horse (Plin. *H.N.* 10. 57).

ASBOLUS was a centaur who could prophesy from the flight of birds.

ASTERIA. Zeus was enamored with her, but she, being metamorphosed through her prayers into a bird, flew across the sea. She was then changed into a rock, which for a long time lay under the surface of the sea; but at the request of Leto, it rose and received Leto, who was pursued by Python. Leto then gave birth to Apollo, who slew Python (Ov. *Met.* 6. 370; Aristot. *H.A.* 6. 35; Athen. 15. 701; Apollon.Rhod. 2. 707).

CARDEA was a Roman divinity who protected little children in their cradles from witches who changed themselves into night birds.

CIRIS (See SCYLLA)

CLEINIS of Babylon, against the wishes of Apollo, persisted in sacrificing asses to the god, whereupon Apollo caused the animals to attack the family of Cleinis. The other gods took pity and changed the family into various birds.

DEIANEIRA. When Meleager died, Artemis turned his grieving sisters, except Deianeira and Gorge, into birds (Ov. *Met.* 8. 532; Apollod. 1. 8.3).

HARPALYCE was changed into a bird because she served the flesh of her brother to her father, Clymenus, who had raped her.

HARPIES. These monsters were described by later writers as birds with the heads of maidens, long claws on their hands, and faces pale with hunger (Virg. *Aen.* 3. 216; Ov. *Met.* 7. 4; Ov. *Fast.* 6. 132).

HERACLES. The sixth labor of Heracles consisted of expelling the Stymphalian birds. These voracious creatures had brazen claws, wings, and beaks, and they killed men and beasts. Heracles accomplished his labor by startling the birds with a brazen rattle given him by Athena and then killing them with arrows (Apollod. 2. 5.6).

HIERAX was a youth who warned Argus that Hermes was stealing Io, whereupon Hermes changed him into a bird of prey.

IAMUS, the seer, was given the power to understand and explain the voices of birds.

IDAS was one of the companions of Diomedes metamorphosed into birds by the anger of Aphrodite (Ov. *Met.* 14. 504).

LAIUS, a Cretan, with three other thieves, Aegolis, Celeus, and Cerberus, attempted to steal honey from the sacred cave of bees in Crete and accidentally came upon the cradle of the infant Zeus. The god wanted to destroy them with a flash of lightning but was dissuaded by the Moirae and Themis, because no one was allowed to be killed on the sacred spot. He metamorphosed them into birds instead (Plin. *H.N.* 10. 60, 79).

MELAMPUS. Once while he slept, some serpents which he had reared approached him from either side and cleaned his ears with their tongues. When he awoke, he was amazed to find that he could understand the language of birds and with their assistance could foretell the future (Apollod. 1. 9.11).

MEMNON. His companions, who mourned excessively at his death, were changed by the gods into birds, called Memnonides. According to Ovid (*Met.* 13. 576), Eos implored Zeus to confer an honor on her son to console her for her loss. Accordingly he caused a number of birds to fight in the air over the funeral sacrifice until some of them fell down upon the ashes of the hero and thus formed a funeral offering for him. According to a story on the Hellespont, the Memnonides every year visited the tomb of Memnon, cleared the ground around the area and moistened it with their wings, which they wetted in the waters of the river Aesepus (Paus. 10. 31.2; Plin. *H.N.* 36. 7).

PARNASSUS, son of Cleopompus or Poseidon, was the inventor of the art of foretelling the future from the flight of birds (Paus. 10. 6.1).

PHOENIX was the fabulous bird that periodically died and was reborn from the ashes of its funeral pyre.

PIERUS, a king of Emathia (Macedonia), had nine daughters, whom he named for the nine Muses. They entered into a contest with the Muses, and, being conquered, were metamorphosed into birds called Colymbas, Iynx, Cenchris, Cissa, Chloris, Acalanthis, Nessa, Pipo, and Dracontia (Paus. 9. 29.2; Ov. *Met.* 5. 295).

SCYLLA was the daughter of Nisus, whom she caused to die for her love of Minos. In disgust at her deed, Minos left her in Megara, but she swam after the ship and was metamorphosed into a fish or a bird called ciris (Ov. *Met.* 405).

STYMPHALIDES were rapacious birds near the Stymphalian lake in Arcadia, from which they were driven by Heracles and compelled to take refuge in the island of Aretias in the Euxine, where they were afterwards found by the Argonauts. They are described most commonly as voracious birds of prey which attacked even men, armed with brazen wings from which they could shoot out their feathers like arrows (Apollod. 2. 5.2; Paus. 8. 22.4).

TIRESIAS (TEIRESIAS), a son of Everes (or Phorbas) and Chariclo, was one of the most renowned soothsayers in antiquity. He was blind from an early age, and one account says he became blind from seeing Athena in her bath. Chariclo prayed to Athena to restore his sight, but as the goddess was unable to do this, she conferred upon him the power to understand the voices of birds (Apollod. 3. 6.7; Callim. *Lav.Pall.* 75).

See also: Names of individual birds

Blessings

PANDORA. Later writers speak of a vessel of Pandora containing all the blessings of the gods, which would have been preserved for the human race had not Pandora opened the vessel, so that the winged blessings escaped forever.

Blindness

AEPYTUS, a son of Hippothous and king of Arcadia, was struck blind for entering a sanctuary forbidden to all mortals.

ALCATHOUS, son of Aesyetes and one of the Trojan leaders, was slain by Idomeneus with the help of Poseidon, who struck Alcathous with blindness and paralysis so that he could not flee.

AMPHISSA (See METOPE)

ANCHISES. Some accounts say that he was blinded when he boasted of his intercourse with Aphrodite.

BELLEROPHON. When he was thrown from Pegasus while trying to reach heaven, he became lame or blind in consequence (Pind. *Isth.* 7. 44; Hor. *Carm.* 4. 11.26).

DAPHNIS. A Naiad fell in love with him and made him promise to love no other maiden, warning that if he should, he would become blind. He eventually broke his vow and became blind. One writer says that in his blindness he fell from a steep rock and was killed.

EPHIALTES was one of the giants who in the war against the gods was blinded by Apollo and Heracles (Apollod. 1. 6.2).

EROS, the god of love, was often represented with eyes covered so that he acted blindly (Theocrit. 10. 20).

ERYMANTHUS, son of Apollo, was blinded by Aphrodite because he had seen her in the bath. Apollo, in revenge, metamorphosed himself into a boar and killed Adonis.

ILUS. When the temple that housed the Palladium was consumed by fire, Ilus rescued the statue but became blind, as no one was permitted to see it. He propitiated the goddess and recovered his sight (Plut. *Paral.Gr.et Rom.* 17).

LYCURGUS was a son of Dryas and king of the Edones in Thrace. For having persecuted Dionysus and his worship on the sacred mount of Nyseion, he was blinded by Zeus, and died shortly afterwards (Hom. *Il.* 6. 130).

METOPE (AMPHISSA). When she yielded to the embraces of her lover, Aechmodicus, she was blinded by her father, Echetus, the cruel king of Epirus. He gave his daughter iron barley corns, promising to restore her sight if she would grind them into flour (Hom. *Od.* 18. 83, 21. 307; Apollon.Rhod. 4. 1093).

OEDIPUS. When he learned that he had killed his father and married his mother and fathered children by her, he put out his eyes (Apollod. 3.

5.8; Soph. *Oed. Tyr.* 447, 713, 731, 774). When he was exiled, he wandered to Attica, guided by Antigone, his daughter. Some accounts say that he was blinded as an infant by Polybus, who rescued him from a chest which floated on the sea to Sicyon.

ORION, the giant hunter, once visited Oenopion, king of Chios, and sued for the hand of his daughter, Merope (Aero, Aerope, Haero, or Maerope). On one occasion, Orion became intoxicated and raped her. Oenopion blinded him and expelled him from the island. Being informed by an oracle that he would recover his sight if he went towards the east and exposed his eyeballs to the rays of the rising sun, Orion, following the sound of a Cyclops' hammer, went to Lemnos, where Hephaestus gave Cedalion to him as his guide. According to others, Orion stole a boy, whom he carried on his shoulders and who told him the roads. Orion was afterwards cured of his blindness and returned to Chios to take vengeance on Oenopion (Apollod. 1. 4.3).

PHINEUS, son of Agenor and king of Salmydessus in Thrace, was a blind soothsayer. Various accounts of his blindness are given: he was blinded by the gods for revealing to mortals the divine counsels of Zeus about the future (Apollod. 1. 9.21); Aeetes, on hearing that the sons of Phrixus had been saved by Phineus, cursed him, and Helios, father of Aeetes, carried the curse into effect by blinding Phineus; Boreas or the Argonauts blinded him for his inhuman conduct towards his sons. Phineus had punished his sons, when they were falsely accused by his second wife of improper conduct to her. According to most accounts, he put out their eyes (Soph. *Antig.* 973). The sons had their sight restored by the sons of Boreas or by Asclepius.

PHOENIX was a son of Amyntor. His stepmother accused him of making improper advances to her, whereupon Amyntor put out his eyes. Afterwards, he became the companion of Achilles and later had his sight restored to him by Cheiron, the centaur, at the request of Peleus, who also made him king of the Dolopes (Apollod. 3. 13.8; Lycoph. 421; Hom. *Il.* 9. 438, 480).

PLUTUS, the personification of wealth, was described as a son of Iasion and Demeter (Hes. *Theog.* 969; Hom. *Hymn. in Cer.* 491; Hom. *Od.* 5. 125). Zeus was said to have blinded him in order that he would not bestow his favors on righteous men exclusively but so that he would distribute his gifts blindly and without regard to merit (Aristoph. *Plut.* 90).

POLYMESTOR (POLYMNESTOR), king of the Thracian Chersonesus, killed Polydorus, a son of Priam, for treasure that had been entrusted to him for safekeeping. He tossed the body into the sea, and it washed upon the coast. Hecuba and other Trojan captives took vengeance on Polymestor by killing his two children and putting out his eyes (Eurip. *Hec.* 3, 1050; Virg. *Aen.* 3. 49; Ov. *Met.* 13. 432, 536).

POLYPHEMUS. In order to escape his cave, Odysseus contrived to make the Cyclops drunk with wine, and then with a burning pole he destroyed his one eye. Odysseus and his men escaped by hanging on the underside of the sheep which Polyphemus let one by one out of the cave to graze. The blind Cyclops felt only the backs of the sheep as they left the cave.

STESICHORUS had been struck blind after writing a derogatory poem about Helen. She sent word to Autoleon that the poet's vision would be restored if he recanted. He composed a poem in praise of her, and his vision returned. Pausanias (3. 9.11) relates the same story about Leonymus.

THAMYRIS, an ancient Thracian bard, was the son of Philammon and the nymph, Argiope. He went so far in his conceit as to think he could surpass the Muses in song, so they deprived him of his sight and of the power of singing (Hom. *Il.* 2. 595; Apollod. 1. 3.3; Paus. 4. 33.4, 10. 7.2; Eurip. *Rhes.* 925). He was represented with a broken lyre in his hand (Paus. 9. 30.2).

TIRESIAS (TEIRESIAS) was a son of Everes (or Phorbas) and Chariclo and one of the most renowned soothsayers in antiquity. He was blind from his seventh year but lived to a very old age. His blindness was believed to have been caused by his revealing to men things which, according to the will of the gods, they ought not to know or by his seeing Athena while she was bathing, on which occasion the goddess is said to have blinded him by sprinkling water into his face. Chariclo prayed to Athena to restore his sight, but as the goddess was unable to do this, she conferred on him the power to understand the voices of birds and gave him a staff, with the help of which he could walk as safely as if he had his eyesight (Apollod. 3. 6.7; Callim. *Lav.Pall.* 75). According to another tradition, he saw a male and female serpent in the act of mating once on Mt. Cithaeron. He struck them with his staff and, as he happened to kill the female, he himself was changed into a woman. Seven years later, he again saw two serpents together and, now killing the male, he again became a man. It was for this reason that Zeus and Hera, when they were discussing whether a man or a woman enjoyed sexual intercourse more, referred the matter to Tiresias, who could judge for both. Tiresias agreed with Zeus that women derived more pleasure from sex. Hera, indignant at the answer, blinded him, but Zeus gave him the power of prophecy and granted him a life which was to last for seven or nine generations (Apollod. 3. 6.7; Ov. *Met.* 3. 320; Pind. *Nem.* 1. 91).

Blood

ADONIS. After he was killed by a wild boar, Aphrodite, who loved him desperately, caused a blood-red anemone to sprout from his blood.

AESON, father of Jason, killed himself by drinking bull's blood when it seemed evident that the Argonauts would not return (Diod. 4. 50).

AJAX. When he died, a purple flower grew from his blood with the letters *ai* on its petals.

ASCLEPIUS, the god of healing, received from Athena blood that had flowed from the veins of the monster, Gorgo; this blood had the power to restore life.

BELLONA was a Roman goddess of war. When they offered sacrifices to her, her priests, the Bellonarii, had to wound their own arms or legs and either offer up the blood or drink it themselves, in order to become inspired with warlike enthusiasm (Lucan, 1. 565; Mart. 12. 57).

CARDEA, a Roman divinity, protected little children in their cradles from witches who changed themselves into formidable night birds and sought to tear the children from their beds and suck the blood from them.

DEMIPHON. Upon being directed by an oracle to sacrifice a noble maiden each year to avert a pestilence, he did not offer his own daughters to draw lots for the sacrifice. Mastusius, whose daughter had been sacrificed, killed the king's daughters and gave their blood in a cup to the father to drink.

ERINYES, the avenging divinities, sprang from the blood shed when Cronus castrated his father, Uranus.

ERYSICHTHON, son of Triopas, once cut down an oak tree in a grove sacred to Demeter. Since a Dryad lived in the tree, blood ran out from the cuts made by the ax.

EUMENIDES were considered to be the daughters of Gaea, who conceived them in the drops of blood that fell upon her from the body of Uranus (Hes. *Theog.* 185; Apollod. 1. 1.4). They were represented with blood dripping from their eyes.

GIANTS. When Cronus emasculated Uranus, the giants sprang from the spilled blood.

HECATE was a spectral being who at night sent from the lower world the demons and phantoms who dwelt near the blood of murdered persons.

HYACINTHUS. When Apollo accidentally killed him with a thrown discus, he caused a flower to spring from the blood of the slain youth.

ION. When Creusa, his mother, tried to poison him with a cup of poisonous blood from a dragon, her treachery was discovered when Ion poured a libation to the gods before drinking. A pigeon drank of it and died on the spot.

MARSYAS, a Phrygian satyr, challenged Apollo to a musical contest. After being defeated by the god, he was flayed alive, and the blood which ran from his wounds was changed into the river Marsyas.

MELIAE (MELIADES) were the nymphs who, along with the giants and Erinyes, sprang from the drops of blood that fell when Uranus was castrated (Hes. *Theog.* 187).

MIDAS was said to have killed himself by drinking the blood of an ox (Strab. 1. 61; Plut. *De Superst.* 7).

NESSUS was a centaur who was shot with an arrow by Heracles for trying to rape Deianeira, Heracles' wife. Dying, he told her to preserve his blood and use it to guarantee the continued love of her husband. Years later, when Heracles brought Iole home from Oechalia, Deianeira, in order to regain his love, smeared the blood on a garment which she sent Heracles for the wedding. The centaur's blood caused his death, and Deianeira killed herself.

POLYDORUS, son of Priam and Hecuba, was treacherously killed by his brother-in-law, Polymestor and buried in the Thracian Chersonese. Later, Aeneas and his men stopped in the area, and the men gathered cornel and myrtle boughs from the unmarked grave. They noticed that the wood was bleeding, and the voice of Polydorus called out from the grave. They hastily sacrificed to the spirit and left.

Bloodthirst

ERIS, goddess of war, was insatiable in her desire for bloodshed, and after all the other gods withdrew from the battlefield, she remained rejoicing over the havoc that had been made (Hom. *Il.* 5. 518, 11. 3, 73).

Boar

ADMETUS. Pelias promised his daughter, Alcestis, to Admetus if he would come to her in a chariot drawn by lions and boars. Admetus did so with the assistance of Apollo.

ADONIS died from a wound by Apollo metamorphosed into a boar during a chase. (See also APOLLO)

ANCAEUS was killed by the Calydonian boar (Apollod. 1. 9.16, 23; Apollon. Rhod. 2. 894; Ov. *Met.* 8. 400). For a variation, see ANCAEUS under WINE.

APOLLO. When Erymanthus, his son, saw Aphrodite in the bath and was blinded by the goddess, Apollo metamorphosed himself into a boar and killed Adonis, who was beloved by Aphrodite.

APOLLO EPICURUS is a surname meaning helper, under which he was worshipped at Bassae in Arcadia for having delivered the country from a pestilence. Every year, a wild boar was sacrificed to him in his temple on Mt. Lycaeus (Paus. 8. 38.6, 41.5).

ARTEMIS. The boar was sacred to her.

ATYS. Cybele conceived such an attachment for him that Zeus, in his anger at it, sent a wild boar into Lydia that killed many of the inhabitants, including Atys.

HELIOS. Sacrifices to the sun god consisted of boars.

HERACLES. The fourth labor of Heracles consisted of bringing back alive the Erymanthian boar to Mycenae. He did so by chasing it through deep snow until it was exhausted; then he caught it in a net (Apollod. 2. 5.4). After he became deified, boars were sacrificed to him.

HYAS, the brother of the Hyades, was killed in Libya by a boar, according to some traditions.

IDAS. During the Argonauts' expedition, he killed the boar that had destroyed Idmon in the kingdom of Lycus.

IDMON, son of Apollo and one of the Argonauts, was killed in the country of the Mariandynians by a boar or a serpent; or, according to others, he died of a disease (Apollod. 1. 9.23; Apollon. Rhod. 1. 140, 443, 2. 815; Val. Flacc. 5. 2).

MELEAGER. After he killed the Calydonian boar, Artemis created a dispute about the animal's head and skin among the Calydonians and Curetes, which led to various battles. Meleager was depicted as wearing a boar's head (Philostr. *Imag.* 15).

Meleager

ODYSSEUS. When he was staying with his grandfather, Autolycus, on Mt. Parnassus, he was wounded by a boar on a chase. It was by the scar left from that wound that Odysseus was recognized by his aged nurse when he returned from Troy (Paus. 10. 8.4; Ov. *Met.* 11. 295).

OENEUS once neglected to sacrifice to Artemis, who punished him by sending a monstrous boar into the territory of Calydon. This creature became the object of the famous Calydonian boar hunt, which included Meleager and various other heroes (Hom. *Il.* 9. 532).

POSEIDON. Wild boars were sacred to him.

TYDEUS was a fugitive from Calydon to Argos, where Adrastus inferred by the boar device on his shield that he was the fulfillment of an oracle that said one of his daughters would marry a boar.

Boat

CHARON, son of Erebus, was the aged dirty ferryman who conveyed in his boat the shades of the dead.

HELIOS. Later poets described this sun god as sailing in a golden boat round half of the earth to arrive in the east at the point from which he would begin his trip across the heavens.

HEPHAESTUS built the golden boat in which Helios sailed to cause the rising and setting of the sun (Athen. 11. 469; Apollod. 2. 5.10).

HERACLES, annoyed with the heat of the sun, shot arrows at it, and Helios so much admired his boldness that he presented him with a golden boat. Once back in Tartessa, he returned the golden boat to Helios.

MELIBOEA was an Ephesian maiden who loved Alexis. When she was on the point of being married to another, she threw herself from the roof of her house. Uninjured, she escaped to a boat nearby, and its ropes became untied of their own accord. The boat carried her to the self-exiled Alexis, and the happy lovers dedicated a sanctuary to Aphrodite, surnamed Automate and Epidaetia.

SEMELE. The inhabitants of Brasiae in Laconia related that she, after having given birth to Dionysus, was thrown by her father, Cadmus, in a boat upon the sea, and that her body was driven to the coast of Brasiae, where it was buried; Dionysus, whose life was saved, was brought up at Brasiae (Paus. 3. 24.3).

Boatman

CHARON, son of Erebus, was the aged dirty ferryman who conveyed in his boat the shades of the dead across the rivers of the underworld.

PHAON was an old, ugly boatman at Mitylene who very willingly and without accepting payment carried Aphrodite across the sea, for which the goddess gave him youth and beauty. After this, Sappho is said to have fallen in love with him (Lucian, *Dial. Mort.* 9).

Boisterousness

DIONYSUS BACCHUS, "a noisy or riotous god," was originally a Roman surname of Dionysus; this name does not occur till after the time of Herodotus.

Bone

DEUCALION. When after the Flood he prayed to Themis to restore mankind, he and his wife, Pyrrha, were instructed to throw the bones of their mother behind them while walking from the temple. They interpreted bones to mean stones of their mother earth. They threw the stones, and men and women sprang up.

OSSIPAGA (OSSIPANGA, OSSILAGO, or OSSIPAGINA) was a Roman divinity invoked to harden and strengthen the bones of infants.

PELOPS. While the Greeks were engaged in the siege of Troy, they were informed by an oracle that the city could not be taken unless one of the bones of Pelops was brought from Elis to Troas. The shoulder bone accordingly was fetched from Letrina or Pisa but was lost when the ship in which it was carried sank off the coast of Euboea. Many years later it was dragged up from the bottom of the sea by a fisherman, Demarmenus of Eretria, who concealed it in the sand and then consulted the Delphic oracle about it. At Delphi he met ambassadors of the Eleians, who had come to consult the oracle respecting a plague which was ravaging their country. The Pythia requested Demarmenus to give the shoulder bone of Pelops to the Eleians. This was done, and the Eleians appointed Demarmenus to guard the venerable relic (Paus. 5. 13.3). According to some, the Palladium was made of the bones of Pelops (Clem. Alex. *Protrept.* 30; comp. Plin. *H.N.* 28. 4).

Book

ALBUNEA was the tenth Sibyl, who was represented at Tibur holding a book in one hand.

AMALTHEA, one of the Sibyls, is said to have sold the celebrated Sibylline books to King Tarquinius.

CLIO, the Muse of history, appears in a sitting position with an open chest of books.

CLOTHO, one of the Moirae, or Fates, is sometimes represented with a roll (the book of fate).

SIBYLLA, the Cumaean Sibyl, according to tradition, appeared before King Tarquinius, offering him the Sibylline books for sale (Plin. *H.N.* 13. 28; Gell. 1. 10).

TAGES was a mysterious Etruscan being who is described as a boy with the wisdom of an old man. He was the son of a genius (protecting spirit), Jovialis, and grandson of Jupiter. He is said to have instructed the Etruscans in the art of haruspicy. The Etruscans afterwards wrote down all he had said, creating the books of Tages which, according to some, were twelve in number (Cic. *De Div.* 2. 23; Ov. *Met.* 15. 588).

Booty

APOLLO DECATEPHORUS, "the god to whom the tenth part of the booty is dedicated," was his surname at Megara (Paus. 1. 42.5).

ASTYNOME (See CHRYSEIS)

BRISEIS, daughter of Briseus of Lyrnessus, was captured by Achilles, but later was seized by Agamemnon. From this circumstance arose the dire feud between the two greatest Greek heroes in the Trojan War. "Briseis" was a patronymic; her proper name was Hippodameia.

CASSANDRA. When the Greeks divided the booty of Troy, she was given to Agamemnon, who took her with him to Mycenae (Aeschyl. *Agam.* 1260; Paus. 2. 16.5; Hom. *Il.* 13. 365, 24. 699; Hom. *Od.* 11. 420).

CHRYSEIS, daughter of Chryses, a priest of Apollo, was taken prisoner by Achilles and in the division of booty was given to Agamemnon, who, however, was obliged to restore her to her father to soothe the anger of Apollo (Hom. *Il.* 1. 378). Her proper name was Astynome.

CLYMENE, companion of Helen, was given to Acamas when Trojan booty was distributed (Paus. 10. 26.1).

HIPPODAMEIA (See BRISEIS)

JUPITER FERETRIUS. Some believe this surname came from the circumstance that people dedicated to him the spoils that they had plundered (Liv. 1. 10; Propert. 4. 10.46).

PANOPEUS, son of Phocus, accompanied Amphitryon on his expedition against the Taphians or Teleboans and took an oath by Athena and Ares not to embezzle any part of the booty. But he broke his oath, and, as a punishment, his son, Epeius, became unwarlike.

Boundaries

HERMES, the messenger god, was also guardian of boundaries.

JUPITER TERMINUS was his surname at Rome as protector of boundaries, not only of personal property but also of the state.

SILVANUS was a Latin divinity of the fields and forests. He was called the protector of boundaries of fields (Hor. *Epod.* 2. 22) because he was the first to set up stones to mark them. Every estate had three Silvani (gods presiding over the points at which an estate began).

TERMINUS was a Roman divinity presiding over boundaries and frontiers. His worship is said to have been instituted by Numa, who ordered that everyone should mark the boundaries of his landed property by stones to be consecrated to Jupiter and at which every year sacrifices were to be offered at the festival of the Terminalia (Dionys. 2. 9, 74).

Bow

APOLLO. At his birth he was fed nectar and ambrosia and immediately sprang up and demanded a lyre and a bow. (See also EURYTUS)

ARTEMIS. The Arcadian Artemis was represented carrying a bow.

ARTEMIS AGROTERA. At Agrae, she had a temple with a statue carrying a bow.

EURYTUS, son of Melaneus and Stratonice, was king of Oechalia in Thessaly and a skillful archer. He was said to have instructed Heracles in the use of the bow (Theocrit. 24. 105; Apollod. 2. 4.9). He offered his daughter, Iole, as prize to whoever could conquer him and his sons in shooting with the bow. Heracles won the prize, but Eurytus and his sons refused to give up Iole, whereupon Heracles marched on Oechalia and slew Eurytus and his sons (Apollod. 2. 7.7). According to Homeric poems, Eurytus was killed by Apollo, whom he presumed to rival in using the bow.

HERACLES. For defeating the forces of Erginus, he was presented with a bow by Apollo. (See also EURYTUS)

IPHITUS, son of Eurytus, gave Odysseus his father's famous bow while both the young men were seeking stolen livestock in Messene.

MERIONES. When Diomedes chose Odysseus for his companion on the exploring expedition to the Trojan camp, Meriones gave the latter his bow, quiver, sword, and famous helmet (Hom. *Il.* 10. 662). At the funeral games of Patroclus, Meriones won the first prize in shooting with the bow.

ODYSSEUS received from Iphitus the famous bow of Eurytus. This bow Odysseus used only at Ithaca, regarding it as too great a treasure to be employed in the field. It was so strong that none of the suitors of Penelope was able to handle it (Hom. *Od.* 21. 14). They were subsequently slain by the same bow. (See also MERIONES)

PHILOCTETES was a son of Poeas and friend of Heracles, who instructed him in the use of the bow and bequeathed him his bow with the never-erring poisoned arrows. After the Trojan War, he founded a sanctuary of Apollo Alaeus in Crimissa in Italy, where he dedicated the bow (Strab. 6. 254).

SCYTHES, son of Heracles and Echidna, became the king of the Scythians—according to his father's arrangement—because he was able to manage the bow which Heracles had left behind and to use his father's girdle (Herod. 4. 8–10).

TEUTARUS was the original owner of the bow that was used by Heracles (Lycoph. 56).

VENUS CALVA was the surname under which Venus had two temples in the neighborhood of the Capitoline Hill. Some believed that one of them had been built as a monument to a patriotic act of the Roman women, who, during the siege of the Gauls, cut off their hair and gave it to the men to make strings for their bows. *Calva* means a bald head.

Box

PANDORA. Her curiosity led her to open a forbidden box, from which all earth's ills escaped.

PERSEPHONE. In works of art she appears as a mystical divinity with a sceptre and a little box.

See also: CHEST

Boxing

AMYCUS was king of the Bebryces. When the Argonauts landed on his coast, he challenged the bravest of them to a boxing match. Polydeuces, who accepted the challenge, killed him (Apollod. 1. 9.20).

EPEIUS, son of Panopeus, was the only one to conquer Euryalus in any contest at the funeral games of Oedipus; this contest was in boxing (Hom. *Il.* 23. 675–99).

EUTHYMUS, hero of Locri in Italy, was a son of Astycles and famous for his strength and skill in boxing. He gained several victories at Olympia (Pind. *Ol.* 74, 76, 77).

HERMES was said to have invented boxing.

PHORBAS, son of Lapithes, was described as a bold boxer.

POLYDEUCES, one of the Dioscuri, was famous for his skill in boxing. (See also AMYCUS)

Brain

TYDEUS was a son of Oeneus and Periboea. When Tydeus was mortally wounded at the battle of Thebes, Athena appeared with a remedy which was to make him immortal, but Amphiaraus, who hated Tydeus, brought him a different remedy: the head of the vanquished enemy, Melanippus. Tydeus cut it in two and ate the brain, or devoured some of the flesh. Athena, seeing this, shuddered and did not apply the remedy which she had brought (Apollod. 3. 6.8). Tydeus died and was buried at Mecon (Paus. 9. 18.2).

Brass

EMPUSA was a monster which was sent by Hecate to frighten strangers. It was believed usually to appear with one leg of brass and the other of an ass (Aristoph. *Ran.* 294; Aristoph. *Eccles.* 1094).

TALOS, a man of brass, was the work of Hephaestus. This creature was given to Minos by Zeus or Hephaestus and watched the island of Crete by walking around the island three times each day. Whenever he saw strangers approaching, he made himself red-hot in fire, then embraced them when they landed. He had in his body only one vein, which ran from the head to the ankles and was closed at the top with a nail. When he attempted to keep the Argonauts from Crete by throwing stones at them, Medea, by her magic powers, threw him into a state of madness and took the nail out of his vein causing him to bleed to death (Apollon. Rhod. 4. 1638).

Bravery

ACHILLES was the bravest of the Greeks at Troy.

DEIPHOBUS, son of Priam, was, next to Hector, the bravest of the Trojans.

DIOMEDES, next to Achilles, was the bravest of the Greeks at Troy.

EURYALUS accompanied Diomedes to Troy, where he was one of the bravest heroes and slew a great number of Trojans (Hom. *Il.* 2. 565, 6. 20; Paus. 2. 30.9).

HECTOR, son of Priam, was the bravest of the Trojans.

IDOMENEUS, king of Crete, was one of the bravest heroes in the Trojan War, even though he was older than most of his companions.

NERIO (NERIENE or NERIENIS) was the wife of the Roman god Mars. Little is known about her, but her name is said to be of Sabine origin and to be synonymous with *virtus* or *fortitudo* (Plaut. *Truc.* 2. 6.24).

VIRTUS was the Roman personification of manly valor. She was represented with a short tunic, her right breast exposed, a helmet on her head, a spear in her left hand, a sword in her right, and standing with her right foot on a helmet.

Bread

ARCAS, son of Zeus and Callisto, after succeeding to the government of Arcadia, taught his subjects the art of breadmaking (Paus. 8. 4.1).

FORNAX was a goddess at Rome who presided over baking of bread.

JUPITER PISTOR, "the baker," was Jupiter's surname at Rome, because, according to tradition, when the Gauls were besieging Rome, the god suggested to the Romans the idea of throwing loaves of bread among the enemies to make them believe that the Romans had plenty of provisions and thus caused them to give up the siege (Ov. *Fast.* 6. 359, 394).

Breast

AMAZONS. All female children of the Amazons had their right breast cut off, so that when they became warriors the breast would not interfere with their pulling a bowstring.

GAEA EURYSTERNOS, "the goddess with the broad chest," was the surname under which Gaea had a sanctuary on the Crathis near Aegae in Achaia (Paus. 5. 14.8, 7. 25.8).

PISTAS was a personification of faithful attachments, love, and veneration among the Romans. She was sometimes represented as a female figure offering her breast to an aged parent.

Breastplate

ATHENA. After Perseus cut off the head of Medusa, he gave it to Athena, who placed it in the center of her shield or breastplate.

Bribery

BATTUS. When he observed Hermes stealing the cattle of Apollo, the god bribed him to keep the secret, but, not trusting Battus, returned later in disguise and bribed the old man to reveal it. When Battus did, he was changed by Hermes into a stone (Ov. *Met.* 2. 688).

INO by her artifices brought about a famine. When Athamas, her husband, sent messengers to Delphi to consult the oracle, she bribed them to report that Phrixus, his son by Nephele, must be sacrificed to end the famine.

MYRTILUS was the charioteer of Oenomaus, king of Pisa, who forced all suitors of his daughter, Hippodameia, to compete with him in a chariot race, which he invariably won. Pelops bribed Myrtilus to remove the nails from Oenomaus' chariot so that he was able to win the race and marry Hippodameia.

Brick

HYPERBIUS, a mythical artist of Corinth, was said to be, in conjunction with Agrolas or Euryalus, the inventor of brick walls.

LATERANUS was a Roman divinity protecting hearths built of bricks (*lateres*).

Bride

FORTUNA VIRGINENSIS was the surname under which Fortuna was worshipped by newly married women, who dedicated their maiden garments and girdles in her temple.

JUNO DOMIDUCA was Juno's surname at Rome as the goddess of marriage, who conducted the bride into the house of the bridegroom (August. 7. 3, 9. 6).

JUPITER DOMIDUCUS was Jupiter's surname at Rome as the god of marriage, who conducted the bride into the house of the bridegroom.

VENUS CALVA. This name probably refers to the fact that on her wedding day the bride, either actually or symbolically, cut off a lock of hair to sacrifice to Venus. *Calva* means a bald head.

See also: MARRIAGE

Bridge

DIONYSUS. In his wanderings he built a bridge to cross a river, but a tiger sent to him by Zeus carried him across the river, which was then called Tigris.

Bridle

ATHENA invented the bridle for horses. (See also BELLEROPHON)

ATHENA CHALINITIS was a surname describing the goddess as the tamer of horses by means of the bridle. Under this name she had a temple at Corinth. She was said to have so tamed Pegasus before she gave him to Bellerophon (Paus. 2. 4.1).

BELLEROPHON desired to obtain possession of the winged horse, Pegasus. The soothsayer Polyidus of Corinth advised him to spend a night in the temple of Athena and, as Bellerophon was sleeping, the goddess appeared to him in a dream, commanded him to sacrifice to Poseidon, and gave him a golden bridle. When he awoke he found the bridle, offered the sacrifice, and caught Pegasus (Pind. *Ol.* 13. 90; Strab. 8. 379).

NEMESIS, the goddess of retribution, sometimes is represented in a pensive mood, holding in her left hand a bridle or a branch of an ash tree and in her right hand a wheel, along with a sword or a scourge.

PELETHRONIUS was the reputed inventor of the bridle and saddle. (Plin. *H.N.* 7. 56).

POSEIDON taught men the art of managing horses by the bridle.

Bull

ACHELOUS. In a contest with Heracles, Achelous assumed the form of a bull, but his horn was broken off and, to recover it, he had to surrender the horn of Amalthea.

ANDROGEUS, son of Minos, was sent by Aegeus to fight the Marathonian bull, which killed him. This event occasioned the payment by Attica of the fearful tribute to Crete—the sacrifice of youths and maidens to the Minotaur.

ARGUS PANOPTES slew a fierce bull that ravaged Arcadia, and afterwards appeared wearing its hide.

ARTEMIS TAURIONE (TAURO, TAUROPOLOS, or TAUROPOS). Under these names she was identified with the Taurian goddess. The name is explained either by the idea of the goddess protecting the country of Tauris or the goddess to whom bulls are sacrificed. Others interpret it to mean a goddess riding on bulls, drawn by bulls, or killing bulls. All ideas indicate that the bull was central to the ancient bloody worship of the Taurian divinity (Eurip. *Iphig.Taur.* 1457).

ATHENA. Sacrifices offered to her included bulls, rams, and cows.

ATHENA TAURIONE (TAURO, TAUROPOLOS, or TAUROPOS) was sometimes identified with the Taurian goddess. The name symbolizes either the goddess protecting the country of Tauris or the goddess to whom bulls are sacrificed (Eurip. *Iphig.Taur.* 1457).

CYCNUS imposed on his persistent admirer, Phyllius, three tasks, one of which was to lead with his own hands a bull to the altar of Zeus. Later, in accordance with a request from Heracles, Phyllius refused to give Cycnus the bull, which he had received as a prize, and Cycnus, in exasperation, leaped into a lake.

DEMETER. Sacrifices to her included bulls.

DIDO. Landing on the coast of Carthage, she negotiated to buy as much land as could be covered with the hide of a bull. She had the hide cut into the thinnest possible strips and with them she surrounded a great extent of the country, which she called Byrsa, the hide of a bull (Virg. *Aen.* 1. 367). In laying the foundations for the city that was to become Carthage, the head of a bull was found, and this was thought to be a favorable sign.

DIONYSUS. When the sisters Alcathoe, Leucippe, and Arsippe, refused to attend his revels, he assumed different forms—one of them a bull—and drove them mad.

DIONYSUS TAUROCEPHALUS was the surname, meaning bull's head, of the god in the Orphic mysteries.

DIONYSUS TAURUS, his surname meaning the bull (Eurip. *Bacch.* 918; Athen. 11. 476; Plut. *Quaest.Gr.* 36; Lycoph. 209).

DIRCE. In vengeance for her ill-treatment of Antiope, their mother, Amphion and Zethus tied Dirce to a bull, which dragged her until she was dead.

EUROPA, daughter of Agenor and sister of Cadmus, was carried from Phoenicia to Crete by Zeus, who had metamorphosed himself into a bull (Apollod. 3. 1. 1; Mosch. 2. 7; Herod. 1. 173; Paus. 7. 4.1, 9. 19.1).

HELIOS. Sacrifices to the sun god included bulls.

HERACLES. The seventh labor of Heracles was to bring the Cretan bull alive to Eurystheus. This bull was, according to some, the one that brought Europa to Crete. According to others, it had been sent by Poseidon to be sacrificed by Minos, who because of the bull's extraordinary beauty refused to sacrifice it. Poseidon punished Minos by having the bull go mad and cause great destruction in Crete. Heracles caught the bull and later let it go; after that it figured in the Theseus stories. Heracles was also said to have instituted an annual festival at Syracuse at the well of Cyane, where a bull was sunk into the well as a sacrifice (Diod. 5. 4). After Heracles was deified, sacrifices to him included bulls.

HERACLES BUPHAGUS was a name given from his having eaten a whole bull at once (Apollod. 2. 5.11, 7.7).

HIPPOLYTUS, cursed by his father, Theseus, for allegedly making improper advances to Phaedra, his step-mother, was thrown and dragged to death when a bull appeared from the sea and frightened the horses which drew the chariot in which he was riding.

IPHIGENEIA. When she was on the point of being sacrificed by the Greeks at Aulis, Artemis carried her away and, according to some, substituted a bull for the sacrifice.

JASON. One of the tasks Aeetes imposed on him in promised exchange for the golden fleece was the yoking of brazen-footed and fire-breathing bulls to a plow.

MA (See RHEA)

MELICERTES. When his body, washed up on the shore of the Corinthian isthmus, was found by his uncle, Sisyphus, it was carried to Corinth. On the command of the Nereids, Sisyphus instituted the Isthmian games and sacrifices of black bulls in honor of Melicertes, who was deified under the name Palaemon (Philostr. *Imag.* 2. 16; Paus. 2. 1.3).

MINOS. After the death of Asterius, Minos wanted to be king of Crete, claiming that it was destined to him by the gods. As he was offering a sacrifice to Poseidon, he prayed that a bull might come forth from the sea and promised to sacrifice the animal. The bull appeared, and Minos became king of Crete; but he refused to sacrifice the beautiful animal, so Poseidon caused Pasiphae, the wife of Minos, to conceive a passion for the animal. She concealed herself in an artificial cow made by Daedalus and impregnated by the bull, became the mother of the Minotaur. (See also HERACLES)

MINOTAUR, offspring of Pasiphae and a bull, was the fearful creature imprisoned in the Cretan labyrinth. He had the head of a bull and the body of a man. Attic youths and maidens were thrust into the labyrinth and devoured by him, until Theseus killed him.

PALAEMON (See MELICERTES)

PARIS found out about his true parentage in the following way: Priam was going to celebrate a funeral solemnity for Paris, whom he believed to be dead, so he ordered a bull to be fetched from the herd, to be given as a prize to the victor in the games. The king's servants took the favorite bull of Paris, who therefore followed his pet, took part in the games, and conquered his brothers. Deiphobus drew his sword against him, but Paris fled to the altar of Zeus Herceius, and there Cassandra declared him to be her brother, and Priam received him as his son.

POSEIDON. Sacrifices to him generally consisted of black and white bulls (Hom. *Od.* 3. 6;

Hom. *Il.* 20. 404; Pind. *Ol.* 13. 93; Virg. *Aen.* 5. 237). (See also MINOS)

POSEIDON TAUREUS was a surname given because bulls were sacrificed to him or because he was the divinity who gave green pasture to bulls on the sea coast (Hes. *Scut.Herc.* 104; Hom. *Od.* 3.6).

RHEA was called Ma by the Lydians, and bulls were sacrificed to her. From this custom the name of the town Mastaura was derived.

THESEUS. Among his early enterprises was the destruction of the Marathonian bull, a feat in which Androgeus, the son of Minos, had perished, resulting in the demand of tribute of seven youths and seven maidens from Attica to be sacrificed to the Minotaur.

ZEUS, in the form of a bull, carried off Europa and landed at Gortyn in Crete, where he was worshipped under the name of Hecatombaeus. Bulls were sacred to him.

ZEUS ATABYRIUS. This surname was derived from Mt. Atabyrius, or Atabyrion, in Rhodes, where the Cretan, Althemenes, was said to have built a temple to him (Apollod. 3. 2.1). Upon this mountain there were, it is said, brazen bulls which roared when anything extraordinary was going to happen.

Burial

AETOLUS. When he died in childhood, his parents, Oxylus and Pieria, were instructed by an oracle to bury him neither within nor without the town of Elis, so he was buried under the gate where the road led to Olympia.

ANTIGONE. When she defied the edict of Creon against the burial of the slain in the battle of the Seven against Thebes, she was buried alive in the tomb where she had placed her brother, Polyneices (Apollod. 3. 7.1).

ATYS. An oracle commanded that his body be buried in order to avert a plague, but the body was already in a state of decomposition, so funeral honors were paid to an image of him (Diod. 3. 58).

CREON was the king of Thebes who refused to allow burial of the bodies of the fallen heroes after the battle of the Seven against Thebes.

LEUCOTHOE, daughter of Orchamus and Eurynome, was beloved by Apollo; but her love was betrayed by the jealous Clytia to her father, who buried her alive, whereupon Apollo metamorphosed her into an incense shrub (Ov. *Met.* 4. 208).

LIBITINA was an ancient Italian divinity associated with the dead and their burial. Her temple at Rome was a repository of everything necessary for burials, where persons might either buy or hire those things.

MANES were Roman divinities of the dead and were thought to hover over burial places.

SISYPHUS. Before he died, he asked his wife not to bury him. She complied with his request, but in the lower world Sisyphus complained of being neglected and desired the rulers of the underworld to allow him to return to the upper world to punish his wife. When this request was granted, he refused to return to the lower world, until Hermes carried him back by force. This piece of treachery is said to have accounted for his special punishment in the lower world (Hor. *Carm.* 2. 24.20).

See also: FUNERAL

Butterfly

PSYCHE was the beloved of Amor (Cupid). In works of art, she is represented as a maiden with the wings of a butterfly.

Buttocks

APHRODITE CALLIPYGOS was a surname meaning beautiful buttocks (Athen. 12. 554; Alciph. 1. 39).

Cake

CECROPS abolished human sacrifices in Attica by substituting cakes (Paus. 8. 2.1; Strab. 9. 397).

HERMES. Cakes were among the sacrifices offered to him.

IRIS was the goddess of the rainbow. The Delians offered cakes made of wheat and honey and dried figs to her.

JANUS. Cakes were among the sacrifices offered to him.

PRIAPUS was the son of Dionysus and Aphrodite and god of the fructifying powers and manifestations of nature. Sacrifices to him included cakes.

TERMINUS was a Roman divinity presiding over boundaries and frontiers. Sacrifices of cakes, meal, and fruit were offered at the stone boundary markers each year, since it was unlawful to stain the boundary stones with blood.

ZEUS HYPATUS, "the most high." An altar of Zeus Hypatus existed at Athens in front of the Erechtheum, and only cakes could be offered to him at the altar (Paus. 1. 26.6, 8. 2.1). Zeus Hypatus was also worshipped at Sparta (Paus. 3. 17.3) and at Glisas near Sparta (Paus. 9. 19.3).

Calamity

CONSENTES DII were the twelve Etruscan gods who formed the council of Jupiter. He consulted them when he intended to announce great calamities to mankind (Senec. *Quaest.Nat.* 2. 41).

Calf

MINERVA. Her sacrifices included calves that had not borne the yoke or felt the sting of a whip.

Canal

EUROTAS, son of Myles, was said to have carried the waters stagnating in the plain of Lacedaemon into the sea by means of a canal, and to have called the river that arose Eurotas, after his own name (Paus. 3. 1.2).

Cannibalism

ANTHROPOPHAGI were Scythians who fed on human flesh.

ANTIPHATES, king of Lamus in Telepylos, ruled over the Laestrygones, who were cannibals. Odysseus escaped from them with only one ship (Hom. *Od.* 10. 80).

CLYMENUS was served the flesh of his own son by his daughter, Harpalyce, whom he had raped.

CRONUS was the youngest of the Titans. When Rhea, his wife, delivered children to him, he devoured them so that his rule would not be overthrown by one of his offspring.

CYCLOPES. In Homeric poems, the Cyclopes are a gigantic, insolent, and lawless race of shepherds who lived in Sicily and devoured human beings (Hom. *Od.* 6. 5, 9. 106, 190, 240, 10. 200).

DIONYSUS. When the people of Argos refused to acknowledge him as a god, he drove the Argive women mad to such a degree that they killed their own babies and devoured their flesh (Apollod. 3. 5.2).

EMPUSA was a monstrous spectre who was believed to devour human beings. The Lamiae and Mormotyceiae, who assumed the form of handsome women for the purpose of attracting young men and then sucked their blood like vampires and ate their flesh, were reckoned among the Empusae (Philostr. *Vit.Apoll.* 4. 25).

EURYNOMUS was a daemon of the lower world. At Delphi there was a tradition that he devoured the flesh of dead human bodies and left nothing but the bones. He was represented sitting on the skin of a vulture (Paus. 10. 28.4).

MINEIDES were daughters of Minyas who, because they derided the orgies of Dionysus, were afflicted with the unconquerable desire to eat human flesh.

MINOTAUR, offspring of Pasiphae and a bull, was the fearful creature, half-man, half-bull, penned in the labyrinth, where he fed on human flesh.

POLYPHEMUS, the Cyclops, son of Poseidon and Thoosa, devoured six of the companions of Odysseus and kept Odysseus and his other companions as prisoners in his cave for future meals.

POLYTECHNUS. His son, Itys, was killed and served to him by Aedon and Chelidonis after Polytechnus had raped Chelidonis and forced her to pose as a slave to Aedon, his wife.

SCYLLA was the monster who inhabited one of the rocks between which Odysseus was forced to sail. She devoured six of his companions (Hom. *Od.* 12. 73, 235).

TANTALUS, a favorite of the gods, once invited them to a feast. For that occasion, he slaughtered Pelops, his son, and, having boiled him, set the flesh before the gods. They divined what it was and did not touch it. Demeter alone, absorbed with grief for the loss of Persephone, consumed the shoulder of Pelops. The gods ordered Hermes to put the limbs of Pelops into a cauldron and restore him to life and former appearance. When the process was over, Clotho, one of the Fates, found that the shoulder devoured by Demeter was missing. Demeter supplied one made of ivory in its place. His descendants the Pelopidae, as a mark of their origin, were believed to have one shoulder as white as ivory (Pind. *Ol.* 1. 37; Virg. *Georg.* 3. 7; Ov. *Met.* 6. 404).

TEREUS. When Procne, his first wife, learned that he had hidden away and then raped and cut out the tongue of her sister, Philomela, she killed Itys, her son by Tereus, and served his flesh to Tereus.

THYESTES was served the flesh of his two sons, Tantalus and Pleisthenes, by Atreus, his brother, in revenge for the many outrages committed on him by Thyestes.

TYDEUS was a son of Oeneus and Periboea. When Tydeus was mortally wounded at the battle of Thebes, Athena appeared with a remedy which was to make him immortal, but Amphiaraus, who hated Tydeus, brought him a different remedy: the head of the vanquished enemy, Melanippus. Tydeus cut it in two and ate the brain, or devoured some of the flesh. Athena, seeing this, shuddered and did not apply the remedy which she had brought (Apollod. 3. 6.8). Tydeus died and was buried at Mecon (Paus. 9. 18.2).

ZEUS. When Metis prophesied that she would give birth to a girl who was destined to rule the world, he devoured her when she was pregnant with Athena. Lycaon, the Arcadian king, once served the flesh of Arcas, his son, to Zeus to test his divine character. Zeus destroyed Lycaon's house and restored Arcas to life. Maenalus, a descendant of Lycaon, with his kinsmen invited Zeus to a repast, and the hosts mixed in one of the dishes set before him the entrails of a boy whom they had murdered. According to Ovid, Zeus recognized these deceptions and changed Lycaon and his sons into wolves.

Cap

GANYMEDE was frequently represented in works of art as a beautiful youth with the Phrygian cap.

HEPHAESTUS, god of fire, was represented in art wearing an oval cap.

JUPITER. The color white was sacred to Jupiter, and his priests wore white caps.

LIBERTAS, the Roman divinity of freedom, was sometimes represented holding the Phrygian cap in her hand (Dio Cass. 47. 25, 63. 29; Suet. *Ner.* 57). This cap, called a pileus, was a symbol of liberty.

MIDAS. When he decided in favor of Pan over Apollo in a musical contest, Apollo punished him by changing his ears into those of an ass. Midas concealed them under his Phrygian cap, but the servant who cut his hair discovered them (Ov. *Met.* 11. 146; Aristoph. *Plut.* 287).

ODYSSEUS. In works of art he was commonly represented as a sailor wearing the semi-oval cap of a sailor (Plin. *H.N.* 35. 36; Paus. 10. 26.1, 29.2).

PARIS. In works of art he was represented wearing a Phrygian cap.

See also: HAT

Care

CURA, in Rome, was a personification of care.

Carpentry

DAEDALUS was the reputed inventor of carpentry.

Cat

GALINTHIAS (GALANTHIS). When she deluded the goddesses of childbirth so that Alcmena, her friend, was able to give birth to Heracles, she was punished by being metamorphosed into a weasel or cat.

LIBERTAS was the Roman divinity of freedom. The cat was sacred to her.

Cattle

APOLLO, for displeasing Zeus, was required to work for Laomedon by guarding his cattle in the valleys of Mt. Ida (Hom. *Il.* 21. 488).

BATTUS observed Hermes stealing the cattle of Apollo, and the god bribed Battus to keep the secret. When Battus did not, he was changed into a stone (Ov. *Met.* 2. 688).

CACA, sister of Cacus, betrayed the place where the cattle were concealed which Cacus had stolen from Heracles or Recaranus.

CACUS, a giant son of Vulcan, stole part of the cattle of Heracles or Recaranus and dragged the animals into his cave by their tails so that they left no tracks.

ELECTRYON. Taphius and the sons of Pterelaus quarreled with Electryon and stole his cattle. In recovering them, Electryon was accidentally killed by Amphitryon.

FAUNUS, son of Picus and king of the Laurentes, promoted agriculture and the breeding of cattle among his subjects (Plin. *H.N.* 9. 6; Propert. 4. 2.34).

HECATE was a mysterious divinity who bestowed prosperity to flocks of cattle.

HERACLES was sent by Amphitryon to attend his cattle to prevent further insane outbursts, such as Heracles' slaying of Linus. The fifth labor of Heracles consisted of cleansing the Augean stables. He stipulated that a reward of one tenth of the cattle be given for the task. The debt was not paid, and Heracles killed Augeus and his sons.

SILVANUS was a Latin divinity of the fields and forests. He is described as the divinity protecting flocks and cattle, warding off wolves, and promoting the fertility of flocks (Virg. *Aen.* 8. 601; Tibull. 1. 5.27; Cato 83).

See also: CALF, COW, HEIFER, BULL, OX

Cauldron

DIONYSUS. According to one story, his body was cut up and thrown into a cauldron by the Titans, and he was restored by Rhea or Demeter (Paus. 8. 37.3; Diod. 3. 62).

MEDEA. In order to take vengeance on Pelias for all the crimes he had committed against Jason, she persuaded the daughters of Pelias to cut their father into pieces and boil his limbs in a cauldron, thus making him young again. She had demonstrated the process earlier by changing a ram into a lamb. But Pelias remained dead.

MELICERTES, son of Athamas and Ino, according to some traditions, died in a cauldron filled with boiling water (Plat. *Sympos.* 5. 3; Ov. *Met.* 4. 505, 520).

PELEUS once observed his wife, Thetis, holding the infant Achilles over a fire (or in a cauldron of boiling water), in order to destroy in him those parts that he had inherited from his father and which were, therefore, mortal. Peleus was terror-struck and screamed so loud that she was prevented from completing her work.

PELOPS was killed and dismembered by his father, but the gods ordered Hermes to put the limbs into a cauldron and thereby restore his life and former appearance.

Cave

AEOLUS was keeper of the winds, which he confined in a cave until they were needed.

ANIGRIDES were nymphs of the river Anigrus in Elis. In a grotto there, persons suffering from skin diseases were cured by prayers and sacrifices to the nymphs.

ANTIGONE. According to Sophocles, she was shut up in a subterranean cave for defying Creon's edict that the slain agressors in the battle of the Seven against Thebes should not be buried.

CACUS. When he stole the cattle of Heracles or Recaranus, he dragged them into a cave by their tails so they would leave no tracks.

DIONYSUS was carried as an infant to a cave in the neighborhood of Nysa on a lonely island formed by the river Triton. He was brought up by Nysa, the daughter of Aristaeus.

ECHIDNA, the monster, lived with her husband Typhon in a cave. She stole Heracles' horses once, and when he came to her cave and demanded them back, she promised to restore them if he would stay with her awhile. He complied and became by her father of Agathyrsus, Gelonus, and Scythes.

EILEITHYIA (ELEUTHO), goddess of birth, was believed to have been born in a cave in the territory of Cnossus.

HEPHAESTUS. Upon being cast from Olympus, he was rescued by the marine divinities, Thetis and Eurynome, with whom he dwelt in a grotto for nine years (Hom. *Il.* 18. 394).

ION, son of Apollo by Creusa, was born at Athens in the cave under the Propylaea, where he was also conceived. He was also exposed by his mother in the cave but was rescued by his father and conveyed to Delphi.

LINUS was a son of Apollo. His image stood in a hollow rock formed in the shape of a grotto near Mt. Helicon. There, every year, a funeral sacrifice was offered to him, and dirges were sung in his honor.

OREIADES were nymphs associated with mountains and grottoes.

PALINURUS. The Sibyl commanded Aeneas to atone for the murder of his helmsman Palinurus, by erecting a tomb for him and dedicating a cave to him (Virg. *Aen.* 6. 337; Strab. 6. 252).

POLYPHEMUS, the Cyclops, kept Odysseus and his companions prisoners in his cave in Sicily, until Odysseus put out his single eye and escaped with his men.

SPHRAGITIDES was a surname of a class of prophetic nymphs on Mt. Cithaeron in Boeotia, where they had a grotto (Plut. *Aristid.* 9; Paus. 9. 3; Plut. *Quaest. Conviv.* 1. 10).

Cedar

ARTEMIS CEDREATIS was her surname in Orchomenus because her images were hung on lofty cedars.

Chain

ANDROMEDA was chained to a rock to be devoured by a sea monster but was rescued by Perseus (Apollod. 2. 4.3; Ov. *Met.* 4. 663).

ARES was chained by the Aloidae, who kept him prisoner until Hermes freed him (Hom. *Il.* 5. 385). A statue of him at Sparta depicted him with chained feet to express the idea that victory and courage would always remain in the city (Paus. 1. 22.4, 3. 15.5).

ENYALIUS, in the *Iliad,* was an epithet of Ares, but in later times Enyalius and Ares were distinguished as two separate gods of war. Enyalius was thought to be the son of Ares and Enyo. Near the temple of Hipposthenes at Sparta there stood an ancient fettered statue considered by some (Paus 3. 15.5) to be that of Enyalius. (Cf. ARES)

HERA. In conjunction with Poseidon and Athena, she contemplated putting Zeus into chains (Hom. *Il.* 8. 408, 1. 399). For this or a similar act, Zeus once hung her up in the clouds with her hands chained and with two anvils suspended from her feet (Hom. *Il.* 8. 400, 477, 15. 17).

HESIONE was the daughter of Laomedon, who was commanded by an oracle to chain her to a rock to be eaten by wild beasts in order to stop a plague sent on Troy.

IXION. As punishment for his lust for Hera, he was chained by Hermes to a wheel, which is described as winged or fiery; it is said to have rolled perpetually in the air (or in the lower world).

LYCURGUS of Thrace was put in chains and torn to pieces by horses for having brought a famine on the land of the Edones by inhospitable treatment of Dionysus, when the Edones were told that the famine would end only with his death.

OTUS and his brother, Ephialtes, put Ares in chains and kept him imprisoned for thirteen months (Hom. *Il.* 5. 385).

SISYPHUS. Some say that Zeus, in order to take revenge on the treachery of Sisyphus, sent Death to Sisyphus, who, however, succeeded in putting Death in chains, so that no man died until Ares delivered death. When this happened, Sisyphus himself expired.

Chair

HEPHAESTUS, son of Zeus and Hera, wished to find out his parentage and so constructed a chair that those who sat on it could be released only at his command. Having thus trapped Hera, he forced her to tell him who his parents were.

PEIRITHOUS was a king of the Lapiths and a friend of Theseus. He rashly decided to abduct Persephone, queen of the underworld, and he and Theseus came to Hades to announce their intention. Hades invited them to sit, and the unsuspecting interlopers were unable to rise from the chairs provided. Theseus was eventually rescued by Heracles, but Peirithous remained a prisoner forever (Apollod. 1. 8.2; Hom. *Il.* 14. 317; Paus. 1. 2.1, 3. 18.15, 10. 29.9; Ov. *Met.* 12. 210).

Chamois

ARTEMIS AEGINAEA was a surname meaning, according to some, huntress of the chamois (Paus. 3. 14.3).

BONA DEA. The chamois was sacred to her.

See also: GOAT

Chance, see Luck

Chaos

CHAOS, one of the oldest of the gods, was the rude and shapeless mass which existed before the formation of the universe.

Charcoal

ASOPUS, the river god, was confined by one of Zeus' thunderbolts to his river bed, after he had tried to revolt because of Zeus' abduction of his daughter, Aegina. Pieces of charcoal later found in the river were believed to have been produced by this lightning (Paus. 2. 5.1). Three rivers in Greece had this name, but it is likely that this river was located in the Peloponnesus and emptied into the Gulf of Corinth.

Chariot

ADMETUS. Pelias promised his daughter, Alcestis, to Admetus if he would come to her in a chariot drawn by lions and boars. Admetus did so with assistance from Apollo.

AETOLUS. At the funeral games of Azan, he ran his chariot over Apis, the son of Jason, and was expelled from the kingdom of Elis.

ATALANTA (ATALANTE). When she and her husband, Meilanion or Hippomenes, consummated their marriage in a grove sacred to Cybele, she metamorphosed them into lions and yoked them to her chariot (Ov. *Met.* 8. 318, 10. 565).

ATHENA invented the chariot. (See also ENCELADUS)

BITON and his brother Cleobis, when the oxen failed to arrive in time to pull the chariot which was bearing their mother, Cydippe, a priestess, to the temple of Athena, dragged the chariot with their mother a distance of forty-five stadia to the temple. The priestess prayed to the goddess to grant them what was best for mortals, and Athena put them to sleep never to waken (Herod. 1. 31).

CENTAURS. In later times they were described as drawing the chariot of Dionysus.

CHRYSIPPUS, son of Pelops, was carried off while still a boy by Laius of Thebes, who instructed him in driving the chariot (Apollod. 3. 5.5).

CITHAERON. In order to settle a quarrel between Zeus and Hera, he persuaded Zeus to take into his chariot a wooden statue and dress it up so as to make it resemble Plataea, the daughter of Asopus. As Zeus was riding along with his pretended bride, Hera, overcome with jealousy, ran up and tore the covering from the suspected bride and became reconciled with Zeus (Paus. 9. 1.2, 3.1).

CLEITUS, beloved by Pallene, daughter of Sithon, entered into combat with Dryas for the hand of the beautiful maiden. She induced the charioteer of Dryas to remove the nails from his master's wheels, enabling Cleitus to overcome and kill his rival. When her father learned of the trick, he erected a funeral pyre, on which he intended to burn the body of Dryas along with his daughter. But when Aphrodite appeared and brought a shower of rain to extinguish the fire, Sithon changed his mind and gave his daughter to Cleitus.

DIOMEDES. At the funeral games of Patroclus, he conquered in the chariot race.

ENCELADUS, one of the hundred-armed giants who made war upon the gods, was killed, according to some, by the chariot of Athena (Paus. 8. 47.1).

EOS was goddess of the dawn. At night's end, she rose from her couch and in a chariot drawn by swift horses, ascended to heaven to announce the coming light of the sun (Hom. *Od.* 5. 1, 23. 244; Virg. *Aen.* 4. 129; Virg. *Georg.* 1. 446).

ERICHTHONIUS was the first to use a chariot with four horses, for which reason he was placed among the stars as Auriga (Virg. *Georg.* 1. 205, 3. 113). He is sometimes called the inventor of the chariot.

EUMELUS was a son of Admetus and distinguished for his excellent horses. He would have gained the prize at the funeral games of Patroclus if his chariot had not been broken (Hom. *Il.* 2. 711, 764, 23. 375, 536; Hom. *Od.* 4. 798; Strab. 9. 436).

HADES. When he carried Persephone away to the lower world, he rode in a golden chariot drawn by four black, immortal horses (Ov. *Met.* 5. 404; Hom. *Hymn.in Cer.* 19; Claud. *Rapt. Proserp.* 1).

HARMONIA. She and Cadmus, her husband, were metamorphosed into dragons and transferred to Elysium; or, according to others, they were carried there in a chariot drawn by dragons (Apollod. 3. 5.4; Eurip. *Bacch.* 1233; Ov. *Met.* 4. 562).

HEBE, daughter of Zeus and Hera, assisted Hera in harnessing the horses to her chariot (Hom. *Il.* 5. 722).

HECTOR. After killing him, Achilles tied Hector's body to his own chariot and dragged him into the camp of the Greeks.

HELIOS. During the daily course of the sun, Helios drove a chariot drawn by horses (Ov. *Met.* 2. 106; Pind. *Ol.* 7. 71).

HERA rode in a chariot drawn by two horses, in the harnessing and unharnessing of which she was assisted by Hebe and the Horae (Hom. *Il.* 4. 27, 5. 720, 8. 382, 433). (See also CITHAERON)

HERACLES was instructed by Amphitryon in riding in a chariot.

HIPPODAMEIA, the daughter of Oenomaus, wished to be won by Pelops. She persuaded

Myrtilus, the charioteer, to take the nails out of her father's chariot wheels, so that Pelops could win the race that Oenomaus imposed on all suitors of his daughter.

HIPPOLYTUS. Cursed by Theseus, his father, for allegedly making improper advances to Phaedra, his step-mother, Hippolytus was killed when a bull appeared from the sea and frightened the horses pulling the chariot in which he was riding. He was dragged to death.

IDAS, son of Aphareus, eloped with Marpessa, daughter of Evenus, with the assistance of Poseidon, who gave him a winged chariot.

JUPITER. The color white was sacred to him, and his chariot was drawn by four white horses.

MEDEA killed her children by Jason and fled in a chariot drawn by winged dragons.

MENELAUS. At the funeral games of Patroclus, he competed with Antilochus in the chariot race but voluntarily gave up the second prize and was satisfied with the third (Hom. *Il.* 23. 293, 401, 516–609).

MERIONES. At the funeral games of Patroclus, he won the fourth prize in the chariot race.

NYX. The goddess of night in later accounts is described as riding in a chariot.

OENOMAUS was a son of Ares. An oracle had declared that he would die if his daughter married. Therefore he made it a condition that those who came forward as suitors for Hippodameia's hand compete with him in a chariot race. If the suitor won, he would marry her, but if he lost, he would die. (See also PELOPS)

PELOPS. Since Oenomaus challenged each of Hippodameia's suitors to a chariot race and declared he would give his daughter to the winner but would kill the losers, Pelops gained the favor of Myrtilus, the charioteer of Oenomaus, and, in exchange for a promise to give him half the kingdom, had him fasten the wheels of Oenomaus' chariot in such a way that it would be upset during the race. Thus he conquered Oenomaus and gained Hippodameia. According to Pindar (*Ol.* 1. 109), Pelops in the chariot race with Oenomaus did not gain the victory by any strategem but called upon Poseidon for assistance, who gave him the chariot and horses by which he overcame Oenomaus.

PHAETHON, son of Helios, was presumptuous and ambitious enough to persuade his father to allow him to drive the chariot of the sun across heaven. Phaethon, being too weak to check the horses, came down so close to the earth that he almost set it on fire. Zeus, therefore, killed him with a flash of lightning.

PHILOMELUS. A son of Iasion and Demeter, was said to have invented the chariot. This invention so pleased his mother that, when he died, she placed him among the stars as Bootes.

POSEIDON rode in a chariot over the waves of the sea, which became smooth as he approached, and the monsters of the deep recognized him and played around his chariot (Hom. *Il.* 13. 27; comp. Virg. *Aen.* 1. 147, 5. 817; Apollon. Rhod. 3. 1240). His chariot was drawn over the surface of the sea by sea-horses, or hippocampi. Generally, he himself harnessed his horses to his chariot, but sometimes he was assisted by his wife, Amphitrite (Apollon. Rhod. 1. 1158, 4. 1325; Eurip. *Androm.* 1011; Virg. *Aen.* 5. 817). Horse and chariot races were held in his honor on the Corinthian isthmus (Pind. *Nem.* 5. 66).

PROTEUS, the old man of the sea, is often represented riding through the sea in a chariot drawn by hippocampi (Virg. *Georg.* 4. 389).

RHEA, mother of the gods, is sometimes seen in works of art riding in a chariot drawn by lions.

ROMULUS. One day as he was reviewing his people in the Campus Martius, the sun suddenly eclipsed, darkness overspread the earth, and a dreadful storm dispersed the people. When daylight returned, Romulus had disappeared, for his father, Mars, had carried him up to heaven in a fiery chariot (Hor. *Carm.* 3. 3; Ov. *Fast.* 2. 496).

SELENE, the moon goddess, rode across the heavens in a chariot drawn by two white horses, cows, or mules (Ov. *Fast.* 3. 110, 4. 374; Ov.

Rem.Am. 258; Claud. *Rapt. Proserp.* 3. 403; Nonn. 7. 244).

TRIPTOLEMUS. When Demeter accidentally killed his brother, Demophon, she gave Triptolemus a chariot with winged dragons and seeds of wheat. (In works of art he is represented on a chariot drawn by dragons.) After receiving the dragon chariot he rode in it all over the earth, acquainting men with the blessings of agriculture.

Charioteer

AMPHISTRATUS was the charioteer of the Dioscuri.

AUTOMEDON was the charioteer and companion of Achilles (Hom. *Il.* 9. 209).

BATON was the charioteer of Amphiaraus.

CEBRIONES, son of Priam and charioteer of Hector, was slain by Patroclus (Hom. *Il.* 8. 318, 11. 521, 16. 736).

CILLAS (See SPHAERUS)

COERANUS was the charioteer of Meriones and was slain by Hector (Hom. *Il.* 7. 165, 17. 610).

EURMEDON was son of Ptolemaeus and charioteer of Agamemnon (Hom. *Il.* 4. 228).

HERMES was charioteer to Zeus.

IOLAUS, son of Iphicles, was a relative of Heracles and also his companion and charioteer.

LAODOCUS was the friend and charioteer of Antilochus (Hom. *Il.* 17. 699).

MOLION, a Trojan, was the charioteer of Thymbraeus (Hom. *Il.* 11. 322).

MYRTILUS, son of Hermes by Cleobule or Clytia, was charioteer to Oenomaus, king of Elis. He conspired with Pelops to cause Oenomaus to lose the chariot race that Oenomaus forced all suitors of his daughter, Hippodameia, to engage in with him. Pelops thus won the race and the hand of Hippodameia.

OILEUS, a Trojan, was charioteer of Bianor (Hom. *Il.* 11. 93).

PERIERES was the charioteer of king Menoeceus in Thebes (Apollod. 2. 4.11).

POLYPHONTES (POLYPHETES or POLYPOETES) was the charioteer of Laius. When he and Laius met Oedipus on the road between Delphi and Daulis, he tried to push Oedipus out of the way. In the ensuing scuffle, he and Laius were slain by Oedipus.

POSEIDON was regarded as the protector and friend of charioteers (Pind. *Ol.* 1. 63).

PTOLEMAEUS, a son of Peiraeas, accompanied Agamemnon to Troy as charioteer (Hom. *Il.* 4. 228).

RHECAS was the brother of Amphistratus and, with him, charioteer of the Dioscuri.

SPHAERUS was the charioteer of Pelops; there was a monument of him in the island of Sphaeria or Hiera near Troezen (Paus. 2. 33.1; 5. 10.2). He was sometimes referred to by the name Cillas.

Chase, see Hunting

Chasm, see Engulfment

Chastity, see Virginity

Chest

ADONIS was concealed as an infant by Aphrodite in a chest and entrusted to Persephone because he was so beautiful. Persephone refused to give him up and Zeus had to arbitrate by allowing the boy to spend an equal part of the year with each goddess.

CLIO, the Muse of history, appears in a sitting position with an open chest of books.

DIONYSUS, according to some traditions, at birth was shut in a chest with his mother, Semele, by her father, Cadmus, and thrown into the sea to perish. He was rescued by Poseidon.

DIONYSUS ASYMNETES. In Troy, there was an ancient image of him kept in a chest. When Troy fell, Cassandra left the chest, knowing that it would bring harm to the one possessing the image. The chest fell to Eurypylus, who went mad when he opened it. He was restored to health by surrendering the chest to the town of Aroe to remove an ancient curse from its inhabitants.

ERICHTHONIUS, son of Hephaestus by Gaea or Atthis, was half serpent, half man. Athena became his guardian and concealed him in a chest, which she had Agraulos, Pandrosos, and Herse guard. She forbade them to open the chest, but they did, and, observing the child in the form of a serpent, they were thrown into madness and flung themselves from the acropolis of Athens or into the sea (Apollod. 3. 14.6; Paus. 1. 2.5, 18.2; Eurip. *Ion* 260; Ov. *Met.* 2. 554).

OEDIPUS. Some accounts state that Laius, his father, cast the infant on the sea in a chest because of a dire prophecy. These accounts say that he was blinded by Polybus, who rescued him when the chest floated to Sicyon.

PANDORA. Her curiosity caused her to open a forbidden box, or chest, from which all the earth's ills escaped.

PERSEUS. When Acrisius found that his daughter, Danae, had given birth to a son, he threw both mother and child into a chest and put them out to sea. But Zeus caused the chest to land on the island of Seriphos, where Dictys, a fisherman, found them and carried them to his brother, king Polydectes.

RHOEO, a daughter of Staphylus and Chrysothemis, was beloved by Apollo. When her father discovered that she was pregnant, he put her in a chest and exposed her to the waves of the sea. The chest floated to the coast of Euboea, where Rhoeo gave birth to Anius (Diod. 5. 62).

TENES (TENNES) was a son of Cycnus. His stepmother, Philonome, fell in love with him and, when she was unable to win his love, accused him before his father of improper conduct toward her. Cycnus threw both his son and daughter, Hemithea, into a chest and set them adrift at sea. The chest was carried to the island of Leucophrys, where Tenes was eventually made king.

Childbirth

ANTEVORTA and Postvorta had altars at Rome, where they were invoked by pregnant women hoping to avert the dangers of childbirth.

APHRODITE GENETYLLIS was a surname describing the goddess as protectress of births (Aristoph. *Nub.* 52).

APOLLO. When Leto gave birth to him, the island of Delos became sacred, so that afterwards it was not lawful for any human being to be born or die on the island. Every pregnant woman was conveyed to the neighboring island of Rheneia in order not to pollute Delos (Strab. 10. 486).

ARTEMIS presided over women in labor.

ARTEMIS APANCHOMENE, "the strangled (goddess)," was a name derived from an incident which took place at Caphyae in Arcadia. Some boys in their play put a string on the statue of Artemis Condyleatis in a sacred grove and said they were strangling her. When discovered at this, they were stoned to death. Thereafter, all the women at Caphyae had stillbirths until the boys were honorably buried. An annual sacrifice to their spirits was commanded by an oracle (Paus. 8. 23.5). The surname Condyleatis was changed to Apanchomene.

ARTEMIS CONDYLEATIS (See ARTEMIS APANCHOMENE)

ARTEMIS GENETYLLIS, protectress of births, was a name of the goddess to whom women sacrificed dogs. (Aristoph. *Lys.* 2).

ARTEMIS LOCHEIA was a surname designating the goddess as protectress in childbed (Plut. *Quaest. Conviv.* 3. 10).

ARTEMIS MELISSA was a surname of Artemis, under which she alleviated the suffering of women in childbed.

ARTEMIS UPIS was a surname referring to the goddess in her role of assisting women in childbirth (Callim. *Hymn. in Dian.* 240).

DEVERRA was one of three symbolic beings—their names were Pilumnus, Intercidona, and Deverra—whose influence was sought by the Romans at the birth of a child, as a protection for the mother against the vexations of Sylvanus (August. 6. 9).

DIANA LUCINA was goddess of light, or rather the goddess who brings the light, and hence the goddess who presides over the birth of children (Varr. *De Ling. Lat.* 5. 69; Catull. 34. 13; Hor. *Carm. Saec.* 14; Ov. *Fast.* 2. 441, 6. 39; Tibull. 3. 4.13).

EILEITHYIA (ELEUTHO) was the goddess of birth, who came to the assistance of women in labor. When she was kindly disposed, she furthered the birth, but when she was angry, she protracted the labor and delayed the birth.

ELIONIA was worshipped at Argos as the goddess of birth (Plut. *Quaest. Rom.* 49). Probably, she was the same as Eileithyia.

EPIDOTAE were certain Greek divinities who presided over the birth and growth of children.

FASCINUS, the early Latin divinity, protector from evil daemons, was especially invoked to protect women in childbed and their offspring (Plin. *H.N.* 28. 4, 7).

GALINTHIAS (GALANTHIS) was a daughter of Proteus of Thebes and a friend of Alcmene. When Hera was endeavoring via the Moirae and Eileithyia to delay the birth of Heracles, Galinthias rushed in with the false report that Alcmene had given birth to a son, and thus broke the charm and enabled Alcmene to give birth.

GENETYLLIDES (GENNAIDES) were a class of divinities presiding over generation and birth and companions of Aphrodite Colias (Aristoph. *Thes.* 130; Paus. 1. 1.4; Alciph. 3. 2).

HEMITHEA, a daughter of Staphylus, formerly named Molpadia, had a temple erected to her in Castabus in the Chersonesus. She was worshipped as a divinity who gave relief to women in childbed (Diod. 5. 52, 63).

HERA was the Olympian goddess of childbirth. As such, she was able to delay the birth of Heracles, so that Eurystheus would rule over the race of Perseus (Hom. *Il.* 19. 90; Ov. *Met.* 9. 273).

HISTORIS, a daughter of Tiresias, was engaged in the service of Alcmene. By her cry that Alcmene had already given birth, she induced the Pharmacides to withdraw and thus enabled her mistress to give birth to Heracles (Paus. 9. 11.2). Some attribute this act to Galinthias.

ILITHYIA was the Roman goddess of childbirth. She was identified with Juno Lucina, and identical with the Greek Eileithyia.

IPHIGENEIA. In Attica, veils and costly garments that had been worn by women who died in childbirth were offered up to her (Eurip. *Iphig. Taur.* 1464; Diod. 4. 44).

JUNO LUCINA was goddess of light, or rather the goddess who brings the light, and hence the goddess who presides over the birth of children (Varr. *De Ling. Lat.* 5. 69; Catull. 34. 13; Hor. *Carm. Saec.* 14; Ov. *Fast.* 2. 441, 6. 39; Tibull. 3. 4.13).

LEVANA was a goddess at Rome who presided over the action of the person who took up from the ground a newly-born child after it had been placed there by the midwife.

MOIRAE (MOERAE) are goddesses of birth who spin the thread of beginning life and prophesy the fate of the newly-born. They are mentioned along with Eileithyia, who is called their companion (Paus. 8. 21.2; Pind. *Ol.* 6. 70; Pind. *Nem.* 7. 1).

MOLPADIA (See HEMITHEA)

NASCIO was a Roman divinity presiding over the birth of children and, accordingly, a goddess assisting Lucina in her functions; she was analagous to the Greek Eileithyia, and had a sanctuary in the neighborhood of Ardea (Cic. *De Nat.Deor.* 3. 18).

NIXI DII was a general term which seems to have been applied by the Romans to divinities who assisted women at the time they were giving birth (Ov. *Met.* 9. 294).

NUMERIA was probably a deity of some importance in Rome, as the pontifex mentioned her in the ancient prayers. Women in childbirth were accustomed to pray to her.

PHARMACIDES, "witches or sorceresses," was the name by which the Thebans designated the divinities who delayed the birth of Heracles (Paus. 9. 11.2).

Children

CARDEA was a Roman divinity who protected little children in their cradles against formidable witches metamorphosed into night birds to attack children, tear them from their cradles and suck their blood. Cardea exercised her power with whitethorn and other magical substances.

CATIUS was a Roman divinity who was invoked under the name of *divus Catius pater* to grant prudence and thoughtfulness to children at the time when their consciousness was beginning to awaken (August. 4. 21).

CUBA, Cunina, and Rumina were three Roman genii, who were worshipped as the protectors of infants sleeping in their cradles. Libations of milk were offered to them.

EDULICA (EDUSA) was a Roman divinity who was worshipped as the protectress of children and was believed to bless their food, just as Patina and Cuba blessed their drinking and their sleep (August. 4. 11).

EPIDOTAE were Greek divinities who presided over the birth and growth of children.

FASCINUS, an early Latin divinity, protector from evil daemons, was especially invoked to protect women in childbed and their offspring (Plin. *H.N.* 28. 4, 7).

LAMIA was a female phantom by which children were frightened. According to tradition, she was originally a Libyan queen of great beauty and a daughter of Belus. She was beloved by Zeus, and Hera in her jealousy robbed her of her children. Lamia, from revenge and despair, robbed others of their children and murdered them.

LEVANA was a Roman divinity who derived her name from the custom of the father picking up his newborn child from the ground, by which symbolic act he declared his intention not to kill the child but to bring it up (August. 4. 11).

MANIA was an ancient and formidable Italian, probably Etruscan, divinity. Originally, human sacrifices were made to her. In later times, the plural, Maniae, occurs as the designation of terrible, ugly, and deformed spectres with which nurses used to frighten children.

MATUTA. Certain ceremonies observed at her festival, the Matralia, which took place on the 11th of June, seem to have been intended to enjoin people to take care of the children of deceased brothers and sisters, as if they were their own, and not leave them to the mercy of slaves or hirelings (Plut. *Quaest.Rom.* 16, 17).

MORMO was a female spectre with which the Greeks used to frighten little children (Aristoph. *Acharn.* 582; Aristoph. *Pax* 474). She was one of the same class of bugbears as Empusa and Lamia.

MORMOLYCE (MORMOLYCEION) was the same type of phantom or bugbear as Mormo and used for the same purpose (Philostr. *Vit.Apoll.* 4. 25; Aristoph. *Thes.* 417; Strab. 1. 19).

NUNDINA (NONA DIES) was a goddess whom the Romans invoked when they named their children.

OPS was a female Roman divinity of plenty and fertility. As she was believed to give to human beings both their place of abode and their food, newly-born children were recommended to her care (August. 4. 11, 21).

ORBONA was a female Roman divinity who

was invoked by parents who had been deprived of their children and desired to have others. She was also invoked to protect against the dangerous maladies of children (Cic. *De Nat.Deor.* 3. 25; Plin. *H.N.* 2. 7).

OSSIPAGA (OSSIPANGA, OSSILAGO, or OSSIPAGINA) was a Roman divinity, who was asked to harden and strengthen the bones of infants.

PICUMNUS, brother of Pilumnus, was believed to give newborn infants strength and prosperity.

PIETAS was a Roman personification of faithful attachments, love, and veneration. Her attributes are a stork and children.

PILUMNUS, a rustic divinity of the ancient Romans, was believed to ward off the sufferings of newborn infants and children with his *pilum,* with which he also taught men to pound grain. A couch was prepared for him and his brother Picumnus in the house in which there was a newly-born child.

STATINUS (STATILINUS) was a Roman divinity to whom sacrifices were offered at the time when a child began to stand or run alone (August. 4. 21).

See also: INFANT EXPOSURE

Chisel

PERDIX, nephew of Daedalus, was inventor of the chisel.

Chiton, see Garment

Choral Music

PHILAMMON, a mythical poet and musician who lived after the Homeric period, was the son of Apollo and the nymph, Chione. He is closely associated with the worship of Apollo at Delphi and with the music of the cithara. He is said to have established the choruses of girls, who, in the Delphian worship of Apollo, sang hymns in which they celebrated the births of Leto, Artemis, and Apollo; some ascribe the invention of choral music in general to him.

Cicada

EUNOMUS was a cithara player of Locri in Italy. When one of the strings of his cithara was broken in a musical contest at the Pythian games, a cicada perched on the instrument, and by its notes supplied the deficiency (Strab. 6. 260; Clem.Alex. *Protrept.* 1).

Cithara

EUNEUS. The Euneidae, a famous family of cithara players in Lemnos, traced their origin to Euneus.

EUNOMUS was a cithara player of Locri in Italy. When one of the strings of his cithara was broken in a musical contest at the Pythian games, a cicada perched on the instrument, and by its notes supplied the deficiency (Strab. 6. 260; Clem.Alex. *Protrept.* 1.).

PHILAMMON, a mythical poet and musician who lived after the Homeric period, was the son of Apollo and the nymph, Chione. He is closely associated with the worship of Apollo at Delphi and with the music of the cithara.

Civic Affairs

JUNO CURIATA. A surname of Juno as presider over public affairs.

JUNO POPULONIA. A surname of Juno as protectress of the whole Roman people.

Civilization

DIONYSUS was regarded as the promoter of civilization.

TRIPTOLEMUS, a son of Celeus and Metaneira and a favorite of Demeter, invented the plow and agriculture and thus, indirectly, civilization.

Claws

GORGONS were described as having wings and claws (Aeschyl. *Prom.* 794; Aeschyl. *Choeph.* 1050).

Clemency

CLEMENTIA, a personification of clemency, was worshipped as a divinity at Rome. She was represented holding a patera in her right hand and a lance in her left hand (Claud. *De Consul.Stil.* 2. 6; Stat. *Theb.* 12).

Cloak, see Garment

Cloud

AGENOR, one of the bravest of the Trojans, ventured to fight with Achilles. When he was wounded, Apollo rescued him by concealing him in a cloud.

CENTAURS were offspring of the Magnesian mares and Centaurus, who was begotten by Ixion on a cloud (Pind. *Pyth.* 80).

HECTOR. In order to protect his body from being devoured by dogs, Apollo protected it by a cloud.

HERA. Once after she tried to put Zeus in chains, he hung her up in the clouds with her hands chained and with two anvils suspended from her feet (Hom. *Il.* 8. 400, 477, 15. 17).

HERACLES. While his funeral pyre was burning, a cloud came down from heaven and amid peals of thunder carried him to Olympus, where he was honored with immortality (Hes. *Theog.* 949; Apollod. 2. 7.7; Diod. 4. 38).

NEPHELE, the mother of Phrixus and Helle, was changed into a cloud.

ODYSSEUS. When the Phaeacians returned him by ship to Ithaca, he did not recognize his native land, for Athena had enveloped him in a cloud so that he would not be recognized.

PARIS. In single combat with Menelaus, he was seized by the helmet and dragged to the camp of the Achaeans, but Aphrodite loosened the helmet and wrapped her favorite in a cloud, enabling him to escape from the enemy (Hom. *Il.* 3. 325, 4. 12).

Club

AREITHOUS, king of Arne in Boeotia, fought in the Trojan War armed only with a club (Hom. *Il.* 7. 8).

HERACLES cut a club for himself in the neighborhood of Nemea; according to others, the club was of brass and the gift of Hephaestus (Apollon.Rhod. 1. 1196; Diod. 4. 14). He used his club, along with arrows and a sickle, to cut off the Hydra's heads. In works of art he is often represented carrying a club.

MELPOMENE, the Muse of tragedy, often appears bearing the club of Heracles.

ORION. After his death, he was placed among the stars (Hom. *Il.* 18. 486, 22. 29; Hom. *Od.* 5. 274), where he appears as a giant with a girdle, a sword, a lion's skin, and a club.

PERIPHETES, son of Hephaestus, and surnamed Corynetes, that is, club-bearer, was a robber at Epidaurus; he slew travelers with an iron club. Theseus killed him and took his club for his own use (Apollod. 3. 16.1; Plut. *Thes.* 8; Paus. 2. 1.4; Ov. *Met.* 7. 437).

Coals

ARCHELAUS. King Cisseus promised him succession to his throne for assistance against neighboring enemies but regretted his promise and tried to kill Archelaus by digging a hole, filling it with burning coals, and covering it with branches. Cisseus himself was thrown into the pit by Archelaus.

Coast

APOLLO EPACTAEUS (EPACTIUS) was a surname of Apollo as the god worshipped on the coast (Apollon.Rhod. 1. 404).

Heracles

Cock

ALECTRYON was a youth set guard during the love-making of Ares and Aphrodite. Forgetting his watch, he was changed into a cock, which still answers the approach of the sun.

APOLLO. The cock was sacred to him.

ASCLEPIUS. Those cured in his temples offered the sacrifice of a cock.

ATHENA. The cock was sacred to her.

EROS. The cock was sacred to him.

HELIOS. The cock was especially mentioned as sacred to the sun god (Paus. 5. 25.5).

IDOMENEUS. On his statue at Olympia, a cock was represented on his shield.

NYX. The cock was sacred to her.

Coin

CHARON. For his services as ferryman of the dead across the rivers of the lower world, he was paid by each shade with a coin (an obolus or danace); to provide payment a coin was placed in the mouth of every dead body previous to its burial (Paus. 10. 28.1; Juv. 3. 267).

Colonization

APOLLO ARCHEGETES was a surname that refers to the god either as protector of colonies or as founder of towns in general.

Comedy

THALIA, the Muse of comedy and of merry or idyllic poetry, appears with the comic mask, a shepherd's staff, or a wreath of ivy.

Comet

ELECTRA. When she saw Troy perishing in flames, she tore out her hair for grief and was placed among the stars as a comet.

MENIPPE and her sister Metioche, daughters of Orion, in order to avert a plague in Aonia, where they lived, offered themselves as a sacrifice (in response to an oracle). Hades and Persephone metamorphosed them into comets (Ov. *Met.* 13. 685).

Commerce

FERONIA was regarded by some in Italy as the goddess of commerce and traffic, because these things were carried on to a great extent during the festival that was celebrated in her honor in the town of Feronia.

HERMES was the promoter of commerce.

HERMES AGORAEUS (AGORAIOS). This surname of Hermes as god of commerce referred to the agora or marketplace.

HERMES CERDEMPOROS (DEMPOROS or PALENCAPELOS) was a surname of Hermes as god of commerce.

MERCURIUS MALEVOLUS, "the ill-willed," was the surname under which he had a statue in Rome. This statue had a purse in its hand to indicate his commercial function. His festival was celebrated on the 25th of May.

Compass

PERDIX, nephew of Daedalus, was inventor of the compass.

Constellations, see Stars and Constellations

Contest

AGON, a personification of solemn contests, was represented with a statue at Olympia.

APOLLO AGONIUS was a surname of Apollo as helper in struggles and contests.

HERMES AGONIUS was a surname of Hermes as presider over solemn contests.

ZEUS AGONIUS was a surname of Zeus as helper in struggles and contests.

Cornucopia

AMALTHEA. The broken horn of the goat whose milk nourished Zeus was filled by the nymph, Amalthea, with fresh herbs and fruits (Ov. *Fast.* 5. 115). This horn was later used as the symbol of plenty.

EIRENE (IRENE), the goddess of peace, was pictured on coins carrying in her left arm a cornucopia.

FELICITAS, the personification of happiness, is often seen on Roman medals in the form of a matron with a staff and a cornucopia.

FORTUNA. The cornucopia was sometimes an attribute of the goddess of fortune (Paus. 4. 30.4, 7. 26.3).

GENIUS. On Roman monuments, a genius (guardian spirit) commonly appears as a youth dressed in the toga, with a patera or cornucopia in his hands and his head covered.

HONOR (HONOS), the personification of honor, is represented as a male figure bearing a cornucopia in his left hand and a spear in his right.

PLUTUS, the personification of wealth, commonly appears as a boy with a cornucopia.

PRIAPUS, son of Dionysus and Aphrodite, was sometimes represented carrying a cornucopia.

THEMIS, daughter of Uranus and Gaea, is often represented on coins with a cornucopia and a pair of scales (Gell. 14. 4).

TYCHE was the personification of chance or luck. With Plutus, or the horn of Amalthea, she was the symbol of the plentiful gifts of fortune. At Smyrna, her statue, the work of Buphalus, held a globe on her head with one hand and in the other she carried the horn of Amalthea (Paus. 4. 30.4).

ZEUS was often represented holding a cornucopia in his hand.

Cothurnus, see Garment

Couch

PILUMNUS, a rustic divinity of the ancient Romans, was believed to ward off the sufferings of newborn infants and children with his *pilum,* with which he also taught men to pound grain. A couch was prepared for him and his brother, Picumnus, in any house in which there was a newly-born child.

Council

CONSUS was a deity at Rome who presided over councils.

Counsel

ARTEMIS ARISTOBULE, "the best advisor," was a surname of Artemis, to whom Themistocles built a temple at Athens and in it dedicated his own statue (Plut. *Them.* 22).

DIONYSUS EUBULEUS was a surname designating Dionysus as providing good counsel.

HADES EUBULEUS (EUBULUS) was a surname of Hades as a god of good counsel (Plut. *Quaest.Conviv.* 7. 9).

Court

ATHENA maintained the authority of law, justice, and order in the courts and the assembly of the people. She was believed to have instituted the ancient court of the Areiopagus. In cases where the votes of the judges were equally divided, she cast the deciding one in favor of the accused (Aeschyl. *Eum.* 753).

Courtesan, see Prostitute

Cow

ARGUS was appointed by Hera as guardian of Io after she had been metamorphosed into a cow. He was selected for this job because he had one hundred eyes, some of them always awake.

ATHENA. Sacrifices to her included bulls, rams, and cows.

CADMUS. The Delphic oracle commanded him to cease searching for Europa, to follow a cow of a certain kind, and to build a town on the spot where the cow should lie down (Paus. 9. 12.1).

DAEDALUS made a wooden cow for Pasiphae to conceal herself in and satisfy her lust for the bull in Minos' herd to which she was attracted.

DEMETER. Sacrifices to her included cows.

HERMES was commissioned by Zeus to dispatch Argus, the hundred-eyed guardian of Io, who had been changed into a cow.

HESTIA. Because she was a virgin goddess, cows which were only one year old were sacrificed to her.

ILUS. The king of Phrygia gave him a cow of different colors as a prize in a wrestling contest, requesting Ilus to build a town on the spot where the cow should lie down. Eventually she lay down at the foot of the Phrygian hill, Ate, and it was here that Ilus founded Ilion (Troy).

IO, daughter of Inachus, was metamorphosed by Zeus into a white cow to hide his relationship with her from Hera. Hera saw through the trick and seized the cow, placing her under the care of Argus Panoptes, who tied her to an olive tree in the grove of Hera at Mycenae. Zeus commissioned Hermes to deliver Io, which he did by killing Argus with a stone or by lulling him to sleep with flute music and cutting off his head. Hera then sent a gadfly to torment Io. It chased her around the world until at length she found peace on the banks of the Nile (Apollod. 2. 1.2).

PAN. Sacrifices to him included cows.

POLYIDUS of Argos was summoned, along with other soothsayers, by Minos to locate his missing son, Glaucus. Minos had been advised that someone who could compare one of his cows that had changed color from white to red to black to any other object would lead him to the missing boy. Polyidus compared the cow to a mulberry, which is at first white, then red, and finally black. He used his prophetic powers to find the child, who had been drowned in a vat of honey (Aelian. *De Nat.Anim.* 5. 2).

SELENE, the moon goddess, rode across the heavens in a chariot drawn by two white cows (or horses or mules).

TAYGETE, one of the Pleiades, daughters of Atlas and Pleione (Apollod. 3. 10.1), according to some traditions, refused to yield to the embrace of Zeus, and, in order to secure her against him, Artemis metamorphosed her into a cow.

TELLUS, among the Romans, was a name by which the earth was personified. A festival was celebrated in her honor on the 15th of April. It was called Fordicidia or Hordicalia, from *hordus* or *fordus,* a bearing cow (Ov. *Fast.* 4. 633; Hor. *Epist.* 2. 1.143).

ZEUS. Cows were sacrificed to him.

Cowardice

EPEIUS was a son of Panopeus. When Panopeus broke an oath to Amphitryon, his punishment was that his son, Epeius, became unwarlike. Epeius' cowardice in the Trojan War is said to have been so great that it became proverbial.

PARIS. When he came unrecognized to his brothers and conquered them all in the contest for his favorite bull, Deiphobus drew his sword against him and Paris fled to the altar of Zeus Herceius. When the Greeks first appeared before Troy, Paris was bold and courageous (Hom. *Il.* 3. 16), but when Menelaus advanced against him, he took flight. As Hector upbraided him for his cowardice, he offered to fight in single combat with Menelaus for the possession of Helen (Hom. *Il.* 3. 70). Menelaus accepted the challenge, and Paris, though conquered, was removed from the field of battle by Aphrodite (Hom. *Il.* 3. 380).

VENUS MURTIA was a surname denoting cowardice. The goddess, worshipped under this name, had a temple at the foot of the Aventine Hill, and as she patronized indolence, laziness, and cowardice, her statues were generally covered with moss to represent inactivity (Plin. *H.N.* 15.121; August. 4).

Cowherd

APOLLO. As a punishment from Zeus, Apollo was required to work for one year as a hireling to a mortal. He chose Admetus, king of Pherae in Thessaly, and worked for him as a cowherd. Admetus was a very good master, and Apollo conferred many favors upon him.

PHILOETIUS was the celebrated cowherd of Odysseus. He assisted Odysseus in his attack on the suitors and slew Ctesippus (Hom. *Od.* 20. 288, 12. 285).

Crab

HERACLES. While he was trying to sever the Hydra's heads, a gigantic crab came to the assistance of the Hydra and wounded Heracles.

Cradle

CARDEA was a Roman divinity who protected little children in their cradles from witches.

CUBA, Cunina, and Rumina were three Roman genii who were worshipped as the protectors of infants sleeping in their cradles and to whom libations of milk were offered.

HERMES. In the first hour of his birth, he escaped from his cradle, went to Pieriria and carried off some of the oxen of Apollo (Hom. *Hymn. in Merc.* 17).

ROMULUS. When his mother, Silvia, a vestal virgin, gave birth to him and his twin, Remus, the mother and babies were set adrift to drown. The mother was rescued by the river god, Anio, but the twins floated in their cradle into the Tiber, where eventually they landed and were adopted and suckled by a she-wolf.

Crane

GERANA was a Pygmaean woman who incurred the wrath of Artemis and Hera because of her vanity about her beauty. They metamorphosed her into a crane (Ov. *Met.* 6. 90).

MEGARUS was a son of Zeus. In the Deucalionian flood, he is said to have escaped to the summit of Mt. Gerania by following the cries of cranes (Paus. 1. 40.1).

PYGMIES were a fabulous nation of dwarves, who, according to Homer, every spring waged war against the cranes on the banks of Oceanus (Hom. *Il.* 3. 5). Later writers usually place them near the sources of the Nile, where the cranes are said to have migrated every year to take possession of the fields of the Pygmies (Aristot. *H.A.* 8. 12; Strab. 1. 42, 17. 821).

Creation

ERICAPAEUS (See PHANES)

EROS (See PHANES)

METIS (See PHANES)

PHANES, a mystic divinity in the system of the Orphics, is also called Eros, Ericapaeus, Metis, and Protogonus. He is said to have sprung from the mystic mundane egg and to have been the father of all gods and the creator of men.

PROMETHEUS. One account states that he created men out of earth and water at the very beginning of the human race or after the flood of Deucalion, when Zeus is said to have ordered him and Athena to make men out of mud, and the winds to breathe life into them (Apollod. 1. 7.1; Ov. *Met.* 1. 81). Prometheus is said to have given to men some of each of the qualities possessed by the other animals (Hor. *Carm.* 1. 16.13).

PROTOGONUS (See PHANES)

Cremation, see Immolation

Crescent

SELENE was the moon goddess, sister of Helios, the sun. In works of art, her veil forms an arch above her head, and above it there is the crescent.

Cricket

TITHONUS. When Eos, goddess of the dawn, prayed to Zeus to grant her beloved Tithonus immortality, she forgot to ask for eternal youth. So he lived, growing older and weaker, until eventually he dried up and was metamorphosed by Eos into a cricket (Hom. *Hymn. in Ven.* 218; Hor. *Carm.* 1. 228, 2. 16.30; Apollod. 3. 12.4).

Crime

EUMENIDES, also called Erinyes, originally were only the personification of curses pronounced upon a guilty criminal. Later they were conceived of as angry goddesses who hunted, pursued, and punished evildoers. The crimes they punished were disobedience toward parents, violation of the respect due to old age, perjury, murder, violation of the law of hospitality, and improper conduct toward suppliants.

LITAE, daughters of Zeus and the personification of prayers offered up in repentance, followed closely behind crime and endeavored to make amends for what had been done.

Crocus

CROCUS, the unrequited lover of Smilax, was changed by the gods into a crocus or a saffron plant (Ov. *Met.* 4. 283).

Crone

IPHIGENEIA. When she was on the point of being sacrificed by the Greeks at Aulis, Artemis carried her away and, according to some, substituted an old woman for the sacrifice.

MOIRAE, the Fates, were sometimes described by the poets as aged and hideous women.

TIRESIAS (TEIRESIAS). When he awarded the prize for beauty to Cale, one of the Charites, Aphrodite changed him into an old woman.

Crossroads

ARTEMIS TRIVIA was a surname given to Artemis because she presided over all places where three roads met. At these crossroads her image was placed with three faces, one looking each way. At the new moon, the Athenians offered her sacrifices and a sumptuous entertainment, and food was generally distributed among the poor.

HECATE. Crossroads were regarded as her province.

LARES. The *Lares publici,* divinities of public places in Rome, presided over the *compita,* or the points where two or more streets crossed each other.

Crow

APOLLO. The crow was sacred to him.

ATHENA. At Corone in Messenia, her statue bore a crow in its hand.

CORONIS, daughter of Phoroneus, when pursued by Poseidon, implored the protection of Athena, who turned her into a crow (Ov. *Met.* 2. 550).

Crown

ARIADNE. Dionysus is said to have placed her, and the crown he gave her at their marriage, among the stars (Hes. *Theog.* 949).

HERA, queen of the gods, was represented wearing a diadem.

MEDEA (MEDEIA). When Jason deserted her for Creon's daughter, Glauce (or Creusa), she sent a poisoned garment and diadem to the bride. When Glauce put these on, she and her father were consumed by the poisonous fire which issued from the vestments.

MOIRAE. Plato (*De Re Pub.* 617) mentions the Fates as wearing crowns.

NEMESIS. The Rhamnusian statue of Nemesis wore on its head a crown adorned with stags and an image of victory.

RHEA, mother of the gods, in works of art is usually represented sitting on a throne, adorned with the mural crown, from which a veil hangs down.

SELENE, the moon goddess, was represented with a golden diadem (Hom. *Hymn. in Sol.* 32. 1.7).

Crucifixion

ASBOLUS, a centaur, was nailed to a cross by Heracles. He had engaged with the other centaurs in the battle with the Lapithae.

CHALCON of Cyparissus was in love with the Amazon, Penthesileia, but, on hastening to her assistance, was killed by Achilles, and the Greeks nailed his body to a cross.

Crutches

HEPHAESTUS was the god of fire. Owing to the weakness of his legs, he was held up when he walked by artificial supports, skillfully made of gold (Hom. *Il.* 18. 410; Hom. *Od.* 8. 311, 330).

Cunning

AUTOLYCUS, son of Hermes, was a famous thief who was renowned for his cunning and oaths (Ov. *Met.* 11. 311).

HERMES. As the messenger god and god of thieves, he was endowed with ingenuity and was regarded also as the god of cunningness.

Cup

ALPHEIUS. It was believed that a cup thrown into the Alpheius river would make its reappearance in the fountain of Arethusa in Ortygia. The river and the fountain were supposed to be connected subterraneously (Strab. 6. 270, 8. 343). Alpheius, the god of this Peloponnesan river, fell in love with the nymph Arethusa, whom he pursued. Artemis changed her into a fountain on the island of Ortygia at Syracuse, but Alpheius pursued her beneath the sea, so that their waters would mingle.

ANCAEUS was a vinegrower. A seer warned him that he would not live to taste the wine from his vineyard. As he lifted the cup of his vineyard's first wine to his lips, he scorned the prediction, but the seer remarked: "There is many a slip between the cup and the lip." A tumult arose outside, and when Ancaeus went out to investigate, he was killed by a wild boar.

CLEMENTIA, the Roman goddess of clemency, was represented holding a patera (shallow cup) in her right hand (Claud. *De Consul.Stil.* 2. 6; Stat. *Theb.* 12).

DEMIPHON. An oracle told King Demiphon that pestilence would be averted if he sacrificed a noble maiden each year, but he did not offer his own daughters to draw lots for the sacrifice. Mastusius, whose daughter was sacrificed, killed the king's daughters and gave their blood in a cup to the father to drink. When Demiphon discovered the deed, he ordered Mastusius and the cup to be thrown into the sea.

GANYMEDE. In works of art he is shown being carried off by an eagle or giving food to an eagle from a patera.

GENIUS. On Roman monuments, a genius (guardian spirit) commonly appears as a youth dressed in the toga with a patera or cornucopia in his hands and with his head covered.

HAGNO, an Arcadian nymph, was represented carrying in one hand a pitcher and in the other a patera.

HERACLES, annoyed with the heat of the sun, shot arrows at it, and Helios, the sun god, so much admired his boldness that he presented him with a golden cup. Once back in Tartessa, Heracles returned the cup to Helios.

HYGIEIA was goddess of health. Her usual symbol is a serpent, which she is shown feeding from a cup.

NEMESIS. The Rhamnusian statue of Nemesis held a patera in its right hand.

PYGMIES. When Heracles came into their country, these tiny creatures used ladders to climb to the edge of his goblet to drink (Philostr. *Imag.* 2. 21).

SALUS was the Roman personification of public welfare and was represented with a rudder, a globe at her feet, and pouring from a patera a libation upon an altar, around which a serpent is winding itself.

SATYRS. This class of beings is always described as fond of wine. They often appear either with a cup or with a thyrsus in their hand (Athen. 11. 484).

STYX was the divinity by whom the most solemn oaths were sworn. When one of the gods was to take an oath by Styx, Iris, the messenger of the gods, fetched a cup of water from the river Styx, and the god, while taking the oath, poured out the water (Hes. *Theog.* 775).

Cupbearer

CYATHUS, youthful cupbearer of Oeneus, was killed by Heracles because he failed to discharge his duty properly. He was honored at Phlius with a sanctuary near the temple of Apollo (Paus. 2. 13.8).

GANYMEDE was a son of Tros. Being the most beautiful of mortals, he was carried off by the gods so that he might fill the cup of Zeus and live among the eternal gods (Hom. *Il.* 20. 231; Pind. *Ol.* 1. 44). Ganymede was a name sometimes given to handsome slaves who officiated as cupbearers (Petron. 91; Mart. 9. 37; Juv. 5. 59). The idea of Ganymede being the cupbearer of Zeus subsequently gave rise to his identification with the divinity who was believed to preside over the sources of the Nile (Philostr. *Vit.Apoll.* 6. 26; Pind. *Fragm.* 110) and of his being placed by astronomers among the stars under the name of Aquarius (Virg. *Georg.* 3. 304).

HEBE, daughter of Zeus and Hera, filled the cups of the gods with nectar (Hom. *Il.* 4. 2).

HEPHAESTUS. Upon his return to Olympus, he acted for a time as cupbearer to the gods.

HERMES was one of the cupbearers to Zeus.

Cymbals

CYBELE. When her father discovered her liaison with Atys, he put him to death and, maddened with grief, Cybele roamed around the country, her lamentations accompanied by the sound of cymbals (Diod. 3. 58).

Cypress

CYPARISSUS, a youth of Cea, son of Telephus, was beloved by Apollo and Zephyrus or Silvanus. When he inadvertently killed his favorite stag, he was seized with immoderate grief and metamorphosed into a cypress (Ov. *Met.* 10. 120).

SILVANUS was a Latin divinity of the fields and the forests. He is represented carrying the trunk of a cypress (Virg. *Georg.* 1. 20). Silvanus was in love with the youth, Cyparissus, who died from grief over the death of his favorite stag and was metamorphosed into a cypress.

Daffodil, see Asphodel

Dam

ARCAS, son of Zeus and Callisto, rescued Chrysopeleia, a Hamadryad, when a mountain torrent threatened to undermine the oak tree in which she lived. He accomplished this by diverting the torrent with a dam.

HERACLES. His fifth labor was cleansing the stables of Augeus in one day. He accomplished this by diverting with dams the flow of the rivers Alpheius and Peneius so they ran through the stables.

Dance

ARTEMIS CORDACA, a surname in Elis, was

derived from an indecent dance called *kordax*, which the companions of Pelops are said to have performed in honor of the goddess after a victory (Paus. 6. 22.1).

DEMETER CIDARIA, a surname of the Eleusinian Demeter at Peneus in Arcadia, was derived either from an Arcadian dance called *kidaris* or from a royal headdress of the same name (Paus. 8. 15.1).

DIONYSUS ENORCHES was a surname either from Enorchus, son of Thyestes, who built a temple to him, or from description of the god as a dancer.

IAMBE, daughter of Pan and Echo, was believed to have given the name to iambic poetry, for some say that she cheered Demeter by a dance in the iambic metre.

MUSES. Dancing was one of the occupations of the Muses.

PAN. He is often depicted in art in the act of dancing.

SILENUS (SEILENUS), one of the satyrs, was a son of Hermes or Pan by a nymph. A special kind of dance was named *silenus* after him (Anacr. 38.11; Paus. 3. 25.2).

TERPSICHORE, the Muse of choral dance and song, appears with the lyre and plectrum.

Darkness

EREBUS (EREBOS) was the son of Chaos. The name signifies darkness and is therefore applied to the dark and gloomy space under the earth through which the shades pass into Hades (Hom. *Il.* 8. 368).

Dawn

AURORA was the Roman goddess of dawn.

EOS was the Greek goddess of dawn.

MATUTA, commonly called Mater Matuta, is usually believed to be the goddess of the dawn or morning. Her name is connected with *maturus* or *matutinus* (Lucret. 5. 655; August. 4. 8).

Deafness

VEIOVIS was an Etruscan divinity of a destructive nature, whose fearful lightnings produced deafness in those who were struck by them (Amm. Marc. 17. 10).

Death

AGAMEDES. After building the temple of Apollo at Delphi, Agamedes and his brother, Trophonius, prayed to the god to grant them what was best for man. The god promised on a certain day to do this and, when the day arrived, both brothers died.

APOLLO. When Leto gave birth to him, the island of Delos became sacred, so that afterwards it was not lawful for any human to be born or die on the island. In another connection, sudden deaths were thought to be the effect of his arrows.

ARCHEMORUS was a son of the Nemean king, Lycurgus. When the seven heroes on their expedition against Thebes stopped at Nemea to take in water, the nurse of the child Opheltes left the child alone to show the way to the seven. The child was killed by a dragon and was buried by the seven heroes. Amphiaraus saw in this accident an omen boding destruction to him and his companions. He called the child Archemorus, meaning "forerunner of death," and instituted the Nemean games in honor of him (Apollod. 3. 6.4).

ARTEMIS. Like Apollo, she sent plague and death among men and animals. Sudden death was believed to be the effect of her arrows.

ATHENA AMBULIA was a surname under which the goddess was worshipped at Sparta. The meaning may have been "delayer of death" (Paus. 3. 13.4).

BITON. He and his brother, Cleobis, performed an act of outstanding filial devotion for their mother, who prayed that Athena grant her sons what was best for mortals. Athena caused them to sleep and never waken. (Cf. AGAMEDES)

CHARON, son of Erebus, was the aged dirty ferryman who took in his boat the shades of the dead across the river Styx into Hades.

DIOSCURI AMBULI was their surname at Sparta. It may have meant "delayers of death" (Paus. 3. 13.4).

HERMES CATAEBATES was a surname from his office of conducting the shades of the dead to the underworld.

HERMES NECROPOMPOS. As HERMES CATAEBATES.

HERMES PSYCHOGOGOS. As HERMES CATAEBATES.

HERMES PSYCHOPOMPOS. As HERMES CATAEBATES.

LARVAE were spirits of the dead worshipped at Rome.

LIBITINA was an ancient Roman divinity who presided over the burial of the dead. Roman poets frequently employed her name to mean death itself (Hor. *Carm.* 3. 30.6; Hor. *Sat.* 2. 6.19; Hor. *Epist.* 2. 1.49; Juv. 14. 122).

MANES, i.e., "the good ones," was the general name by which the Romans designated the souls of the departed. At certain seasons, which were looked upon as sacred days, sacrifices were offered to the spirits of the departed with the observance of various ceremonies. But an annual festival, which belonged to all of the Manes in general, was celebrated on the 19th of February, under the name of Feralia or Parentalia, because it was more especially the duty of children and heirs to offer sacrifices to the shades of their parents and benefactors (Ov. *Fast.* 2. 535).

PERSEPHONE was the daughter of Zeus and Demeter and was the infernal goddess of death and the dead.

SISYPHUS. Some say that Zeus, in order to take revenge on the treachery of Sisyphus, sent Death to Sisyphus, who, however, succeeded in putting Death into chains, so that no man died until Ares delivered Death, whereupon Sisyphus himself expired.

THANATOS was a personification of death.

ZEUS AMBULIUS was a surname of Zeus at Sparta, perhaps meaning "delayer of death" (Paus. 3. 13.4).

Debauchery

COTYLLO was a goddess of debauchery whose festivals were celebrated during the night.

Decapitation

ALCMENA was the mother of Heracles. After he was raised to the rank of a god, she and his sons, in dread of Eurystheus, fled to Trachis and then to Athens. When Hyllus cut off the head of Eurystheus, Alcmena obtained her revenge by picking the eyes out of his head (Apollod. 2. 8.1).

HERMES. When Io was metamorphosed into a cow, Hera set the hundred-eyed Argus to guard her. Zeus, however, sent Hermes to kill the monster. Hermes lulled Argus to sleep by playing on the flute and then cut off his head.

LITYERSES was a son of Midas who compelled strangers to assist him in the harvest. If they did not surpass him, he cut off their heads and concealed their bodies in sheaves.

MEDUSA was one of the Gorgons. After Perseus cut off her head, Athena had it placed in the center of her shield or breastplate.

MOLUS was a son of Minos. When he attempted to violate a nymph, he was afterwards found without a head. At a certain festival in Crete, they showed the image of a man without a head, who was called Molus (Plut. *De Def. Orac.* 13).

TYDEUS was a son of Oeneus and Periboea. When Tydeus was mortally wounded at the battle of Thebes, Athena appeared with a remedy which was to make him immortal, but Amphiaraus, who hated Tydeus, brought him a different remedy: the head of the vanquished enemy, Melanippus. Tydeus cut it in two and ate the brain, or devoured some of the flesh. Athena, seeing this, shuddered and did not apply the remedy which she had brought (Apollod. 3. 6.8). Tydeus died and was buried at Mecon (Paus. 9. 18.2).

Deception

APHRODITE APATURIA, "the deceitful," was a surname of Aphrodite at Phanagoria and other places in the Chersonesus. By deceit she lured giants who had attacked her to a cave where Heracles killed them (Strab. 11. 495). This name was said to have been given her by Aethra (Paus. 2. 33.1).

Deer, see Hind, Stag

Delight

THELXINOE was one of four Muses mentioned as a daughter of Zeus and Plusia and as Muse of the heart delighting.

Deliverance

ZEUS ELEUTHERIUS was a surname describing Zeus as a deliverer (Plut. *Quaest. Conviv.* 7; Pind. *Ol.* 12. 1; Strab. 9. 412; Tacit. *Ann.* 15. 64).

Deluge, see Flood

Desecration

ATALANTA (ATALANTE). When she was caught in a footrace and thus married Meilanion (or Hippomenes), they embraced in a grove sacred to Zeus and, having profaned the sanctity of the place, were both metamorphosed into lions (Apollod. 3. 9.2). Another account says the grove was sacred to Cybele and that she changed them into lions and yoked them to her chariot (Ov. *Met.* 8. 318, 10. 565).

AUGE. When her father learned from an oracle that something unholy was profaning the temple of Athena and thereby causing a famine, he found Auge's illegitimate son in the temple and exposed the child on Mt. Parthenion (Apollod. 2. 7.4, 3. 9.1).

Destiny, see Fate

Destruction

ARES. As god of war, he delighted in the destruction of cities.

VEIOVIS was an Etruscan deity of a destructive nature, whose fearful lightnings produced deafness to those who were struck by them (Amm. Marc. 17. 10).

Dew

EOS, goddess of the dawn and mother of Memnon, wept for her dead son every morning, and the dewdrops which appear in the morning are the tears of Eos (Virg. *Aen.* 8. 384; Ov. *Met.* 13. 622).

Diadem, see Crown

Diamastigosis, see Scourging

Dice

CHARITES. As companions of Apollo, they always carried dice, the god's favorite game.

HERACLES BURAICUS. At his oracle in a cave near Bura, persons threw four dice outside the cave and had the meaning explained with the help of a painting hung inside the cave (Paus. 7. 25.6).

HERMES was taught by Apollo the art of prophesying by means of dice. He also presided over the game of dice as the god of good luck.

PALAMEDES, son of Nauplius, was described as the inventor of dice.

PATROCLUS. While yet a boy, he involuntarily slew Clysonymus, a son of Amphidamas, during a game of dice.

THERSITES, a son of Agrius, was the ugliest and most impudent talker among the Greeks at Troy. In Delphi he was represented by Polygnotus in the act of playing dice with Palamedes (Paus. 10. 31.1; Soph. *Phil.* 442).

Dirge

IALEMUS, son of Apollo and Calliope, was said to be the inventor of the dirge, a song sung on the most mournful occasions (Aeschyl. *Suppl.* 106; Eurip. *Herc.Fur.* 109; Eurip. *Suppl.* 283).

LINUS was the personification of a dirge or lamentation. He was a son of Apollo and a Muse or Psamathe (Apollod. 1. 3.2; Paus. 1. 43.7, 2. 19.7). When his mother was put to death by her father, Apollo was propitiated by Argive women singing dirges. According to some legends, Linus was killed by his father, and every year dirges were sung in his honor. Linus is called the inventor of dirges.

NAENIA. At Rome, she was a goddess and the personification of a dirge or lamentation. Her chapel was outside the city close to the Porta Viminalia.

Disappearance

HARPIES. When a person disappeared from the earth, it was said that he had been carried off by the Harpies (Hom. *Od.* 16. 371).

NEPHELE became so enraged over her husband Athamas' love for Ino that she disappeared, and Ino became his wife.

Discord

ERIS was the goddess who calls for war and discord. She threw the golden apple inscribed "for the fairest" among the assembled gods which, in effect, perpetrated the Trojan War.

DISCORDIA was goddess of malevolence and discord. According to Roman myth, she threw the apple of discord at the wedding feast of Peleus and Thetis.

Discus

CROCUS was metamorphosed into a saffron plant by his friend Hermes, who had killed him in a game of discus (Ov. *Met.* 4. 283).

HYACINTHUS was a beautiful youth beloved by Apollo, who unintentionally killed him during a game of discus (Apollod. 1. 3.3). Some relate that Zephyrus (or Boreas) from jealousy of Apollo, drove the discus of the god against the head of the youth and thus killed him (Lucian *Dial.Deor.* 14; Philostr. *Imag.* 1. 24; Ov. *Met.* 10. 184).

PALAMEDES, son of Nauplius, was described as the inventor of the discus.

PELEUS. With Telamon he slew his stepbrother, Phocus, with a discus.

PERSEUS. According to some traditions, he killed his grandfather, Acrisius, during the funeral games celebrated for Polydectes by throwing a discus, which was caught by the wind and struck the head of Acrisius.

Disease

ANGERONA (ANGERONIA). When sacrifices were vowed to her, the disease called angina disappeared.

ANIGRIDES were nymphs of the river Anigrus in Elis. In a grotto there, persons suffering from skin diseases were cured by prayers and sacrifices to the nymphs.

CER. Ceres were the goddesses presiding over the necessity of death. Epidemic diseases were often personified as the Ceres.

DIONYSUS. At his oracle of Amphicleia in Phocis, he cured diseases by revealing the remedies to the sufferers in their dreams (Paus. 10. 33.5). He was invoked as a savior from raging diseases (Soph. *Oed.Tyr.* 210; Lycoph. 206).

MACHAON, son of Asclepius, had his tomb at Gerenia in Messenia, where a sanctuary was dedicated to him in which sick persons sought relief from their sufferings.

ORBONA was a female Roman divinity who was invoked by parents who had been deprived of their children and desired to have others. She was also invoked to protect against the dangerous maladies of children (Cic. *De Nat.Deor.* 3. 25; Plin. *H.N.* 2. 7).

Disfigurement

BROTEAS, son of Vulcan and Minerva, burnt himself so that he might not be taunted for his ugliness (Ov. *Ib.* 517).

Disguise

ANNA PERENNA. When Mars was in love with Minerva, he invoked the aged Anna, a Roman divinity, for assistance. She appeared before him, disguised as Minerva, and when the god took hold of her veil and wanted to kiss her, she laughed him to scorn (Ov. *Fast.* 3. 657).

APHRODITE visited Anchises in the guise of a daughter of the Phrygian king, Otreus. When she revealed herself, she exacted a promise not to betray her identity on the pain of being struck by lightning (Hom. *Hymn.in Ven.* 45).

APOLLO. In order to encourage Hector, he assumed the appearance of Mentes, leader of the Cicones in the Trojan War. He also assumed the appearance of Asius when he wanted to stimulate Hector to fight against Patroclus (Hom. *Il.* 16. 715).

ATHENA assumed the appearance of Deiphobus in order to urge Hector to take a stand against Achilles, from whom he had fled (Hom. *Il.* 22. 227). After the gods in council had determined that Odysseus should return home from the island of Ogygia, Athena, assuming the appearance of Mentes, king of the Taphians, went to Ithaca and advised Telemachus to eject his mother's troublesome suitors from his house, and then to go to Pylos and Sparta to gather information concerning his father. In the form of Mentor, son of Alcimus and friend of Odysseus (Hom. *Od.* 2. 269, 402, 3. 13, 4. 654), she accompanied him to Pylos, where they were hospitably received by Nestor, who assisted them in the eventual fulfillment of the prophecy of Proteus concerning Odysseus (Hom. *Od.* 1 – 4). Athena also assumed the appearance of Iphthime, sister of Penelope, when she appeared to the unfortunate mother of Telemachus (Hom. *Od.* 4. 797).

CEPHALUS, husband of Procris, was beloved by Eos, whom he rejected; so Eos bade him test the fidelity of his wife. She metamorphosed him into a stranger and gave him rich presents to tempt Procris. She succumbed and, upon discovery of his true being, fled to Crete and sought the advice of Artemis. (See also PROCRIS)

HERA, stimulated by jealousy, appeared to Semele in the form of Beroe, her aged nurse, and induced her to pray to Zeus to visit her in the same splendor and majesty with which he appeared to Hera. She also appeared to Zeus in disguise and urged him to fulfill Semele's prayer. He did so; Semele was terrified and consumed in flames, whereupon she gave premature birth to Dionysus (Apollon.Rhod. 4. 1137). Another time, when Hippolyte, queen of the Amazons, promised Heracles her girdle, Hera, disguised as an Amazon, spread the report that the queen had been robbed by a stranger. The Amazons rose against him, and Heracles slew Hippolyte and took her girdle (Apollod. 2. 5.9).

HERMES. When Battus observed him stealing the cattle of Apollo, he bribed Battus to keep the secret, but, not trusting him, Hermes returned in disguise and bribed him to reveal the secret. When he did, Hermes changed him into a stone (Ov. *Met.* 2. 688).

INO was a daughter of Cadmus and Harmonia. After her supposed death, she came back in disguise to the abode of her husband, Athamas, whose new wife, Themisto, had resolved to kill Ino's children. She ordered one of her slaves at night to cover her own children with white and Ino's children with black so that she would know which were which. The slave was Ino in disguise, who did just the opposite, so that Themisto killed her own children. When Themisto discovered what she had done, she hanged herself.

IRIS. Assuming the appearance of Beroe, wife of Doryclus, Iris persuaded the women to set fire to the ships of Aeneas on the coast of Sicily (Virg. *Aen.* 5. 620).

IXION. When he fell in love with Hera, Zeus made a phantom resembling Hera, and by it Ixion became the father of a centaur.

LEUCIPPUS was in love with Daphne and, disguised as a maiden, hunted with her. But Apollo's jealousy caused his discovery during the bath, and he was killed by the nymphs (Paus. 8. 20.2).

ORESTES pretended to be a messenger of Strophius to Argos to announce his own death, and brought ashes of the deceased (Soph. *Elect.* 1110). He also visited the tomb of Agamemnon, his father, in disguise and sacrificed upon it a lock of his hair.

PARIS. Some say that Aphrodite deceived Helen by giving Paris the appearance of Menelaus.

POSEIDON knew that Tyro was in love with the river god, Enipeus. In order to seduce her, he metamorphosed into the form of Enipeus and fathered her twins, Pelias and Neleus (Apollod. 1. 9.8). Ovid (*Met.* 6. 116) relates that Poseidon, in the form of Enipeus, begot by Iphimedeia two sons, Otus and Ephialtes. In the Trojan War, he sided with the Greeks and sometimes assumed the appearance of a mortal hero to encourage the Greeks (Hom. *Il.* 13. 12, 44, 209, 351, 357, 677, 14. 136, 510).

PROCRIS, disguised as a youth, hunted with her dog and spear (neither of which ever missed the quarry) in the company of Cephalus. This was after he had tested her by seducing her in disguise. Cephalus wanted to buy the dog and spear, but she refused to part with them at any price but love. He agreed to the bargain, whereupon she revealed herself, and they were reconciled. (See also CEPHALUS)

ZEUS disguised as Amphitryon, husband of Alcmena, fathered her son, Heracles.

See also: TRANSVESTISM

Dish

PATELLARII DII, divinities to whom sacrifices were offered in dishes (*patellae*), were perhaps the same as the Lares (Plaut. *Cistell.* 2. 1.45; Ov. *Fast.* 2. 634).

Dishonesty

HERMES was the god of dishonest people.

Dismemberment

ABSYRTUS. When Aeetes pursued Jason, Medea, and the Argonauts as they were fleeing with the golden fleece, Medea dismembered the body of her brother, Absyrtus, and scattered his limbs on the water, so that Aeetes was detained while he gathered the pieces and buried them.

ASTYDAMEIA. When Peleus besieged Iolcus, he slew Astydameia and led his warriors into the city over the scattered limbs of her body (Apollod. 3. 13.7; Apollon. Rhod. 1. 91).

AURA. When she became by Dionysus the mother of twins, Aura was seized at the moment of their birth with madness, tore one of her children to pieces, and then threw herself into the sea (Nonn. 260).

DIONYSUS. According to one story, his body was cut up and thrown into a cauldron by the Titans, but he was restored and cured by Rhea or Demeter (Paus. 8. 37.3; Diod. 3. 62).

DIONYSUS ZAGREUS was the surname of the mystic Dionysus. He was torn to pieces by the Titans, though he defended himself bravely and assumed various forms. Athena carried his heart to Zeus.

GLAUCUS. According to some writers, he was torn to pieces by his flesh-eating mares after they were seized with madness from drinking from a sacred well in Boeotia or from eating a herb called hippomanes (Paus. 9. 8.1).

HIPPASUS was given up by his mother, Leucippe, to be torn to pieces. She committed this act in a blind frenzy to atone to Dionysus for avoiding his rites.

LYCURGUS, king of Thrace, having brought a famine on the land of the Edones by inhospitable treatment of Dionysus, was put in chains and led to Mt. Pangaeum, where he was torn to pieces by horses. An oracle had told the Edones that the country would not be restored to fertility unless they did this. Another story states that for having tried to destroy all the vines of his country, he was driven mad by Dionysus. In this state he killed his wife and son and cut off one (some say both) of his legs; or, according to others, he killed himself.

MEDEA (MEDEIA). In order to take vengeance on Pelias for all the crimes he had committed against Jason, she persuaded the daughters of Pelias to cut their father into pieces and boil his limbs in a cauldron, promising them it would make him young again. She had demonstrated the process earlier by changing a ram into a lamb. But Pelias remained dismembered and dead. (See also ABSYRTUS)

ORPHEUS. His grief for his lost wife led him to treat with contempt the Thracian women, who in revenge tore him to pieces under the excitement of their Bacchanalian orgies. The Muses collected the fragments of his body and buried them at Leibethra at the foot of Mt. Olympus.

PELOPS was called an Arcadian by some. They state that he slew the Arcadian king, Stymphalus, and scattered the limbs of his body (Apollod. 3. 12.6).

PENTHEUS was a king of Thebes, who was opposed to the introduction of the worship of Dionysus in his kingdom. He was torn to pieces by his mother, Agave, and two other Maenads, Ino and Autonoe, who in their Bacchic frenzy believed him to be a wild beast (Ov. *Met.* 3. 513; Eurip. *Bacch.* 1215; Philostr. *Imag.* 1. 1; Apollod. 3. 5.2).

PHILOTTUS. In one story, Niobe was the daughter of Assaon and wife of Philottus. When she boasted about her children, Philottus was torn to pieces during the chase.

PROCRUSTES (See SINIS)

SINIS (SINNIS), often called Procrustes, was a robber on the isthmus of Corinth. He killed travellers by tying them to the tops of fir trees which he curled and then let spring up again. He himself was killed in this manner by Theseus (Apollod. 3. 16.2; Plut. *Thes.* 8; Paus. 2. 1.3; Diod. 4. 59; Eurip. *Hippol.* 977; Ov. *Met.* 7. 440).

Disobedience

EUMENIDES, the avenging deities, punished disobedience.

Distaff

PALLADIUM. This image of Pallas Athena held a spear in its right hand and a spindle and distaff in its left (Apollod. 3. 12.3; Dionys. 1. 69).

Ditamy, see Herb

Dog

ACTAEON. Pausanias (9. 2.3) relates that Actaeon was in love with Semele and that Artemis caused him to be torn to pieces by his dogs to prevent his marrying her. The usual story is that this punishment was as a result of his accidentally observing the goddess bathing naked in a stream. She changed him into a stag, and his dogs destroyed him. (See also TELCHINES)

AGRE, one of Actaeon's dogs, killed him when he was changed into a stag.

AIDONEUS, a king of the Molossians, thinking that Theseus and Peirithous were suitors for his daughter's hand, promised to give her to Peirithous if he would fight and conquer his dog, Cerberus.

AMPHITRYON. A wild fox which he was ordered to destroy could not be overtaken by anyone, so Amphitryon went to Cephalus of Athens, who owned a dog that overtook any animal it pursued.

ANTILOCHUS, son of Nestor, was exposed on Mt. Ida and suckled by a dog.

ARES (See ENYALIUS)

ARTEMIS. The dog was sacred to her.

ARTEMIS GENETYLLIS was a surname of Artemis as protectress of births. Under this name women sacrificed dogs to her (Aristoph. *Lys.* 2).

ASCLEPIUS. On being exposed at birth, he was fed by a goat and watched by a dog. Sometimes statues of him show a dog lying at his side.

AURA was the name of one of Actaeon's dogs.

CANACE. Her offspring by her brother, Macareus, was thrown to the dogs by their father, Aeolus.

CEPHALUS was persuaded by Amphitryon to give up his dog to hunt the fox which was ravaging the Cadmean territory. (See also LAELAPS and PROCRIS)

CERBERUS (1) was the many-headed dog that guarded the entrance of Hades (Hom. *Il.* 8. 368; Hom. *Od.* 11. 623).

CERBERUS (2) (See AIDONEUS)

CRIMISSUS, the river god, in the shape of a bear or dog, begot by Segesta, daughter of Phoenodamas, a son called Aegestus (Egestus or Acestes), by whom Egesta in Sicily was built (Dionys. 1. 52).

ENYALIUS. The youths of Sparta sacrificed young dogs to Ares under the name of Enyalius (Paus. 3. 14.9).

HECATE. As goddess of purifications and expiations, she was accompanied in the underworld by Stygian dogs (Apollon. Rhod. 3. 1211; Lycoph. 1175; Hor. *Sat.* 1. 8.35; Virg. *Aen.* 6. 257). She wandered about on the earth with the souls of the dead, and her approach was announced by the whining and howling of dogs. Sacrifices to Hecate consisted of dogs. She was often described as having three heads, one of them that of a dog.

HECUBA (HECABE). In accordance with a prophecy by Polymestor, she was metamorphosed into a dog and leapt into the sea at a place called Cynosema (Thuc. 8. 104). According to Ovid (*Met.* 13. 423–575), this prophecy was fulfilled in Thrace, the inhabitants of which stoned her; but she was metamorphosed into a dog, and in this form howled through the country for a long time.

HERACLES. The twelfth labor of Heracles was to fetch from Hades the multiheaded dog, Cerberus. (See also ORTHRUS)

HYLAEUS was one of the dogs of Actaeon (Ov. *Met.* 3. 213).

IPHICLUS kept a ferocious dog to guard his cattle; the beast could be approached by neither man nor animal. When Melampus tried to steal the cattle for Neleus on behalf of his brother, Bias, who wished to marry Neleus' daughter, he was caught and imprisoned with the help of the dog (Apollod. 1. 9.12).

LAELAPS was the dog of Procris. She had received this extremely swift animal as a present either from Artemis or Minos and afterward left it to her husband, Cephalus. To deliver the city of Thebes from a monster fox, the dog was sent out. The dog overtook the fox and both animals were changed by Zeus into stone (Apollod. 2. 4.6; Ov. *Met.* 7. 771).

LARES. The dog was the ordinary sacrifice offered to the Lares.

LINUS was exposed by Psamathe, his mother. He was found by shepherds, who brought him up, but the child was later torn to pieces by dogs.

MAERA (MERA) was the faithful dog of Icarius, who led his daughter, Erigone, to Icarius' grave. Maera was placed among the constellations as the Dog-Star.

NELEUS and his brother, Pelias, were exposed as infants by their mother. Neleus was suckled by a she-dog. Both were brought up by a shepherd.

ODYSSEUS in the guise of a beggar was recognized by his old dog when he arrived home.

ORESTHEUS was a son of Deucalion and king of the Ozolian Locrians in Aetolia. His dog is said to have given birth to a piece of wood, which Orestheus concealed in the earth. In the spring, a vine grew forth from it, from the sprouts of which he derived the name of his people, *Ozolae* (Paus. 10. 38.1).

ORTHRUS was the dog of Geryones, who was begotten by Typhon and Echidna (Hes. *Theog.* 293; Apollod. 2. 5.10). During the performance of his tenth labor, Heracles overcame the dog, Orthrus, who guarded the red oxen of Geryones in Erytheia. Orthrus was also credited with fatherhood of the Sphinx and the Nemean lion.

PANDAREUS, son of Merops of Miletus, is said to have stolen the golden dog which Hephaestus had made from the temple of Zeus in Crete and to have carried it to Tantalus. When Zeus sent Hermes to Tantalus to claim the dog back, Tantalus declared it was not in his possession. The god, however, took the amimal by force and threw Mt. Sipylus upon Tantalus. Some say that his severe punishment in the lower world resulted from this deception.

PROCRIS, wife of Cephalus, was given by Artemis a dog which always found its quarry and a spear that never missed its mark. After she and Cephalus were reconciled over her infidelity (and his), she followed him often to the hunt because she feared that Eos would try to seduce him again. On a hunt, Cephalus accidentally killed her with the never-erring spear.

RHADAMANTHYS. A law ascribed to him said man should not swear by the gods but by a goose, a dog, or a ram.

SCYLLA, daughter of Crateis, was a monster who dwelt on a rock on the Italian coast opposite Sicily. She barked like a dog, had twelve feet, six long necks and mouths, each of which contained three rows of sharp teeth. One tradition says that through trickery Scylla, once a beautiful maiden, was metamorphosed in such a manner that the upper part of her body remained that of a woman, while the lower part was changed into the tail of a fish or serpent surrounded by dogs (Ov. *Met.* 13. 732, 905, 14. 40; Tibull. 3. 4.89).

TELCHINES were a mysterious race of artisans and magicians. Some state that these beings were originally the dogs of Actaeon and were changed into men. The following are mentioned as the names of individual Telchines: Mylas, Atabyrius, Antaeus, Megalesius, Hormenus, Lycus, Nicon, Simon, Chryson, Argyron, and Chalcon.

Dog Grass

ARES. Dog grass was sacred to him.

Dolphin

ALCIMEDON was one of the Tyrrhenian sailors who wanted to carry off the infant Dionysus from Naxos, but he and his companions were metamorphosed into dolphins.

APOLLO DELPHINIUS was a surname derived from his having shown Cretan colonists the way to Delphi while riding on a dolphin or metamorphosing himself into a dolphin. Under this name he had temples at Athens, Cnossus, Didyma, and Massilia.

ARETHUSA. Her head was represented on coins of Syracuse surrounded by dolphins.

ARION was a semi-legendary Greek bard and great master of the lyre. When robbed by sailors, he invoked the gods on his lyre, leapt overboard and was carried by a dolphin to shore (Herod. 1. 24; Gell. 16. 19; Paus. 3. 25.5).

DIONYSUS. For a voyage from Icaria to Naxos he hired a ship, which belonged to Tyrrhenian pirates; but instead of landing at Naxos the men steered toward Asia to sell him there. The god, however, changed the mast and oars into serpents and himself into a lion; he filled the vessel with ivy and the sound of flutes. The sailors were seized with madness and leaped into the sea, where they were metamorphosed into dolphins (Apollod. 3. 5.3; Ov. *Met.* 3. 582). The dolphin was sacred to Dionysus.

ENALUS. When his beloved was chosen by lot to be sacrificed to Amphitrite, he leapt with her into the sea. They were saved by dolphins.

ICADIUS was a Cretan, who, guided by Apollo in the form of a dolphin, came to Mt. Parnassus and there gave Delphi and Crissa their names.

INO. When she leapt into the sea with her son, Melicertes, to escape the murderous insanity of her husband, Athamas, the two were carried by a dolphin to the coast of Corinth.

LIBYS was one of the Tyrrhenian pirates whom Dionysus changed into dolphins (Ov. *Met.* 3. 617).

MELANTHO, daughter of Deucalion, became the mother of Delphus by Poseidon, who seduced her in the form of a dolphin (Ov. *Met.* 6. 120).

MELANTHUS was one of the Tyrrhenian pirates who tried to carry off young Dionysus but were metamorphosed into dolphins (Ov. *Met.* 3. 671).

MELAS was one of the Tyrrhenian pirates who tried to carry off young Dionysus but were metamorphosed by him into dolphins (Ov. *Met.* 3. 671).

MELICERTES. When Ino, his mother, leapt with him into the sea, he was carried by dolphins into a port on the Corinthian isthmus (Paus. 1. 44.11, 2. 1.3; Plut. *Quaest.Conviv.* 5. 32). In works of art, Melicertes (or Palaemon, as he was known after he was changed into a marine deity) is represented as a boy carried by marine deities or dolphins (Philostr. *Imag.* 2. 16).

OPHELTES was one of the Tyrrhenian pirates who tried to carry off Dionysus and were therefore metamorphosed into dolphins.

PALAEMON (See MELICERTES)

POSEIDON. In works of art, he is often represented in the company of dolphins. (See also MELANTHO)

TARAS, a son of Poseidon by a nymph, is said to have crossed the sea from the promontory of Taenarum to the south of Italy riding on a dolphin and to have founded Tarentum in Italy (Paus. 10. 10.4, 13.5), where he was worshipped as a hero (Strab. 6. 279).

THETIS was a daughter of Nereus and Doris and one of the marine deities. Some accounts say she pursued the mortal, Peleus, on Mt. Pelion, not telling him that she was immortal and a sea deity. But Peleus saw her playing with dolphins and recognized her, thereafter shunning her presence. She reminded him of various other mortal/immortal relationships and promised him a son who would be more illustrious than any mortal, and so persuaded him to be her husband.

TRITON was a son of Poseidon and Amphitrite. He was described as riding over the sea on horses or sea-monsters. Often referred to in the plural, Tritons were sometimes described as having a tail like that of dolphins instead of feet.

Domesticity

HESTIA was regarded as the goddess of domestic life and the giver of domestic happiness and blessings.

LARES were, with the Penates, the household gods of the Romans.

Door

CARDEA. A Roman divinity presiding over and protecting the hinges of doors.

JANUS. The Roman god of gates, doors, and thresholds.

Dove

APHRODITE. The dove was sacred to her.

OENOTROPAE were the daughters of Anius of Delos. Because of their power to change water into wine and anything else into corn and olives, Agamemnon wanted to carry them off by force, so that they might provide for the army of the Greeks at Troy; but they implored Dionysus for assistance, and were metamorphosed into doves (Ov. *Met.* 13. 640).

PELEIA, wife of Melus, hanged herself along with her husband when Adonis died, and she was metamorphosed into a dove by Aphrodite.

PLEIADES were daughters of Atlas and Pleione. According to one story, they were virgin companions of Artemis and, together with Pleione, were pursued by the hunter, Orion, in Boeotia. Their prayer to be rescued from him was heard by the gods, and they were metamorphosed into doves and placed among the stars (Pind. *Nem.* 2. 17).

ZEUS. The fertile doves were sacred to him at Dodona and in Arcadia.

Dowry

DARDANUS. He consulted an oracle, which told him that the town Dardanus would remain invincible as long as the sacred dowry of his wife was kept in the country under the protection of Athena. After his death, the palladia were carried to Troy by his descendants.

Dragon

AEACUS. When three dragons rushed against the newly built walls of Troy, only the part built by Aeacus gave way. It was therefore prophesied that the Aeacids, the descendants of Aeacus, would conquer Troy.

AEETES. Half the teeth of the dragon slain by Cadmus were given to Aeetes, king of Colchis, by Athena (Apollon. Rhod. 3. 1183; Apollod. 1. 9.23). (See also JASON)

AEGINA. Hera sent a dragon to destroy the population of the island Aegina because of Zeus' infidelity with Aegina, the mother of Aeacus. Zeus restored the population by changing ants into men, creating the Myrmidons.

AGAMEMNON. While the Greeks were assembled at Aulis, a dragon crawled from under a tree and devoured a nest containing eight young birds and their mother. Calchas prophesied that the war would go on for nine years and that Troy would be taken in the tenth year.

AJAX (the Lesser). According to Philostratus, Ajax had a tame dragon five cubits long, which followed him everywhere like a dog.

APOLLO. Shortly after his birth, he killed the dragon, Python, on Mt. Parnassus.

APOLLO DELPHINIUS was a surname of Apollo derived, according to some, from his slaying the dragon, Delphine, or Delphyne (usually called Python).

APOLLO PYTHIUS was a surname meaning the Pythian, from Pytho, the ancient name of Delphi, where the god's most famous oracle was located (Hom. *Hymn. in Apoll.* 373). The name Pytho was derived from Python, the dragon which was slain by the god.

ARCHEMORUS was the infant son of the Nemean king, Lycurgus. Left alone by his nurse, who was supplying water for the seven heroes on their way to Thebes, he was killed by a dragon (Apollod. 3. 6.4).

ARISTODEME mated with Asclepius in the form of a dragon (serpent) and so became the mother of Aratus.

ARTEMIS DELPHINA, the surname of Artemis at Athens, was the female form of Delphinius, which was applied to Apollo.

ASCLEPIUS. His image was brought in the form of a dragon from Epidaurus to Sicyon by Echetimus of Sicyon on a car drawn by mules (Paus. 2. 10.3). Asclepius is sometimes represented with his hand resting on the head of a dragon. (See also ARISTODEME)

CADMUS. When some of the men he sent to fetch water at the well of Ares were killed by a dragon, he slew the dragon and, on the advice of Athena, sowed the teeth of the monster, from which armed men grew up and fought each other (Apollod. 3. 1.1). Cadmus and his wife Harmonia were finally changed into dragons and were removed by Zeus to Elysium (Apollod. 3. 1.1). According to others, they were carried to Elysium in a chariot drawn by dragons (Eurip. *Bacch.* 1233).

CECROPS, the first king of Athens, was the son of Gaea. His upper body was human, while the lower part was that of a dragon.

CHIMAERA, the monster, had three heads, one of a dragon, one of a goat, and one of a lion. Some accounts say that the hind part of her body was that of a dragon.

CYCHREUS (CENCHREUS) was honored on the island of Salamis (called after him Cychreia) as a hero, because he delivered the island from a dragon (Apollod. 3. 12.7; Diod. 4. 72). Other traditions hold that Cychreus himself was called a dragon because of his savage nature. Still others say that Cychreus had raised a dragon, which was expelled by Eurylochus (Strab. 9. 393). There was a tradition that while the battle of Salamis was going on, a dragon appeared in one of the Athenian ships and that an oracle declared this dragon to be Cychreus (Paus. 1. 36.1; Plut. *Thes.* 10).

ECHION was one of the five surviving Spartae that had grown up from the dragon's teeth which Cadmus had sown (Apollod. 3. 4.1; Ov. *Met.* 3. 126).

ELEPHENOR. After the fall of Troy, which, according to some accounts, he survived, he went to the island of Othronos near Sicily and was driven away by a dragon (Lycoph. 1029).

GIANTS. Gaea, indignant at the fate of her children, the Titans, gave birth to monstrous and unconquerable giants with fearful countenances and the tails of dragons (Ov. *Fast.* 4. 7, 17).

HYPERENOR, one of the Spartae that grew up from the dragon's teeth sown by Cadmus, was worshipped as a hero at Thebes (Apollod. 3. 4.1; Paus. 9. 5.1).

ION. Creusa, his mother, tried to poison him by giving him a cup of the poisonous blood of a dragon. When a pigeon drank a drop of the blood, it died on the spot, warning Ion and so saving his life.

JASON was set the task by Aeetes of plowing a field with brazen-footed, fire-breathing bulls and then sowing the furrows with the teeth of a dragon. The golden fleece was nailed to a tree in Colchis and guarded by a dragon. When Aeetes refused to surrender the fleece in return for the tasks that Jason perfomed, Medea put the dragon to sleep, and Jason was able to take the fleece and sail away in the Argo.

LADON, the dragon, and the Hesperides guarded the golden apples that Heracles was sent to fetch as his eleventh labor.

MEDEA (MEDEIA) killed her children by Jason, Mermerus and Pheres, and fled in a chariot drawn by winged dragons. (See also JASON)

ORPHEUS, one of the Argonauts, lulled the Colchian dragon that guarded the golden fleece to sleep with his lyre.

PYTHON, the famous dragon who guarded the oracle at Delphi, is described as a son of Gaea. He lived in the caves of Parnassus and was killed by Apollo, who then took possession of the oracle (Apollod. 1. 4.1; Strab. 9. 422).

SPARTAE (SPARTI) comes from the verb *speiro,* and signifies "the sown men." It was the name given to the armed men who sprang from the dragon's teeth sown by Cadmus. They were believed to be the ancestors of the five oldest families at Thebes (Apollod. 3. 4.1; Paus. 9. 5.1, 10.1; Ov. *Met.* 3. 101).

TELEPHUS was a son of Heracles and Auge. When he unwittingly proposed to marry his own mother, she without knowing that he was her son, would hear nothing of the marriage, and resolved to murder him because he had won her hand by assisting her father in a siege. A dragon sent by the gods prevented this crime. When she confessed her intention to Telephus, he resolved to kill her, but as he invoked the aid of Heracles, the relation between them was discovered, and Telephus led his mother back to his own country.

TILPHUSA was a surname of the Erinys, with whom Ares fathered the dragon that was slain by Cadmus.

TRIPTOLEMUS. When Demeter accidentally killed his brother, Demophon, she gave Triptolemus a chariot with winged dragons and seeds of wheat. (In works of art, he is represented on a chariot drawn by dragons.) After receiving the dragon chariot, he rode it all over the earth, acquainting men with the blessings of agriculture.

ZEUS. In the form of a dragon he is said to have begotten Zagreus by Persephone, before she was carried off by Hades (Ov. *Met.* 6. 114; Nonn. 6. 264).

See also: SERPENT

Dream

AESACUS, son of Priam, learned the art of interpreting dreams from his mother, Arisbe. During Hecuba's pregnancy with Paris, he interpreted her dream of giving birth to a burning piece of wood as her giving birth to a son who would be the ruin of the city of Troy.

BRIZO was a prophetic goddess of Delos who sent dreams and revealed their meaning to men.

CASSANDRA (See PASIPHAE)

DAPHNE (See PASIPHAE)

HERMES brought to man the dreams sent by Zeus.

ICELUS, son of Somnus and brother of Morpheus, was believed to shape the dreams which came to man, and from this role he derived his name. (See also ONEIROS)

MORPHEUS was the son of Sleep and the god of dreams. His name signifies the fashioner or molder, because he shaped or formed dreams. (Ov. *Met.* 11. 635). (See also ONEIROS)

ONEIROS (pl. ONEIRATA) was a personification of a dream. Ovid (*Met.* 11. 633) mentions three of them: Morpheus, Icelus (Phobetor), and Phantasus. According to Homer, dreams dwell on the dark shores of the western Oceanus (*Od.* 24. 12), and the deceitful dreams come through an ivory gate, while the true dreams issue from a gate made of horn (*Od.* 19. 562).

PASIPHAE, an oracular goddess at Thalamae in Laconia, was believed to be a daughter of Atlas, or to be the same as Cassandra or Daphne, the daughter of Amyclas. People used to sleep in her temple for the purpose of receiving revelations in dreams (Plut. *Agis* 9; Cic. *De Div.* 1. 43).

PHANTASUS (See ONEIROS)

PHOBETOR (See ONEIROS)

Drink

POTINA was a Roman divinity who was worshipped as the protectress of children and was believed to bless their drink just as Edulica blessed their food (August. 4. 11).

Drought

ARISTAEUS saved the inhabitants of Cos from a destructive drought by erecting an altar to Zeus Icmaeus.

ICARIUS was murdered when he tried to introduce cultivation and worship of the vine to the Athenians. His murderers fled from Athens to Cos where a drought promptly descended. The inhabitants were told to propitiate Icarius with many sacrifices and to beg Zeus to send the winds called Etesiae. Zeus granted their prayers by making the winds blow at the rising of the dog star for forty days (Apollod. 3. 14.7; Paus. 1. 2.4).

POSEIDON. When Inachus, Cephissus, and Asterion gave Hera the possession of Argos, Poseidon was angry and caused the rivers of these three river gods to dry up (Paus. 2. 15.5; Apollod. 2. 1.4). Water was restored to them only during the rainy season.

Drowning

ALCYONE. When her husband, Ceyx, perished in a shipwreck, she threw herself into the sea but was changed by the gods into a bird.

ANNA PERENNA was a Roman divinity. After

the death of her sister, Dido, she came to Italy and was kindly received by Aeneas. She became jealous of Lavinia and threw herself into the river Numicius (Virg. *Aen.* 4).

AURA. When she became the mother of twins by Dionysus, she was seized at the moment of their birth with madness, tore one of her children to pieces, and then threw herself into the sea (Nonn. 260).

BUTES was struck mad by Dionysus for having abducted Coronis and threw himself into a well (Diod. 5. 50).

CAICUS, son of Hermes, threw himself into the river Astraeus; thereafter the river was called Caicus.

HECUBA (HECABE). Some accounts say that after she murdered Polymestor, she was given as a slave to Odysseus and that in despair she leapt into the Hellespont.

LEANDER, the famous youth of Abydos, using the light from the lighthouse of Sestus to guide him, swam across the Hellespont every night to meet his love, Hero, the priestess of Aphrodite in Sestus. One stormy night the light was extinguished, causing him to drown. The next morning Hero saw his body, which had been washed up on shore, and threw herself into the sea. (Ov. *Her.* 18. 19; Stat. *Theb.* 6. 535; Virg. *Georg.* 3. 258).

MYRTILUS was the charioteer of Oenomaus who assisted Pelops in winning Hippodameia. On their journey home, Pelops threw Myrtilus into the sea in order to keep from giving him half the kingdom which he had promised him. As Myrtilus drowned, he cursed Pelops and his whole race (Diod. 4. 73).

NARCISSUS. According to one account, he had a beloved twin sister who died, whereupon he looked at his own image reflected in a well to satisfy his longing for his sister. Some say that Narcissus was drowned in the well.

PALAMEDES, son of Nauplius, falsely accused of treason by Agamemnon, Diomedes, and Odysseus during the Trojan War, was, according to some traditions, drowned by Diomedes and Odysseus (Paus. 10. 31.1).

SCYLLA arranged for the death of her father, King Nisus, because of her love for his enemy, Minos. Her unfilial act horrified Minos, who had her tied to the rudder of his ship, and she was drowned in the Saronic Gulf. (Apollod. 3. 15.5, 6, 8).

TIBERINUS, one of the mythical kings of Alba, is said to have been drowned crossing the river Alba, which was thereafter called Tiberis after him, and of which he became the guardian god (Liv. 1.3; Dionys. 1. 71; Cic. *De Nat. Deor.* 3. 20).

Drunkenness, see Intoxication

Dust

ZEUS CONIUS, "the god who excites or makes dust," was a surname from an unearthed temple in the arx of Megara (Paus. 1. 40.5).

Dwarf

PYGMAEUS was a being whose length is a *pygme,* that is the distance from the elbow to the hand. The Pygmaei (plural) is the name of a fabulous nation of dwarves, who, according to Homer, every spring had to sustain a war against the cranes on the banks of Oceanus (Hom. *Il.* 3. 5). Later writers usually place them near the sources of the Nile, where the cranes are said to have migrated every year to take possession of the fields of the Pygmies (Aristot. *H.A.* 8. 12; Strab. 1. 42).

Eagle

AJAX. When Heracles offered a prayer to Zeus to send a brave son to his friend Telamon, an eagle appeared as a favorable omen. A son was born and was named Ajax (Aias) for the eagle.

GANYMEDE, the most beautiful of mortals, was carried off, according to most traditions, by Zeus in the form of an eagle. Some say that Zeus sent his eagle to fetch Ganymede into heaven (Apollod. 3. 12.2; Virg. *Aen.* 5. 253; Ov. *Met.* 10. 255; Lucian *Dial.Deor.* 4). In works of art he is represented as being carried off by an eagle or giving food to an eagle from a shallow cup.

GRIFFIN (See GRYPS)

GRYPS (GRYPHUS). The body of the griffin was that of a lion, while the head and wings were those of an eagle.

MEROPS, king of Cos, about to commit suicide from grief for his dead wife, was changed into an eagle by Hera and placed among the stars (Eurip. *Hel.* 384).

NISUS. According to some legends, he was changed into an eagle when his daughter, Scylla, betrayed him for love of Minos. When Minos left her in Megara in disgust for what she had done to her father, she leaped into the sea and swam after his ship, whereupon Nisus, in the form of an eagle, dived down upon her, and she was metamorphosed into either a fish or a bird called ciris (Ov. *Met.* 8. 145).

PERICLYMENUS was one of the sons of Neleus, king of Pylos. His grandfather, Poseidon, gave him the power to change his shape at will in battle. When Heracles attacked Pylos, Periclymenus fought him in many forms. At one point he became an eagle and tore at Heracles' face, but Heracles shot him down with an arrow (Ov. *Met.* 12. 556– 72).

PERIPHAS was an Attic autochthon and priest of Apollo. He was honored as highly as Zeus, who jealously planned to destroy him, but Apollo prevailed on Zeus to change him into an eagle instead (Ov. *Met.* 7. 400).

PROMETHEUS. For stealing fire from heaven he was punished by being chained to a pillar. Daily an eagle consumed his liver which, in the succeeding night was restored. Later, Heracles killed the eagle and freed the sufferer.

SPHINX. Sometimes the monster appears with the forepart of its body that of a lion and the lower part that of a man, with the claws of a vulture and the wings of an eagle.

ZEUS. The eagle was sacred to him. In the form of an eagle he visited Asteria and also abducted Ganymede.

Ear

CASSANDRA. The ears of Cassandra and her brother, Hellenus, were purified by serpents in the sanctuary of Apollo, thereby enabling them to understand the future.

HERACLES once met the heralds of Erginus, who were going to demand an annual tribute of oxen from Thebes. He cut off their ears and noses, tied their hands behind their backs, and sent them to Erginus, saying that this was his trubute (Apollod. 2. 4.11; Diod. 4. 10; Strab. 9. 414).

MELAMPUS. Once while he slept, some serpents that he had reared licked his ears with their tongues. When he woke, he was amazed to find that he could understand the language of birds and that with their assistance he could foretell the future (Apollod. 1. 9.11).

MIDAS. When he decided in favor of Pan over Apollo in a musical contest, Apollo changed his ears into those of an ass. Midas concealed them under his cap, but the servant who cut his hair discovered them. The secret so plagued the man that he dug a hole in the ground and whispered into it, "King Midas has ass's ears." He then filled up the hole, but a reed grew up on the same spot, which in its whispers betrayed the secret to the world (Ov. *Met.* 11. 146; Aristoph. *Plut.* 287).

SATYRS. This class of beings was represented as having ears pointed at the top like those of animals.

Earth

DEMETER. Her name was explained by some as *ge meter*—i.e., mother earth.

DEMETER CHTHONIA was a surname of Demeter meaning the subterranean, or goddess of the earth, or protectress of the fields (Herod. 2. 123; Apollon. Rhod. 4. 987).

FERONIA. Regarded in Italy by some as a goddess of the earth or the lower world, she was said to have given to her son three souls, so that he had to be killed three times before he was dead (Virg. *Aen.* 2. 564).

GAEA (GE) was a personification of the earth.

HECATE CHTHONIA. As DEMETER CHTHONIA (Apollon. Rhod. 4. 148).

MELINOE CHTHONIA. As DEMETER CHTHONIA.

NYX CHTHONIA. As DEMETER CHTHONIA.

OPS was a female Roman divinity of plenty and fertility. Her abode was in the earth, therefore those who invoked her or made vows to her used to touch the ground.

POSEIDON GAEEOCHUS was a surname designating Poseidon as "holder of the earth" (Hom. *Od.* 11. 240). Near Therapne in Laconia he had a temple under this name (Paus. 3. 20.2).

RHEA was one of the Titans and a goddess of the earth.

RUSOR, a Roman divinity, was probably an attribute of Tellus, personifying the power of the earth to bring to light the seeds entrusted to her.

TELLUMO was a Latin divinity to whom the priests prayed when sacrifices were offered to the female divinity, Tellus.

TELLUS, among the Romans, was a name by which the earth was personified (cf. Gaea among the Greeks). She is often mentioned in contrast with Jupiter, the god of heaven, and connected with Dis and the Manes. A festival was celebrated in her honor on the 15th of April, and it was called Fordicidia or Hordicalia, from *hordus* or *fordus*, a bearing cow (Ov. *Fast.* 4. 633; Hor. *Epist.* 2. 1.143).

Earthquake

ANCHURUS, son of Midas, leaped into a chasm to save his father's kingdom from an earthquake.

Echo

CANENS was a nymph, who, when her husband was changed into a bird, pined away and became only a voice.

ECHO was a nymph, who, because she diverted Hera's attention from Zeus' dalliances with other nymphs by constant chatter, was changed into an echo. The most famous story about her is that she was in love with Narcissus, who, because he was in love with his own image, did not return her love. She pined away till only her voice was left.

HYLAS. When Heracles went searching for him and came to the well where Hylas had disappeared, the voice of Hylas was heard from the bottom of the well like a faint echo. Some say that he was actually metamorphosed into an echo.

Eclipse

ROMULUS. One day as he was reviewing his people in the Campus Martius, the sun was suddenly eclipsed, darkness spread over the earth, and a dreadful storm dispersed the people. When daylight returned, Romulus had disappeared, for his father, Mars, had carried him up to heaven in a fiery chariot (Hor. *Carm.* 3. 3; Ov. *Fast.* 2. 496).

Effeminacy

MIDAS, son of Gordius, was a wealthy but effeminate king of Phrygia. His effeminacy is described by Philostratus (*Imag.* 1. 22) and by Athenaeus (12. 516).

PARIS. In works of art, Paris was represented as a beardless youthful man of almost feminine beauty.

Egg

ENORCHES, a son of Thyestes by his sister Daeta, was hatched from an egg.

ERICAPAEUS (See PHANES)

EROS. In the ancient cosmogonies and in Orphic poetry, he was described as the first of the gods, who sprang from the world's egg. (See also PHANES)

EURYTUS and his brother, Cteatus, sons of Actor and Molione, according to later traditions, were hatched from an egg (Athen. 2. 58). It is further stated that the two brothers were grown together so that they had only one body, but two heads, four arms and four legs (Athen. 2. 58; Plut. *De Frat.Am.* 1).

LEDA of Sparta, wife of Tyndareus, was visited by Zeus in the disguise of a swan, and produced two eggs, from one of which issued Helen and from the other the Dioscuri, Castor and Polydeuces (Ov.*Her.* 17. 55; Paus. 3. 16.1; Hor.*Ars Poet.* 147).

METIS (See PHANES)

NEMESIS. An allegorical tradition held that Zeus begot by Nemesis at Rhamnus an egg, which Leda found and from which Helen and the Dioscuri sprang, and for this reason Helen is called Rhamnusis (Callim. *Hymn.in Dian.* 232; Paus. 1. 33.7).

PHANES, a divinity in the system of the Orphics, is also called Eros, Ericapaeus, Metis, and Protogonus. He is said to have sprung from the mystic mundane egg and to have been the father of all gods and the creator of men.

PHOENIX. This fabulous bird was reputed to make a large egg of myrrh and seal its dead father inside.

PROTOGONUS (See PHANES)

Elm

PROTESILAUS. His tomb was shown near Eleus in the Thracian Chersonesus (Strab. 13. 595; Paus. 1. 34.2). There was a belief that nymphs had planted elm trees around his grave and that those branches that grew on the Trojan side were sooner green than the others, but that, at the same time, their foliage faded and died earlier; or it was said that the trees, when they had grown so high as to see Troy, died away and that fresh shoots then sprang from their roots (Plin. *H.N.* 16. 99).

Eloquence

HERMES. As herald of the gods, he is the god of skill in the use of speech and of eloquence in general (Hom.*Il.* 4. 193, 7. 279, 385, 8. 517, 9. 684; Aelian. *De Nat.Anim.* 10. 29; Hor. *Carm.* 1. 10.1).

NESTOR was regarded by the Greeks at Troy as eminently wise, just, brave, knowledgeable about war, and eloquent.

Emasculation

AECHMODICUS was castrated by Echetus, the father of his lover, Metope (or Amphissa) (Hom. *Od.* 18. 83, 21. 307; Apollon.Rhod. 4. 1093).

AGDISTIS, a divinity of Phrygia, both male and female and feared by the gods, was unmanned. From its severed member an almond tree grew.

ATYS was beloved of Agdistis. He fell into a fit of madness and emasculated himself when the divinity appeared to him at his wedding ceremony. Others say that when he broke his vow of chastity, Cybele threw him into a state of madness, during which he unmanned himself. Another account says that as a priest of Cybele he fled into the forest to escape the voluptuous embraces of a Phrygian king, but was overtaken, and in the ensuing struggle unmanned the king, who in turn inflicted the same calamity on Atys.

CRONUS emasculated Uranus, his father, and out of his father's blood sprang the Erinyes.

Embroidery

AEDON. In a contest with her husband, Polytechnus, she finished a piece of embroidery before he finished a chair he was making and received a female slave as a prize.

Enchantment

CIRCE, daughter of Helios, was an enchantress celebrated for her knowledge of magic and spellbinding herbs. When Odysseus, returning from the Trojan War, visited her on Aeaea, she changed his men into swine.

MEDEA, daughter of Aeetes and niece of Circe, was a powerful enchantress. She aided Jason in obtaining the golden fleece, restored Jason's aged father, Aeson, to youth, and caused the death of Glauce.

SIRENS (SIRENES), were mythical beings who were believed to have the power of enchanting and charming by their song anyone who heard them. When Odysseus, in his wanderings through the Mediterranean, came near their island, on the advice of Circe he stuffed the ears of his companions with wax and tied himself to the mast of his vessel until he was so far off that he could no longer hear their song (Hom. *Od.* 12. 39, 166).

Enemy

PELLONIA was a Roman divinity who was believed to protect mortals from their enemies (August. 4. 21).

Energy

HORME was the personification of energetic activity (Paus. 1. 17.1).

Engulfment

ALTHEMENES. When he learned that he had unknowingly killed his father, Catreus, he prayed to the gods and, accordingly, was swallowed up by the earth (Apollod. 3. 2.1).

AMPHIARAUS. Pursued by the enemy, he and his chariot were swallowed up by the earth (Pind. *Nem.* 9. 57; Pind. *Ol.* 6. 21).

ANCHURUS. When a great chasm opened in the kingdom of his father, Midas, an oracle said it could be closed by throwing into it the most precious thing Midas owned. Midas threw gold and silver into it without effect, but when Anchurus leapt on horseback into the chasm, it promptly closed (Plut. *Paral. Gr.et Rom.* 5).

BATON. Along with Amphiaraus, he was swallowed up by the earth after the battle of Thebes (Apollod. 3. 6.8).

DAPHNE. Pursued by Apollo, she prayed to her mother, Gaea, who opened the earth and received her.

LAODICE, a daughter of Priam and Hecuba, was so stricken with grief when her son Munitus died that she was swallowed up by the earth.

THALEIA, daughter of Hephaestus, prayed to be swallowed up by the earth out of fear of Hera after Zeus impregnated her. This was done, but in due time she delivered up from the earth twin boys, who were called Palici.

TROPHONIUS. While he and his brother, Agamedes, were robbing a treasury, Agamedes became ensnared, and, to conceal his identity, Trophonius cut off his brother's head. He was immediately swallowed up by the earth.

Entombment

ANTIGONE. When her brothers slew each other in single combat in the battle of the Seven against Thebes, she performed funeral rites for Polyneices against the order of her uncle, Creon, king of Thebes, and was ordered by him to be buried alive.

POLYIDUS. Glaucus, the son of Minos of Crete, died by drowning in a cask of honey. Polyidus, the soothsayer, divined where the body was, and Minos ordered him to restore the boy to life. When Polyidus was unable to perform this miracle, Minos ordered him entombed with the dead boy. In the tomb, Polyidus observed a serpent crawling toward the boy's body and killed it. Another serpent emerged with a herb in its mouth and laid it on the body of the dead snake, whereupon the snake came back to life. Polyidus did this with the dead boy and achieved the same result. He was given rich gifts and allowed to return to his homeland (Apollod. 3. 10.3).

Circe

Entrails

CARNA (CARDINEA) was a divinity at Rome who presided over entrails and the secret parts of the human body.

SORANUS was a Sabine divinity of the lower world. During a sacrifice to him, wolves snatched away the entrails of the offering from the altar. Shepherds chased the wolves into a cave filled with poisonous vapors, which caused a pestilence among them, but the shepherds were saved when an oracle ordered them to live like wolves on prey. They were called Hirpini Sorani (the wolf-people of the god Soranus). At his festival on Mt. Soracte they walked with bare feet on glowing coals carrying the entrails of sacrificed victims (Plin. *H.N.* 7. 2; Stil.Ital. 5. 174; Strab. 5. 226).

TAGES was a mysterious Etruscan being, who is described as a boy with the wisdom of an old man. He was the son of a genius, Jovialis, and a grandson of Jupiter. He is said to have instructed the Etruscans in the art of haruspicy (divination from the entrails of sacrificial victims). The Etruscans afterwards wrote down all he had said, and thus arose the books of Tages, which, according to some, were twelve in number (Cic. *De Div.* 2. 23; Ov. *Met.* 15. 588).

Envy

FASCINUS. Roman generals who entered the city in triumph had the symbol (a phallus) of Fascinus, the averter of evil, fastened under their chariots, that he might protect them from envy of others, for envy was believed to exercise an injurious influence on those who were envied (Plin. *H.N.* 28. 4, 7).

INVIDIA, the personification of envy, is described as a daughter of Pallas, the giant, and Styx (Ov. *Met.* 2. 760).

Epidemic, see Plague

Epilepsy

ALEXIDA was the daughter of Amphiaraus, from whom certain divinities called Elasii (averters of epileptic fits) were believed to be descended (Plut. *Quaest.Gr.* 23).

Eunuch

CYBELE demanded that all her priests be eunuchs.

Evil

APOLLO. His name was thought to signify a god who drives away evil.

APOLLO ACESIUS, averter of evil, was a surname of Apollo in Elis, where he had a temple.

APOLLO ALEXICACUS was another surname of the god as averter of evil, particularly by the Athenians, who believed he had stopped a plague that raged during the Peloponnesian War.

APOTROPAEI were certain divinities the Greeks invoked to avert danger and evil (Paus. 2. 11.2).

ATE, daughter of Zeus, was an avenger of evil deeds.

CARDEA was a Roman divinity who had the power of preventing evil daemons from entering houses.

FASCINUS, an early Latin divinity, protector from evil daemons, was represented by a phallus. This symbol was believed to be the most efficient in averting evil influences.

HERACLES ALEXICACUS was a surname of Heracles meaning the averter of evil.

ZEUS ALASTOR was a surname of Zeus as an avenger of evil deeds.

ZEUS ALEXICACUS was a surname of Zeus as an averter of evil.

Ewe

HERA. The ewe was sacred to her.

Expiation, see Atonement

Eye

ARGES (See CYCLOPES)

ARGUS PANOPTES was a surname of Argus meaning the all-seeing because he had a hundred eyes, some of which were always awake.

ATHENA GLAUCOPIS was a surname frequently given to Athena from the blueness of her eyes.

BRONTES (See CYCLOPES)

CYCLOPES—Arges, Brontes, and Steropes—were sons of Uranus and Gaea; each had only one eye on his forehead. These monsters later were in the service of Zeus and Hephaestus. Another group of one-eyed giants lived as shepherds and included Polyphemus, who imprisoned Odysseus and his men. They managed to escape when Odysseus put out Polyphemus' single eye with a burning stake.

EPHIALTES, one of the giants in the war against the gods, was deprived of his left eye by Apollo and of the right by Heracles (Apollod. 1. 6.2).

GRAEAE, the ancient daughters of Phorcys and Ceto and sisters of the Gorgons, were described as having one eye among the three of them which they passed around as needed. Perseus, by temporarily depriving them of this eye, forced them to reveal the whereabouts of Medusa, one of the Gorgons.

LAMIA was the phantom queen of Libya who frightened children. Zeus gave her the power of taking her eyes out of her head and putting them in again (Diod. 20. 41; Plut. *De Curios.* 2; Strab. 1. 19).

OXYLUS, son of Andraemon, was three-eyed and was made commander of the Heracleidae in their Peloponnesian expedition by order of an oracle (Paus. 8. 5.4).

POLYPHEMUS (See CYCLOPES)

STEROPES (See CYCLOPES)

THERSITES, a son of Agrius, was the ugliest and most impudent talker among the Greeks at Troy. According to later poets, he plucked the eyes out of the dead body of Penthesileia, the queen of the Amazons, who had been killed by Achilles.

Faith

FIDES was the Roman goddess of faith, oaths, and honesty.

ZEUS PISTIUS was a surname of Zeus as god of faith and fidelity (Dionys. 2. 49; Eurip. *Med.* 170).

Falcon

DAEDALION, son of Lucifer, was so grieved at the death of Philonis that he threw himself from the top of Mt. Parnassus and was changed into a falcon.

Fame

FAMA was the Roman goddess of fame.

Family

HESTIA, the eldest child of Cronus and Rhea, was guardian of the hearth and its fire. She was, consequently, the goddess of the home, the family, and the community.

VESTA was the Roman counterpart of Hestia, identical in all her attributes.

ZEUS was regarded as the god who presided over every house and family.

Famine

ALCMAON, son of Amphiaraus, while fleeing the Erinyes, went to Phegeus, the Arcadian king, and was purified by him and married his daughter, Arsinoe. But the country was visited by a famine because of his being a matricide, and he had to leave the country.

ATREUS. After avenging himself on his brother, Thyestes, famine came to Mycenae, in accordance with Thyestes' curse.

ATYS. After Atys was murdered by the father of Cybele, Phrygia was visited by an epidemic and famine (Diod. 3. 58).

AUGE, a priestess of Athena, caused a famine to come on the land because she hid her newborn illegitimate son in the temple.

AUXESIA. After she and Damia were stoned to death during an insurrection of Troezen, famine came to the land. The Delphic oracle directed the inhabitants to erect statues of them out of olivewood; having done so, the people were freed from the famine.

BUSIRIS was a king of Egypt whose country had been visited for nine years with a famine. He consulted a seer, who instructed him each year to sacrifice a foreigner to Zeus.

DEMETER. She brought famine on earth when she realized that Zeus had assisted Hades in the rape of Persephone. She would not listen to entreaties from Olympus, and swore not to restore fertility to the earth until her daughter was restored.

DIONYSUS. Because Lycurgus was inhospitable to him, he brought famine on the land of the Edones. Dionysus stated that the famine would cease only when Lycurgus died, so the Edones put him in chains, and Dionysus had him torn to pieces by horses.

ERICHTHONIUS. According to some traditions, he was an Egyptian who, during a famine, brought grain to Athens and instituted the worship of Demeter and the Eleusinian mysteries.

HYACINTHUS, a Lacedaemonian, in compliance with an oracle, went to Athens and caused his daughters to be sacrificed on the tomb of Cyclops Geraestus for the purpose of delivering the city from famine and plague.

INO, by her artifices, brought about a famine and when Athamas, her husband, sent messengers to Delphi to consult the oracle, she bribed them to report that Phrixus, his son by Nephele, must be sacrificed to end the famine.

MELANIPPUS profaned the temple of Artemis in Patrae by having intercourse with one of her priestesses, Comaetho. In consequence he and his beloved were put to death, and plague and famine came to the whole of Achaia. The oracle of Delphi revealed the cause of these calamities and ordered the inhabitants to sacrifice to Artemis every year the handsomest youth and the most beautiful maiden (Paus. 7. 19.2).

MENELAUS. When a famine came to Sparta, Menelaus, on the advice of an oracle, went to Troy to propitiate the sons of Prometheus, Lycus and Chimaereus, who were buried there. Paris accompanied him from Troy back to Greece (Lycoph. 132).

PHRASIUS, a Cyprian soothsayer, advised Busiris, the Egyptian king, to sacrifice strangers that came to his dominions to avert a famine. Phrasius himself became the first victim of his own advice (Apollod. 2. 5.11).

PRAXITHEA and her sisters, Theope and Eubule, daughters of Leos, were sacrificed by their father at the direction of the Delphic oracle to halt a plague or famine in Athens.

SCEPHRUS was a son of Tageates and Maera. When he was murdered by his brother, Leimon, the country of the Tageatans was visited by a famine, which ended only when Scephrus was honored with funeral solemnities at the order of the Delphian oracle.

STYMPHALUS was a son of Elatus and Laodice. Pelops, unable to conquer him in war, murdered him by strategem and cut his body in pieces. For this crime, Greece was visited with a famine, which, however, was averted by the prayer of Aeacus (Apollod. 3. 12.6).

Fasting

DEMETER. When her daughter, Persephone, was abducted, Demeter wandered about in search of her for nine days without taking any nectar or ambrosia and without bathing.

Fate

APOLLO MOIRAGETES was a surname designating the god as the guide or leader of fate at Delphi (Paus. 10. 24.4).

ATROPOS (See MOIRAE)

CLOTHO (See MOIRAE)

EUMENIDES, together with Zeus and the Moirae (or Parcae), were considered to be in control of men's fate (Hom. *Il.* 19. 87; Hom. *Od.* 15. 234).

HEIMARMENE was the personification of fate.

LACHESIS (See MOIRAE)

MOIRAE were the deities who assigned to every man his fate or his share. Homer usually speaks of only one Moira, and only once mentions the Moirae in the plural (*Il.* 24. 29). Hesiod (*Theog.* 217, 904) and Apollodorus (2. 3.1) distinguish three fates: Clotho, the spinning fate; Lachesis, the one who assigns to man his fate; and Atropos, the fate that cannot be avoided.

NECESSITAS was a Roman divinity who presided over the destinies of mankind.

NEMESIS was a divinity who was a check upon extravagant favors conferred upon man by Tyche, or Fortune. From this function arose the idea of her being an avenging and punishing power of fate, who sooner or later overtakes the reckless sinner (Apollon.Rhod. 4. 1043; Soph. *Phil.* 518; Eurip. *Orest.* 1362; Catull. 50).

PARCAE (See EUMENIDES)

PEPROMENE, "the share destined by fate," occurs also as a proper name in the same sense as Moira, or Fate (Paus. 8. 21.2; Hom. *Il.* 3. 309).

TYCHE AUTOMATIA, a surname of Tyche, characterizes her as the goddess who manages things according to her own will, without any regard to the merit of man.

ZEUS MOIRAGETES was a surname of Zeus as the guide or leader of fate, at Delphi (Paus. 10. 24.4). Fate itself was subordinate to Zeus.

Fear

ANGERONA (ANGERONIA) was a Roman goddess of anguish and fear.

DEIMA was the personification of fear. She was represented in the form of a fearful woman on the tomb of Medea's children at Corinth (Paus. 2. 3.6).

DEIMUS was brother to Phobus. He was a personification of fear, particularly during war.

METUS (See PHOBUS)

PALLOR, "paleness or pale fear," or a personification of it, was, together with Pavor, Fear, a companion of Mars among the Romans.

PERSEPHONE EPAINE. Homer (*Il.* 9. 457) uses this surname in the sense of "the fearful."

PHOBUS (METUS), the personification of panic, is the son of Ares and Cythereia, a brother of Deimus, and one of the companions of Ares (Hom. *Il.* 11. 37, 13. 299, 15. 119; Hes. *Theog.* 934).

Feast

COMUS was the god of feasting and revelry.

NEOPTOLEMUS, son of Achilles and Deidameia, was worshipped at Delphi as a hero, presiding over sacrificial repasts.

Feather

MUSES defeated the Sirens in a contest, took the feathers from the Sirens' wings and put them on as ornaments. In some representations, the Muses are seen with feathers on their heads, alluding to this contest.

STYMPHALIDES, the rapacious birds near the Stymphalian lake in Arcadia, were armed with brazen wings from which they could shoot out their feathers like arrows (Apollod. 2. 5.2; Paus. 8. 22.4).

February

FEBRUUS was an ancient Italian divinity to whom the month of February was sacred, for in the latter half of that month, great and general purifications and lustrations were celebrated. Februus was also regarded as the god of the lower world. The festival of the dead (Feralia) was celebrated in February (Ov. *Fast.* 2. 535).

JUNO. The month of February was sacred to Juno as the goddess of marriage.

Fecundity, see Fertility

Feet

LABDA was a daughter of the Bacchiad, Amphion (Herod. 5. 92). According to some, her name was derived from the fact that her feet were turned outward so that they resembled the letter L (lambda).

OEDIPUS. Because an oracle had stated that any son born to Laius would cause him to lose his life, he had the child born to Jocasta exposed on Mt. Cithaeron with its feet pierced and bound together. When the boy was discovered by a shepherd, he was called Oedipus because of his swollen feet.

SCYLLA was a monster who lived on a rock on the Italian coast opposite Sicily. She barked like a dog, had twelve feet, and had six long necks and mouths, each of which contained three rows of sharp teeth.

Ferocity

ARES THEREITAS. According to Pausanias: "They surname him Theritas, from Thero; for they say that Thero was the nurse of Ares. But perhaps they learned the name Thereitas from the Colchians; for certainly the Greeks know of no nurse of Ares called Thero. However, it seems to me that Ares got the name Thereitas, not because of his nurse, but because a man must be fierce when he fights a foe. . . ." Pausanias associated the name with *ther,* a wild beast (3. 19.8).

Ferryman, see Boatman

Fertility

AMPHION. The Tithoraeans believed they could make their fields more fruitful by taking, at a certain time of the year, a piece of earth from Amphion's grave and putting it on the grave of Antiope (Paus. 9. 17.3).

DEMETER. The notion of her being the giver of the earth's fertility was extended to that of fertility in general, and she was accordingly also regarded as the goddess of marriage.

DIONYSUS PHLEON, "the giver of plenty," was a surname describing the god as promoting the fertility of plants and trees.

EILEITHYIA was the goddess of birth, but frequent births were displeasing to her.

FEBRUUS was an ancient Italian divinity whose rites were celebrated to produce fertility among men as well as beasts.

HORAE, the seasons, promoted the fertility of the earth by the various kinds of weather they sent down (Hom. *Od.* 24. 343; Hom. *Il.* 5. 749, 8. 393).

OPS was a female Roman divinity of plenty and fertility.

PRIAPUS, the son of Dionysus and Aphrodite, was regarded as the promoter of fertility both of the vegetation and of all animals connected with an agricultural life. In this capacity he was worshipped as the protector of flocks of sheep and goats, of bees, the vine, all garden produce, and of fishing (Paus. 9. 31.2; Virg. *Ecl.* 7. 33; Virg. *Georg.* 4. 110).

SILVANUS was a Latin divinity of the fields and forests. He is described as the divinity protecting flocks of cattle, warding off wolves, and promoting the fertility of flocks (Virg. *Aen.* 8. 601; Tibull. 1. 5.27; Cato 83; Nonn. 2. 324).

TYCHON, an obscene daemon, is mentioned as a companion of Aphrodite and Priapus. The name seems to signify "the producer" or "the fructifier."

Festival

CHARITES. The festivals of the gods were the work of the Charites, or Graces.

Fever

FEBRIS was the Roman goddess of fever, or rather the averter of fever. In her sanctuaries, amulets were dedicated which people had worn during a fever (Cic. *De Leg.* 2. 11; Cic. *De Nat.Deor.* 3. 25).

Fidelity

CABEIRI were obscure divinities of Phrygia and the islands of Samothrace, Lemnos, and Imbros. They were particularly honored in the Samothracian mysteries. Lovers swore by the Cabeiri in promising fidelity to one another (Juv. 3. 144).

FIDES was the personification of fidelity or faithfulness (Cic. *De Off.* 3. 29).

PIETAS was a personification of faithful attachments, love, and veneration among the Romans. At first she had a small sanctuary in Rome, but in B.C. 191, a larger one was built (Plin. *H.N.* 7. 36; Liv. 40. 34).

ZEUS PISTIUS was a surname of Zeus as the god of faith and fidelity (Dionys. 2. 49; Eurip. *Med.* 170).

Field

APOLLO NOMIUS was a surname designating the god as protector of pastures and shepherds.

ARISTAEUS NOMIUS. As APOLLO NOMIUS.

DEMETER CHLOE was a surname meaning the blooming, as protectress of green fields. Under this name she had a sanctuary at Athens cojointly with Gaea Curotrophos (Paus. 1. 22.3).

DEMETER CHTHONIA was a surname meaning the subterranean, that is, the goddess of the earth and protectress of the fields (Herod. 2. 123; Apollon. Rhod. 4. 987).

HECATE CHTHONIA. As DEMETER CHTHONIA (Apollon. Rhod. 4. 148).

HERMES NOMIUS. As APOLLO NOMIUS.

MARS SILVANUS was a surname designating Mars as the protector of fields and flocks.

MELINOE CHTHONIA. As DEMETER CHTHONIA.

NYX CHTHONIA. As DEMETER CHTHONIA.

PAN. In Arcadia he was god of forests and pastures as well as flocks and shepherds (Eurip. *Ion* 501; Ov. *Met.* 14. 515).

PAN NOMIUS. As APOLLO NOMIUS.

PERSEPHONE AUXESIA was a surname of Persephone as the goddess who grants growth and prosperity to fields.

See also: AGRICULTURE

Fig

CALCHAS, the soothsayer, was defeated by Mopsus in not being able to state the number of figs on a wild fig tree (Strab. 14. 642, 668).

CHARYBDIS lived under an immense fig tree growing on a rock on the Sicilian coast opposite Italy. Three times a day she swallowed down the waters of the sea and three times a day she threw them up again.

DIONYSUS. The fig tree was sacred to him.

IRIS was the goddess of the rainbow. The Delians offered cakes made of wheat, honey, and dried figs to her.

JUNO CAPRATINA was a surname of Juno at Rome. When an invading army threatened to destroy Rome unless women were sent out to them, the female slaves volunteered to pose as free women and meet the demand. Later, while the sated and drunken invaders slept, the slaves gave a signal from a wild fig tree (*cap-*

rificus), and the Romans attacked and defeated the enemy. This event gave rise to an annual festival (Varr. *De Ling.Lat.* 6. 18; Plut. *Romul.* 29; Plut. *Camil.* 33).

PHYTALUS was an Eleusinian hero who is said to have kindly received Demeter on her wanderings and was rewarded by the goddess with a fig tree (Paus. 1. 37.2).

ROMULUS. When he and his twin, Remus, were set adrift in their cradle and left to die, they eventually floated into the Tiber. Finally the cradle lodged in the root of a wild fig tree, and a she-wolf, coming to the river to drink, found them and adopted and suckled them.

Fin

TELCHINES were a family, a class of people, or a tribe said to have been descended from Thalassa or Poseidon (Diod. 5. 55; Nonn. 14. 40). They are described as marine beings with fins in place of hands.

Finance

JUNO was the guardian of finances, and under the name of Moneta she had a temple on the Capitoline Hill, which contained the mint (Liv. 4. 20).

See also: MONEY

Fingers

DACTYLI. Their name is accounted for by their number being five or ten, or by their serving Rhea as the fingers serve the hand, or by their having lived at the foot of Mt. Ida (Strab. 10. 473).

Fir

ARTEMIS. The fir tree was sacred to her.

ATYS. Dying from loss of blood as a result of emasculation by an amorous suitor (or by self-emasculation), he was found under a fir tree by the priests of Cybele. He wanted to end his life, but Cybele changed him into a fir tree (Ov. *Fast.* 4. 221).

CYBELE. The fir tree was sacred to her.

DIONYSUS. The fir tree was sacred to him.

PAN. Fir trees were sacred to him.

PITYS, a nymph beloved by Pan, was changed into a fir tree (Lucian *Dial.Deor.* 22.4; Virg. *Ecl.* 7. 24).

PROCRUSTES (See SINIS)

SATYRS were dressed with the skins of animals and wore wreaths of vine, ivy, or fir.

SINIS (SINNIS), often called Procrustes, was a robber on the isthmus of Corinth. He killed travelers by tying them to the tops of fir trees, which he curled and then let spring up again. He himself was killed in this manner by Theseus (Apollod. 3. 16.2; Plut. *Thes.* 8; Paus. 2. 1.3; Diod. 4. 59; Eurip. *Hippol.* 977; Ov. *Met.* 7. 440).

Fire

AEGINA, daughter of Asopus, was mother of Zeus' son, Aeacus. She was changed by Zeus into a flame of fire.

AETHILLA, sister of Priam, when captured by Protesilaus and sailing for Greece, persuaded fellow prisoners to set fire to the fleet.

ASCLEPIUS. When the body of Coronis was to be burnt, Apollo (or, according to others [Paus. 2. 26.5], Hermes) saved the child, Asclepius, from the flames and carried him to Cheiron, who instructed the boy in the art of healing.

ATHENA acquainted men with the art of making fire.

CAANTHUS was a son of Poseidon. Failing in his attempt to rescue his sister, Melia, from Apollo, who had carried her off, he threw fire into Apollo's sacred grove, called the Ismenium. The god killed Caanthus with an arrow (Paus. 9. 10.5).

CACA. For revealing the place where the stolen cattle of Heracles or Recaranus were concealed, she was rewarded with divine honors. In her sanctuary, a perpetual flame was kept up.

CAECULUS was an Italian hero of Praeneste. He was born as a result of a spark of fire falling into the lap of his mother. He was exposed near the temple of Jupiter and was found by maidens who came to fetch water. Since he lay near a fire when found, he came to be considered the son of Vulcan. When he built the town of Praeneste, he tried to get people to settle there by claiming to be the son of Vulcan. They disbelieved him, and he prayed to Vulcan to send a sign. A bright flame suddenly surrounded the whole assembly, and the people decided to obey the request.

CHIMAERA was a fire-breathing monster of divine origin. She ravaged the country of Lycia, destroying cattle and starting fires, until she was killed by Bellerophon.

DACTYLI were fabulous beings who were believed to have discovered iron and the art of working it by means of fire.

DEMOPHON, son of Celeus and Metaneira and brother of Triptolemus, was entrusted to the care of Demeter, who at night placed him in fire to secure eternal youth for him. She was observed by Metaneira, who disturbed the goddess with her cries, and the child was consumed by the flames (Apollod. 1. 5.1; Ov. *Fast.* 4. 512; Hom. *Hymn.in Cer.* 234).

HECATE BRIMO was a surname of Hecate meaning the angry or terrifying. Some derive the name from *bromos,* so that it would refer to the crackling of fire, as Hecate was pictured bearing a torch.

HEPHAESTUS was the Olympian god of fire.

HERACLES established the worship of fire in the west.

HERMES rescued Dionysus from the flames which consumed the infant's mother, Semele. (See also ASCLEPIUS)

HESTIA was the Olympian goddess of the hearth, or rather the fire burning on the hearth. She was also regarded as the goddess of the sacred fire of the sacrificial altar.

ILUS. When the temple that housed the Palladium was consumed by fire, Ilus rescued the statue but became blind, as no one was permitted to see it. He propitiated the goddess and recovered his sight (Plut. *Paral.Gr.et Rom.* 17).

IODAMEIA, a priestess of Athena, was changed to stone from seeing the head of Medusa in Athena's sanctuary. In commemoration of this event, a fire was kindled every day on the altar of Iodameia by a woman, accompanied by the exclamation "Iodameia lives and demands fire!" (Paus. 9. 34.1).

IRIS assumed the appearance of Beroe, wife of Doryclus, and persuaded the women to set fire to the ships of Aeneas on the coast of Sicily (Virg. *Aen.* 5. 620).

IXION. When Deioneus demanded of Ixion the bridal gifts he had promised, Ixion treacherously invited him to a banquet and contrived to make him fall into a pit of fire. Later, as punishment for his lust for Hera, Ixion was chained by Hermes to a wheel, which is described as winged or fiery and said to have rolled perpetually in the air or in the lower world.

JASON. One of the tasks Aeetes imposed on him in exchange for the golden fleece was the yoking of brazen-footed, fire-breathing bulls to a plow.

LAODAMEIA. Her husband Protesilaus had been killed in the Trojan War and briefly resurrected. After his second death, she made an image of him and paid it divine honors. When her father, Acastus, commanded her to burn the image, she herself leaped into the flames.

MEDEA (MEDEIA). When Jason deserted her for Creon's daughter, Glauce (or Creusa), she sent to the bride a poisoned garment and diadem. When Glauce put these on, she and her father were consumed by the poisonous fire which issued from the garment (Apollod. 1. 9.28; Diod. 4. 55).

MELEAGER. When he was seven days old, the Moirae appeared, declaring that the boy would die as soon as a piece of wood burning on the hearth was consumed. His mother, Althaea, immediately extinguished the firebrand and concealed it in a chest. He therefore became invulnerable as long as the wood remained unburned, but when he killed his mother's brothers, she lighted the piece of wood, and Meleager died.

NAUPLIUS was the father of Palamedes, who after his son was sacrificed to the artifice of Odysseus in the Trojan War, lighted fires on the cliffs of Euboea to draw the ships to destruction. Some say he failed and threw himself into the fire.

PARIS. Previous to his birth, his mother, Hecuba, dreamed that she had given birth to a firebrand, whose flames spread over the whole city. The dream was interpreted to mean that Hecuba should give birth to a son who should bring about the ruin of his native city, Troy.

PELEUS once observed his wife, Thetis, holding the infant Achilles over a fire (or in a cauldron of boiling water), in order to destroy in him those parts that he had inherited from his father and which were, therefore, mortal. Peleus was terror-struck and screamed so loud that she was prevented from completing her work. Later writers state that she had already destroyed six of their children by fire, and that as she attempted the same with Achilles, her seventh child, she was prevented by Peleus (Apollon.Rhod. 4. 816; Lycoph. 178).

PENATES. On the hearth of each household in Rome a perpetual fire was kept up in honor of the Penates, the household gods.

PERSEPHONE BRIMO. As HECATE BRIMO.

PHOENIX was the fabulous bird, which, when it arrived at a very old age, committed itself to the flames (Lucian *De Mort.Per.* 27; Philostr. *Vit.Apoll.* 3. 49).

PROMETHEUS. When he practiced a deception on Zeus, the king of the gods avenged himself by withholding fire from mortals, but Prometheus stole it in a hollow tube and gave fire to men and taught them to use it (Aeschyl. *Prom.* 110). He is said to have ascended heaven with the assistance of Athena and there secretly to have lighted his torch at the chariot of Helios.

SEMELE. Hera, jealous of Zeus' attention to Semele, in disguise persuaded her to request Zeus to appear to her in the same glory and majesty in which he was accustomed to approach his own wife, Hera. Under protest Zeus complied and appeared to Semele in lightning and thunder, which not only terrified her but caused her to be consumed in flames, whereupon she gave premature birth to Dionysus (Apollon.Rhod. 4. 1137).

SORANUS was a Sabine divinity of the lower world. The Sabine people were ordered by an oracle to live like wolves on prey and were called the Hirpini Sorani (the wolf-people of the god Soranus). At his festival on Mt. Soracte, the Sabines walked with bare feet on glowing coals, carrying the entrails of the victims (Plin. *H.N.* 7. 2; Sil.Ital. 5. 174; Strab. 5. 226).

STATA MATER was a Roman divinity whose image at one time stood in the forum, where fires were lighted every night. After the forum was paved, the fires were kindled in other parts of the town in order not to spoil the stones.

TALOS was a man of brass, the work of Hephaestus. He was given to Minos by Zeus or Hephaestus and guarded Crete by walking round the island three times every day. Whenever he saw strangers approaching, he made himself red-hot with fire and then embraced the strangers when they landed.

VESTA was not represented in her temple in Rome by a statue but by the eternal fire burning on the hearth or altar. Brought to Rome from Troy by Aeneas, the eternal fire was tended by the vestals, her virgin priestesses. Vesta was regarded as chaste and pure as her fire, which every year on the 1st of March was renewed. (Ov. *Fast.* 3. 143).

VULCAN was the Roman god of fire.

VULCAN MULCIBER. This surname seems to have been given to the god as a euphemism and for the sake of a good omen, that he might not consume by ravaging fire the habitations and property of men, but might kindly and benevolently aid men in their pursuits (Ov. *Met.* 2. 5; Ov. *Ars Am.* 2. 562).

Fish

AEGIPAN, son of Zeus by the nymph Aex or the goat Boetis, was sometimes represented as half-goat, half-fish.

APHRODITE. During the battle between the giants and the gods, she metamorphosed herself into a fish.

ARES. During the contest between the giants and the gods, he fled with the other gods to Egypt, where he changed himself into a fish.

ARTEMIS. Fish were sacred to her (Diod. 5. 3).

ARTEMIS EURYNOME was a surname of Artemis at Phigaleia in Arcadia. Here she was represented as half-woman, half-fish (Paus. 8. 41.4).

GLAUCUS, the marine deity, was described as having his lower body ending in the tail of a fish (Philostr. *Imag.* 2. 15).

HIPPOCAMPUS, the mythical sea horse, had the upper body of a horse but from the breast down was a fish. The horses which drew Poseidon's chariot over the surface of the sea were represented as sea horses.

ICHTHYOCENTAURI were fabulous beings; the upper part of their bodies was human, the lower part fish, with horse's hooves in place of hands.

NAIS was one of the Oceanides, who turned her lovers into fishes. Later, she herself was turned into a fish by Apollo.

PRIAPUS was the son of Dionysus and Aphrodite and the god of the fructifying powers and manifestations of nature. Sacrifices to him included fish.

SCYLLA (1). Circe, the enchantress, jealous of Scylla's beauty, threw herbs into a well where Scylla bathed that caused her to be metamorphosed in such a manner that the upper part of her body remained that of a woman, while the lower part was changed into the tail of a fish.

SCYLLA (2) was the daughter of Nisus, whom she caused to die for her love of Minos, the king of Crete. In disgust for her deed, Minos left her in Megara, but she swam after the ship and was metamorphosed into a fish (or a bird) called ciris (Ov. *Met.* 8. 145).

TRITON was a son of Poseidon and Amphitrite. He was described as riding over the sea on horses or sea-monsters. Sometimes described in the plural, Tritons are human in the upper part of their bodies, while the lower part is like a fish.

Fisherman

BRITOMARTIS was a Cretan divinity of hunters and fishermen.

DEMARMENUS was an Eretrian fisherman, who dragged up the shoulder bone of Pelops which had been lost with the ship carrying it from Elis to Troy. On the advice of the Delphic oracle, he restored the bone to the Eleians to avert a plague that was ravaging the country. They appointed him guardian of the venerable relic (Paus. 5. 13.3).

DICTYS was the fisherman who found the chest in which Danae and the infant Perseus had been set adrift.

GLAUCUS of Athedon in Boeotia was a fisherman who had the good luck to eat a part of a divine herb that Cronus had sown and which made Glaucus immortal (Claud. *De Nupt.Mar.* 10. 158). Later, as a marine deity, he was paid homage by fishermen.

PAN. Fishermen owed their success to him (Theocrit. 5. 15).

PRIAPUS, son of Dionysus and Aphrodite, was worshipped as the protector of fishing.

Flaying

ASCUS was flayed and a bag was made of his

skin for throwing the chained Dionysus into a river.

DAMASCUS was flayed alive by Dionysus for opposing the introduction of the vine, which Dionysus was believed to have discovered.

MARSYAS. When he challenged Apollo to a contest on the flute, the god won, and for his presumption Marsyas was bound to a tree and flayed alive.

PALLAS was a giant, who, in the fight with the gods, was slain and flayed by Athena (Apollod. 1. 6.2).

Fleece

AEETES, a son of Helios and Perseis and king of Colchis, killed Phrixus to obtain the fleece of the golden ram, which he nailed to a tree and set a dragon to guard. (See also JASON, PHRIXUS, and THEOPHANE)

ARES. The grove in Colchis where the golden fleece was suspended was sacred to him.

JASON was sent by King Pelias to fetch the golden fleece from Colchis in order to placate the spirit of Phrixus (Pind. *Pyth.* 4. 109; Diod. 4. 40). When the Argonauts arrived and demanded the fleece, King Aeetes promised to surrender it if Jason performed certain difficult tasks. Jason successfully completed the tasks but was forced to steal the fleece, which he did with the help of Medea, daughter of Aeetes.

PHRIXUS, the son of Athamas and Nephele, and his sister, Helle, escaped being sacrificed by riding away in the air on the ram with the golden fleece. Helle fell into the sea but Phrixus arrived safely in Colchis and sacrificed the ram to Zeus Phyxius (or Laphystius) (Paus. 1. 24.2) and gave its skin to King Aeetes, who fastened it to an oak tree in the sacred grove of Ares.

THEOPHANE, a daughter of Bisaltes, was abducted by Poseidon because of her extraordinary beauty to the isle of Crinissa, where in order to escape her suitors, he changed her into a sheep and himself into a ram. Thus, he became by her the father of the ram with the golden fleece, which carried Phrixus to Colchis.

Flint

ZEUS, and more particularly the Roman Jupiter, was sometimes represented holding a flintstone instead of a thunderbolt.

Flock

APOLLO. As a punishment from Zeus, he was required to work for one year for King Laomedon of Troy, tending the king's flocks on Mt. Ida (Hom. *Il.* 21. 446).

ARTEMIS was the protectress of flocks.

HERMES. Apollo conferred on him the office of protecting flocks and pastures (Hom. *Hymn.in Merc.* 568; Lucian *Dial.Deor.* 7; Ov. *Met.* 2. 683).

MALIADES were nymphs who were worshipped as the protectors of flocks and fruit trees.

MARS SILVANUS was a surname designating Mars as the protector of fields and flocks.

NYMPHS were often thought of as protectors of herds and flocks (Apollon.Rhod. 4. 1218).

PALES was a Roman divinity of flocks and shepherds. His festival was celebrated on the 21st of April.

PAN was the great god of flocks and shepherds among the Greeks.

PARIS distinguished himself as a valiant defender of flocks and shepherds.

PELEUS gave Acastus a flock as an indemnity for the murder of his son, Actor. The sheep were killed by a wolf, which was turned into stone by Thetis. Another account says that Acastus abandoned Peleus during a hunt and that Peleus killed Eurytion and then offered his father, Irus, a flock as an indemnity, but Irus refused the sheep. Peleus allowed the sheep to wander about unshepherded until they were attacked by a wolf. This wolf was sent by Psamathe to avenge the murder of Phocus, but she herself afterwards, at the request of Thetis, changed him into a stone.

PHAETHUSA, a daughter of Helios, and her sister, Lampetia, guarded the flocks of her father in Thrinacia (Hom. *Od.* 12. 132; Apollon. Rhod. 4. 971).

Flood

ANDROMEDA. When her mother boasted that Andromeda was more beautiful than the Nereids, Poseidon flooded the land and sent a sea monster to ravage it.

CHRYSOPELEIA. A Hamadryad, who, when a mountain torrent threatened to undermine the oak tree in which she lived, was rescued by Arcas, who diverted the torrent by a dam.

DEUCALION followed the advice of his father, Prometheus, and built a ship, filling it with provisions. When Zeus, who had resolved to destroy mankind, flooded the world, everyone was killed but Deucalion and his wife, Pyrrha.

HERA HYPERCHEIRA, "a goddess who holds her hand over what she protects," was the surname under which Hera had a sanctuary at Sparta, erected to her at the command of an oracle when the country was inundated by the river Eurotas (Paus. 3. 13.6).

NYCTIMUS, a son of Lycaon, was the only one spared by Zeus when he killed Lycaon and his other sons. However, some say that the flood of Deucalion occurred during the reign of Nyctimus as a punishment of the crimes of the Lycaonides (Apollod. 3. 8.1).

PHILEMON, an aged Phrygian and husband of Baucis, kindly received Zeus and Hermes, when they traveled in the guise of ordinary mortals. For this favor Zeus rescued them from a flood and appointed them guardians of one of his temples (Ov. *Met.* 8. 621).

POSEIDON. When the gods assigned Attica to Athena, Poseidon was indignant and caused the country to be inundated (Herod. 8. 55; Apollod. 3. 14.1; Paus. 1. 24.3).

TELCHINES, a mysterious tribe of people said to have been descended from the marine gods, migrated from Crete to Cyprus and then to Rhodes, which became their principal territory. Eventually, foreseeing that the island would be inundated, they abandoned Rhodes and scattered in different directions. Despite their efforts, Zeus caused their destruction by a flood (Ov. *Met.* 7. 367).

Flour

EUNOSTUS was a goddess of mills. Her image was set up in mills and she was believed to keep watch over the just weight of flour.

Flower

AJAX. From his blood sprang up a purple flower which bore the letters *ai* on its leaves.

APHRODITE. After she sprang from sea foam, flowers bloomed under her feet as she walked on the shores of Cythera and Cyprus.

APHRODITE ANTHEIA, "the blooming," or "the friend of flowers," was a surname under which Aphrodite was worshipped at Cnossus.

ARES. Some traditions say that Hera conceived Ares by touching a certain flower (Ov. *Fast.* 5. 255).

CHLORIS was the wife of Zephyrus and the goddess of flowers. She is identical with the Roman Flora (Ov. *Fast.* 5. 195).

FLORA was the Roman goddess of flowers, gardens, and spring.

GENIUS. Every man at Rome had his own genius, whom he worshipped as *sanctus sanctissimus deus,* especially on his birthday, with libations of wine and garlands of flowers (Tibull. 2. 2.5; Ov. *Trist.* 3. 13.18, 5. 5.11).

HERA ANTHEIA, "the blooming," or "the friend of flowers," was a surname under which Hera had a temple at Argos.

HORAE, the seasons, adorned Aphrodite with flowers as she rose from the sea; they also made a garland for Pandora as one of the gifts from the gods.

SILENUS (SEILENUS) was one of the satyrs,

a son of Hermes or Pan and a nymph. When he was drunk and asleep, he was in the power of mortals who might compel him to prophesy and sing by surrounding him with chains of flowers (Philostr. *Imag.* 1. 22; Philostr. *Vit.Apoll.* 6. 27; Ov. *Met.* 11. 91).

SPES, the personification of hope among the Romans, was represented holding a flower in her right hand.

See also: Names of individual flowers

Flute

APOLLO. The invention of the flute was attributed to him. (See also MARSYAS and PAN)

ARDALUS, son of Hephaestus, was also said to be the inventor of the flute.

ATHENA. In Libya, she was credited with the invention of the flute. (See also MARSYAS)

ATYS. In works of art, he is represented as a shepherd with flute and staff.

BORMUS was a beautiful youth who was pulled into a well by admiring nymphs. The Bithynians celebrated his memory each year at harvest time by singing plaintive songs with flute accompaniment (Athen. 14. 620; Aeschyl. *Pers.* 94).

DAPHNIS tried to console himself for his blindness by songs and playing on the flute.

DIONYSUS. When Tyrrhenian pirates attempted to abduct him to Asia to sell him, he changed himself into a lion, filled the ship with the sound of flutes, and performed other magical feats. The sailors were driven mad and leaped overboard to be metamorphosed into dolphins (Apollod. 3. 5.3).

EUTERPE, the Muse of lyric poetry, often appears with a flute. By some she was regarded as its inventor.

HERMES lulled Argus Panoptes, the guardian of Io, to sleep with flute music and then cut off his head.

MARSYAS was the son of Hyagnis, Oeagrus, or Olympus. When Athena threw away her flute, Marsyas found it and was able to produce godlike music on it. He challenged Apollo to a musical contest, and when the god won, Marsyas was bound to a tree and flayed alive for his presumption. He is sometimes regarded as inventor of the flute.

MOLPUS. No flute player was allowed to enter the temple of Tenes in Tenedos because the flute player, Molpus, had borne false witness against Tenes to please Tenes' stepmother, Philonome (Plut. *Quaest.Gr.* 28).

MUSES. In earliest representations, they are shown with a flute or other musical instrument.

OLEN was a mythical flute player who is represented as the earliest Greek lyric poet.

OLYMPUS was a disciple of Marsyas and a celebrated flute player of Phrygia.

PAN. Once when he vied in a contest with a flute against Apollo and a lyre, Midas was the judge and voted for Pan, whereupon Apollo punished Midas by changing his ears into those of an ass.

SATYRS usually appear with flutes, the thyrsus, syrinx, the shepherd staff, and cups or bags filled with wine.

SILENUS (SEILENUS), one of the satyrs, a son of Hermes or Pan and a nymph, is mentioned along with Marsyas and Olympus as the inventor of the flute, which he is often seen playing (Strab. 10. 470).

Fly

MYIAGRUS (MYIODES), "the fly-catcher," was the name of a hero, who was invoked at Aliphera at the festival of Athena as the protector against flies (Paus. 5. 14.2, 8. 26.4).

ZEUS APOMYSIUS, "who drives away the flies," was his surname from Heracles' having sacrificed to Zeus to get rid of flies at Olympia. Thereafter, the Eleans sacrificed to Zeus under this name (Paus. 5. 14.2).

Foam

APHRODITE. Some traditions state that she sprang from the foam of the sea gathered around the mutilated parts of Uranus which had been thrown into the sea by Cronus after he castrated his father (Hes. *Theog.* 190).

APHRODITE ANADYOMENE was a surname given the goddess, alluding to her birth from the foam of the sea.

GRAEAE, regarded by some as marine divinities and personifications of the white foam seen on the waves of the sea, were the ancient daughters of Phorcys and Ceto and sisters of the Gorgons.

Food

ARES APHNEIUS, "the giver of food or plenty," was the surname under which Ares had a temple on Mt. Cnesius, near Tegea, in Arcadia. The surname may allude to the time when Ares allowed Aeropus, his son, to suckle from the breast of his mother, Aerope, after she had died during childbirth.

EDULICA (EDUSA), a Roman divinity, was worshipped as the protectress of children and was believed to bless their food (August. 4. 11).

PHINEUS, son of Agenor and king of Salmydessus in Thrace, was a blind soothsayer. He was tormented by the Harpies, who stole his food when he tried to eat and soiled the rest, so that he was slowly starving to death until he was rescued by the Argonauts.

Footprint

HERMES. When he stole the oxen of Apollo, he put on sandals so that his footprints could not be identified. (Hom. *Hymn. in Merc.* 125; Diod. 1. 16).

Footrace, see Race

Footstool

ANTINOUS, one of the suitors of Penelope, threw a footstool at Odysseus when he appeared in the guise of a beggar (Hom. *Od.* 18. 42).

Force

ARES was a personification of bold force.

BIA, daughter of Styx and the Titan, Pallas, was the personification of mighty force.

Forest

DRYADS (See NYMPHS)

FERONIA, a divinity in Italy, presided over woods and groves.

NYMPHS of forests, groves, and glens were believed sometimes to appear and frighten solitary travelers. They were sometimes designated as Alseides, Hyleoroi, Auloniades, and Napaiai (Apollon. Rhod. 1. 1066, 1227; Theocrit. 13. 44; Ov. *Met.* 20. 490; Virg. *Georg.* 4. 535). Dryads and Hamadryads are often placed in this category as well.

PAN. In Arcadia he was god of forests and pastures as well as flocks and shepherds (Eurip. *Ion* 501; Ov. *Met.* 14. 515).

QUERQUETULANAE, nymphs presiding over the green oak forests near the *porta querquetularia,* or *querquetulana,* were believed to have prophetic powers (Plin. *H.N.* 16. 10, 15.37).

SILVANUS was a Latin divinity of the fields and forests.

SILVIUS, son of Ascanius, may have been given this name because he was born in a wood.

Forethought

PROMETHEUS. His name means forethought.

Fortitude, see Bravery

Fortress

ATHENA was defender of fortresses.

Fortune, see Luck

Fountain, see Well

Four

HERMES. The number four was sacred to him.

MERCURY QUADRATUS. The number four, according to Plutarch, was sacred to Mercury, because he was born on the fourth day of the month.

Fox

AMPHITRYON. Creon, his uncle, agreed to assist him in avenging the slaughter of Alcmene's brothers by the Taphians if he would first kill a wild fox which was plaguing Thebes.

DIONYSUS BASSAREUS was a surname taken, perhaps, from the word fox, *bassaris,* the skin of which originally was used in making the long robes worn by the god and the Maenads.

LAELAPS was the dog of Procris and, later, Cephalus. The Teumessian fox was sent as a punishment to the Thebans, to which they had to sacrifice a boy every month. Eventually, Cephalus sent Laelaps, his swift dog, against the fox. The dog overtook the fox, but Zeus changed both animals to stone (Apollod. 2. 4.6; Ov. *Met.* 7. 771).

Frankincense

LEUCOTHEA, daughter of Orchamas, was beloved by Apollo. When the affair was revealed to her father, she was buried alive and changed into the tree which bears frankincense.

Fratricide, see Murder (of Brother)

Fraud

HERMES. Fraud was one of his attributes.

Freedom, see Liberty

Friendship

ACHILLES. The friendship between Achilles and Patroclus was one of the important themes in the *Iliad.* Patroclus withdrew from the war when Achilles did, as a result of Agamemnon's insult, but reentered the battle when the Trojans attacked the Greek ships. Dressed in Achilles' armor, he led the Greeks up to the walls of Troy, but was killed by Hector. Achilles refused to bury the body until he had avenged himself on Hector and the Trojans. At Patroclus' funeral he killed twelve Trojan men on the grave. He directed that after his death, which had been foretold, his ashes be mixed with those of his friend. (See also ANTILOCHUS)

ANTILOCHUS, son of Nestor and Anaxibia, was distinguished for his beauty and bravery, and was one of the close friends of Achilles.

ARGENNUS was a favorite of Agamemnon, who, after his friend's death, built a sanctuary to Aphrodite Argennis on the river Cephissus (Athen. 13. 608).

DIOMEDEA was the friend of Briseis and had grown up in the house of her playmate's father, Briseus. When Briseis was given to Achilles after the sack of Lyrnessus, Diomedea refused to be parted from her friend.

GALANTHIS was an attendant and friend of Alcmena. At the birth of Heracles, Galanthis tricked Eileithyia and the Pharmacides, who were preventing the delivery, and Alcmena was thus able to give birth. Galanthis was punished for this act of devotion to her friend by being changed by Eileithyia into a cat or weasel.

HERACLES, during his many adventures, usually was accompanied by a friend, or, in a few cases, a lover. Iolaus, his nephew, was one of the faithful companions assisting him on some of his labors, particularly the one in which Heracles killed the Hydra. Iolaus was so devoted to Heracles, even after his master's death, that he prayed to the gods to be made young again, so that he could protect the dead hero's sons, who were still being persecuted by Eurystheus. Ceyx, King of Trachis, was also a friend of Heracles and assisted him against Eurystheus. Iphitus, son of Eurytus, was also one of the hero's friends, taking his side in many disputes, even against his own father, who did not honor his promise to deliver his daughter, Iole, to Heracles for winning an archery contest against him and his sons. Unfortunately, Heracles in a fit of madness killed Iphitus by hurling him from the walls of Tiryns. Philoctetes, son of Poeas, lighted Heracles' funeral pyre, and Heracles gave him his bow and arrows as a reward.

ODYSSEUS. According to Homer, Iphitus and Odysseus became acquainted while searching for the mares of Pheneus in Arcadia, and they became close friends. Iphitus gave Odysseus his father's bow, which Odysseus used against the suitors of Penelope. Odysseus, in turn, gave Iphitus a sword and a spear.

ORESTES grew up in the home of Strophius, husband of Agamemnon's sister, and formed a close and intimate friendship with Pylades, his cousin, which has almost become proverbial. Pylades assisted him in his vengeance on Clytemnestra and his attempted murder of Helen. He also accompanied him on his trip to the land of the Taurians. He married Electra, Orestes' sister, and appears in most of the dramas of Orestes' adventures.

PEISISTRATUS, son of Nestor and Anaxibia, was a friend and companion of Telemachus, whom he accompanied on his journey to Sparta from Pylos to enlist help against the suitors of Penelope.

THESEUS, the young king of Athens, became a very close friend of Peirithous, king of the Lapiths. The friends hunted the Calydonian boar together, and Peirithous helped Theseus abduct Antiope, the Amazon. Theseus assisted the Lapiths in their battle with the Centaurs. Peirithous helped Theseus kidnap Helen from Sparta, and, in turn, Theseus accompanied Peirithous to Hades in an ill-fated effort to steal Persephone. Theseus, with the help of Heracles, managed to escape, but Peirithous remained a prisoner eternally in the underworld.

Frivolity

COTYS (COTYTTS) was a Thracian divinity whose rites were connected with licentious frivolity.

Frog

LETO, insulted by the peasants of Caria when she asked them for water, changed them into frogs.

Fruit

CORA CARPOPHOROS (See DEMETER CARPOPHOROS)

DEMETER. Sacrifices to her consisted of fruit.

DEMETER CARPOPHOROS was a surname, which she shared with Cora (Persephone), under which they were worshipped at Tegea as the Carpophori (Paus. 8. 53.3), fruit-bearers.

EUMOLPUS was sometimes described as having invented the cultivation of fruit trees (Hom. *Hymn. in Cer.* 476).

FIDES, goddess of fidelity, was represented as a matron carrying a basket of fruit.

HESTIA. Sacrifices to her consisted of the first fruits produced in each harvest.

MALIADES were nymphs who were worshipped as the protectors of flocks and fruit trees.

PENATES. The family table was sacred to these household gods, and the table always contained the saltcellar and fruit (Plut. *Quaest. Conviv.* 7. 4; Liv. 26. 36).

PERSEPHONE CARPOPHOROS (See DEMETER CARPOPHOROS)

POMONA was the Roman divinity of the fruit of trees.

TERMINUS was a Roman divinity presiding over boundaries and frontiers. Sacrifices of cakes, meal, and fruit were offered at the stone boundary markers each year, since it was unlawful to stain the boundary stones with blood.

See also: Names of individual fruits

Fugitive

APOLLO PHYXIUS was a surname describing the god as a protector of fugitives.

ZEUS PHYXIUS, "the god who protects fugitives," was a surname of Zeus in Thessaly (Paus. 2. 21.3, 3. 17.8).

Funeral

LIBITINA was a divinity at Rome who presided over funerals.

NAENIA was a divinity at Rome who presided over funerals.

See also: BURIAL

Fur

SATYRS were dressed with the skins of animals and wore wreaths of vine, ivy, or fir.

Furnace

VULCAN was the Roman god of fire. The most ancient festival in honor of him seems to have been the Fornacalia or Furnalia.

Future

CARMENATA ANTEVORTA was a surname describing the Roman goddess Carmenata as looking into the future. Carmenata Postverta (or Postvorta) described her as turning to look backward at the past, which she revealed to poets and other mortals. In like manner, the prophetic power with which she looked into the future is indicated by Antevorta, Prorsa (Proversa) and Porrima. Poets, however, have personified these attributes of Carmenata and thus describe them as companions of the goddess (Ov. *Fast.* 1. 633; Gell. 16. 16).

CARMENATA PORRIMA (See CARMENATA ANTEVORTA)

CARMENATA PRORSA (PROVERSA) (See CARMENATA ANTEVORTA)

Gadfly

IO, daughter of Inachus, was metamorphosed by Zeus into a white cow to hide from Hera his relationship with Io. Hera asked for and obtained the cow and put Argus Panoptes to guard her. Hermes slew Argus and set Io free to wander over the whole earth, but always pursued and tormented by a gadfly sent by Hera (Apollod. 2. 1.2).

PEGASUS. When Bellerophon endeavored to rise up to heaven on the winged steed, the horse threw him off his back when he was stung by a gadfly sent by Zeus (Pind. *Isth.* 7. 6).

Games

ADRASTUS, king of Sicyon, is said to have instituted the Nemean games.

AETOLUS. At the funeral games of Azan, he ran his chariot over Apis, the son of Jason, and was expelled from the kingdom of Elis.

AGAMEMNON. At the funeral games of Patroclus, he excelled in throwing the spear.

AMPHIARAUS with other heroes in the expedition of the Seven against Thebes instituted the Nemean games (Apollod. 3. 6.4).

AMYTHAON was reported to be among those who restored the Olympian games (Paus. 5. 8.1).

ANDROGEUS, son of Minos, conquered all his opponents in the games of the Panathenaea at Athens.

ARCHEMORUS. Amphiaraus instituted the Nemean games in his honor after he was killed by a dragon (Apollod. 3. 6.4).

ATALANTA (ATALANTE) took part in the games which were celebrated in honor of Pelias.

AZAN. The funeral games celebrating his death were believed to have been the first in Greece (Paus. 8. 4.2, 3, 5. 1.6).

CHRYSOTHEMIS, son of Carmanor, was a priest of Apollo at Tarrha in Crete. He is said by a hymn on Apollo to have been a poet and to have won the first victory in the Pythian games (Paus. 10. 7.2).

CLYMENUS, son of Cardis in Crete, is said to have restored in Elis the Olympic games.

DIOMEDES instituted the Pythian games at Troezen.

DIOSCURI were regarded as the presidents ot the public games (Pind. *Ol.* 3. 38; Pind. *Nem.* 10. 53).

EUMELUS, son of Admetus, participated in the funeral games of Patroclus and would have gained the horse race if his chariot had not broken down (Hom. *Il.* 2. 711, 764, 23. 375, 536; Hom. *Od.* 4. 798; Strab. 9. 436).

EURYALUS. At the funeral games of Oedipus he conquered all his competitors except Epeius, who excelled him in boxing (Hom. *Il.* 23. 675–99).

HERACLES (1). After he had slain Augeas and his sons for non-payment of the debt for cleansing the Augean stables, he instituted the Olympian festival and games (Apollod. 2. 7.2).

HERACLES (2) was one of the Idaean Dactyls, who cared for the infant Zeus. At Olympia he contended with his brother Dactyls in a foot race and adorned the victor with a wreath of olive. In this manner he is said to have founded the Olympian games (Paus. 5. 7.4).

IPHITUS was a son of Haemon, Praxonides, or Iphitus. At the command of the Delphic oracle, he restored the Olympian games and instituted the cessation of all war during their celebration (Paus. 5. 4.5).

JUPITER CAPITOLINUS was a surname of Jupiter under which the Roman games and the Feriae Latinae were celebrated.

JUPITER LATIALIS. As JUPITER CAPITOLINUS.

NELEUS. Pausanias (2. 2.2) says that he, in conjunction with Nestor, restored the Olympian games.

NEOPTOLEMUS was worshipped at Delphi as a hero presiding over public games.

NEREIDES. When Ino leapt into the sea with her son, Melicertes, the boy was saved by the Nereides. They also ordered the institution of the Isthmian games in honor of the deified Palaemon.

PELIAS is mentioned as one of the first who celebrated the Olympian games (Paus. 5. 8.1).

PELOPS. When he made himself master of Olympia, he restored the Olympian games with greater splendor than they had ever had before (Pind. *Ol.* 9. 16; Paus. 5. 1.5, 8).

POSEIDON ISTHMIUS was the god worshipped on the Isthmus of Corinth, in honor of whom the Isthmian games were celebrated (Paus. 2. 9.6).

PRONAX was a son of Talaus and Lysimache. According to some traditions, the Nemean games were instituted in his honor (Paus. 3. 18.7).

SISYPHUS. When Ino and her son Melicertes were carried to Corinth by a dolphin, they came under the protection of Ino's brother-in-law, Sisyphus, who instituted the Isthmian games and an annual sacrifice in honor of her and her son. Another story says that he found the body of Melicertes on the coast of Corinth and buried it on the isthmus, whereupon he founded the Isthmian games in honor of him (Paus. 2. 1.3; Apollod. 3. 4.3).

THESEUS. After destroying the isthmian robber, Sinis, he propitiated the spirit of Sinis by instituting in his honor the Isthmian games (Plut. *Thes.* 25).

Garden

DOLIUS was an aged slave of Penelope who took care of her garden.

FLORA was the Roman goddess of flowers, gardens, and spring.

VENUS was said to have presided over gardens (Varr. *De Re Rus.* 1. 1; Plin. *H.N.* 19. 4).

VERTUMNUS was an Etruscan deity to whom gardeners offered the first product of their gardens and garlands of budding flowers (Propert. 4. 2.18, 45).

Garlic

MANIA was an ancient and formidable Italian, probably Etruscan, divinity of the lower world. Boys are said to have been sacrificed to her on behalf of the families to which they belonged. The consul Junius Brutus afterwards abolished the human sacrifices and substituted garlic and the heads of poppies for them.

Garment

ALCMAON. When his mother, Eriphyle, received from Thersander, the son of Polyneices, the peplus of Harmonia, she induced her son to join the Epigoni against Thebes. He first gave the peplus and necklace to Arsinoe, his first wife. When he wanted to give the articles to his second wife, he was slain by his ex-brother-in-law, Agenor.

ARTEMIS CHITONE was a surname representing the goddess with her chiton girt up.

CADMUS. When he married Harmonia, he presented her with the famous peplus and necklace which he had received from Hephaestus or from Europa (Apollod. 3. 1.1).

CALLIRRHOE induced her husband, Alcmaon, to procure for her the peplus and necklace of Harmonia.

DIONYSUS BASSAREUS was a surname taken, perhaps, from the long robe worn by the god and the Maenads.

HARMONIA. Upon her marriage to Cadmus, he presented her with a peplus and necklace, both of which he had received either from Hephaestus or from Europa (Apollod. 3. 4.2).

HEPHAESTUS, god of fire, is represented in art as wearing a chiton which leaves the right shoulder and arm uncovered.

HERACLES. For defeating the forces of Erginus, he was presented with a peplus by Athena. Deianeira, his second wife, unwittingly killed him when she sent him a garment soaked in the blood of the centaur Nessus. This garment, Nessus had told her, had the power to restore the love of an errant husband. (See also LICHAS)

LAODICE, daughter of Agenor, founded a sanctuary of the Paphian Aphrodite at Tegea and sent to Athena Alea a peplus from Cyprus (Paus. 8. 5.2, 53.2).

LICHAS was an attendant of Heracles. He brought to his master the deadly garment which killed him, and as a punishment was thrown into the sea, where the Lichadian islands, between Euboea and the coast of Locris, were believed to have derived their name (Ov. *Met.* 9. 155, 211; Strab. 9. 426, 10. 447).

MEDEA (MEDEIA). When Jason deserted her for Creon's daughter, Glauce (or Creusa), she sent to the bride a poisonous garment and diadem. When Glauce put these on, she and her father were consumed by the poisonous fire which issued from the vestment (Apollod. 1. 9.28; Diod. 4. 55).

MELPOMENE, the Muse of tragedy, is often represented wearing the cothurnus.

PHILOMELA. When Tereus, who first married her sister, Procne, concealed his first wife in order to marry Philomela, he cut out Philomela's tongue. When Philomela learned the truth, she made it known by a few words which she wove into a peplus.

SOSIPOLIS, the boy-hero of the Eleans, was represented wearing a military cloak and carrying the horn of Amalthea in his hand (Paus. 3. 25.4, 6. 20.2).

Gas

MEPHITIS was a Roman divinity who had a grove and temple in the Esquiliae on a spot which it was thought fatal to enter (Plin. *H.N.* 2. 93; Varr. *De Ling.Lat.* 5. 49). It is probable that she was invoked against the influence of the gaseous exhalations of the earth in the grove of Albunea.

Gate

AETOLUS was a son of Oxylus. When he died, an oracle enjoined his parents to bury him neither within nor without the gates of Elis, so he was buried under the gate, where the road to Olympia commenced.

CERBERUS, the many-headed dog, kept watch at the gates of Hades.

CHIMAERA. After her slaying by Bellerophon, she was placed by Virgil (*Aen.* 6. 288) with other monsters at the entrance to Orcus.

HADES kept the gates of the lower world closed that no shade might be able to escape or return to the region of light.

HADES PYLARTES was a surname derived from his keeping the gates to the lower world closed.

HORAE. As ministers of Zeus, they guarded the doors of Olympus.

JANUS, a Latin divinity, was regarded as the god of all entrances and gates. He was also described as the god who had power over the entrance of heaven (Ov. *Fast.* 1. 125).

ONEIROS (pl. ONEIRATA). According to Homer, dreams dwell on the dark shores of the western Oceanus (*Od.* 24. 12), and the deceitful dreams come through an ivory gate, while the true dreams issue from a gate made of horn (*Od.* 19. 562).

PEISIDICE was a daughter of a king of Methymnia in Lesbos, who, out of love for Achilles, opened to him the gates of her native city, but was stoned to death at the command of Achilles by his soldiers.

Generation

GENETYLLIDES (GENNEIDES; pl. GENETYLLIS) were a class of divinities presiding over generation and birth, companions of Aphrodite Colias (Aristoph. *Thes.* 130; Paus. 1. 1.4; Alciph. 3. 2).

GENIUS was a protecting spirit connected with generation. The bridal bed was sacred to him.

METIS, a male being, was a mystic personification of the power of generation, similar to Phanes and Ericapaeus among the so-called Orphics.

See also: CHILDBIRTH

Generosity

ZEUS EPIDOTES, the "liberal giver," was a surname of Zeus at Mantineia and Sparta (Paus. 8. 9.1.)

Genitals

CONISALUS (CONISALTUS) was worshipped at Athens with Priapus.

FASCINUS, the early Latin divinity, protector from evil daemons, was represented in the form of a phallus, this symbol being believed to be the most efficient in averting all evil influences. Roman generals who entered the city in triumph had the symbol of Fascinus fastened under their chariots, that they might be protected from envy, for envy was believed to exercise an injurious influence on those who were envied (Plin. *H.N.* 28. 4, 7).

Cerberus

MUTUNUS (MUTINUS), was believed to be the most powerful averter of daemons. Mutunus was a Roman divinity identified with Priapus.

PRIAPUS was the son of Dionysus and Aphrodite. Hera, unhappy with Aphrodite's conduct with Adonis while Dionysus was in India, caused her to give birth to a child of extreme ugliness and with unusually large genitals. In art, he was represented with grotesquely large genitals.

TARCHETIUS was a mythical king of Alba, who, in some traditions, was connected with the founders of Rome. Once, a phallus was seen rising above one of his flocks. In compliance with an oracle, he ordered one of his daughters to approach the phallus; but she sent one of her maidservants, who became pregnant and gave birth to the twins, Romulus and Remus. Tarchetius ordered them exposed, but they were suckled by a she-wolf and brought up by a shepherd, and when they grew to manhood they dethroned Tarchetius (Plut. *Romul.* 2).

See also: EMASCULATION

Gift

GAEA ANESIDORA, "the goddess who sends gifts," was a surname of Gaea.

PANDORA received gifts from all the gods when she was created. Also, she herself was given as a gift to Epimetheus.

Girdle

AETHRA, mother of Theseus, introduced among the maidens of Troezen the custom of dedicating their girdles to Athena Apaturia on the day of their marriage.

APHRODITE possessed a magic girdle which had the power of inspiring love and desire for those who wore it (Hom. *Il.* 14. 214).

ARTEMIS LYSIZONA was a surname of Artemis at Athens, meaning the goddess who loosens the girdle (Theocrit. 17. 60.)

BYBLIS, daughter of Miletus, was loved by her brother Caunus with more than brotherly affection, so he fled from home and was followed by Byblis, who, on not finding him, hanged herself by means of her girdle.

EILEITHYIA LYSIZONA. As ARTEMIS LYSIZONA.

FORTUNA VIRGINENSIS. Under this name Fortuna was worshipped by newly-married women, who dedicated their maiden garments and girdles in her temple.

HERA once borrowed from Aphrodite the girdle, the giver of charm and fascination, to excite the love of Zeus (Hom. *Il.* 14. 215).

HERACLES. The ninth labor of Heracles consisted of bringing back to Admete, the daughter of Eurystheus, the girdle of Hippolyte, the queen of the Amazons. At first he was received kindly by Hippolyte, who promised him her girdle, but Hera, in the disguise of an Amazon, spread the report that the queen had been robbed by a stranger. The Amazons rose against him, and, believing that Hippolyte had plotted against him, he killed her and took her girdle.

OENEUS, king of Pleuron and Calydon, hospitably received Bellerophon, to whom he gave a costly girdle (Hom. *Il.* 6. 216).

SCYTHEA, son of Heracles and Echidna, became the king of the Scythians according to his father's arrangement, because he was the only one among the three brothers who was able to manage the bow which Heracles had left behind and to use his father's girdle (Herod. 4. 8. – 10).

Globe

FORTUNA. When she entered Rome, she put off her wings and shoes and threw away the globe, as she intended to live permanently among the Romans.

HONOR (HONOS), the personification of honor, is represented as a male figure standing on a globe.

SALUS, Roman personification of public welfare, was represented with a rudder, a globe at his feet, and pouring from a patera a libation upon an altar, around which a serpent is winding itself.

URANIA, the Muse of astronomy, in works of art points with a little staff to a celestial globe.

ZEUS. Adrasteia gave the infant Zeus a globe to play with. On some Cretan coins Zeus is represented sitting on a globe.

Glory

EUCLEIA was a divinity worshipped at Athens to whom a sanctuary was dedicated there out of the spoils the Athenians had taken in the battle of Marathon (Paus. 1. 14.4). She was a personification of the glory which the Athenians had reaped on the day of that battle.

Glue

DAEDALUS was the reputed inventor of glue.

Goat

AEGIPAN was the son of Zeus and a goat or Zeus and Aex, and, according to some, the father of Pan. He was often regarded as identical to Pan. He was sometimes represented as half-goat and half-fish.

AEGISTHUS was exposed at birth but was found by shepherds and was suckled by a goat.

AMALTHEA was the goat whose milk fed the infant Zeus on Mt. Ida in Crete, where he was reared by nymphs (Callim. *Hymn.in Jov.* 49). Some called Amalthea a nymph, who fed Zeus milk of a goat (Apollod. 2. 7.5).

APHRODITE PANDEMOS. Her worship occurred at Athens, Megalopolis, and at Thebes. The sacrifice offered to her consisted of white goats (Lucian *Dial.Meret.* 7).

APOLLO. When Cleinis of Babylon wanted to sacrifice asses to the god, Apollo demanded that only sheep, goats, and heifers should be sacrificed to him.

ARCHELAUS built the town of Aegae on the spot to which he was led by a goat.

ARTEMIS. White goats were sacrificed to her.

ARTEMIS AEGINAEA was a surname of Artemis at Sparta, meaning either huntress of chamois or wielder of the javelin.

ASCLEPIUS was exposed as an infant but was fed by a goat. Those cured in his temples sometimes offered a goat as sacrifice.

CHIMAERA. The monster had three heads, one a dragon, one a goat, and one a lion. Some accounts say that the middle part of her body was that of a goat.

DIONYSUS. The goat was sacrificed to him because of its propensity for killing the vine.

DIONYSUS AEGOBOLUS was a surname of Dionysus, meaning the goat-killer, at Potniae in Boeotia.

FAUNUS. Eventually the worship of this single god gave rise to a plurality of fauns, who are described as monsters, half goat and with horns (Ov. *Fast.* 5. 99; Ov. *Her.* 4. 49). Faunus came to be identified with the Arcadian Pan, and the fauns seen as identical to the Greek satyrs.

HELIOS. Sacrifices to the sun god consisted of goats.

HERA AEGOPHAGUS, meaning the goat-eater, was a surname under which Hera was worshipped by the Lacedaemonians.

HERMES. Young goats were among the sacrifices offered to him.

NYMPHS. Sacrifices to them consisted of goats.

PAN, the great god of flocks and shepherds, had horns, beard, pug nose, tail, goats' feet and was covered with hair.

PAN AEGOCERUS was a surname of Pan describing his goat horns.

PRIAPUS, son of Dionysus and Aphrodite, was worshipped as the protector of flocks of goats.

ZEUS. Goats were sacrificed to him.

ZEUS AEGIDUCHOS (AEGIOCHOS) was a surname of Zeus from his being suckled by a goat.

Goatherd

MELANTHIUS, son of Dolius, was a goatherd of Odysseus. Because he sided with the suitors of Penelope, he was cruelly killed by Odysseus (Hom. *Od.* 17. 212, 21. 176, 22. 474).

Goblet, see Cup

Gold

ANCHURUS. His father Midas tried to close a great chasm in his kingdom by throwing in gold as token of the most precious thing he owned, but the chasm was closed only when Anchurus leapt into it (Plut. *Paral. Gr.et Rom.* 5).

ARNE betrayed her country for gold and was metamorphosed into a jackdaw (Ov. *Met.* 7. 465).

DAEDALUS made a honeycomb of gold for the temple of Aphrodite on Mt. Eryx.

GRIFFIN (See GRYPS)

GRYPS (GRYPHUS), the griffin, a fabulous bird-like species of animal, was said to have been the guardian of the gold of the north—later, of India. The Arismaspians mounted on horseback and attempted to steal the gold, and hence arose the hostility between the horse and the griffin.

HERA. Proteus' daughters, Iphinoe, Lysippe, and Iphianassa, were seized with madness because they had, according to some, stolen gold from the statue of Hera. They were cured by Melampus, the soothsayer.

MIDAS. When Dionysus granted him a wish in exchange for a favor, Midas asked that everything he touched be turned to gold (comp. Plut. *Parall.Min.* 5). The request was granted; but when even his food turned to gold, he implored the god to take his favor back. Dionysus accordingly ordered him to bathe in the source of the Pactolus near Mt. Tmolus. This bath saved Midas, but the river from that time on had an abundance of gold in its sand (Ov. *Met.* 11. 90; Virg. *Ecl.* 6. 13). (See also ANCHURUS)

PANDAREUS, son of Merops of Miletus, is said to have stolen the golden dog, which Hephaestus had made, from the temple of Zeus in Crete and to have carried it to Tantalus. When Zeus sent Hermes to Tantalus to claim the dog back, Tantalus declared it was not in his possession. The god, however, took the animal by force and threw Mt. Sipylus upon Tantalus. Some say that his severe punishment in the lower world resulted from this deception.

ZEUS in the form of a shower of gold visited Danae in the apartment where she had been locked and by her fathered Perseus.

See also: FLEECE

Goldfinch

AEDON was a daughter of Pandarus. She was jealous of the son of Niobe, her sister-in-law, and sought to kill him but killed her own son Itylus by mistake. She was changed into a goldfinch as she sought to kill herself.

Goldsmith

LAERCES was a mythical artist in gold, mentioned by Homer (Hom. *Od.* 3. 425).

Good

MANA (MANA GENITA) was an ancient Italian divinity. According to ancient etymology the name Mana is the same root as Manes and like *manis* originally signified good.

MANES, i.e., "the good ones," was the general name by which the Romans designated the souls of the departed. At certain seasons, which were looked upon as sacred days, sacrifices were offered to the spirits of the dead with the observance of various ceremonies. But an annual festival, which belonged to all the Manes in general, was celebrated on the 19th of February under the name of Feralia or Parentalia, because it was especially the duty of children and heirs to offer sacrifices to the shades of their parents and benefactors (Ov. *Fast.* 2. 535).

Goose

HERA. The goose was sacred to her.

HERCYNA was a daughter of Trophonius. Once when she was playing with Cora, daughter of Demeter, she let a goose which she carried in her hand fly away. When she found it in a cave concealed by a block of stone, she pulled the bird forth, and a spring gushed out from under the stone. A statue of a girl carrying a goose was later erected at the site.

RHADAMANTHYS. A law ascribed to him said man should not swear by the gods but by a goose, a dog, or a ram.

Gossip

LARUNDA (LARA), one of the Naiads, was talkative and revealed Zeus' amours to Hera. Zeus punished her by having her tongue cut out.

Grace

CHARITES were the personification of grace and beauty.

Grain

DEMETER. Her name was explained by some as derived from the Cretan word for barley, so that Demeter would be the mother or giver of barley or of food generally. In artistic representations, she often wore a garland of wheat ears, and sometimes she carried them in her hand. She was regarded as the goddess of grain.

DEMETER SITO was a surname describing Demeter as the giver of food or grain (Athen. 3. 109, 10. 416).

EIRENE (IRENE), goddess of peace, is sometimes represented carrying wheat ears in her hand or upon her head.

ERICHTHONIUS, according to some traditions, was an Egyptian who during a famine brought grain to Athens and instituted the worship of Demeter and the Eleusinian mysteries.

FIDES, the Roman goddess of fidelity, was represented as a matron carrying wheat ears in her hand.

FORNAX, a Roman goddess, is said to have been worshipped so that she would ripen the wheat and prevent its being burned in baking in the oven.

HYPEROCHE was one of the maidens who were sent by the Hyperboreans to Delos with certain sacred offerings enclosed in stalks of wheat (Herod. 4.33–35).

IRIS was the goddess of the rainbow. The Delians offered to her cakes made of wheat, honey, and dried figs.

JANUS. Barley was sacred to him.

MIDAS was a wealthy king of Phrygia. When he was a child, ants carried grains of wheat into his mouth to indicate that one day he would be the richest of mortals.

MOLAE were Roman divinities whose name indicates that they were in some way connected with the pounding or grinding of grain.

NODOTUS (NODUTUS) was a divinity who presided over the knots in the stems of plants producing grain. This was possibly a surname of Saturnus (August. 4. 8).

OENOTROPAE was the name of the three or four daughters of king Anius in Delos, because they had received from Dionysus the power of changing water into wine and anything else they chose into grain and olives.

OPS RUNCINA. By this name Ops was invoked by the people of Italy to prevent the growth of weeds among the grain and to promote the harvest (August. 4. 8).

PATELLA (PATELLANA) was a Roman divinity, or perhaps only a surname of Ops, by which she was described as opening the stem of the wheat plant, so that the ears would be able to grow (August. 4. 8).

PILUMNUS, a rustic divinity of the ancient Romans, was believed to ward off the sufferings of newborn infants and children with his *pilum,* with which he also taught men to pound grain.

PYGMIES were reported to have cut down separate ears of wheat with axes. They were conceived as an agricultural people living near the sources of the Nile.

ROBIGUS was described by some Latin writers as a divinity worshipped for the purpose of averting blight or too great heat from the grain fields. The festival of the Robigalia was celebrated on the 25th of April and was said to have been instituted by Numa (Varr. *De Ling.Lat.* 6. 16; Gell. 5. 12; Ov. *Fast.* 4. 907, 911).

SILVANUS was a Latin divinity of the forests and fields. Sacrifices to him included ears of wheat.

TRIPTOLEMUS. When Demeter accidentally killed his brother, Demophon, she gave Triptolemus a chariot with winged dragons and seeds of wheat. After receiving the dragon chariot, he rode it all over the earth, acquainting man with the blessings of agriculture. He first sowed barley in the Rharian plain, and from there the cultivation of grain spread to the rest of the world. In works of art Triptolemus is represented as a youthful hero, sometimes holding in his hands ears of wheat.

ZEUS POLIEUS, "the protector of the city," was a surname under which Zeus had an altar on the acropolis of Athens. Upon this altar, barley and wheat were strewn, which were consumed by the bull about to be sacrificed to the god.

Grapevine

ANCAEUS was a vineyard grower whom a seer warned that he would not live to taste the wine of his vineyard. As he lifted a cup to his lips, he scorned the seer, and the seer remarked: "There is many a slip between the cup and the lip." A tumult arose outside, and Ancaeus went out in time to be killed by a wild boar.

ARISTAEUS was worshipped as protector of vine and olive plantations.

DIONYSUS. The grapevine was sacred to him.

ICARIUS. For his hospitality to Dionysus, he was taught by the god the cultivation of the vine. He killed a ram for having injured his vines, made a bag of its skin and performed a dance on it.

LYCURGUS, son of Dryas and king of the Edones in Thrace, being intoxicated, sought to destroy all the vines of his country. For this reason or because of ill treatment of Dionysus and his Bacchantic followers, the god visited Lycurgus with madness, in which he killed his wife and son and cut off one (some say both) of his legs; or, according to others, he killed himself. He killed his son, Dryas, in the belief that he was cutting down a vine.

PRIAPUS, son of Dionysus and Aphrodite, was worshipped as the protector of the vine.

SILVANUS was a Latin divinity of the fields and forests. Sacrifices to him included grapes.

See also: WINE

Grasshopper

APOLLO. The grasshopper was sacred to him.

TITHONUS, son of Laomedon, king of Troy, was so beautiful that Eos, goddess of the dawn, carried him away. She prayed that he be granted immortality, but forgot to ask for eternal youth. As he grew decrepit and infirm with old age, he begged Eos to remove him from the world. Since he had been made immortal, he could not die, so the goddess changed him into a grasshopper.

Grief

ALCYONE (See CLEOPATRA)

ARGANTHONE. When her husband, Rhesus, was slain at Troy, she died in grief.

CALCHAS. A soothsayer who, upon being defeated by Mopsus in predictions, died from grief (Strab. 14. 642, 668).

CLEOPATRA, daughter of Idas and wife of Meleager (Hom. *Il.* 9. 556), hanged herself after her husband's death, or died of grief. Her proper name was Alcyone (Apollod. 1. 8.3).

CYANE, a Sicilian nymph and playmate of Proserpina, was changed through grief at the loss of Proserpina into a well (Ov. *Met.* 5. 412).

CYBELE. When her father discovered her liaison with Atys, he put him to death, and, maddened with grief, Cybele traversed the country amid loud lamentations and the sound of cymbals (Diod. 3. 58).

CYCNUS was a son of Sthenelus and friend of Phaethon. While he was lamenting the death of Phaethon on the banks of the Eridanus, he was metamorphosed by Apollo into a swan and placed among the stars (Ov. *Met.* 2. 366; Paus. 1. 30.3).

CYPARISSUS was a youth of Cea beloved by Silvanus, the Latin divinity of forests. Once Silvanus by accident killed a hind belonging to the youth, who died from grief and was metamorphosed into a cypress.

DAEDALION. When his daughter, Chione, was killed by Artemis, in his grief he threw himself from a rock of Parnassus, but in falling he was changed by Apollo into a hawk (Ov. *Met.* 11. 300).

ECHO, a nymph, fell in love with Narcissus, who did not return her love, so she pined away until nothing was left but her voice (Ov. *Met.* 3. 356–401).

ELECTRA. When she saw Troy perishing in flames, she tore out her hair for grief and was placed among the stars as a comet.

EOS, goddess of the dawn and mother of Memnon, wept for her dead son every morning, and the dewdrops which appear in the morning are the tears of Eos (Ov. *Met.* 13. 622).

HARPALYCE was a maiden who died because her love for Iphiclus was not returned. In commemoration of her fate, a contest in songs was celebrated by maidens.

HIPPOLYTE. With an army of Amazons she marched into Attica to take vengeance on Theseus for having carried off Antiope, but being conquered by Theseus, she fled to Megara, where she died of grief.

LAODICE was a daughter of Priam and Hecuba. When her son, Munitus, died, she was so striken with grief that she leaped to her death from a precipice (Lycoph. 497).

LUCTUS, a personification of grief and mourning, was a son of Aether and Terra.

MELEAGER. When he died, his sisters, called Meleagrides, wept unceasingly, until Artemis changed them into guinea hens. They were transferred to the island of Leros, where they continued to mourn during a certain part of the year.

PALAESTINUS was a son of Poseidon and father of Haliacmon. From grief at the death of his son, Palaestinus threw himself into a river, which was called Palaestinus after him.

PLEIADES, the seven daughters of Atlas and sisters of the Hyades, made away with themselves from grief at the death of the Hyades or at the fate of Atlas and were afterwards placed as stars at the back of Taurus.

POLYDORA, daughter of Meleager and Cleopatra, was married to Protesilaus, after whose death she was so much affected by grief that she killed herself (Paus. 4. 2.5).

PROCNE. According to Megarian tradition, she and her sister, Philomela, after exacting revenge on their husband, Tereus, by killing Itys, Tereus' son by Procne, and serving his flesh to the father, escaped to Attica, where they wept themselves to death (Paus. 1. 41.8).

SELEMNUS, a shepherd youth, pined away with grief when Argyra, a nymph, forsook him. He was changed into the river Selemnus, where unhappy lovers could bathe and be freed from their grief (Paus. 7. 23.2).

Griffin

APOLLO. The griffin was sacred to him.

Grotto, see Cave

Guardian

CHALION. An oracle warned his father that Antilochus should be guarded against an Ethiopian, so at the Trojan War he was given Chalion as his constant attendant and bodyguard.

GENIUS. Each man was said to have been born with a genius, a guardian angel, which accompanied him to the afterlife. Some ancients believed in two genii, one good and one evil, the moral complements of every man.

REDICULUS was a Roman divinity, who had a temple near the Porta Capena and who was believed to have received his name from having induced Hannibal, when he was near the gates of the city, to return (*redire*) southward. This divinity was probably one of the Lares of the city of Rome, for he was sometimes called Tutanus, "the god who keeps safe."

TUTANUS (See REDICULUS)

Guide

CEDALION. When Orion, for having violated Oenopion's daughter, was blinded and expelled from Chios by him, he wandered eventually to Lemnos, where Hephaestus gave to him Cedalion as a guide.

CORYTHUS was a son of Paris and Oenone. According to some, he was afterwards sent off by his mother to serve the Greeks as guide on their voyage to Troy.

Guinea Hen

MELEAGER. When he died, his sisters, called Meleagrides, wept unceasingly, until Artemis changed them into guinea hens. They were transferred to the island of Leros, where they continued to mourn during a certain part of the year.

Gymnastics

CHEIRON the centaur was renowned for his skill in gymnastics.

HERMES was said to have invented gymnastics.

Hail

TELCHINES, a group of mysterious beings described as sorcerers and envious daemons, had the power to bring on hail, rain, and snow, and to assume any form they pleased (Diod. 5. 55).

Hair

ACHILLES PYRRHA was a surname meaning "golden locks." Pyrrha was the name Achilles used when disguised as a maiden to escape the Trojan War.

AMPHITRITE in ancient works of art was represented with a net over her hair.

AMPHITRYON was unable to subdue the Taphians as long as Pterelaus lived. Pterelaus had one golden hair which rendered him immortal. Comaetho, his daughter, was in love with Amphitryon, so she cut off the golden hair and thus allowed Amphitryon to conquer the Taphians.

ANTIGONE, daughter of Laomedon, boasted of excelling Hera in the beauty of her hair and was punished by being changed into a stork (Ov. *Met.* 6. 93).

APOLLO ACERSECOMES was a surname of Apollo describing his beautiful hair, which was never cut or shorn.

APOLLO INTONSUS , "the unshorn," was a surname of the god, alluding to his eternal youth, since Greek youths allowed their hair to grow until they attained the age of manhood.

BACCHUS INTONSUS. As APOLLO INTONSUS.

ELECTRA (1). When Orestes came back to Argos, he left a lock of his hair on Agamemnon's grave, and this was a sign to Electra that her brother was near and would carry out revenge for the death of their father.

ELECTRA (2), one of the Pleiades, when she saw Troy perishing in flames, tore out her hair for grief and was placed among the stars as a comet.

ERGINUS. When he took part in the funeral games which Hypipyle celebrated at Lemnos in honor of her father, Thoas, he was ridiculed by the Lemnian women, because, though still young, he had gray hair.

GORGONS were represented as girded with serpents or with serpents for hair. Medusa was the only one of the three who was mortal, but her hair was changed into serpents by Athena. Her head was then of so fearful an appearance that everyone who looked at it was changed into stone. Athena gave Heracles a lock of Medusa's hair, which he later give to Sterope as a protection for the town of Tegea, since sight of the lock was enough to put the enemy to flight (Paus. 8. 47.4; Apollod. 2. 7.3).

GRAEAE, the ancient daughters of Phorcys and Ceto, had gray hair from their birth.

IPHINOE, a daughter of Alcathous, died a virgin. The women of Megara previous to their marriage offered to her a funeral sacrifice and dedicated a lock of hair to her (Paus. 1. 43.4).

MEDUSA (See GORGONS)

NEOPTOLEMUS was known by the name of Pyrrhus, which was given to him by Lycomedes because he had fair hair, or because Achilles, his father, while disguised as a girl, had borne the name of Pyrrha (Paus. 10. 26.1).

NISUS was a son of Pandion and father of Scylla. He was king of Megara, and when Minos on his expedition against Athens took Megara, Nisus died, because his daughter, Scylla, who had fallen in love with Minos, had pulled out the purple or golden hair growing on the top of her father's head on which his life depended (Apollod. 3. 15.5, 6, 8).

ORESTES. When he returned to Argos in disguise, he visited the tomb of his father (Agamemnon) and sacrificed upon it a lock of his hair.

PYRRHUS (See NEOPTOLEMUS)

TIRESIAS (TEIRESIAS). When he awarded the prize for beauty to Cale, one of the Charites, Aphrodite changed him into an old woman, but Cale rewarded him with a beautiful head of hair and took him to Crete.

TRITON was a son of Poseidon and Amphitrite. He was described as riding over the sea on horses or sea monsters. Often referred to in the plural, Tritons were sometimes described as having green hair (Paus. 9. 21.1).

VENUS CALVA was a name under which Venus had two temples in the neighborhood of the Capitoline Hill. Some believed that one of them had been built as a monument of a patriotic act of the Roman women, who during the siege of the Gauls cut off their hair and gave it to the men to make strings for their bows. But it probably refers to the fact that on her wedding day the bride, either actually or symbolically, cut off a lock of hair to sacrifice to Venus.

Halcyon

ALCYONE. Upon the death of her husband, Ceyx, she threw herself into the sea, and she and Ceyx were changed into sea birds, known as alcyones, or halcyons. The modern equivalent is kingfisher.

CINYRAS. When he was killed by Apollo, his fifty daughters leaped into the sea and were metamorphosed into halcyons.

Hammer

CYCLOPES. As assistants to Hephaestus they worked with such ardor that Sicily and neighboring islands resounded with their hammering.

DAMNAMENEUS, one of the Dactyli, presided over the hammer.

HEPHAESTUS, god of fire, was represented in art carrying a hammer.

ORION. Having been blinded by Oenopion, he was instructed by an oracle how to recover his vision. Orion followed the sounds of a Cyclops' hammer and arrived in Lemnos, where Hephaestus gave him Cedalion as his guide.

Hand

APHRODITE. In the Trojan War, when she endeavored to rescue Aeneas from a fight, she was wounded in the hand by Diomedes.

HERA HYPERCHEIRA, a goddess who holds her protecting hand over a thing, was a surname under which Hera had a sanctuary at Sparta, which had been erected to her at the command of an oracle, when the country was inundated by the river Eurotas (Paus. 3. 13.6).

Hanging

ALCYONE (See CLEOPATRA)

ALTHAEA was the mother of Meleager. When she burned the piece of wood which had kept him alive as long as it remained unburned, her son died, and she hanged herself (Apollod. 1. 8.2; Diod. 4. 34; Ov. *Met.* 8. 450, 531).

AMATA was the wife of Latinus. When she learned that Turnus had fallen in battle, she hanged herself (Virg. *Aen.* 12. 600).

ANTIGONE, wife of Peleus, hanged herself when she received a letter from Astydameia falsely stating that Peleus was on the point of marrying Sterope, daughter of Acastus.

ARCEOPHON (See IPHIS)

BRISEUS, the father of Briseis, hanged himself when his daughter was taken from him.

BYBLIS, daughter of Miletus, was loved incestuously by her brother, Caunus. He fled from home and was followed by Byblis, who hanged herself with her girdle when she could not find him.

CLEITE was the wife of Cyzicus, who, when the Argonauts murdered her husband, hanged herself. The tears of the nymphs who lamented her death were changed into the well named Cleite (Apollon. Rhod. 1. 967, 1063).

CLEOPATRA, daughter of Idas and wife of Meleager, hanged herself after her husband's death, or died of grief. Her proper name was Alcyone (Apollod. 1. 8.3).

CLYMENUS. After being served the flesh of his son by his daughter, Harpalyce, whom he had raped, he hanged himself.

DEIANEIRA hanged herself after unwittingly causing the death of Heracles by providing him with a poison-soaked garment (Apollod. 2. 7.5, 6.7; Diod. 4. 34).

ERIGONE. When her father, Icarius, was killed, she hanged herself on the tree under which he was buried. Dionysus punished the Athenians, who had killed Icarius, by a mania, which caused all the Athenian maidens to hang themselves as Erigone had done (Gell. 15. 10).

IPHIS hanged himself in despair when Anaxarete did not return his love (Ov. *Met.* 14. 698). Some writers called the ill-fated pair Arsinoe and Arceophon.

JOCASTA (IOCASTE) was the mother of Oedipus. When she learned that her son had both killed his father, her husband, and also married her and had children by her, she hanged herself.

MELANTHO was the daughter of Dolius and, like her brother, Melanthius, sided with the suitors of Penelope. She was hanged by Odysseus (Hom. *Od.* 18. 321; Paus. 10. 25.1).

MELUS, friend and companion of Adonis, hanged himself when Adonis died. His wife Peleia, in grief for their friend, did likewise.

NICAEA, a nymph, the daughter of the river god Sangarius and Cybele, was made intoxicated by Dionysus, who made her the mother of Telete, whereupon she hanged herself.

OENONE. At first refusing to heal her husband Paris' wound, she later changed her mind and hastened after him with remedies. But Paris was already dead, and in her grief she hanged herself (Apollod. 3. 12.6).

PHYLLIS, a daughter of king Sithon in Thrace, hanged herself when Demophon was prevented from keeping his promise to marry her by the agreed-on time.

THEMISTO. When in an attempt to murder Ino's children she killed her own by mistake, she hanged herself.

Happiness

FELICITAS was the personification of happiness. She is frequently seen on Roman medals in the form of a matron with the staff of Mercury and a cornucopia.

Harbor

APHRODITE LIMENIA (LIMENITES, LIMENITIS, or LIMENOSCOPUS), was a surname describing Aphrodite as protector or superintendent of the harbor (Paus. 2. 34.11).

ARTEMIS LIMENIA (LIMENITES, LIMENITIS, or LIMENOSCOPUS). As APHRODITE LIMENIA (Callim. *Hymn.in Dian.* 259).

ATHENA was defender of harbors.

ATHENA PROMACHORMA, "the protectress of the bay," was a surname of Athena under which she had a sanctuary on Mt. Buporthmos near Hermione (Paus. 2. 34.9).

BRITOMARTIS was protectress of harbors.

PORTUNUS (PORTUMNUS) was the protecting genius of harbors among the Romans. At his temple, an annual festival, the Portunalia, was celebrated on the 17th of August (Varr. *De Ling.Lat.* 6. 19; Cic. *De Nat.Deor.* 2. 26; Virg. *Aen.* 5. 241).

POSEIDON ASPHALIUS (ASPHALEIUS) was a name under which Poseidon was worshipped in various towns of Greece. It describes him as the god who grants safety to ports and to navigation in general (Strab. 1. 57; Paus. 7. 21.3).

PRIAPUS LIMENIA (LIMENITES, LIMINITIS, or LIMENOSCOPUS). This surname described him as protector or superintendent of the harbor.

ZEUS LIMENIA (LIMENITES, LIMINITIS, or LIMENOSCOPUS) was a surname of Zeus as protector or superintendent of the harbor.

Hare

EROS. The hare was sacred to him.

Harm

HERMES ACACESIUS was a surname of Hermes, possibly from Greek *kakos,* meaning the god who cannot be hurt or who does not hurt.

Harp, see Lyre

Haruspicy, see Entrails

Harvest

BORMUS was a beautiful youth who was pulled into a well by admiring nymphs. The Bithynians celebrated his memory each year at harvest by singing plaintive songs with flute accompaniment (Athen. 14. 620; Aeschyl. *Pers.* 94).

DEMETER was the goddess of harvests.

LITYERSES was a son of Midas who compelled strangers to assist him in harvest, and, if they did not surpass him, he cut off their heads and concealed their bodies in sheaves, accompanying his deed with songs. Phrygian reapers used to celebrate his memory in a harvest-song which bore the name of Lityerses (Athen 10. 615; 14. 619).

TELLUS was a name by which the earth was personified among the Romans. In private life, sacrifices were offered to Tellus at the beginning of sowing and at harvest time.

TUTELINA was an agricultural divinity among the Romans, or perhaps an attribute of Ops.

She is described as the goddess protecting the fruits brought in at harvest time from the fields.

Hat

DIOSCURI. In art they are usually represented in egg-shaped hats, or helmets, crowned with stars, and with spears in their hands (Paus. 3. 18.8, 5. 19.1; Catull. 37.2; Val.Flacc. 5. 36).

HERMES was represented in a traveling hat with a broad brim, which was later adorned with two little wings.

TRIPTOLEMUS. In works of art he is represented as a youthful hero, sometimes with the petasus, or broad-brimmed traveler's hat.

Hawk

APOLLO. The hawk was sacred to him.

CHIONE was changed by Artemis into a hawk for preferring her own beauty to that of the goddess.

DAEDALION. When his daughter Chione was taken away by Artemis, in his grief he threw himself from a rock of Parnassus, but in falling he was changed by Apollo into a hawk (Ov. *Met.* 11. 300).

HERA. The hawk was sacred to her.

NISUS. When his daughter, Scylla, brought about the fall of his kingdom, he killed himself and was changed into a hawk.

TEREUS. When his wives, Procne and Philomela, killed his son, Itys, and served his flesh to him, he pursued them with an ax, and they were all changed into birds. According to some, he became a hawk.

Head

ALALCOMENIA (See PRAXIDICAE)

ATHENA. When Metis was pregnant by Zeus with Athena, he swallowed her. Later, Athena sprang from his head (Hes. *Theog.* 924). (See also MEDUSA)

ATHENA TRITO (TRITOGENEIA or TRITONIS). The surname possibly was derived from *trito,* which, in the dialect of the Athamanians, is said to signify "head," so that it would be the goddess born out of the head of her father (Hes. *Theog.* 924).

ATLAS bore heaven on his head and shoulders.

AULIS (See PRAXIDICAE)

CERBERUS, the monster dog which guarded the gates of Hades, had many heads (some writers say three) with a mane consisting of heads of various snakes (Apollod. 2. 5.12; Virg. *Aen.* 6. 417; Ov. *Met.* 4. 449).

CHIMAERA, the fire-breathing monster, had three heads: one a dragon, one a goat, and one a lion.

ECHIDNA, a three-headed monster, was a daughter of Chrysaor and Callirrhoe (Hes. *Theog.* 295).

GERYON, son of Chrysaor and Callirrhoe, was a fabulous king of Hesperia and is described as a being with three heads and possessing magnificent oxen on the island of Erytheia. He plays a prominent part in the stories of Heracles (Apollod. 2. 5.10).

HECATE was often described as having three heads: one of a horse, one of a dog, and one of a lion.

HEPHAESTUS is accounted with splitting the head of Zeus and thus assisting him in giving birth to Athena.

HYDRA. The second labor of Heracles consisted of killing the Lernean Hydra, which had nine heads, the middle one being immortal. When Heracles with burning arrows and with club and sickle cut off the heads, two new ones grew in their place. With the aid of Iolaus, he burned away the heads and buried the ninth under a stone (Apollod. 2. 5.2). He dipped his arrows in the poison and thereafter the arrows had no antidote when one was struck by them.

JANUS QUADRIFRONS. It is said that after the conquest of the Faliscans, an image of Janus was found with four foreheads. The fact of the god being represented with four heads was considered by the ancients to indicate that he was the divinity presiding over the four seasons (August. 7. 4).

MANIA was an ancient and formidable Italian (probably Etruscan) divinity of the lower world. The festival of the Compitalia was celebrated as a propitiation to Mania and the Lares. According to an ancient oracle that heads should be offered to her, boys are said to have been sacrificed. The consul Junius Brutus afterwards abolished the human sacrifices and substituted garlic and the heads of poppies.

MEDUSA. Polydectes, king of Seriphos, made Danae his slave and courted her in vain. In order to gain undisturbed possession of her, he sent off Perseus, her son, to fetch the head of Medusa, one of the Gorgons. When Perseus cut off the head of Medusa, the monsters Chrysaor and Pegasus sprang forth from it. Perseus gave the severed head to Athena, who put it on her shield or breastplate.

PRAXIDICAE were the goddesses who carried out the objects of justice. Their images consisted of heads, and their sacrifices of heads of animals. Their names were Alalcomenia, Aulis, and Thelxinoea.

SCYLLA, daughter of Crataeis, was a monster who dwelt on a rock on the Italian coast opposite Sicily. She barked like a dog, had twelve feet, six long necks and mouths, each of which contained three rows of sharp teeth. Some described her with six heads of different animals or with only three heads.

THELXINOEA (See PRAXIDICAE)

Headdress

DEMETER CIDARIA was a surname of the Eleusinian Demeter at Pheneus in Arcadia, derived either from an Arcadian dance called *kidaris* or from a royal headdress of the same name (Paus. 8. 15.1).

Healing

APOLLO ACESTOR was a surname of Apollo as god of healing.

ARISTAEUS learned from Cheiron and the Muses the arts of healing and prophecy.

ARTEMIS cured and alleviated the suffering of mortals.

ARTEMIS PAEONIA, "the healing goddess," was a surname under which Artemis had a statue at Athens and an altar in the temple of Amphiaraus at Oropus (Paus. 1. 2.4, 34.2).

ASCLEPIUS, son of Apollo by Coronis, was the god of healing and medicine. He was physician to the Argonauts.

BONA DEA was regarded as a goddess possessing healing powers.

CHEIRON the centaur was noted for his knowledge of medicine and healing.

DIONYSUS. At his oracle of Amphicleia in Phocis, he cured diseases by revealing the remedies to the sufferers in their dreams (Paus. 10. 33.5). He was invoked against raging diseases (Soph. *Oed. Tyr.* 210; Lycoph. 206).

GORGASUS was a son of Machaon and grandson of Asclepius. He followed the example of his grandfather by practicing the art of healing, for which he received divine honors after his death (Paus. 4. 30.2).

HEPHAESTUS was believed to have great healing powers, and Lemnian earth *(terra Lemnia)* from the spot on which he had fallen from Olympus was believed to cure madness, the bites of snakes, and hemorrhage.

IAPIS, son of Iasus and a favorite of Apollo, turned down the gift of prophecy in favor of the art of healing.

IONIDES was a name borne by four nymphs believed to possess healing powers. They had a temple on the river Cytherus in Elis, and derived their name from a mythical Ion, a son of Gargettus, who was believed to have led a colony from Athens to those districts.

Perseus and Medusa

JUTURNA was the nymph of a well in Latium famous for its excellent healing qualities.

OENONE, wife of Paris, possessed prophetic powers. She cautioned him not to sail to the country of Helen; but as he did not follow her advice (Hom. *Il.* 5. 64), she promised to heal him if he were wounded, as that was the only aid she could give him (Apollod. 3. 12.6).

PANACEIA, "the all-healing," was a daughter of Asclepius, who had a temple at Oropus (Paus. 1. 34.2; Aristoph. *Plut.* 702).

See also: HEALTH, MEDICINE, SURGERY

Health

AEGLE, daughter of Asclepius, derived her name from the splendor of the healthy human body.

ANNA PERENNA was the Roman goddess of health.

ATHENA HYGIEIA was a surname of Athena, designating her as giver or protectress of (mental) health (Paus. 1. 23.5).

CARNA (CARNEA) was a Roman divinity whose name is probably connected with *caro,* flesh, for she was regarded as the protector of the well-being of man.

HERACLES. Among the Sabines, Heracles was regarded as the giver of health.

HYGIEIA, daughter of Asclepius, was the goddess of health (Paus. 1. 23.5, 31.5)

LATOBIUS was god of health among the Corinthians.

SALUS was the personfication of health, prosperity, and the public welfare among the Romans. She was worshipped publicly on the 30th of April (Ov. *Fast.* 3. 811).

Heart

CARNA (CARNEA). The heart, lungs, and liver were entrusted to the protection of this Roman divinity.

DIONYSUS ZAGREUS was the surname of the mystic Dionysus. He was torn to pieces by the Titans, though he defended himself bravely and assumed various forms. Athena carried his heart to Zeus.

Hearth

AMPHINOME. About to be murdered by Pelias after he had killed Aeson, her husband, and Promachus, her son, she fled to Pelias' hearth so that his crime would be greater by his murdering her on a sacred spot (Diod. 4. 50; Apollon.Rhod. 1. 45).

CAECULUS, a divinity of the hearth because he was the son of Vulcan, was conceived by a priestess of the hearth and was found near a hearth (fire).

HEPHAESTUS. The Greeks frequently placed small dwarf-like statues of the god near the hearth, and these figures seem to have been very ancient (Herod. 3. 37; Aristoph. *Av.* 436; Callim. *Hymn.in Dian.* 60).

HESTIA was the Olympian goddess of the hearth.

LARES were the Roman divinities who presided over the hearth.

LATERANUS, according to some, was a divinity protecting hearths built of bricks (*lateres*).

PENATES. The Penates, or private household gods, had their place at the hearth of every house; the hearth was sacred to them.

VESTA, one of the great Roman divinities, was identical with the Greek Hestia. She was the goddess of the hearth and therefore inseparably connected with the Penates, for Aeneas was believed to have brought the eternal fire of Vesta from Troy, along with the images of the Penates. The praetors, consuls, and dictators, before entering upon their official functions, sacrificed not only to the Penates but also to Vesta at Lavinium (Virg. *Aen.* 2. 296, 5. 259).

Heaven

ATLAS bore heaven on his head and shoulders. He was also credited with first teaching man that heaven had the form of a globe (Diod. 3. 60, 4. 27; Paus. 9. 20.3). (See also HERACLES)

ATLAS TELAMON was a surname describing him, according to some, as the sufferer or bearer of heaven.

HERACLES sent Atlas to fetch the golden apples of the Hesperides and meanwhile bore the weight of the heavens on his back. Atlas, upon returning, refused to take the weight of the heavens again, but Heracles contrived by a strategem to get the apples and went back to Eurystheus with them.

JANUS CLUSIUS (CLUSAVIUS). As JANUS PATULCUS.

JANUS PATULCUS (PATULCIUS) was a surname of Janus pertaining to his power over the entrance to heaven (Ov. *Fast.* 1. 129).

SUMMANUS was an ancient Roman or Etruscan divinity, who was equal to or higher in rank than Jupiter. As Jupiter was the god of heaven in the bright day, so Summanus was the god of the nocturnal heaven, and lightning at night was regarded as his work (August. 4. 23; Plin. *H.N.* 2. 53).

URANUS, the most ancient of all the gods, was the ruler of the heavens and father by Gaea of the twelve Titans.

ZEUS. When Zeus and his brothers distributed among themselves the government of the world by lot, he obtained the heavens and the upper regions.

Heel

ACHILLES. When Thetis dipped Achilles in the Styx to make him immortal, she held him by the heel (or ankle) which remained vulnerable. A wound in this heel in the Trojan War caused his death.

Heifer

APOLLO. When Cleinis of Babylon wanted to sacrifice asses to the god, Apollo demanded that only sheep, goats, and heifers should be sacrificed to him.

IO was beloved by Zeus, who changed her into a heifer to disguise his affair with her from Hera.

Helmet

AMYNTOR. The helmet which was stolen from him by Autolycus was later worn by Meriones in the Trojan War (Hom. *Il.* 10. 266).

APHRODITE. When represented as the victorious goddess, she had the attributes of Ares—a helmet, a shield, and a sword—or a lance and an image of Victory.

ATHENA was usually represented in art wearing a helmet.

CYCLOPES. For his part in assisting in their release from Tartarus, they provided Hades with a helmet (Apollod. 1. 1; Hes. *Theog.* 503).

CYCNUS, in the Trojan War, was killed by Achilles by being strangled with the thong of his helmet or by being struck by him with a stone; he could not be killed with iron.

DARDANUS. In Italian traditions, in a battle with the Aborigines he lost his helmet. Although already defeated, he went back to recover the helmet and in this fresh attack won the battle. He called the place Corythus.

DIOSCURI. In art they are usually represented in egg-shaped hats or helmets.

HADES possessed a helmet which rendered the wearer invisible. Later traditions stated that this helmet was given him as a present by the Cyclopes after their delivery from Tartarus (Apollod. 1. 2.1). Perseus wore this helmet when he went to slay Medusa.

HERACLES. After killing the Cithaeronian lion, he wore its skin as his ordinary garment and its mouth and head as his helmet.

MENELAUS. In single combat with Paris, he seized him by the helmet and dragged him to the camp of the Achaeans, but Aphrodite loosened the helmet and wrapped her favorite in a cloud in which he escaped from the enemy (Hom. *Il.* 3. 325; 4. 12).

MERIONES. When Diomedes chose Odysseus for his companion on the exploring expedition to the Trojan camp, Meriones gave the latter his bow, quiver, sword, and famous helmet (Hom. *Il.* 10. 662).

MINERVA was represented with a helmet, shield, and coat of mail.

PERSEUS. For his mission to fetch Medusa's head, the nymphs provided him with the helmet of Hades, which rendered him invisible, so that he could approach the Gorgons undetected (Hes. *Scut.Herc.* 220, 222).

VIRTUS was the Roman personification of manly valor. She is often represented with a helmet on her head and standing with her right foot on a helmet.

Helmsman

ANCAEUS, son of Poseidon, became helmsman of the Argo (Appollon. Rhod. 2. 867).

AZORUS was helmsman of the Argo.

BAEUS was the helmsman of Odysseus.

CANOBUS was the helmsman of Menelaus (Strab. 17. 801).

ERGINUS succeeded Tiphys as helmsman of the Argo.

EUPHEMUS, son of Poseidon, was the helmsman of the Argo.

PALINURUS, son of Jasus, was helmsman of Aeneas.

PHARUS was the helmsman of Menelaus.

PHRONTIS, son of Onetor, was the helmsman of Menelaus (Hom. *Od.* 3. 282; Paus. 10. 25.2).

TIPHYS, son of Agnius, or of Phorbas and Hyrmine of Siphae, or Tiphae in Boeotia, was the helmsman of the ship Argo (Apollon. Rhod. 1. 105; Paus. 9. 32.3; Apollod. 1. 9.22).

Hemorrhage

HEPHAESTUS was believed to have great healing powers, and Lemnian earth (*terra Lemnia*) from the spot on which he had fallen from Olympus was believed to cure hemorrhage.

Hen

BONA DEA. Hens were sacrificed to her, except for black ones (Plin. *H.N.* 10. 77).

Herald

AETHALIDES, a son of Hermes, was herald to the Argonauts.

COPREUS, son of Pelops, was a friend and herald of Eurystheus. He was employed to tell Heracles of the labors he had to perform (Hom. *Il.* 15. 639; Apollod. 1. 5.1).

EURYBATES was a herald of Odysseus, who followed his master to Troy.

HERMES. Zeus made him his own herald and herald also of the gods of the lower world.

IDAEUS was a herald of the Trojans (Hom. *Il.* 3. 247, 7. 276, 381, 413, 24. 325).

LEOS was the herald of Aegeus. He betrayed to his master the plot of the sons of Pallas to overthrow Theseus, to whom Aegeus had ceded the kingdom of Athens, whereupon they were destroyed.

MEDON, the herald of the palace of Odysseus, was spared when Odysseus slew the suitors and faithless servants on his return to Ithaca.

MULIUS from Dulichium was a servant and herald in the house of Odysseus (Hom. *Od.* 18. 422).

ODIUS was a herald in the camp of the Greeks at Troy (Hom. *Il.* 9. 170).

PEISENOR was a herald of Telemachus in Ithaca (Hom. *Od.* 2. 38).

PERIPHAS, son of Epytus, was a herald of Aeneas (Hom. *Il.* 17. 323).

STENTOR was a herald of the Greeks at Troy, whose voice was as loud as that of fifty other men together (Hom. *Il.* 5. 783; Juv. 13. 112).

TALTHYBIUS was the herald of Agamemnon at Troy (Hom. *Il.* 1. 320; Ov. *Her.* 3. 9).

Herb

AMPHITRITE threw magic herbs into the well where Scylla bathed and caused her to be changed into a monster.

ARTEMIS. Ditamy (dittany) was sacred to her.

GIANTS. Gaea discovered an herb which would save the giants from being killed by mortal hands (as had been foretold), but Zeus was able to acquire the herb and prevent its use.

GLAUCUS (1). According to some writers, his flesh-eating mares tore him to pieces after being seized with madness from eating an herb called hippomanes, or from drinking from a sacred well in Boeotia (Paus. 9. 8.1).

GLAUCUS (2) of Anthedon in Boeotia was a fisherman who had the good luck to eat part of a divine herb which Cronus had sown and which made Glaucus immortal (Claud. *De Nupt.Mar.* 10. 158). Later, as a marine deity, he was paid divine homage by fishermen.

SCYLLA. One tradition relates that she was originally a beautiful maiden beloved by the marine god, Glaucus. He applied to Circe for means to make Scylla return his love; but Circe, jealous of the fair maiden, threw magic herbs into the well where Scylla bathed, and by these herbs she was metamorphosed into a sea-monster, half fish and half woman.

Herdsman

MENOETIUS was Hades' herdsman in the underworld, with whom Heracles fought after killing one of the cattle in order to give the shades blood to drink.

Hermaphroditism

AGDISTIS, a mythical being of Phrygian origin and offspring of Zeus by the Earth, was both male and female.

HERMAPHRODITUS was a son of Hermes and Aphrodite. When the nymph Salmacis fell in love with him and her love was unreturned, she prayed to the gods, while he was bathing in her spring, to unite her with him forever, which the gods did by joining them in one body. Hermaphroditus, on becoming aware of the change, prayed that in the future everyone who bathed in the spring should be metamorphosed into a hermaphrodite (Ov. *Met.* 4. 285; Diod. 4. 6; Lucian *Dial.Deor.* 15.2; Vitruv. 2. 8). Hermaphroditus was usually represented as having the head, breasts, and body of a female but with the sexual parts of a man.

PALES, a Roman divinity of flocks and shepherds, is described by some as a male and by others as a female divinity, whence some modern writers have inferred that Pales was a combination of both sexes.

Hero

ATHENA was the protectress of heroes.

Hilarity

IAMBE was the daughter of Pan and Echo. The extravagant hilarity displayed at the festivals of Demeter in Attica was traced to her, for when Demeter in her wandering in search of Persephone arrived in Attica, Iambe cheered the mournful goddess with her jokes (Hom. *Hymn.in Cer.* 202; Apollod. 1. 5.1; Diod. 5. 4).

Hill

ANTAEUS. The tomb of Antaeus was said to be a hill in the shape of a man stretched out at full length (Strab. 17. 829).

NAPAEAE were Roman divinities who presided over hills and woods.

Hind

ATALANTA (ATALANTE) was represented in ancient art as holding a hind.

CYPARISSUS was a youth who accidentally killed his favorite hind and, dying from grief, was metamorphosed into a cypress.

TAYGETE, a daughter of Atlas and Pleione, was one of the Pleiades. She showed her gratitude to Artemis, who helped her evade the embraces of Zeus, by dedicating to the goddess the Cerynitian hind with golden antlers.

TELEPHUS, a son of Heracles and Auge, was reared by a hind.

Hinges

CARDEA (CARDINIA or CARNA) was a Roman divinity presiding over and protecting the hinges of doors.

History

CLIO, the Muse of history, appears in a sitting attitude with an open roll of paper or an open chest of books.

Hole

MIDAS. When he decided in favor of Pan over Apollo in a musical contest, Apollo punished him by changing his ears into those of an ass. Midas concealed them under his cap, but the servant who cut his hair discovered them. The secret so plagued this man that, as he could not betray it to a human, he dug a hole in the earth and whispered into it: "King Midas has ass's ears." He then filled up the hole, but on the same spot a reed grew up, which in its whispers betrayed the secret to the world (Ov. *Met.* 11. 146; Aristoph. *Plut.* 287).

PYRAMUS and Thisbe, the ill-fated Babylonian lovers, were not allowed by their families to marry one another. They communicated by whispering through a chink in the wall between their houses. In this manner they arranged the meeting at the tomb of Ninus which proved fatal for both of them (Ov. *Met.* 4. 55).

Homosexuality

ABDERUS, son of Hermes, was a favorite of Heracles. After he was torn to pieces by the mares of Diomedes, Heracles built the town of Abdera in his honor.

ACHILLES. The famous friendship between Achilles and Patroclus was regarded by some as a homosexual relationship. Athenaeus in the *Deipnosophistae* (13. 601) refers to their love as the theme of Aeschylus' *Myrmidons.*

APOLLO CARNEIUS was a surname of Apollo from Carnus or Carneius, son of Zeus and Europa, who was a favorite of the god (Paus. 3. 13.3).

ARCHIAS. Actaeon was a son of Melissus, who had fled from Argos to Corinth for fear of the tyrant, Pheidon. Archias, a Corinthian, enamored with the beauty of Actaeon, endeavored to carry him off; but in the struggle which ensued between Melissus and Archias, Actaeon was killed (Plut. *Amat.Narr.* 772).

ATYMNIUS, son of Zeus and Cassiopeia, was a beautiful boy, who was beloved by Sarpedon (Apollod. 3. 1.2).

ATYS, priest of Cybele, fled into the forest to escape the voluptuous embraces of a Phrygian king, but was overtaken and in the ensuing struggle unmanned the king, who in turn inflicted the same calamity on Atys.

BRITOMARTIS was a huntress who was beloved by Artemis.

CEPHALUS. After he disguised himself as a stranger and seduced his wife Procris to test her fidelity, she retaliated by disguising herself as a handsome youth and joining his hunting expeditions. She possessed a dog and spear—neither of which ever missed its quarry—given to her by Artemis. Cephalus wanted to buy the dog and spear, but she refused to part with them at any price but love. He agreed to the bargain, whereupon she revealed herself and they were reconciled.

CYCNUS, son of Apollo by Thyria, a handsome hunter, repulsed all lovers except Phyllius, who persisted and was given various tasks by Cycnus, who eventually was thwarted.

CYPARISSUS, a youth of Cea, son of Telephus, was beloved by Apollo and Zephyrus or Silvanus. When his favorite stag was inadvertently killed, he was seized with immoderate grief and was metamorphosed into a cypress.

DAPHNIS, a Sicilian poet, was called the beloved of Hermes.

GANYMEDE. The early legend simply states that he was carried off to be the cupbearer of Zeus, in which office he was thought to have succeeded Hebe (Diod. 4. 75; Virg. *Aen.* 1. 28); but later writers describe him as the beloved and favorite of Zeus, without allusion to his office (Eurip. *Orest.* 1392; Plat. *Phaedr.* 255; Xenoph. *Sympos.* 8. 30; Cic. *Tusc.* 4. 33). Zeus made Ganymede immortal and exempt from old age. The Romans called Ganymede by a corrupt form of his name, Catamitus (Plaut. *Men.* 1. 2.34). (See also TANTALUS)

HYACINTHUS, a youth of extraordinary beauty, was beloved by Thamyris and Apollo and, according to some traditions, by the wind god Boreas or Zephyrus. Apollo unintentionally killed him during a game of discus (Apollod. 1. 3.2). Some relate that Zephyrus (or Boreas) from jealousy of Apollo, drove the discus of the god against the head of the youth and thus killed him (Lucian *Dial.Deor.* 14; Philostr. *Imag.* 1. 24; Ov. *Met.* 10. 184).

HYLAS was a beautiful youth who was taken by Heracles to Colchis on the Argo. On the way he was pulled into a well by admiring nymphs. Heracles sought him everywhere and finally abandoned the Argonautic expedition to continue the search.

LAIUS of Thebes carried off Chrysippus, son of Pelops, while he was still a boy and instructed him in driving the chariot (Apollod. 3. 5.5).

MACAREUS, son of Aeolus, was beloved of Apollo and became his priest after he had an incestuous relationship with his sister, Canace.

MELES, an Athenian, was beloved by Timagoras but refused to listen to him and ordered him to leap from the rock of the acropolis, which Timagoras did. Meles, repenting his cruel command, likewise threw himself from the rock (Paus. 1. 30.1).

MILETUS was a son of Apollo and Areia of Crete. Being beloved by Minos and Sarpedon, he attached himself to the latter and fled from Minos to Caria, where he built a town, which he named after himself (Apollod. 3. 1.2; Paus. 7. 2.3).

MYRMEX was an Athenian maiden who was beloved by Athena but later was changed by her into an ant.

NARCISSUS. According to some traditions, he sent a sword to one of his lovers, Ameinius, who killed himself with it at the very door of Narcissus' house and called upon the gods to avenge his death. Narcissus, tormented by love of himself and by repentance, put an end to his own life.

NESTOR. Heracles is said to have become more attached to Nestor than even to Hylas and Abderus.

PATROCLUS is said to have taken part in the expedition against Troy on account of his attachment to Achilles.

POSEIDON. Pindar (*Ol.* 1. 46) states that Poseidon, being in love with the beautiful boy, Pelops, carried him off, whereupon Pelops, like Ganymede, for a time stayed with the gods (Eurip. *Iphig.Taur.* 387; Philostr. *Imag.* 1. 17; Lucian *Charid.* 7; Tibull. 1. 4.57).

SILVANUS was a Latin divinity of the fields and

the forests. He is represented carrying the trunk of a cypress. Silvanus was in love with Cyparissus, who died from grief over the death of his favorite hind and was metamorphosed into a cypress.

SOSTRATUS was a youth beloved by Heracles, to whom funeral sacrifices were offered in Achaia, and whose tomb was in the neighborhood of the town of Dyme (Paus. 7. 17.4).

TANTALUS, king of Lydia, was in love with Ganymede and engaged with Ilus in a contest for the possession of the youth.

Honesty

FIDES was the Roman goddess of faith, oaths, and honesty.

Honey

DEMETER. Sacrifices to her included honey-cakes.

EUMENIDES. Sacrifices offered to them consisted of nephalia (a drink of honey mixed with water).

GLAUCUS, the young son of Minos and Pasiphae, while playing ball or while chasing a mouse (Apollod. 3. 3.1) fell into a cask full of honey and died.

HECATE. Sacrifices to her consisted of honey (Plut. *Quaest.Rom.* 49; Apollon.Rhod. 3. 1032).

HEMITHEA (See MOLPADIA)

HERMES. Honey was among the sacrifices offered to him.

IAMUS, son of Apollo, was deserted by his mother, Evadne, and was fed with honey by two serpents.

IRIS was the goddess of the rainbow. The Delians offered to her cakes made of wheat, honey, and dried figs.

LAIUS was a Cretan who with three other thieves, Aegolis, Celeus, and Cerberus, attempted to steal honey from the sacred cave of bees and accidentally came upon the cradle of the infant Zeus. The god metamorphosed them into birds (Plin. *H.N.* 10. 60, 79).

MACRIS, daughter of Aristaeus, fed the infant Dionysus with honey after he was brought to her in Euboea by Hermes (Apollon.Rhod. 4. 540, 990, 1131).

MELISSA was the nymph who discovered and taught the use of honey and from whom bees were believed to have received their name.

MELLONA (MELLONIA) was a Roman divinity who was believed to protect honey (August. 4. 34).

MOLPADIA, daughter of Staphylus, under the name of Hemithea, had a temple erected to her in Castabus in the Chersonesus. There, libations were offered to her consisting of honey and water.

MUSES. Sacrifices to them consisted of honey.

PAN. Sacrifices to him consisted of honey.

PERSEPHONE MELITODES, "sweet as honey," occurs as a euphemistic surname (Theocrit. 15. 94).

PRIAPUS was the son of Dionysus and Aphrodite and god of the fructifying powers and manifestations of nature. Sacrifices to him included honey.

ZEUS was reared by nymphs on Crete. They fed him the milk of the goat Amalthea, and the bees of the mountain provided him with honey (Apollod. 1. 1.6).

See also: BEE

Honeycomb

DAEDALUS made a honeycomb of gold for the temple of Aphrodite on Mt. Eryx.

Honor

HONOR (HONOS) was the personification of honor at Rome.

Hoof

PEGASUS. With his hoof he called forth the inspiring spring Hippocrene.

Hoopoe

TEREUS. When his wives, Procne and Philomela, killed his son, Itys, and served his flesh to him, he pursued them with an ax, and they were all changed into birds. According to some, he became a hoopoe (Ov. *Met.* 6. 424).

Hope

ELPIS, the Greek personification of hope, was worshipped by the Greeks. When Epimetheus opened the vessel brought to him by Pandora, from which all manner of evils were scattered over the earth, Hope (Elpis) alone remained behind (Hes. *Op.et D.* 96).

PANDORA. When she opened the box of ills, hope was the only thing that remained when she closed the lid.

PROMETHEUS taught men the art of prophecy. Later he deprived them of their knowledge of the future and gave them hope instead (Aeschyl. *Prom.* 248).

SPES, the Latin personification of hope, was worshipped at Rome, where she had several temples.

Horn (Instrument)

CENTAURS were in later times described as in the train of Dionysus playing the horn or lyre.

Horns

ACHELOUS. While he was disguised as a bull, one of his horns was broken off by Heracles. This was changed by the Naiads into the horn of plenty. Some accounts say he recovered his horn by exchanging for it the horn of Amalthea.

AMALTHEA. The broken horn of the goat whose milk suckled Zeus was filled by the nymph Amalthea with fresh herbs and fruits (Ov. *Fast.* 5. 115). This horn was later used as the symbol of plenty. Zeus is said also to have been fed from the horn. Amalthea is often used as the name of the goat which suckled Zeus.

ONEIROS (pl. ONEIRATA). According to Homer, dreams (Oneirata) dwell on the dark shores of the western Oceanus (*Od.* 24. 12), and deceitful dreams come through an ivory gate, while the true dreams issue from a gate made of horn (*Od.* 19. 562).

PAN, the great god of flocks and shepherds among the Greeks, had horns, beard, pug nose, tail, and goat's feet, and was covered with hair.

SABAZIUS, a Phrygian agricultural divinity and son of Rhea or Cybele, was represented with horns because he was said to be the first to yoke oxen to the plow for agriculture (Diod. 4. 4).

SATYRS. This class of beings was represented as having little horns.

SELENE was the moon goddess. At Elis there was a statue of her with two horns (Paus. 6. 24.5).

SOSIPOLIS, the boy-hero of the Eleans, was represented wearing a military cloak and carrying the horn of Amalthea in his hand (Paus. 3. 25.4, 6. 20.2).

Horoscope

LACHESIS, one of the Moirae, or Fates, is sometimes represented pointing with a staff to the horoscope on a globe of the firmament.

Horror

ARES was god of the horrors of war.

Horse

ABDERUS was a favorite of Heracles and was torn to pieces by the mares of Diomedes. Or, he was killed by Heracles along with his master and the man-devouring horses.

ACAMAS was a son of Theseus and Phaedra. Virgil (*Aen.* 2. 262) lists him among the Greeks concealed in the wooden horse at the taking of Troy. On his return home, he was detained in Thrace by his love for Phyllis; but after leaving Thrace and arriving in the island of Cyprus, he was killed by a fall from his horse onto his own sword.

ACHILLES inherited the immortal horses, Balius and Xanthus, from Peleus, his father.

AETHON (1) was one of the horses of the sun.

AETHON (2) was one of the horses of Athena.

ALASTOR was one of Pluto's horses.

ANTHUS, son of Autonous and Hippodameia, was torn to pieces by his father's horses. He was metamorphosed into a bird which imitated the neighing of a horse but always fled from the sight of a horse (Plin. *H.N.* 10. 57).

APOLLO reared the swift steeds of Eumelus Pheretiades in Pieria (Hom. *Il.* 2. 766).

AREION was the horse of Adrastus which saved him by its swiftness in the battle of the Seven against Thebes.

ARION was a horse, the son of Poseidon by Demeter, who had taken the form of a mare to escape from him. Poseidon assumed the form of a horse and thereby deceived her. She later gave Arion to Oncus, son of Apollo (Paus. 8. 25.4).

ARTEMIS HEURIPPE, "the finder of horses," was a surname of Artemis, to whom Odysseus was said to have built a temple at Pheneus in common with Poseidon Hippius, when at length he found his lost horses there (Paus. 8. 14.4).

ATHENA took care of the breeding of horses and taught men how to tame them by the bridle.

ATHENA CHALINITIS was a surname describing the goddess as the tamer of horses by means of the bridle, under which name she had a temple at Corinth. She was said to have so tamed Pegasus before she gave him to Bellerophon (Paus. 2. 4.1).

BALIUS was one of the horses of Achilles, offspring of Zephyrus and Podarge. (See also PELEUS)

BARGYLUS, a friend of Bellerophon, was killed by Pegasus.

CASTOR, one of the Dioscuri, was famous for his skill in taming and managing horses.

CENTAURS were usually described as partly human and partly horse. According to some, Zeus metamorphosed himself into a horse and begot the Centaurs by Dia, the wife of Ixion (Nonn. 16. 240; 14. 193).

CYLLARUS was the horse of Castor (Virg. *Georg.* 3. 90; Val.Flacc. 1. 426).

DIDO. While the foundations were being laid for the city of Carthage, the head of a horse was found, and this was a highly favorable sign (Virg. *Aen.* 1. 443).

DIOSCURI. When they appeared they were seen riding on magnificent white steeds. In Rome, they were worshipped as the patrons of the equestrian order, and every year they were honored with a splendid horseback procession.

ECHIDNA, the monster, once stole Heracles' horses and promised to return them only if he would stay with her awhile. He complied and became by her the father of Agathyrsus, Gelonus, and Scythes.

EETION. When he fell in battle, Achilles' booty from the town of Eetion included the horse Pedasus and the phorminx with a silver neck, on which Achilles played in his tent (Hom. *Il.* 16. 153; 9. 186).

EPONA, a Roman divinity, was regarded as the protectress of horses. Images of her were frequently seen in stables. She was said to be the daughter of Fulvius Stellus by a mare (Juv. 8. 157; Plut. *Paral.Gr.et Rom.* 312).

EUMELUS, son of Admetus, was distinguished for his excellent horses which had once been under the care of Apollo and with which Eumelus would have gained the prize at the funeral games of Patroclus, if his chariot had not been broken (Hom. *Il.* 23. 375, 536; Hom. *Od.* 4. 798; Strab. 9. 436).

GANYMEDE. Zeus compensated Ganymede's father for his loss with the present of a pair of divine horses (Hom. *Il.* 5. 266; Hom. *Hymn.in Ven.* 202; Apollod. 2. 5.9; Paus. 5. 24.1).

GLAUCUS. It was believed that the shade of Glaucus haunted the Corinthian isthmus and frightened horses during the race (Paus. 6. 20.9).

GRYPS (GRYPHUS), the griffin, a fabulous birdlike species of animal, was said to have been the guardian of the gold of the north—later of India. The Arismaspians mounted on horseback and attempted to steal the gold, and hence arose the hostility between the horse and the griffin.

HADES. When he carried Persephone away to the lower world, he rode in a golden chariot drawn by four black, immortal horses (Ov. *Met.* 5. 404; Hom. *Hymn.in Cer.* 19; Claud. *Rapt.Proserp.* 1).

HEBE, daughter of Zeus and Hera, assisted Hera in putting the horses to her chariot (Hom. *Il.* 5. 722).

HECATE was often described as having three heads, one of them that of a horse.

HELIOS. During the daily course of the sun, Helios drove a chariot drawn by horses (Ov. *Met.* 2. 106; Pind. *Ol.* 7. 71). Sacrifices to him consisted of horses, especially white ones.

HERACLES. On his return from his ninth labor, he landed in Troas, where he rescued Hesione from a sea monster and was promised a reward of the horses which Laomedon, her father, had received from Zeus as a compensation for Ganymede. Laomedon did not keep his word, whereupon Heracles sailed against Troy and killed Laomedon and all his sons (except Priam) (Hom. *Il.* 5. 649; Diod. 4. 42; Apollod. 2. 5.9, 3. 12.7).

HIPPOCAMPUS. The mythical sea horse had the upper body of a horse, but from the breast down was a fish. The horses which drew Poseidon's chariot over the surface of the sea were later represented as sea horses.

HIPPONA was a goddess who presided over horses.

HIPPOTHOUS, son of Alope and Poseidon, was exposed twice by his grandfather, Cercyon, but in both instances was suckled by a mare and survived to become a hero.

IASION, son of Zeus and Electra, according to some was killed by his own horses.

IASUS. At the first Olympian games, he won the prize at the horse race (Paus. 5. 8.1, 8. 4).

ICHTHYOCENTAURIS was a fish-centaur, or a particular kind of Triton. Ichthyocentauri were fabulous beings; the upper part of their bodies were human, the lower part fish, with horse's hooves in place of hands. (See TRITON)

JUPITER. The color white was sacred to Jupiter, and his chariot was thought to be drawn by four white horses.

LAMPUS (1) was a horse which belonged to Hector (Hom. *Il.* 8. 185).

LAMPUS (2) was one of the horses which drew the chariot of Eos, goddess of the dawn (Hom. *Od.* 23. 246).

LYCURGUS of Thrace, having brought famine on the land of the Edones by inhospitable treatment of Dionysus, was put in chains and led by the Edonians to Mt. Pangaeum, where he was torn to pieces by horses. An oracle had declared that his country would not be restored to fertility unless he were killed.

MARS. The horse was sacred to him and was, with the wolf, his favorite sacrifice.

MESSAPUS, a son of Neptune and king of Etruria, was invulnerable and a famous trainer of horses (Virg. *Aen.* 7. 691).

MONYCHUS was a giant with the feet of a horse.

NELEUS, son of Tyro by Poseidon, was exposed with his brother, Pelias, but they were found and reared by horse herds. When he was grown, he once sent a team of four horses to the Olympian games, but Augeas intercepted them and kept them for himself (Hom. *Il.* 11. 699).

NEPTUNE EQUESTOR. Neptune had created the horse, and in his honor horse races were held (Liv. 1. 9; Paus. 5. 15.4).

NIKE (NICE). In works of art, she is often seen together with other divinities, such as Zeus and Athena, and with conquering heroes, whose horses she guides.

PEGASUS was the famous winged horse which Bellerophon rode to kill the monster Chimaera.

PEIRITHOUS received his name because when Zeus tried to seduce his mother, Dia, he ran around her in the form of a horse.

PELEUS. Upon his marriage to Thetis, he was presented the immortal horses, Balius and Xanthus, by Poseidon (Apollod. 3. 13.5).

PELOPS. In the earliest traditions, Pelops was described as a native of Greece and not as a foreign immigrant; and in these traditions he is called the tamer of horses and the favorite of Poseidon (Hom. *Il.* 2. 104; Paus. 5. 1.5, 8.1; Pind. *Ol.* 1. 38).

PHAETHON (1) was the son of Helios, and one day he insisted on driving the chariot of the sun across the heavens. On the way, he lost control of the horses, and the sun came so close to the earth that it almost burned it. Zeus killed him with a thunderbolt.

PHAETHON (2) was one of the horses of Eos, goddess of the dawn (Hom. *Od.* 23. 246).

PHLEGON was one of the horses of Sol (Ov. *Met.* 2. 154).

POSEIDON. The horse was sacred to him, and there are many associations between him and the horse. According to some legends, he was not swallowed at birth by his father, Cronus, but was concealed among a flock of lambs, and his mother pretended to have given birth to a young horse, which she gave to Cronus to devour. At his palace in the sea near Aegae in Euboea (Hom. *Il.* 13. 21; Hom. *Od.* 5. 381), he kept his horses with brazen hooves and golden manes. With these horses he rode in a chariot over the waves of the sea. He was further regarded as the creator of the horse and was accordingly believed to have taught men the art of managing horses by the bridle and to have been the originator and protector of horse races (Hom. *Il.* 23. 307, 584; Pind. *Pyth.* 6. 50; Soph. *Oed.Col.* 712). He was also represented on horseback or riding in a chariot drawn by two or four horses. He even metamorphosed himself into a horse for the purpose of deceiving Demeter. The common tradition about Poseidon creating the horse is as follows: when Poseidon and Athena disputed as to which of them should give the name to the capital of Attica, the gods decided that it should receive its name from the one who could bestow on man the most useful gift. Poseidon then created the horse, and Athena called forth the olive tree, for which the honor was given to her. According to others, however, Poseidon did not create the horse in Attica but in Thessaly, where he also gave the famous horses to Peleus (Lucan 6. 396; Hom. *Il.* 23. 277; Apollod. 3. 13.5). In Argolis, bridled horses were thrown into the well Deine as a sacrifice to him (Paus. 8. 7.2), and horse and chariot races were held in his honor on the Corinthian isthmus (Pind. *Nem.* 5. 66). (See also ARION and HIPPOCAMP.US)

RHESUS was a son of King Eioneus in Thrace and an ally of the Trojans. He possessed horses white as snow and swift as the wind, which were carried off at night by Odysseus and Diomedes, the latter of whom murdered Rhesus in his sleep (Hom. *Il.* 10. 435, 495; Virg. *Aen.* 1. 469).

SELENE, the moon goddess, rode across the heavens in a chariot drawn by two white horses (or cows or mules). She was represented on the pedestal of the throne of Zeus at Olympia riding on a horse or mule (Paus. 5. 11.3).

STHENIUS was one of the horses of Poseidon.

TRITON was a son of Poseidon and Amphitrite, who dwelt with his father and mother in the golden palace at the bottom of the sea. He was described as riding over the sea on horses or sea monsters. Tritons were sometimes represented with two horse's feet instead of arms,

Pegasus

and they were often called Centaur-Tritons or Ichthyocentauri.

TROS, king of Phrygia, gave up his son Ganymede to Zeus for a present of horses (Paus. 5. 24.1; Apollod. 3. 12.2).

XANTHUS (1) was the name of one of Achilles' horses, offspring of Zephyrus and Podarge, one of the Harpies (Hom. *Il.* 16. 149). (See also PELEUS)

XANTHUS (2) was the name of one of Hector's horses (Hom. *Il.* 8. 185).

Hospitality

ALCINOUS. Both in the story of the Argonauts and the *Odyssey* he is represented with his wife, Arete, as giving extraordinarily hospitable treatment to the heroes.

ATHENA XENIA was a surname designating Athena as presiding over the laws of hospitality and protecting strangers (Paus. 3. 11; Hom. *Od.* 14. 389; Cic. *Ep.ad Q.Frat.* 2. 12).

BAUBO received Demeter kindly while she was searching for Persephone, and offered her something to drink.

BUPHAGUS received the wounded Iphicles into his house and cared for him until he died.

CELEUS. When Demeter in search of Persephone came to Eleusis, she stayed at his house and tried to repay him for his kindness by making his son Demophon immortal. At night she put him in the fire but was discovered by Metaneira, the mother, who screamed and caused the child to be consumed by flames (Apollod. 1. 5.1).

CHEIRON the centaur received the Argonauts kindly when they came to his residence during their voyage.

DAUNUS hospitably received Diomedes and gave him his daughter Evippe in marriage (Plin. *H.N.* 3. 11).

DEMETER. In her wanderings in search of her daughter Persephone, she dwelt among men, confering presents and blessings wherever she was kindly received and severely punishing those who repulsed her. (See also BAUBO, CELEUS, DEMO, MYSIUS, PELASGUS, and PHYTALUS)

DEMO, daughter of Celeus and Metaneira, together with her sisters, kindly received Demeter at the well Callichoros in Attica (Hom. *Hymn.in Cer.* 109). The name Demo was sometimes applied to Demeter.

DIOSCURI were the protectors of the law of hospitality, the violation of which they severely punished (Paus. 3. 16.3).

EMPANDA (PANDA) was a Roman goddess, who had a sanctuary near the gate called the Porta Pandana after her (Varr. *De Ling.Lat.* 5. 42). Her temple was always open, and suppliants who came were privided with food from temple funds. Anyone who wanted protection was admitted.

EUMENIDES were the avenging deities who punished violation of the law of hospitality.

HOSPITALIS was the guardian or protector of the law of hospitality. We find the title of *dii hospitales* applied to a distant class of gods, though their names are not mentioned (Tacit. *Ann.* 15. 52; Liv. 39. 51; Ov. *Met.* 5. 45).

ICARIUS hospitably received Dionysus on his arrival in Attica.

IPHINOE was one of the Lemnian women who received the Argonauts on their arrival in Lemnos (Apollon.Rhod. 1. 702; Val.Flacc. 2. 162, 327).

JUPITER HOSPITALIS was a surname of Jupiter at Rome as protector of hospitality (Cic. *Ep.ad Q.Frat.* 2. 12).

LYCUS, son of Dascylus and king of the Mariandynians, was connected with Heracles and the Argonauts by ties of hospitality (Apollod. 1. 9.23, 2. 5.9; Apollon.Rhod. 2. 139).

MIDAS. During the expedition of Dionysus from Thrace to Phrygia, Silenus, in a state of intoxication, went astray and was caught by country people in the rose gardens of Midas. He was bound in wreaths of flowers and led before the king. Midas received him kindly, conversed with him and after treating him hospitably for ten days, led him back to his divine pupil, Dionysus, who in his gratitude granted Midas a favor.

MOLORCHUS was the mythical founder of Molorchia near Nemea. He hospitably received Heracles when he went out to slay the Nemean lion (Apollod. 2. 5.1).

MYSIUS was an Argive who received Demeter kindly during her wanderings and built a sanctuary to her. A temple at Pellene was eventually built, and the Mysian Demeter was worshipped here (Paus. 2. 18.3; 7. 27.9).

PELASGUS, son of Triopas and founder of the city of Argos, received Demeter in her wanderings and taught the people agriculture (Paus. 1. 14.2, 2. 22.2).

PHILEMON, an aged Phrygian, and his wife Baucis kindly received Zeus and Hermes, who traveled in the guise of ordinary mortals. For this favor Zeus rescued them from a flood and appointed them guardians of one of his temples. He granted them the favor of letting them die at the same moment and metamorphosed them into trees (Ov. *Met.* 8. 621).

PHYTALUS was an Eleusinian hero who is said to have kindly received Demeter on her wanderings and was rewarded by the goddess with a fig tree (Paus. 1. 37.2).

THETIS received Dionysus on his flight from Lycurgus, and the god in his gratitude presented her with a golden urn (Hom. *Il.* 6. 135; Hom. *Od.* 24. 75). When Hephaestus was thrown down from heaven, he was likewise received by Thetis.

ZEUS EUXEINOS (EUXENUS). Zeus was worshipped at Cape Genetus on the Black Sea by this name, which meant "the hospitable." He had a sanctuary here (Apollon.Rhod. 2. 378, 1009; Val.Flacc. 5. 148; Strab. 12. 548).

ZEUS XENIOS was a surname of Zeus as presiding over the laws of hospitality and protecting strangers (Paus. 3. 11; Hom. *Od.* 14. 389; Cic. *Ep.ad Q.Frat.* 2. 12).

Household, see Domesticity

Human Sacrifice

AEGLEIS, daughter of Hyacinthus, with her three sisters, Lytaea, Orthaea, and Antheis, was sacrificed on the tomb of Geraestus, the Cyclops, to avert a pestilence in Athens.

AGRAULOS sacrificed herself by leaping from the acropolis, when an oracle declared that a long war on Athens would cease when one of its inhabitants sacrificed his life for the good of the country. She was worshipped in Cyprus, where human sacrifices were offered to her.

ARES. In Sparta and in Scythia human sacrifices were offered to him.

ARTEMIS. Orgiastic worship of the Taurian Artemis was connected with human sacrifices. Strangers shipwrecked on the coast in Tauris were sacrificed to her. The Lacedaemonians maintained that the carved image of Artemis, which Iphigeneia and Orestes had carried away from Tauris, existed at Sparta and was worshipped there in the Limnaeon under the name of Artemis Orthia (Paus. 3. 16). The image was said to have thrown the beholders into a state of madness. Once, at a celebration of her festival, a quarrel arose which ended in bloodshed, and an oracle commanded that in the future, human sacrifices should be offered to her. That in Attica, also, human sacrifices were offered to her (at least in early times) may be inferred from the fact that it was customary to shed human blood in the worship in honor of Orestes (Eurip. *Iphig.Taur.* 1446). (See also TAURICA [DEA])

ATHENA. Locrian maidens or children are said to have been sacrificed to her every year as an atonement for the crime committed by the Locrian Ajax upon Cassandra.

BUSIRIS, an Egyptian king, was instructed by a seer to sacrifice a foreigner to Zeus every year in order to deliver the country from famine. He sacrificed the seer and, afterwards, all foreigners who entered Egypt.

CECROPS abolished human sacrifices in Attica by substitution of cakes (Paus. 8. 2.1; Strab. 9. 397).

CORESUS, a priest of Dionysus, sacrificed himself in lieu of his beloved, Callirrhoe, who for spurning the love of Coresus had been ordered by an oracle to be sacrificed to Dionysus (Paus. 7. 21.1).

DEMIPHON, king of Phlagusa, in order to avert a pestilence, was commanded by an oracle to sacrifice a noble maiden every year.

DIONYSUS. Among the sacrifices which were offered to him in the earliest times, human sacrifices were also mentioned (Paus. 7. 21.1). When the oracle of Delphi gave advice to cure Eurypylus from madness brought on by bringing from Troy a chest containing the image of Dionysus, Eurypylus journeyed to Aroe, where the inhabitants were obliged to offer human sacrifices each year because of defiling a temple of Artemis. The oracle had said that when he saw men performing a strange sacrifice, he should dedicate the chest. The inhabitants had also been told by the oracle that they would be relieved of the curse when a foreign king should bring a foreign divinity. Thus was instituted the festival of Dionysus Aesymnetes.

DIONYSUS OMADIUS, "the flesh-eater," was a surname of Dionysus, to whom human sacrifices were offered in Chios and Tenedos.

ELECTRA. Receiving a false report that her brother Orestes had been sacrificed to Artemis, she went to Delphi to learn the facts. Orestes and their sister Iphigeneia arrived there at the same time, but another false message arrived that Orestes had been sacrificed by Iphigeneia, and Electra seized a firebrand to put out her sister's eyes. But Orestes appeared, and they all traveled to Mycenae, where Orestes killed Aletes, the usurper of his father's throne.

ENALUS. When the first settlers of Lesbos were commanded to sacrifice a virgin to Amphitrite, lots were cast, and the daughter of Smintheus was chosen for the sacrifice. When she was about to be thrown into the sea, her lover, Enalus, embraced her and leapt with her. They were saved by dolphins.

ERICHTHONIUS. His daughters agreed to die together. When Poseidon or an oracle decreed that one of his daughters be sacrificed, the others accompanied her in death (Apollod. 3. 15.4; Plut. *Paral.Gr.et Rom.* 2).

HERACLES. In the west, Heracles abolished human sacrifice among the Sabines.

HESIONE, daughter of Laomedon, was either chosen by lot or commanded by an oracle to be chained to a rock as sacrifice to a sea monster which had been sent by Poseidon to ravage Troy because of non-payment of wages owed to him by Laomedon. Some say she was chained to a rock to be devoured by wild beasts to stop a plague sent on Troy. In either case, she was delivered from the sacrifice by Heracles.

HIPPOTES (See PHOENODAMAS)

HYACINTHUS was a Lacedaemonian, who in compliance with an oracle went to Athens and caused his daughters to be sacrificed on the tomb of Cyclops Geraestus for the purpose of delivering the city from famine and plague.

IDOMENEUS. Once, in a storm at sea, he vowed to Poseidon to sacrifice to him whatever he should meet first on his landing, if the god would grant him a safe return. The first person he met on his landing was his son, whom he accordingly sacrificed.

IPHIGENEIA. Her father Agamemnon killed a stag in the grove of Artemis or vowed in the year in which Iphigeneia was born that he would sacrifice to Artemis the most beautiful thing produced that year and failed to keep his vow; one of these circumstances caused the Greek fleet to lie becalmed in the port of Aulis when the Greeks wanted to sail against Troy. The seer, Calchas, declared sacrificing Iphigeneia was the only way to propitiate Artemis, so she was fetched on the pretext of marriage to Achilles. On the point of being sacrificed, she was carried away in a cloud by Artemis to Tauris, where she was made to serve the goddess as a priestess. (See also TAURICA [DEA])

IPPOTEUS (See PHOENODAMAS)

IPSOSTRATUS (See PHOENODAMAS)

LAELAPS, the dog of Procris and later

Cephalus, was sent to deliver Thebes from a monster fox to which the Thebans had been forced to sacrifice a boy each month. The dog overtook the fox, but Zeus changed both animals into stone (Apollod. 2. 4.6; Ov. *Met.* 7. 771).

LYCAON sacrificed a child on the altar to Zeus, and during the sacrifice he was changed into a wolf (Paus. 8. 2.1; Ov. *Met.* 1. 237).

MANIA was an ancient and formidable Italian (probably Etruscan) divinity of the lower world. Boys are said to have been sacrificed to her on behalf of the families to which they belonged. The consul Junius Brutus afterwards abolished the human sacrifices and substituted garlic and the heads of poppies.

MELANIPPUS. Because he profaned the temple of Artemis in Patrae by having intercourse with one of her priestesses, Melanippus and his beloved were put to death, and plague and famine visited the whole of Achaia. The oracle of Delphi revealed the cause of these calamities and ordered the inhabitants to sacrifice to Artemis every year the handsomest youth and most beautiful maiden (Paus. 7. 19.2).

MENIPPE and her sister Metioche, daughters of Orion, offered themselves as a sacrifice in order to avert a plague in Aonia, where they lived (Ov. *Met.* 13. 685).

MERCURY TEUTAS (TEUTATES) was a name of Mercury among the Gauls, probably the same as the Troth of the Egyptians. The people offered human sacrifices to this deity.

MINOS. In order to avenge the wrong done to his son, Androgeus at Athens, he made war against the Athenians and Megarians. He subdued Megara and compelled the Athenians either every year or every nine years to send as a tribute seven youths and seven maidens, who were devoured in the labyrinth by the Minotaur (Apollod. 3. 15.8; Paus. 1. 27.9, 44.5; Plut. *Thes.* 15; Diod. 4. 61).

ORESTES. When he arrived in Tauris to carry the image of Artemis to Attica, he was, with his companion, Pylades, about to be sacrificed in the temple, according to the custom of the country, but was recognized by his sister, the priestess Iphigeneia, who fled with him and the statue of the goddess. (See also ELECTRA and IPHIGENEIA)

PALAEMON was a marine deity, to whom, it is said, children were sacrificed in the island of Tenedos (Hom. *Od.* 3. 6).

PALICI were Sicilian daemons, twin sons of Zeus and the nymph, Thaleia. They were worshipped in the neighborhood of Mt. Aetna, near Palice; in the earliest times, human sacrifices were offered to them.

PHOENODAMAS (others call him Hippotes, Ippoteus, or Ipsostratus), a Trojan, had three daughters. When he was compelled by Laomedon to expose one of them to the marine monster which was ravaging the country, he called the people together and induced them to force Laomedon, whose guilt had brought the monster to the country, to expose his own daughter, Hesione.

PHRASIUS was a Cyprian soothsayer, who advised Busiris to sacrifice the strangers that came to his dominions, for the purpose of averting a famine; but Phrasius himself fell a victim to his advice (Apollod. 2. 5.11).

PHRIXUS was the son of Athamas and Nephele. Because of the intrigue of his stepmother, Ino, he was to be sacrificed to Zeus; others state that he offered himself. But Nephele removed him and Helle, his sister, and the two of them rode away through the air on the ram with the golden fleece.

POLITES was an evil spirit which victimized the town of Temessa and demanded that a fair maiden be sacrificed to him each year. The town was delivered by Euthymus.

POLYXENA was a daughter of Priam and Hecuba, beloved by Achilles. When the Greeks were preparing to leave Troy, the shade of Achilles appeared to them demanding that Polyxena be sacrificed to him. Neoptolemus accordingly sacrificed her on the tomb of his father (Eurip. *Hec.* 40; Ov. *Met.* 13. 448).

PRAXITHEA and her sisters, Theope and

Eubule, daughters of Leos, were sacrificed by their father at the directions of the Delphic oracle to halt a plague and famine in Athens.

SINON was a Greek spy who infiltrated the Trojan ranks, pretending that he was hated by Odysseus and had been selected by him to be sacrificed because Apollo had ordered a human sacrifice to be offered that the Greeks might safely depart from the coast of Troy, and that he had escaped death by flight.

TAURICA (DEA) was "the Taurian goddess," commonly called Artemis. Her image was believed to have been carried from Tauris by Orestes and Iphigeneia and to have been conveyed to Brauron, Sparta, or Aricia. Worship of this Taurian goddess, identified with Artemis and Iphigeneia, was carried on with orgiastic rites and human sacrifices and seems to have been very ancient in Greece (Paus. 3. 16.6; Herod. 4. 103).

ZEUS LAPHYSTIUS. This surname, according to some, signified "the voracious," in reference to the human sacrifices offered to him in early times (Paus. 1. 24.2, 9. 34.4).

ZEUS LYCAEUS was so named by Lycaon, a son of Pelasgus, who built the first and most ancient town of Lycosura. He erected a temple there and instituted the festival of the Lyceia in honor of him. He further offered to him bloody sacrifices and, among others, his own son, in consequence of which he was metamorphosed into a wolf (Paus. 8. 2.1, 38.1; Callim. *Hymn.in Jov.* 4; Ov. *Met.* 1. 218).

Hunchback

EURYBATES, the herald of Odysseus, was described as a hunchback, brown complexioned, and curly haired (Hom. *Il.* 1. 319, 2. 184, 9. 170; Hom. *Od.* 19. 246).

Hunger

ANNA PERENNA was a Roman divinity. When the plebs had seceded to the *Mons Sacer* and were in need of food, she came to them as an aged woman and distributed cakes among the hungry, who later built a temple to her.

ERYSICHTHON, son of Triopas, cut down trees in a grove sacred to Demeter, for which he was punished by the goddess with fearful hunger (Callim. *Hymn.in Cer.* 34; Ov. *Met.* 8. 738). He even sold his daughter, Mestra, so that he could buy food to satisfy his hunger.

FAMES (See LIMUS)

LIMUS (FAMES) was the personification of hunger.

MIDAS, king of Phrygia, was granted a wish that all things he touched be turned to gold. He discovered that this included food and drink and begged to have the wish taken back, because he was about to starve to death.

PHINEUS, a king of Thrace, was blinded by the gods. The Harpies stole and spoiled his food until he was on the point of utter starvation. His brothers-in-law, Zetes and Calais, overcame the Harpies and delivered him.

TANTALUS, a wealthy king, betrayed the divine counsels of Zeus. He was punished by being placed in the midst of a lake in the nether world. Branches laden with fruit hung over his head, but when he stretched out his hand to reach the fruit, the branches withdrew (Hom. *Od.* 11. 582).

See also: FAMINE

Hunting

ACTAEON. According to some legends, he was changed into a stag for boasting that he excelled Artemis in hunting.

AMARYNTHUS was a hunter and companion of Artemis; from him a town in Euboea derived its name (Strab. 10. 448).

APOLLO AGRAEUS was a surname of Apollo as hunter.

ARGANTHONE of Mysia hunted alone in the forest and was met and wooed by Rhesus.

ARISTAEUS was worshipped as the deity who taught men the skill of hunting.

ARISTAEUS AGREUS was a surname of Aristaeus from his love of hunting (Pind. *Pyth.* 9. 115; Apollon.Rhod. 3. 507; Diod. 4. 81).

ARTEMIS was the Arcadian goddess of hunting and the chase.

ARTEMIS AGRAEA was a surname of Artemis as huntress. (Cf. APOLLO AGRAEUS)

ARTEMIS AGROTERA was a surname of Artemis as huntress, at Agrae and Aegeira.

ATALANTA (ATALANTE) was identified by ancient writers with the chase.

BRITOMARTIS was a Cretan divinity of hunters and fishermen.

CALLISTO was a huntress and companion of Artemis.

CAMILLA, as a servant of Diana, was accustomed to the chase.

CANDAON (See ORION)

CHEIRON the centaur was renowned for his skill in hunting.

CYCNUS, son of Apollo by Thyria, was a handsome hunter living in the district between Pleuron and Calydon. He repulsed all lovers except Phyllius, who persisted and was given various tasks by Cycnus, all of which Phyllius accomplished. Cycnus finally in exasperation leaped into a lake and was changed into a swan.

EUMENIDES were sometimes represented in the richly adorned attire of huntresses with bands of serpents around their heads.

FAUNUS, son of Picus and king of the Laurentes, promoted agriculture and the breeding of cattle among his subjects and also distinguished himself as a hunter (Plin. *H.N.* 9. 6; Propert. 4. 2.34).

GANYMEDE. Some legends report that he was killed during the chase and buried on the Mysian Olympus (Strab. 13. 587).

HECATE was a mysterious divinity who bestowed good luck on hunters.

HYLEUS was a hunter who was killed by the Calydonian boar (Apollod. 1. 8.2; Ov. *Met.* 8. 312).

ORION was a son of Hyrieus or Hyria in Boeotia. He was a very handsome giant and hunter and was said to have been called Candaon by the Boeotians (Hom. *Od.* 11. 309; Strab. 9. 404). He fell in love with Aero (Merope), daughter of Oenopion of Chios, and cleared the island of wild beasts, bringing the spoils of the hunt to his beloved. He was blinded by Oenopion for violating his daughter, but later recovered his vision and went to Crete, where he lived as a hunter with Artemis (Apollod. 1. 4.3).

PAN was a hunter, and hunters owed their success to him, who at the same time might prevent their being successful. In Arcadia, hunters used to scourge the statue of Pan if they hunted in vain (Theocrit. 7. 107).

PELEUS. Having been accused by Astydameia of attempting to seduce her, Peleus was taken to Mt. Pelion by Acastus, her husband, where they hunted wild beasts. When Peleus, overcome with fatigue, fell asleep, Acastus left him alone and concealed his sword so that he would be destroyed by wild beasts.

ZETHUS. While his twin, Amphion, preferred music and song, he preferred hunting and shepherdry (Hor. *Epist.* 1. 18.41).

Hurricane

TYPHON (TYPHOEUS), a monster of the primitive world, is described sometimes as a destructive hurricane and sometimes as a fire-breathing giant.

Hyacinth

HYACINTHUS. When Apollo accidentally killed him with a discus, he caused a flower known as the hyacinth to spring from the blood of the slain youth.

Hymn

POLYMNIA (POLYHYMNIA) was the Muse of the sublime hymn.

Hypochondria

DEIPHOBUS. His body, which remained unburied, was believed to have been changed into a plant used against hypochondria.

Ice Bird

ALCYONIDES were daughters of Alcyoneus. After their father's death, they threw themselves into the sea and were changed into ice birds.

Idleness

VENUS MURTIA was a surname of Venus as the goddess of idleness (August. 4. 16).

Image, see Statue

Immolation

BROTHEUS, a son of Hephaestus and Athena, burned himself to avoid the ridicule to which his deformity subjected him.

CREUSA, daughter of Creon of Corinth, was burned to death in a poisoned robe given to her by Medea upon Creusa's betrothal to Jason. She was called Glauce by some writers.

DEMOPHON, the brother of Triptolemus, in the process of being made immortal by Demeter by being placed in a fire, was discovered by his mother, who screamed and caused him to be consumed by the flames.

DIDO. In order to avoid marriage with the barbarian king Hiarbas, she raised a funeral pyre, ostensibly to sacrifice animals, and then on the pyre she stabbed herself with a sword and was burned. In the *Aeneid* she does the same thing, but because she was deserted by Aeneas, with whom she was in love.

ELPENOR. In the underworld Odysseus met the shade of Elpenor, who implored him to burn his body and to erect a monument to him (Hom. *Od.* 11. 57). When Odysseus returned to the island of Circe, he performed this service.

EVADNE. When her husband, Capaneus, perished in the campaign against Thebes, she threw herself on the pyre with him.

GLAUCE (See CREUSA)

HERACLES. In his agony from putting on a poisoned garment, he climbed Mt. Oeta, raised a pile of wood, ascended it, and ordered it to be set on fire. Eventually, Poeas, a shepherd, was prevailed on to set fire to the pile. (See also PHILOCTETES)

LAODAMEIA. After the second death of her husband, Protesilaus, she made an image of him, which she worshipped, and when her father, Acastus, ordered her to burn it, she threw herself with the image into the flames.

LEOS, son of Orpheus, immolated his three daughters for the good of Athens.

MENIPPE and Metioche were daughters of Orion. They gave themselves as sacrifices to be burned to save Boeotia from pestilence.

OENONE. According to some, in her grief at her husband Paris' death, she rushed into the flames of the funeral pyre on which his body was burning (Lycoph. 65; Q.Smyrn. 10. 467).

PALLENE, daughter of Sithon, loved Cleitus, who entered into combat with Dryas for the hand of the beautiful maiden. She induced the charioteer of Dryas to remove the nails from his master's wheels, whereupon Cleitus was able to overcome and kill his rival. When her father learned of the trick, he erected a funeral pyre on which he intended to burn the body of Dryas along with his daughter. But when Aphrodite appeared, bringing a shower of rain to extinguish the fire, Sithon changed his mind and gave his daughter to Cleitus.

PATROCLUS. When his funeral pyre would not burn, Achilles promised to offer sacrifices to the winds, and Iris was sent to find them as they feasted in the palace of Zephyrus in Thrace.

Boreas and Zephyrus, at the invitation of Iris, hastened across the Thracian sea into Asia to make the fire blaze (Hom. *Il.* 23. 185).

PHILOCTETES, friend of Heracles, received the hero's bow and arrows for having erected and set fire to the pyre on Mt. Oeta, where Heracles burned himself (Diod. 4. 38; Ov. *Met.* 9. 230). According to others, it was Poeas, Morsimus, Hyllus, or Zeus who performed that service to Heracles (Apollod. 2. 7.7).

Immortality

ACHILLES. Thetis, his mother, sought to make him immortal by concealing him in fire at night and anointing him with ambrosia during the day. She also sought immortality for him by dipping him in the river Styx.

ADMETUS was a son of Pheres and Clymene and king of Thessaly. Apollo, after tending his flocks for nine years, promised him immortality if another person laid down his life for him. His wife, Alcestis, did so, and thus Admetus gained immortality.

AENEAS, half immortal by birth, was said to have disappeared at the instant of his death and reappeared among the immortals.

AMPHIARAUS. After being swallowed up by the earth after the battle of the Seven against Thebes, he was made immortal by Zeus (Pind. *Nem.* 9. 57; Pind. *Ol.* 6. 21).

ATYS. Agdistis, the hermaphroditic divinity who caused his death, obtained from Zeus the promise that the body of Atys would neither decompose nor disappear.

CALYPSO promised Odysseus eternal youth and immortality if he would remain with her (Hom. *Od.* 5. 28, 7. 254).

CHEIRON. During a struggle between Heracles and the centaurs, Cheiron was struck by a poisoned arrow. Although immortal, he would not live any longer and gave his immortality to Prometheus.

DEMOPHON, son of Celeus and Metaneira, was entrusted to the care of Demeter. She fed him her own milk and ambrosia and at night she placed him in fire to secure to him eternal youth; but once she was observed by Metaneira, who disturbed the goddess with her cries, and the child was consumed by the flames (Apollod. 1. 5.1; Ov. *Fast.* 4. 512; Hom. *Hymn. in Cer.* 234).

ENDYMION. According to some legends, Zeus granted him a request, and Endymion begged for immortality, eternal sleep, and everlasting youth (Apollod. 1. 7.5).

GANYMEDE was the beloved of Zeus, who made him immortal and exempt from old age.

GLAUCUS of Anthedon in Boeotia was a fisherman who had the good luck to eat part of a divine herb which Cronus had sown and which made Glaucus immortal (Athen. 7. 48; Claud. *De Nupt. Mar.* 10. 158). Later, as a marine deity, he was paid homage by fishermen.

HERACLES. While his funeral pyre was burning, a cloud came down from heaven and amid peals of thunder carried him to Olympus, where he was honored with immortality (Hes. *Theog.* 949; Apollod. 2. 7.7; Diod. 4. 38).

IPHIGENEIA. Some traditions state that she did not die but was endowed by Artemis with immortality and eternal youth, and under the name of Oreilochia she became the wife of Achilles on the island of Leuce.

JUTURNA was a nymph beloved by Jupiter, who rewarded her with immortality and the rule over waters (Virg. *Aen.* 12. 140, 878; Ov. *Fast.* 2. 585, 606).

MEMNON. After he was killed at Troy, his mother Eos prayed to Zeus to grant her son immortality.

MENELAUS. According to the prophecy of Proteus, Menelaus and Helen were not to die, but the gods were to conduct them to Elysium (Hom. *Od.* 4. 561).

ODYSSEUS. When he floated to the island of Calypso after his ship had been destroyed, she received him with kindness and wanted him to marry her, promising him immortality and eternal youth if he would consent.

OREILOCHIA (See IPHIGENEIA)

PERSEPHONE. In the mysteries of Eleusis, the return of Cora (Persephone) from the lower world was thought a symbol of immortality.

PHILONOE, a daughter of Tyndareus, was rendered immortal by Artemis (Apollod. 3. 10.6).

POLYDEUCES (POLLUX), one of the Dioscuri, according to some traditions, was the son of Zeus and Leda and was immortal, while Castor, the son of Tyndareus and Leda, was subject to old age and death like any other mortal (Pind. *Nem.* 10. 80; Theocrit. 24. 130; Apollod. 3. 10.7). When Castor was killed by Idas, Pollux prayed to be permitted to die with him. Zeus left him the option either to live as an immortal or to share his brother's fate, and to live alternately one day under the earth and the other in the heavenly abode of the gods (Hom. *Il.* 3. 243).

PSYCHE. After many discouraging misadventures in seeking to recover Amor's love, she eventually succeeded in overcoming the jealousy and hatred of Venus, became immortal, and was united with Amor forever (Apul. 4. 28).

SEMELE. After her death, she was led by her son Dionysus out of the lower world and carried up to Olympus as Thyone (Pind. *Ol.* 2. 44; Pind. *Pyth.* 11. 1; Paus. 2. 31.2, 37.5; Apollod. 3. 5.3).

THYONE (See SEMELE)

TITHONUS was a son of Laomedon, beloved of Eos, who obtained for him from the gods immortality but not eternal youth, in consequence of which he lived, growing older and weaker until he eventually dried up and was metamorphosed by Eos into a cricket (Hom. *Hymn.in Ven.* 218; Hor. *Carm.* 1. 22.8, 2. 16.30; Apollod. 3. 12.4).

TYDEUS was a son of Oeneus and Periboea. When Tydeus, at the battle of Thebes, was mortally wounded, Athena appeared with a remedy which was to make him immortal, but Amphiaraus, who hated Tydeus, brought him a different remedy, the head of the vanquished enemy, Melanippus. Tydeus cut it in two and ate the brain, or devoured some of the flesh. Athena, seeing this, shuddered and did not apply the remedy which she had brought (Apollod. 3. 6.8). Tydeus then died and was buried at Mecon (Paus. 9. 18.2).

Impartiality

APOLLO ISODETES was a surname designating him as the god who binds all equally, thereby expressing his impartiality.

DIONYSUS ISODAETES was a surname designating the god as one who distributes his gifts equally to all (Plut. *De E ap.Delph.* 9.)

HADES ISODETES. As APOLLO ISODETES.

Impersonation, see Disguise

Imposter

LAVERNA was the protecting divinity of thieves and imposters; her name was probably connected with the Latin word *levator,* thief.

Impotence

ATYS. According to Pausanias (7. 17.5) Atys, the son of Calaus, was by nature incapable of propagating his race. When he grew up, he went to Lydia and introduced the worship of Cybele.

Imprisonment, see Prison

Impudence

THERSITES, a son of Agrius, was the ugliest and most impudent talker among the Greeks at Troy. Once, when he had spoken in the assembly in an unbecoming manner against Agamemnon, he was chastised by Odysseus (Hom. *Il.* 2. 212; Apollod. 1. 8.6).

Incense

HERMES. Incense was among the sacrifices offered to him.

JANUS. Incense was sacred to him.

LEUCOTHOE, daughter of Orchamas and Eurynome, was beloved by Apollo; but her love was betrayed by the jealous Clytia to her father, who buried her alive, whereupon Apollo metamorphosed her into an incense shrub (Ov. *Met.* 4. 208).

PIETAS was a personification of faithful attachments, love, and veneration among the Romans. She is seen represented on Roman coins as a matron throwing incense upon an altar.

Incest

ASTRAEUS had sexual intercourse with Alcippe, without realizing that she was his sister. When he learned the truth, he threw himself into a river.

BYBLIS, daughter of Miletus, and her brother Caunus were in love with each other. Caunus fled from home but was followed by Byblis who, when she could not find him, hanged herself with her girdle. Another tradition says she was in love with her brother and tried to kill herself by leaping into the sea, but was changed into a Hamadryad.

CANACE, daughter of Aeolus and Enarte, was passionately attracted to her brother, Macareus (Macar) and persuaded him to commit incest with her. According to some accounts, he killed himself in consequence.

CINYRAS had sexual intercourse with Smyrna (Myrrha) without realizing she was his daughter. Adonis was born from this union. Cinyras, on learning the truth, killed himself (Ov. *Met.* 10. 310).

CLYMENUS was passionately attracted to his daughter, Harpalyce, and committed incest with her. Later he gave her in marriage to Alastor and then took her from him and lived with her again.

DAETA was the mother of Enorches by her brother, Thyestes, and Enorches was born out of an egg.

LEUCIPPUS was passionately attracted to his sister and was finally discovered in her embrace by their father. The father killed her on the spot, and Leucippus killed his father.

LYCAON was father of Dryops by Dia, his own daughter, who concealed her newborn infant in a hollow oak tree.

MENEPHRON, an Arcadian, was said to have lived in an incestuous relationship with both his mother, Blias, and his daughter, Cyllene (Ov. *Met.* 7. 386).

NARCISSUS. According to one account, he had a beloved twin sister who died. He looked at his own image reflected in a pool to satisfy his longing and desire for his sister. Some say that Narcissus drowned in the pool.

NIOBE. In one story, she was the daughter of Assaon and wife of Philottus. When she boasted about her children, Philottus was torn to pieces during the chase, and Assaon fell in love with Niobe. She rejected him, and he in revenge burned all her children, causing Niobe to throw herself from a rock in grief.

NYCTIMENE was a daughter of Epopeus, king of Lesbos. Pursued and raped by her father, she concealed herself in the shade of forests, where she was metamorphosed by Athena into an owl (Ov. *Met.* 2. 590).

OEDIPUS. When he solved the riddle of the Sphinx, he obtained the kingdom of Thebes and unknowingly married his mother, Jocasta (Iocaste), by whom he became the father of Eteocles, Polyneices, Antigone, and Ismene.

OENEUS was said by some to have been the father of Tydeus by his own daughter Gorge (Apollod. 1. 8.4; Diod. 4. 35).

OENOMAUS, king of Pisa, challenged suitors of his daughter, Hippodameia, to a chariot race, because he himself was in love with her.

PALLAS. According to some traditions, he was the father of Athena, who slew him when he was on the point of raping her (Cic. *De Nat.Deor.* 3. 23).

PELOPIA bore a son, Aegisthus, by her own father, Thyestes, and the son was exposed at birth.

PHLEGYAS was a king of the Lapithae, son of Ares and Chryse. By his own mother he became the father of Coronis, who became by Apollo the mother of Asclepius.

POLYMELA, a daughter of Aeolus, was beloved by Odysseus, but afterwards married her brother, Diores.

SMYRNA (MYRRHA) was the mother of Adonis by her own father, Theias, to whom, as a result of a curse by Aphrodite, she was lustfully attracted. Others call her the daughter of Cinyras.

TELEPHUS was a son of Heracles and Auge. When King Teuthras was about to lose his kingdom to Idas, he solicited the aid of Telephus and promised him his throne and the hand of his daughter, Auge, if he would deliver him from his enemy. Telephus did so, and therefore unwittingly married his own mother.

TUCCIA, a vestal virgin, was accused of incest and appealed to the goddess to prove her innocence. She was given the power to carry a sieve full of water from the Tiber to the temple (Plin. *H.N.* 28. 2; Dionys. 2. 69; August. 10. 16).

VALERIA of Tusculum, according to Roman tradition, became the mother of Aegipan by her own father, Valerius.

Independence, see Liberty

Indigestion

PANDAREUS was an Ephesian upon whom Demeter conferred the benefit of never suffering from indigestion, regardless of how much food he should eat.

Industry

ATHENA. Industry was under her care.

Infant Exposure

AECHMAGORAS, son of Heracles by Phillo, daughter of Alcimedon, was exposed by his grandfather but saved by Heracles.

AEGISTHUS, son of Pelopia by Thyestes, her father, was exposed at birth.

AMPHION. After Antiope gave birth to Amphion and Zethus, her twin sons by Zeus, her uncle, Lycus, exposed them.

ANTILOCHUS, son of Nestor, was exposed on Mt. Ida and suckled by a dog.

ASCLEPIUS. When he was exposed in Thelpusa, he was found and brought up by Autolaus (Paus. 8. 4.2, 25.6). He had been exposed on Mt. Tittheion to conceal the fact of his birth from Coronis' father.

ATALANTA (ATALANTE). Her father wanted a son when she was born, so he exposed her on the Parthenian hill. She was suckled by a she-bear.

CAECULUS was an Italian hero of Praeneste. He was exposed near the temple of Jupiter and was found by maidens who came to fetch water. Since he lay near a fire when found, he came to be considered the son of Vulcan.

CYBELE was exposed at infancy by her father, Maeon, the Phrygian king, but was fed by panthers and brought up by shepherdesses, and afterwards married Atys (Diod. 3. 58).

CYCNUS, son of Poseidon, was exposed on the seacoast where he was found by shepherds, who, seeing a swan descending upon him, called him Cycnus.

DAPHNIS. His mother exposed him in a laurel grove, but he was found and brought up by nymphs and shepherds.

HERACLES. He was exposed in a field near

Thebes by his mother, Alcmene, who feared the wrath of Hera.

HIPPOTHOUS, son of Alope and Poseidon, was exposed twice by his grandfather, Cercyon, but was suckled each time by a mare and managed to achieve manhood and heroic fame.

IAMUS, son of Apollo, was deserted by his mother, Evadne, and was fed with honey by two serpents.

ION was exposed by Creusa, his mother, in the cave under the Propylaea at Athens. Apollo, his father, conveyed the child to Delphi and there had him educated by a priestess.

LINUS was exposed by his mother, Psamathe. He was found by shepherds who brought him up, but the child was later torn to pieces by dogs.

MELITEUS, son of Zeus by an Othreian nymph, was exposed by his mother in a wood, lest Hera should discover the affair. Zeus took care that he was reared by bees, and the boy was saved.

OEDIPUS. Because an oracle had stated that any son born to Laius would cause him to lose his life, he had the child born to Jocasta exposed on Mt. Cithaeron with its feet pierced and bound together. When the boy was discovered by a shepherd, he was called Oedipus because of his swollen feet. Some accounts say he was cast on the sea in a chest and rescued by Polybus.

PARIS. Because it had been foretold that he would bring about the ruin of Troy, Priam, his father, exposed him. The task was entrusted to a shepherd, Agelaus, who left the child on Mt. Ida but returned five days later to find him alive and suckled by a she-bear. He took the child and raised it as his own (Eurip. *Troad.* 921).

PELIAS and his brother, Neleus, were exposed as infants by their mother, and one of them was struck by a mare which passed by, so that his face became black, and a shepherd who found the child called him Pelias; the other child, which was suckled by a she-dog, was called Neleus, and both were brought up by the shepherd.

PERSEUS, son of Zeus and Danae, was cast into the sea with his mother in a chest by Acrisius, Danae's father. They were rescued by Dictys, a fisherman.

ROMULUS. When his mother Silvia, a vestal virgin, gave birth to him and his twin, Remus, her father, Amulius, doomed the guilty vestal and her babies to be drowned by being set adrift. Silvia was changed into a goddess and became the wife of the river god, Anio. The stream carried the cradle with the twins into the Tiber, where it eventually lodged in the root of a wild fig tree. A she-wolf adopted the infants and suckled them.

TELEPHUS, son of Auge, a priestess of Athena, was exposed as an infant on Mt. Parthenion by his grandfather, Aleus, and there he was suckled by a hind.

Infanticide, see Murder (of Children)

Injustice, see Justice

Insanity

AJAX. When he lost the contest over the armor of Achilles to Odysseus, he went mad and slew the sheep of the Greek army.

ALCATHOE (ALCITHOE). When she and her sisters, Leucippe and Arsippe, refused to join the Bacchic revels in Boeotia, Dionysus appeared to them successively as a maiden, a bull, a lion, and a panther. They were seized with madness and became his ardent followers. (See IPHINOE for a similar account.)

ALCMAON became mad as a result of slaying his mother, Eriphyle, and was pursued by the Erinyes.

ANTIOPE was thrown into a state of madness by Dionysus on account of the vengeance her sons, Amphion and Zethus, had taken on Dirce.

ARTEMIS. The Lacedaemonians maintained that the carved image of Artemis, which Iphigeneia and Orestes had carried away from Tauris, existed at Sparta and was worshipped there in the Limnaeon under the name of Artemis Orthia (Paus. 3. 16). The image was said to have been found in a bush and to throw beholders into a state of madness.

ASTRABACUS with his brother, Alopecus, found a statue of Artemis Orthia in a bush and became mad at the sight of it.

ATHAMAS was driven insane by Hera for his actions concerning Nephele and Phrixus and Helle. He killed his son by Ino (Learchus) in a fit of madness. (See also INO)

ATYS. When he broke his vow of chastity, the goddess Cybele threw Atys into a state of madness during which he castrated himself.

AURA. When she became by Dionysus the mother of twins, she was seized at the moment of their birth with madness, tore one of her children to pieces, and then threw herself into the sea (Nonn. 260).

AUXESIA. When the Athenians threw ropes around the statues of Auxesia and Damia and attempted to drag them from Aegina, thunder and lightning ensued, and the Athenians were seized with madness (Herod. 5. 82–86; Paus. 2. 30.5).

BIAS acquired through his brother, Melampus, a third of the kingdom of Argos, since Melampus refused to cure the daughter of Proteus and other Argive women of madness without this condition.

BUTES. For having abducted Coronis, he was struck mad by Dionysus and threw himself into a well (Diod. 5. 50).

CALLIRRHOE of Calydon rejected the love of Coresus, a priest of Dionysus, who prayed to the god to punish the cruel maid. The people of Calydon were visited with a general madness (Paus. 7. 21.1).

CARYA and her two sisters, Orphe and Lyco, daughters of Dion, were seized with madness after they failed to keep a promise to Apollo.

CASSANDRA. Because of her prophecies during the Trojan War, she was thought to be mad by her father, Priam, and was shut up and guarded.

DIONYSUS. When he had grown up, Hera threw him into a state of madness, in which he wandered about through many countries. Later, when the people of Argos refused to acknowledge him as a god, he drove the Argive women mad to such a degree that they killed their own babies and devoured their flesh (Apollod. 3. 5.2). When Tyrrhenian pirates attempted to take him to Asia to sell him, he changed himself into a lion and performed other magical feats which drove the sailors to madness so that they leapt overboard and were changed into dolphins (Apollod. 3. 5.3; Ov. *Met.* 3. 582).

ERICHTHONIUS was a son of Hephaestus by Gaea or Atthis and was a half-serpent, half-man. Athena became his guardian and concealed him in a chest which she put Agraulos, Pandrosos, and Herse to guard. She forbade them to open the chest, but they did, and, observing the child in the form of a serpent (or entwined with serpents), they were thrown into madness and flung themselves from the acropolis or into the sea (Apollod. 3. 14.6; Paus. 1. 2.5, 18.2; Eurip. *Ion* 260; Ov. *Met.* 2. 554).

EURYPYLUS, a Thessalian, was seized by a fit of madness upon opening the chest which contained the image of Dionysus Aesymnetes.

HEPHAESTUS was believed to have great healing powers, and Lemnian earth (*terra Lemnia*) from the spot on which he had fallen from Olympus was believed to cure madness.

HERACLES. While searching with Iphitus for the stolen cattle of Eurytus, he was seized with a fit of madness at Tiryns and threw his friend down from the wall and killed him. According to some traditions, after his return from Hades he was seized with madness, in which he killed his wife, Megara, and his children by her and also two children of Iphitus. This madness was a calamity sent to him by Hera, because he had slain Lycus, king of Thebes, who, in the belief that Heracles would not return from Hades, had attempted to murder Megara and her children. Finally, when he put on the garment poisoned by the blood of Nessus the centaur, he was driven mad by the flaming pain and threw into the sea his companion, Lichas, who had delivered the garment.

INO and her husband, Athamas, were visited with madness by Hera for bringing up Dionysus. In his rage, Athamas killed his son, Learchus, and was on the point of killing Melicertes, but Ino fled from him and threw herself and the boy into the sea.

IPHINOE and her sisters, Lysippe and Iphianassa, daughters of Proteus, were seized with madness because they opposed the worship of Dionysus (Diod. 4. 68; Apollod. 1. 9.12). Some say they were seized with madness because they boasted of equaling Hera in beauty, or because they had stolen the gold from the statue of the goddess. They were cured by Melampus, the soothsayer.

LYCURGUS, son of Dryas and king of the Edones in Thrace, attempted to destroy all the vines of his country while intoxicated. Dionysus then visited him with madness. Others say that he was driven mad by Dionysus because of ill treatment of him and his Bacchantic followers. Lycurgus killed his own son, whom he mistook for a vine, or, according to others, he cut off his own legs in the belief that he was cutting down some vines.

MELAMPUS, the soothsayer, cured the women of Argos of madness on the condition that he and his brother, Bias, receive part of the kingdom of Argos (Paus. 2. 18.4; Diod. 4. 68). Others relate that the daughters of Proteus, king of Argos, were seized with madness. Melampus said he would cure them if the king would give him one-third of the kingdom. This was refused, and the madness seized the other Argive women. Proteus applied to Melampus for help, whereupon Melampus asked two-thirds of the kingdom. This time the terms were complied with (Apollod. 2. 2.2; Strab. 8. 346; Ov. *Met.* 15. 322; Paus. 2. 7.8, 8. 18; Herod. 9. 34).

ODYSSEUS did not want to join the Greeks against Troy (Hom. *Od.* 24. 116). When Palamedes came to persuade him, Odysseus pretended to be mad: he yoked an ass and an ox to a plow and began to sow salt. Palamedes, to try him, placed the infant Telemachus before the plow, whereupon the father could not continue to play his part.

ORESTES. After his murder of his mother, he became mad and took flight from her Erinyes.

SPHINX. Some say that she was one of the women who, together with the daughters of Cadmus, were thrown into madness, and then she was metamorphosed into the monstrous figure which terrorized Thebes.

Inspiration

DIONYSUS THYONEUS was a surname from *thyo,* "to rage, be inspired" (in the sense of Bacchantic frenzy) (Ov. *Met.* 4. 13; Hor. *Carm.* 1. 17.23).

MUSES were the inspiring goddesses of song, poetry, the arts and sciences. They were originally regarded as the nymphs of inspiring wells, near which they were worshipped.

NYMPHS. Many of the nymphs presided over waters or springs which were believed to inspire those who drank from them, and hence the nymphs themselves were thought to be endowed with prophetic or oracular power, to inspire men with the same and to confer upon them the gift of poetry (Paus. 4. 27.2, 9. 3.5, 34.3; Plut. *Aristid.* 11; Theocrit. 7. 92).

Insult

EMPUSA was a monster sent by Hecate to frighten strangers. Whenever a traveler addressed the monster with insulting words, it used to flee and utter a shrill sound (Philostr. *Vit.Apoll.* 2. 4).

Intoxication

BONA DEA. She was said to have intoxicated herself by emptying a large vessel of wine, whereupon Faunus killed her with a myrtle staff, but afterwards raised her to the rank of goddess.

COMUS, the Roman divinity of joy and mirth, was often represented as drunk and languid after a repast.

ELPENOR, companion of Odysseus, fell asleep intoxicated on the roof of Circe's residence, fell off and broke his neck (Hom. *Od.* 10. 550).

ENTORIA. When her father, a Roman nobleman, taught his neighbors to make wine, they became intoxicated and, thinking he had poisoned them, stoned him to death.

ICARIUS. For his hospitality to Dionysus he was taught by the god the cultivation of the vine. He was given bags filled with wine. When he distributed these to his neighbors, some of them became intoxicated, and their friends, thinking he had poisoned them, slew him and threw his body in the well Angyrus, or buried it under a tree.

LYCURGUS, son of Dryas and king of the Edones in Thrace, became intoxicated with wine and attempted to rape his mother. He then sought to destroy all the vines of his country.

NICAEA, a nymph, the daughter of the river god Sangarius and Cybele, was made intoxicated by Dionysus, who impregnated her with Telete, whereupon she hanged herself.

ORION. His marriage to Aero (Merope) being constantly deferred by her father, Oenopion, the handsome young giant one day became intoxicated and forced his way into the chamber of the maiden. For this act he was blinded by Oenopion.

POLYPHEMUS. In order to escape his cave, Odysseus contrived to make the Cyclops drunk with wine and then with a burning pole put out his one eye.

SILENUS (SEILENUS), one of the satyrs, the son of Hermes or Pan and a nymph, was generally represented as intoxicated. He usually rode an ass, since he couldn't trust his own legs. When he was drunk he was in the power of mortals, who might compel him to prophesy and sing by surrounding him with chains of flowers (Philostr. *Imag.* 1. 22; Philostr. *Vit.Apoll.* 6. 27; Ov. *Met.* 11. 91). On an expedition with Dionysus from Thrace to Phrygia, Silenus in a state of intoxication strayed into the rose gardens of Midas, who received him hospitably and delivered him back to his divine pupil, Dionysus, who in appreciation requested Midas to ask a favor. Silenus had a temple at Elis, where Methe (Drunkenness) stood by his side handing him a cup of wine.

Invention

APHRODITE MECHANITIS. At Megalopolis, this surname connoted skill in invention.

ATHENA. Inventions were under her care.

ATHENA MECHANITIS was a surname describing Athena as skilled in inventing, at Megalopolis (Paus. 8. 31.3, 36.3).

DAEDALUS was the famous inventor of the labyrinth. He was also the inventor of the ax, the wedge, the awl, the level, sails of ships, and many other things.

TALOS was the son of Perdix, the sister of Daedalus. He was a disciple of Daedalus and is said to have invented several instruments used in the mechanical arts; but Daedalus, mad with envy, thrust him down the rock of the acropolis at Athens. The Athenians worshipped him as a hero (Apollod. 3. 15.9; Diod. 4. 76; Lucian *Pisc.* 42).

ZEUS MECHANEUS was a surname at Argos describing his skill in inventing (Paus. 2. 22.3).

Invisibility

ELECTRA (See STEROPE)

HADES, god of the underworld, possessed a helmet which rendered the wearer invisible.

PERSEUS acquired the invisible helmet of Hades for the purpose of approaching the Gorgons undetected in order to cut off Medusa's head.

STEROPE, one of the Pleiades, became invisible from shame because she alone among her sisters had had intercourse with a mortal man. Some writers call her Electra and make her disappear from the choir of her sisters on account of her grief at the destruction of the house of Dardanus.

Invulnerability

ACHILLES. His mother made him invulnerable by dipping him at birth into the river Styx. He became invulnerable except for the heel she held him by.

ALCYON, one of the giants, was immortal as long as he fought in his native land. The gods were informed that they would not be able to kill him unless they were assisted by some mortal in their fight. Heracles was able to kill him by dragging him away from his native land.

GIANTS. Gaea, indignant at the fate of her former children, the Titans, gave birth to the giants, monstrous and unconquerable creatures with fearful countenances and the tails of dragons (Ov. *Trist.* 4. 7, 17).

HYDRA, the monstrous serpent of the Lernaean lake, had several heads, one of them invulnerable. Heracles was able to destroy the other heads but had to bury the immortal one under a rock.

JASON was given an ointment by Medea to protect him from the brazen-footed and fire-breathing bulls which Aeetes had set him to yoke for plowing in exchange for the golden fleece.

MESSAPUS, a son of Neptune and king of Etruria, was invulnerable and a famous tamer of horses (Virg. *Aen.* 7. 691).

Iron

CYCNUS. In the Trojan War he could not be slain by iron and so was strangled by Achilles with the thong of his helmet or by being struck with a stone (Diod. 5. 83; Strab. 13. 604; Ov. *Met.* 12. 144).

DACTYLI were fabulous beings to whom the discovery of iron and the art of working it by means of fire were ascribed.

ECHETUS, king of Epirus, blinded his daughter, Metope, for yielding to her lover, Aechmodicus, and then gave his daughter iron barleycorns, promising to restore her sight if she would grind them into flour (Hom. *Od.* 18. 83, 21. 307; Apollon.Rhod. 4. 1093).

Ivory

PELOPS was slaughtered by his father, Tantalus, and served at a repast to the gods. They refused to eat, except for Demeter, who, absorbed in grief for the loss of her daughter, consumed the shoulder of Pelops. When the gods restored him to life, the shoulder consumed by Demeter was lacking; Demeter supplied in its place one made of ivory; his descendants (the Pelopidae), as a mark of their origin, were believed to have one shoulder as white as ivory (Pind. *Ol.* 1. 37; Virg. *Georg.* 3. 7; Ov. *Met.* 6. 404).

Ivy

DIONYSUS. When Tyrrhenian pirates attempted to take him to Asia to sell him, he changed himself into a lion, filled the ship with ivy, and performed various other magical feats which drove them to madness, so that they jumped overboard and were changed into dolphins (Apollod. 3. 5.3; Ov. *Met.* 3. 582). Ivy was sacred to Dionysus.

SATYRS were dressed with the skins of animals and wore wreaths of vine, ivy, or fir.

THALIA, the Muse of comedy and of merry or idyllic poetry, appears with the comic mask, a shepherd's staff, or a wreath of ivy.

Iynx, see Wryneck

Jackdaw

ARNE, who betrayed her country for gold, was metamorphosed into a jackdaw.

Javelin

AGELAUS was one of the suitors of Penelope and was killed by a javelin hurled by her husband Odysseus.

ARTEMIS AEGINAEA was a surname of Artemis at Sparta, meaning either huntress of chamois or wielder of the javelin.

ARTEMIS AETOLE. In Naupactus, a white marble statue showed the goddess hurling a javelin.

MELEAGER, son of Oeneus and one of the most famous Aetolian heroes of Calydon, was distinguished for skill in throwing the javelin.

MERIONES. At the funeral games of Patroclus, he won the second prize in throwing the javelin.

Joy

CHARITES were the goddesses who gave festive joy.

COMUS, a later Roman divinity, was represented as the god of joy.

Judge

ACHILLES, according to some, after his death became a judge in the lower world.

AEACUS, son of Zeus and Aegina, was one of the judges in Hades, especially (according to Plato) for Europeans.

MINOS, son of Zeus and Europa, after his death became one of the judges of Hades (Hom. *Il.* 13. 450, 14. 322; Hom. *Od.* 11. 321, 567, 17. 523, 19. 178).

RHADAMANTHYS (RHADAMANTHUS) was a son of Zeus and Europa. In consequence of his justice throughout his life, he became one of the judges in the lower world after his death and took up his abode in Elysium (Apollod. 3. 1.2, 2. 4.11; Hom. *Od.* 4. 564, 7. 323; Pind. *Ol.* 2. 137).

Justice

ADRASTEIA (NEMESIS) was a daughter of Zeus and Necessity and was responsible for punishing injustice.

ALALCOMENIA (See PRAXIDICAE)

ASTRAEA, a daughter of Zeus and Themis, was the goddess of justice.

ATHENA maintained the authority of justice.

AULIS (See PRAXIDICAE)

HORAE were the personification or goddesses of order in general and of justice. Hesiod describes them as giving a state good laws, justice, and peace (*Theog.* 901).

NEMESIS (See ANDRASTIA)

PERSEPHONE PRAXIDICE. In writings of the Orphic poets, Praxidice is the surname of Persephone, meaning the goddess who carries out the objects of justice.

PRAXIDICAE were the goddesses who carried out the objects of justice or watched that justice was done to men. Near Haliartus in Boeotia they were worshipped (Paus. 9. 33.2) as daughters of Ogyges, and called Alalcomenia, Thelxinoea, and Aulis (Paus. 9. 33.4).

THELXINOEA (See PRAXIDICAE)

ZEUS, particularly as Jupiter, was regarded as protector of justice.

Key

GAEA. Her statue at Athens represented her holding a key.

PORTUNUS (PORTUMNUS), the protecting genius of harbors among the Romans, was represented with a key in his hand, *portus* (or *porta*) signifying a place which can be closed.

Kindness

CHARITES, or the three Graces, presided over kindness.

Kingfisher, see Halcyon

Knee

AUXESIA. When the statues of Auxesia and Damia were being dragged from Aegina by the Athenians, the statues fell upon their knees and remained forever in that attitude (Herod. 5. 82–86; Paus. 2. 30.5).

ODYSSEUS. As a young man, while engaged in the chase during a visit to his grandfather Autolycus near Mt. Parnassus, he was wounded in the knee. By the scar of this wound he was recognized by his nurse Eurycleia upon his return to Ithaca.

Knife

IPHICLUS. In order to cure his sterility, he was advised by Melampus, the soothsayer, to take rust from the knife with which Phylacus, his father, had once cut him, and drink it in water over a period of ten days.

Labyrinth

ARIADNE, daughter of Minos, gave Theseus the twine by means of which he found his way out of the labyrinth at Crete after slaying the Minotaur.

DAEDALUS. When Pasiphae, wife of King Minos of Crete, gave birth to the Minotaur, Daedalus constructed the labyrinth at Cnossus, in which the monster was kept.

MINOS was a powerful king of Crete about thirty-five years before the Trojan War. For him Daedalus, the famous inventor and architect, constructed the labyrinth to house the Minotaur.

MINOTAUR. This monster, with a bull's head and a man's body, was the offspring of Pasiphae, queen of Crete, and a bull. He was shut up in the Cnossian labyrinth, where he was fed on the bodies of the youths and maidens whom the Athenians at fixed times were obliged to send to Minos as tribute (Paus. 1. 24.2, 27, 3. 18.7; Apollod. 3. 1.4, 15.8).

THESEUS. When he volunteered to be one of the sacrifices to the Cretan Minotaur, Ariadne, the daughter of Minos, king of Crete, fell in love with him and provided him with a sword to kill the creature. She also provided him with a length of thread by which he found his way out of the labyrinth which housed the Minotaur.

Ladder

CAPANEUS, one of the Seven against Thebes, was struck by lightning as he was ascending a ladder in the siege of the city (Apollod. 3. 6.7; Ov. *Met.* 9. 404).

PYGMIES. When Heracles came into their country, they climbed with ladders to the edge of his goblet to drink. When they attacked the hero, a whole army of them made an assault on his left hand, while two others made the attack on his right hand (Philostr. *Imag.* 2. 21).

Lake

ARTEMIS LIMNAEA (LIMNETES or LIMNEGENES) was a surname meaning "inhabiting or born in a lake or marsh" or "having a temple near a lake." Artemis was so addressed at Sicyon near Epidaurus (Paus. 2. 7.6, 3. 23.10), on the frontiers between Laconia and Messenia (Paus. 3. 2.6, 7.4; Strab. 8. 362; Tacit. *Ann.* 4. 43), near Calamae (Paus. 4. 31.3), at Tegea (Paus. 8. 53.11) and Patrae (Paus. 7. 20.7).

DIONYSUS. In his wanderings, he was on his way to the oracle of Dodona, but his passage was cut off by a lake. One of two asses he met there carried him across the water, and the grateful god placed both animals among the stars; asses henceforth remained sacred to him.

Minotaur

DIONYSUS LIMNAEA (LIMNETES or LIMNEGENES) was a surname describing the god as inhabiting or born near a lake or marsh or having a temple near a lake. Dionysus was thus addressed at Athens (Thuc. 2. 15; Aristoph. *Ran.* 216; Athen. 10. 437, 11. 465).

NYMPHAE LIMNAEA (LIMNETES or LIMNEGENES) was a surname of nymphs that dwell in lakes or marshes.

Lamb

ATREUS was robbed by Thyestes, his brother, of the lamb with the golden fleece, the gift of Hermes.

HECATE. Sacrifices to her consisted of black female lambs (Plut. *Quaest.Rom.* 49; Apollon.Rhod. 3. 1032).

HELIOS. Sacrifices to the sun god included lambs.

HERACLES. Sacrifices to him included lambs.

HERMES. Lambs were among the sacrifices offered to him.

JUNO. Lambs were sacrificed to Juno at the first of every month.

MEDEA. In order to take vengeance on Pelias for all the crimes he had committed against Jason, she persuaded the daughters of Pelias to cut their father into pieces and boil his limbs in a cauldron, thus supposedly making him young again. She had demonstrated the process earlier by changing a ram into a lamb. But Pelias remained dead.

NYMPHS. Sacrifices to them included lambs.

PAN. Sacrifices to him included lambs.

POSEIDON. According to some legends, he was not swallowed at birth by his father, Cronus, but was concealed by Rhea among a flock of lambs, and his mother pretended to have given birth to a young horse, which she gave to Cronus to devour. A well in the neighborhood of Mantineia, where this is said to have happened, was believed, from this circumstance, to have derived the name of the "Lamb's Well" or Arne (Paus. 8. 8.2).

VENTI. Black lambs were sacrificed to the destructive winds, and white ones to the favorable or good winds (Aristoph. *Ran.* 845; Virg. *Aen.* 3. 117).

Lameness

ANCHISES. Some say that he was lamed when he boasted of intercourse with Aphrodite.

BELLEROPHON. When he was thrown from Pegasus while trying to reach heaven, he was made lame or blind in consequence (Pind. *Isth.* 7. 44; Hor. *Carm.* 4. 11.26).

HEPHAESTUS was thrown from Olympus twice—once by Hera, his mother, for being physically a weakling, and the second time by Zeus for Hephaestus' siding with Hera in an argument. The second fall was said to have caused him to be lame.

HEPHAESTUS AMPHIGYEEIS was a surname meaning lame or limping on both feet; Hephaestus was lamed when Zeus threw him from Olympus (Hom. *Il.* 1. 599; Apollod. 1. 3.5).

MOIRAE, the Fates, were sometimes described by the poets as aged and hideous women, and as lame to indicate the slow march of fate (Catull. 64, 306; Ov. *Met.* 15. 781).

Lamentation

LINUS, the personification of a dirge or lamentation, was a son of Apollo and a Muse or Psamathe (Apollod. 1. 3.2; Paus. 1. 43.7, 2. 19.7). When his mother was killed by her father, Apollo was propitiated by having Argive women sing dirges. According to some legends, Linus was killed by his father, and every year dirges were sung in his honor. Linus is called the inventor of dirges.

MUSES. At the funeral of Patroclus, they sang lamentations (Hom. *Od.* 24. 60; Pind. *Isth.* 8. 126).

NAENIA. At Rome, Naenia was a goddess and the personification of a dirge or lamentation. Her chapel was outside the city near the Porta Viminalis.

Lamp

PSYCHE. Prompted by her jealous sisters to discover the identity of the mysterious lover who visited her nightly, she took a lamp and found him to be the handsomest and youngest of the gods—Amor himself. In her excitement, she spilled a drop of hot oil on the shoulder of the god, who awoke and, censuring her for her mistrust, fled.

Lance

APHRODITE. When represented as the victorious goddess, she had the attributes of Ares—a helmet, a shield, and a sword—or a lance, and an image of Victory.

ATHENA was usually represented in art as carrying a lance.

BENDIS, the Thracian moon goddess, was described as carrying two lances.

CLEMENTIA, the Roman goddess of clemency, was represented holding a lance in her left hand (Claud. *De Consul.Stil.* 2. 6; Stat. *Theb.* 12).

JANUS QUIRINUS. According to Dionysus of Halicarnassus (2. 48), this surname came from a Sabine word and perhaps was derived from *quiris,* a lance or spear.

LAOCOON. When the Greeks left behind the wooden horse and pretended to sail home, Laocoon cautioned the Trojans against the danger of pulling the horse into Troy. While thus warning them, he thrust his lance into the side of the horse (Virg. *Aen.* 2. 40).

MARS. A lance was honored at Rome and at Praeneste as the symbol of Mars (Liv. 24. 10).

MARS QUIRINUS. As JANUS QUIRINUS.

PELEUS. Upon his marriage to Thetis, he was presented a lance by Cheiron, the centaur (Hom. *Il.* 16. 143, 24. 61). However, according to Pindar (*Nem.* 3. 56), Peleus made the lance himself.

PENATES. The public (as distinguished from the private) Penates of the city of Rome had a chapel somewhere about the center of the city. They were represented as two youths with lances in their hands.

ROMULUS QUIRINUS. As JANUS QUIRINUS. It occurs as the name of Romulus after he had been raised to the rank of a divinity, and the festival celebrated in his honor bore the name of Quirinalia (Virg. *Aen.* 1. 292; Cic. *De Nat.Deor.* 2. 24; Ov. *Amor.* 3. 8.51; Ov. *Fast.* 4. 56, 808, 6. 375; Ov. *Met.* 15. 862).

See also: SPEAR

Lark

SCYLLA, daughter of Nisus, having brought about the capture of her father's kingdom because of her love of Minos, the enemy, was changed into a lark when Minos spurned her love.

Laurel

AMYCUS. On his tomb grew a species of laurel (*Laurus insana*) which when taken on shipboard, caused general havoc till thrown overboard (Plin. *H.N.* 16. 89).

APOLLO. The first temple of Apollo at Delphi was said to have been made of branches of the wild laurel from Tempe. (See also DAPHNE)

APOLLO DAPHNAEUS was a surname of Apollo derived from laurel, which was sacred to him.

ARTEMIS. Laurel was sacred to her.

ARTEMIS DAPHNAEA. This surname might have been an allusion to her statue being made of laurel wood (Paus. 3. 24.6).

DAPHNE was pursued by Apollo and was, on her own request, swallowed by the earth. To console Apollo, Gaea created the laurel tree, from the boughs of which Apollo made himself a wreath. According to Ovid (*Met.* 1. 452), Daphne in her flight from Apollo was metamorphosed into a laurel.

DIONYSUS. The laurel was sacred to him.

FIDES, the Roman goddess of fidelity, was represented as a matron with a wreath of laurel leaves.

LIBERTAS, the Roman divinity of freedom, was represented as a matron with a wreath of laurel.

VESTA was the Roman goddess of the hearth. Every year on the first of March, her sacred fire and the laurel tree which shaded her hearth were supposed to be renewed (Ov. *Fast.* 3. 143).

Law

ATHENA maintained the authority of law.

DEMETER was represented as the friend of peace and as a lawgiving goddess (Callim. *Hymn.in Cer.* 138; Virg.*Aen.* 4. 58; Hom.*Il.* 5. 500; Ov. *Met.* 5. 341; Paus. 8. 15.1).

DEMETER THESMIA (THESMOPHOROS) was a surname meaning the lawgiver, in honor of whom the Thesmophoria were celebrated at Athens in the month of Pyanepsion (Herod. 2. 171, 6. 16; Aristoph. *Thes.* 303).

DIONYSUS was regarded as a lawgiver.

HORAE. Hesiod describes the Horae, goddesses of the seasons, as giving to a state good laws, justice, and peace *(Theog.* 901).

JUPITER (See ZEUS)

MINOS, king of Crete, was said to have been instructed in the art of lawgiving by Zeus himself. The Cretans traced their legal and political institutions to him, and the Spartan Lycurgus was believed to have taken the legislation of Minos as his model (Paus. 3. 4.2; Plut. *De Ser.Num.Vind.* 4).

NEMESIS was a personification of the moral reverence for law, of the natural fear of committing a culpable action, and hence of conscience (Hes. *Theog.* 223; Hes. *Op.et D.* 183).

NOMOS, a personification of law, was described as the ruler of gods and men.

PERSEPHONE THESMIA (THESMOPHOROS), "the lawgiver," was a surname of Persephone under which the Thesmophoria were celebrated at Athens in the month of Pyranepsion (Herod. 2. 171, 6. 16; Aristoph. *Thes.* 303).

SAON, a mythical lawgiver of Samothrace, is said to have been a son of Zeus by a nymph. He united the scattered inhabitants of Samothrace into one state, which he regulated by laws (Diod. 5. 48).

THEMIS was a daughter of Uranus and Gaea. In the Homeric poems, she is the personification of the order of things established by law, custom, and equity, whence she is described as reigning in the assemblies of men (*Od.* 2. 68) and as convening, by the command of Zeus, the assembly of the gods (*Il.* 20. 4).

ZEUS was regarded as the founder of kingly power, of law and of order. As Jupiter he was regarded as protector of the law.

See also: JUDGE, JUSTICE

Lead

BELLEROPHON was said to have killed the Chimaera by fixing lead to an arrow and shooting it into the fire-breathing monster's mouth, where it melted and choked the Chimaera.

Leadership

APOLLO AGETOR was a surname of Apollo meaning the leader of men.

ARTEMIS HEGEMONE, leader or ruler, was a surname of Artemis at Sparta and in Arcadia (Paus. 3. 14.6, 8. 36.7, 47.4; Callim. *Hymn.in Dian.* 227).

ATHENA AGELEIA was a surname designating the goddess as leader or protectress of the people.

Leisure

VACUNA was a Sabine divinity whose name the Romans derived from the word *vacuus*. They paid tribute to her when through with harvest and at leisure (Ov. *Fast.* 6. 307; Plin. *H.N.* 3. 17).

Letter

PALAMEDES, son of Nauplius, during the Trojan War was accused of treason by Agamemnon, Diomedes, and Odysseus, who were jealous of his fame. They conspired to plant a forged letter from Priam in his tent, and when it was discovered, they stoned him to death (Ov. *Met.* 13. 56).

PROETUS. Believing that Bellerophon had attempted to seduce his wife, he sent him with a sealed letter to his father-in-law, Iobates, instructing him to kill Bellerophon.

Level

DAEDALUS was said to have been the inventor of the level.

Liberty

FERONIA was an ancient Italian divinity who by some was considered the goddess of liberty, because at Terracina slaves were emancipated in her temple, and because on one occasion the freedmen at Rome collected a sum of money for the purpose of offering it to her as a donation (Liv. 22. 1).

LIBERTAS, a personification of liberty, was worshipped at Rome as a divinity. Her temple was set up on the Aventine but successively destroyed until eventually it was newly built by Asinius Pollio as a repository for the first public library in Rome.

Library

APOLLO PALATINUS was a surname of Apollo at Rome, where Augustus, in commemoration of the battle of Actium, dedicated a temple to the god on the Palatine Hill, in which subsequently a library was established (Hor. *Carm.* 1. 31; Hor. *Epist.* 1. 317; Propert. 4. 6. 11; Ov. *Ars Am.* 3. 389).

LIBERTAS, a personification of liberty, was worshipped at Rome as a divinity. Her temple was set up on the Aventine but successively destroyed until eventually it was newly built by Asinius Pollio as a repository for the first public library in Rome.

Licentiousness

PRIAPUS, son of Dionysus and Aphrodite, was connected in Attic legends with such sensual and licentious beings as Conisalus, Orthanes, and Tychon (Strab. 13. 587; Aristoph. *Lys.* 982; Diod. 4. 6).

Light

APOLLO LYCEGENES. This surname describes the god as either born in Lycia or as the god of light (Hom. *Il.* 4. 101, 119).

APOLLO LYCEIUS. Similar to APOLLO LYCEGENES.

DIANA LUCINA was a surname of Diana as goddess of light, or rather the goddess who brings the light, and hence the goddess that presides over the birth of children (Varr. *De Ling.Lat.* 5. 69; Catull. 34. 13; Hor. *Carm. Saec.* 14; Ov. *Fast.* 2. 441, 6. 39; Tibull. 3. 4.13).

JUNO LUCERIA (LUCETIA), "giver of light," was a surname of Juno used especially among the Oscans.

JUNO LUCINA, goddess of light. As DIANA LUCINA.

JUPITER LUCERIUS (LUCETIUS), "giver of light," was a surname of Jupiter, especially among the Oscans.

THEIA, a daughter of Uranus and Gaea, and one of the Titans, became by Hyperion the mother of Helios, Eos, and Selene, and was thus regarded as the deity from whom all light proceeded (Hes. *Theog.* 135, 371; Pind. *Isth.* 5. 1; Apollod. 1. 1.3, 2.2; Catull. 66.44).

Lighthouse

LEANDER, the famous youth of Abydos, using the light from the lighthouse of Sestus to guide him, swam across the Hellespont every night to meet his love, Hero, the priestess of Aphrodite in Sestus. One stormy night the light was extinguished, causing him to drown. The next morning Hero saw his body, which had been washed up on shore, and threw herself into the sea.

PALAMEDES, son of Nauplius, was described as inventor of lighthouses.

Lightning

AJAX (the Lesser). Athena struck him dead with a bolt of lightning for dragging Cassandra from her temple where she had fled during the sack of Troy.

ALIPHERUS, one of the sons of Lycaon, was killed by Zeus with a flash of lightning for insolence (Apollod. 3. 8.1).

ANCHISES was warned by Aphrodite not to reveal her identity as his lover. He was struck by lightning when he boasted of his intercourse with the goddess. Some say the bolt killed him, others that he was blinded or lamed.

ARISTODEMUS, a descendant of Heracles, was killed by lightning just as he was setting out on an expedition to the Peloponnesus (Apollod. 2. 8.2; Paus. 3. 1.5).

ASCLEPIUS was exposed as an infant and discovered by a shepherd, who saw the boy surrounded by a luster like that of lightning. Zeus killed Asclepius with a flash of lightning because he feared that through Asclepius' ability to restore life, men would eventually cease to die.

ASOPUS, the river god, when he revolted against Zeus for carrying away his daughter, Aegina, was struck by Zeus with a thunderbolt and confined to his original (river) bed.

AUXESIA. When the Athenians tried to drag the statues of Auxesia and Damia from Aegina, thunder and lightning ensued and they were struck with madness (Herod. 5. 82–86; Paus. 2. 30.5).

CAPANEUS, one of the Seven against Thebes, was struck by lightning while scaling the walls during the siege (Apollod. 3. 6.7; Ov. *Met.* 9. 404).

CHARYBDIS was a daughter of Poseidon and Gaea and a voracious woman who stole oxen from Heracles and was hurled by the thunderbolt of Zeus into the sea, where, as a whirlpool, she retained her voracious nature.

CYCLOPES. Because Zeus released them from Tartarus, where they had been thrown by first their father and then their brother, Cronus, they provided him with lightning (Apollod. 1.1; Hes. *Theog.* 503).

ENCELADUS, son of Tartarus and Gaea, was one of the hundred-armed giants who made war upon the gods and was killed by Zeus, according to some, by a flash of lightning (Virg. *Aen.* 3. 578).

ERICHTHONIUS. Zeus killed him, at the request of Poseidon, with a flash of lightning (Apollod. 3. 15.4).

FAUNUS. He and his father, Picus, were compelled by Numa to reveal the secret of calling down lightning from heaven and of purifying things struck by lightning (Plut. *Num.* 15; Ov. *Fast.* 3. 291).

FULGORA was a Roman goddess of lightning.

HERACLES. At Delphi, while trying to find a remedy for an illness, he entered a struggle with Apollo which Zeus had to break up by sending a flash of lightning between them.

IASION. When he became the father of Pluton or Plutus by Demeter, Zeus killed him with a flash of lightning (Hom. *Od.* 5. 125; Hes. *Theog.* 969; Diod. 5. 49, 77).

IDAS. In the battle between Idas and Lynceus and the Dioscuri, when Polydeuces killed Lynceus with a spearthrust, Idas in turn hit Polydeuces so hard with a stone that he fell, whereupon Zeus slew Idas with a bolt of lightning (Apollod. 3. 11.2; Ov. *Fast.* 5. 700).

JUPITER ELICIUS was a surname of Jupiter at Rome having to do with the Etruscan prayers and sacrifices which called forth (*eliciebant*) lightning or invited Jupiter to send lightning.

JUPITER LAPIS, "the stone," was a surname of Jupiter at Rome. The pebble or flint stone was regarded as the symbol of lightning. In some representations of Jupiter he held a stone in his hand instead of a thunderbolt.

LYCAON. According to some legends, he and his sons, when they tried to serve Zeus human flesh, were killed by him by a flash of lightning. Arcas was the son who was killed and whose flesh was served.

MENOETIUS, a son of Iapetus and Clymene, was killed by Zeus with a flash of lightning in the fight of the Titans, and thrown into Tartarus (Hes. *Theog.* 507, 514; Apollod. 1. 2.3).

MIMAS was a giant who is said to have been killed by Ares or by Zeus with a flash of lightning (Apollon. Rhod. 3. 1227; Eurip. *Ion* 215).

MINERVA was sometimes said by the Romans to have wielded the thunderbolts of Jupiter.

NOVENSILES DII were Roman divinities mentioned in a solemn prayer repeated by the pontifex before he devoted himself to death for his country (Liv. 8. 9). It is said that the Novensiles were nine gods, to whom Jupiter gave permission to hurl his lightnings.

ODYSSEUS. He and his men were detained on the island of Helios by storms, and his companions, in spite of an oath not to touch the sacred cattle of Helios, devoured some of the finest. The storm abated and they sailed away, but another storm came on, and their ship was destroyed by Zeus with a flash of lightning. All were drowned except Odysseus.

OENOMAUS was the king of Pisa (in Greece) who vied with the suitors of his daughter, Hippodameia, in a chariot race, which he invariably won. After Pelops finally won the race and the daughter, Oenomaus' house was destroyed by lightning, and only one pillar remained standing (Paus. 5. 14.5, 20.3).

PEGASUS, the winged horse, carried thunder and lightning for Zeus.

PHAETHON, son of Helios, was presumptuous and ambitious enough to persuade his father to allow him to drive the chariot of the sun across heaven. Phaethon, being too weak to check the horses, came down so close to the earth that he almost set it on fire. Zeus, therefore, killed him with a flash of lightning.

PORPHYRION, one of the giants, was killed by the combined efforts of Zeus and Heracles, the one using a flash of lightning and the other his arrows (Pind. *Pyth.* 8. 19).

PROMETHEUS knew that by a certain woman Zeus would beget a son who was to dethrone his father, but Prometheus refused to reveal the decree of fate, whereupon Zeus by a thunderbolt sent Prometheus, together with the rock to which he was chained, into Tartarus (Hor. *Carm.* 2. 18, 35).

SALMONEUS, son of Aeolus and Enarte, presumed to claim equality with Zeus and was destroyed by the god with a thunderbolt and punished in the lower world (Apollod. 1. 9.7; Lucian *Tim.* 2; Virg. *Aen.* 6. 585; Claud. *In Rufin.* 514).

SEMELE. When she was induced by the disguised Hera to ask Zeus to visit her in the same splendor and majesty with which he appeared to Hera, Semele was consumed by the fire of lightning, at the same time giving premature birth to Dionysus (Apollon. Rhod. 4. 1137).

SUMMANUS was an ancient Roman or Etruscan divinity, who was of rank equal to or higher than Jupiter. As Jupiter was the god of heaven in the bright day, so Summanus was the god of the nocturnal heaven, and lightnings plying in the night were regarded as his work (August. 4. 23; Plin. *H.N.* 2. 53).

TITYUS, a son of Gaea, was a giant in Euboea. Instigated by Hera, he made an assault upon Leto or Artemis when she passed through Panopaeus to Pytho, but was killed by the arrows of Artemis or Apollo, or, according to others, Zeus killed him with a flash of lightning (Paus. 3. 18.9; Pind. *Pyth.* 4. 160; Hor. *Carm.* 4. 6.2).

TYPHOEUS was a monster who wanted to acquire the sovereignty of gods and men but was subdued, after a fearful struggle, by Zeus with a thunderbolt (Hes. *Theog.* 821).

VEIOVIS was an Etruscan divinity of a destructive nature, whose fearful lightnings produced deafness in those who were struck by them (Amm. Marc. 17. 10).

ZEUS was armed with thunder and lightning, and the shaking of his aegis produced storm and tempest. He was said to have been provided with lightning by the Cyclopes, whom he delivered from the bonds with which they had been fettered by Cronus. (See also ENCELADUS)

ZEUS CATAEBATES was a surname of Zeus as the god who descends in thunder and lightning. Under this name he had an altar at Olympia (Paus. 5. 14.8; Lycoph. 1370). Places which had been struck by lightning were sacred to him.

Lion

ADMETUS. Pelias promised his daughter, Alcestis, to Admetus if he would come to her in a chariot drawn by lions and boars. He did so with assistance of Apollo.

AJAX. Some accounts say that Heracles made the infant Ajax invulnerable by wrapping him in his lion's skin.

ALCATHOUS conquered the Cithaeronian lion and won, as promised, the kingdom and daughter of Megarius, whose son, Euaechme, had earlier been killed by the beast.

APOLLO was the slayer of the lion of Cithaeron, according to some.

ATALANTA (ATALANTE). When she and her husband, Meilanion (or Hippomenes) consummated their marriage in a grove sacred to Zeus, they were metamorphosed into lions (Apollod. 3. 9.2).

CHIMAERA, the monster, had three heads, one a dragon, one a goat, and one a lion. Some say that the fore part of her body was that of a lion.

CYCNUS imposed on his persistent admirer, Phyllius, three tasks, one of which was to kill a lion without weapons.

CYRENE, the mother of Aristaeus, was found fighting a lion by Apollo, who carried her to Libya, where Cyrene was named for her.

DIOMEDES sometimes wore a lion's skin (Hom. *Il.* 8. 195, 10. 177).

DIONYSUS. When the sisters Alcathoe, Leucippe, and Arsippe refused to attend his revels, he assumed different forms—one of them a lion—and drove them mad. Another time, when Tyrrhenian pirates attempted to take him to Asia to sell him, he changed himself into a lion and performed various other magical feats which drove them to madness, so that they jumped overboard and were changed into dolphins (Apollod. 3. 5.3; Ov. *Met.* 3. 582).

EVIPPUS was the son of Megareus who was killed by the Cithaeronian lion (Paus. 1. 41.4).

GRIFFIN (See GRYPS)

GRYPS (GRYPHUS). The body of the griffin was that of a lion, while the head and wings were those of an eagle.

HECATE was often described as having three heads, one of them that of a lion.

HERACLES killed the lion of Cithaeron, which made havoc among the flocks of Amphitryon. After slaying the lion, he wore its skin as his ordinary garment and its mouth and head as his helmet. His first labor consisted of bringing to Eurystheus the skin of the lion which plagued Nemea. After having in vain used his club and arrows against the monster, he blocked up one of the entrances to the den, and, entering by the other, he strangled the animal with his own hands (Apollod. 2. 5.1).

HYAS, the brother of the Hyades, was killed in Libya by a lion, according to some traditions.

MERMERUS (MACAREUS or MORMORUS), son of Medea and Jason, was, according to some, killed during the chase by a lioness (Paus. 2. 3.7).

OLYNTHUS. When he was killed during the chase by a lion, his brother, Brangas, buried him on the spot where he died and called the town built there Olynthus.

ORION. After his death he was placed among the stars (Hom. *Il.* 18. 486, 22. 29; Hom. *Od.* 5. 274), where he appears as a giant with a girdle, a sword, a lion's skin, and a club.

PHOBUS, son of Ares and Cythereia and the personification of fear, is often represented in works of art with the head of a lion (Paus. 5. 19.1).

POLYNEICES was a fugitive from Thebes to Argos, where Adrastus recognized him by the lion on his shield as part of the fulfillment of an oracle which said that one of his daughters would marry a lion.

RHEA. The lion was sacred to the mother of the gods. In works of art she is shown with lions crouching on the right and left of her throne, and sometimes riding in a chariot drawn by lions.

SPHINX. The common idea of a Greek (as opposed to Egyptian or Ethiopian) Sphinx is the winged body of a lion, having the breast and upper part of a woman (Aelian. *De Nat.Anim.* 12. 7; Apollod. 3. 5.8), or the fore part of the body may be that of a lion and the lower part that of a man with the claws of a vulture and the wings of an eagle.

THISBE, a beautiful maiden in Babylon, was beloved by Pyramus. The lovers were forbidden by their parents to marry. They agreed to meet at night by the tomb of Ninus, and Thisbe, arriving first, observed a lioness killing an ox. She fled, leaving her garment in the blood. When Pyramus arrived, he thought her dead and stabbed himself under a mulberry tree, the fruit of which henceforth was red as blood. Thisbe, who later found the body of her lover, likewise killed herself (Ov. *Met.* 4. 55–165).

Liver

CARNA. The heart, lungs, and liver were entrusted to the protection of this Roman divinity.

PROMETHEUS. For stealing fire from heaven, he was punished by being chained to a pillar, where an eagle daily consumed his liver, which in the succeeding night was restored. Later, Heracles, during his eleventh labor, killed the eagle (some accounts say vulture) and delivered the sufferer.

TITYUS, a son of Gaea, was a giant in Euboea. For assaulting Leto (or Artemis), he was cast into Tartarus, where he lay outstretched on the ground. Two vultures or snakes devoured his liver (Hom. *Od.* 11. 576).

Lizard

ABAS was changed into a lizard when he mocked Demeter for drinking eagerly to quench her thirst at his mother's house. In some traditions he is called Ascabulus.

ASCABULUS (See ABAS)

GALEUS, "the lizard," was a son of Apollo and Themisto. In pursuance of an oracle of the Dodonean Zeus, Galeus emigrated to Sicily, where he built a sanctuary to his father, Apollo. The Galeotae, a family of Sicilian soothsayers, derived their origin from him. (Cic. *De Div.* 1.20).

Locust

APOLLO PARNOPIUS, "the expeller of locusts," was a surname of the god under which he had a statue on the acropolis at Athens (Paus. 1. 24.8).

Longevity

TIRESIAS (TEIRESIAS) was a son of Everes (or Phorbas) and Chariclo and one of the most renowned soothsayers in antiquity. He was blind from an early age but lived to a very old age. Since he had been metamorphosed at one time into a woman, he was once called on to settle a dispute between Zeus and Hera as to whether a man or a woman had more enjoyments. Tiresias agreed with Zeus that women had more enjoyments. Hera, indignant at the answer, blinded him, but Zeus gave him the power of prophecy and granted him a life which was to last for seven or nine generations (Apollod. 3. 6.7; Ov. *Met.* 3. 320; Pind. *Nem.* 1. 91).

Lotus

APHRODITE. The lotus was sacred to her.

APOLLO. The lotus was sacred to him.

DRYOPE was a maiden of Oechalia who was ravaged by Apollo. She was later changed with her son, Amphissus, into a lotus.

LOTIS was a nymph who, in her escape from the embrace of Priapus, was metamorphosed into a tree called lotus. (Ov. *Met.* 9. 347).

LOTOPHAGI were a people of Africa who subsisted upon the lotus. (See also ODYSSEUS)

ODYSSEUS. When his ship was driven onto the coast of Libya, the home of the Lotophagi, some of his companions were so much delighted with the taste of the lotus that they wanted to remain in the country; but Odysseus compelled them to embark again, and they continued the voyage (Hom. *Od.* 9. 67, 84, 94).

VULCAN was the Roman god of fire. Some say his temple was built by Romulus himself, who also planted by it the sacred lotus tree, which still existed in the days of Pliny (*H.N.* 16. 44).

Love

ABDERUS, son of Ares and Aphrodite, was god of mutual love and tenderness.

AMOR was god of love and harmony. (See also CUPIDO)

APHRODITE was the Olympian goddess of love.

CUPIDO, like Amor and Voluptus, was a Roman modification of Eros, whose worship was carried to Rome from Greece.

EROS, the son of Zeus and Aphrodite, was the god of love.

HIMERUS, the personification of longing love, is first mentioned by Hesiod (*Theog.* 201), where he and Eros appear as the companions of Aphrodite.

IYNX, daughter of Pierus (or of Peitho and Pan), was changed into the bird iynx, the symbol of passionate and restless love. The bird was given by Aphrodite to Jason, who, by turning it round and pronouncing certain magic words, excited the love of Medea (Pind. *Pyth.* 4. 380).

PIETAS was a personification of faithful attachment, love, and veneration among the Romans. At first she had a small sanctuary in Rome, but in B.C. 191 a larger one was built (Plin. *H.N.* 7. 36; Liv. 40. 34).

POTHOS, a personification of love or desire, was represented along with Eros and Himerus in the temple of Aphrodite at Megara by the hand of Scopas (Paus. 1. 43.6; Plin. *H.N.* 36. 4, 7).

VENUS was the goddess of love among the Romans, especially sensual love.

Luck

FORTUNA was the goddess of chance or luck among the Romans.

HECATE was a mysterious divinity who bestowed good luck on sailors and hunters.

NEMESIS was a divinity who was a check upon extravagant favors conferred upon man by Tyche or Fortune, and from this idea arose that of her being an avenging and punishing power of fate, who sooner or later overtakes the reckless sinner (Apollon. Rhod. 4. 1043; Soph. *Phil.* 518; Eurip. *Orest.* 1362; Catull. 50).

NORTIA was a name given to the goddess of fortune among the Etrurians.

TYCHE, the personification of chance or luck, the Fortuna of the Romans, is called by Pindar (*Ol.* 12) a daughter of Zeus the Liberator.

TYCHON, a god of chance or accident, was, according to Strabo (13. 588), worshipped at Athens.

ZEUS CLARIUS describes the god as distributor of things by lot (Aeschyl. *Suppl.* 360). A hill near Tegea was sacred to him under this name.

Lung

CARNA. The heart, lungs, and liver were entrusted to the protection of this Roman divinity.

Lust

APHRODITE APOTROPHIA, "the expeller," was a surname of Aphrodite under which she was worshipped at Thebes and which described her as the goddess who expelled desire after sinful pleasure and lust from the hearts of men (Paus. 9. 16.2).

Lustration, see Purification

Lute

LINUS, son of Apollo and a Muse, is said to have received from his father the three-stringed lute.

Lynx

DIONYSUS. The lynx was sacred to him.

LYNCUS (LYNCAEUS), a king of Scythia or, according to others, of Sicily, wanted to murder Triptolemus, who came to him with the gifts of Ceres, in order to secure the merit to himself, but he was metamorphosed by the goddess into a lynx (Ov. *Met.* 5. 650).

Lyre

AMPHION was given a lyre by Hermes and became adept at song and music (Hor. *Epist.* 1. 18.41). By playing his lyre he caused stones to move and fit themselves together to form the walls of Thebes (Apollon. Rhod. 1. 740, 755).

APOLLO. At his birth he was fed with nectar and ambrosia and immediately sprang up and demanded a lyre and a bow. Later tradition says he received the lyre from Hermes, but generally he is credited with the invention of the flute and lyre. Ovid (*Her.* 16. 180) makes Apollo build the walls of Troy by playing on the lyre. When he helped Alcathous rebuild the walls of Megara, he used to lay his lyre on a stone. Even in late times, the stone when struck was supposed to give off lyre-like tones. Once when Pan and Apollo were engaged in a musical contest on the flute and lyre, Midas was chosen to decide between them. He decided in favor of Pan, and Apollo punished him by changing his ears into those of an ass. (See also HERMES)

ARION was a semi-legendary Greek bard and great master of the cithara (lyre). When robbed by sailors, he invoked the gods on his lyre, leapt overboard and was carried by a dolphin to shore (Herod. 1. 24; Gell. 16. 19; Paus. 3. 25.5).

CENTAURS were in later times described as in the train of Dionysus playing the horn or lyre.

ERATO, the Muse of erotic poetry and mimic imitation, appears often with the lyre.

HERACLES was instructed by Linus in singing and playing the lyre. Linus was killed by his pupil with the lyre because he had censured him (Apollod. 2. 4.9). At Rome, Hercules was associated with the Muses and represented with a lyre.

HERMES took a tortoise's shell, drew strings across it, and thus invented the lyre and plectrum. The number of strings of his new invention is said to have been three or seven, and they were made of the guts either of oxen or of sheep (Diod. 1. 16, 5. 75; Hor. *Carm.* 1. 10.6). When Apollo heard the sounds of the lyre, he forgave Hermes the theft of his cattle.

HYPATE (See MUSES [1])

MESE (See MUSES [1])

MUSES (1). Quite early, three Muses were recognized at Delphi—Nete, Mese, and Hypate, their names being identified with the lowest, middle, and highest chord of the lyre (Plut. *Quaest.Conviv.* 9. 14).

MUSES (2) in earliest representations are shown with a lyre, barbiton, or other musical instruments. (See also ORPHEUS)

NETE (See MUSES [1])

ORPHEUS was presented the lyre by Apollo and instructed by the Muses in its use. He enchanted with its music not only the wild beasts but the trees and rocks upon Olympus, so that they moved from their places to follow the sound of his golden harp. The power of his music caused the Argonauts to seek his aid, which contributed materially to the success of their expedition in the following ways: at the sound of his lyre, the Argo glided down into the sea; the Argonauts tore themselves away from the pleasures of Lemnos; the Symplegadae, or moving rocks, which threatened to crush the ship between them, were fixed in their places; and the Colchian dragon, which guarded the golden fleece, was lulled to sleep. He followed his lost wife to the abode of Hades, where the charms of his lyre suspended the torments of the damned and won back his wife. The astronomers taught that the lyre of Orpheus was placed by Zeus among the stars, at the intercession of Apollo and the Muses.

TERAMBUS, a son of Euseirus and Eidothea, was a distinguished musician and played both the syrinx and the lyre.

TERPSICHORE, the Muse of choral dance and song, appears with the lyre and plectrum.

THAMYRIS, an ancient Thracian bard, was the son of Philammon and the nymph, Argiope. He went so far in his conceit as to think he could surpass the Muses in song, in consequence of which he was deprived of his sight and of the power of singing (Hom. *Il.* 2. 595; Apollod. 1. 3.3; Paus. 4. 33.4, 10. 7.2; Eurip. *Rhes.* 925). He was represented with a broken lyre in his hand (Paus. 9. 30.2).

Magic

HECATE was the goddess of magic, witches, and enchantments.

Magnet

CELMUS, one of Zeus' nurses, was changed into a magnet stone for saying that Zeus was mortal.

MAGNES was the discoverer of the magnet. According to others, he was a slave of Medea, who changed him into a magnet.

Magpie

ARES. The magpie was sacred to him.

DIONYSUS. The magpie was sacred to him, because at his triumphs people were permitted to speak with a free tongue.

PIERIDES, daughters of Pierus, were changed, according to some, into magpies, when their father dared to compare them with the nine Muses.

Malevolence

MERCURIUS MALEVOLUS, "the ill-willed," was a surname under which Mercury had a statue in what was called the *vicus sobrius* (or the sober street, in which no shops were allowed to be kept), and milk was offered to him instead of wine. This statue had a purse in its hand to indicate his function (commerce). His festival was celebrated on the 25th of May.

Manufacturing

HEPHAESTUS. He gave skill to mortal artists and was believed to have taught men the arts which embellish and adorn life (Hom. *Od.* 6. 233, 23. 160; Hom. *Hymn.in Vulc.* 2).

Manure

PICUMNUS, a rustic divinity of the ancient Romans, was believed, under the name of Sterquilinius, to have discovered the use of manure for the fields.

STERQUILINIUS (See PICUMNUS)

Mare

CAMILLA, daughter of Metabus, was suckled by a mare.

DEMETER ERINYS was a surname applied to Demeter after she had changed herself into a mare to escape the embraces of Poseidon. He had turned himself into a horse and mated with her, producing the horse Arion (Paus. 8. 25.4). The surname refers to her Fury-like wrath toward Poseidon.

DIOMEDES, son of Ares, was killed by Heracles because he fed his mares on human flesh (Apollod. 2. 5.8). (See also HERACLES)

ECHEPOLUS was a Sicyonian, who made Agamemnon the present of a mare, Aethe, in order not to be obliged to accompany him to Troy (Hom. *Il.* 23. 293).

EPONA, a Roman divinity, was said to be the daughter of Fulvius Stellus by a mare (Juv. 8. 157; Plut. *Paral.Gr.et Rom.* 312).

ERICHTHONIUS, son of Dardanus, was declared to be the wealthiest of mortals, for three thousand mares grazed in his fields. The mares were so beautiful that Boreas, the god of the north wind, fell in love with them.

EVIPPE (See MELANIPPE)

GLAUCUS, son of Sisyphus, did not allow his mares to breed so that they would be stronger for the horse race. He was also reported to feed them with human flesh in order to make them spirited and warlike. He took part in the funeral games of Pelias with a chariot (Paus. 3. 18.9, 5. 17.4; Apollod. 1. 9.28; Nonn. 11. 143). According to others, they tore Glaucus to pieces after being seized with madness from drinking from a sacred well in Boeotia. Others describe their madness as a consequence of eating an herb called hippomanes (Paus. 9. 8.1).

HERACLES. The eighth labor of Heracles consisted of fetching the flesh-eating mares of Diomedes of Thrace back to Mycenae. After he had seized the mares, he was overtaken by the Bistones, the subjects of Diomedes, and in the ensuing fight he entrusted the mares to Abderus, his friend, who was devoured by them. Heracles killed Diomedes and threw his body to the mares, who, after eating him, became tame. They were later set free and destroyed on Mt. Olympus by wild beasts (Apollod. 2. 5.8; Diod. 4. 15; Eurip. *Alcest.* 483, 493).

MELANIPPE, daughter of Cheiron, is also called Evippe. When she became pregnant by Aeolus, she fled to Mt. Pelion, and, when her father made a search for her, she prayed to be metamorphosed into a mare. Artemis granted the prayer, and, in the form of a mare, Melanippe was placed among the stars (Aristoph. *Thes.* 512).

PELIAS and his brother, Neleus, were exposed as infants by their mother, and Pelias was kicked in the face by a mare which passed by, so that his face was bruised. A shepherd who found the children called the injured one Pelias.

Mariner, see Sailor

Marjoram

AMARACUS, an officer of Cinyras, was changed into the herb called marjoram.

Marksmanship

APHRODITE HECAERGE, "hitting at a distance," was a surname of Aphrodite at Iulis in Cos.

APOLLO HECAERGES, "hitting at a distance," was a surname of Apollo, referring to his marksmanship (Hom. *Il.* 1. 147).

ARTEMIS HECAERGE. As APOLLO HECAERGES.

Marriage

AETHRA, mother of Theseus, introduced among the maidens of Troezen the custom of dedicating their girdles to Athena Apaturia on the day of their marriage.

APHRODITE. Marriages were called by Zeus the work of Aphrodite, and the matter to which she should devote her attention (Hom. *Il.* 5. 429). (See also GAMELII)

CECROPS was author of the first elements of civilized life, such as marriage, the political division of Attica, and abolition of human sacrifices by substitution of cakes.

DEMETER. As goddess of fertility, she was also looked upon as the goddess of marriage. Her priestesses initiated young married people into the duties of their new situation.

EUCLEIA, daughter of Heracles and Myrto, died as a maiden and was worshipped in Boeotia and Locris, where she had an altar and a statue in every marketplace, on which persons on the point of marrying used to offer sacrifices to her.

GAEA was classed with the divinities presiding over marriage.

GAMELII were the divinities protecting and presiding over marriage. Plutarch (*Quaest. Rom.* 2) says that those who married required (the protection of) five divinities: Zeus, Hera, Aphrodite, Peitho, and Artemis.

HERA was the Olympian goddess of marriage. (See also GAMELII)

HERA ZYGIA was a name describing her as presiding over marriage.

HYMEN (HYMENAEUS) was the god of marriage. He rescued some Attic maidens from pirates and was afterward praised by them in their bridal songs, which were called, after him, hymeneal songs.

JUNO CINXIA was a surname of Juno as the goddess of marriage, alluding to her symbolic untying of the girdle of newly married women.

JUNO DOMIDUCA was a surname of Juno at Rome as the goddess of marriage who conducted the bride into the house of the bridegroom (August. 7. 3, 9. 6).

JUNO FEBRUATA (FEBRUTIS) was a surname of Juno as goddess of marriage (cf. Februus, the Italian divinity).

JUNO FLUONIA was a name under which Juno was invoked by newly-married people.

JUNO INTERDUCA. As JUNO DOMIDUCA.

JUNO JUGA was a surname of Juno as goddess of marriage, under which name she had a temple in the forum at Rome.

JUNO JUGALIS. As JUNO JUGA.

JUNO LUCINA. As JUNO FLUONIA.

JUNO PERTUNDA. As JUNO FLUONIA.

JUNO PREMA. As JUNO FLUONIA.

JUNO PRONUBA. She was so named in Rome because she presided over marriage (Virg. *Aen.* 4. 166, 7. 319; Ov. *Her.* 6. 43).

JUNO VIRIPLACA, "the goddess who soothes the anger of man," was a surname describing Juno as the restorer of peace between married people.

JUPITER DOMIDUCUS was a surname of Jupiter at Rome as the god of marriage who conducted the bride into the house of the bridegroom.

LARES. When a young bride entered the house of her husband, her first duty was to offer a sacrifice to the Lares, Roman deities presiding over households.

PICUMNUS and his brother, Pilumnus, were

regarded as the beneficent gods of matrimony in the rustic religion of the ancient Romans.

PUDICITIA, a personification of modesty, was worshipped both in Greece and at Rome. In Rome, no woman who had married twice was allowed to touch her statue.

VENUS CALVA. This surname, in use at Rome, has been traced to the real or symbolical cutting off of the hair of brides on their wedding day.

VENUS CLOACINA was a surname which designated her as presiding over and purifying sexual intercourse in marriage.

ZEUS ZYGIUS was a surname of Zeus as presiding over marriage.

Mask

MELPOMENE, the Muse of tragedy, appears with a tragic mask.

THALIA, the Muse of comedy and of merry or idyllic poetry, appears with the comic mask, a shepherd's staff, or a wreath of ivy.

Mast

DAEDALUS. The invention of the ship's mast was ascribed to him.

ODYSSEUS was able to escape the fatal attraction of the voices of the Sirens by filling the ears of his companions with wax and lashing himself to the mast of his ship (Hom. *Od.* 12. 39, 166). When his last ship was destroyed by Zeus, he escaped drowning by means of the mast and planks, on which he floated to safety.

Mathematics

PROMETHEUS brought the knowledge of mathematics to men.

Matricide, see Murder (of Mother)

May

MAIA was a Roman divinity to whom sacrifices were offered on the first of May.

Meal

TERMINUS was a Roman divinity presiding over boundaries and frontiers. Sacrifices of cakes, meal, and fruit were offered at the stone boundary markers each year, since it was unlawful to stain the boundary stones with blood.

Measures

HERMES was said to have invented measures.

PALAMEDES, son of Nauplius, was described as inventor of measures.

Medicine

AGAMEDE, daughter of Augeias, was acquainted with the healing powers of all plants that grew upon the earth.

APOLLO ACESTOR was a surname of Apollo as god of the healing art.

ARABUS was a son of Apollo and Babylone, who first invented medicine and taught it in Arabia.

ARTEMIS PAEONIA, "the healing goddess," was a surname of Artemis under which she had a statue at Athens and an altar in the temple of Amphiaraus at Oropus (Paus. 1. 2.4, 34.2).

ASCLEPIUS, son of Apollo, was god of the medical art.

CHEIRON the centaur was renowned for his skill in medicine.

EURYBATES was a son of Teleon and one of the Argonauts. He was skilled in the medical art and dressed the wound which Oileus received from one of the Stymphalian birds (Apollon. Rhod. 1. 73, 2. 1040; Val. Flacc. 1. 402).

MACHAON, son of Asclepius, was physician to the Greeks during the Trojan War.

MEDITRINA was the goddess of medicine at Rome.

MELAMPUS, son of Amythaon, was looked upon by the ancients as the person who first practiced the medical art.

PODALEIRIUS was a son of Asclepius and brother of Machaon. Like them, he was skilled in the medical art (Hom. *Il.* 11. 832).

POLEMOCRATES, son of Machaon, like his father was a skillful physician (Paus. 2. 38.6).

PROMETHEUS brought the knowledge of medicine to men.

TELESPHORUS, "the completing," was the name of a medical divinity who is mentioned now and then in connection with Asclepius.

See also: HEALING

Meditation

MELETE was one of the originally recognized three Muses, who were worshipped on Mt. Helicon. She presided over meditation.

Melody

LINUS, son of Apollo, was called the inventor of new melodies.

Memory

AETHALIDES received from his father, Hermes, the faculty for remembering everything, even in Hades.

MNEME, "memory," was one of the three Muses who were in early times worshipped at Ascra in Boeotia (Paus. 9. 29.2). There was also a tradition that she was the mother of the Muses, for her name could be an abridged form of Mnemosyne.

MNEMOSYNE, "memory," a daughter of Uranus and one of the Titanides, became by Zeus the mother of the Muses (Hom. *Hymn.in Merc.* 429; Hes. *Theog.* 54, 915; Diod. 5. 67; Cic. *De Nat.Deor.* 3. 21).

Mental Health

HYGIEIA was sometimes conceived as the giver or protectress of mental health (Aeschyl. *Eum.* 522).

Mercy

ELEOS, the personification of pity or mercy, had an altar in the agora at Athens (Paus. 1. 17.1)

Mermaid

NEREIDES were nymphs of the Mediterranean and were often identified with mermaids, half-fish and half-maiden.

Messenger

ARNAEUS (See IRUS)

FAMA (See OSSA)

HERMES was herald and messenger to Zeus.

IRIS, daughter of Thaumas and Electra and minister of the Olympian gods, carried messages from Ida to Olympus, from gods to gods and from gods to men (Hom. *Il.* 15. 144, 24. 78, 95; Hom. *Hymn.in Apoll.* 102).

IRUS. His proper name was Arnaeus, but he was called Irus because he was employed by the suitors of Penelope as the messenger and Irus, according to ancient lexicographers, signifies a messenger (Hom. *Od.* 18. 5, 239).

ORESTES pretended to be a messenger of Strophius to Argos to announce his own death, and he brought the ashes of the deceased (Soph. *Elect.* 1110).

Hermes

OSSA was the personification of rumor or report, the equivalent of the Latin Fama. As it is often impossible to trace a rumor or report to its source, it is said to come from Zeus, and hence Ossa is called the messenger of Zeus (Hom. *Od.* 1. 282, 2. 216, 24. 412; Hom. *Il.* 2. 93).

Metal

HADES was regarded as the possessor and giver of all metals contained in the earth (Hes. *Op.et D.* 435; Aeschyl. *Prom.* 805; Strab. 3. 147; Lucian *Tim.* 21).

ITONUS was the inventor of a method for polishing metal.

PROMETHEUS brought the knowledge of metallurgy to men.

Metamorphosis

AUTOLYCUS, the famous robber, had the power of metamorphosing not only stolen goods but also himself (Hom. *Il.* 10. 267; Apollod. 2. 6.2).

DIONYSUS ZAGREUS was the surname of the mystic Dionysus. He was torn to pieces by the Titans, though he defended himself bravely and assumed various forms. Athena carried his heart to Zeus.

HYPERMESTRA (See MESTRA)

MESTRA. In order to escape the slavery into which she had been sold by her father, she prayed to Poseidon, who loved her, and he conferred on her the power of metamorphosing herself whenever she was sold, and of thus each time returning to her father (Ov. *Met.* 8. 847). She was also called Hypermestra.

NEREUS, son of Pontus and Gaea, was believed to have the power of appearing to mortals in different forms.

PERICLYMENUS, son of Neleus and Chloris, was one of the Argonauts. Poseidon gave him the power of changing himself into different forms and conferred on him great strength (Apollod. 1. 9.9, 2. 7.3; Apollon.Rhod. 1. 156; Ov. *Met.* 13. 556), but he was nevertheless slain by Heracles at the taking of Pylos.

PROTEUS was the prophetic old man of the sea. Anyone wishing to compel him to foretell the future was obliged to catch hold of him at the time he kept his usual form, for he had the power of assuming every possible shape in order to escape the necessity of prophesying. Whenever he saw that his endeavors were in vain, he resumed his usual appearance and told the truth (Hom. *Od.* 4. 410, 455; Ov. *Ars Am.* 1. 761; Ov. *Fast.* 1.369; Philostr. *Vit.Apoll.* 1. 4).

TELCHINES, a group of mysterious beings described as sorcerers and envious daemons, had the power to bring hail, rain, and snow, and to assume any form they pleased (Diod. 5. 55).

THETIS, like certain other marine deities, had the power of assuming different shapes to elude captors. Peleus, her suitor, instructed by his friend, Cheiron the centaur, would not release her until she again assumed her proper form (Apollod. 3. 13.5; Pind. *Nem.* 3. 60; Paus. 8. 18.1).

VERTUMNUS was an Etruscan deity whose worship was introduced at Rome by an ancient Vulsinian colony, occupying at first the Caelian Hill and afterwards the vicus Tuscus (Propert. 4. 2.6; Ov. *Met.* 14. 642). The name evidently signifies "the god who changes or metamorphoses himself." When he was in love with Pomona, he assumed all possible forms, at last gaining his end by metamorphosing into a youth (Propert. 4. 2.21; Ov. *Met.* 14. 642).

Metempsychosis

AETHALIDES, son of Hermes and herald of the Argonauts, was possessed of total recall in memory. Even after death, his soul remembered that it had successively migrated into the bodies of Euphorbus, Hermotius, Pyrrhus, and at last into that of Pythagoras, in whom it still retained the recollection of its former migrations (Apollon.Rhod. 1. 54, 640; Val.Flacc. 1. 437).

Midwifery

EILEITHYIA, the goddess of birth, came to the assistance of women in labor.

Military Campaigns

HERMES AGETOR. Under this name he was invoked by Athenian generals setting out on expeditions.

HERMES HEGEMONIUS. As HERMES AGETOR.

Milk

BONA DEA. At her festivals, wine was present and the women drank of it, but they avoided calling it wine and called it milk instead.

CUBA, Cunina, and Rumina were three Roman genii who were worshipped as the protectors of infants in their cradles and to whom libations of milk were offered.

HARPALYCE, daughter of Harpalycus of Thrace, was brought up by her father on the milk of cows and mares and was trained in all manly exercises.

HERA. Hermes carried the infant Heracles to Olympus and put him on the breast of the sleeping Hera, but as she awoke she pushed him away, and the milk thus spilled produced the Milky Way.

MERCURIUS MALEVOLUS, "the ill-willed," was a surname under which Mercury had a statue in what was called the *vicus sobrius* (or the sober street, in which no shops were allowed to be kept), and milk was offered to him instead of wine.

MUSES. Sacrifices to them consisted of milk.

NYMPHS. Sacrifices to them consisted of milk.

PAN. Sacrifices to him consisted of milk.

PRIAPUS was a son of Dionysus and Aphrodite and god of the fructifying powers and manifestations of nature. Sacrifices to him included milk.

ZEUS. On Crete he was reared by the Curetes and the nymphs, Adrasteia and Ida, the daughters of Melisseus. They fed him the milk of the goat Amalthea, and the bees of the mountain provided him with honey (Apollod. 1. 1.6).

Mill

EUNOSTUS was a goddess of mills. Her image was set up in mills and she was believed to keep watch over the just weight of flour.

MOLAE were Roman divinities, whose name indicates that they were in some way connected with the pounding or grinding of grain.

MYLES, son of Lelex and king of Lacedaemon, was regarded as the inventor of mills (Paus. 3. 1.1, 20.2, 4. 1.2).

Mind

MENS, a personification of mind, was worshipped by the Romans. A festival in honor of Mens was celebrated on the 8th of June.

Minstrel, see Bard

Mint

MINTHA (MINTHO or MENTHA), a Cocythian nymph beloved by Hades, was metamorphosed by Demeter or Persephone into a plant called after her *minthe* or, according to others, was changed into dust, from which Hades caused the mint plant to grow (Strab. 8. 344; Ov. *Met.* 10. 728).

Mirror

PERSEUS. For his mission to fetch Medusa's head, Athena provided him with a mirror so that he would not have to regard the monster directly and thus be turned to stone (Hes. *Scut.Herc.* 220, 222).

Mirth

COMUS was a later Roman divinity who was represented as the god of mirth.

Misandry

BONA DEA. Her worship was confined exclusively to women, and men were not even allowed to know her name.

DIANA, the Roman goddess, so hated the sight of male beings that no man was allowed to enter her temple, and she herself remained a virgin (Hor. *Epist.* 2. 1.454).

Misery

ACHLYS was the personification of misery and sadness.

Misfortune

ERIS, goddess of war, was the mother of a variety of allegorical beings, who were the causes or representatives of man's misfortunes (Hes. *Theog.* 225).

Misogyny

EUNOSTUS was falsely accused of attempted seduction by Ochne and thereby slain. He had a sanctuary at Tanagra in a sacred grove, which no woman was allowed to approach (Plut. *Quaest.Gr.* 40).

MARS. Females were excluded from his worship. He presided more particularly over those occupations of country life which belonged to the male sex (Cato 83).

Mockery

MOMUS, son of Nyx, was a personification of mockery and censure (Hes. *Theog.* 214).

Modesty

PENELOPE. When her father, Icarius, entreated her not to follow Odysseus to whom she was betrothed, Odysseus demanded that she give a decided answer as to what she meant to do. She modestly covered her face and declared that she would follow her husband. Icarius then desisted from further entreaties and erected a statue of Modesty on the spot (Paus. 3. 20.10).

PUDICITIA, a personification of modesty, was worshipped both in Greece and at Rome.

Money

JUNO MONETA was a surname of Juno in Rome as the guardian of the mint. In the war with Pyrrhus and the Tarentines, the Romans, needing money, prayed to Juno and were told by the goddess that money would not be lacking so long as they fought with arms of justice. As the Romans by experience found the truth of these words, they called her Juno Moneta. Her festival was celebrated on the first of June (Ov. *Fast.* 6. 183).

JUPITER PECUNIA was a surname of Jupiter at Rome by which he was characterized as the protector of money.

Monkey

CERCOPES were the droll and thievish gnomes who were located by some writers on the islands called Pithecusae, which derived their name from the Cercopes, who were changed into monkeys by Zeus for having cunningly deceived him (Ov. *Met.* 14. 90).

EPIMETHEUS was eventually changed by the gods into a monkey and sent to the island of Pithecusa.

Months

LUNUS (See MEN)

MEN was a Phrygian god who presided over the months (Strab. 12. 557, 577). The Latin translation was Lunus.

MENE was a female divinity presiding over the months (Apollon. Rhod. 3. 533, 4. 55; August. 7. 2).

Moon

ARTEMIS was the Olympian goddess of the moon.

ARTEMIS MELISSA was a surname of Artemis as goddess of the moon, in which capacity she alleviates the suffering of women in childbed.

ARTEMIS ORTHIA was a surname of Artemis as goddess of the moon. It was at the altar of Artemis Orthia that Spartan boys had to undergo the rite of flagellation (Herod. 4. 87). She had temples also at Brauron, in the Cerameicus at Athens, in Elis, and on the coast of Byzantium.

ARTEMIS PHOEBE. This surname was used in her capacity as the goddess of the moon, the moon being regarded as the female Phoebus or sun (Virg. *Georg.* 1. 431; Virg. *Aen.* 10. 215; Ov. *Her.* 20. 229).

BENDIS was a Thracian divinity in whose name the moon was worshipped.

BRITOMARTIS, identified with the moon, was pictured on Roman coins with a crescent.

ENDYMION was a beautiful shepherd who slept on Mt. Latmus, where he was visited nightly by Selene, goddess of the moon.

HECATE. As a goddess of the moon, she is regarded as the mystic Persephone (Hom. *Hymn. in Cer.* 25; Paus. 1. 43.1).

HERA. Some ancients regarded her as the goddess of the moon (Plut. *Quaest. Rom.* 74).

IO. The ancients believed Io to be the moon, and there is a tradition that the Argives called the moon Io. Various things related to her refer to the phases and phenomena of the moon.

JANA, an ancient Latin divinity, was worshipped at first as the moon (Cic. *De Nat. Deor.* 2. 27).

LUNA was the Roman goddess of the moon, but her worship never occupied any prominent place in their religion.

MENE (See SELENE)

PERSEPHONE (See HECATE)

SELENE, also called Mene, or Latin Luna, was the goddess of the moon, or the moon personified into a divine being. She was called a daughter of Hyperion and Theia, and accordingly a sister of Helios and Eos (Hes. *Theog.* 371; Apollod. 1. 2.2).

Morning

JANUS MATUTINUS was so called because he presided over the beginning of every day.

Moss

VENUS MURTIA was a surname denoting cowardice. The goddess worshipped under this name had a temple at the foot of the Aventine hill, and as she patronized indolence, laziness, and cowardice, her statues were generally covered with moss to represent inactivity (August. 4).

Mountain

ARTEMIS CORYPHAEA was a surname of Artemis as the goddess who inhabits the summit of mountains. Under this name she had a temple on Mt. Coryphaeon near Epidaurus (Paus. 2. 28.2).

ATLAS. For refusing shelter to Perseus, he was metamorphosed into a mountain by being shown the head of Medusa (Ov. *Met.* 4. 630). Some say he was thus changed by Zeus for aiding the giants in their war against the gods.

HAEMUS was a son of Boreas and husband of Rhodope. He and his wife presumed to assume the names of Zeus and Hera and were metamorphosed into mountains (Ov. *Met.* 6. 87).

NYMPHS. The Oreiades were nymphs associated with mountains and grottoes.

ZEUS. The summits of mountains were sacred to him.

Mourning

LUCTUS, a personification of grief or mourning, was a son of Aether and Terra.

Mouse

APOLLO SMINTHEUS. This surname is derived by some from *sminthos,* a mouse. The mouse was regarded by the ancients as inspired by the vapors arising from the earth and as the symbol of prophetic power. In the temple of Apollo at Chryse, there was a statue of the god by Scopas, with a mouse under its foot (Strab. 13. 604), and on coins Apollo is represented carrying a mouse in his hands.

GLAUCUS, young son of Minos and Pasiphae, while chasing a mouse (Apollod. 3. 3.1) fell into a cask of honey and died.

Mouth

ANGERONA (ANGERONIA) was the Roman goddess of anguish, who was represented with her mouth bound and sealed up.

SCYLLA was a monster who dwelt on a rock on the Italian coast opposite Sicily. She barked like a dog, had twelve feet, six long necks and mouths, each of which contained three rows of sharp teeth.

Mud

ARTEMIS. When pursued by Alpheius, the river god, she fled to Letrini and covered her face and the faces of her nymph companions with mud, so that Alpheius could not distinguish her (Paus. 6. 22.5).

Mulberry

POLYIDUS of Argos was summoned along with other soothsayers by Minos, king of Crete, to locate his missing son, Glaucus. Minos had been advised that someone who could devise an appropriate comparison between a cow which could assume three different colors and any other object would lead him to the missing boy. Polyidus likened the cow to a mulberry, which is at first white, then red, and finally black. He then, by his prophetic powers and by guidance from an owl, and bees, found the child, who had been drowned in a vat of honey (Aelian. *De Nat.Anim.* 5. 2).

PYRAMUS was the lover of Thisbe, a beautiful Babylonian maiden. The lovers were forbidden by their parents to marry. They agreed to meet at night at the tomb of Ninus, and Thisbe, arriving first, observed a lioness killing an ox. She fled, leaving her garment in the blood. When Pyramus arrived, he thought her dead and stabbed himself under a mulberry tree, the fruit of which henceforth was as red as blood. Thisbe, who later found the body of her lover, likewise killed herself (Ov. *Met.* 4. 55–165).

Mule

ECHETIMUS of Sicyon brought the image of Asclepius in the form of a dragon from Epidaurus to Sicyon on a car drawn by mules (Paus. 2. 10.3).

SELENE, the moon goddess, rode across the heavens in a chariot drawn by two white mules (or horses or cows). She was represented on the pedestal of the throne of Zeus at Olympia riding on a horse or mule (Paus. 5. 11.3).

Murder

EUMENIDES were the avenging deities who punished murder.

ROMULUS. In the newly founded city of Rome, he found his people too few in numbers, so he set apart, on the Capitoline Hill, an asylum, or a sanctuary in which homicides and runaway slaves might take refuge and thereby populate the city.

TISIPHONE, one of the Erinys, was the avenger of murder.

Murder (of Brother)

ATREUS and Thyestes, sons of Pelops, were prevailed upon by Hippodameia, their mother, to kill their younger brother, Chrysippus. They accomplished their crime and threw the body of their murdered brother into a well.

BELLEROPHON slew his own brother, Deliades (Peiren or Alcimenes) (Apollod. 2. 3.1).

LEIMON, thinking that Apollo plotted with his brother, Scephrus, murdered his brother and was punished by Artemis with sudden death.

MEDEA. When she and Jason fled with the Argonauts from Cochis, the fleet of her father, Aeetes, was about to overtake them. She dismembered her brother, Absyrtus, and strewed his limbs on the water, so that Aeetes was detained while he gathered the pieces and buried them.

PYGMALION, brother of Sychaeus (Sichaeus), who was a wealthy Phoenician and husband of Dido, was anxious to secure the treasures of Sychaeus and treacherously murdered him (Virg. *Aen.* 1. 347, 4. 20, 502, 532, 632, 6. 474).

ROMULUS. When he was raising the walls of Rome, his twin brother Remus, resenting having been defeated in the choice of the city's site, leaped over the wall in scorn, whereupon Romulus slew him.

TEREUS. Warned by an oracle that his son, Itys, would be killed by a relative, he suspected his own brother Dryas after the murder took place, and killed him (Apollod. 1. 8.2).

TYDEUS, son of Oeneus and Periboea, was said by some to have killed his brother, Olenias.

Murder (of Children)

HERACLES. After the battle with the Minyans (or, according to some traditions, after his return from Hades), Hera inflicted Heracles with madness, in which he killed his own children by Megara and two of the children of Iphicles.

MEDEA murdered her sons, Mermerus (or Macareus or Mormorus) and Pheres at Corinth (Apollod. 1. 9.28; Diod. 4. 54) and then fled in a chariot drawn by winged dragons.

THEMISTO in attempting to kill Ino's children killed her own. Ino, disguised as a slave, had covered Themisto's children with black bedclothes instead of white, as directed, and Themisto, thinking her children were Ino's, killed them. When she discovered the mistake, she killed herself.

Murder (of Father)

ALTHEMENES. When Catreus, king of Crete, sailed to Crete in a desire to see his son, who an oracle had predicted would slay him, the son mistook him and his crew for pirates and fatally shot his father (Apollod. 3. 2.1).

ASTEROPEIA, daughter of Pelias, in conjunction with her sisters, murdered her father (Paus. 8. 11.2).

ATHENA. Some accounts of her birth say her father was Pallas, the winged giant, whom she afterwards killed because he attempted to violate her chastity.

CALLIAS and his brothers hired killers to slay their father, since the father preferred his son-in-law to his own sons (Apollod 2. 8.5).

EPEIGEUS, a Myrmidon and son of Agacles, having killed his father, was obliged to flee from Budeion. He joined Achilles in the Trojan War and was killed by Hector (Hom. *Il.* 16. 570).

EVANDER killed his father at the instigation of his mother and had to leave Arcadia on that account.

OEDIPUS. On the road between Delphi and Daulis, he met his real father, Laius, and as Polyphontes (Polyphetes or Polypoetes), the charioteer of Laius, tried to push him out of the way, a scuffle ensued in which Oedipus slew both Laius and Polyphontes.

SCYLLA was a daughter of Nisus of Megara who, in her love of Minos, cut off the single golden hair from her father's head and thereby caused his death (Apollod. 3. 15.8).

TELEGONUS was a son of Odysseus and Circe. When Odysseus returned to Ithaca, Circe sent Telegonus to search for his father. A storm cast his ship on the coast of Ithaca, and, being pressed by hunger, he began to plunder the fields. Odysseus and Telemachus, on being informed of the ravages of the stranger, went out to fight against him and Telegonus ran Odysseus through with a spear which he had received from his mother (Ov. *Trist.* 1. 1.114).

Murder (of Father-In-Law)

LYNCEUS. According to some, he slew Danaus and all the sisters of Hypermnestra in revenge for his brothers, who had been slain by their wives on their wedding night.

PELEUS accidentally killed Eurytion during the Calydonian Boar Hunt (Apollod. 3. 13.1).

Murder (of Grandchild)

AEOLUS. When his daughter, Canace, bore a child by her brother, Macareus, Aeolus threw it to the dogs.

Murder (of Grandfather)

ELEPHENOR, son of Chalcodon, killed his grandfather, Abas, without being aware of it, and as a consequence was obliged to leave Euboea.

PERSEUS accidentally killed his grandfather, Acrisius, by a quoit which went astray while he was throwing it.

Murder (of Husband)

AGAVE killed her husband, Lycotherses, in order to gain his Illyrian kingdom for her father, Cadmus.

CASSIPHONE, daughter of Odysseus by Circe, murdered Telemachus, her husband (and half-brother), because he had put her mother to death.

CLYTEMNESTRA with her lover, Aegisthus, murdered her husband Agamemnon upon his return from the Trojan War.

DANAIDES were the fifty daughters of Danaus, who were betrothed to the fifty sons of Aegyptus. They were compelled by their father to kill their husbands the first night with the swords which Danaus gave them.

ILIONA and her brother Polydorus, when they learned that her husband Polymnestor had killed his own son Deiphylus (believing him to be Polydorus), put out Polymnestor's eyes and then slew him (Hor. *Sat.* 2. 3, 64; Cic. *Acad.* 2. 27; Cic. *Tusc.* 1. 44).

Murder (of Mother)

ALCMAON slew his mother, Eriphyle, for her earlier infidelity to his father; some accounts say he was aided by his brother, Amphilochus.

ELECTRA, daughter of Agamemnon and Clytemnestra, became an accomplice to her brother, Orestes, in the murder of their mother.

ORESTES. To avenge the death of his father, Agamemnon, he slew his mother, Clytemnestra, and her lover, his uncle Aegisthus (Soph. *Elect.* 1405; Aeschyl. *Choeph.* 931; comp. Eurip. *Elect.* 625, 671, 774, 969, 1165, who differs in several points with Sophocles).

Murder (of Nephew)

AEGISTHUS murdered Agamemnon on his return from Troy.

DAEDALUS instructed his sister's son, Calos (Talos or Perdix) in sculpture, until the nephew came to pass him in skill and ingenuity, and Daedalus killed him in envy.

PRIAM put Cilla, his sister, and her infant son, Menippus, to death in lieu of Hecuba, pregnant with Paris, to satisfy a prophecy that calamity would come if mother and child were not put to death (Apollod. 3. 12.8).

Murder (of Sister)

ALTHEMENES. On Rhodes, his sister Anemosyne was raped by Hermes. Althemenes did not believe her, and in a rage killed her (Apollod. 3. 2.1).

PRIAM put Cilla, his sister, and her infant son, Menippus, to death in lieu of Hecuba, pregnant with Paris, to satisfy a prophecy that calamity would come if mother and child were not put to death (Apollod. 3. 12.8).

Murder (of Sister-In-Law)

LYNCEUS. According to some, he slew Danaus and all the sisters of Hypermnestra, his wife, in revenge for his brothers, who had been slain by their wives on their wedding night.

Murder (of Son)

AEDON, daughter of Pandareos, was jealous of the many children of her brother-in-law, Amphion, and determined to murder one of his sons, Amaleus, but in the night she mistook her own son for her nephew and killed him. Some add that she afterwards killed her own son from fear of vengeance of her sister-in-law, Niobe. When she discovered that she had killed Itylus, her son, she was changed by Zeus into a nightingale to relieve her grief.

AGAVE was the mother of Pentheus. When her son sought to stop the riotous proceedings of the women who followed Dionysus, he was mistaken by Agave for an animal, and in her Bacchic frenzy she helped tear him apart (Theocrit. 26; Eurip. *Bacch.* 1142; Ov. *Met.* 3. 714).

ALCATHOUS slew his son, Callipolis, with a piece of wood which the son had pulled away from the altar, where Alcathous was sacrificing to Apollo. Callipolis had hastened to tell his father of the death of the other son, Echepolis, and felt it improper to tell his father while he was sacrificing. He was purified of this murder at Megara by Polyidus, the celebrated soothsayer (Apollod. 3. 3.1).

ATHAMAS, husband of Ino, driven mad by Hera for bringing up Dionysus, killed his son, Learchus.

ATREUS slew Pleisthenes, his son, who was sent as an emissary (and murderer) to Mycenae by Thyestes, who had reared him. Atreus was unaware that Pleisthenes was his son.

HERACLES killed his son, Deicoon, during a fit of madness (Apollod. 2. 7.8).

IDOMENEUS. Once in a storm at sea he vowed to Poseidon to sacrifice to him whatever he met first on his landing, if the god would grant him a safe return. The first person he met on his landing was his son, whom he accordingly sacrificed.

INO. According to Plutarch (*Quaest.Rom.* 13) she killed Melicertes, her son, as she had become mad from jealousy of an Aetolian slave named Antiphera.

LYCURGUS was a son of Dryas and king of the Edones in Thrace. For having tried to destroy all the vines of his country, he was driven mad by Dionysus. In this state he killed his wife and also his son, whom he mistook for a vine.

MEDEA. When Jason wanted to marry Glauce, Medea killed her two sons, Alcimenes and Tisander. The names of the sons are also given as Mermerus (Macareus or Mormorus) and Pheres.

OENEUS was said to have killed his son, Toxeus.

PARIS was said to have killed his son, Corythus (by Oenone), out of jealousy, because he found him with Helen.

PELOPS. According to some legends, Chrysippus was killed by his father, Pelops (Paus. 6. 20.4).

POEMANDER, son of Chaeresilaus, inadvertently killed his own son and was purified by Elephenor.

POLYMNESTOR (POLYMESTOR). Polydorus was reared as the son of his sister, Iliona, who was married to Polymnestor, king of Thracian Chersonesus. However, she made everyone believe that her own son, Deiphilus (Deipylus) was Polydorus. When the Greeks bribed Polymnestor to kill Polydorus as the last of the male line of Priam, the king slew his own son instead (Hor. *Sat.* 2. 361; Cic. *Tusc.* 1. 44; Cic. *Acad.* 2. 27).

PROCNE was the first wife of Tereus. When she learned that he had hidden her away and then married her sister, Philomela, and cut out her tongue, she killed Itys, her son by Tereus, and served his flesh to Tereus.

TANTALUS invited the gods to a repast and slaughtered his own son, Pelops, setting the flesh before the gods to eat.

Murder (of Uncle)

ORESTES murdered his uncle Aegisthus to avenge the death of his father, Agamemnon.

PYGMALION, brother of Dido, murdered her husband and uncle, Acerbas, for his treasure (Virg. *Aen.* 1. 349).

TLEPOLEMUS was a son of Heracles by Astyoche and king of Argos. After slaying his uncle, Lycimnius, he was obliged to take flight, and settled on the island of Rhodes.

TYDEUS, son of Oeneus and Periboea, was said by some to have killed his father's brother, Melas (Lycopeus or Alcathous); others said he killed his mother's brother, Thoas (Aphareus).

Murder (of Wife)

CYCNUS. When he learned that his wife Philonome had falsely accused his son, Tenes, of improper conduct toward her (his stepmother), resulting in his exposing the son and daughter in a chest at sea, he killed Philonome and went to join his children at Tenedos, where they had been carried by the waves (Paus. 10. 14.2; Diod. 5. 83; Strab. 14. 640).

HERACLES. According to some traditions, after his return from Hades he was seized with madness, in which he killed his wife, Megara, and his children by her.

LYCURGUS was a son of Dryas and king of the Edones in Thrace. For having tried to destroy all the vines of his country, he was driven mad by Dionysus. In this state he killed his wife and also his son, whom he mistook for a vine.

Music

AMPHION. While his twin brother, Zethus, preferred hunting and shepherdry, he preferred song and music (Hor. *Epist.* 1. 18.41).

APOLLO was the Olympian god of fine arts, music, poetry and eloquence.

CHEIRON the centaur was renowned for his skill in music.

DACTYLI were reported to have introduced music from Phrygia into Greece, and to have invented rhythm, especially the dactylic rhythm (Plut. *De Mus.* 5).

DIOSCURI were believed to have invented the war dance and warlike music.

EUMOLPUS, the bard, is said to have instructed Heracles in music (Theocrit. 24. 108; Apollod. 2. 5.12).

EVANDER. In Italy, he was said to have taught his neighbors the art of music.

HERMES was said to have invented music.

HIERAX was a musician of the mythic period before the Trojan War. He is said to have invented the Hieracian measure and to have been the friend and disciple of Olympus, the musician.

LINUS, son of Apollo, is said to have instructed Heracles in music and to have been killed by the hero (Apollod. 2. 4.9; Theocrit. 24. 103; Diod. 3. 67; Athen. 4. 164). Another legend says that he was killed by his father because he had ventured into a musical contest with the god (Paus. 9. 29.3).

MUSES, according to the earliest writers, were the inspiring goddesses of song. They also, according to later notions, presided over the different kinds of poetry, and over the arts and sciences. They are often represented carrying musical instruments.

SILENUS (SEILENUS), one of the satyrs and son of Hermes or Pan, like all satyrs was unusually fond of music.

ZAREX was a hero who was believed to have been instructed in music by Apollo. He had a shrine near Eleusis.

Musical Instruments

CHARITES. As companions of Apollo, they always carried musical instruments.

MINERVA was believed to have been the inventor of musical instruments, especially wind instruments.

See also: Names of individual instruments

Myrrh

PHOENIX. This fabulous bird was reputed to make a large egg of myrrh and seal its dead father inside. One version of the regeneration story of this bird relates that when Phoenix arrived at the age of five hundred years he built for himself a funeral pyre consisting of spices, settled upon it, and died. Out of the decomposing body he then rose again, and having grown up, he wrapped the remains of his old body up in myrrh, carried them to Heliopolis and burnt them (Stat. *Silv.* 2. 4.36).

SMYRNA (MYRRHA) was changed into a myrrh tree after being discovered in an incestuous relationship with her father, Cinyras.

Myrtle

APHRODITE. Myrtle was sacred to her.

BONA DEA. She was said to have intoxicated herself, thereby incurring the wrath of Faunus, who killed her with a myrtle staff, but afterwards raised her to the rank of a goddess. Myrtle was forbidden in any of her temples.

CHARITES. As companions to Apollo, they always carried myrtle.

IACCHUS. At the celebration of the Eleusinian mysteries, he was represented carrying a torch and adorned with a myrtle wreath.

VENUS MURCIA (MURTEA or MURTIA) was a surname of Venus at Rome, where she had a chapel in the circus with a statue (Apul. 6. 395; Tertull. *De Spect.* 8; Varr. *De Ling.Lat.* 5. 154; August. 4. 16; Liv. 1. 33). This surname, which is said to be the same as Myrtea (from *myrtus,* a myrtle) was believed to indicate the fondness of the goddess for the myrtle tree, and in ancient times there is said to have been a myrtle grove in the front of her chapel at the foot of the Aventine (Plin. *H.N.* 15. 36; Plut. *Quaest.Rom.* 20).

Mysteries

DYSAULES was the father of Triptolemus and Eubuleus. According to tradition, he had been expelled from Eleusis by Ion and had come to Phlius, where he introduced the Eleusinian mysteries (Paus. 1. 14.2, 2. 14.2).

EUMOLPUS, son of Poseidon, is credited with founding the Eleusinian mysteries and as the first priest of Demeter and Dionysus.

IASION, inspired by Demeter and Cora, traveled about in Sicily and other countries and taught the people the mysteries of Demeter. Some say that Zeus himself instructed him in the mysteries (Dionys. 1. 61; Diod. 5. 48).

IDAEUS instituted in Phrygia the worship and mysteries of the Phrygian mother of the gods (Dionys. 1. 61).

LYCUS was said to have raised the mysteries of the great goddesses to greater celebrity and to have introduced them from Attica to Andania in Messenia (Paus. 4. 1.4).

MESSENE, wife of Polycaon, was said to have

introduced the Eleusinian mysteries to Messenia (Paus. 4. 1.2, 3.6, 27.4, 31.9).

Nail

HIPPODAMEIA, the daughter of Oenomaus, wished to be won by Pelops. She persuaded Myrtilus, the charioteer of Oenomaus, to take the nails out of her father's chariot wheels, so that Pelops could win the race which Oenomaus imposed on all suitors of his daughter.

NORTIA was an Etruscan divinity who was worshipped at Volsinii, where a nail was driven every year into the wall of her temple, for the purpose of marking the number of years (Liv. 7. 3; Juv. 10. 74).

TALOS was a man of brass, the work of Hephaestus. He guarded Crete and killed all who landed there by embracing them after he had heated himself red-hot. He had in his body only one vein, which ran from the head to the ankles and was closed at the top with a nail. When he attempted to keep the Argonauts from Crete, Medea by her magic powers threw him into a state of madness and took the nail out of his vein, causing him to bleed to death (Apollon. Rhod. 4. 1638).

Names

NUNDINA (NONA DIES) was a goddess whom the Romans invoked when they named their children.

Narcissus

EUMENIDES. The narcissus was sacred to them.

LINUS, son of Apollo, was considered by some to have originally been the name of a flower (a species of narcissus).

NARCISSUS. When he pined away for love of his own image in the water, he was metamorphosed into the flower called narcissus after him (Ov. *Met.* 3. 341).

Navigation

ATHENA invented the science of navigation.

ATHENA AETHYIA. In Megara, she was worshipped under this name for having taught there the art of navigation.

BRITOMARTIS was protectress of navigation.

NAUPLIUS of Argos, son of Poseidon and Amymone, was a famous navigator (Apollon. Rhod. 1. 136).

ODYSSEUS. At an early age he was noted for his skill in navigation.

POSEIDON ASPHALIUS (ASPHALEIUS) was a name under which Poseidon was worshipped in various towns of Greece. It describes him as the god who grants safety to ports and to navigation in general (Strab. 1. 57; Paus. 7. 21.3).

PROMETHEUS brought the knowledge of navigation to men.

Navy

LARES. The *Lares marini* or *permarini,* Roman divinities of the sea, had a sanctuary dedicated to them by P. Aemilius in remembrance of his naval victory over Antiochus (Liv. 40. 52).

MINOS. During his reign, Crete was a powerful maritime state, and Minos not only checked the piratical pursuits of his contemporaries but made himself master of the Greek islands of the Aegean (Thuc. 1. 4; Strab. 1. 48).

Neck

SCYLLA was a monster who dwelt on a rock on the Italian coast opposite Sicily. She barked like a dog, had twelve feet, and six long necks and mouths, each of which contained three rows of sharp teeth.

Necklace

AGENOR went to Delphi with his brother, Pronous, to dedicate the necklace and peplus of Harmonia, which they had received from their father, Phegeus, but they were killed by the sons of Alcmaon.

ALCMAON. Eriphyle, his mother, was bribed by the gift of Harmonia's necklace to persuade her husband, Amphiaraus, to join the expedition against Thebes. When they grew up, Alcmaon and his brother, Amphilochus, killed their mother at Amphiaraus' entreaty. The necklace came into Alcmaon's possession, and he gave it and the peplus to Arsinoe, his first wife. Later, when he wanted to give them to his second wife, he was slain by his ex-brother-in-law, Agenor.

AMPHOTERUS and Acarnan, sons of Alcmaon, received from their father the fatal necklace and peplus of Harmonia, which they dedicated in the temple of Athena Pronaea at Delphi (Apollod. 3. 7.5– 7).

CADMUS. When he married Harmonia, he presented her with the famous peplus and necklace, which he had received from Hephaestus or from Europa (Apollod. 3. 1.1).

CALLIRRHOE induced her husband, Alcmaon, to procure for her the peplus and necklace of Harmonia.

ERIPHYLE, daughter of Talaus and Lysimache, received from Polyneices the necklace of Harmonia so that she could persuade her husband, Amphiaraus, to undertake the expedition against Thebes (Apollod. 3. 6.2).

IPHIS was a son of Alector and king of Argos. He advised Polyneices to induce Amphiaraus to take part in the expedition against Thebes by giving the famous necklace of Harmonia to Eriphyle, wife of Amphiaraus (Apollod. 3. 6.2).

MENELAUS. When he consulted the Delphic oracle about the expedition against Troy, he dedicated the necklace of Helen to Athena Pronaea.

PHAYLLUS, the tyrant, stole the necklace of Harmonia from the temple of Athena Pronaea at Delphi to gratify his mistress, the wife of Ariston. She wore it for a time, but at last her youngest son was seized with madness and set fire to the house, in which she perished with all her treasures (Athen. 6. 232).

Necromancy

ELPENOR, companion of Odysseus, was said to have been killed by Odysseus himself for necromantic purposes.

Nectar

APOLLO. After his birth, his mother Leto was not able to nurse him, so Themis gave him nectar and ambrosia.

PATROCLUS. Thetis prevented his body from decomposing by anointing it with nectar and ambrosia.

TANTALUS. Some say that his severe punishment in the lower world resulted from his stealing nectar and ambrosia from the table of the gods and giving them to his friends (Pind. *Ol.* 1. 98).

Net

AGAMEMNON. According to some, Clytemnestra threw a net over him while he was at bath and either slew him herself or assisted Aegisthus in doing so.

AMPHITRITE. In ancient works of art she was represented with a net over her hair.

BRITOMARTIS. Fleeing from pursuit of Minos, she threw herself into the sea and became entangled in nets set by fishermen but was rescued by Artemis, who made her a goddess.

BRITOMARTIS DICTYMNA (DICTYNNA) was a surname of Britomartis from the word for net (Diod. 5. 76).

DICTYMNA (DICTYNNA) was a nymph who invented hunting nets.

HERACLES succeeded in catching the Erymanthian boar by chasing it through deep snow and exhausting it, after which he caught it in a net (Apollod. 2. 5.4).

New Year's Day

JANUS. The first day of the year was particularly sacred to him as god of beginnings.

Night

ACHLYS was, according to some ancient cosmogonies, the eternal night, and the first created being, who existed even before Chaos.

NYX was night personified. She was one of the first created beings and is described as the daughter of Chaos and the sister of Erebus.

SUMMANUS was an ancient Roman or Etruscan divinity, who was equal to or higher than Jupiter in rank. As Jupiter was the god of heaven in the bright day, so Summanus was the god of the nocturnal heaven, and lightnings plying in the night were regarded as his work (August. 4. 23; Plin. *H.N.* 2. 53).

Nightingale

AEDON. When she slew her son, Itylus, by accident, she was changed by Zeus into a nightingale to relieve her grief.

ORPHEUS was the famous lyre player, by whose grave nightingales sang with greater melody than anywhere else.

PHILOMELA. When pursued with her sister, Procne, by their husband, Tereus, she and her sister prayed to the gods to change them into birds. She was changed into a nightingale and Procne into a swallow. Ovid (*Met.* 6. 424 – 675) reverses Procne and Philomela in this regard.

Noise

PAN had a terrific voice and by it frightened the Titans in their fight with the gods. He was fond of noise and riot.

Nose

PAN, the great god of flocks and shepherds, had a pug nose.

Nudity

CHARITES. In later representations, the Charites always appear naked (Paus. 9. 35.2).

Numbers

ATHENA, the goddess of wisdom, invented numbers.

HERMES was said to have invented numbers.

MINERVA was thought by the Romans to have invented numbers.

NUMERIA was a divinity at Rome who presided over numbers.

Nurse(s) of

AENEAS
Caieta, according to some accounts, was the nurse of Aeneas (Virg. *Aen.* 7. 1; Ov. *Met.* 14. 442) and, according to others, the nurse of Creusa or Ascanius.

APOLLO
Themis. After Apollo's birth, his mother Leto was not able to nurse him, so Themis gave him nectar and ambrosia.

ARCAS
Maia. Arcas, the son of Zeus by Callisto, was given to Maia to be reared (Hom. *Od.* 14. 435; Hom. *Hymn. in Merc.* 3; Hes. *Theog.* 936; Apollod. 3. 10.2, 8.2; Hor. *Carm.* 1. 10.1, 2.42).

ARES
Thero was the nurse of Ares, from whom he was believed to have received the surname of Thereitas.

ARTEMIS
Upis was a nymph who is said to have reared Artemis.

DEMETER

Baubo of Eleusis is called by some the nurse of Demeter.

DEMOPHON

Demeter, the goddess of agriculture, when she arrived in Eleusis, undertook to nurse Demophon, a brother of Triptolemus. She tried to make Demophon immortal by putting him into a fire, but was discovered one night by Metaneira, the child's mother, who screamed and caused him to be consumed by the flames.

DIONYSUS

Bacche was a nymph on Mt. Nysa who was a nurse of Dionysus.

Bassarae were nurses of Dionysus.

Bromia (*Bromie*) (See *Nyseides*)

Cisseis (See *Nyseides*)

Cleis was a nurse of Dionysus.

Coronis was a nurse of Dionysus.

Erato (See *Nyseides*)

Eriphia (See *Nyseides*)

Hermes was a nurse of Dionysus after he rescued him from the flaming body of Semele.

Hippia nursed Dionysus on Mt. Tmolus.

Hyades were nymphs who were appointed by Zeus to bring up Dionysus.

Lydae were nurses of Dionysus.

Ma was a nymph in the suite of Rhea, to whom Zeus entrusted the bringing up of the infant Dionysus.

Macetae were nurses of Dionysus.

Macris, daughter of Aristaeus, fed the infant Dionysus with honey, after he was brought to her in Euboea by Hermes (Apollon. Rhod. 4. 540, 990, 1131).

Mimallones were nurses of Dionysus.

Muses were nurses of Dionysus.

Mystis was a nurse of Dionysus, and also instructed him in the mysteries (Nonn. 13. 140).

Nysa, daughter of Aristaeus, was believed to have brought up the god Dionysus in the island formed by the river Triton. She was one of the Nyseides.

Nyseides (*Nysiades*), the nymphs of Nysa, are said to have reared Dionysus. Their names are Cisseis, Nysa, Erato, Eriphia, Bromia, and Polyhymnia (Apollod. 3. 4.3; Ov. *Met.* 3. 314; Ov. *Fast.* 3. 769).

Philia, a nymph of Naxos, was one of the nurses of Dionysus.

Polyhymnia (See *Nyseides*)

HERA

Acraea, daughter of the river Asterion, was one of the nurses of Hera (Paus. 2. 7.1; Plut. *Quaest. Conviv.* 3. 9). Her sisters, Euboea and Prosymna, assisted her in this duty.

Horae were said to have been nurses of Hera (Paus. 2. 13.3).

HYLLUS

Abia was a nurse of Hyllus, son of Heracles.

HYPSIPYLE

Polyxo was the nurse of queen Hypsipyle in Lemnos; she was celebrated as a prophetess (Apollon. Rhod. 1. 668; Val. Flacc. 2. 316).

MUSES

Eupheme was nurse of the Muses. She brought up her son Crotus with them. There was a statue of her in the grove of the Muses near Helicon (Paus. 9. 29.3).

ODYSSEUS

Eurycleia, daughter of Ops, was the nurse of Odysseus. She recognized Odysseus when he returned home in the disguise of a beggar from a scar on his knee which he had received as a child. Afterwards, she faithfully assisted him against the suitors of Penelope (Hom. *Od.* 1. 429, 4. 742, 19. 385).

ORESTES

Geilissa was the nurse of Orestes, who spirited the child away and thus saved him from being murdered by Aegisthus (Aeschyl. *Choeph.* 732).

POSEIDON

Arne was the nurse of Poseidon.

ROMULUS

Acca Laurentia was a nurse of Romulus and Remus after they had been taken from the she-wolf which at first suckled them.

SEMELE

Beroe was the nurse of Semele.

TELEMACHUS

Eurycleia, daughter of Ops, brought up Telemachus as she had his father, Odysseus.

ZEUS

Adrasteia was one of the daughters of Melisseus, an ancient king of Crete, and Amalthea. Rhea entrusted to her and her sister, Ida, the infant Zeus to be brought up in the Dictaean grotto (Apollod. 1. 1.6).

Aega was a nurse of Zeus in Crete.

Amalthea was a daughter of King Melisseus of Crete; according to some, she fed the infant Zeus goat's milk. According to others, Amalthea was the name of the goat itself.

Celmus, one of Zeus' nurses, was changed into a magnet stone for saying Zeus was mortal.

Curetes were nurses of Zeus on Crete.

Cynosura was an Idaean nymph and one of the nurses of Zeus.

Helice, daughter of Olenus, with her sister Aega, was said to have brought up Zeus.

Heracles was one of the Idaean Dactyls who cared for the infant Zeus at Olympia.

Hyades. As nymphs of Dodona, they were said, in some traditions, to have brought up Zeus.

Meliae (*Melissae*) were the nymphs who nursed Zeus (Callim. *Hymn.in Jov.* 47; Apollod. 1. 1.3).

Neda, an Arcadian nymph, was believed, conjointly with Theisoa and Hagno, to have nursed the infant Zeus (Callim. *Hymn.in Jov.* 38; Paus. 8. 38.3). In a Messenian tradition, Neda and Ithome were called nurses of Zeus (Paus. 4. 33.2).

Oenoe was an Arcadian nymph who is said to have been one of those who brought up the infant Zeus (Paus. 8. 47.2).

Nut Tree

CARYA, daughter of Dion, went mad as a consequence of betraying Apollo, and was changed into a nut tree.

Nymph

ARTEMIS was the Arcadian goddess of the nymphs.

Oak

CHRYSOPELEIA was a Hamadryad, who, when a mountain torrent threatened to undermine the oak tree in which she dwelt, was rescued by Arcas, who diverted the torrent by a dam.

DRYOPS was a son of Lycaon by Dia, the daughter of Lycaon, who concealed her newborn infant in a hollow oak tree.

LYCASTUS and his twin brother, Parrhasius, sons of Ares, were thrown into the river Erymanthus by their mother, Philonome, from fear of her father. The river god carried them into a hollow oak tree, where they were suckled by a she-wolf until the shepherd, Tyliphus, found them and carried them home.

LYNCEUS, brother of Idas, had extremely keen vision, so that in the battle with the Dioscuri he could see through the trunk of an oak tree where Castor and Polydeuces were lying in ambush (Apollod. 3. 11.2; Ov. *Fast.* 5. 700).

QUERQUETULANAE were nymphs presiding over the green oak forests near the *porta querquetularia,* or *querquetulana,* and were believed to be possessed of prophetic powers (Plin. *H.N.* 16. 10, 15.37).

RHEA. In Greece, the oak was sacred to her.

ZEUS. The oak tree was sacred to him.

ZEUS DODONAIS. At Dodona, Zeus was mainly a prophetic god, and the oak tree was sacred to him. The Dodonaean Zeus is often represented as wearing a wreath of oak leaves.

Oath

AGRAULOS. When she sacrificed herself to end a war against Athens, a temple was erected to her. Young Athenians on receiving their first armor took an oath in the temple to defend their country to the last.

ALALCOMENIA (See PRAXIDICAE)

AULIS (See PRAXIDICAE)

FIDES was the Roman goddess of faith, oaths, and honesty.

GAEA was invoked by persons taking oaths

(Hom. *Il.* 3. 278, 15. 36, 19. 259; Hom. *Od.* 5. 124).

HORCUS, the personification of an oath, is described by Hesiod as the son of Eris and as the avenger of perjury (*Theog.* 231; *Op. et D.* 209).

JUPITER was regarded as protector of the sanctity of an oath.

JUPITER FERETRIUS was a surname of Jupiter probably derived from *ferire,* "to strike," since persons who took an oath called upon Jupiter, if they swore falsely, to strike them as they struck the victim they sacrificed to him.

PALICI were Sicilian daemons, twin sons of Zeus and the nymph, Thaleia. Near their sanctuary there gushed from the earth two sulphurous springs called Deilloi, at which solemn oaths were taken. These oaths were written on tablets and thrown into one of the springs. If the tablet floated, the oath was considered to be true, but if it sank, the oath was regarded as perjury, which was believed to be punished instantaneously (Diod. 11. 89; Strab. 6. 275; Cic. *De Nat. Deor.* 3. 22; Virg. *Aen.* 9. 585; Ov. *Met.* 5. 406).

PRAXIDICAE. The three divinities, Alalcomenia, Thelxinoea, and Aulis, watched over oaths and saw that they were not taken rashly or thoughtlessly.

STYX was the name by which the most solemn oaths were sworn (Hes. *Theog.* 383; Hom. *Od.* 5. 185, 15. 37; Apollod. 1. 2. 5; Apollon. Rhod. 2. 191). When one of the gods was to take an oath by Styx, Iris fetched a cup full of water from the river Styx, and the god poured out the water while taking the oath (Hes. *Theog.* 775).

THALLO, one of the Attic Horae, was invoked in the political oath which the citizens of Athens had to take (Paus. 9. 35.1).

THELXINOEA (See PRAXIDICAE)

ZEUS was regarded as the god who watched over the sanctity of the oath.

ZEUS ASBAMAEUS was the protector of the sanctity of oaths.

Oblivion

LETHE, the personification of oblivion, is called by Hesiod (*Theog.* 227) a daughter of Eris.

Octopus

ENALUS. Once when the sea around Lesbos rose in high billows and no one ventured to approach it, Enalus alone had the courage to do so, and when he returned from the sea he was followed by octopi, the greatest of which was carrying a stone, which Enalus took from it and dedicated in a temple.

Oil

HESTIA. Oil was sacred to her.

NYMPHS. Sacrifices to them consisted of oil.

OENOTROPAE were the daughters of Anius; Dionysus had given them the power of producing at will any quantity of wine, grain, and oil. Their names were Oeno, Spermo, and Elais.

SATURN. The statue of Saturn was hollow and filled with oil, probably to denote the fertility of Latium in olives (Plin. *H.N.* 20. 7.7).

Ointment

JASON was given an ointment by Medea to rub on himself and his armor to make him invulnerable to the fire-breathing bulls which Aeetes had set him the task of yoking and plowing.

Old Age

APHRODITE AMBOLOGERA was a surname of Aphrodite denoting "delaying old age." There was a statue at Sparta under this name (Paus. 3. 18.1).

EUMENIDES were the avenging deities who punished violation of respect due to old age.

POSEIDON appeared as an old man to

Agamemnon when he was ready to flee from the Trojan War.

TITHONUS was a son of Laomedon, beloved by Eos, who obtained for him from the gods immortality but not eternal youth, in consequence of which he completely shrunk together in his old age, whence any old, decrepit man was proverbially called Tithonus (Hom. *Hymn.in Ven.* 219; Hes. *Theog.* 984; Apollod. 3. 12.4; Hom. *Carm.* 1. 28.8; Ov. *Fast.* 1. 461).

See also: LONGEVITY

Olive

ARISTAEUS, son of Apollo and Cyrene, was worshipped as protector of vines and of olive plantations.

ATHENA created the olive tree which remained sacred to her. She was the patron goddess of Athens. In a contest with Poseidon for patronage of Athens, she gave the olive as the most profitable gift to the inhabitants of the city, while Poseidon gave the horse. The gods decreed that peace was more profitable than war and awarded Athena the prize.

AUXESIA. After she and Damia were stoned to death in Troezen, an oracle directed the inhabitants to erect statues of them out of olivewood in order to rid the land of famine.

CECROPS. When Athena, in her contest with Poseidon for patronage of Athens, planted an olive tree, she took Cecrops as witness and thus won the contest.

EIRENE (IRENE), goddess of peace, was pictured on coins carrying in her right arm an olive branch.

FIDES was represented as a matron wearing a wreath of olive leaves.

HERACLES was one of the Idaean Dactyls who cared for the infant Zeus at Olympia. He contended with his brother Dactyls in a footrace and adorned the victor with a wreath of olive. In this manner he is said to have founded the Olympian games (Paus. 5. 7.4).

HERMES is said to have discovered the cultivation of the olive tree.

IO. When she was transformed into a cow, she was tied by her guardian, Argus Panoptes, to an olive tree.

OENOTROPAE, "the changers of or into wine," was the name of the three or four daughters of King Anius in Delos, because they had received from Dionysus the power of changing water into wine and anything else they chose into grain and olives.

SATURN. The statue of Saturn was hollow and filled with oil, probably to denote the fertility of Latium in olives (Plin. *H.N.* 15. 7.7).

ZEUS. The Olympian Zeus sometimes wears a wreath of olive.

ZEUS MORIUS was a surname of Zeus as the protector of the sacred olive trees (Soph. *Oed.Col.* 705).

Omen

HELIOS PANOMPHAEUS was a surname of Helios as the author of all signs and omens (Q.Smyrn. 5. 624).

ZEUS PANOMPHAEUS was a surname of Zeus as the author of all signs and omens. Under this name he had a sanctuary on the Hellespont between capes Rhaeteum and Sigeum (Hom. *Il.* 8. 250; Ov. *Met.* 11. 198).

Omniscience

HELIOS was described as the god who sees and hears everything; he was therefore able to betray to Hephaestus the faithlessness of Aphrodite and to reveal to Demeter the abduction of her daughter (Hom. *Od.* 8. 271; Hom. *Hymn.in Cer.* 75; Hom. *Hymn.in Sol.* 10).

Order

JUPITER STATOR. In Rome, this name described him as protecting the Romans in their flight from an enemy and generally in preserving the order of things (Liv. 1. 12, 10. 37; Cic. *Cat.* 1. 13; Senec. *De Benef.* 4. 7; Plin. *H.N.* 2. 53; August. 3. 13).

THEMIS was a daughter of Uranus and Gaea. In the Homeric poems she is the personification of the order of things established by law, custom, and equity, whence she is described as reigning in the assemblies of men (Hom. *Od.* 2. 68) and as convening, by the command of Zeus, the assembly of the gods (Hom. *Il.* 20.4).

ZEUS was regarded as the founder of kingly power, of law, and of order.

Owl

ALOEIDAE, the giants Otus and Ephialtes, were tied to a pillar in Hades and perpetually tormented by the shriek of an owl.

ASCALAPHUS was a son of Acheron by Gorgyra. When Heracles freed him from the huge stone under which Demeter had buried him for revealing that Persephone had eaten part of a pomegranate while in Hades, Demeter changed Ascalaphus into an owl (Apollod. 2. 5.12). According to Ovid, Persephone herself changed him into an owl by sprinkling him with the water of the river Phlegethon.

ATHENA. The owl was sacred to her.

DIONYSUS hated the sight of an owl (Paus. 8. 39.4; Theocrit. 26. 4; Plut. *Quaest.Conviv.* 3. 5).

EPHIALTES (See ALOEIDAE)

NYCTIMENE was a daughter of Epopeus, king of Lesbos. Pursued and dishonored by her amorous father, she concealed herself in the shade of forests, where she was metamorphosed by Athena into an owl (Ov. *Met.* 2. 590).

OTUS (See ALOEIDAE)

POLYIDUS, the soothsayer from Argos, was by his prophetic powers and by guidance from an owl and bees able to find Minos' missing son, Glaucus, who had drowned in a vat of honey (Aelian. *De Nat.Anim.* 5. 2).

Ox

ACHELOUS changed himself first into a serpent, then into an ox, in a contest with Heracles, who broke off one of his horns, which was taken up by the nymphs and filled with fruits and flowers; this cornucopia was presented to the goddess of plenty.

AESON. According to one account, he was forced to kill himself by drinking ox's blood.

ALCYONES was one of the giants who carried off the oxen of Helios from Erytheia.

AMPHITRYON restored the oxen which the Taphians had stolen from Electryon, but when one of them turned wild, he struck at it and killed Electryon instead.

ATHENA taught people to yoke oxen to the plow.

AUGEAS was supposed to have given Heracles one-tenth of his oxen when Heracles finished cleansing the stables in which the oxen were kept.

BIAS sought to marry Pero, but Neleus, her father, refused to allow this until the suitor brought him the oxen of Iphicles.

CHARYBDIS, a daughter of Poseidon and Gaea and a voracious woman, stole oxen from Heracles and was hurled by the thunderbolt of Zeus into the sea, where, as a whirlpool, she retained her voracious nature.

DANAUS. At Argos, a dispute arose between him and Gelanor about the government. While a settlement was being reached, a wolf rushed among the cattle and killed one of the oxen. This occurrence symbolized to the Argives how the dispute should terminate, and Danaus was accordingly made king (Paus. 2. 19.3).

DIOSCURI. In conjunction with Idas and Lynceus they carried away a herd of oxen from Arcadia, and it was left up to Idas to divide the

Athena

booty. He cut up a bull into four parts and declared that whichever of them first succeeded in eating his share would receive half the oxen, and the second would have the other half. Idas not only ate his own quarter but devoured his brother's in addition, and then drove the whole herd to his home in Messene (Pind. *Nem.* 10. 60; Apollod. 3. 11.2). The Dioscuri then invaded Messene, drove away the cattle of which they had been deprived and many more in addition. This caused a war between the Dioscuri and the sons of Aphareus.

ERGINUS. When his father, Clymenus, was killed by Perieres at the festival of the Onchestian Poseidon, Erginus, the eldest son, who succeeded him as king of Orchomenos, undertook to avenge his father's death. He marched against Thebes and forced them to sign a treaty in which they were bound for twenty years to pay him an annual tribute of one hundred oxen. (See also HERACLES)

EURYLOCHUS was a companion of Odysseus. It was on his advice that the companions carried off the oxen of Helios (Hom. *Od.* 10. 203, 11. 23, 12. 339).

EURYTUS. After failing to deliver his daughter, Iole, to Heracles as his prize in an archery contest, Eurytus' oxen were stolen, and he suspected Heracles. But Iphitus, the son of Eurytus, defended Heracles and persuaded him to help look for the stolen oxen.

GERYON, son of Chrysaor and Callirrhoe, a fabulous king of Hesperia, is described as a being with three heads and possessing magnificent oxen in the island of Erytheia. He plays a prominent part in the stories of Heracles (Apollod. 2. 5.10).

HADES was believed to have herds of oxen in the lower world and in the island of Erytheia, which were attended to by Menoetius (Apollod. 2. 5.10, 12).

HELIOS. In spite of his omniscience, he was unaware of the fact that the companions of Odysseus had stolen his oxen until he was informed of it by Lampetia (Hom. *Od.* 12. 375). Oxen were sacred to him. His herd of oxen numbered three hundred and fifty head and never increased or diminished. They were guarded by his daughters, Phaetusa and Lampetia (Hom *Od.* 12. 128, 261; Apollon. Rhod. 4. 965).

HERACLES. The tenth labor of Heracles consisted of fetching back to Mycenae the red oxen of Geryon from Erytheia. He sailed to Erytheia and overcame the giant, Eurytion, and the dog, Orthrus, who guarded the cattle; he slew Geryon and then sailed back. In the neighborhood of Rhegium, one of the oxen escaped, and Eryx, the son of Poseidon, caught it and put it among his herds. Heracles went in search of it and in recovering it had to kill Eryx. The oxen later were driven mad by Hera, and Heracles spent time in pursuing them but later brought them intact to Eurystheus, who sacrificed them to Hera (Hes. *Theog.* 287; Apollod. 2. 5.10). On his way home two princes, Alebion and Dercynus, attempted to carry off his oxen, but they were slain by him. Other stories about Heracles and oxen are: while proceeding across the country of the Dryopes, he took one of the oxen of Theiodamas and consumed it all; another time, having delivered Theseus and Ascalaphus in the underworld, he killed one of the oxen of Hades in order to give the shades the blood to drink, and he fought with Menoetius, the herdsman; again he met the envoys of King Erginus of Orchomenos who were going to fetch the annual tribute of one hundred oxen which they compelled the Thebans to pay, and he cut off their ears and noses and sent them back to Erginus. When Erginus marched to Thebes, Heracles defeated the enemy and demanded double the tribute formerly received from the Thebans. (See also AUGEAS, CHARYBDIS, EURYTUS, LATINUS, and SCYLLA)

HERMES. In the first hour of his birth, he escaped from his cradle, went to Pieiria and carried off some of the oxen of Apollo (Hom. *Hymn. in Merc.* 17). Other accounts refer the theft of the oxen to a more advanced period of his life (Apollod. 3. 10.2). In order not to be discovered by his footprints, he put on sandals and drove the oxen to Pylos, where he killed two and hid the remainder in a cave. The skins of the slaughtered animals were nailed to a rock, and part of their flesh was prepared and consumed and the rest burnt at the same time he offered sacrifices to the twelve gods (Hom. *Hymn. in Merc.* 125; Diod. 1. 16). Apollo by his divinative powers discovered the thief and eventually took the young boy before Zeus and demanded back his oxen. Hermes denied he had stolen the cattle, but finally was forced to lead Apollo to Pylos and restore the stolen cattle. When Apollo heard the sounds of the lyre Hermes had invented, he forgave Hermes and allowed him to keep the animals.

IPHICLES, son of Phylacus, possessed large herds of oxen which he gave to Melampus, who had given him a favorable prophecy about his progeny (Hom. *Il.* 2. 705; Hom. *Od.* 11. 289).

LATINUS. It is related that Latinus was slain by Heracles for having taken away from him the oxen of Geryon.

MELAMPUS. His brother, Bias, was a suitor for Pero, whose father, Neleus, had promised her as a prize to anyone who could bring him the oxen of Iphicles. These oxen were guarded by a dog which neither man nor animal could approach. Melampus agreed to the task of procuring the oxen, although he knew his mission would fail and he would be thrown in prison. But by demonstrating his prophetic powers to Iphicles, he was released and presented with the cattle, thereby gaining Pero for his brother (Apollod. 1. 9.12; Paus. 4. 36.2). (See also IPHICLES)

MENOETIUS, son of Ceuthonymus, was guardian of the oxen of Hades in the lower world and in the island of Erytheia (Apollod. 2. 5.10). (See also HERACLES)

ODYSSEUS did not want to join the Greeks against Troy (Hom. *Od.* 24. 116). When Palamedes came to persuade him, Odysseus pretended to be mad: he yoked an ass and an ox to a plow and began to sow salt. Palamedes, to test him, placed the infant Telemachus before the plow, whereupon the father could not continue to play his part. Eventually, on his return from Troy, he descended to the underworld to consult Tiresias, the seer, who told him that the voyage would turn out well if he and his companions would leave the sacred herds of Helios alone. Odysseus made his men swear not to touch any of the cattle, but they were overcome by hunger and killed the finest of the cattle while Odysseus slept. For this impiety their ship was destroyed by a flash of lightning from Zeus, and all perished except Odysseus.

RECARANUS was a fabulous Italian shepherd of gigantic bodily strength and courage. Cacus, a wicked Italian robber, once stole eight oxen from the herd of Recaranus, who was able to trace them, although they had been dragged backwards by the tails to disguise their tracks. He entered the hiding place, a cave on Mt. Aventine, slew the robber and dedicated to Jupiter a tenth part of the booty.

SABAZIUS, a Phrygian agricultural divinity and son of Rhea or Cybele, was said to be the first to yoke oxen to the plow (Diod. 4. 4).

SCYLLA. Heracles is said to have killed her because she had stolen some of the oxen of Geryon; but Phorcys restored her to life.

See also: CATTLE

Painting

HERACLES BURAICUS. At his oracle in a cave near Bura, persons threw four dice outside the cave and had the meaning explained with the help of a painting which hung inside the cave (Paus. 7. 25.6).

Palm

HERMES. The palm tree was sacred to him.

NIKE (NICE) was the goddess of victory. In appearance she resembles Athena, but carries a palm.

Panther

ANTENOR. When Troy was plundered, the skin of a panther was hung up at the door of Antenor's house as a sign for the Greeks not to commit any outrage upon it (Paus. 10. 17; Strab. 13. 608).

CYBELE was exposed at infancy but was fed by panthers and brought up by shepherdesses (Diod. 3. 58).

DIONYSUS. When the sisters Alcathoe, Leucippe, and Arsippe refused to attend his revels, he assumed various forms—including a panther—and drove them mad. The panther was sacred to him.

Pantomime

ERATO, the Muse of erotic poetry and mimic imitation, appears often with the lyre.

Paralysis

ALCATHOUS, son of Aesyetes and one of the bravest and handsomest of the Trojans, was slain by Idomeneus with the help of Poseidon, who struck Alcathous with blindness and paralysis so that he could not flee.

Parricide, see Murder (of Father)

Partridge

PERDIX. His skill at inventing excited the jealousy of his uncle, Daedalus, who threw him headlong from the temple of Athena on the acropolis, but the goddess caught him in his fall and changed him into the bird which was named after him *perdix,* the partridge (Paus. 1. 21.6, 26.5; Diod. 4. 76; Apollod. 3. 15.9; (Ov. *Met.* 8. 241).

Past

CARMENATA POSTVERTA (POSTVORTA) was a surname describing the Roman goddess, Carmenata as turning backward and looking at the past, which she revealed to poets and other mortals. In like manner, the prophetic power with which she looked into the future is indicated by Antevorta, Prorsa (Proversa), and Porrima. Poets, however, have personified these attributes of Carmenata and thus describe them as companions of the goddess (Ov. *Fast.* 1. 633; Gell. 16. 16).

POSTVORTA was an attribute (but later a separate personification) of the Roman goddess, Carmenta, meaning knowledge of the past.

Pasture, see Field

Patera, see Cup

Patricide, see Murder (of Father)

Patriotism

AGRAULOS. When an oracle declared that a long protracted war with Athens would cease if one of its inhabitants would sacrifice himself for the good of the country, Agraulos threw herself from the acropolis.

ANCHURUS, son of Midas, leaped into a chasm to save his father's kingdom from an earthquake.

ANDROCLEA, a daughter of Antipoenus of Thebes, with her sister Alcida, sacrificed herself for the victory of Thebes.

CODRUS was the son of Melanthus and king of Athens, where he reigned, according to tradition, some time after the conquest of the Peloponnesus by the Dorians. Once when the Dorians invaded Attica, they were told by an oracle that they would be victorious if the life of the Attic king was spared. The Dorians accordingly took the greatest precautions not to kill the king. But when Codrus was informed of the oracle, he resolved to sacrifice himself, and thus to deliver his country. In the disguise of a common man, he entered the camp of the enemy, where he began quarreling with the soldiers and was slain in the struggle. When the Dorians discovered the death of the Attic king, they abstained from further hostilities and returned home.

MENIPPE and her sister, Metioche, daughters of Orion, in order to avert a plague in Aonia, where they lived, offered themselves as a sacrifice (in response to an oracle) (Ov. *Met.* 13. 685).

MENOECEUS. In the war of the Seven against Thebes, Tiresias (or the Delphic oracle) declared that the Thebans should conquer if Menoeceus would sacrifice himself for his country. Menoeceus accordingly killed himself outside the gates of Thebes (Eurip. *Phoen.* 913, 930; Apollod. 3. 6.7).

PRAXITHEA and her sisters, Theope and Eubule, daughters of Leos, were sacrificed by their father at the direction of the Delphic oracle to halt a plague or famine in Athens. The maidens were afterwards honored by the Athenians, who erected the Leucorium to them (Plut. *Thes.* 13; Paus. 1. 5.2; Diod. 15. 17).

Peace

CONCORDIA was the Roman goddess of peace and concord.

DEMETER was represented as the friend of peace and as a law-giving goddess (Callim. *Hymn. in Cer.* 138; Virg. *Aen.* 4. 58; Hom. *Il.* 5. 500; Ov. *Met.* 5. 341; Paus. 8. 15.1).

DIONYSUS was regarded as a lover of peace.

EIRENE (IRENE) was the Greek goddess of peace.

HERMES was regarded as the maintainer of peace among men.

HESYCHIA was the personification of tranquility and peace.

HORAE. Hesiod describes them as giving to a state good laws, justice, and peace (*Theog.* 901).

JUPITER FERETRIUS. Some derived this surname from *ferre,* because he was the bringer of peace.

PAX was the personification of peace at Rome, where a festival was celebrated in her honor on the 30th of April (Ov. *Fast.* 1. 711; Juv. 1. 115; Plin. *H.N.* 36. 5; Gell. 16. 8).

Peacock

ARGUS was the hundred-eyed giant set to guard Io. After he was decapitated by Hermes, Hera transplanted his hundred eyes to the tail of a peacock (Apollod. 2. 1, 2; Ov. *Met.* 1. 264).

HERA. The peacock was sacred to her.

Pelican

POLYTECHNUS was changed by Zeus into a pelican to end a running feud between him and his wife Aedon and her relatives.

Peplus, see Garment

Perjury

EUMENIDES were the avenging deities who punished perjury.

HERMES. Perjury was one of his attributes.

HORCUS was the personification of an oath and is described by Hesiod as the son of Eris and the avenger of perjury (*Theog.* 231; *Op. et D.* 209).

JUPITER punished persons guilty of perjury.

PALICI were Sicilian daemons, twin sons of Zeus and the nymph, Thaleia. Near their sanctuary there gushed from the earth two sulphurous springs called Deilloi, at which solemn oaths were taken. These oaths were written on tablets and thrown into one of the springs. If the tablet floated, the oath was considered to be true, but if it sank, the oath was regarded as perjury, which was believed to be punished instantaneously (Diod. 11. 89; Strab. 6. 275; Cic. *De Nat.Deor.* 3. 22; Virg. *Aen.* 9. 585).

ZEUS punished persons guilty of perjury.

Persuasion

PEITHO, the personification of persuasion, was worshipped as a divinity at Sicyon, where she was honored with a temple in the agora.

SUADA was the Roman personification of persuasion, equivalent to the Greek Peitho. She was also called by the diminutive Suadela (Hor. *Epist.* 1. 6.38; Cic. *Brut.* 15).

Petasus, see Hat

Phallus, see Genitals

Phantom

HELEN. According to later traditions, Helen did not reach Troy at all, for Zeus and Hera allowed only a phantom resembling her to accompany Paris to Troy, while the real Helen was carried to Proteus in Egypt and remained there until she was fetched by Menelaus (Eurip. *Elect.* 1280; Eurip. *Hel.* 33, 243, 584, 670; Herod. 2. 118, 120; Lycoph. 113; Philostr. *Vit. Apoll.* 4. 16).

Phorminx

APOLLO delighted the immortal gods with his play on the phorminx during their repast.

EETION. When Eetion fell in battle, Achilles' booty from the town of Eetion included the horse Pedasus and the phorminx with a silver neck, on which Achilles played in his tent (Hom. *Il.* 15. 153, 9. 186).

Physician, see Medicine

Pickpocket

HERMES was the god of pickpockets.

Pig

CALCHAS. As soothsayer he was defeated by Mopsus in not being able to state the number of pigs which a sow was going to give birth to (Strab. 14. 642, 668).

CIRCE was the sorceress on the island of Aeaea who changed the men of Odysseus into swine.

DEMETER. Sacrifices to her consisted of pigs.

ELPENOR was one of the companions of Odysseus who were metamorphosed into swine and afterwards back into men by Circe.

HEMITHEA (See MOLPADIA)

HERMES. Pigs were among the sacrifices offered to him.

JUNO. Pigs were sacrificed to her at the first of every month.

MOLPADIA was a daughter of Staphylus. When she allowed her father's wine to be spoiled by swine, she threw herself from a rock, but Apollo saved her. He transferred her under the name of Hemithea to Castabus in the Chersonesus. There, a temple was erected to her, which no one was allowed to enter who had touched a swine.

SILVANUS was a Latin divinity of the fields and forests. Sacrifices to him included pigs.

Pigeon

ION. Upon growing up, he was thought by his mother, Creusa, to be a son to her husband by a former beloved, and she tried to poison the youth by a cup of venomous blood from a dragon, but her object was discovered when Ion, before drinking, poured a libation to the gods. A pigeon drank of it and died on the spot.

Pileus, see Cap

Pillar

ALOEIDAE, the giants Otus and Ephialtes. In Hades they were tied with serpents to a pillar.

EPHIALTES (See ALOEIDAE)

HERACLES. On the frontiers of Libya and Europe he erected two pillars (Calpe and Abyla) on the two sides of the straits of Gibraltar.

OTUS (See ALOEIDAE)

PROMETHEUS. For stealing fire from heaven, he was punished by being chained to a pillar, where an eagle daily consumed his liver, which, in the succeeding night, was restored. Later, Heracles killed the eagle and delivered the sufferer.

Pilot

ACOETES was pilot of the ship which took Dionysus from Naxos. After the ship's crew was destroyed, he returned with Dionysus to Naxos and became a priest.

TIPHYS was a pilot of the Argo.

Pirate

ACOETES. He and his crew were Tyrrhenian pirates.

ADMETE. When she took the image of Hera from Argos to Samos, pirates were sent to recover it but failed because their ship would not move.

AEACUS was believed by the Aeginetans to have surrounded their island with high cliffs to protect it against pirates.

BUTES (See PANCRATIS)

DIONYSUS. For a voyage from Icaria to Naxos, he hired a ship which belonged to Tyrrhenian pirates, who steered instead toward Asia to sell him. The god by various magical feats drove the sailors insane, so that they jumped overboard and were changed into dolphins (Apollod. 3. 5.3; Ov. *Met.* 3. 582).

GLAUCUS of Anthedon in Boeotia, in the battle of the Argonauts with the Tyrrhenians, alone remained unhurt. He sank to the bottom of the sea, became a marine deity, and was of service to the Argonauts.

HERACLES. When he returned from Troy, he landed at Cos, was mistaken for a pirate and attacked by the inhabitants with stones (Apollod. 2. 7.1, 8).

HYMEN (HYMENAEUS) was a youth of Argos, who delivered some Attic maidens from Pelasgian pirates and was afterward praised by them in their bridal songs, which were called, after him, hymeneal songs.

IPHIMEDEIA. She and her daughter, Pancratis, while celebrating the orgies of Dionysus on Mt. Drius, were carried off by Thracian pirates to Naxos or Strongyle; but both were delivered by the sons of Iphimedeia.

LIBYS was one of the Tyrrhenian pirates whom Dionysus changed into dolphins (Ov. *Met.* 3. 671).

MELANTHUS. As LIBYS.

MELAS. As LIBYS.

OPHELTES. As LIBYS.

PANCRATIS, daughter of Aloeus and Iphimedeia, was carried off along with her mother and other women from Mt. Drius, where they were solemnizing a festival of Dionysus, by Thracian pirates under Butes.

THEONOE, a daughter of Thestor, was carried off by pirates and sold to King Icarus in Caria.

Pit

ARCHELAUS. King Cisseus promised him succession to his throne for assistance against neighboring enemies but regretted his promise and tried to kill Archelaus by digging a hole, filling it with burning coals and covering it with branches. Cisseus himself was thrown into the pit by Archelaus.

Pitcher

HAGNO, an Arcadian nymph, was represented as carrying in one hand a pitcher and in the other a patera.

IRIS, the goddess of the rainbow, was represented as carrying a pitcher in her hands.

Pity

ELEOS, the personification of pity and mercy, had an altar in the agora at Athens (Paus. 1. 17.1).

Plague

AESCULAPIUS (See ASCLEPIUS)

APOLLO had the power of visiting men with plagues and epidemics, and he was also able to deliver them from these evils. He sent a plague on Argos to punish the father of Psamathe, who had been put to death by him for bearing Linus to Apollo. Propitiation was achieved by sacrifices and matrons and virgins singing dirges.

APOLLO ALEXICACUS was a surname of the god as averter of evil, particularly by Athenians, who believed he had stopped a plague which had raged during the Peloponnesian War.

APOLLO CARNEIUS. This surname might have been connected with Carnus, an Acarnanian soothsayer, whose murder by Hippotes provoked Apollo to send a plague on the army of Hippotes.

APOLLO EPICURUS was a surname meaning helper, under which he was worshipped at Bassae in Arcadia. He had received the surname because he had at one time delivered the country from a pestilence (Paus. 8. 38.6, 41.5).

APOLLO LIBYSTINUS, "the Libyan," was a surname under which Apollo was worshipped by the Sicilians, because he was believed to have destroyed by a pestilence a Libyan fleet which sailed against Sicily.

APOLLO LOEMIUS was a surname describing the god as the deliverer of plague, in Lindus in Rhodes.

ARES was responsible for plagues and epidemics that resulted from war.

ARTEMIS, like Apollo, sent plague and death among men and animals. She also had the power to remove these misfortunes.

ASCLEPIUS. His worship was introduced in Rome at the command of the Delphic oracle for the purpose of averting a pestilence. At Rome he was called Aesculapius.

ATHENA HELLOTIA (HELLOTIS). This surname might have come from Hellotia, one of the daughters of Timander, who fled into the temple of Athena when Corinth was burned down by the Dorians; she was destroyed in the temple with her sister, Eurytione. Soon after, a plague broke out at Corinth, and the oracle declared that it would not cease until the souls of the maidens were propitiated and a sanctuary erected to Athena Hellotis.

ATYS. After Atys was murdered by the father of Cybele, Phrygia was visited by an epidemic and famine (Diod. 3. 58).

CHRYSES, when his offer of ransom was refused and he suffered insult from Agamemnon, he prayed to Apollo for revenge, and the god sent a plague into the camp of the Greeks (Hom. *Il.* 1. 10).

DEMARMENUS was an Eretrian fisherman, who dragged up the shoulder bone of Pelops which had been lost with the ship carrying it from Elis to Troy. On the advice of the Delphic oracle, he restored the bone to the Eleians to avert a plague which was ravaging the country, and they appointed him guardian of the venerable relic (Paus. 5. 13.3).

DEMIPHON, king of Phlagusa, in order to avert a pestilence, was commanded by an oracle to sacrifice a noble maiden every year.

ENTORIA. When the Romans were visited by a plague, they were told by the Delphic oracle that the plague was a punishment for the murder of Entoria's father. Latatius Catulus caused a temple to be erected to Cronus on the Tarpeian rock, and in it an altar with four faces (Plut. *Paral.Gr.et Rom.* 9). (See also under INTOXICATION)

HESIONE. When Troy was visited by a plague and a monster on account of Laomedon's breach of promise, he chained his daughter, Hesione, to a rock in accordance with the command from an oracle, where she was supposed to be devoured by wild beasts. She was rescued by Heracles.

HYACINTHUS, a Lacedaemonian, in compliance with an oracle, went to Athens and caused his daughters to be sacrificed on the tomb of Cyclops Geraestus for the purpose of delivering the city from famine and plague.

IDOMENEUS. When he sacrificed his son in accordance with a promise to Poseidon, Crete was visited by a plague, and the Cretans expelled Idomeneus.

MELANIPPUS. He profaned the temple of Artemis in Patrae by having intercourse with one of her priestesses, Comaetho. As a consequence they were put to death, and plague and famine visited the whole of Achaia. The oracle of Delphi revealed the cause of these calamities and ordered the inhabitants to sacrifice to Artemis every year the handsomest youth and loveliest maiden (Paus. 7. 10.2).

MENIPPE and her sister, Metioche, daughters of Orion, in order to avert a plague in Aonia, where they lived, offered themselves as a sacrifice (in response to an oracle) (Ov. *Met.* 13. 685).

OEDIPUS. As a result of his unknowingly incestuous marriage to his mother, a plague came on Thebes. Oedipus, the king, pronounced a curse on the unknown murderer of Laius, whom an oracle demanded to be expelled. Tiresias, the seer, revealed that Oedipus himself was both the parricide and the husband of his own mother.

PAN LYTERIUS, "the deliverer," was a surname under which Pan had a sanctuary at Troezen, because he was believed, during a plague, to have revealed in dreams the proper remedy against the disease (Paus. 2. 35.5).

PRAXITHEA and her sisters, Theope and Eubule, daughters of Leos, were sacrificed by their father at the direction of the Delphic oracle to halt a plague or famine at Athens.

TIRESIAS (TEIRESIAS) was the famous Theban soothsayer. The oracle connected with his tomb lost its power and became silent at the time of the Orchomenian plague.

Plank

ODYSSEUS escaped drowning when his last ship was destroyed by Zeus by means of its mast and planks, on which he floated to safety.

Plectrum

TERPSICHORE, the Muse of choral dance and song, appears with the lyre and plectrum.

Plenty, see Abundance

Plow

ANDROGEUS was worshipped under the name of Eurygyes, he who plows or possesses extensive fields.

ATHENA. As protectress of agriculture, she is represented as the inventor of the plow.

BUTES, son of Teleon, was renowned as an Athenian plowman.

ECHETLUS was a mysterious being who appeared in the garb of a rustic among the Greeks at the battle of Marathon and slew many of the barbarians with his plow. After the battle he was not to be found, and an oracle commanded the Greeks to worship the hero with the plow (Paus. 1. 15.4, 32.4).

JASON. One of the tasks Aeetes imposed on him in exchange for the golden fleece was the yoking of brazen-footed and fire-breathing bulls to a plow.

MYRMEX was an Athenian maiden who was beloved by Athena. When the goddess invented the plow, Myrmex boastfully pretended to have made the discovery herself, whereupon she was metamorphosed into an ant.

ODYSSEUS did not want to join the Greeks against Troy (Hom. *Od.* 24. 116). When Palamedes came to persuade him, Odysseus pretended to be mad: he yoked an ass and an ox to a plow and began to sow salt. Palamedes, to test him, placed the infant Telemachus before the plow, whereupon the father could not continue the deception.

ROMULUS. When he marked the boundary of Rome, he yoked a bullock and a heifer to a plow and drew a deep furrow around the foot of the Palatine. The plow was carried over the spaces where the gates were to be, so that nothing unclean could ever enter the city, as the track of the plow was holy.

SABAZIUS, a Phrygian agricultural divinity and son of Rhea or Cybele, was said to be the first to yoke oxen to the plow (Diod. 4. 4).

TRIPTOLEMUS, a son of Celeus and Metaneira, was a favorite of Demeter and inventor of the plow.

Plumb Line

DAEDALUS was the reputed inventor of the plumb line.

Poetry

APOLLO was god of poetry.

ARETHUSA was the divinity who inspired pastoral poetry.

ARION is called the inventor of the dithyrambic poetry (Herod. 1. 23).

CALLIOPE, the Muse of epic poetry, appears with a tablet and stylus and sometimes with a roll of paper.

CHARITES. Poetry was the art especially favored by the Charites, or Graces.

CHRYSOTHEMIS, son of Carmanor, was a priest of Apollo at Tarrha in Crete. He is said to have been a poet and to have won the first victory in the Pythian games by a hymn to Apollo (Paus. 10. 7.2).

DAPHNIS, shepherd son of Hermes, was a Sicilian hero, to whom the invention of bucolic poetry is ascribed.

ERATO, the Muse of erotic poetry and mimic imitation, appears often with the lyre.

EUTERPE, the Muse of lyric poetry, appears with a flute.

IAMBE, daughter of Pan and Echo, was believed to have given the name to iambic poetry, for some say that she cheered Demeter by a dance in the iambic metre.

MUSES. The Muses were divinities who presided over the different kinds of poetry.

NYMPHS. Many of the nymphs presided over waters or springs which were believed to inspire those who drank from them. Hence the nymphs themselves were thought to be endowed with prophetic or oracular power, to inspire men with the same, and to confer upon them the gift of poetry (Paus. 4. 27.2, 9. 3.5, 34.3; Plut. *Aristid.* 11; Theocrit. 7. 92).

OLEN was a mythical personage, who is represented as the earliest Greek lyric poet and the first author of sacred hymns in hexameter verse.

PALAMEDES, son of Nauplius, was described by the tragic poets as a poet.

PHANOTHEA was the wife of Icarius and inventor of the hexameter (Clem. Alex. *Strom.* 1. 366).

PHEMONOE, a mythical Greek poetess of the ante-Homeric period, was said to have been the daughter of Apollo and the first priestess at Delphi, and the inventor of the hexameter verse (Paus. 10. 5.7, 6.7; Strab. 9. 419; Plin. *H.N.* 7. 57; Clem. Alex. *Strom.* 1. 323, 334).

THALIA, the Muse of comedy and of merry or idyllic poetry, appears with the comic mask, a shepherd's staff, or a wreath of ivy.

Poison

CERBERUS. When Heracles brought him to the upper world, the multiheaded dog could not stand the light and spat forth the poisonous plant called aconitum.

HARCALO was a man famous for his knowledge of poisons and his resistance to them.

HERACLES. About to sacrifice to Zeus, he sent his companion Lichas to fetch a white garment which his wife Deianeira, in order to preserve Heracles' love as directed, had steeped in a preparation made from the blood of Nessus, the centaur. When Heracles put on the garment, he was consumed in pain by the poisoned blood. In his agony, he threw Lichas into the sea. Deianeira, upon seeing what she had unwittingly done, hanged herself. (See also HYDRA)

HYDRA. From the wounds of its severed heads poison came forth, and Heracles dipped his arrows in the poison. Thereafter the arrows had no antidote when one was struck.

ILUS was a son of Mermerus. When Odysseus came to him in Ephyra to fetch poison for his arrows, Ilus refused it from fear of vengeance of the gods (Hom. *Od.* 1. 259, 2. 328; Strab. 8. 338).

ION, upon growing up, was thought by his mother, Creusa, to be a son to her husband by a former lover. She tried to poison the youth by a cup of venomous blood from a dragon, but her object was discovered when Ion, before drinking, poured a libation to the gods. A pigeon drank of it and died on the spot.

LICHAS, an attendant of Heracles, brought to his master the deadly garment prepared by Deianeira, and as a punishment was thrown by Heracles into the sea, from which the Lichadian islands, between Euboea and the coast of Locris were believed to have derived their name (Ov. *Met.* 9. 155, 211; Strab. 9. 426, 10. 447).

MEDEA. When Jason deserted her for Creon's daughter, Glauce (Creusa), she sent to the bride a poisoned garment and diadem. When Glauce put these on, she and her father were consumed by the poisonous fire which issued from the vestment. Later, when Medea was the wife of Aegeus, Theseus came to Athens. When Medea recognized Theseus, she laid a plot for poisoning him at a banquet to which he was invited, but she failed in the attempt and was forced to flee.

MERMERUS, son of Pheres and grandson of Jason and Medea, was skilled in the art of preparing poison (Hom. *Od.* 1. 260).

NESSUS, the centaur, was killed with a poisoned arrow by Heracles for attempting to steal Deianeira from the hero. The centaur in turn gave Deianeira a tunic dipped in the poisoned blood, telling her that it was a charm to guarantee fidelity. Heracles' death was brought about when he put on the poisoned garment.

ODYSSEUS went to Thesprotian Ephyra to fetch from Ilus poison for his arrows, but as he could not get it there he obtained it from Anchialus of Taphus (Hom. *Od.* 1. 259).

PHARMACEIA was a nymph of a well with poisonous powers, near the river Ilissus in Attica.

Pole

POLYPHEMUS. In order to escape from the cave of the Cyclops, Odysseus contrived to make him drunk with wine and then with a burning pole deprived him of his one eye.

Pomegranate

ASCALAPHUS. When Pluto gave Persephone permission to return to the upper world, Ascalaphus declared that she had eaten part of a pomegranate, thereby causing her to have to remain in Hades for half of each year.

PERSEPHONE. Because she ate part of a pomegranate given to her by Hades, she was compelled to spend part of every year in the underworld.

Pool, see Well

Poplar

AEGLE (AEGIALE). In her grief at the death of her brother, Phaethon, she and her sisters were changed into poplars (Ov. *Met.* 1. 755).

HELIADES, sisters of Phaethon, were so grieved by his death that they were changed into poplar trees.

HERACLES. The white poplar was sacred to him.

LEUCE, a nymph, daughter of Oceanus, was carried off by Pluto; after her death she was changed into a white poplar in Elysium.

Poppy

APHRODITE. The poppy was sacred to her.

ARTEMIS. The poppy was sacred to her.

DEMETER. The poppy was sacred to her.

MANIA was an ancient and formidable Italian, probably Etruscan, divinity of the lower world. Boys are said to have been sacrificed to her on behalf of the families to which they belonged. The consul Junius Brutus abolished the human sacrifices and substituted garlic and the heads of poppies.

MECON was the name of an Athenian whom Demeter loved and who was metamorphosed into a poppy plant (Callim. *Hymn.in Cer.* 45; Theocrit. 7).

Potter's Wheel

HYPERBIUS, a mythical artist of Corinth, was said to have been the inventor of the potter's wheel (Paus. 1. 26.3; Plin. *H.N.* 7. 56).

PERDIX, nephew of Daedalus, was the inventor of the potter's wheel.

Prayer

CYBELE ANTAEA was a surname suggesting a goddess whom man may approach in prayer.

DEMETER ANTAEA. As CYBELE ANTAEA.

RHEA ANTAEA. As CYBELE ANTAEA.

Pregnancy

AEGERIA (EGERIA), one of the Camenae in Roman mythology, was regarded as a prophetic divinity and also as the giver of life, whence she was invoked by pregnant women.

Prison

ANTIOPE was imprisoned by Lycus, her uncle, during which time she gave birth to twin sons, Amphion and Zethus (Apollod. 3. 5.5).

DANAE, daughter of Acrisius, was shut up by her father in a subterranean apartment, when he learned from an oracle that if she bore a son, he would kill his grandfather.

MELAMPUS. For attempting to steal the cattle of Iphicles for his brother to give to Neleus in exchange for the hand of Pero, he was thrown into prison but released when he demonstrated his prophetic powers. From the woodworms in the walls of the prison he knew the building would collapse and demanded to be let out.

Promiscuity

JUNO despised unchastity and the inordinate love of sexual pleasures.

Property

HERMES CTESIUS was a surname of Hermes referring to him as protector of property (Paus. 1. 31.2).

JUPITER HERCIUS was a surname of Jupiter at Rome as protector of property (from *herctum,* property).

JUPITER TERMINUS was a surname of Jupiter at Rome as protector of boundaries, not only of personal property but also of the state.

ZEUS CTESIUS was a surname describing Zeus as a protector of property, at Phlyus (Athen. 11. 473).

Prophecy

ABARIS was a priest of Apollo who because of his oracles was held in high esteem in Greece. He traveled about Greece, carrying with him an arrow, as symbol of Apollo, and gave prophecies. Some say that he rode the arrow through the air.

AEGERIA (EGERIA) (See CAMENAE)

ALBUNEA was a prophetic nymph or Sibyl to whom in the neighborhood of Tibur a grove was consecrated.

ALCMAON had prophetic powers ascribed to him.

AMPHIARAUS, son of Oicleus and father of Alcmaon, had prophetic insight. He was one of the Argonauts.

ANCHISES was believed to have prophetic powers and provided wise counsel on the voyage of Aeneas.

ANIUS was the son of Apollo and Rhoeo. Having been cast adrift in a chest by her father, Staphylus, Rhoeo floated to Delos, where she gave birth to Anius. She placed the child on the altar of Apollo, praying that the god would save the child. Apollo accordingly concealed the boy and taught him the art of prophecy (Diod. 5. 62).

ANTEVORTA (See CAMENAE)

APOLLO exercised his power of prophecy through his numerous oracles, especially the one at Delphi.

APOLLO LOXIAS. This surname, deriving from his intricate and ambiguous oracles, describes the god as the prophet or interpreter of Zeus (Herod. 1. 91, 8. 136; Aeschyl. *Eum.* 19; Aristoph. *Plut.* 8).

ARISTAEUS learned from Cheiron and the Muses the arts of healing and prophecy.

ASBOLUS was a centaur who could prophesy from the flight of birds.

BONA DEA was a Roman divinity worshipped from earliest times as a chaste and prophetic divinity. She was also called Fauna, Fatua, or Oma.

BRANCHUS, son of Apollo, was endowed by his father with prophetic powers, which he exercised at Didyma, near Miletus.

BRIZO was a prophetic goddess of Delos, who sent dreams and revealed their meaning to men.

CAMENAE were Roman divinities whose name is connected with *carmen* (an oracle or prophecy). Their names were Antevorta, Postvorta, Carmenata, and Aegeria. (See also CARMENATA ANTEVORTA)

CARMENATA (See CAMENAE)

CARMENATA ANTEVORTA was a surname describing the Roman goddess Carmenata as looking into the future. Carmenata Postverta, or Postvorta, described her as turning backward at the past, which she revealed to poets and other mortals. In like manner, the prophetic power with which she looked into the future is indicated by Antevorta, Prorsa (Proversa) and Porrima. Poets, however, have personified these attributes of Carmenata and thus described them as companions of the goddess (Ov. *Fast.* 1. 633; Gell. 16. 16).

CARMENATA PORRIMA (See CARMENATA ANTEVORTA)

CARMENATA PRORSA (PROVERSA) (See CARMENATA ANTEVORTA)

CASSANDRA, daughter of Priam and Hecuba, was renowned for her prophetic powers. When she grew up, she spent the night in the temple of Apollo, who approached her. When she resisted, he punished her by causing her prophecies, though true, to be disbelieved by men. (See also HELENUS)

CHEIRON, the centaur, was renowned for his skill in the art of prophecy.

CREUSA, wife of Aeneas, became separated from him at the fall of Troy. When he went to search for her, she appeared to him as a shade and revealed to him his future fate.

DION. Apollo conferred on his three daughters, Orphe, Lyco, and Carya, the gift of prophecy on the condition that they not betray the gods nor search for forbidden things. This gift was earned by Dion's hospitality to the god.

DIONYSUS was regarded as a god who had the power of revealing the future to man by oracles. He is said to have had as great a share in the Delphic oracle as Apollo (Eurip. *Bacch.* 300), and he himself had an oracle in Thrace (Paus. 9. 30.5).

ERATO was a nymph who became a prophetic priestess of the Arcadian Pan (Paus. 8. 27.9).

FATUA (See BONA DEA)

FAUNA (FAULA) (See BONA DEA)

FAUNUS in Italy was worshipped as an oracular and prophetic divinity.

GLAUCUS, the marine deity, visited once a year all the coasts and islands of Greece, accompanied by marine monsters, and gave prophecies (Paus. 9. 22.6). He was believed to dwell in Delos, where he gave oracles. His prophetic power was said to be greater even than that of Apollo.

HELENUS, son of Priam and Hecuba, once was left in the temple of the Thymbraean Apollo as a child with his sister Cassandra. As they fell asleep, snakes came and cleaned their ears, whereby they acquired the gift of prophecy. Helenus was a skillful observer of auguries and knew the counsel of the gods (Hom. *Il.* 6. 76, 7. 44; Apollod. 3. 12.5).

HERA was able to confer the power of prophecy (Hom. *Il.* 19. 407).

HERMES. According to some, Apollo refused to teach Hermes the art of prophecy and referred him to the three sisters (Muses) dwelling on Mt. Parnassus.

IAMUS, son of Apollo and Evadne, was initiated in the art of prophecy by his father and was regarded as the ancestor of the famous family of seers, the Iamidae at Olympia (Paus. 6. 2.3; Pind. *Ol.* 6. 43; Cic. *De Div.* 1. 41).

LAVINIA was a daughter of Anius who married Aeneas and followed him to Italy. Like her father, she was endowed with prophetic powers (Dionys. 1. 59).

MANTO was a daughter of the Theban soothsayer, Tiresias. She herself was a prophetess, first of the Ismenian Apollo at Thebes, where monuments of her existed (Paus. 9. 10.3), and subsequently of the Delphian and Clarian Apollo. Another Manto was a daughter of Heracles and likewise was a prophetess.

MARS was looked upon as a god with prophetic powers. In the neighborhood of Reate there had been a very ancient oracle of the god (Dionys. 1. 41), in which the future was revealed through a woodpecker (*picus*), which was sacred to him.

MELAMPUS, son of Amythaon, was looked upon by the ancients as the first mortal endowed with prophetic powers. He is said to have acquired his gift of prophecy in the following way: An oak tree before his house in Pylos contained a serpent's nest, and his servants killed the old serpents, but Melampus reared the young ones. One day after they had grown up and Melampus was asleep, they approached from both sides and cleaned his ears with their tongues. When he awoke, he was amazed to find that he could understand the language of the birds and that with their assistance he could foretell the future. He also acquired the power of prophesying from the victims which were offered to the gods, and, after having an interview with Apollo on the banks of the Alpheius, he became a most renowned soothsayer (Apollod. 1. 9.11).

MOIRAE. Being goddesses of fate, they must necessarily know the future, which at times they reveal and thus become prophetic divinities (Ov. *Met.* 8. 454; Ov. *Trist.* 5. 3.25; Tibull. 1. 8.1; 4. 5.3; Catull. 64.307).

MOPSUS, son of Ampyx (Ampycus), was the famous prophet of the Argonauts.

MUSES had prophetic power because they were connected with Apollo, the prophetic god of Delphi. Hence, they instructed Aristaeus in the art of prophecy (Apollon. Rhod. 2. 512).

NEREUS, son of Pontus and Gaea, was believed, like other marine divinities, to have the power of prophesying.

NYMPHS. Those who inhabited bodies of water were thought to be endowed with prophetic powers and to inspire those who drank from them.

OENONE, wife of Paris, possessed prophetic powers. She cautioned Paris not to sail to the country of Helen; but even though he did not follow her advice (Hom. *Il.* 5. 64), she promised to heal him if he were wounded, as that was the only aid she could give him (Apollod. 3. 12.6). She also predicted the fall of Troy.

OLEN was a mythical personage closely related with the worship of Apollo, of whom, in one legend, he was made the prophet.

OMA (See BONA DEA)

PAN was believed to be possessed of prophetic powers and to have even instructed Apollo in this art (Apollod. 1. 4.1).

PARNASSUS, son of Cleopompus or Poseidon, was the inventor of the art of foretelling the future from the flight of birds (Paus. 10. 6.1).

PICUS, a Latin prophetic divinity, son of Saturn or Sterculus, was often called the first king of Italy.

POLYMESTOR. After Hecuba had murdered his two sons and gouged out his eyes, he prophesied that she would be metamorphosed into a she-dog and leap into the sea at a place called Cynosema (Thuc. 8. 104).

POLYXO, the nurse of Hypsipyle in Lemnos, was celebrated as a prophetess (Apollon. Rhod. 1. 668; Val.Flacc. 2. 316).

POSTVORTA (See CAMENAE)

PRIAPUS, son of Dionysus and Aphrodite, was believed to be possessed of prophetic powers.

PROMETHEUS taught men the art of prophecy. Later he deprived them of their knowledge of the future and gave them hope instead (Aeschyl. *Prom.* 248). Io came to him, and he foretold the wanderings and sufferings which were yet in store for her, as well as her final relief (Aeschyl. *Prom.* 703). Prometheus also knew that by a certain woman Zeus would beget a son who was to dethrone his father, but Prometheus refused to reveal the decree of fate, whereupon Zeus by a thunderbolt sent Prometheus together with the rock to which he was chained into Tartarus (Hor. *Carm.* 2. 18, 35).

PROTEUS, the prophetic old man of the sea, occurs in the earliest legends as a subject of Poseidon (Hom. *Od.* 4. 365, 385, 400; Virg. *Georg.* 4. 392; Theocrit. 2. 58; Hor. *Carm.* 1. 2.7; Philostr. *Imag.* 2. 17). Anyone wishing to compel him to foretell the future was obliged to catch hold of him at the time he kept his usual form, for he had the power of assuming every possible shape in order to escape the necessity of prophesying, but whenever he saw that his endeavors were in vain, he resumed his usual appearance and told the truth (Hom. *Od.* 4. 410, 455; Ov. *Ars Am.* 1. 761; Ov. *Fast.* 1. 369; Philostr. *Vit.Apoll.* 1. 4).

QUERQUETULANAE, nymphs presiding over the green oak forests near the *porta querquetularia*, or *querquetulana*, were believed to be possessed of prophetic powers.

SIBYLLA was the name by which several prophetic women are designated who occurred in various countries and at different times in antiquity. The first Sibyl, from whom all the rest are said to have derived their name, is said to have been a daughter of Dardanus and Neso. Ten Sibyls are mentioned: the Babylonian, the Libyan, the Delphian, the Cimmerian, the Erythraean, the Samian, the Cumaean, the Hellespontian or Trojan, the Phrygian, and the Tiburtian.

SILENUS (SEILENUS), one of the satyrs, a

son of Hermes or Pan and a nymph, was conceived of as an inspired prophet, who knew all the past and the most distant future. When he was drunk and asleep, he was in the power of mortals who might compel him to prophesy and sing by surrounding him with chains of flowers (Philostr. *Imag.* 1. 22; Philostr. *Vit.Apoll.* 6. 27; Ov. *Met.* 11. 91).

SPHRAGITIDES was a surname of a class of prophetic nymphs on Mt. Cithaeron in Boeotia, where they had a grotto (Plut. *Aristid.* 9; Paus. 9. 3; Plut. *Quaest.Conviv.* 1. 10).

THEMIS was a daughter of Uranus and Gaea. She is described as an ancient prophetic divinity and is said to have been in possession of the Delphic oracle after Gaea and before Apollo (Ov. *Met.* 1. 321; 4. 642; Apollon.Rhod. 4. 800; Apollod. 1. 4.1; Paus. 10. 5.3.).

TIRESIAS (TEIRESIAS) was a son of Everes (or Phorbas) and Chariclo and one of the most renowned soothsayers in antiquity. He was blind from an early age, and one account says that his blindness came as a result of seeing Athena while she was bathing. Chariclo prayed to Athena to restore his sight, but as the goddess was unable to do this, she conferred upon him the power to understand the voices of birds. Another account says that he was blinded by Hera for deciding an argument between Zeus and Hera in favor of Zeus. Hera blinded him, but Zeus gave him the power of prophecy. In the war of the Seven against Thebes, he declared that Thebes would be victorious if Menoeceus would sacrifice himself (Apollod. 3. 6.7); and during the war of the Epigoni, when the Thebans had been defeated, he advised them to commence negotiations of peace and to avail themselves of the opportunity thus afforded them to take flight.

ZEUS was the original source of all prophetic power and from whom all prophetic signs and sounds proceeded (Hom. *Il.* 8. 250; comp. Aeschyl. *Eum.* 19; Callim. *Hymn.in Jov.* 69).

ZEUS DODONAIS. At Dodona, Zeus was mainly a prophetic god.

Propitiation, see Atonement

Prosperity

ARTEMIS. The mortal upon whom she looked graciously was prosperous in his fields and flocks, his household was thriving, and he died in old age (Callim. *Hymn.in Dian.* 129).

HECATE was a mysterious divinity who bestowed prosperity to youth and to flocks of cattle.

SALUS was the personification of health, prosperity, and the public welfare among the Romans. She was worshipped publicly on the 30th of April (Ov. *Fast.* 3. 881).

Protector, see Guardian

Prostitute

JUNO. A law of Numa ordained that a prostitute should not touch the altar of Juno, and that if she had done so, she should, with dishevelled hair, offer a female lamb to Juno (Gell. 4. 3).

VENUS. Courtesans regarded the 23rd of April as a holiday of their own and on that day worshipped Venus in a temple outside Rome (Ov. *Fast.* 4. 865).

Prudence

CATIUS was a Roman divinity who was invoked under the name of *divus Catius pater* to grant prudence and thoughtfulness to children at the time when their consciousness was beginning to awaken (August. 4. 21).

HERMES. As the messenger god, he was also god of prudence and skill in all relations of social intercourse (Hom. *Il.* 20. 35; 24. 282; Hom. *Od.* 2. 38).

METIS was the personification of prudence. She was a daughter of Oceanus and Tethys.

Pruning Knife

SATURN. His statue held in its hand a crooked pruning knife (Virg. *Aen.* 7. 179; Mart. 11. 6.1).

Public Welfare

SALUS was the personification of health, prosperity, and public welfare among the Romans. She was worshipped publicly on the 30th of April (Ov. *Fast.* 3. 881).

Pumice

BATTUS violated a promise to Hermes that he would not reveal the theft of Admetus' cattle and so was changed into a pumice stone.

Punishment

ATE was avenger of evil deeds and inflicter of just punishments upon the offenders and their posterity (Aeschyl. *Choeph.* 381).

Purification

AMPHITRYON was purified of his accidental slaying of Electryon by his uncle, Creon.

CARMANOR, a Cretan of Tarrha, was said to have received and purified Apollo and Artemis after they had slain the monster Python.

CIRCE subsequently purified Jason and the Argonauts for the murder of Absyrtus, brother of Medea.

DEIPHOBUS, son of Hippolytus at Amyclae, purified Heracles after the murder of Iphitus (Apollod. 2. 6.2; Diod. 4. 31).

FEBRUUS was the Italian divinity whose name is connected with *februare* (to purify) and *februae* (purification) (Varr. *De Ling.Lat.* 6. 13; Ov. *Fast.* 2. 31).

HECATE was regarded as the goddess of purifications.

HERACLES was initiated by Eumolpus into the Eleusinian mysteries in order to purify him from the murder of the centaurs. (See also DEIPHOBUS and NELEUS).

LUA was a goddess at Rome who presided over things which were purified by lustrations.

NELEUS. When Heracles had killed Iphitus, he went to Neleus to be purified, but Neleus, who was a friend of Eurytus, the father of Iphitus, refused to purify him (Diod. 4. 31).

PELEUS. After being exiled from Aegina, he went to Phthia in Thessaly, where he was purified for the murder of his step-brother by Eurytion (Hom. *Il.* 16. 175; Apollod. 3. 13.1). After accidentally killing Eurytion during the Calydonian Boar Hunt, he fled from Phthia to Iolcus, where he was again purified by Acastus (Apollod. 3. 12.2).

PHYTALUS. When Theseus killed Sinis the robber on the Isthmus of Corinth, he tore him apart by bending fir trees together, tying the victim, and then letting the trees spring back—a device the robber had used on his victims. Theseus then caused himself to be purified by Phytalus at the altar of Zeus Meilichios, because Theseus was related to Sinis (Paus. 1. 37.3); or, according to others, he propitiated the spirit of Sinis by instituting in his honor the Isthmian games (Plut. *Thes.* 25).

POEMANDER, son of Chaeresilaus, inadvertently killed his own son and was purified by Elephenor.

POLYIDES, the celebrated soothsayer at Corinth, purified Alcathous when he murdered his son, Callipolis, at Megara (Apollod. 3. 3.1).

TYDEUS, son of Oeneus and Periboea, was purified by Adrastus at Argos, where he fled after the murder of one of his relatives.

VENUS CLOACINA (CLUACINA) was a surname of Venus under which she is mentioned in Rome from very early times (Liv. 3. 48). The name is probably best explained by the purification rites the forces of Tatius and Romulus undertook when the Sabine women prevented them from bloodshed. They purified themselves with myrtle branches, and the spot was afterwards the site of a temple of Venus Cloacina.

ZEUS CATHARSIUS, "the purifier" or "atoner," was a name under which Zeus, in conjunction with Nike, had a temple at Olympia (Paus. 5. 14.6).

Purse

HERMES was represented sometimes as holding a purse in his hands.

MERCURIUS MALEVOLUS, "the ill-willed," was a surname under which Mercury had a statue in what was called the *vicus sobrius*. This statue had a purse in its hand to indicate his function (commerce). His festival was celebrated on the 25th of May.

Pyre, see Immolation

Quail

ASTERIA, daughter of Ceus, in order to escape the embraces of Zeus, was metamorphosed into a quail (Apollod. 1. 2.2).

HERACLES. The quail was sacred to him.

LETO. Zeus changed her into a quail, and in this state she arrived at the floating island of Delos, which was afterwards called Ortygia. There she gave birth to Apollo and Artemis.

Quarrel

AGAMEMNON. An oracle said that Troy would fall when the two most distinguished among the Greeks should quarrel. This occurred in the tenth year of the war when Agamemnon and Achilles quarreled over Breseis, who had fallen to Achilles as part of the spoils when Lyrnessus was taken. Agamemnon, upon losing his own concubine, appropriated Briseis.

AMYCUS. On his tomb grew a species of laurel (*Laurus insana*) which when taken on shipboard caused quarreling among the crew and general havoc till thrown overboard (Plin. *H.N.* 16. 89).

Quiver

ARTEMIS was represented carrying a quiver.

EROS was represented carrying a golden quiver.

MERIONES. When Diomedes chose Odysseus for his companion on the exploring expedition to the Trojan camp, Meriones gave the latter his bow, quiver, sword, and famous helmet (Hom. *Il.* 10. 662).

Race

AJAX (the Lesser) contended in a footrace with Odysseus and Antilochus at the funeral games of Patroclus, but Athena, who favored Odysseus, caused Ajax to stumble and fall.

ALEXIDAMUS. Antaeus, a king of Irasa, promised his daughter, Alceis (Barce) to whoever should conquer in the footrace. Alexidamus won the prize (Pind. *Pyth.* 9. 183).

ATALANTA (ATALANTE). When her father desired that she marry, she made it the condition that every suitor who wanted to win her should first contend with her in a footrace. If he conquered her, she would marry him, but if he lost, he was to be put to death by her. Many suitors lost, since Atalanta was extremely fleet of foot. Eventually Meilanion (or Hippomenes) won the race by the device of throwing golden apples in her path, which she stopped to pick up, causing her to delay and thus lose the race.

CHLORIS, daughter of Amphion and Niobe, according to an Olympian legend, once gained the prize during a footrace at the festival of Hera at Olympia (Paus. 5. 16.3).

ENDYMION, king of Elis, caused his sons to engage in the race course at Olympia and promised the victor the succession to his kingdom. Epeius thus conquered his brothers and succeeded Endymion as king of Elis.

ERGINUS. Although ridiculed for having gray hair at an early age, he still conquered the sons of Boreas in the footrace at the funeral games of Thoas in Lemnos (Pind. *Ol.* 4. 29).

ETEOCLES, son of Iphis, was said to have won a prize in the footrace at the Nemean games (Apollod. 3. 6.4, 8).

HERACLES was one of the Idaean Dactyls who cared for the infant Zeus at Olympia. He contended with his brother Dactyls in a footrace and adorned the victor with a wreath of olive. In this manner he is said to have founded the Olympian games (Paus. 5. 7.4).

ODYSSEUS. According to some, he gained Penelope by conquering his competitors in a footrace (Apollod. 3. 10.9; Paus. 3. 12.2).

OEONUS, son of Lycimnius of Midea in Argolis, was the first victor at Olympia in the footrace (Pind. *Ol.* 11. 76; Apollod. 2. 7.3; Paus. 3. 15.3).

Radiance

APOLLO AEGLETES was a surname of Apollo meaning radiant.

Raft

ODYSSEUS. When the gods commanded Calypso to dismiss Odysseus, she taught him to build a raft, on which he left the island (Hom. *Od.* 5. 140, 234, 263).

Rain

ANTAEUS. It was believed that whenever a piece of the hill tomb of Antaeus was removed, the rain would fall until the hole was filled up again.

HYADES. When this constellation rose simultaneously with the sun, rainy and stormy weather was forecast. The name of the constellation is derived from the Greek word for rain.

JUPITER. When Italy needed rain, the help of Jupiter was sought by a sacrifice called *aquilicium* (Tertull. *Apol.* 40).

JUPITER PLUVIUS, "the sender of rain," was a surname of Jupiter among the Romans, and sacrifices were offered to him under this name during protracted droughts.

ORION. The rising and the setting of the constellation Orion were believed to be accompanied by storms and rain.

TELCHINES were a group of mysterious beings described as sorcerers and envious daemons, and they had the power to bring on hail, rain, and snow, and to assume any form they pleased (Diod. 5. 55).

ZEUS HYES, "the moist or fertilizing god," was a surname of Zeus as the sender of rain.

ZEUS HYETIUS, "the moist or fertilizing god," was a surname of Zeus as the sender of rain. Under this name he had an altar at Argos and a statue in the grove of Trophonius near Lebadeia (Paus. 2. 19.5, 9. 39.3).

ZEUS OMBRIUS, "the rain-giver" was a surname of Zeus under which he had an altar on Mt. Hymettus in Attica (Paus. 1. 32.3; comp. Hes. *Op. et D.* 587, 620).

Rainbow

IRIS was the goddess of the rainbow, which was regarded as the swift minister of the gods. She was originally thought to be the personification of the rainbow. Some writers regarded the rainbow as the road on which Iris traveled, which therefore appeared only when she needed it and vanished as soon as it was no longer needed.

Rake

ATHENA. As protectress of agriculture, she is represented as the inventor of the rake.

Ram

AGAMEDES. At the location of the oracle of his brother Trophonius, those who consulted the oracle first offered a ram to Agamedes.

APHRODITE PANDEMOS. She was represented at Elis by Scopas as riding on a ram (Paus. 6. 25.2).

ATHENA. Sacrifices to her consisted of bulls, rams, and cows.

DIONYSUS. Zeus, in order to protect the child Dionysus, changed him into a ram and carried him to the nymphs of Mt. Nysa, who brought him up in a cave. The animal most commonly sacrificed to him was a ram (Virg. *Georg.* 2. 380, 395; Ov. *Fast.* 1. 357).

EROS. The ram was sacred to him.

HELIOS. Sacrifices to the sun god consisted of white rams.

HERACLES. Sacrifices offered to him consisted of rams.

ICARIUS. For his hospitality to Dionysus he was taught by the god the cultivation of the vine. Once he killed a ram for having injured his vines, made a bag of its skin and then performed a dance on it.

JUPITER. Rams were sacrificed to Jupiter on the ides of every month. Another sacrifice consisting of a ram was offered to him in the regia at the beginning of every week.

MEDEA (MEDEIA). In order to take vengeance on Pelias for all the crimes he had committed against Jason, she persuaded the daughters of Pelias to cut their father into pieces and boil his limbs in a cauldron, thus supposedly making him young again. She had demonstrated the process earlier by changing a ram into a lamb. But Pelias remained dead.

OENOMAUS, son of Ares, contested with suitors of his daughter, Hippodameia, in a chariot race, which if he won he killed the suitor. He always first sacrificed a ram to Zeus and then hastened with his swift chariot and four horses, guided by Myrtilus, after the suitor, always overtaking and slaying him.

PAN visited Selene, the moon goddess, in the shape of a white ram (Virg. *Georg.* 3. 391). Sacrifices to him consisted of rams.

PELOPS. An annual sacrifice to him in Elis consisted of a black ram.

PHRIXUS was a son of Athamas and Nephele. In consequence of the intrigues of his stepmother, Ino, he was to be sacrificed to Zeus; but Nephele removed him and Helle, his sister, and the two of them rode away through the air on the ram with the golden fleece. Helle lost her hold and fell into the sea. Phrixus, upon arrival in Colchis, sacrificed the ram to Zeus Phyxius or Laphystius (Paus. 1. 24.2) and gave its skin to king Aeetes, who fastened it to an oak tree in the grove of Ares.

POSEIDON carried off Theophane, a daughter of Bisaltes, because of her extraordinary beauty and because she was beleaguered by lovers. She was followed by the lovers to the isle of Crinissa, where Poseidon changed her into a sheep and himself into a ram to elude them. Thus, he became by her the father of the ram with the golden fleece, which carried Phrixus to Colchis. Rams were sacred to Poseidon.

PRIAPUS was the son of Dionysus and Aphrodite and god of the fructifying powers and manifestations of nature. Sacrifices to him included rams.

RHADAMANTHYS. A law ascribed to him said man should not swear by the god but by a goose, a dog, or a ram.

ZEUS was worshipped in the form of a ram as Ammon. Sometimes he was worshipped as a human being with the head of a ram.

Ransom

ANTIPHUS was restored to freedom by payment of a ransom when he was captured by Achilles.

CHRYSES was a priest of Apollo at Chryse, who was insulted by Agamemnon when he offered to ransom his daughter, Astynome (Chryseis).

PRIAM, the famous king of Troy at the time of the Trojan War and son of Laomedon, had his name changed from Podarces (swiftfooted) to Priam, which meant "the ransomed," because he was the only surviving son of Laomedon and was ransomed by his sister, Hesione, after he had fallen into the hands of Heracles (Apollod. 2. 6.4; 3. 12.3). After the death of his son, Hector, Priam, accompanied by Hermes, went to the tent of Achilles to ransom Hector's body for burial and was able to obtain it (Hom. *Il.* 24. 470).

Rashness

ATE was an ancient Greek divinity who led both gods and men to rash and inconsiderate actions and to consequent suffering.

Rattle

HERACLES startled the Stymphalian birds with a brazen rattle given him by Athena and then killed them with arrows (Apollod. 2. 5.6).

Raven

CORONIS. While she was pregnant with Asclepius, her child by Apollo, she became enamored of Ischys, and Apollo sent a raven to spy on her.

Recovery

ACESIUS (See TELESPHORUS)

EUAMERION (See TELESPHORUS)

IASO, daughter of Asclepius and sister of Hygieia, was worshipped as the goddess of recovery (Paus. 1. 34.2; Aristoph. *Plut.* 701).

SALUS (See SOTERIA)

SOTERIA was the personification of safety or recovery (Lat. *Salus)* and was worshipped as a divinity in Greece, with a temple and a statue at Patrae (Paus. 7. 21.2, 24.2).

TELESPHORUS was a boy sometimes represented with Asclepius in statues as the genius of recovery. He was called also Euamerion or Acesius.

Reed

CALAMITES was mentioned by Demosthenes (129) as the hero of the art of surgery, or a being well skilled in handling the reed, which was used in dressing fractured arms and legs.

MIDAS. When he decided in favor of Pan over Apollo in a musical contest, Apollo punished him by changing his ears into those of an ass. Midas concealed them under his Phrygian cap, but the servant who cut his hair discovered them. The secret so much harrassed this man that, as he could not betray it to a human being, he dug a hole in the earth and whispered into it, "King Midas has ass's ears." He then filled up the hole, but on the same spot a reed grew up, which in its whispers betrayed the secret to the world (Ov. *Met.* 11. 146; Aristoph. *Plut.* 287).

SYRINX was an Arcadian nymph, who, being pursued by Pan, fled into the river Ladon and at her own request was metamorphosed into a reed, of which Pan then made his flute (Ov. *Met.* 1. 690).

Reflection

NARCISSUS. When he spurned the love of all those who tried to approach him, he was punished by falling in love with his own image in the water.

Regeneration

PHOENIX was the fabulous bird which, when its life drew to a close, built a nest for itself in Arabia, to which it imparted the power of generation, so that after its death a new phoenix rose out of it. One version of this regeneration story relates that when Phoenix arrived at the age of five hundred years, he built for himself a funeral pyre consisting of spices, settled upon it, and died. Out of the decomposing body he then rose again, and having grown up, he wrapped the remains of his old body up in myrrh, carried them to Heliopolis and burned them (Stat. *Silv.* 2. 4.36).

Rejuvenation

AESON, the father of Jason, by herbs and incantations was made young again by Medea on the return of the Argonauts from Colchis (Ov. *Met.* 7. 162).

HEBE was a divinity who had it in her power to make persons of an advanced age young again (Ov. *Met.* 9. 400).

HYADES were nymphs who nursed Dionysus and were later placed among the stars. They had been old, but were made young again by Medea at the request of Dionysus (Ov. *Met.* 7. 295).

LAERTES, father of Odysseus, after the death of Penelope's suitors, was led out of rural retirement and made young again by Athena.

MEDEA (MEDEIA). In order to take vengeance on Pelias for all the crimes he had committed against Jason, she persuaded the daughters of Pelias to cut their father to pieces and boil his limbs in a cauldron, thus supposedly making him young again. She had demonstrated the process earlier by changing a ram into a lamb. But Pelias remained dead.

PHAON was a boatman at Mitylene and already of an advanced age and of ugly appearance; but on one occasion he very willingly and without accepting payment carried Aphrodite across the sea, for which she gave him youth and beauty. After this, Sappho is said to have fallen in love with him (Lucian *Dial. Mort.* 9).

Repentance

LITAE were daughters of Zeus and the personification of prayers offered up in repentance.

Reservoir

DAEDALUS was credited with the structure of the reservoir from which the Alabon river flowed into the sea.

Resurrection

ALCESTIS, wife of Admetus, who died in his stead, is said to have been brought back from the underworld by Heracles or Persephone.

ANDROGEUS. Propertius (2. 1.64) relates that he was restored to life by Asclepius. He was the son of Minos, king of Crete, and had been killed by the Marathonian bull.

ASCLEPIUS was reputed to have the ability to restore the dead to life; he was said to have learned this power from a serpent.

CAPANEUS was one of those heroes whom Asclepius was believed to have called back to life (Apollod, 3. 10.3).

DIONYSUS. According to one mystical story, his body was cut up and thrown into a cauldron by the Titans, and later he was restored and cured by Rhea or Demeter (Paus. 8. 37.3; Diod. 3. 62).

DIOSCURI. Although they were buried, says Homer, yet they came to life every other day, and they enjoyed honors like those of the gods.

EURYDICE, wife of Orpheus, died from the bite of a serpent and went to the underworld. Orpheus followed his lost wife to the abode of Hades, where the charms of his lyre won back his wife from the most inexorable of all deities; but his prayer was only granted on the condition that he not look back upon his restored wife till they had arrived in the upper world. At the very moment they were about to pass the gate, the anxiety of love overcame him. He looked round to see that Eurydice was following him; only to see her caught back into the infernal regions.

GLAUCUS, son of Minos, died by drowning in a cask of honey. When Polyidus, the soothsayer, divined where the body was, Minos ordered him to restore the boy to life, but Polyidus was unable to perform this miracle. Minos ordered him entombed with the dead boy. In the tomb, Polyidus observed a serpent crawling toward the boy's body and killed it. Another serpent emerged with an herb in its mouth and laid it on the body of the dead snake, whereupon the snake came back to life. Polyidus did this with the dead boy and achieved the same result. He was given rich gifts and allowed to return to his homeland (Apollod. 3. 10.3).

HYMEN (HYMENAEUS). According to Orphic legends, the youth was killed on his wedding day when his house caved in on him. The deceased youth was restored to life by Asclepius (Apollod. 3. 10.3).

LYCURGUS was mentioned among those whom Asclepius called to life again after their death (Apollod. 3. 10.3).

PELOPS was killed by his father, Tantalus, but the gods ordered Hermes to put the limbs of Pelops into a cauldron and thereby restore to him his life and former appearance.

PROTESILAUS. His wife, Laodameia, sued for the favor of the gods to be allowed to converse for only three hours with her husband, who was the first Greek killed in the Trojan War. Her request was granted, and when Protesilaus died a second time, she died with him.

SCYLLA. Heracles is said to have killed her because she had stolen some of the oxen of Geryon, but Phorcys restored her to life.

VIRBIUS was an ancient king of Aricia and a favorite of Diana, who, when he died, called him back to life and entrusted him with the care of the nymph, Aegeria.

Retaliation

POENA, a personification of retaliation, is sometimes mentioned as one being, sometimes in the plural. They belonged to the train of Dice and are akin to the Erinyes (Aeschyl. *Choeph.* 936, 947; Paus. 1. 43.7).

Retreat

JUPITER STATOR was a surname of Jupiter as the stayer of flight. When the Sabines drove the Romans before them and all seemed lost, Romulus prayed to Jupiter Stator, whereupon the Romans took courage and returned again to combat.

Retribution

NEMESIS was the goddess of retribution for evil deeds or undeserved good fortune.

Revelry

BACCHUS, as god of wine, was associated with revelry and feasting.

COMUS was the Roman god of revelry and feasting.

DIONYSUS BROMIUS was a surname of Dionysus explained by some from the noise of the Bacchantic processions — *bromiazomai* —meaning to rage like a Bacchant (Apollod. 2. 1.5).

Rhetoric

PITTHEUS, son of Pelops and king of Troezen, was said to have taught the art of speaking and even to have written a book upon it (Paus. 2. 31.4).

Rhythm

DACTYLI were reported to have introduced music from Phrygia into Greece, and to have invented rhythm, especially the dactylic rhythm (Plut. *De Mus.* 5).

Ribbon

SATURN. The feet of his statue were surrounded with a woolen ribbon (Virg. *Aen.* 7. 179; Mart. 11. 6.1).

Riddle

OEDIPUS solved the riddle of the Sphinx, the monster which tormented Thebes. The riddle was: "A being with four feet has two feet and three feet, and only one voice; but its feet vary, and when it has most it is weakest." Oedipus solved the riddle by saying it was man, and the Sphinx, in frustration, threw herself from the rock on which she sat.

POLYIDUS of Argos was summoned along with other soothsayers by Minos to locate his missing son, Glaucus. Minos had been advised that someone who could devise an appropriate comparison between one of his cows which had changed color from white to red to black and any other object would lead him to the missing boy. Polyidus compared the cow to a mulberry, which is at first white, then red, and finally black. He then by his prophetic powers found the child, who had been drowned in a vat of honey (Aelian. *De Nat.Anim.* 5. 2).

SPHINX. The famous riddle which this Theban monster proposed she was said to have learned from the Muses (Apollod. 3. 5.8); or Laius (who, some claim, was her father) himself taught her the mysterious oracles which Cadmus had received at Delphi (Paus. 9. 26.2). (See also OEDIPUS)

Ridicule

MOMUS was the god of pleasantry, satire, and ridicule.

Ring

SARPEDON, son of Zeus by Laodameia, became prince of Lycia when his uncles were quarreling over the government, and it was proposed that they shoot through a ring placed on the breast of a child. Laodameia, their sister, gave up her own son, Sarpedon, for this purpose, who was thereupon honored by his uncles with the kingdom to show their gratitude to their sister.

River

NAIADS were nymphs who presided over rivers, springs, wells, and fountains.

Road

ARTEMIS TRIVIA was a surname given to Artemis, because she presided over all places where three roads met, where her image was placed with three faces, one looking towards each way. At the new moon, the Athenians offered her sacrifices and a sumptuous entertainment, which was generally distributed among the poor.

HECATE was regarded as a spectral being who at night sent from the lower world all kinds of demons and phantoms, who dwelt in places where two roads crossed. Statues of Hecate stood where two roads crossed, and food was left at the end of each month at the crossroads to be consumed by the poor.

HERMES was regarded as the god of roads.

Robber

AUTOLYCUS, son of Hermes, was renowned for his cunning and thievery. He once broke into the house of Amyntor and stole a beautiful helmet, which later fell into the hands of Meriones, who wore it during the Trojan War (Hom. *Il.* 10. 266).

CACUS was a wicked Italian robber who stole eight oxen from the herd of Recaranus, the legendary shepherd of gigantic bodily strength and courage. Recaranus was able to trace them, although they had been dragged backwards by the tails to disguise their tracks. He entered the hiding place, a cave on Mt. Aventine, slew the robber and dedicated to Jupiter a tenth part of the booty.

CAECULUS, the ancient Italian hero, upon becoming a man, lived for a time as a robber together with a number of comrades who were shepherds.

CORYNETES (See PERIPHETES)

EMATHION was a famous robber destroyed by Heracles.

FURINA was the Roman goddess of robbers.

HARPALYCE was a daughter of Harpalycus of Thrace. After her father's death, she spent her time in the forests as a robber, being so swift in running that horses were unable to overtake her.

HERMES was characterized as a cunning thief and was the god of thieves (Hom. *Il.* 5. 390, 24. 24).

HYMEN (HYMENAEUS). When he fell in love with a girl who refused to listen to him, he put on the disguise of a girl and followed her to Eleusis to the festival of Demeter. He, together with the other girls, was carried off by robbers into a distant and desolate country. While the robbers slept, they were killed by Hymen, who then returned to Athens, requesting the citizens to give him his beloved in marriage in exchange for the rescued maidens. His request was granted, and the resultant marriage was happy.

LACINIUS was an Italian hero and fabulous robber, by whom Heracles, on his expedition to Italy, is said to have been robbed of some of the oxen of Geryon, and who was killed by the hero in consequence. After Heracles had killed the robber, he built a temple to Juno, surnamed Lacinia (Diod. 4. 24).

LAOGORAS was king of the Dryopes, and he accustomed all his subjects to become robbers. He was killed by Heracles.

LAVERNA was the protecting divinity of thieves and imposters; her name was probably connected with the Latin word *levator,* thief.

PERIPHETES, son of Hephaestus, was surnamed Corynetes, "club-bearer," and was a robber at Epidaurus, who slew travelers he met with an iron club. He was eventually overcome by Theseus (Apollod. 3. 16.1; Plut. *Thes.* 8; Paus. 2. 1.4; Ov. *Met.* 8. 437).

PITYOCAMPTES (See SINIS)

PROCRUSTES (See SINIS)

SCIRON was a famous robber who haunted the frontier between Attica and Megaris and not only robbed travelers who passed through the country but compelled them to wash his feet on the Scironian rock, during which operation he kicked them into the sea. At the foot of the rock there was a tortoise which devoured the bodies of the victims. He was slain by Theseus in the same manner in which he had killed others (Plut. *Thes.* 10; Diod. 4. 59; Strab. 9. 391; Paus. 1. 44.12; Ov. *Met.* 7. 445).

SINIS (SINNIS) was a son of Polypemon, Pemon, or Poseidon by Sylea. He was surnamed, according to some, Pityocamptes, and according to others, Procrustes. He dwelt on the Isthmus of Corinth as a robber, destroying the travelers whom he had conquered by fastening them to the tops of fir trees, which he curved and then let spring up again. He himself was killed in this manner by Theseus (Apollod. 3. 16.2; Plut. *Thes.* 8; Paus. 2. 1.3; Diod. 4. 59; Eurip. *Hippol.* 977; Ov. *Met.* 7. 440).

Robe, see Garment

Rock

ACIS was crushed beneath a rock by Polyphemus.

ACTAEON. Near Orchomenos there was a rock on which Actaeon rested and saw Artemis bathing. His spectre haunted the rock, and the Orchomenians built an iron image of Actaeon and offered annual sacrifices.

AEGAEON. He and his brother Uranids could with their hundred arms each hurl three hundred rocks at the Titans.

AEGEUS, father of Theseus, threw himself from a high rock into the sea, when he believed his son dead.

AGRAULOS. With her sisters, Herse and Pandrosos, she threw herself from a rock in a fit of madness after they saw Erichthonius in a chest which they had been forbidden to open.

AJAX (the Lesser). On the return from Troy, his vessel was wrecked on the Whirling Rocks, but he escaped upon a rock with the assistance of Poseidon; but when he used presumptuous words about being able to survive without immortal assistance, Poseidon split the rock with his trident and Ajax drowned. Some say Athena struck him dead for dragging Cassandra from her temple. His body washed up on the rocks on the coast of Euboea, and the rocks came to be called the Rocks of Ajax.

ANDROMEDA was chained to a rock to be devoured by a sea monster, but was rescued by Perseus (Apollod. 2. 4.3; Ov. *Met.* 4. 663).

ASTERIA. Zeus was enamored with her, but she, metamorphosed through her prayers into a bird, flew across the sea; she was then changed into a rock, which for a long time lay under the surface of the sea; but at the request of Leto, it rose and received her when she was pursued by Python. Leto then gave birth to Apollo, who slew Python (Ov. *Met.* 6. 370; Aristot. *H.A.* 6. 35; Athen. 15. 701; Apollon.Rhod. 2. 707).

ATALANTA (ATALANTE). A spring is supposed to have gushed from a rock near the ruins of Cyphanta when she struck it with her spear (Paus. 3. 24.2).

BYBLIS. Conceiving a passion for her brother, she tried to throw herself into the sea from a rock but was kept back by nymphs and changed by them into a Hamadryad. The stream which came down the rock was referred to by neighboring people as the tears of Byblis.

CHARYBDIS was the name of a rock on the Sicilian coast across from Italy. On this rock was an immense fig tree, under which dwelt the monster, Charybdis, who thrice every day swallowed down the waters of the sea and thrice threw them up again. She was described as a daughter of Poseidon and Gaea, and as a voracious woman who stole oxen from Heracles and was hurled by Zeus into the sea, where she retained her voracious nature. She preyed on ships which passed between her and a rock on the Italian side under which dwelt the fearful monster, Scylla (Hom. *Od.* 12. 73, 235).

DAEDALION. When his daughter, Chione, was killed by Artemis, in his grief he threw himself from a rock of Parnassus, but in falling he was changed by Apollo into a hawk (Ov. *Met.* 11. 300).

DAPHNIS. While wandering about in his blindness, he fell from a steep rock and was killed.

HESIONE was a daughter of Laomedon, who was commanded by an oracle to chain her to a rock to be devoured by wild beasts in order to stop a plague sent on Troy.

LINUS was a son of Apollo. His image stood in a hollow rock formed in the shape of a grotto near Mt. Helicon. Here, every year, a funeral sacrifice was offered to him, and dirges were sung in his honor.

LYCOMEDES was king of the Dolopians on the island of Scyros near Euboea. Once when Theseus came to him, Lycomedes, dreading the influence of the stranger upon his subjects, thrust him down a rock (Plut. *Thes.* 35; Paus. 1. 17; Soph. *Phil.* 243).

LYCURGUS. For his various impieties he was entombed in a rock (Soph. *Antig.* 955; comp. Ov. *Trist.* 5. 3, 39).

MELES was an Athenian who was beloved by Timagoras but refused to listen to him and ordered him to leap from the rock of the acropolis, which Timagoras did. Meles, repenting of his cruel command, likewise threw himself from the rock (Paus. 1. 30.1).

OCHNE, daughter of Colonus, caused the death of Eunostus when she accused him of trying to seduce her because he had failed to return her love. Later she confessed the truth and threw herself down a rock (Plut. *Quaest.Gr.* 40).

ORPHE and Lyco, her sister, daughters of Dion, went mad as a consequence of betraying Apollo and were changed into rocks.

ORPHEUS. He enchanted with his music not only the wild beasts but the trees and rocks upon Olympus, so that they moved from their places to follow the sound of his golden harp. On the expedition of the Argonauts, by playing his lyre he caused the Symplegadae, or moving rocks, which threatened to crush the ship between them, to become fixed in their places.

PROMETHEUS. When he continued to defy the will of Zeus, he was again chained to a rock, first in Scythia, where he continued to give out prophecies, except for one concerning the dethronement of Zeus. For this reason he was sent still chained into Tartarus. Later he returned to the upper world and was fastened to Mt. Caucasus, where an eagle daily devoured his liver, which was restored at night (Apollon.Rhod. 2. 1247, 3. 853; Strab. 15. 688; Philostr. *Vit.Apoll.* 2. 3; Aeschyl. *Prom.* 1015).

SCIRON was a famous robber who haunted the frontier between Attica and Megaris, and not only robbed travelers who passed through the country but compelled them to wash his feet on the Scironian rock, during which operation he kicked them into the sea. At the foot of the rock there was a tortoise which devoured the bodies of the victims. He was slain by Theseus in the same manner in which he had killed others (Plut. *Thes.* 10; Diod. 4. 59; Strab. 9. 391; Paus. 1. 44.12; Ov. *Met.* 7. 445).

SCYLLA was the name of a rock on the Italian coast across from Sicily. In the midst of this rock there dwelt Scylla, a daughter of Crataeis, a fearful monster, who preyed on ships which passed between her and a rock on the Sicilian side, under which dwelt the dreadful whirlpool, Charybdis (Hom. *Od.* 12. 73, 235).

SIRENS. When their singing was surpassed by Orpheus so that they failed to lure the Argonauts to their death, they threw themselves into the sea and were metamorphosed into rocks.

SISYPHUS, son of Aeolus and king of Corinth, was punished in the lower world for his wickedness by having to roll uphill a huge marble block, which as soon as it reached the top always rolled down again (Cic. *Tusc.* 1.5; Virg. *Georg.* 3. 39; Ov. *Met.* 4. 459; Ov. *Ib.* 175; Lucret. 3. 1013). Some say that the reason for this particular punishment was because he attacked travelers and killed them with a huge block of stone.

SPHINX. When Oedipus solved the riddle of the monster, she threw herself from a rock.

TALOS was a son of Perdix, sister of Daedalus. He was a disciple of Daedalus and is said to have invented several instruments used in the mechanical arts; but Daedalus, incensed by envy, thrust him down the rock of the acropolis at Athens. The Athenians worshipped him as a hero (Apollod. 3. 15.9; Diod. 4. 76; Lucian *Pisc.* 42).

TANTALUS, a wealthy king, was celebrated in ancient stories for the severe punishment inflicted upon him after his death in the lower world. In addition to being within reach of ever-retreating water to slake his thirst and ever-withdrawn branches of fruit to appease his hunger, a huge rock was suspended over his head, ever-threatening to fall and crush him (Pind. *Ol.* 1. 90; Pind. *Isth.* 8. 21; Eurip. *Orest.* 5; Diod. 5. 74).

TARPEIA was the daughter of the commander of the fortress on the Saturnian (later Capitoline) hill, where the city of Rome was being invaded by the Sabines. She betrayed her people with promise of a reward of ornaments but was killed when the Sabines heaped their shields on her. Her memory was preserved by the name of the Tarpeian rock, from which traitors were afterwards hurled down.

ZEUS STHENIUS, "the powerful," or "the strengthening," was a surname under which Zeus had an altar in a rock near Hermione, where Aegeus concealed his sword and shoes, which were found there by Theseus after he had lifted up the rock (Paus. 2. 32.7, 34.6).

See Also: STONE

Roof

ELPENOR, companion of Odysseus, one day fell asleep intoxicated on the roof of Circe's residence, fell off, and broke his neck (Hom. *Od.* 10. 550).

MELIBOEA was an Ephesian maiden who loved Alexis, and when she was on the point of being married to another, she threw herself from the roof of her house. Uninjured, she escaped to a boat nearby, and its ropes came untied of their own accord. The boat carried her to the self-exiled Alexis, and the happy lover dedicated a sanctuary to Aphrodite, surnamed Automate and Epidaetia.

Rope

AUXESIA. When the Athenians demanded the surrender of the statues of Auxesia and Damia from Aegina and were refused, they put ropes around the statues and tried to drag them away (Paus. 2. 30.5; Herod. 5. 82–86).

MELIBOEA was an Ephesian maiden who loved Alexis, and when she was on the point of being married to another, she threw herself from the roof of her house. Uninjured, she escaped to a boat nearby, and its ropes came untied of their own accord. The boat carried her to the self-exiled Alexis, and the happy lover dedicated a sanctuary to Aphrodite, surnamed Automate and Epidaetia.

TENES was a son of Cycnus. After Cycnus learned hat his son had been innocent of trying to seduce his step-mother, he went to Tenedos to join him. Tenes would not allow him to land, but cut the rope with which Cycnus had fastened his ship to the coast (Paus. 10. 14.2).

Rose

APHRODITE. The rose was sacred to her.

EROS. The rose was sacred to him.

Rudder

SALUS, the Roman personification of public welfare, was represented with a rudder, a globe at her feet, pouring a libation from a patera upon an altar, around which a serpent is winding itself.

TYCHE, the personification of chance or luck, equivalent to the Fortuna of the Romans, is called by Pindar (*Ol.* 12) a daughter of Zeus the Liberator. She was conceived of as the divinity guiding and conducting the affairs of the world with a rudder (Paus. 7. 26.3).

Rumor

FAMA (See OSSA)

OSSA was the personification of rumor or report, equivalent to the Latin Fama. As it is often impossible to trace a rumor or report to its source, it is said to come from Zeus, and hence Ossa is called the messenger of Zeus (Hom. *Od.* 1. 282, 2. 216, 24. 412; Hom. *Il.* 2. 93).

Rust

IPHICLUS. In order to cure his sterility, he was advised by Melampus, the soothsayer, to take the rust from the knife with which Phylacus, his father, had once cut his son and drink it with water over a period of ten days.

TELEPHUS was a king of Mysia at the time of the Trojan War. When the Greeks invaded Mysia, he repelled them. He was, however, wounded by Achilles. The wound could not be healed, and when he consulted the oracle he received the answer that only he could cure him who had wounded him. The Greeks had received an oracle that without the aid of Telephus they could not reach Troy. A reconciliation was brought about, and Achilles cured Telephus by means of the rust of the spear by which the wound had been inflicted; Telephus in return pointed out to the Greeks the road which they had to take (Ov. *Met.* 12. 112; Ov. *Trist.* 5. 2, 15; Ov. *Rem.Am.* 47; Ov. *Ep.ex Pont.* 2. 26).

Sacrifice

HERMES was considered the inventor of divine worship and sacrifices; he was also the protector of sacrificial animals.

Saddle

PELETHRONIUS was the reputed inventor of the bridle and saddle for horses (Plin. *H.N.* 7. 56).

Sadness

ACHLYS was the personification of misery and sadness.

Safety

SOTERIA was the personification of safety or recovery (Lat. *Salus*) and was worshipped as a divinity in Greece, with a temple and a statue at Patrae (Paus. 7. 21.2, 24.2).

Saffron

CROCUS, the unrequited lover of Smilax, was changed by the gods into a saffron plant. According to another tradition, he was metamorphosed by his friend, Hermes, who had killed him in a game of discus (Ov. *Met.* 4. 283).

Sail

AEOLUS taught the natives of the Aeolian Islands the use of sails in navigation.

DAEDALUS. The invention of sails was ascribed to him.

THESEUS. After slaying the Minotaur and sailing for Athens, he failed to hoist the white sail, which was to have been the signal that the expedition had been successful. Aegeus, his father, king of Athens, consequently threw himself in despair from a cliff into the sea.

Sailor

BRITOMARTIS, the Cretan goddess, was protectress of sailors.

DIOSCURI. Castor and Polydeuces were protectors of sailors.

GLAUCUS, the marine deity, was paid homage by sailors.

HECATE bestowed good luck on sailors.

NEREIDES, nymphs of the Mediterranean Sea, were believed to be propitious to all sailors.

Salt

ODYSSEUS did not want to join the Greeks against Troy (Hom. *Od.* 24. 116). When Palamedes came to try to persuade him, Odysseus pretended to be mad. He yoked an ass and an ox to a plow and began to sow salt. Palamedes, to test him, placed the infant Telemachus before the plow, whereupon the father could not continue to play his part.

PENATES. The family table was sacred to these household gods of the Romans, and the table always contained the saltcellar and fruit (Plut. *Quaest.Conviv.* 7. 4; Liv. 26. 36).

Sandal

HERMES. When he stole the oxen of Apollo, he put on sandals so that his footprints could not be distinguished (Hom. *Hymn.in Merc.* 125; Diod. 1. 16). His golden sandals carried him across land and sea with the rapidity of the wind. The sandals were later represented as winged.

JASON. Pelias was advised by an oracle to be on his guard against a man with only one sandal. Jason came to a sacrifice which Pelias was offering to Poseidon, and on the way he lost a sandal while crossing a river. Thus Pelias recognized him as an enemy and plotted to send him on the quest for the Golden Fleece.

PERSEUS. For his mission to fetch Medusa's head, the nymphs provided him with winged sandals, with which he flew to the lair of the Gorgons (Hes. *Scut.Herc.* 220, 222).

THESEUS was son of Aegeus, king of Athens, and Aethra. When he reached maturity, he took the sword and sandals, the tokens which had been left by Aegeus under a heavy stone near Troezen, and proceeded to Athens to seek recognition from his father. By means of the sword and sandals Theseus was recognized by Aegeus, acknowledged as his son, and declared his successor. (See also ZEUS STHENIUS)

ZEUS STHENIUS, "the powerful," or "the strengthening," was a name under which he had an altar in a rock near Hermione, where Aegeus concealed his sword and shoes, which were found there by Theseus after he had lifted up the rock (Paus. 2. 32.7, 34.6).

Satire

MOMUS was the god of pleasantry, satire, and ridicule.

Saw

DAEDALUS was the reputed inventor of the saw.

PERDIX, nephew of Daedalus, was said to be the inventor of the saw. The idea was suggested to him by the backbone of a fish or the teeth of a serpent.

Scales

ATROPOS, one of the Moirae, or Fates, is sometimes represented with a pair of scales.

MEMNON. While he was fighting with Achilles, Zeus weighed the fate of the two heroes and the scale containing that of Memnon sank (Pind. *Ol.* 2. 148; Pind. *Nem.* 3. 110, 6. 83; Q.Smyrn. 2. 224; Philostr. *Imag.* 2. 7; Plut. *De Aud.Poet.* 2).

PALAMEDES, son of Nauplius, was described as the inventor of scales.

THEMIS is often represented on coins as resembling the figure of Athena, with a cornucopia and a pair of scales (Gell. 14. 4).

Scales (Fish)

TRITON, a son of Poseidon and Amphitrite, was described as riding over the sea on horses or sea monsters. Often referred to in the plural, the Tritons were sometimes described as having very fine and hard scales.

Scar

ODYSSEUS. As a young man, while engaged in the chase during a visit to his grandfather, Autolycus, near Mt. Parnassus, he was wounded in his knee by a boar, by which scar he was subsequently recognized, even though disguised as a beggar, by his old nurse, Eurycleia, upon his return to Ithaca from Troy (Hom. *Od.* 1. 429, 4. 742; Paus. 10. 8.4; Ov. *Met.* 11. 295).

Sceptre

AGAMEMNON. The emblem of his power as commander of the Greek forces at Troy was a sceptre made by Hephaestus, which Zeus gave to Hermes, who in turn gave it to Pelops, from whom it descended to Agamemnon.

DEMETER. In artistic representations, she often carried a sceptre.

HERA. As queen of the gods, she was often represented as holding a sceptre.

MOIRAE, the Fates, were represented by early artists with staffs or sceptres.

PELOPS received his sceptre from Hermes and bequeathed it to Atreus (Hom. *Il.* 2. 104).

PERSEPHONE. In works of art she appears as a mystical divinity with a sceptre and a little box.

TRIPTOLEMUS. In works of art, he is represented as a youthful hero, sometimes holding in his hand a sceptre.

ZEUS. As king of the gods, the sceptre was one of his attributes.

Science

MUSES presided over the sciences.

Scorpion

ORION, the giant hunter, boasted that he would conquer every animal and would clear the earth of all wild beasts; but the earth sent forth a scorpion by which he was killed (Ov. *Fast.* 5. 539). Some say that for a transgression against Artemis, she sent a monstrous scorpion which killed him (Hor. *Carm.* 2. 4.72; Apollod. 1. 4.5).

Scourging

ARTEMIS ORTHIA was a surname of Artemis as the goddess of the moon. It was at her altar that Spartan boys had to undergo the ritual scourging, in such a manner that the altar became sprinkled with blood (Herod. 4. 87).

BELLONA, Roman goddess of war, is described as armed with a bloody scourge (Virg. *Aen.* 8. 703).

IXION was said to have been scourged and compelled to exclaim: "Benefactors should be honored." This was a result of his having repaid Zeus' hospitality by trying to seduce Hera.

NEMESIS was the goddess of retribution. Sometimes she was represented holding in her right hand a wheel with a sword or a scourge.

PELOPS. Every year, the ephebi of Pisa scourged themselves at the tomb of Pelops, shedding their blood as a funeral sacrifice to the hero.

PHINEUS. When his sons by a first marriage were falsely accused of improper conduct toward his second wife, Phineus punished them by having them scourged and then half buried in the earth (Diod. 4. 44).

Scroll

CALLIOPE, the Muse of epic poetry, appears sometimes with a scroll.

CLIO, the Muse of history, appears in a sitting attitude with an open roll of paper.

CLOTHO, one of the Moirae, or Fates, is sometimes represented with a roll (the book of fate).

Sculpture

CORE of Corinth is mentioned as the mystic inventor of sculpture.

DAEDALUS. Under his name the Greeks personified the earliest development of the art of sculpture.

PYGMALION, a king of Cyprus, was said to have fallen in love with the ivory image of a maiden, which he himself had made, and therefore to have prayed to Aphrodite to breathe life into it. When the request was granted, Pygmalion married his beloved and became by her the father of Paphus (Ov. *Met.* 10. 243).

Sea

AMPHITRITE was wife of Poseidon and goddess of the sea.

AMPHITRITE HALSODYNE. This surname means "sea-fed" or "the sea-born" goddess (Hom. *Od.* 4. 404).

APHRODITE. Since she sprang from the sea, she was mentioned by some writers as having some influence over the sea (Virg. *Aen.* 8. 800; Ov. *Her.* 15. 213).

APHRODITE ANADYOMENE was a surname of Aphrodite from the story of her having been born from the foam of the sea.

DIOSCURI were worshipped as the protectors of travelers by sea, for Poseidon had rewarded their brotherly love by giving them power over wind and waves, that they might assist the shipwrecked (Eurip. *Hel.* 1511; Hor. *Carm.* 1. 3.2).

DORIS was a daughter of Oceanus and Tethys and mother by Nereus of the Nereides. The Latin poets sometimes used her name for the sea itself (Virg. *Ecl.* 10. 5).

EUPHEMUS was a son of Poseidon. By a power which his father had granted him, he could walk on the sea just as on firm ground (Apollon. Rhod. 1. 182).

EURYNOME was a daughter of Oceanus. When Hephaestus was expelled by Hera from Olympus, Eurynome and Thetis received him into the bosom of the sea (Hom. *Il.* 18. 395; Apollod. 1. 2.2).

GALENE was a personification of the calm sea and was perhaps identical with Galateia, one of the Nereides.

GLAUCE was one of the Nereides, and her name was perhaps a personification of the color of the sea (Hom. *Il.* 18. 39).

GLAUCUS of Anthedon in Boeotia, in the battle of the Argonauts with the Tyrrhenians, alone remained unhurt; he sank to the bottom of the sea, became a marine deity and was of service to the Argonauts.

GRAEAE were regarded by some as marine divinities and personifications of the white foam seen on the waves of the sea.

HALIA. After leaping into the sea, she received the name of Leucothea and was worshipped as a divine being by the Rhodians (Diod. 5. 55).

IPHIMEDEIA was a daughter of Triops and wife of Aloeus. Being in love with Poseidon, she often walked to the sea and collected its waters in her lap or sprinkled water on her bosom, whence she became by Poseidon the mother of the Aloeidae, Otus and Ephialtes.

MATUTA. Sometimes this Roman divinity was identified with the Greek Leucothea and was therefore regarded as a marine deity (Plut. *Camil.* 5; Ov. *Fast.* 6. 551; Cic. *De Nat.Deor.* 3. 19; Cic. *Tusc.* 1. 12).

MELICERTES. When Ino, his mother, was driven mad, she threw herself with her son from the Molurian rock into the sea, and both were changed into marine deities. Ino became Leucothea, and Melicertes, Palaemon (Apollod. 3. 4.3; Ov. *Met.* 4. 520, 13. 919). The apotheosis was effected by the Nereides, who saved Melicertes and also ordered the institution of the Nemean games. The body of Melicertes, according to the common tradition, was washed by the waves or carried by dolphins into a port on the Corinthian isthmus (Paus. 1. 44.11, 2. 1.3; Plut. *Quaest.Conviv.* 5. 3).

NEPTUNE was the chief maritime divinity of the Romans. His name is probably connected with the verb *nato* and a contraction of *navitunus*. His day was probably the 23rd of July.

NEREIDES, daughters of Nereus and Doris, were regarded by the ancients as marine nymphs of the Mediterranean, as distinguished from the Oceanids, or the nymphs of the great ocean.

NEREUS was the son of Pontus and Gaea and husband of Doris, by whom he became the father of the fifty Nereides. He is described as the wise and unerring old man of the sea, at the bottom of which he dwelt (Hom. *Il.* 18. 141; Hom. *Od.* 24. 58; Hes. *Theog.* 233; Apollod. 1. 2.6).

NYMPHS of bodies of water were divided into the following classes: (1) Oceanides, daughters of Oceanus—nymphs of the ocean; (2) Nereides, daughters of Nereus—nymphs of the Mediterranean or inner sea; (3) Potameides—nymphs named for individual rivers; (4) Naiades—nymphs of fresh water; and (5) *Nymphae infernae paludis* or Avernales—nymphs presiding over rivers of the lower regions.

PALAEMON (See MELICERTES)

PHORCUS (PHORCYS or PHORCYN). According to Homeric poems, he was an old man ruling over the sea, or "the old man of the sea," to whom a harbor in Ithaca was dedicated.

PONTUS, a personification of the sea, was described as the son of Gaea and father of certain marine deities by his mother (Hes. *Theog.* 132, 233; Apollod. 1. 2.6).

POSEIDON was the god of the sea; it was determined by lot that he should rule over the sea (Hom. *Il.* 14. 156, 15. 187; Hes. *Theog.* 456).

PROTEUS, the prophetic old man of the sea, occurs in the earliest legends as a subject of Poseidon and tending the flocks of Poseidon (seals) (Hom. *Od.* 4. 365, 385, 400; Virg. *Georg.* 4. 392; Theocrit. 2. 58; Hor. *Carm.* 1. 2.7).

SALACIA was the female divinity of the sea among the Romans and was the wife of Neptune (Varr. *De Ling.Lat.* 5. 72).

TELCHINES were a family, a class of people, or a tribe said to have been descended from Thalassa or Poseidon (Diod. 5. 55; Nonn. 14. 40). They are described as marine beings without feet, the place of the hands being occupied by fins.

TETHYS was a daughter of Uranus and Gaea and wife of Oceanus, by whom she was thought to be the mother of of the Oceanides and the numerous river gods (Hes. *Theog.* 136, 337; Apollod. 1. 1.3).

THALASSA, a personification of the sea, is described as a daughter of Aether and Hemera (Lucian *Dei Marin.* 11).

THETIS, daughter of Nereus and Doris and mother of Achilles, was one of the marine deities, and she dwelt like her sisters, the Nereids, in the depth of the sea (Hom. *Il.* 1. 358, 18. 36, 20. 207).

THETIS HALSODYNE. As AMPHITRITE HALSODYNE (Hom. *Il.* 20. 207).

TRITON was a son of Poseidon and Amphitrite, who dwelt with his father and mother in a golden palace at the bottom of the sea. He was described as riding over the sea on horses or sea monsters. Sometimes Tritons are mentioned in the plural and as serving other marine divinities in riding over the sea.

VENILIA was a Roman divinity connected with the winds and the sea (Virg. *Aen.* 10. 75; Ov. *Met.* 14. 334).

VENUS SALACIA was a surname of Venus derived possibly from her having risen from the sea.

ZEUS OGOA was the Carian name of Zeus at Mysala, in whose temple a sea wave was seen from time to time (Paus. 8. 10.3). Strabo (14. 659) calls the god of Mysala, in the Carian dialect, Osogo.

Sea Eagle

PANDAREUS, son of Merops and father of Aedon, was changed by Zeus into a sea eagle.

Sea Horse

HIPPOCAMPUS, the mythical sea horse, according to a description of Pausanias (2. 1), was a horse, but the part of its body down from the breast was that of a sea monster or fish. The horse appears even in the Homeric poems as the symbol of Poseidon, whose chariot was drawn over the surface of the sea by swift horses. The later poets and artists conceived and represented the horses of Poseidon and other marine divinities as a combination of a horse and a fish (Hom. *Il.* 13. 24, 29; Eurip. *Androm.* 1012; Virg. *Georg.* 4. 389; Philostr. *Imag.* 1. 8; Stat. *Theb.* 2. 45).

PROTEUS, the old man of the sea, is often represented as riding through the sea in a chariot drawn by Hippocampi (Virg. *Georg.* 4. 389).

Seal

PROTEUS, the prophetic old man of the sea, occurs in the earliest legends as a subject of Poseidon and tending the flocks of Poseidon (seals) (Hom. *Od.* 4. 365, 385, 400; Virg. *Georg.* 4. 392; Theocrit. 2. 58; Hor. *Carm.* 1. 2.7; Philostr. *Imag.* 2. 17).

Seashell, see Shell

Seasons

ADONIS was allowed to spend four months by himself, four with Aphrodite, and four with Persephone. His return each year from Hades betokens spring.

CARPO, daughter of Zephyrus, was one of the seasons.

HORAE were the personification or goddesses of the order of nature and the seasons.

JANUS QUADRIFRONS. It is said that after the conquest of the Faliscans, an image of Janus was found with four foreheads. The fact of the god being represented with four heads was considered by the ancients to be an indication of his being the divinity presiding over the year with its four seasons (August. 7. 4).

PERSEPHONE, the daughter of Zeus and Demeter, was carried away to the lower world by Hades. Demeter searched for her everywhere, neglecting her responsibility for the earth's crops, until Zeus promised to restore the lost maiden, on the condition that Persephone had eaten nothing in the underworld. But she had eaten six pomegranate seeds and was compelled to spend six months every year with Hades and six months on the earth with her mother. Her return to earth every year coincided with the return of spring.

VERTUMNUS was an Etruscan deity. The name is evidently connected with *verto*; for this reason the Romans connected Vertumnus with all occurrences to which the verb *verto* applies, such as the change of seasons.

Seaweed

GLAUCUS, the marine deity, was described as being covered on his chest by seaweed (Philostr. *Imag.* 2. 15).

NEREUS. In works of art, Nereus, like other sea gods, is represented with pointed seaweeds taking the place of hair in the eyebrows, the chin, and the breast.

Seduction

ANTEIA, wife of Proetus, fell in love with Bellerophon and tried to seduce him. When she failed, she told her husband that Bellerophon had made improper advances to her and insisted that their guest be put to death.

BIADICE (DEMODICE), wife of Cretheus, tried to seduce Phrixus and, failing, accused him before Athamas, who attempted to kill his son.

DEMODICE (See BIADICE)

EUNOSTUS of Tanagra, son of Elinus, failed to return the love of Ochne, who accused him before her brother of improper conduct toward her, and Eunostus was slain (Plut. *Quaest. Gr.* 40).

HIPPOLYTUS, son of Theseus, was accused by Phaedra, his step-mother, of improper conduct toward her, since he would not return the passion she felt for him.

PELEUS. During his stay at Iolcus, Astydameia, the wife of his host, Acastus, fell in love with him and made proposals to him, which he rejected. In order to take vengeance on him, she sent a message to his wife at Phthia, that he was on the point of marrying Sterope, the daughter of Acastus. On receiving this information, the wife of Peleus hanged herself. Astydameia further charged Peleus before her husband with having made improper proposals to her, which caused Acastus to try to bring about the death of his friend. Instead of Astydameia, some writers mention Hippolyte, daughter of Crethus (Pind. *Nem.* 4. 92).

TENES (TENNES) was a son of Cycnus. His stepmother, Philonome, fell in love with him, and when she was unable to win his love, she accused him before his father of improper conduct toward her. Cycnus threw both his son and daughter, Hemithea, into a chest and exposed them on the waves of the sea, but the chest was carried to the island of Leucophrys, where Tenes was eventually made king.

Seed

SEGETIA was a Roman divinity, who, together with Setia (Seja) and Semonia, was invoked by the early Italians at seed time, for Segetia, like the other two names, is connected with *sero* and *seges* (Plin. *H.N.* 18. 2.2; August. 4. 8; comp. Tertull. *De Spect.* 8).

TELLUS, Roman goddess of the earth, personified the power of nature (the earth) of bringing forth to light the seeds entrusted to her.

Seer

AMPHIARAUS foresaw the unfortunate outcome of the expedition of the Seven against Thebes, in which he participated (Apollod. 3. 6.2). He also participated in the Calydonian Boar Hunt and the Argonautica. He has been called one of the seven great soothsayers of antiquity.

AMPHICTYON was a son of Deucalion and Pyrrha. He was the first man to divine from omens, to interpret dreams, and to give prophecies.

AMPHILOCHUS was a son of Amphiaraus. He was one of the Epigoni, and he took part in the Trojan War. He was a celebrated soothsayer.

ASTYLUS was a seer among the centaurs and is mentioned as trying to dissuade the centaurs from fighting against the Lapithae (Ov. *Met.* 12. 308).

CALCHAS was the wisest of the soothsayers among the Greeks at Troy (Hom. *Il.* 1. 69, 13. 70). An oracle had declared that he would die if he met with a soothsayer superior to himself, and this came to pass when he met Mopsus (Strab. 14. 642, 668).

CARNUS was an Acarnanian soothsayer whose murder by Hippotes, one of the Heracleidae, provoked Apollo to send a plague on the army of Hippotes.

GALEUS, son of Apollo, was the ancestor of the Galeotae, a family of Sicilian soothsayers (Cic. *De Div.* 1.20).

HALITHERSES, son of Mastor of Ithaca, was a soothsayer, and, during the absence of Odysseus, he assisted Telemachus against the suitors of Penelope (Hom. *Od.* 2. 157, 253, 24. 451).

IDMON was a son of Apollo and Asteria and one of the soothsayers who accompanied the Argonauts. He knew beforehand that he would die on the trip.

MACAREUS (MACAR) (See MEROPS)

MELAMPUS, son of Amythaon, could understand the language of birds and could foretell the future. He also acquired the power of prophesying from the victims that were offered to the gods, and, after having had an interview with Apollo on the banks of the Alpheius, he became a most renowned soothsayer (Apollod. 1. 9.11).

MEROPS, king of Rhindacus, or Percote, on the Hellespont, is also called Macar, or Macareus. He was a celebrated soothsayer (Hom. *Il.* 2. 831, 11. 329; Apollon. Rhod. 1. 975; Strab. 13. 586; Apollod. 3. 12.5).

MOPSUS, son of Ampyx (Ampycus) by the nymph Chloris, was also called a son of Apollo because he was a seer (Hes. *Scut.Herc.* 181; Val. Flacc. 1. 384; Stat. *Theb.* 3. 521). He participated in both the Calydonian Boar Hunt and the expedition of the Argonauts.

NAUTES was a Trojan soothsayer, who comforted Aeneas when his ships had been burned at Sicily.

PHINEUS, son of Agenor and king of Salmydessus in Thrace, was a blind soothsayer, who had received his prophetic powers from Apollo (Apollon. Rhod. 2. 180).

PHRASIUS was a Cyprian soothsayer, who advised Busiris to sacrifice the strangers that came to his dominions in order to avert a famine. Phrasius, also called Thrasius, was the first victim of his own advice (Apollod. 2. 5.11).

PICUS, a Latin prophetic divinity, son of Saturnus or Sterculus, was often called the first king of Italy.

POLYIDUS, a son of Coeranus, a grandson of Abas, and a great-grandson of Melampus, was, like his ancestor, a celebrated soothsayer at Corinth and Argos. He was summoned along with other soothsayers by Minos, king of Crete, to locate his missing son, Glaucus. Minos had been advised that someone who could devise an appropriate comparison between one of his cows which had changed color from white to red to black and any other object would lead him to the missing boy. Polyidus compared the cow to a mulberry, which is at first white, then red, and finally black. He then by his prophetic powers found the child, who had been drowned in a vat of honey (Aelian. *De Nat.Anim.* 5. 2).

SCIRUS, a soothsayer of Dodona, came to Salamis in the reign of Erechtheus and was afterwards honored in the island as a hero (Paus. 1. 36.3; Strab. 9. 393).

TELEMUS, a son of Eurymus, was a celebrated soothsayer (Hom. *Od.* 9. 509; Ov. *Met.* 13. 731; Theocrit. 6. 23).

TENERUS, son of Apollo by Melia and a brother of Ismenius, was a soothsayer (Paus. 9. 10.5, 26.1).

THEOCLYMENUS, a son of Polypheides of Hyperasia and a descendant of Melampus, was a soothsayer, who, in consequence of a murder, was obliged to take flight. He came with Telemachus to Ithaca from Pylos and tried to warn the suitors of Penelope of the doom which awaited them, but they only laughed at him (Hom. *Od.* 15. 256, 507, 17. 151, 350).

THRASIUS (See PHRASIUS)

TIRESIAS (TEIRESIAS) was a son of Everes (or Phorbas) and Chariclo and one of the most renowned soothsayers in all antiquity. Even in the underworld he was believed to retain his powers of perception, and there also he continued to use his golden staff (Hom. *Od.* 10. 492, 11. 190; Lycoph. 682; Cic. *De Div.* 1. 40; Paus. 9. 33). Before Odysseus could leave the island of Circe, she begged him to descend into the underworld to consult the famous seer (Hom. *Od.* 10. 135).

See also: PROPHECY

Sensuality

APHRODITE APOTROPHIA, "the expeller," was a surname under which Aphrodite was worshipped at Thebes, which described her as the goddess who expelled from men's hearts the desire for sinful pleasure and lust (Paus. 9. 16.2).

APHRODITE PANDEMOS was a surname of Aphrodite meaning "common to all people," describing her as the goddess of low sensual pleasures, as *Venus vulgivaga* or *popularis,* in opposition to Venus (Aphrodite) Urania, or the heavenly Aphrodite (Plat. *Sympos.* 180; Lucret. 4. 1067).

VENUS LIBENTINA (LUBENTINA or LUBENTIA) was a surname of Venus by which she was described as the goddess of sexual pleasure (*dea libidinis*) (Varr. *De Ling.Lat.* 5. 6; Cic. *De Nat.Deor.* 2. 23; August. 4. 8; Nonn. 1. 324; Plaut. *Asin.* 2. 2.2).

VOLUPIA, the personification of sensual pleasure among the Romans, was honored with a temple near the Porta Romanula (Plin. *Epist.* 8. 20; Plin. *H.N.* 3. 5; Varr. *De Ling.Lat.* 5. 164; August. 4. 8). She is also called Voluptas (Cic. *De Nat.Deor.* 2. 23).

Sentinel

PALAMEDES, son of Nauplius, was described as the inventor of the sentinel.

Serpent

ACHELOUS. In a contest with Heracles, one of the forms assumed by Achelous was that of a serpent.

ADMETUS. When he failed to sacrifice to Artemis on his wedding day, he found in his bridal chamber a coil of snakes.

AEPYTUS was killed during a chase on Mt. Sepia by the bite of a venomous snake.

ALCON was a skillful archer, who, when a serpent entwined his son, shot it without injuring the child (Val.Flacc. 1. 399).

ALOEIDAE, the giants Otus and Ephialtes, in Hades were tied to a pillar with serpents, their faces turned away from each other.

ANGITIA (ANGUITIA) was a goddess worshipped by the Marsians and Marrubians, who taught the people remedies against the poison of snakes. She was identified with Medea, and accounts say that Medea came with Jason to the shores of Italy and taught the above-mentioned remedies.

ANTINOE (AUTONOE). When she led the inhabitants from the old to the new townsite of Mantineia, she was guided by a serpent (Paus. 8. 8.3, 9.2).

APOLLO soon after his birth destroyed the serpent Python, whom Hera had sent to devour Leto.

ARCHEMORUS (See OPHELTES)

ARGUS slew the serpent Echidna, which rendered the roads unsafe.

ASCLEPIUS. A serpent twined around a staff on which he was leaning, and he killed it; another serpent came bearing an herb, which restored the first serpent to life. From this, Asclepius learned the art of restoring life. The serpent was sacred to him.

ATHENA. When Medusa was killed, her sisters lamented her death, and plaintive sounds issued from the mouths of the serpents which surrounded their heads. Athena imitated these sounds on a reed and thus invented the flute (Pind. *Pyth.* 12. 19). The serpent was sacred to her.

BONA DEA. Faunus (her brother, husband, or father) himself had not been able to overcome her aversion to men, except by changing her into a serpent (Cic. *De Harusp.Resp.* 17). Her statues had a serpent surrounding the feet.

BOREAS, the north wind, is represented on the chest of Cypselus, with serpents in the place of legs (Paus. 5. 19.1).

CANOBUS was the helmsman of Menelaus, who on his return from Troy died in Egypt in consequence of a snake bite (Strab. 17. 801).

CASSANDRA. Having been left with her brother, Helenus, by their parents in the sanctuary of the Thymbraean Apollo, they were found the next morning entwined by serpents, which were purifying the children's ears, so as to render them capable of understanding the divine sounds of nature and thereby learning the future.

CERBERUS was described by some writers as a monster with three heads, the tail of a serpent, and a mane consisting of heads of various snakes (Apollod. 2. 5.12; Eurip. *Herc.Fur.* 24, 611; Virg. *Aen.* 7. 417; Ov. *Met.* 4. 449).

DIONYSUS. When Tyrrhenian pirates attempted to take him to Asia to sell him, he changed the mast and oars of their ship into serpents and performed additional magical feats, which drove them to madness so that they jumped overboard and were changed into dolphins (Apollod. 3. 5.3; Ov. *Met.* 3. 582). The serpent was sacred to Dionysus.

DRYOPE. She was admired by Apollo, who, in order to gain possession of her, metamorphosed himself into a tortoise. Her nymph companions played with the animal, and Dryope took it into her lap. The god then changed himself into a serpent, which frightened the nymphs away, so that he remained alone with Dryope (Ov. *Met.* 9. 325).

ECHIDNA, the monstrous daughter of Tartarus and Gaea, was half maiden and half serpent. She was killed by Argus.

EPHIALTES (See ALOEIDAE)

ERICHTHONIUS, son of Hephaestus by Gaea or Atthis, was half serpent, half man. Athena became his guardian and concealed him in a chest, which she put Agraulos, Pandrosos, and Herse to guard. She forbade them to open the chest, but they did, and, observing the child in the form of a serpent (or entwined by serpents) they were thrown into madness and flung themselves from the acropolis or into the sea. The serpent escaped into the shield of Athena and was protected by her (Apollod. 3. 14.6; Paus. 1. 2.5, 18.2; Eurip. *Ion* 260; Ov. *Met.* 2. 554).

EUMENIDES were represented with serpents twined in their hair. Sometimes they carried serpents in their hands.

EURYDICE, wife of Orpheus, died from the bite of a serpent and went to the underworld, where Orpheus followed to attempt to persuade Hades to restore her to him.

GENIUS. Every place had its genius, and each local genius, when he made himself visible, appeared in the form of a serpent: that is, the symbol of renovation or of a new life. The genius of a place is usually represented in art in the form of a serpent eating fruit placed before him.

GLAUCUS was a son of Minos who drowned in a cask of honey. When Polyidus, the soothsayer, divined where the body was, Minos ordered him to restore the boy to life, but Polyidus was unable to perform this miracle. Minos ordered him entombed with the dead boy. In the tomb, Polyidus observed a serpent crawling toward the boy's body and killed it. Another serpent emerged with a herb in its mouth and laid it on the body of the dead snake, whereupon the snake came back to life. Polyidus did this with the dead boy and achieved the same result. He was given rich gifts and allowed to return to his homeland (Apollod. 3. 10.3).

GORGONS were represented as girded with serpents or with serpents for hair. Medusa was the only one of the three who was mortal, but her hair was changed into serpents by Athena. (See also ATHENA)

HEPHAESTUS was believed to have great healing powers, and Lemnian earth (*terra Lemnia*) from the spot on which he had fallen from Olympus was believed to cure the bites of snakes.

HERACLES. When he was only two months

old, Hera sent two serpents into the apartment where Heracles and his brother Iphicles were sleeping, but Heracles killed the serpents with his own hands (Apollod. 2. 4.8). After his twelve labors were done, he also killed a serpent on the river Sygaris.

HERMES. The herald's staff which he carried originally had white ribbons, but these were later represented by artists as serpents.

HESPERIA was stung by a viper while fleeing the advances of Aesacus.

HYAS, the brother of the Hyades, was killed in Libya by a serpent's bite, according to some traditions.

HYGIEIA was the goddess of health. Her ordinary attribute is a serpent, which she is feeding from a cup.

IAMUS, son of Apollo, was deserted by his mother, Evadne, and was fed with honey by two serpents.

IDMON, son of Apollo and one of the Argonauts, was killed in the country of the Mariandynians by a boar or a serpent; or, according to others, he died of a disease (Apollod. 1. 9.23; Apollon.Rhod. 1. 140, 443; Val.Flacc. 5. 2).

LAOCOON. When he opposed bringing the wooden horse into Troy, he prepared to sacrifice a bull to Poseidon, and suddenly two fearful serpents appeared swimming toward the Trojan coast from Tenedos. The serpents entwined Laocoon and his two sons, and all three were killed (Virg. *Aen.* 2. 199 – 227; comp. Q.Smyrn. 12. 398; Lycoph. 347). The serpents then hastened to the acropolis of Troy and disappeared behind the shield of Tritonis.

MEDEA (See ANGITIA)

MELAMPUS was said to have acquired his gift of prophecy in the following way: An oak tree before his house in Pylos contained a serpent's nest, and his servants killed the old serpents, but Melampus reared the young ones. One day, after they had grown up and Melampus was asleep, they approached from both sides and cleansed his ears with their tongues. When he was thus aroused, he was amazed to find that he could understand the language of birds, and that with their assistance he could foretell the future (Apollod. 1. 9.11).

MELANTHUS was one of the sons of Laocoon, who, with his father and brother, was killed by serpents at Troy to punish Laocoon's blasphemy.

MOPSUS, the famous seer of the Argonauts, was said to have died in Libya by the bite of a snake and to have been buried there by the Argonauts (Apollon.Rhod. 1. 80, 4. 1518).

MYAGRUS was a divinity who was entreated to prevent harm from serpents.

OPHELTES, a son of Lycurgus, was killed by a snake at Nemea, as his nurse, Hypsipyle, had left him alone (Apollod. 1. 9.14; Paus. 2. 15.3). His name was changed, after his death, to Archemorus, and the seven heroes in their expedition against Thebes instituted the Nemean games in his honor.

OPHIUCHUS (See PHORBAS)

ORESTES died in Arcadia of the bite of a snake.

OTUS (See ALOEIDAE)

PHILOCTETES was a son of Poeas and Demonassa. On the voyage to Troy, as leader of seven ships, he was left behind by his men in the island of Lemnos, because he was ill of a wound which he had received from the bite of a snake (Hom. *Il.* 2. 716).

PHORBAS was a son of Lapithes and Orsinome. The Rhodians, in response to an oracle, are said to have invited him to their island to deliver it from snakes and afterwards to have honored him with heroic worship (Diod. 5. 58). From this circumstance he was called Ophiuchus and is said to have been placed among the stars.

POENE was a serpent sent by Apollo to avenge Argos but was killed by Coroebus.

SABAZIUS. Serpents were sacred to this Phrygian agricultural divinity, a son of Rhea or Cybele (Theophrast. 16).

SALUS was the Roman personification of public welfare and was represented with a rudder, a globe at her feet, and pouring from a patera a libation upon an altar, around which a serpent is winding itself.

SCYLLA. Circe, the enchantress, jealous of Scylla's beauty, threw herbs into a well where Scylla bathed and caused her to be metamorphosed in such a manner that the upper part of her body remained that of a woman, while the lower half was changed into the tail of a fish or serpent surrounded by dogs (Ov. *Met.* 13. 732, 905, 14. 40; Tibull. 3. 4.89).

SOSIPOLIS, "the savior of the state," was the name of a hero among the Eleans. Once when the Arcadians invaded Elis and the Eleans had marched out to meet them, there appeared among the Eleans a woman with a boy at her breast, declaring that after she had given birth to the child, she had had a vision in a dream to offer the child as a champion to the Eleans. The commanders of the Eleans placed the child naked among their ranks, and when the Arcadians began the attack, the child was metamorphosed into a serpent. The Arcadians fled in dismay, and the Eleans pursued them and gained the victory (Paus. 6. 20.2, 3. 25.4).

SPHINXES. They appear with the face of a maiden, the breast, feet, and claws of a lion, the tail of a serpent, and the wings of a bird (Soph. *Oed. Tyr.* 391; Athen. 6. 253).

TIRESIAS (TEIRESIAS) was a son of Everes (or Phorbas) and Chariclo and one of the most renowned soothsayers in antiquity. He was blind from an early age but lived to a very old age. One tradition accounts for his blindness in the following way. Once, on Mt. Cithaeron, he saw a male and female serpent in the act of mating; he struck them with his staff and, as he happened to kill the female, he himself was changed into a woman. Seven years later, he again saw two serpents together and, now killing the male, he again became a man. It was for this reason that Zeus and Hera, when they were discussing whether a man or a woman enjoyed sexual intercourse more, referred the matter to Tiresias, who could judge for both. Tiresias agreed with Zeus that women derived more pleasure from sex. Hera, indignant at the answer, blinded him, but Zeus gave him the power of prophecy and granted him a life which was to last for seven or nine generations (Apollod. 3. 6.7; Ov. *Met.* 3. 320; Pind. *Nem.* 1. 91).

TITYUS was a son of Gaea and a giant in Euboea. For assaulting Leto (or Artemis) he was cast into Tartarus, where he lay outstretched on the ground. Two vultures or snakes devoured his liver (Hom. *Od.* 11. 576).

See also: DRAGON

Seven

APOLLO. The number seven was sacred to him. On the seventh day of every month sacrifices were offered to him.

APOLLO HEBDOMAGETES was a surname of Apollo derived from the fact of sacrifices being offered to him on the seventh of every month, the seventh of some month being looked upon as the god's birthday. Others connect the name with the fact that at the festivals of Apollo, the procession was led by seven boys and seven maidens (Aeschyl. *Sept.* 804; Herod. 6. 57).

Sewer

VENUS CLOACINA. According to some, this name was derived from the fact that an image of Venus was found in the great sewer (*cloaca*) of Rome and was set up by the Sabine king, T. Tatius, in a temple near the forum (Liv. 3. 48; Plaut. *Curcul.* 4. 1.10).

Sexual Intercourse

VENUS CLOACINA was a surname of Venus, which designated her as presiding over and purifying sexual intercourse in marriage.

Shadow

ZEUS LYCAEUS (LYCEUS) was a name given to Zeus from his being worshipped on Mt. Lycaeus in Arcadia; he had a sanctuary there in which the festival of the Lycaea was celebrated. No one was allowed to enter the temple, and if anyone forced his way in, he was believed to stay within the temple for one year and to lose his shadow (Paus. 8. 2.1, 38.4; Pind. *Ol.* 13. 154).

Shame

AIDOS, the personification of shame, was often mentioned along with Nemesis (Hes. *Theog.* 223).

MEROPE was one of the Pleiades and wife of Sisyphus of Corinth, by whom she became the mother of Glaucus. In the constellation of the Pleiades she is the least visible star, because she is ashamed of having had intercourse with a mortal (Apollod. 1. 9.3, 3. 10.1; Ov. *Fast.* 4. 175). She is also called Sterope.

STEROPE (See MEROPE)

Sharpsightedness

LYNCEUS was son of Aphareus and brother of Idas. He was one of the Argonauts and famous for his sharpsightedness. His vision was so keen that in the battle with the Dioscuri he could see through the trunk of an oak tree to where Castor and Polydeuces were lying in ambush. He pointed them out to Idas, who slew Castor. Polydeuces pursued them and slew Lynceus with a spear thrust (Apollod. 3. 11.2; Ov. *Fast.* 5. 700).

Shearing

MELUS, son of Melus and Peleia, after his parents' death, was ordered by Aphrodite to return with a colony to Delos, where he founded the town of Delos. There, the sheep were called *mela* because he first taught the inhabitants to shear them and make cloth out of their wool.

Shears

ATROPOS, one of the Moirae, or Fates, is sometimes represented with a shears or other cutting instrument.

Sheep

AJAX. When he lost the contest with Odysseus for Achilles' armor, he went mad and slew the Greek army's sheep, thinking that they were enemies.

APOLLO tended the flocks of Admetus at Pherae in Thessaly (Apollod. 1. 9.15; Eurip. *Alcest.* 8; Tibull. 2. 3.11; Virg. *Georg.* 3. 2). When Cleinis of Babylon wanted to sacrifice asses to the god, Apollo demanded that only sheep, goats, and heifers should be sacrificed to him.

ARISTAEUS was worshipped as the protector of flocks and shepherds.

ATHAMAS. An oracle declared that he should settle wherever he found hospitality from animals. He came upon wolves devouring a sheep, and they ran away, leaving the sheep. He founded the town of Athamania at that place.

DRYOPE was the daughter of King Dryops. While she tended the flocks of her father on Mt. Oeta, she became the playmate of the Hamadryads, who taught her to sing hymns to the gods and to dance.

EUMENIDES. Sacrifices to them consisted of black sheep.

FAUNUS. In his worship as a prophetic divinity, the person consulting him had to sleep for one night in the skin of the sacrificial sheep, during which the god gave answers to questions, either in a dream or by supernatural voices.

GAEA. Black sheep were sacrificed to her (Hom. *Il.* 3. 104).

HADES. The sacrifices which were offered to him and Persephone consisted of black male and female sheep.

HELIOS. Sheep were sacred to him. The sun god owned a flock of three hundred and fifty sheep, and this number never increased or diminished. They were guarded by his daughters, Phaetusa and Lampetia (Hom. *Od.* 12. 128, 261; Apollon. Rhod. 4. 965).

HERMES was believed to increase the fertility of sheep (Hom. *Hymn. in Merc.* 567; Hom. *Il.* 14. 490, 16. 180; Hes. *Theog.* 444).

IRUS. During the Calydonian Boar Hunt, Peleus unintentionally killed Eurytion, son of Irus, and endeavored to soothe him by offering him his flocks, but Irus would not accept them, and at the command of an oracle, Peleus allowed them to run wherever they pleased. A wolf devoured the sheep but was thereupon changed into a stone.

LUPERCUS was an ancient Italian divinity who was worshipped by shepherds as the promoter of fertility among sheep.

MELUS, son of Melus and Peleia, after his parents' death was ordered by Aphrodite to return with a colony to Delos, where he founded the town of Delos. There, the sheep were called from him *mela* because he first taught the inhabitants to shear them and make cloth out of their wool.

NOX. Black sheep were sacrificed to the goddess of night.

ODYSSEUS. When the Messenians had carried off some sheep from Ithaca, Laertes sent young Odysseus to Messene to demand reparation, for the youth had already shown a fine sense of diplomacy. Much later, on his return from Troy, in order to escape from the cave of the blinded Cyclops, he concealed himself and his men under the bodies of the sheep which the Cyclops let out of his cave each day, and Odysseus with part of the flock, reached his ship.

PRIAPUS, son of Dionysus and Aphrodite, was worshipped as the protector of flocks of sheep.

THEOPHANE was a daughter of Bisaltes, who, in consequence of her extraordinary beauty, was beleaguered by lovers, but was carried off by Poseidon to the isle of Crinissa. As the lovers followed her even there, Poseidon metamorphosed the maiden into a sheep and himself into a ram. He became by her the father of the ram with the golden fleece, which carried Phrixus to Colchis.

See also: EWE, LAMB, RAM

Shell

DAEDALUS was the famous inventor of the labyrinth in Crete. When he fled the island after assisting Theseus in his escape from the labyrinth, Minos, the king, went in pursuit of him. Minos gave a spiral seashell to rulers in all the countries he touched, asking them to thread it. No one could do so, until Minos reached Sicily. There, King Cocalus was able to have this accomplished, and Minos knew that his search was over, as Daedalus was the only one who was ingenious enough to do it. Daedalus had been able to manage the feat by tying a thread to an ant, which crawled through the labyrinthine shell.

PAN. Cnossus in Crete is said to have originally been inhabited by Titans, who were hostile to Zeus, but they were driven away by Pan with the fearful sounds of his shell trumpet (Hom. *Hymn. in Apoll.* 336; Diod. 3. 57, 5. 66).

TRITON was a son of Poseidon and Amphitrite. He was described as riding over the sea on horses or sea monsters. The chief characteristic of Tritons in poetry as well as in art is a trumpet consisting of a shell (*concha*) which they blew at the command of Poseidon to soothe the restless waves of the sea (Ov. *Met.* 1. 333). In the fight with the giants, this trumpet served to frighten the enemies.

Shepherd

AEGISTHUS, exposed at birth, was found and reared by shepherds.

AENEAS. Prior to his entrance into the Trojan War he was a shepherd on Mt. Ida near Troy.

AGELAUS. When Priam had the infant Paris exposed, the task was left to the shepherd, Agelaus, who left the child on Mt. Ida but returned five days later to find the child alive and suckled by a she-bear. He took the child and raised it as his own (Eurip. *Troad.* 921).

ALEXANDER (See PARIS)

AMPHION with his twin brother, Zethus, was exposed shortly after birth. They were found and brought up by shepherds.

ANTIPHUS was a son of Priam and Hecuba. He was captured by Achilles while tending his flocks on Mt. Ida.

APOLLO was the god of flocks and herds. He was obliged to serve as a shepherd to King Admetus for nine years for killing one of the Cyclops. He assumed the shape of a shepherd to court Isse.

APOLLO NOMIUS was a surname designating the god as protector of pastures and shepherds.

ARESTHANAS, a shepherd, found the exposed infant, Asclepius, on Mt. Tittheion.

ARISTAEUS was worshipped as protector of flocks and shepherds.

ARISTAEUS NOMIUS was a surname of Aristaeus as protector of pastures and shepherds.

ATYS, son of Nana, was a beautiful shepherd in Phrygia beloved by Cybele. In works of art he is represented as a shepherd with flute and staff.

BATTUS was a shepherd of Neleus, who saw Hermes driving away the cattle he had stolen from Apollo (Ov. *Met.* 2. 688).

BUTES, son of Teleon, was renowned as an Athenian shepherd.

CACUS was an Italian shepherd, who stole the cattle of Heracles or Recaranus.

CYBELE was exposed at infancy but was fed by panthers and brought up by shepherdesses (Diod. 3. 58).

CYCLOPES. In Homeric poems, the Cyclopes are a gigantic, insolent and lawless race of shepherds, who lived in Sicily and devoured human beings (Hom. *Od.* 6. 5, 9. 106, 190, 240, 10. 200).

CYCNUS, son of Poseidon, was exposed on the seacoast, where he was found by shepherds.

DAPHNIS was called by Ovid (*Met.* 4. 275) an Idaean shepherd. He was brought up by nymphs and shepherds and became a shepherd himself.

ENDYMION was usually described as a shepherd on Mt. Latmus, where Selene, the moon goddess, came and lay with him while he slumbered (Apollon. Rhod. 4. 57).

FAUNUS, in Italy, was worshipped as the god of fields and shepherds.

FAUSTULUS was the royal shepherd of Amulius and husband of Acca Laurentia. He found Romulus and Remus as they were nursed by the she-wolf and carried the twins to his wife to be brought up (Liv. 1. 5).

GARANUS (See RECARANUS)

HERMES was especially worshipped by shepherds.

HERMES NOMIUS was a surname of Hermes designating him as protector of pastures and shepherds.

ISUS was a brother of Antiphus and also a shepherd on Mt. Ida.

PALES was a Roman divinity of flocks and shepherds. His festival was celebrated on the 21st of April.

PAN was the great god of flocks and shepherds among the Greeks.

PAN NOMIUS was a surname designating Pan as a divinity who protected pastures and shepherds.

PARIS. When he grew up, as Agelaus' son, he distinguished himself as a valiant defender of flocks and shepherds, and thereby received the name of Alexander, i.e., the defender of men. (See also AGELAUS)

RECARANUS, also called Garanus, was a fabulous Italian shepherd of gigantic bodily strength and courage. He overcame the wicked robber, Cacus, and is often identified with the Greek Heracles.

ZETHUS. While his twin brother, Amphion, preferred song and music, he preferred hunting and shepherdry (Hor. *Epist.* 1. 18.41). (See also AMPHION)

Shield

ACHLYS, the personification of misery and sadness, was represented on the shield of Heracles.

APHRODITE. When she was represented as the victorious goddess, she had the attributes of Ares—a helmet, a shield, and a sword or a lance, and an image of Victory.

ATHENA. When she killed the winged giant, Pallas, she used his skin as her aegis. Perseus gave Medusa's head to her, and she put it on her shield or breastplate. In art, Athena was usually represented carrying a shield.

ATHENA PALLAS (PALLAS ATHENA) derived the surname, according to Plato (*Cratyl.* 406) from *pallein,* to brandish, in reference to the goddess brandishing the spear or aegis.

DIONYSUS MELANAEGIS was a surname meaning armed or clad with a black aegis, at Eleutherae (Paus. 1. 38.8) and at Athens (Paus. 2. 35.1).

ERICHTHONIUS, son of Hephaestus by Gaea or Atthis, was half serpent, half man. After Agraulos, Pandrosos, and Herse opened the chest in which he had been concealed by Athena, he escaped into the shield of Athena and was protected by her (Apollod. 3. 14.6; Paus. 1. 2.5, 18.2; Eurip. *Ion* 260; Ov. *Met.* 2. 554).

ERINYS MELANAEGIS was a surname designating the Erinys as the goddesses armed or clad with a black aegis (Aeschyl. *Sept.* 700).

EUPHORBUS was slain in the Trojan War by Menelaus (Hom. *Il.* 7. 1–60), who subsequently dedicated the shield of Euphorbus in the temple of Hera, near Mycenae (Paus. 2. 17.3). It is a well-known story that Pythagoras asserted that he had once been the Trojan Euphorbus, that from a Trojan he had become an Ionian, and from a warrior a philosopher (Philostr. *Vit.Apoll.* 1.1; Ov. *Met.* 15. 161).

EURYSACES, son of the Telamonian Ajax and Tecmessa, was named after the broad shield of his father (Soph. *Ajax* 575).

HERA. The shield which Abas received from his grandfather, Danaus, was sacred to her.

HIPPOLYTE. Her tomb at Megara had the form of an Amazon's shield (Paus. 1. 41.7).

IDOMENEUS. On his statue at Olympia, a cock was represented on his shield.

LYNCEUS. When he received the news of the death of his father-in-law, Danaus, from his son, Abas, Lynceus gave to Abas the shield of Danaus, which had been dedicated in the temple of Hera, and instituted games in honor of Hera, in which the victor received a shield as a prize.

MEDUSA was one of the Gorgons. After Perseus cut off her head, Athena had the head placed in the center of her shield.

MINERVA was represented with a helmet, shield, and coat of mail.

NIKE (NICE), goddess of victory, resembled Athena in appearance; she was represented as engaged in inscribing the victory of a conqueror on a shield (Paus. 5. 10.2, 11.1, 2, 6. 18.1).

PALLAS ATHENA (See ATHENA PALLAS)

TARPEIA was the daughter of the commander of the fortress on the Saturnian (later Capitoline) Hill. When the city of Rome was invaded by the Sabines in retaliation for the abduction of their women, she betrayed the hill to them in return for the ornaments which they wore on their left arms, and thus opened the gates and let them in. When she claimed her reward, they threw upon her their shields, which they carried on their left arms, and thus crushed her to death.

TRITONIS. After the serpents strangled Laocoon and his sons, they crawled to the acropolis of Troy and disappeared behind the shield of Tritonis.

TYCHIUS of Hyle was a mythical artisan mentioned by Homer as the maker of Ajax's shield of seven ox hides covered with a plate of brass.

ZEUS as king of the gods was armed with thunder and lightning, and the shaking of his aegis produced storm and tempest.

ZEUS AEGIDUCHOS (AEGIOCHOS) described Zeus as the bearer of the aegis.

Shield Bearer

CHALCON of Cyparissus was the shield bearer of Antilochus.

Ship

AMYCUS. On his tomb grew a species of laurel (*Laurus insana*) which when taken on shipboard caused general havoc till thrown overboard (Plin. *H.N.* 16. 89).

APOLLO EMBASIOUS was a surname of Apollo employed in much the same sense as Apollo Epibaterius (Apollon. Rhod. 1. 404).

APOLLO EPIBATERIUS was a surname of Apollo meaning the god who conducts men on board a ship. Diomedes on his return from Troy built the god, under this name, a temple at Troezen (Paus. 2. 32.1).

BRIZO was a Delian goddess to whom prayers were offered to protect ships. Sacrifices were made to her in the form of boats.

DANAUS. Fearing his nephews, sons of Aegyptus, were plotting against him, he built a large ship and embarked with his fifty daughters, first to Rhodes and then to the Peloponnesus.

DEUCALION, son of Prometheus, when Zeus resolved to destroy mankind, built a ship on the advice of his father, and stored it with provisions. When the flood came which destroyed all the inhabitants, Deucalion and his wife Pyrrha alone were saved (Apollod. 1. 7.2).

DIONYSUS. For a voyage from Icaria to Naxos, he hired a ship which belonged to Tyrrhenian pirates; but the men, instead of landing at Naxos, passed by and steered toward Asia to sell him there. The god, however, on perceiving this, changed the mast and oars into serpents and himself into a lion; he filled the vessel with ivy and the sound of flutes, so that the sailors were seized with madness and leaped into the sea where they were metamorphosed into dolphins (Apollod. 3. 5.3; Ov. *Met.* 3. 582).

HECTOR. After being cured by Apollo of the wound which Ajax inflicted on him, he returned to battle, repelled Ajax, and set fire to the ships of the Greeks (Hom. *Il.* 15. 253, 16. 114).

IRIS assumed the appearance of Beroe, wife of Doryclus, and persuaded the women to set fire to the ships of Aeneas on the coast of Sicily (Virg. *Aen.* 5. 620).

JASON. According to some he was crushed by the poop of the ship Argo, under which he lay down on the advice of Medea, and which fell upon him.

ORPHEUS. The power of his music caused the Argonauts to seek his aid, which contributed materially to the success of their expedition. At the sound of his lyre the Argo glided down into the sea and the Symplegadae, or moving rocks, which threatened to crush the ship between them, were fixed in their places when he played.

PATAECI were Phoenician divinities whose dwarvish figures were attached to Phoenician ships (Herod. 3. 37).

PROTESILAUS. According to some, Protesilaus survived the Trojan War and took with him Aethilla, a sister of Priam, who was his prisoner. When, on his homeward voyage, he landed on the Macedonian peninsula of Pallene, between Mende and Scione, and had gone some distance from the coast to fetch water, Aethylla prevailed upon the other women to set fire to the ships. Protesilaus was thus obliged to remain there and build the town of Scione.

ROMA was a Trojan captive who advised her fellow captives on the coast of Italy to set fire to the fleet of the Greeks (Plut. *Romul.* 1).

Shipbuilding

ARGUS was the builder of the Argo, the ship of the Argonauts.

ATHENA AETHYIA. She was worshipped under this name in Megara for having taught the Megarians the art of shipbuilding.

GLAUCUS was reported to have built the ship Argo.

PHERECLUS, a son of Harmonides, is said to have built the ship in which Paris carried off Helen. Some say the builder was Harmonides, his father.

Shipwreck

ARGUS. En route to Greece, he was shipwrecked and rescued from the island of Aretias by Jason (Apollon. Rhod. 2. 1095).

CEYX. When he perished in a shipwreck, his wife, Alcyone, threw herself into the sea.

DIOSCURI were worshipped as the protectors of travelers by sea, for Poseidon had rewarded their brotherly love by giving them power over wind and waves, so that they could assist the shipwrecked (Eurip. *Hel.* 1511; Hor. *Carm.* 1. 3.2).

NAUPLIUS was king of Euboea and father of Palamedes. His son had been condemned to death by the Greeks during the siege of Troy, and as Nauplius considered his condemnation to be an act of injustice, he watched for the return of the Greeks, and as they approached the coast of Euboea, he lighted torches on the most dangerous part of the coast. The sailors, thus misguided, suffered shipwreck and perished in the waves or by the sword of Nauplius.

ODYSSEUS. He and his men were detained on the island of Helios by storms and his companions, in spite of an oath not to touch the sacred cattle of Helios, devoured some of the finest. The storms abated and they sailed away, but another storm came up, and their ship was destroyed by Zeus with a flash of lightning. All were drowned except Odysseus.

Shoe

FORTUNA. When she entered Rome, she put off her wings and shoes and threw away the globe, as she intended to make her permanent abode among the Romans.

See also: SANDAL

Shoulder

AENEAS. Before Troy fell, Aeneas escaped with his family and carried Anchises, his father, on his shoulders to Mt. Ida (Virg. *Aen.* 2. 687).

ATLAS bore heaven on his head and shoulders.

PELOPS was slaughtered by his father, Tantalus, and served at a repast of the gods. They refused to eat, except for Demeter, who, absorbed in grief for the loss of her daughter, consumed the shoulder of Pelops. When the gods restored him to life, the shoulder consumed by Demeter was lacking, so she supplied in its place one made of ivory. Pelops' descendants, the Pelopidae, as a mark of their origin, were believed to have one shoulder as white as ivory (Pind. *Ol.* 1. 37; Virg. *Georg.* 3. 7; Ov. *Met.* 6. 404).

Shroud

PENELOPE deceived her suitors in Odysseus' absence by declaring that she must finish a large shroud which she was making for Laertes, her aged father-in-law, before she could make up her mind. During the day, she worked on the shroud, and in the night she undid the work of the day (Hom. *Od.* 19. 149; Propert. 2. 9.5).

Shuttle

MENIPPE and her sister Metioche, after the death of their father, Orion, were taught the art of weaving by Athena. To avert a plague in Aonia, where they lived, they offered themselves as a sacrifice (in response to an oracle) and killed themselves with their shuttles. Hades and Persephone metamorphosed them into comets (Ov. *Met.* 13. 685).

Sickle

GAEA. When her children by Uranus were hated by their father, she concealed them in the bosom of the earth. She made a large iron sickle, gave it to her sons, and requested them to take vengeance upon their father. Cronus accordingly emasculated Uranus with the sickle (Hes. *Theog.* 180).

HERACLES used arrows, a club, and a sickle to cut off the Hydra's heads.

PERSEUS. For his mission to fetch Medusa's head, the nymphs provided him with a sickle with which to sever the head (Hes. *Scut.Herc.* 220, 222).

PRIAPUS, son of Dionysus and Aphrodite, was sometimes represented in art as carrying a sickle.

TELCHINES were a mysterious order of artisans who worked in brass and iron and made the sickle of Cronus.

Sieve

DANAIDES. For their crime of murdering their husbands, they were compelled everlastingly to pour water into a vessel full of holes (Ov. *Met.* 4. 462; Hor. *Carm.* 3. 11.25; Tibull. 1. 3.79).

TUCCIA, a vestal virgin accused of incest, appealed to the goddess to prove her innocence, and had the power given to her to carry a sieve full of water from the Tiber to the temple (Plin. *H.N.* 28. 2; Dionys. 2. 69; August. 10. 16).

Sight, see Sharpsightedness

Silence

ANGERONA (ANGERONIA) was the Roman goddess of silence.

CALYPSO was sometimes referred to as a goddess of silence.

HARPOCRATES was a Roman divinity of silence.

LARUNDA (LARA), daughter of Almon, was a nymph who announced to Juno that Jupiter was having an affair with Juturna. Jupiter punished her by depriving her of her tongue (Ov. *Fast.* 2. 599). She is possibly identical with Muta and Tacita.

MUTA was a Roman divinity who presided over silence. (See also LARUNDA)

TACITA, "the silent," was one of the Camenae, whose worship was believed to have been introduced at Rome by Numa. He is, moreover, said to have particularly recommended the worship of Tacita as the most important among the Camenae (Plut. *Num.* 8). (See also LARUNDA)

Silver

ERICHTHONIUS was believed to have acquainted the Athenians with the use of silver.

Skeleton

ANTAEUS. Sertorius is said to have opened the grave of Antaeus, but when he found the skeleton sixty cubits in length, he was struck with horror and had it covered up immediately (Strab. 17. 829; Plut. *Sertor.* 9).

Skin

AEGA was one of the nurses of Zeus. In the battle with the Titans, Zeus was told by an oracle to cover himself with her skin (aegis).

ASCUS. For throwing the chained Dionysus into a river, he was flayed and a bag was made of his skin.

ATHENA. When she killed the winged giant Pallas, she used his skin as her aegis.

MARSYAS. For presuming to challenge Apollo to a musical contest, he was flayed alive by the god, and his skin was hung in the cave out of which the river Marsyas flows.

See also: FLAYING

Skin (Pelt)

MELEAGER. Possession of the skin of the Calydonian boar which he slew became the basis of a war between the Calydonians and Curetes.

Skull

ANTAEUS, the giant, built a house to Poseidon, his father, from the skulls of the victims he overcame in wrestling.

Slaughter

ARES as god of war delighted in slaughter.

Slave

AETHRA, mother of Theseus, carried to Lacedaemon by Castor and Pollux, became the slave of Helen and accompanied her to Troy.

AGELAUS was a slave of Priam who exposed the infant Paris on Mt. Ida. When five days later he found the infant alive, he took him and brought him up.

DIANA, the Roman goddess, was regarded as the protectress of slaves.

HESIONE, daughter of Laomedon, was given as a slave to Telamon. Priam, her brother, sent Teucris to claim her back, and the refusal on the part of the Greeks is mentioned as one of the causes of the Trojan War.

HYPERMESTRA (See MESTRA)

MESTRA. In order to escape the slavery into which she had been sold by her father, she prayed to Poseidon, who loved her and conferred on her the power of metamorphosing herself whenever she was sold, and of thus each time returning to her father (Ov. *Met.* 8. 847). Some call her Hypermestra.

PALICI, Sicilian daemons, were twin sons of Zeus. Their sanctuary was an asylum for runaway slaves.

PSYCHE. In searching to recover Amor's love, she came to the temple of Venus, who enslaved her and forced her to perform all manner of difficult and humiliating labors, in which she was assisted in secret by Amor, who still loved her.

ROMULUS. In the newly founded city of Rome, he found his people too few in number, so he set apart, on the Capitoline Hill, an asylum, or a sanctuary, in which homicides and runaway slaves might take refuge.

TISIPHONE, daughter of Alcmaon, was left for Creon, king of Corinth, to educate. Creon's wife was jealous of her great beauty and sold her as a slave. Her father, not recognizing her, purchased her.

Sleep

BRIZO was a Delian goddess whose name is connected with *brizo,* to fall asleep.

COMUS, the Roman divinity of joy and mirth, was often represented as slumbering in a standing attitude.

CUBA, a Roman divinity, was worshipped as the protectress of children and was believed to bless their sleep, just as Edulica blessed their food (August. 4. 11).

ENDYMION was usually described as a shepherd on Mt. Latmus, where Selene, the moon goddess, came and lay with him while he slumbered (Apollon. Rhod. 4. 57). Some say that Zeus had granted him a request, and that Endymion begged for immortality, eternal sleep, and everlasting youth (Apollod. 1. 7.5). Others state that he was received among the gods of Olympus but that he fell in love with Hera, and Zeus punished him by putting him eternally asleep on Mt. Latmus. Others state that Selene put him to sleep forever, so that she might caress him without being observed (Cic. *Tusc.* 1. 38). It is said that by him she became the mother of fifty daughters (Apollod. 1. 7.5; Cic. *Tusc.* 1. 38; Catull. 66.5; Paus. 5. 1.2).

HERMES had it in his power to send refreshing sleep or to take it away (Hom. *Hymn. in Merc.* 14; Hom. *Il.* 2. 26, 24. 343).

HYPNOS (See SOMNUS)

MORPHEUS was the son of Sleep and the god of dreams. The name signifies the fashioner or molder, because he shaped or formed the dreams which appeared to the sleeper (Ov. *Met.* 11. 635).

MORPHEUS EPIDOTES, the "liberal giver," was a name applied to the god of sleep at Sicyon, where he had a statue in the temple of Asclepius, which represented him in the act of sending a lion to sleep (Paus. 2. 10.3).

ONEIRATA. Ovid (*Met.* 11. 633), who calls dreams the children of Sleep, mentions three of them by name: Morpheus, Icelus or Phobetor, and Phantasus.

ORION. When he violated Aero (Merope), her father Oenopion implored the assistance of Dionysus, who caused Orion to be thrown into a deep sleep by satyrs, in which Oenopion blinded him.

SILENUS (SEILENUS), one of the satyrs, the son of Hermes or Pan by a nymph, was like all satyrs fond of sleep.

SOMNUS, the personification and god of sleep, the Greek Hypnos, is described by the ancients as the brother of Death and as a son of Night (Hes. *Theog.* 211; Virg. *Aen.* 6. 277).

THANATOS was a personification of Death. He and his brother Sleep were usually represented together as slumbering youths.

Smelter

CELMIS was one of the Dactyli and presided over the smelter.

Snake, see Serpent

Snare

HARPALYCE, the fleet-footed Thracian robber, was eventually caught in a snare by shepherds, who killed her.

Snow

HERACLES succeeded in catching the Erymanthian boar by chasing it through deep snow and exhausting it, after which time he caught it in a net (Apollod. 2. 5.4).

TELCHINES were a group of mysterious beings described as sorcerers and envious daemons, and they had the power of bringing on hail, rain and snow and of being able to assume any form they pleased (Diod. 5. 55).

Soil

EUPHEMUS. On the Argonaut he accepted a clod of earth from Triton as a gesture of friendship. This gave him the right to rule over Libya. He accidentally dropped the clod as the ship passed Thera, and the colonization of Libya therefore proceeded from Thera seventeen generations later (Pind. *Pyth.* 4. 1; Apollon. Rhod. 2. 562; Herod. 4. 150).

Song

AMPHION. While his twin brother, Zethus, preferred hunting and shepherdry, he preferred song and music (Hor. *Epist.* 1. 18.41).

AOEDE was one of the originally recognized three Muses, who were worshipped on Mt. Helicon. She presided over song.

CELEDONES, "the soothing goddesses," were believed to be endowed like the Sirens with the magic power of song.

DIONYSUS MELPOMENUS was a surname meaning the singer, at Athens and in the Attic demos of Acharne (Paus. 1. 2.4, 31.3).

HESPERIDES were possessed of the power of sweet song.

LINUS, son of Apollo, was called the inventor of songs in general.

LITYERSES, son of Midas, compelled strangers to assist him in harvest and if they did not surpass him, he cut off their heads and concealed them in sheaves, accompanying his deed with songs. Phrygian reapers used to celebrate his memory in a harvest song, which bore the name Lityerses (Athen. 10. 615, 14. 619).

MUSES according to the earliest writers, were the inspiring goddesses of song.

ORPHEUS. Pindar enumerates him among the Argonauts as the celebrated harp player, father of songs, and as sent forth by Apollo (*Pyth.* 4. 315). (See also SIRENS)

SIRENS were the maidens who attracted sailors with their sweet voices and then destroyed them. When the Argonauts passed by them, the Sirens began to sing, but in vain, for Orpheus rivalled and surpassed them. As it had been decreed that they should pass by unmoved, the Sirens threw themselves into the sea and were metamorphosed into rocks. Later, Odysseus was able to escape them by filling the ears of his companions with wax and lashing himself to the mast of his ship (Hom. *Od.* 12. 39, 166).

TERPSICHORE, the Muse of choral dance and song, appears with the lyre and plectrum.

THAMYRIS, an ancient Thracian bard, was the son of Philammon and the nymph, Argiope. He went so far in his conceit as to think he could surpass the Muses in song, in consequence of which he was deprived of his sight and of the power of singing (Hom. *Il.* 2. 595; Apollod. 1. 3.3; Paus. 4. 33.4; 10. 7.2; Eurip. *Rhes.* 925). He was represented with a broken lyre in his hand (Paus. 9. 30.2).

Soothsayer, see Seer

Sorcery

CIRCE, daughter of Helios and sister of Aeetes, was the sorceress who detained Odysseus on the island of Aeaea during his wanderings.

FASCINUS, an early Latin divinity, was worshipped as the protector from sorcery, witchcraft, and evil daemons.

HECATE was regarded as a spectral being who at night sent from the lower world all kind of demons and phantoms, who taught sorcery and witchcraft, and who dwelt in places where two roads crossed, on tombs, and near the blood of murdered persons. She wandered about with the souls of the dead, and her approach was announced by the whining and howling of dogs (Apollon.Rhod. 3. 168, 861, 4. 829; Ov. *Her.* 12. 168; Ov. *Met.* 14. 405; Stat. *Theb.* 4. 428; Virg. *Aen.* 4. 609).

MEDEA, daughter of Aeetes of Colchis, was a powerful sorceress.

PHARMACIDES, "witches or sorceresses," was the name by which the Thebans designated the divinities who delayed the birth of Heracles (Paus. 9. 11.2).

TELCHINES were a group of mysterious beings described as sorcerers and envious daemons (Strab. 14. 653).

Sororicide, see Murder (of Sister)

Sorrow

DIONYSUS ELEUTHEREUS was a surname of Dionysus referring to the god as the deliverer of man from care and sorrow (Plut. *Quaest.Rom.* 101).

Soul

EVANDER had to kill the son of Feronia three times, since she had given him three souls (Virg. *Aen.* 3. 564).

PSYCHE occurs in the later times of antiquity as a personification of the human soul.

ZALMOXIS (SALMOXIS) was a Getan who had been a slave to Pythagoras in Samos. He was regarded by some as a deity, introducing doctrines regarding the immortality of the soul.

The Getae believed that the departed went to him. Every four years they selected a man by lot to go as a messenger to Zalmoxis and tell him what they needed. The manner in which the man was killed is described by Herodotus (4. 94). The Pythagorean doctrines regarding the soul spread in various forms among the barbaric races who came in contact with the Greeks and seem to have given rise to this fable about Zalmoxis. He was also known as Gebelzeïzis.

Sow

THESEUS. When he reached maturity, he took the sword and sandals, the tokens which had been left by Aegeus, his father, in Troezen and proceeded to Athens to seek recognition from his father. On his way, he destroyed the robbers and monsters that infested the country. These included Phaea, the Crommyonian sow, which had been ravaging the neighborhood (Plut. *Thes.* 9; Eurip. *Suppl.* 316).

Sowing

OPS CONSIVA was a surname from the verb *serere,* to sow.

Space

AETHER was a personification, in Greek cosmogonies, of space, one of the elementary components of the universe.

CHAOS was the personification of vacant and infinite space (Hes. *Theog.* 116).

Spark

CAECULUS was an Italian hero of Praeneste. He was born as a result of a spark of fire falling into the lap of his mother. The spark was believed to have come from Vulcan, the god of fire, making Caeculus his son.

Sparrow

APHRODITE. The sparrow was sacred to her.

Spear

AGAMEMNON. At the funeral games of Patroclus, he excelled in throwing the spear.

AJAX (the Lesser) was especially skilled in throwing the spear.

ATHENA PALLAS (PALLAS ATHENA) derived the surname, according to Plato (*Cratyl.* 406) from *pallein,* to brandish, in reference to the goddess brandishing the spear or aegis.

CAMILLA. When her father, Metabus, was fleeing with her as an infant, he came to a river, tied the child to his spear and hurled it across. He swam across and found the child uninjured.

DIOSCURI. In art they are usually represented as carrying spears in their hands.

ENCELADUS was one of the hundred-armed giants who made war upon the gods; he was killed, according to some, by the spear of Silenus (Eurip. *Cycl.* 7).

HONOR (HONOS), the personfication of honor, is represented as bearing a cornucopia in his left and a spear in his right hand.

JANUS QUIRINUS was a surname of Janus, according to Dionysius of Halicarnassus (2. 48), from a Sabine word *quiris* meaning a lance or spear.

LYNCEUS. In his and Idas' battle with the Dioscuri, he was killed by Polydeuces with a spearthrust (Apollod. 3. 11.2; Ov. *Fast.* 5. 700).

MARS QUIRINUS. As JANUS QUIRINUS.

MELEAGER slew the Calydonian boar and dedicated the spear which made the kill in the temple of Apollo at Sicyon (Paus. 2. 7.8).

PALLADIUM. This image of Pallas Athena held a spear in its right hand and a spindle and distaff in its left (Apollod. 3. 12.3; Dionys. 1. 69).

PALLAS ATHENA (See ATHENA PALLAS)

PELEUS involuntarily killed Eurytion with a spear during the Calydonian Boar Hunt.

PROCRIS, wife of Cephalus, was by Artemis given a dog which always found its quarry and a spear that never missed its mark. After she and Cephalus were reconciled over her infidelity, she followed him often to the hunt because she still feared that Eos would try to seduce him again. Once on a hunt, Cephalus accidentally killed her with the never-erring spear.

ROMULUS QUIRINUS. According to Dionysius of Halicarnassus (2. 48), the surname came from a Sabine word, *quiris,* a lance or spear. It occurs as the name of Romulus after he had been raised to the rank of a divinity, and the festival celebrated in his honor bore the name of Quirinalia (Virg. *Aen.* 1. 292; Cic. *De Nat.Deor.* 2. 24; Ov. *Amor.* 3. 8.51; Ov. *Fast.* 4. 56, 808, 6. 375; Ov. *Met.* 15. 862).

TELEPHUS was a king of Mysia at the time of the Trojan War. When the Greeks invaded Mysia, he repelled them. He was, however, wounded by Achilles. The wound could not be healed, and when he consulted the oracle, he received the answer that only he could cure him who had wounded him. The Greeks received an oracle that without the aid of Telephus they could not reach Troy. A reconciliation was brought about and Achilles cured Telephus by means of the rust of the spear by which the wound had been inflicted; Telephus in return pointed out to the Greeks the road they had to take (Ov. *Met.* 12. 112; Ov. *Trist.* 5. 2, 15; Ov. *Rem.Am.* 47; Ov. *Ep.ex Pont.* 2. 26; Philostr. *Vit.Apoll.* 2. 14).

VIRTUS was the Roman personification of manly valor. She was often represented with a spear in her left hand.

Spectre

LEMURES were the spectres or spirits of the dead, which were believed by the Romans to return to the upper world and injure the living. Some writers describe Lemures as the common name for all the spirits of the dead (Ov. *Fast.* 5. 483).

MANIA was an ancient and formidable Italian, probably Etruscan, divinity. Originally, human sacrifices were made to her. In later times, the plural Maniae occurs as the designators of terrible, ugly, and deformed spectres, with which nurses used to frighten children.

Spider

ARACHNE. For comparing her weaving skill to that of Athena, she was changed into a spider.

Spindle

CLOTHO, one of the Moirae, or Fates, was represented as holding a spindle.

PALLADIUM. This image of Pallas Athena held a spear in its right hand and a spindle and distaff in its left (Apollod. 3. 12.3; Dionys. 1. 69).

Spinning

CLOTHO. Hesiod (*Theog.* 217, 904) distinguishes three Fates, one of them Clotho, who spins out the thread of man's life.

MOIRA. Homer, when he personifies Fate, conceives of her as spinning out the thread of man's future life (*Il.* 24. 209).

OMPHALE was a queen of Lydia for whom Heracles labored after he had killed Eurytus. He was so enamored of the woman that he did household chores for her, notably spinning.

Spoils, see Booty

Spring (Season)

ADONIS. Persephone, queen of Hades, is said to have restored Adonis to life for a part of the year. His resurrection betokens spring.

ANNA PERENNA was the Roman divinity of health and plenty, whose powers were most manifest at the return of spring, when her festival was celebrated.

FLORA was the Roman goddess of flowers and spring.

PERSEPHONE. Because her return to the

upper earth each year signalled the shooting forth of vegetation, she was identified with spring.

See also: SEASONS

Spring, see Well

Spy

DELPHINUS spied on Amphitrite and found her for Poseidon, whom she married.

ECHION. During the expedition of the Argonauts, he acted the part of a cunning spy (Pind. *Pyth.* 4. 179; Ov. *Met.* 8. 311).

SINON was a son of Aesimus and a relation of Odysseus, whom he accompanied to Troy. He allowed himself to be taken prisoner by the Trojans, after he had mutilated himself in such a manner as to make them believe that he had been ill-treated by the Greeks. He told the Trojans that he was hated by Odysseus and had been selected by him to be sacrificed because Apollo had ordered a human sacrifice to be offered that the Greeks might safely depart from the coast of Troy, and added that he had escaped death by flight. When he was asked what was the purport of the wooden horse, he told them that it had been constructed as an atonement for the Palladium which had been carried off, and that if the Trojans ventured to destroy it, their kingdom should fall, but that if they would draw it with their own hands into the city, Asia would gain supremacy over Greece (Virg. *Aen.* 2. 57). The Trojans took his advice, and when the horse was drawn into the city, he gave the prearranged signal, opened the door of the horse, and the Greeks, rushing out, took possession of Troy (Virg. *Aen.* 2. 259).

Stable

BUBONA was a Roman divinity worshipped as protectress of stables.

EPONA, a Roman divinity, was regarded as the protectress of horses. Images of her were frequently seen in stables. She was said to be the daughter of Fulvius Stellus by a mare (Juv. 8. 157; Plut. *Paral.Gr.et Rom.* 312).

HERACLES. The fifth labor of Heracles consisted of cleansing the Augean stables, which he accomplished by diverting the flow of the Alpheius and Peneius rivers through the stables. He stipulated that his reward be a tenth part of the cattle.

Staff

APOLLO presented Hermes with his own golden shepherd's staff.

ASCLEPIUS. A serpent twined around a staff on which he was leaning, and he killed it; another serpent came bearing an herb which restored the other serpent to life. After this, Asclepius began to resurrect the dead.

ATHENA was represented as carrying a golden staff, with which she bestowed youth and majesty on her favorites (Hom. *Od.* 16. 172).

ATYS. In works of art he is represented as a shepherd with flute and staff.

EIRENE (IRENE) is pictured on coins sometimes carrying in her hand the staff of Hermes.

FELICITAS, the personification of happiness, is often seen on Roman medals in the form of a matron with a staff of Mercury and a cornucopia.

HADES. The ensign of his power was a staff with which, like Hermes, he drove the shades into the lower world (Pind. *Ol.* 9. 35).

HERMES was represented as carrying a staff. The white ribbons with which the herald's staff was originally surrounded were changed by later artists into two serpents. (See also APOLLO)

IRIS, the goddess of the rainbow, was represented carrying a herald's staff.

LACHESIS (See MOIRAE)

MOIRAE, the Fates, were represented by early artists with staffs or sceptres. Lachesis is sometimes represented as pointing with a staff to the horoscope or the globe.

SATYRS. Satyrs usually appear with flutes, the thyrsus, syrinx, the shepherd's staff, and cups or bags filled with wine.

THALIA, the Muse of comedy and of merry or idyllic poetry, appears with the comic mask, a shepherd's staff, or a wreath of ivy.

TIRESIAS (TEIRESIAS) was a son of Everes (or Phorbas) and Chariclo and one of the most renowned soothsayers of antiquity. He was blind from an early age, and some attribute his blindness to having seen Athena in her bath. Chariclo prayed to the goddess to restore his sight, but as Athena was not able to do this, she conferred upon him the power to understand the voices of birds and gave him a staff, with the help of which he could walk as safely as if he had his eyesight (Apollod. 3. 6.7; Callim. *Lav.Pall.* 75). In the underworld, Tiresias was believed to retain his powers of perception and there also he continued to use his golden staff (Hom. *Od.* 10. 492, 11. 190; Lycoph. 682; Cic. *De Div.* 1. 40; Paus. 9. 33.1).

URANIA, the Muse of astronomy, appears with a staff pointing to a globe.

Stag

ACTAEON was changed into a stag by Artemis when he accidentally observed her bathing. His hunting dogs thereupon tore him to pieces.

AGAMEMNON once killed a stag in the grove of Artemis or boasted that the goddess herself could not hit better, and this circumstance is said to be one of the causes that the Greek fleet lay becalmed in the port of Aulis when the Greeks wanted to sail against Troy. Sacrifice of Iphigeneia was the only thing that could propitiate the goddess. When, according to some accounts, Artemis saved her, a stag was substituted for the sacrifice.

AMYMONE. On a quest for water during a drought, she shot at a stag but missed and hit a sleeping satyr who pursued her until she was rescued by Poseidon.

ARTEMIS. The stag was sacred to her. She was called the stag-killer. Her chariot was drawn by four stags with golden antlers (Callim. *Hymn.in Dian.* 13, 81, 90). When the Aloeidae sued for her and Hera's hands, she changed herself into a stag and ran between the brothers, who, both aiming at the animal, shot each other dead.

ASCANIUS, son of Aeneas, once while hunting killed a tame stag belonging to Tyrrheus, a shepherd of king Latinus, whereupon the country people took up arms, which was the first conflict in Italy between the natives and the Trojan settlers (Virg. *Aen.* 7. 483; 9. 28).

CYPARISSUS was a youth of Cea. When he had inadvertently killed his favorite stag, he was seized with immoderate grief and was metamorphosed into a cypress (Ov. *Met.* 10. 120).

HERACLES. His third labor consisted of bringing the stag of Ceryneia alive to Mycenae. He pursued the stag for a year and finally succeeded in wounding it with an arrow and bringing it to Mycenae. The stag had golden antlers and brazen feet and was sacred to Artemis (Apollod. 3. 5.3).

NEMESIS. The Rhamnusian statue of Nemesis wore on its head a crown adorned with stags and an image of victory.

TELEPHUS, son of Auge, a priestess of Athena, was exposed as an infant on Mt. Parthenion by his grandfather, Aleus, and there he was cared for by a stag.

ZEUS LYCAEUS (LYCEUS) was a surname from Zeus' being worshipped on Mt. Lycaeus in Arcadia. He had a sanctuary there in which the festival of the Lycaea was celebrated. Entrance was forbidden and, according to some, those who entered there were stoned to death by the Arcadians or were called stags and obliged to take flight to save their lives (Plut. *Quaest.Gr.* 39).

Stars and Constellations

AEGA, one of the nurses of Zeus, was changed into the constellation Capella.

AMALTHEA, the goat (or nymph) who suckled Zeus, was placed among the stars as reward for her services.

ANDROMEDA was placed by Athena among the stars (Arat. 198).

ARCAS. When once he pursued in the chase his mother Callisto, who had been changed into a she-bear, both of them were placed among the stars by Zeus (Ov. *Met.* 2. 410). She became Ursa Major and he Ursa Minor.

ARIADNE. Dionysus is said to have placed her and the crown he gave her on their marriage among the stars (Hes. *Theog.* 949).

ASCLEPIUS. After his death he was placed among the stars by Zeus at Apollo's request.

ASTRAEA, daughter of Zeus and Themis, lived among mortals during the golden age and later was placed among the stars (Ov. *Met.* 1. 149). She became the constellation Virgo.

ASTRAEUS, a Titan, became by Eos, goddess of the dawn, the father of the winds Zephyrus, Boreas, Notus, and of Eosphorus (the morning star), and all the stars of heaven (Hes. *Theog.* 376).

ATLANTIDES (See HYADES)

ATLAS was represented by some as a powerful king who had great knowledge of the courses of the stars and first taught men that heaven had the form of a globe (Diod. 3. 60, 4. 27; Paus. 9. 20.3).

CALLISTO (See ARCAS). Apollodorus says that she was placed among the stars under the name of Arctos (3. 8.2).

CAPRICORNUS was an animal into which Pan made himself when flying before Typhon in the war with the giants. Later this event was commemorated by the constellation Capricorn.

CASSIOPEIA (CASSIEPEIA). She was placed among the stars facing backwards because she had boasted of her beauty.

CASTOR (See DIOSCURI)

CEPHEUS, father of Andromeda and husband of Cassiopeia, was changed by Hermes into a constellation.

CHEIRON, the centaur, was placed by Zeus among the stars (as the constellation Sagittarius).

CROTUS asked the Muses, with whom he had been brought up, to place him among the stars as Sagittarius, as he had been a skillful shooter.

CYCNUS was a son of Sthenelus and friend of Phaethon. While he was lamenting the death of Phaethon on the banks of the Eridanus, he was metamorphosed by Apollo into a swan and placed among the stars (Ov. *Met.* 2. 366; Paus. 1. 30.3).

CYNOSURA, an Idaean nymph and nurse of Zeus, was placed by him among the stars (Arat. 35).

DELPHINUS. For his service in finding Amphitrite for Poseidon, he was rewarded by being placed among the stars.

DIONYSUS. In his wanderings he was carried across a lake by an ass, and the grateful god placed the animal among the stars. Asses henceforth remained sacred to Dionysus. Zeus rewarded the nymphs of Mt. Nysa for bringing up Dionysus by placing them among the stars as the Hyades.

DIOSCURI. During the voyage of the Argonauts the heroes were detained by a vehement storm. When Orpheus prayed to the Samothracian gods, the storm suddenly subsided and stars appeared on the heads of the Dioscuri (Diod. 4. 43; Plut. *De Plac.Philos.* 2. 18; Senec. *Quaest.Nat.* 1. 1). Zeus rewarded the attachment of the two brothers by placing them among the stars as Gemini. In art they are sometimes represented as crowned with stars.

EOSPHORUS, son of Astraeus and Eos and brother of the winds, was the morning star.

ERICHTHONIUS was the first to use a chariot with four horses, for which reason he was placed among the stars as Auriga (Virg. *Georg.* 1. 205, 3. 113) or Bootes.

ERIGONE, daughter of Icarius, hanged herself but was placed by Zeus or Dionysus among the stars as the Virgin.

EVIPPE (EUIPPE) (See MELANIPPE)

GANYMEDE. The idea of his being the cupbearer of Zeus subsequently caused his being placed by astronomers among the stars under the name of Aquarius (Virg. *Georg.* 3. 304).

HELICE, daughter of Lycaon, because she was beloved by Zeus, was metamorphosed by Hera into a she-bear, whereupon Zeus placed her among the stars under the name of the Great Northern Bear.

HERA. Some ancients regarded her as the goddess of the stars (Eurip. *Hel.* 1097).

HESPERUS, the evening star, was the son of Astraeus and Eos and was regarded, even by the ancients, as identical to the morning star.

HYADES. When they saved the infant Dionysus from Lycurgus, Zeus showed his gratitude by placing them among the stars. They are also called Atlantides.

ICARIUS was placed with his wine cup, by Zeus or Dionysus, among the stars as Bootes.

LADON was the dragon who guarded the apples of the Hesperides and who was overcome by Heracles. The famous fight was commemorated by Zeus by placing the antagonists among the stars (Hes. *Theog.* 333; Apollon. Rhod. 4. 1396).

MAERA (MERA), the dog of Icarius, was placed by Zeus or Dionysus among the stars as the dog star.

MELANIPPE, daughter of Cheiron, is also called Evippe. When she became pregnant by Aeolus, she fled to Mt. Pelion, and when her father made a search for her, she prayed to be metamorphosed into a mare. Artemis granted the prayer, and in the form of a horse Melanippe was placed among the stars (Aristoph. *Thes.* 512).

MEROPE was one of the Pleiades and wife of Sisyphus of Corinth, by whom she became the mother of Glaucus. In the constellation of the Pleiades she is the least visible star, because she is ashamed of having had intercourse with a mortal man (Apollod. 1. 9.3, 3. 10.1; Ov. *Fast.* 4. 175).

MEROPS, king of Cos, about to do away with himself from grief over his dead wife, was changed by Hera into an eagle, whom she placed among the stars (Eurip. *Hel.* 384).

MYRTILUS, son of Hermes, after his death was placed among the stars as Auriga.

NAUPLIUS, son of Poseidon and Amymone and a famous navigator, is said to have discovered the constellation of the great bear (Paus. 8. 4815; Strab 8. 368).

OPHIUCHUS (See PHORBAS)

ORION. After his death he was placed among the stars (Hom. *Il.* 18. 486, 22. 29; Hom. *Od.* 5. 274), where he appears as a giant with a girdle, sword, a lion's skin and a club. The rising and setting of the constellation was believed to be accompanied by storms and rain.

ORPHEUS. The astronomers taught that the lyre of Orpheus was placed by Zeus among the stars, at the intercession of Apollo and the Muses. (See also DIOSCURI)

PAN (See CAPRICORNUS)

PARTHENOS was a daughter of Apollo and Chrysothemis, who after her premature death was placed by her father among the stars.

PHORBAS was a son of Lapithes and Orsinome. The Rhodians, in response to an oracle, invited him into their island to deliver it from snakes. Afterwards, they honored him with heroic worship (Diod. 5. 58). From this circumstance he was called Ophiuchus and is said to have been placed among the stars.

PHOSPHORUS, a personification of the morning star, was a son of Astraeus and Eos (Hes. *Theog.* 381), of Cephalus and Eos, or of Atlas.

PLEIADES, the seven daughters of Atlas and

Pleione and sisters of the Hyades, killed themselves from grief at the death of the Hyades or at the fate of Atlas, and were afterwards placed as stars at the back of Taurus. The stars in this constellation are said to have lost their brilliance on seeing the destruction of Troy. (See also MEROPE)

POLYDEUCES (POLLUX) (See Dioscuri)

Statue

ACTAEON. An iron image of him was fashioned by the Orchomenians to lay his ghost to rest.

AEGEUS. There was a statue of him at Delphi and one at Athens. The one at Delphi was made from the tithes of the booty taken by the Athenians at Marathon.

AENEAS left Mt. Ida after the fall of Troy, taking family, friends, and images of the gods, especially that of Pallas, and sailed westward.

AJAX (the Lesser), after the fall of Troy, rushed into the temple of Athena, where Cassandra was embracing the statue of the goddess as a suppliant. He dragged her away, or, according to some accounts, raped her in the temple.

ALALCOMENES advised Zeus to have a figure of oakwood dressed in bridal attire and carried about accompanied by hymeneal songs, in order to change the anger of Hera into jealousy. (See also CITHAERON)

ALMO was a river near Rome, in which the statue of the mother of the gods used to be washed (Cic. *De Nat.Deor.* 3. 20; comp. Varr. *De Ling.Lat.* 5. 71).

ANAXARETE. After her admirer, Iphis, hanged himself because she was indifferent to him, Aphrodite changed her into a stone statue (Ov. *Met.* 14. 698).

APOLLO. In the ancient statues of Apollo at Delos and Delphi, the god carried the Charites, or Graces, on his hand.

ARTEMIS. Orestes and Iphigeneia concealed the image of the Taurian goddess in a bundle of brushwood and carried it to Aricia in Latium. The Lacedaemonians, however, maintained that the carved image of Artemis existed at Sparta and was worshipped there in the Limnaeon under the name of Artemis Orthia (Paus. 3. 16). The image was said to have been found in a bush and to have thrown the beholders into a state of madness; and once, since at the celebration of her festival a quarrel arose which ended in bloodshed, an oracle commanded that in the future human sacrifices should be offered to her.

ARTEMIS LYGODESMA. Her statue had been found by the brothers, Astrabacus and Alopecus, under a bush of willows, by which it was surrounded in such a manner that it stood upright (Paus. 3. 16.7).

ARTEMIS ORTHIA (See ARTEMIS)

ASCLEPIUS. His image in the form of a dragon was brought from Epidaurus to Sicyon on a car drawn by mules (Paus. 2. 10.3).

ASTRABACUS with his brother, Alopecus, found a statue of Artemis Orthia in a bush and became mad at the sight of it.

ATHENA PHRYGIA was given this surname on account of the Palladium, which was brought from Phrygia (Ov. *Met.* 13. 337).

ATYS. In order to halt a plague and famine, an oracle decreed that funeral honors be accorded his body, but decomposition had set in, and the honors were accorded an image of him instead (Diod. 3. 58).

AUTOLYCUS. After the conquest of Sinope by the Romans, the statue of Autolycus was carried by Lucullus from there to Rome (Strab. 12. 546).

AUXESIA. When the Aeginetans and Epidaurans were directed by an oracle to make olivewood statues of Auxesia and Damia, they asked permission of the Athenians to cut an olive tree and were allowed on condition that each year they would offer up sacrifices to Athena Agraulos and Erechtheus. When the Aeginetans separated from Epidaurus, they took the statues, and the Athenians demanded their surrender. They threw ropes around the statues to drag them away, but thunder and lightning ensued and the Athenians were seized with madness. While the statues were being dragged away they fell upon their knees and remained forever in that attitude (Herod. 5. 82–86; Paus. 2. 30.5).

BROTEAS, son of Tantalus, according to a tradition of the Magnetes, had made the most ancient statue of the mother of the gods on the rock of Coddinos (Paus. 3. 22.4).

CELEDONES were a group of divinities whose power of song helped soothe the spirit of man. Hephaestus was said to have made their golden images on the ceiling of the temple at Delphi (Paus. 9. 5.5; Athen. 7. 290; Philostr. *Vit. Apoll.* 6. 11).

CITHAERON. In order to settle a quarrel between Zeus and Hera, Cithaeron persuaded Zeus to take into his chariot a wooden statue and dress it up so as to make it resemble Plataea, the daughter of Asopus. As Zeus was riding along with his pretended bride, Hera, overcome with jealousy, ran up and tore the covering from the suspected bride and became reconciled with Zeus (Paus. 9. 1.2, 3.1). (See also ALALCOMENES)

DIANA FASCELIS was a surname of Diana in Italy, believed to have been received from the circumstance of Orestes having brought her image from Tauris in a bundle of sticks (Sil.Ital. 14. 260).

DIOMEDES with Odysseus entered the acropolis of Troy, slew the guards and carried away the Palladium (Virg. *Aen.* 2. 163), as it was believed that Ilium could not be taken so long as the Palladium was within its walls. Various accounts are given to his later history and that of the Palladium, one of them stating that an oracle warned him of unceasing suffering if the sacred image were not restored to the Trojans. Diomedes was eventually able to restore the Palladium to Aeneas.

DIONYSUS. At Troy there was an ancient image of him kept in a chest, and Cassandra left this chest when Troy was taken, for she knew it would do injury to the one possessing the image. When it fell as part of the spoils to Eurypylus, he went mad but was restored by surrendering the chest and dedicating it in Aroe, which was under an ancient curse and forced to make human sacrifices for atonement. The festival of Dionysus Aesymnetes was instituted from that time. (See also PENTHEUS)

ELECTRA. According to some traditions, she brought the Palladium to Ilium and gave it to her son, Dardanus.

GALATEIA. Pygmalion was a king of Cyprus and was said to have fallen in love with the ivory image of a maiden which he himself had fashioned. He therefore prayed to Aphrodite to bring the statue to life. When the request was granted, Pygmalion married his beloved and became by her the father of Paphus (Ov. *Met.* 10. 243).

HERA. Admete was a priestess of Hera in Argos but fled with the image of the goddess to Samos. Pirates were hired to recover the image but could not sail with the load. The image remained in Samos, but Argos claimed the more ancient worship of Hera. (See also ALALCOMENES and CITHAERON)

IASION. He and his son, Dardanus, were driven from their home by a flood and went from Italy, Crete, or Arcadia to Samothrace, where they carried the Palladium.

ILUS. After having built Ilium, he prayed to Zeus for a sign and found on the next morning the Palladium, a statue of three cubits in height, with its feet close together, holding a spear in its right hand and a distaff in its left. Ilus then built a temple for the statue (Apollod. 3. 12.3). When the temple was consumed by fire, Ilus rescued the statue but became blind, since no one was permitted to see it, but he propitiated the goddess and recovered his sight (Plut. *Paral.Gr.et Rom.* 17).

LINUS, son of Apollo, was reportedly killed by his father for having challenged him to a musical contest. His image stood in a hollow rock formed in the shape of a grotto near Mt. Helicon. Every year, before sacrifices were offered to the Muses, a funeral sacrifice was offered to him, and dirges were sung in his honor.

MINERVA NAUTIA. When an oracle demanded that Diomedes restore the Palladium to the Trojans, Diomedes attempted to deliver the statue to Aeneas, but left it with Nautes when unable to give it to Aeneas. Minerva bestowed many favors on Nautes and his family after him. The image was preserved in the most secret part of the temple of Vesta and was regarded as one of the safeguards of the state (Dionys. 1. 69; Virg. *Aen.* 5. 704; Lucan 1. 598).

ORESTES. When he arrived in Tauris to carry the image of Artemis to Attica, he was, with his companion, Pylades, about to be sacrificed in the temple according to the custom of the country, but was recognized by his sister, the priestess Iphigeneia, who fled with him and the statue of the goddess. This statue was believed to have fallen from heaven. Later, Iphigeneia carried the statue to Brauron near Marathon. According to an Italian legend, Orestes brought the image of the Taurian Artemis to Aricia, whence it was carried in later times to Sparta. (See also ARTEMIS)

PALLADIUM was an image of Pallas Athena, but generally an ancient one, which was kept hidden and secret, and was revered as a pledge of the safety of the town or place where it existed. (See also ILUS)

PELOPS. According to some, the Palladium was made of the bones of Pelops (Plin. *H.N.* 28. 4).

PENTHEUS, king of Thebes, hid in a tree to watch the Bacchic orgies but was discovered and torn to pieces by the women. According to a Corinthian tradition, the women were afterwards commanded by an oracle to find that tree and to worship it like Dionysus himself. Out of the tree two carved images of the god were made (Paus. 2. 2.6).

PROTESILAUS. Laodameia, after the second death of her husband, made an image of him, which she worshipped. When her father, Acastus, ordered her to burn it, she threw herself with the image into the flames. According to others, Protesilaus, on returning from the lower world, found his wife embracing his image, and when he died the second time, he begged her not to follow too late, whereupon she killed herself with a sword. Others again relate that Laodameia, being compelled by her father to marry another man, spent her nights with the image of Protesilaus.

RHEA, earth mother, in Galatia was chiefly worshipped at Pessinus, where her sacred image was believed to have fallen from heaven.

SINON was the Greek spy who infiltrated the ranks of the Trojans, pretending that he had been ill-treated by the Greeks and had escaped death by flight. When he was asked what was the meaning of the wooden horse, he told them that it had been constructed as an atonement for the Palladium, which had been carried off.

STHENELUS, son of Capaneus and Evadne, was a commander of the Argives under Diomedes in the Trojan War. He was one of the Greeks concealed in the wooden horse. At the distribution of the booty, he was said to have received an image of a three-eyed Zeus, which was afterwards shown at Argos (Paus. 2. 45.5, 8. 46.2).

Stature

AJAX was the tallest of the Greeks at Troy.

AJAX (the Lesser) was short in height.

ASTERIUS, son of Anax, measured ten cubits in length.

ASTEROPAEUS was the tallest of all the men in the Trojan War.

OTUS. When Otus and Ephialtes were nine years old, each of their bodies measured nine cubits in breadth and twenty-seven in height. They are said to have grown every year one cubit in breadth and three in height.

Steam

DAEDALUS contrived a steam bath in a cave in the territory of Selinus by means of a vapor which rose from a subterranean fire.

Steersman

CANOBUS was a steersman of Menelaus who died from hunger on the island of Pharos, where Menelaus' crew was detained on the return from Troy.

GLAUCUS of Anthedon in Boeotia accompanied the Argonauts as their steersman.

PHRONTIS was a son of Onetor and the steersman of Menelaus (Paus. 10. 25.2). He is reported to have died on the return trip from Troy.

Sterility

IPHICLUS, son of Phylacus, inquired of the soothsayer, Melampus, how he could become a father, since he had no children. Melampus, on the suggestion of a vulture, advised Iphiclus to take the rust from the knife with which Phylacus had once cut his son and drink it in water during ten days. This done, Iphiclus was cured of his sterility and became the father of Podarces.

Stick

DIANA FASCELIS was a surname of Diana in Italy, believed to have been received because Orestes had brought her image from Tauris in a bundle of sticks (Sil. Ital. 14. 260).

Stone

ACONTEUS, a hunter, was changed into stone by the head of Medusa at the nuptials of Perseus and Andromeda.

AENEAS. In one of the battles of the Trojan War his hip was broken when Diomedes hurled a mighty stone at him.

AGRAULOS. When trying to prevent Hermes from visiting her sister, she was changed by the god into a stone.

AJAX. In the contest between him and Hector he was wounded by a huge stone.

ALCMENA. After her death she went to the Isles of the Blessed, and a stone was placed in her coffin by Hermes. It was so heavy that it could not be lifted by the Heraclids. They erected around it a sanctuary near Thebes.

ALCYONEUS was a giant who crushed twelve wagons and twenty-four of Heracles' men with a huge block of stone on the Isthmus of Corinth.

AMPHION. By playing his lyre, he caused stones to move and fall into place to form the walls of Thebes (Apollon. Rhod. 1. 740, 755).

AMPHITRYON. The uncatchable fox he was supposed to destroy and the inescapable dog which he borrowed for the purpose were changed by Fate into stone.

ANAXARETE. After her admirer, Iphis, hanged himself because she was indifferent to him, Aphrodite changed her into a stone statue (Ov. *Met.* 14. 698).

APOLLO. While assisting Alcathous in rebuilding the walls of Megara, he left his lyre on a stone. Afterwards the stone was supposed to give off a lyre-like sound when struck.

ARES in the Trojan War was thrown to the ground by a mighty stone hurled by Athena (Hom. *Il.* 20. 69; 21. 403).

ARGUS, the many-eyed guardian of Io, according to some was killed by Hermes with a stone.

ASCALAPHUS. For revealing that Persephone had eaten part of a pomegranate while in Hades, he was punished by Demeter, who buried him under a huge stone, which was subsequently removed by Heracles (Apollod. 2. 5.12).

ATLAS. When Perseus came to where Atlas bore the heavens on his shoulders, he showed him the head of Medusa and thus converted the Titan to stone, or the mountain called to this day Atlas (Ov. *Met.* 4. 655).

BAETYLUS was the personification of stones which were believed to be endowed with souls and created by Uranus. They were erected as symbols of the gods and anointed with oil, wine, or blood. The stone given to Uranus to swallow instead of the infant Cronus was called Baetylus.

BATTUS. For revealing that Hermes had stolen the cattle of Apollo, he was changed into a stone (Ov. *Met.* 2. 688).

CHARITES. At Orchomenos, the Charites were worshipped from early times in the form of rude stones, which were believed to have fallen from heaven in the time of Eteocles (Paus. 9. 38.1; Strab. 9. 414).

CLEODOXA, a daughter of Niobe, was changed into a stone for her mother's pride.

CYCNUS in the Trojan War was killed by being struck with a stone by Achilles, since he could not be wounded by iron.

DEUCALION. When, after the Flood, he prayed to Themis to restore mankind, he and his wife, Pyrrha, were instructed to throw the bones of their mother behind them in walking from the temple. They interpreted bones to mean stones of their mother earth. They threw the stones, and men and women sprang up.

ENALUS. Once when the sea around Lesbos rose in high billows and no one ventured to aproach it, Enalus alone had the courage to do so, and when he returned from the sea he was followed by polypi, the greatest of which was carrying a stone, which Enalus took from it and dedicated in a temple.

HECTOR. In the fierce battle in the camp of the Greeks, he was struck with a stone by Ajax and carried away from the field of battle (Hom. *Il.* 14. 402).

HERACLES. On his return from Troy, a storm forced him to land at Cos, where the inhabitants took him for a pirate and received him with a shower of stones. (See also TELAMON.) With the aid of Iolaus, he burned away the Hydra's heads and buried the ninth one, which was immortal, under a stone (Apollod. 2. 5.2). During his labor of bringing Cerberus back from the underworld, he rolled the stone away from Ascalaphus. In his battle with Alebion and Dercynus, who were trying to steal his cattle, he was assisted by Zeus with a shower of stones. When he was bringing back the oxen of Geryon, he reached the river Strymon and had to make himself a road through it by means of huge blocks of stone.

IDAS. When Polydeuces killed Lynceus with a spearthrust, Idas hit him so hard with a stone that he fell, whereupon Zeus slew Idas with a bolt of lightning (Apollod. 3. 11.2; Ov. *Fast.* 5. 700).

IODAMEIA was a priestess of Athena, who once on entering the sanctuary of the goddess by night was changed into a block of stone on seeing the head of Medusa, which was worked into the garment of Athena (Paus. 9. 34.1).

JASON. Medea advised him that from the teeth of the dragon, which Aeetes commanded him to sow, would spring up armed men to rise against him, and that he should throw stones among them so that they would fight among themselves and destroy one another.

JUPITER LAPIS, "the stone," was a surname of Jupiter at Rome. It was formerly believed that Jupiter Lapis was a stone statue of the god, or originally a rude stone serving as a symbol around which people assembled for the purpose of worshipping Jupiter. But it is now generally acknowledged that the pebble or flint stone was regarded as the symbol of lightning, and that, therefore, in some representations of Jupiter, he held a stone in his hand instead of a thunderbolt.

LAELAPS, the dog of Procris and later Cephalus, was sent to deliver Thebes from a monster fox. The dog overtook the fox, but both were changed by Zeus into stones (Apollod. 2. 4.6; Ov. *Met.* 7. 771).

LICHAS, servant to Heracles, was the one who brought the poisoned tunic from Deianeira to Heracles. Heracles in his madness from pain threw Lichas into the sea, where he was turned into a stone.

MEDUSA was one of the Gorgons and the only one of the three who was mortal, but her hair was changed into serpents by Athena. Her head was then of so fearful an appearance that everyone who looked at it was changed into stone. (See also ATLAS, IODAMEIA, PHINEUS, POLYDECTES, and PROETUS.) Perseus was sent to cut off her head and succeeded in doing so. On his return he rescued Andromeda from a sea monster by turning it to stone with the severed head. Later he avenged himself on his enemies by showing them the head.

NIOBE, daughter of Tantalus and wife of Amphion, bragged that she had twelve children while Leto had only two, and Apollo and Artemis slew all her children with arrows. Niobe was metamorphosed into a stone. This stone, located on Mt. Sipylus, always shed tears in the summer (Ov. *Met.* 6. 303; Apollod. 3. 5.6; Paus. 8. 2.3; Soph. *Antig.* 823; Soph. *Elect.* 147).

OLENUS was a person living upon Mt. Ida who wanted to take upon himself the punishment which his wife, Lethaea, had deserved by her pride over her beauty, and was metamorphosed, along with her, into stone (Ov. *Met.* 10. 68).

PANDAREUS. For stealing the golden dog set to guard the temple of Zeus in Crete he was changed into a stone.

PHINEUS, the brother of Cepheus and uncle-in-law to Perseus, was changed to stone when Perseus showed him Medusa's head.

POLYDECTES was the king of Seriphos, who enslaved Danae and sent her son, Perseus, to fetch the head of Medusa. He was changed to stone by looking at the head when Perseus returned, as were his assembled guests at a feast and, some say, the whole island (Pind. *Pyth.* 12. 21; Strab. 10. 487).

PROETUS. For having expelled his brother, Acrisius, the grandfather of Perseus, he was changed by Perseus into a block of stone by means of the head of Medusa.

RHEA. Since her husband Cronus had devoured all her other newborn, when Zeus was born she wrapped a stone like an infant and gave it to Cronus, who swallowed it like the others (Hes. *Theog.* 446; Apollod. 1. 1.5; Diod. 5. 70). At Delphi there was a stone of not very large dimensions, which was every day anointed with oil, and on solemn occasions was wrapped up in white wool; this stone was believed to have been the one which Cronus swallowed when he thought he was devouring Zeus (Paus. 10. 24.5).

TELAMON. On his expedition with Heracles to Troy, he first forced his way into the city, thus arousing the jealousy of Heracles, who determined to kill him; but Telamon quickly collected a pile of stones and pretended that he was building an altar to Heracles (Hom. *Il.* 5. 641, 14. 251, 20. 145; Apollod. 2. 6.4; Diod. 4. 32, 49; Eurip. *Troad.* 802).

TERMINUS was a Roman divinity presiding over boundaries and frontiers. His worship is said to have been instituted by Numa, who ordered that everyone should mark the boundaries of his landed property by stones to be consecrated to Jupiter and where every year sacrifices were to be offered at the festival of the Terminalia (Dionys. 2. 9, 74). At these sacrifices, cakes, meal, and fruit were offered, since it was unlawful to stain the boundary stones with blood.

See also: ROCK

Stoning

ARTEMIS APANCHOMENE, "the strangled (goddess)," was a surname of Artemis from an incident which took place at Caphyae in Arcadia. Some boys in their play put a string on the statue of Artemis Condyleatis in a sacred grove and said they were strangling her. When discovered at this, they were stoned to death. Thereafter, all the women at Caphyae had stillbirths, until the boys were honorably buried. An annual sacrifice to their spirits was commanded by an oracle (Paus. 8. 23.5). The surname Condyleatis was changed to Apanchomene.

ARTEMIS CONDYLEATIS (See ARTEMIS APANCHOMENE)

AUXESIA, with another maiden, Damia, was stoned to death during an insurrection at Troezen.

HECUBA. According to Ovid (*Met.* 13. 423–575) she was stoned by the inhabitants after she landed in Thrace, but was metamorphosed into a dog.

MERMERUS (MACAREUS or MORMORUS), son of Medea and Jason, according to some, was stoned to death by the Corinthians (Paus. 2. 3.6).

ORESTES. After his murder of his mother, Clytemnestra, and her lover, Aegisthus, the Argives wanted to stone him and Electra, his sister, to death.

PALAMEDES, son of Nauplius, was falsely accused of treason by Agamemnon, Diomedes, and Odysseus during the Trojan War. Under the pretext of having discovered a hidden treasure, they let him down into a well and there stoned him to death (Ov. *Met.* 13. 56).

PEISIDICE was a daughter of a king of Methymna in Lesbos, who, out of love for Achilles, opened to him the gates of her native city, but was stoned to death, at the command of Achilles, by his soldiers.

POLYDORUS. When the Greeks attempted to exchange their prisoner, Polydorus, for Helen, they were refused. They stoned him to death under the walls of Troy, and his body was delivered to Helen.

ZEUS LYCAEUS (LYCEUS) was a surname from his being worshipped on Mt. Lycaeus in Arcadia. He had a sanctuary there in which the festival of the Lycaea was celebrated. Entrance was forbidden and, according to some, those who entered there were stoned to death by the Arcadians, or were called stags and obliged to take flight to save their lives (Plut. *Quaest.Gr.* 39).

Stork

ANTIGONE boasted of excelling Hera in the beauty of her hair and was punished by being changed into a stork (Ov. *Met.* 6. 93). Note: She is not to be confused with the daughter of Oedipus.

HERMES. The stork was sacred to him.

PIETAS was a personification of faithful attachments, love, and veneration among the Romans. Her attributes are a stork and children.

Storm

AENEAS, with the remainder of his fleet, was driven by a storm to the coast of Carthage, which was ruled by Dido.

ATHENA plagued the Greeks returning from Troy with storms on account of the manner in which the Locrian Ajax had treated Cassandra in the goddess' temple.

DIOMEDES was believed to have built a temple at Mothone to Athena Anemotis, who subdued the storms as a result of his prayers (Paus. 4. 35.5).

DIONYSUS BROMIUS was a surname explained by some from his having been born during a storm of thunder and lightning (Diod. 4. 5; Dio Chrys. 27).

DIOSCURI. During the voyage of the Argonauts, the heroes were detained by a vehement storm. When Orpheus prayed to the Samothracian gods, the storm suddenly subsided, and stars appeared on the heads of the Dioscuri (Diod. 4. 43; Plut. *De Plac.Philos.* 2. 18; Senec. *Quaest.Nat.* 1. 1).

HARPIES in Homeric poems are personified storm winds (Hom. *Od.* 20. 66, 77).

IDOMENEUS. Once in a storm at sea he vowed to Poseidon to sacrifice to him whatever he should meet first on his landing, if the god would grant him a safe return. The first person he met on his landing was his son, whom he accordingly sacrificed.

LAELAPS. The storm wind is personified by the legend of the dog of Procris which bore this name.

MENELAUS. On the return from Troy, Zeus sent a storm which separated his fleet and cast his ship and five others on the coast of Egypt (Hom. *Od.* 3. 278; comp. Paus. 10. 25.2).

ODYSSEUS was plagued by storms throughout his journey from Troy to his eventual return to Ithaca. Soon after setting sail from Troy, he was thrown by a storm upon the coast of Ismarus. Later, he and his men were detained on the island of Helios by storms and while there his companions, in spite of an oath not to touch the sacred cattle of Helios, devoured some of the finest cattle. Then the storms abated, and they sailed away, but another storm came on, and their ship was destroyed by Zeus with a flash of lightning. All were drowned except Odysseus. Much later, on a raft provided by Calypso, he came in sight of Scheria, the island of the Phaeacians, but Poseidon sent a storm which destroyed the raft, and he was forced to swim ashore (Hom. *Od.* 5. 278, 445, 6. 170).

ORION. The rising and setting of the constellation Orion was believed to be accompanied by storms and rain.

POSEIDON. Being the ruler of the sea, he is described as gathering clouds and calling forth storms. He used the trident for this purpose and also for subduing storms.

ZEUS was armed with thunder and lightning, and the shaking of his aegis produced storm and tempest.

ZEUS MAEMACTES, "the stormy," was a surname from which the name of the Attic month Maemacterion was derived (Plut. *De Ir. Cohib.* 9).

Strangulation

ARTEMIS APANCHOMENE, "the strangled (goddess)," was a surname of Artemis from an incident which took place at Caphyae in Arcadia. Some boys in their play put a string on the statue of Artemis Condyleatis in a sacred grove and said they were strangling her. When discovered at this, they were stoned to death. Thereafter, all the women at Caphyae had stillbirths until the boys were honorably buried. An annual sacrifice to their spirits was commanded by an oracle (Paus. 8. 23.5). The surname Condyleatis was changed to Apanchomene.

ARTEMIS CONDYLEATIS (See ARTEMIS APANCHOMENE)

CYCNUS, in the Trojan War, was strangled by Achilles with the thong of his helmet, since he was invulnerable to iron.

TROILUS was a son of Priam and Hecuba. One account says that Achilles ordered Troilus, who had been made prisoner, to be strangled.

Strategy (Military)

MENESTHEUS, son of Peteus, was an Athenian king, who led the Athenians against Troy and surpassed all other mortals in arranging the war steeds and the men for battle (Hom. *Il.* 2. 552, 4. 327; Paus. 25.6).

NESTOR, king of Pylos, in spite of his advanced age, was brave and bold in battle and was distinguished above all others for drawing up horses and men in battle array in the war with Troy.

Street

APOLLO AGYIEUS was a surname of Apollo as protector of streets and public places. He was worshipped under this name at Acharnae, Mycenae, and Tegea.

ARTEMIS was regarded as founder and protector of towns and streets.

Strength

ALOEIDAE. The giant brothers, Otus and Ephialtes, attempted to pile Pelion upon Ossa to battle the gods.

AMPHISSUS, son of Apollo, was said to be possessed of extraordinary strength.

ARES, god of war, possessed overwhelming physical strength.

ARGUS, the hundred-eyed guardian of Io, possessed superhuman strength.

ATHENA ALALCOMENEIS. The surname is possibly from the verb *alalkein,* signifying the "powerful defender" (Hom. *Il.* 4. 8).

ATHENA ALCIS. The surname means "the strong." She was worshipped by this name in Macedonia.

CRATOS, son of Uranus and Gaea, was the personification of strength.

EPHIALTES (See ALOEIDAE)

GARANUS was a shepherd of gigantic bodily strength, who is said to have come from Greece into Italy in the reign of Evander and to have slain Cacus, the robber. Some call him Recaranus, but most writers agree in identifying him with the Greek Heracles.

HERACLES, son of Zeus and Alcmene, was the strongest hero in all antiquity. Even as a baby in his cradle he strangled two serpents sent by Hera to destroy him. He performed the seemingly impossible twelve labors, the fulfillment of which included a trip to the underworld and the bearing of the heavens upon his shoulders. His sexual prowess included impregnation of the fifty daughters of King Thespiae in as many nights (Apollod. 2. 4.10). His name became synonymous with effort requiring superhuman strength. (See also GARANUS)

LEPREUS, son of Caucon, Glaucon, or Pyrgeus and grandson of Poseidon, was said to be a rival, both in strength and powers of eating, of Heracles, who slew him (Athen. 10. 411).

OTUS (See ALOEIDAE)

PERICLYMENUS, one of the Argonauts, was a son of Neleus and Chloris. Poseidon gave him the power of changing himself into different forms and conferred on him great strength.

RECARANUS (See GARANUS)

STRENUA was a goddess at Rome who gave vigor and energy to the weak and indolent.

Strife

ZELUS, the personification of zeal or strife, is described as the son of Pallas and Styx and a brother of Nike (Hes. *Theog.* 384; Apollod. 1. 2.4).

Stupidity

VENUS MURCIA (MURTEA or MURTIA). Some of the ecclesiastical writers preferred to derive this name from *murcus,* i.e., stupid or awkward (August. 4. 16).

Stylus

CALLIOPE, the Muse of epic poetry, appears with a tablet and stylus.

Suffering

ATE was an ancient Greek divinity, who led both gods and men to rash and inconsiderate actions and to suffering.

Suicide

AEGEUS. If he returned safely from Crete, Theseus was supposed to hoist a white sail on his ship. He failed to remember, and Aegeus, his father, seeing a black sail, leapt to his death from the promontory where he had watched for his son's return.

AESON, father of Jason, was about to be killed by Pelias when it appeared that the Argonauts would never return, but Aeson begged to be permitted to end his own life. He drank the blood of a bull, which he then sacrificed, and thus died (Diod. 4. 50). Aeson's wife also killed herself when her husband died.

AETHRA, mother of Theseus, after being freed of her bondage to Helen at Troy, killed herself from grief at the death of her grandsons in the war.

AGRAULOS, with her sisters, Herse and Pandrosos, threw herself from the acropolis in a fit of madness upon seeing Erichthonius in a chest which they had been forbidden to open.

AJAX killed himself with a sword out of shame and remorse for killing the Greek army's sheep in a fit of madness over losing a contest with Odysseus for Achilles' armor.

ALCYONE (See CLEOPATRA)

AMPHINOME, mother of Jason, killed herself with a sword on the hearth of Pelias, her brother-in-law, who was about to murder her (Diod. 4. 50; Apollon. Rhod. 1. 45).

AMPHION killed himself with a sword from grief at the loss of his children by Niobe (Ov. *Met.* 6. 271).

ANCHURUS, son of Midas, leaped into a chasm to save his father's kingdom from an earthquake.

ANDROCLEA, a daughter of Antipoenus of Thebes, with her sister, Alcida, sacrificed herself for the victory of Thebes.

ANNA PERENNA. Out of jealousy of Aeneas and Lavinia, she threw herself into the river Numicius.

ANTIGONE (1). According to Sophocles, she killed herself after being shut up in a subterranean cave.

ANTIGONE (2), daughter of Eurytion, hanged herself in despair when she received a false message that her husband, Peleus, was on the point of remarrying.

ARIADNE. Some traditions say that she killed herself in despair after being abandoned on Naxos by Theseus.

ASTRAEUS. When he learned that he had unknowingly had intercourse with his sister, Alcippe, he threw himself into a river.

AURA. When she became by Dionysus the mother of twins, she was seized at the moment of their birth with madness, tore one of her children to pieces, and then threw herself into the sea (Nonn. 260).

CALLIRRHOE. After Coresus sacrificed himself in her stead, she put an end to her own life near a well which derived its name from her (Paus. 7. 21.1).

CANACE, daughter of Aeolus, entertained an unnatural love for her brother, Macareus, and put an end to her life.

CEPHALUS put an end to his life by leaping into the sea from Cape Leucas, on which he had built a temple to Apollo, in order to atone for the accidental murder of his wife, Procris (Strab. 10. 452).

CHRYSIPPUS, son of Pelops, according to some, killed himself, although most accounts state that he was murdered.

CINYRAS killed himself when he learned that he had unwittingly caused his son, Adonis, and his daughter, Smyrna, to enter an incestuous relationship (Ov. *Met.* 10. 310).

CLEITE, wife of Cyzicus, when the Argonauts murdered her husband, hanged herself. The tears of the nymphs who lamented her death were changed into the well by the name of Cleite (Apollon. Rhod. 1. 967, 1063).

CLEOPATRA, daughter of Idas and wife of Meleager (Hom. *Il.* 9. 556) hanged herself after her husband's death, or died of grief. Her proper name was Alcyone (Apollod. 1. 8.3).

CLYMENUS. After being served the flesh of his son by his daughter, Harpalyce, whom he had raped, he hanged himself.

ERIGONE, daughter of Aegisthus and Clytemnestra, killed herself when she heard that Orestes was acquitted by the Areiopagus for the murder of her parents.

HAEMON, son of Creon of Thebes, was in love with Antigone and killed himself on hearing that she was condemned by his father to be entombed alive (Soph. *Antig.* 627; Eurip. *Phoen.* 757, 1587).

HERO. When her lover, Leander, was drowned in trying to swim across the Hellespont in a storm to visit her, she threw herself into the sea (Ov. *Her.* 18. 19; Stat. *Theb.* 6. 535; Virg. *Georg.* 3. 258).

IPHIS hanged himself in despair when Anaxarete did not return his love (Ov. *Met.* 14. 698). Some call the ill-fated pair Arsinoe and Arceophon.

JASON, according to Diodorus (4. 55) killed himself after Medea's terrible revenge for his intended marriage to Glauce.

LAODAMEIA, whose husband, Protesilaus, had been killed in the Trojan War and was briefly resurrected, made an image of him after his second death, and paid him divine honors. When her father, Acastus, commanded her to burn the image, she herself leaped into the flames.

LAODICE was a daughter of Priam and Hecuba. When her son, Munitus, died, she was so stricken with grief that she leaped to her death from a precipice (Lycoph. 497).

LYCURGUS was a son of Dryas and king of the Edones in Thrace. For having tried to destroy all the vines in his country, he was driven mad by Dionysus. In this state he killed his wife and son and then cut off one (some say both) of his legs; or, according to others, he killed himself.

MACAREUS (MACAR), son of Aeolus, committed incest with his sister, Canace, and, according to some accounts, then killed himself.

MACARIA, the only daughter of Heracles, killed herself at Marathon, where her name was given to the Macarian spring (Paus. 1. 32.6).

MENIPPE and her sister, Metioche, after the death of their father, Orion, were taught the art of weaving by Athena. To avert a plague in Aonia, where they lived, they offered themselves as a sacrifice (in response to an oracle) and killed themselves with their shuttles (Ov. *Met.* 13. 685).

MENOECEUS. In the war of the Seven against Thebes, Tiresias (or the Delphian oracle) declared that the Thebans would conquer if Menoeceus would sacrifice himself for his country. Menoeceus accordingly killed himself outside the gates of Thebes (Eurip. *Phoen.* 913, 930; Apollod. 3. 6.7).

MOLPADIA, daughter of Staphylus, with her sister, Parthenos, was set to guard their father's wine. But they fell asleep, and swine overturned and spoiled the wine. The sisters on discovering the mischief threw themselves from a rock. Apollo is said to have saved Molpadia.

NARCISSUS, according to some traditions, sent a sword to one of his lovers, Ameinius, who killed himself with it at the very door of Narcissus' house and called upon the gods to avenge his death. Narcissus, tormented by love of himself and by repentance, put an end to his life.

NICAEA, a nymph, the daughter of the river god Sangarius and Cybele, was made intoxicated by Dionysus, who made her the mother of Telete, whereupon she hanged herself.

NYCTEUS. When his daughter, Antiope, fled to escape his vengeance because of her pregnancy by Zeus, he killed himself in despair (Apollod. 3. 5.5).

OCHNE, daughter of Colonus, caused the death of Eunostus when she accused him of trying to seduce her, because he had failed to return her love. Later she confessed the truth and threw herself down a rock (Plut. *Quaest. Gr.* 40).

OENOMAUS, according to some, when Pelops won the hand of his daughter in a chariot race in which Oenomaus thought himself invincible, killed himself.

PELOPIA. When she discovered that she had begotten Aegisthus by her own father, Thyestes, she put an end to her life.

PHAEDRA, wife of Theseus, fell in love with Hippolytus, her step-son, who repulsed her. When he died as a result of her frustrated accusations, she killed herself (Hom. *Od.* 11. 325; Eurip. *Hippol.* 767).

PHYLLIS, daughter of a Thracian king, loved Demophon, who promised to marry her, but when he failed to return when expected, she put an end to her life and was metamorphosed into a tree (Ov. *Ars Am.* 3. 38).

PLEIADES, the seven daughters of Atlas and sisters of the Hyades, killed themselves from grief at the death of the Hyades or at the fate of Atlas and were afterwards placed as stars at the back of Taurus.

POLYDORA, daughter of Meleager and Cleopatra, was married to Protesilaus, after whose death she was so much affected by grief that she killed herself (Paus. 4. 2.5).

POLYXENA was a daughter of Priam and Hecuba. According to some writers, Achilles and Polyxena fell in love with each other at the time when Hector's body was delivered to Priam. After the murder of Achilles, Polyxena fled to the Greeks and killed herself on the tomb of her beloved with a sword (Paus. 1. 22.6, comp. 10. 25.2).

PYRAMUS was the lover of Thisbe, a beautiful Babylonian maiden. The lovers were forbidden by their parents to marry. Once they agreed to meet at night at the tomb of Ninus, and Thisbe, arriving first, observed a lioness killing an ox. She fled, leaving her garment in the blood. When Pyramus arrived, he thought her dead and stabbed himself. Thisbe, who later found the body of her lover, likewise killed herself (Ov. *Met.* 4. 55–165).

SIRENS. When their singing was surpassed by Orpheus, so that they failed to lure the Argonauts to their death, they threw themselves into the sea and were metamorphosed into rocks.

STHENEBOEA, a daughter of Jobates, or Amphianax, or Apheidas, was the wife of Proetus. From love of Bellerophon, she killed herself (Apollod. 2. 2.1, 3. 9.1).

Suitor(s) of

ATALANTA (ATALANTE)

Hippomenes. Atalanta challenged her suitors to a footrace, because she was the swiftest of mortals, and resisted marriage. If she outran them, they would die by her hand; if anyone outran her, she would marry him. Hippomenes outran her by the device of throwing golden apples in her path, so that she lost time by stopping to pick them up. Some call the suitor Meilanion.

CASSANDRA

Coroebus sued for the hand of Cassandra but was killed in the taking of Troy (Paus. 10. 27.1; Virg. *Aen.* 2. 344, 425).

Othryoneus, an ally of King Priam from Cabesus, sued for the hand of Cassandra and promised in return to drive the Greeks from Troy, but he was slain by Idomeneus (Hom. *Il.* 13. 363, 772).

HELEN

Agapenor, king of the Arcadians, was one of the suitors of Helen.

Ajax was one of the suitors of Helen.

Ajax (the Lesser) was one of the suitors of Helen.

Amphimachus, son of Cteatus and Theronice, was one of the suitors of Helen (Apollod. 3. 10.8; Paus. 5. 3.4; Hom. *Il.* 2. 620).

Antilochus was mentioned as one of the suitors of Helen (Apollod. 3. 10.8).

Ascalaphus was one of the suitors of Helen (Apollod. 3. 10.8).

Diomedes was one of the suitors of Helen (Apollod. 3. 10.8).

Elephenor was mentioned as one of the suitors of Helen (Apollod. 3. 10.8).

Enarephorus, son of Hippocoon, was a passionate suitor of Helen when she was quite young (Apollod. 3. 10.5).

Idomeneus, son of Deucalion, was mentioned among the suitors of Helen (Hom. *Il.* 13. 450; Hom. *Od.* 19. 181; Paus. 5. 25.5; Apollod. 3. 3.1).

Meges, son of Phyleus, was mentioned among the suitors of Helen.

Menelaus, brother of Agamemnon, was the successful suitor of Helen.

Odysseus. Some accounts state that he went to Sparta as one of the suitors of Helen, and he is said to have advised Tyndareus to make the suitors swear that they would defend the chosen bridegroom against anyone who should insult him on Helen's account.

Patroclus was mentioned among the suitors of Helen (Apollod. 3. 10.8).

Peneleos was mentioned among the suitors of Helen (Apollod. 1. 9.16, 3. 10.8; Diod. 4. 67; Paus. 9. 5.8; Plut. *Quaest.Gr.* 37).

Phemius was one of the suitors of Helen.

Philoctetes, son of Poeas, was one of the suitors of Helen (Apollod. 3. 10.8).

Polyxenus, son of Agasthenes, was one of the suitors of Helen.

HIPPODAMEIA

Cronius was a suitor of Hippodameia and was killed by Oenomaus, who challenged all suitors of his daughter to a chariot race and killed them as soon as he conquered them (Paus. 6. 21.7).

Eioneus, son of Magnes, was one of the suitors of Hippodameia and was slain by Oenomaus (Paus. 6. 21.7).

Erythrus, son of Leucon, was one of the suitors of Hippodameia.

Euryalus was one of the suitors of Hippodameia (Paus. 6. 21.7).

Eurymachus was one of the suitors of Hippodameia (Paus. 6. 21.6).

Lycurgus, one of the suitors of Hippodameia, was killed by Oenomaus (Paus. 6. 21.7).

Pelagon was one of the suitors of Hippodameia (Paus. 6. 21.7).

Pelops (1) was the successful suitor of Hippodameia. He conspired with Myrtilus, the charioteer of Oenomaus, to remove the nails from the chariot wheels of his master, and he was thereby able to win the race and claim Hippodameia.

Pelops (2) of Opus was one of the suitors of Hippodameia who was unsuccessful and was killed by Oenomaus.

Tricolonus, one of the suitors of Hippodameia, was conquered and killed by Oenomaus (Paus. 6. 21.7).

PENELOPE

Agelaus was the suitor of Penelope who headed and encouraged the other suitors against Odysseus.

Amphimedon, one of the suitors of Penelope, was slain by Telemachus (Hom. *Od.* 22. 284).

Antinous was the suitor of Penelope who tried to take over the Ithacan kingdom (Hom. *Od.* 4. 630, 16. 371, 22. 48).

Arnaeus (See *Irus*)

Ctesippus, son of Polytherses of Same and one of the suitors of Penelope, was killed by Philoetius, the cowherd (Hom. *Od.* 20. 288).

Demoptolemus, one of the suitors of Penelope, was slain by Odysseus after his return (Hom. *Od.* 22. 246, 266).

Eurydamas, one of the suitors of Penelope, was killed by Odysseus (Hom. *Od.* 18. 297, 22. 283).

Eurymachus was one of the suitors of Penelope (Hom. *Od.* 1. 399, 22. 88).

Irus. His proper name was Arnaeus, but he was called Irus because he was employed by the suitors of Penelope as the messenger, since Irus (according to ancient lexicographers) signifies a messenger (Hom. *Od.* 18. 5, 239).

Leiodes, one of the suitors of Penelope, was slain by Odysseus (Hom. *Od.* 21. 144, 22. 328).

Leocritus, son of Evenor and one of the suitors of Penelope, was slain by Telemachus (Hom. *Od.* 2. 242, 22. 294).

Nisus, a noble of Dulichium and father of Amphinomus, was one of the suitors of Penelope (Hom. *Od.* 16. 395, 18. 126, 412).

Odysseus won the footrace in a contest for Penelope's hand. Icarius, her father, had proposed the contest (Paus. 3. 12.2). (See also *Tyndareus*)

Peisander was a son of Polyctor and one of the suitors of Penelope (Hom. *Od.* 18. 298, 22. 268; Ov. *Her.* 1. 91).

Tyndareus. According to some legends, he sued for Penelope's hand in behalf of Odysseus from gratitude for a piece of advice which Odysseus had given him (Apollod. 3. 10.9).

PERO

Bias sought to marry Pero, whom her father refused to give to anyone unless he brought him the oxen of Iphiclus. These Melampus obtained by his courage and skill and won the princess for his brother.

Sulphur

TELCHINES were a mysterious order of sorcerers and envious daemons who mixed Stygian water with sulphur in order to destroy animals and plants (Strab. 14. 654).

Sun

ANTHELII were divinities whose images stood before the doors of houses and were exposed to the sun, whence they derived their name (Aeschyl. *Agam.* 530).

APOLLO PHOEBUS (PHOEBUS APOLLO), "the shining, pure, or bright," occurs both as an epithet and a name of Apollo (Hom. *Il.* 1. 43, 443; Virg. *Aen.* 3. 251; Hor. *Carm.* 3. 21, 24). It may have played a part in later efforts to identify Apollo with the sun, although that had not been one of his original attributes.

BRANCHUS was a son of Apollo. His mother dreamed at the time she gave birth to him that the sun was passing through her body.

HELIOS, son of Hyperion and Theia, brother of Selene and Eos, was god of the sun (Hom. *Od.* 12. 176, 322; Hom. *Hymn. in Min.* 9, 13; Hes. *Theog.* 371).

HERACLES. On his journeys, he became annoyed at the heat of the sun and shot arrows at the sun. Helios so much admired his boldness that he presented him with a golden cup (or boat).

JANUS was an ancient Latin divinity who was worshipped at first as the sun (Cic. *De Nat. Deor.* 2. 27).

ORION. Having been blinded by Oenopion, he was instructed by an oracle that in order to recover his vision he should go towards the east and expose his eyeballs to the rays of the rising sun.

PHAETHON, son of Helios, was presumptuous and ambitious enough to persuade his father to allow him to drive the chariot of the sun across heaven. Phaethon, being too weak to check the horses, came down so close to the earth that he almost set it on fire. Zeus therefore killed him with a flash of lightning. Phaethon's sisters, who had yoked the horses to the chariot, were metamorphosed into poplars and their tears into amber (Eurip. *Hippol.* 737; Apollon. Rhod. 4. 598; Lucian *Dial. Deor.* 25; Virg. *Ecl.* 6. 62; Virg. *Aen.* 10. 190; Ov. *Met.* 1. 755).

PHOEBUS APOLLO (See APOLLO PHOEBUS)

PHOENIX. When this fabulous bird died, a worm crept forth from his body and was developed into a new phoenix by the heat of the sun (Plin. *H.N.* 10. 2; Ov. *Met.* 15. 392).

Sundial

ATROPOS, one of the Moirae, or Fates, is sometimes represented with a sundial.

Sunflower

CLYTIE was a maiden who loved and was deserted by Apollo. She pined away and was changed into a sunflower, which still follows the progress of the sun across heaven.

Suppliant

EUMENIDES were the avenging deities who punished improper conduct towards suppliants.

ZEUS was regarded as the god who watched over the sanctity of the oath and protected suppliants.

Surgery

CALAMITES was mentioned by Demosthenes (129) as the hero of the art of surgery, or a being well skilled in handling the reed, which was used in dressing fractured arms and legs.

ERIBOTES, son of Teleon, one of the Argonauts, acted as surgeon and attended the wounds of Oileus (Apollon. Rhod. 1. 73, 2. 1040).

MACHAON, son of Asclepius by Epeione, was surgeon of the Greeks in the Trojan War.

Swallow

APHRODITE. The swallow was sacred to her.

CHELIDONIS, sister of Aedon, was changed by Zeus into a swallow.

PROCNE. Pursued with her sister, Philomela, by their husband, Tereus, she and her sister

Achilles

prayed to the gods to change them into birds. She was changed into a swallow and Philomela, into a nightingale. Ovid (*Met.* 6. 424–675) reverses Procne and Philomela in this regard.

Swan

APHRODITE. The swan was sacred to her.

APOLLO. The swan was sacred to him.

CYCNUS (1) was a son of Poseidon. At birth he had been exposed on the seacoast, where he was found by shepherds, who, seeing a swan descending on him, called him Cycnus. On growing up, he fought in the Trojan War. When Achilles, after killing him, came to take away his armor, Cycnus was metamorphosed into a swan (Ov. *Met.* 12. 144).

CYCNUS (2), son of Apollo, was refused homage (presentation of a prize bull) by his lover, Phyllius, whereupon he leapt into Lake Canope with his mother, Thyria. They were metamorphosed into swans.

CYCNUS (3), son of Ares, was killed by Heracles and metamorphosed by his father into a swan.

CYCNUS (4), son of Sthenelus, was a friend of Phaethon. While he was lamenting the death of Phaethon on the banks of the Eridanus, he was metamorphosed by Apollo into a swan and placed among the stars (Ov. *Met.* 2. 366; Paus. 1. 30.3).

GRAEAE. Some describe the sisters as having the figures of swans. They were ancient hags, daughters of Phorcys and Ceto.

LEDA of Sparta, wife of Tyndareus, was visited by Zeus in the disguise of a swan, and she produced two eggs, from one of which issued Helen and from the other, Castor and Polydeuces (Ov. *Her.* 17. 55; Paus. 3. 16.1; Hor. *Ars Poet.* 147).

STHENELUS, the father of Cycnus, was metamorphosed into a swan (Ov. *Met.* 2. 368).

Hector

Swiftness

ACHILLES was said to be the swiftest among the Greeks at Troy.

AJAX (the Lesser) was the swiftest of foot, next to Achilles, among the Greeks at Troy.

ATALANTA (ATALANTE) challenged her suitors to a footrace, because she was the swiftest of mortals.

AURA was one of the swiftfooted companions of Artemis.

DOLON was a Trojan and son of Eumedes. He was famous for his swiftness. He was put to death by Diomedes for his treachery.

EUPHEMUS was one of the Argonauts who had such swiftness of foot that he could run over the sea without wetting his feet.

HARPALYCE, the Thracian woman robber, was so swift in running that horses were unable to overtake her.

HARPIES. These winged creatures surpassed winds and birds in the rapidity of their flight (Hes. *Theog.* 267).

HERMES. His golden sandals carried him across land and sea with the rapidity of the wind. The sandals were later represented as winged.

IPHICLES, son of Phylacus, was celebrated for his swift running, which won him a prize at the funeral games of Pelias (Paus. 5. 17.4, 36.2, 10. 29.2).

LAELAPS, the dog of Procris, was extremely swift and was sent to deliver the city of Thebes from a monster fox. The dog overtook the fox, and both animals were changed by Zeus into stones (Apollod. 2. 4.6; Ov. *Met.* 7. 711).

PODARCES (See PRIAM)

PRIAM, son of Laomedon and king of Troy at the time of the Trojan War, was originally named Podarces, "the swiftfooted."

Swine, see Pig

Swineherd

EUMAEUS was the swineherd of Odysseus, who, although not recognizing Odysseus in the guise of a beggar, treated him kindly (Hom. *Od.* 13. 70).

Sword

AEGISTHUS. Pelopia, his mother, stole her father's sword from him when she shared his bed. Later, she gave the sword to Aegisthus, by which his identity was learned. Thus, Thyestes was both father and grandfather to Aegisthus.

AJAX slew himself with the sword exchanged with him by Hector after their initial combat.

AMPHINOME, mother of Jason, killed herself with a sword on the hearth of Pelias, her brother-in-law, who was about to murder her (Diod. 4. 50; Apollon. Rhod. 1. 45).

AMPHION. When his and Niobe's children were slaughtered, he killed himself with a sword (Ov. *Met.* 6. 271).

APHRODITE. When she was represented as the victorious goddess, she had the attributes of Ares—a helmet, a shield, a sword or lance, and an image of Victory.

APOLLO CHRYSAOR was a surname referring to the god with the golden sword or arms (Hom. *Il.* 15. 256).

ARES. In Scythia he was worshipped in the form of a sword, to which cattle, horses, and even humans were sacrificed.

ARTEMIS CHRYSAOR was a surname meaning the goddess with the golden sword or arms (Herod. 8. 77).

CHEIRON, the centaur, restored to Peleus the sword which Acastus had concealed in his attempt to cause the death of Peleus (Apollod. 3. 13.3).

DANAIDES were the fifty daughters of Danaus, who were betrothed to the fifty sons of Aegyptus. They were compelled by their father to kill their husbands the night of their marriage with swords which he gave them.

DEMETER CHRYSAOR. As ARTEMIS CHRYSAOR (Hom. *Hymn. in Cer.* 4).

DIDO. In order to avoid marriage with the barbarian king, Hiarbas, she raised a funeral pyre ostensibly to sacrifice animals and then on the pyre she stabbed herself with a sword and was burned. In the *Aeneid* she does the same thing but because she is deserted by Aeneas, with whom she is in love.

HERACLES. For defeating the forces of Erginus, he was presented with a sword by Hermes.

MACHAEREUS, "the swordsman," a son of Daetus of Delphi, was said to have slain Neoptolemus, son of Achilles, in a quarrel about the sacrificial meat at Delphi (Strab. 9. 421; Pind. *Nem.* 7. 62).

MELPOMENE, the Muse of tragedy, often appears carrying a sword.

MERIONES. When Diomedes chose Odysseus for his companion on the exploring expedition to the Trojan camp, Meriones gave to the latter his bow, quiver, sword, and famous helmet (Hom. *Il.* 10. 662).

NARCISSUS. According to some traditions, he sent a sword to one of his lovers, Ameinius, who killed himself with it at the very door of Narcissus' house and called upon the gods to avenge his death. Narcissus, tormented by love of himself and by repentance, killed himself.

NEMESIS. Sometimes she appears holding in her right hand a wheel, with a sword or a scourge.

ORION. After his death he was placed among the stars (Hom. *Il.* 18. 486, 22. 29; Hom. *Od.* 5. 274), where he appears as a giant with a girdle, sword, a lion's skin, and a club.

PELEUS. Having been accused by Astydameia

of attempted seduction, Peleus was taken to Mt. Pelion by Acastus, the husband, where they hunted wild beasts; and when Peleus, overcome with fatigue, had fallen asleep, Acastus left him alone and concealed his sword, so that he would be destroyed by the wild beasts. Some relate that after Acastus had hidden the sword of Peleus, Cheiron or Hermes brought him another one, which had been made by Hephaestus (Apollon. Rhod. 1. 204; Aristoph. *Nub.* 1055).

THESEUS was the son of Aegeus, king of Athens, and Aethra. When he reached maturity, he took the sword and sandals, the tokens which had been left by Aegeus in Troezen, and proceeded to Athens to seek recognition from his father. By means of the sword, Theseus was recognized by Aegeus, acknowledged as his son, and declared his successor. When Theseus volunteered to be one of the sacrifices to the Cretan Minotaur, Ariadne, the daughter of Minos, king of Crete, fell in love with him and provided him with a sword, with which he slew the Minotaur. (See also ZEUS STHENIUS)

VIRTUS, the Roman personification of manly valor, was often represented with a sword in her right hand.

ZEUS CHRYSAOREUS, "the god with the golden sword or arms," was a name under which he had a temple in Caria (Strab. 14.660).

ZEUS STHENIUS, "the powerful," or "the strengthening," was a name under which he had an altar in a rock near Hermione, where Aegeus concealed his sword and shoes, which were found there by Theseus after he had lifted up the rock (Paus. 2. 32.7, 34.6).

Syrinx

HERMES invented the syrinx and shared the invention with Apollo.

PAN was the inventor of the syrinx, or shepherd's flute, which he himself played in a masterly manner, and in which he instructed others, such as Daphnis (Theocrit. 1.3; Virg. *Ecl.* 1. 32, 4. 58).

SATYRS usually appear with flutes, the thyrsus, syrinx, the shepherd staff, and cups or bags filled with wine.

SILVANUS was a Latin divinity of the fields and forests. The syrinx was sacred to him (Tibull. 2. 5.30).

SYRINX was an Arcadian nymph, who, being pursued by Pan, fled into the river Ladon, and at her own request was metamorphosed by the gods into a reed, of which Pan then made his flute (Ov. *Met.* 1. 690).

TERAMBUS, a son of Euseirus and Eidothea, was a distinguished musician and played both the syrinx and the lyre.

Table

ARCAS. His flesh was served by his father, Lycaon, in a dish on a table before Zeus, who overturned the table, destroyed the house, and restored Arcas to life. The place where this happened was afterwards called Trapezus, from the Greek word for table.

PENATES. The family table was sacred to these household gods, and the table always contained the saltcellar and fruit (Plut. *Quaest. Conviv.* 8. 4; Liv. 26. 36).

Tablet

CALLIOPE, the Muse of epic poetry, appears with a tablet and stylus.

MOIRAE, the Fates, were sometimes described as engraving on indestructible tables the decrees of Zeus (Ov. *Met.* 15. 808).

PALICI were Sicilian daemons, twin sons of Zeus and the nymph, Thaleia. Near their sanctuary there gushed forth from the earth two sulphurous springs called Deilloi, at which solemn oaths were taken. These oaths were written on tablets and thrown into one of the springs. If the tablet floated, the oath was considered to be true, but if it sank, the oath was regarded as perjury, which was believed to be punished instantaneously (Diod. 11. 89; Strab.

6. 275; Cic. *De Nat.Deor.* 3. 22; Virg. *Aen.* 9. 585; Ov. *Met.* 5. 406).

Tail

PAN, the great god of flocks and shepherds, had horns, beard, pug nose, tail, goats' feet, and was covered with hair.

SATYRS. This class of beings was represented as having near the end of the back a little tail like that of a horse or a goat.

Teacher

CHEIRON, the centaur, famous for his knowledge of music, medicine, and shooting, taught mankind the use of all kinds of plants and herbs. He also instructed the greatest heroes: Achilles, Aeneas, Asclepius, Heracles, Jason, Peleus, and others in various arts and skills.

OLYMPUS was a teacher of Zeus, after whom the god is said to have been called the Olympian (Diod. 3. 73).

TEMENUS, a son of Pelasgus, educated Hera at Stymphalus in Arcadia (Paus. 8. 22.2).

TETHYS was a daughter of Uranus and Gaea, wife of Oceanus, and mother of the Oceanids and numerous river gods. She also educated Hera, who was brought to her by Rhea (Hes. *Theog.* 136, 337; Apollod. 1. 1.3; Plat. *Tim.* 40; Ov. *Fast.* 5. 81; Virg. *Georg.* 1. 31).

Tears

BYBLIS. Because of a passion for her brother, she tried to throw herself into the sea from a rock but was kept back by nymphs and changed by them into a Hamadryad. The stream which came down the rock was referred to by neighboring people as the tears of Byblis.

CLEITE was the wife of Cyzicus, who, when the Argonauts murdered her husband, hanged herself. The tears of the nymphs who lamented her death were changed into the well by the name of Cleite (Apollon.Rhod. 1. 967, 1063).

EOS, goddess of the dawn and mother of Memnon, wept for her dead son every morning, and the dewdrops which appear in the morning are the tears of Eos (Ov. *Met.* 13. 622; Virg. *Aen.* 8. 384).

HYRIA (THYRIA). When her son, Cycnus, died, she melted away in tears, causing the Cycnean lake to arise (Ov. *Met.* 7. 371).

NIOBE, daughter of Tantalus and wife of Amphion, bragged that she had twelve children, while Leto had only two. Apollo and Artemis, outraged at such presumption, slew all her children with arrows. Niobe was metamorphosed into a stone. This stone, located on Mt. Sipylus, always shed tears in the summer (Ov. *Met.* 6. 303; Apollod. 3. 5.6; Paus. 8. 2.3; Soph. *Antig.* 823; Soph. *Elect.* 147).

PEIRENE was nymph of the well Peirene near Corinth, which was believed to have arisen out of the tears which she shed in her grief at the death of her son, Cenchrias (Paus. 2. 3.5).

PHAETHON. When he was struck down by Zeus after attempting to drive the chariot of the sun across heaven, his sisters, who had yoked the horses to the chariot, were metamorphosed into poplars and their tears into amber (Ov. *Met.* 1. 755).

THYRIA (See HYRIA)

Teeth

CADMUS. When some men he sent to fetch water at the well of Ares were killed by a dragon, he slew the dragon and, on the advice of Athena, sowed the teeth of the monster, out of which armed men grew up (Apollod. 3. 1.1). Half the teeth of the dragon were later given by Athena to Aeetes, king of Colchis (Apollon.Rhod. 3. 1183; Apollod. 1. 9.23).

GORGONS, the frightful monsters overcome by Perseus, were described as having enormous teeth (Aeschyl. *Prom.* 794, Aeschyl. *Choeph.* 1051).

GRAEAE, the ancient daughters of Phorcys and Ceto, were described as having one tooth among the three of them and passing it around as needed. Perseus stole the tooth and also their single eye and withheld them until the sisters revealed where the Gorgons were.

JASON was set the task by Aeetes of plowing a field with brazen-footed, fire-breathing bulls and then sowing the furrows with the teeth of a dragon, from which sprang up armed men.

SCYLLA was a monster who dwelt on a rock on the Italian coast opposite Sicily. She barked like a dog, had twelve feet, six long necks and mouths, each of which contained three rows of sharp teeth.

SPARTAE were the men that grew forth from the dragon's teeth which Cadmus sowed at Thebes (Apollod. 3. 4.1; Paus. 9. 5.1).

Ten

APOLLO DECATEPHORUS, "the god to whom the tenth part of the body is dedicated," was a surname of Apollo at Megara (Paus. 1. 42.5).

Tent

NEPTUNE. Of his festival little is known, except that the people formed tents (*umbrae*) of the branches of trees, in which they probably rejoiced in feasting and drinking (Varr. *De Ling.Lat.* 6. 19; Hor. *Carm.* 3. 28; Tertull. *De Spect.* 6).

Terror

CHLORIS, daughter of Amphion and Niobe, was originally called Meliboea. She and her brother, Amyclas, were the only children of Niobe not killed by Apollo and Artemis, but she was so terrified by the deaths of her brothers and sisters that she turned perfectly white and was therefore called Chloris.

CYBELE BRIMO was a surname of Cybele signifying the angry or terrifying.

DEMETER BRIMO. As CYBELE BRIMO.

HECATE BRIMO. As CYBELE BRIMO. Some give the derivation from *bromos,* so that it would refer to the crackling of a fire, as Hecate was pictured bearing a torch.

MELIBOEA (See CHLORIS)

PERSEPHONE BRIMO. As HECATE BRIMO.

Theatre

DIONYSUS was regarded as the god of tragic art and protector of theatres.

Thief, see Robber

Thigh

DIONYSUS. When Semele, herself consumed by flames, gave premature birth to him, the child was rescued from the flames and was sewed up in the thigh of Zeus and thus came to maturity.

Thirst

DEMETER. In her wanderings in search of Persephone, she visited the house of Metaneira and drank water eagerly. She was mocked by Abas, the son, whom she changed into a lizard. Another version of the story calls the boy Ascalaphus.

HERACLES. When leading his army through Libya, he was exhausted by thirst and invoked Zeus Ammon. A ram appeared and with its foot scratched open a spring.

TANTALUS was a wealthy king, celebrated in ancient story for the severe punishment inflicted upon him, after his death, in the lower world. For betraying divine counsels of Zeus he was punished by being placed in the nether world in the midst of a lake which withdrew when he stooped to drink.

Thorn

CARDEA was a Roman divinity who used whitethorn and other magical substances to protect children in their cradles from witches.

Thoughtfulness

CATIUS was a Roman divinity who was invoked under the name of *divus Catius pater* to grant prudence and thoughtfulness to children at the time when their consciousness was beginning to awaken (August. 4. 21).

Three

ATHENA TRITO (TRITOGENEIA or TRITONIS). The surname possibly signifies her being born on the third day of the month.

Threshold

JANUS was the Roman god of beginnings, openings, entrances, doorways, and thresholds. January, as the threshold of the year, was named for him, and New Year's day was sacred to him.

LIMA was a Roman divinity protecting the threshold.

LIMENTINUS was the god protecting the threshold (*limen*) of the house (August. 4. 8, 6. 7). Much superstition was connected among the Romans with the threshold and many persons were very scrupulous in always putting the right foot across it first (Petron. 30).

Throne

RHEA, mother of the gods, in works of art is usually represented sitting on a throne. Sometimes lions are crouching right and left.

Thunder

AUXESIA. When the Athenians tried to drag the statues of Auxesia and Damia from Aegina, thunder and lightning ensued, and the Athenians were struck with madness (Herod. 5. 82–86; Paus. 2. 30.5).

HERACLES. While his funeral pyre was burning, a cloud came down from heaven and amid peals of thunder carried him to Olympus, where he was honored with immortality (Hes. *Theog.* 949; Apollod. 2. 7.7; Diod. 4. 38).

IPHIGENEIA. According to some writers, she was saved from being sacrificed at Aulis by the voice of Artemis sounding in a peal of thunder.

PEGASUS, the winged horse, carried thunder and lightning for Zeus.

SEMELE. When, at her insistence, Zeus appeared to her in full majesty, accompanied by lightning and thunder, she gave premature birth to Dionysus and was herself consumed by flames (Apollon. Rhod. 4. 1137).

ZEUS was armed with thunder and lightning, and the shaking of his aegis produced storm and tempest. He was said to have been provided with thunder by the Cyclopes, whom he delivered from the bonds with which they had been fettered by Cronus. (See also PEGASUS and SEMELE)

ZEUS CATAEBATES was a surname describing Zeus as the god who descends in thunder and lightning. Under this name he had an altar at Olympia (Paus. 5. 14.8; Lycoph. 1370).

Thyrsus

SATYRS are described as fond of wine, and they often appear with either a cup or a thyrsus in their hands (Athen. 11. 484).

Tiger

DIONYSUS loved the nymph, Alphesiboea, who would not yield to him until he changed himself into a tiger and compelled her by fear to allow him to carry her across the river later called Tigris. Another story says that in his wanderings he built a bridge to cross the river, but a tiger sent to him by Zeus carried him across the river Tigris. The tiger was sacred to him.

Time

CRONUS, son of Uranus and Gaea and father of the Olympian gods, was regarded as the god of time, as indicated by his name.

EANUS was the name of Janus among the ancient Latins. At that time he was considered the representative of the sun and of time.

Tomb

HECATE was regarded as a spectral being, who at night sent from the lower world all kinds of demons and phantoms, which dwelt on tombs.

LAOMEDON. His tomb at Troy existed in the neighborhood of the Scaean gate, and it was believed that Troy would be safe so long as the tomb remained undisturbed (Ov. *Met.* 11. 696).

Tongue

HERMES. As god of eloquence, the tongues of sacrificial animals were offered to him (Aristoph. *Pax* 1062; Athen. 1. 16).

LARUNDA (LARA), daughter of Almon, was a nymph who reported to Juno that Jupiter was having an affair with Juturna. Jupiter punished her by depriving her of her tongue (Ov. *Fast.* 2. 599).

PHILOMELA. When Tereus, who first married her sister, Procne, concealed his first wife in order to marry Philomela, he cut out Philomela's tongue. When Philomela learned the truth, she made it known by a few words which she wove into a peplus.

Torch

ARTEMIS AMPHIPYROS was a surname of Artemis because she was represented carrying a torch in each hand.

DEMETER in artistic representations often carried a torch.

DIANA FASCELIS was a surname of Diana in Italy. The original name was probably Facelis or Facelina (from *fax*), as the goddess was generally represented with a torch in her hand.

DIANA NOCTILUCA was a surname of Diana. She had a temple under this name at Rome on Mt. Palatine, where torches were generally lighted in the night (Varr. *De Ling.Lat.* 4).

DIONYSUS LAMPTER was a surname of Dionysus meaning the shining or the torch-bearer, under which he was worshipped at Pellene in Achaia, where a festival was celebrated in his honor (Paus. 7. 27.2).

HECATE, with a torch in her hand, accompanied Demeter in her search for Persephone.

HECATE BRIMO was a surname of Hecate meaning the angry or terrifying. Some give the derivation from *bromos,* so that it would refer to the crackling of a fire, as Hecate was pictured bearing a torch.

HYMEN (HYMENAEUS). In works of art, he is represented as a youth carrying in his hand a bridal torch.

IACCHUS. At the celebration of the Eleusinian mysteries, he was represented carrying a torch adorned with a myrtle wreath.

LYNCEUS was the husband of Hypermnestra, who spared his life when all the other Danaids killed their husbands on their wedding night. He escaped to Lyrceia (Lynceia), from where he gave a sign with a torch that he had safely arrived there. Hypermnestra returned the sign from the citadel at Argos, and in commemoration of this event the Argives celebrated every year a festival with torches (Paus. 2. 25.4, comp. 2. 19.6, 20.5, 21.1).

NAUPLIUS was king of Euboea and father of Palamedes. His son had been condemned to death by the Greeks during the siege of Troy, and Nauplius considered his condemnation to be an act of injustice. He watched for the return of the Greeks, and, as they approached the coast of Euboea, he lighted torches on the most dangerous part of the coast. The sailors, thus misguided, suffered shipwreck and perished in the waves or by the sword of Nauplius.

PERSEPHONE BRIMO. As HECATE BRIMO.

PROMETHEUS. At Athens he had a sanctuary in the Academy, from which a torchrace took place in honor of him (Paus. 1. 30.2).

SOMNUS was the Latin personification and god of sleep, equivalent to the Greek Hypnos. In works of art, the brothers Sleep and Death are represented alike, as two youths sleeping or holding inverted torches in their hands.

THANATOS was a personification of death. He and his brother, Sleep, were often represented as genii with torches turned upside down.

Tortoise

CHELONE. For refusing to attend the nuptials of Zeus and Hera, she was thrown by Hermes with her house into a river, and was changed into a tortoise, who had henceforth to carry her house on her back.

DRYOPE was admired by Apollo, who, in order to gain possession of her, metamorphosed himself into a tortoise. Her nymph companions played with the animal, and Dryope took it into her lap. The god then changed himself into a serpent, which frightened the nymphs away, so that he remained alone with Dryope (Ov. *Met.* 9. 325).

GERANA was a Pygmean woman and wife of their king, Nicodamas, by whom she became the mother of Mopsus, or, according to some, of a tortoise.

HERMES took a tortoise's shell, drew strings across it, and thus invented the lyre and plectrum. The tortoise was sacred to him. (See also CHELONE)

SCIRON was a famous robber, who haunted the frontier between Attica and Megara and not only robbed travelers who passed through the country but compelled them, on the Scironian rock, to wash his feet, during which operation he kicked them into the sea. At the foot of the rock there was a tortoise which devoured the bodies of the victims. Sciron was slain by Theseus in the same manner in which he had killed others (Plut. *Thes.* 10; Diod. 4. 59; Strab. 9. 391; Paus. 1. 44.12; Ov. *Met.* 7. 445).

Tower

DANAE was imprisoned by her father, Acrisius, in a tower to prevent her having the opportunity of producing a male offspring who, the oracle said, would slay him. But Zeus in the form of a shower of gold visited her in this tower, and she became by him the mother of Perseus.

OENONE. According to some, in her grief at Paris' death she threw herself from a tower.

Town

ARTEMIS was regarded as founder and protector of towns and streets.

Toy

VENUS LIBENTINA was a surname of Venus from a temple where women at Rome used to dedicate their toys when they became of marriageable age.

Traffic

FERONIA was regarded in Italy by some as the goddess of commerce and traffic, because these things were carried on to a great extent during the festival which was celebrated in her honor in the town of Feronia at the foot of Mt. Soracte.

Tragedy

DIONYSUS was regarded as the god of tragic art and protector of theatres.

MELPOMENE, the Muse of tragedy, appears with a tragic mask, the club of Heracles, or a sword; her head is surrounded by vine leaves, and she wears the cothurnus (Hes. *Theog.* 77).

Tranquility

HESYCHIA was the personification of tranquility and peace.

QUIES, the personification of tranquility, was worshipped as a divinity by the Romans. A chapel dedicated to her stood on the Via Lavicana, probably a pleasant resting place for the weary traveler. Another sanctuary to her was outside the Porta Collina (Liv. 4. 41; August. 4. 16, 21).

Transexualism

CAENIS, daughter of Atrax (or Elatus), by the will of Poseidon, was changed into a man and named Caenus (Ov. *Met.* 12. 190).

HERMAPHRODITUS, son of Hermes and Aphrodite, was combined with Salamacis, a nymph, into a single body, which retained characteristics of both sexes.

IPHIS, daughter of Ligdus and Telethusa of Phaestus in Crete, was brought up as a boy to avoid being killed by her father, who did not want a girl. She was eventually metamorphosed by Isis into a youth when she became betrothed to Ianthe (Ov. *Met.* 9. 665).

LETO PHYTIA, "the creator," was a surname of Leto derived from her changing the daughter of Galateia into a male, in order to escape her being killed by her father, who desired a son.

LEUCIPPUS, the daughter of Galateia, was raised as a boy to prevent her being killed by her father, who wanted a son. When she grew up, Galateia prayed in the temple of Leto for the girl to be changed into a boy, and the request was granted.

TIRESIAS (TEIRESIAS) was a son of Everes (or Phorbas) and Chariclo and one of the most renowned soothsayers in antiquity. He was blind from an early age but lived to be very old. The cause of his blindness was accounted for by some in the following way: once, on Mt. Cithaeron, he saw a male and female serpent in the act of mating; he struck them with his staff and, as he happened to kill the female, he himself was changed into a woman. Seven years later, he again saw two serpents together and, now killing the male, he again became a man. It was for this reason that Zeus and Hera, when they were discussing whether a man or a woman enjoyed sexual intercourse more, referred the matter to Tiresias, who could judge for both. Tiresias agreed with Zeus that women derived more pleasure from sex. Hera, indignant at the answer, blinded him, but Zeus gave him the power of prophecy and granted him a life which was to last for seven or nine generations (Apollod. 3. 6.7; Ov. *Met.* 3. 320; Pind. *Nem.* 1. 91). Another time, when Aphrodite and the three Charites disputed about their beauty with one another, Tiresias awarded the prize to Cale, and he was changed by Aphrodite into an old woman.

Transmigration of Soul, see Metempsychosis

Transvestism

ACHILLES. When Thetis knew her son would perish in the Trojan War, she disguised him as a girl.

ACHILLES PYRRHA was a surname of Achilles derived from the name he used when disguised as a maiden.

DIONYSUS. After his birth he was taken to Ino and Athamas at Orchomenos, who were persuaded to bring him up as a girl to hide him from Hera. In later years, he appeared before Alcathoe, Leucippe, and Arsippe in the form of a maiden and invited them to participate in the Dionysiac mysteries. When they refused, he changed into a bull, a lion, and a panther, and the sisters were seized with madness.

EPIPOLE, daughter of Trachion of Carystus in Euboea, went in the disguise of a man with the Greeks against Troy, but when Palamedes discovered her sex, she was stoned to death by the Greek army.

HERACLES. Some writers state that during

his service for queen Omphale, he put on the garments of a woman.

HYMEN (HYMENAEUS). When he fell in love with a girl who refused to listen to him, he put on the disguise of a girl and followed her to Eleusis to the festival of Demeter. He, together with the other girls, was carried off by robbers into a distant and desolate country. While the robbers slept he killed them. He then returned to Athens and requested the citizens to give him his beloved in marriage in exchange for the rescued maidens. His request was granted, and the resultant marriage was happy. For this reason, he was invoked in hymeneal songs.

IPHIS was the daughter of Ligdus and Telethusa of Phaestus in Crete. She was brought up as a boy, because previous to her birth, her father had ordered the child to be killed if it was a girl. When Iphis grew up, she was betrothed to Ianthe. The difficulty thus arising was removed by the favor of Isis, who had before advised the mother to treat Iphis as a boy, and now metamorphosed her into a youth (Ov. *Met.* 9. 665).

LEUCIPPE was a daughter of Thestor. Her sister, Theone, was carried off by pirates and sold to King Icarus in Caria. Thestor went in search of her and was shipwrecked and taken prisoner in Caria. Leucippe went in search of them. She had been instructed by the oracle of Delphi to go in the attire of a priest of Apollo. When she came to Caria, her sister fell in love with her, but when the love was not returned, ordered her killed. Thestor received the order and was on the point of carrying it out when he recognized his daughter. The three of them were allowed to return home.

LEUCIPPUS (1). When Galateia, her mother, was ordered by her husband to kill any girl child born to her, she brought up the daughter as a boy under the name of Leucippus.

LEUCIPPUS (2) was in love with Daphne and approached her in the disguise of a maiden and thus hunted with her. But Apollo's jealousy caused his discovery during the bath, and he was killed by the nymphs (Paus. 8. 20.2).

PROCRIS was the wife of Cephalus. Eos, goddess of the dawn, fell in love with Cephalus and tried to seduce him but to no avail. Eos, however, induced him to test Procris' fidelity by posing as a handsome stranger and tempting her with rich presents. Procris was induced by the brilliant presents to break her vow of fidelity, and when she learned the truth, she fled to Crete and appealed to Artemis. The goddess made her a present of a dog and a spear, which were never to miss their object, and then sent her back to Cephalus. Procris returned home in the disguise of a youth, and went out with Cephalus to chase. When he perceived the excellence of her dog and spear, he proposed to buy them from her, but she refused to part with them for any price except for love. When he promised to love her, she revealed herself to him, and they became reconciled.

Traveler

APOLLO CATAEBATES. The god was invoked under this name to grant a happy return home to those who were traveling abroad (Eurip. *Bacch.* 1358).

ATHENA XENIA was a surname designating the goddess as presiding over the laws of hospitality and protecting strangers (Paus. 3. 11; Hom. *Od.* 14. 389; Cic. *Ep.ad Q.Frat.* 2. 12).

DIOSCURI were worshipped as the protectors of travelers by sea, for Poseidon had rewarded their brotherly love by giving them power over wind and waves, so that they could assist the shipwrecked (Eurip. *Hel.* 1511; Hor. *Carm.* 1. 3.2).

FORTUNA REDUX was a surname of Fortuna as the divinity who leads the traveler back to his home in safety (Mart. 8. 85; Claud. *De Consul.Hon.* 6. 1).

HERMES was regarded as the protector of travelers. He punished those who refused to assist travelers who had mistaken their way (Hom. *Il.* 7. 277; Theocrit. 25. 5; Aristoph. *Plut.* 1159).

LARES. The *Lares Viales,* divinities of roads, were worshipped on the highroads by travelers (Plaut. *Merc.* 5. 2.22).

PAN, who dwelt in forests, was dreaded by

travelers, to whom he sometimes appeared and startled with a sudden awe and terror (Eurip. *Rhes.* 36).

QUIES, the personification of tranquility, was worshipped as a divinity by the Romans. A chapel dedicated to her stood on the Via Lavicana, probably a pleasant resting place for the weary traveler. Another sanctuary to her was outside the Porta Collina (Liv. 4. 41; August. 4. 16, 21).

ZEUS XENIOS. As ATHENA XENIA.

Treachery

FRAUS was the Roman goddess of treachery.

Treason

ANTENOR was a Trojan whose friendship for the Greeks, just before the taking of Troy, assumed the character of treachery toward his own country. When sent to Agamemnon to negotiate peace, he devised with him and Odysseus a plan of delivering the city, and even the Palladium, into their hands.

ARNE was a woman who betrayed her country for gold and was metamorphosed into a jackdaw (Ov. *Met.* 7. 465).

HELENUS was a son of Priam and Hecuba. According to some accounts, he deserted his countrymen and joined the Greeks by his own free will; other accounts relate that he was ensnared by Odysseus (Soph. *Phil.* 605, 1338; Ov. *Met.* 13. 99, 723). Others relate that he was taken prisoner by the Greeks.

PALAMEDES, son of Nauplius, during the Trojan War was accused of treason by Agamemnon, Diomedes, and Odysseus, who were jealous of his fame. They conspired to plant a forged letter from Priam in his tent, and when it was discovered, they stoned him to death (Ov. *Met.* 13. 56).

PEISIDICE was a daughter of a king of Methymna in Lesbos, who, out of love for Achilles, opened to him the gates of her native city, but was stoned to death at the command of Achilles by his soldiers.

SCYLLA was the daughter of Nisus, king of Megara. When Minos, on his expedition against Athens, took Megara, Nisus died, because his daughter, who had fallen in love with Minos, had pulled out the purple or golden hair which grew on the top of her father's head, on which his life depended (Apollod. 3. 15.5, 6, 8). Even though Scylla's act assisted Minos in the taking of Megara, he was horrified and had her put to death.

TARPEIA was the daughter of the commander of the fortress on the Saturnian (later Capitoline) hill, when the city of Rome was invaded by the Sabines in retaliation for the abduction of their women. She betrayed the hill to them in return for ornaments which they wore on their left arms, and thus opened the gates and let them in. When she claimed her reward, they threw upon her the shields, which they carried on their left arms, and thus crushed her to death. Her memory was preserved by the name of the Tarpeian rock, from which traitors were afterwards hurled.

Treasury

AGAMEDES. When he and his brother, Trophonius, constructed the treasury of Hyrieus, they contrived to place a stone in a way to gain admission. They consistently robbed the treasury, until Agamedes became ensnared one night, whereupon, to conceal his identity, Trophonius cut off his brother's head.

HECUBA. When she discovered that Polymnestor had murdered her last son, Polydorus, she pretended that she was going to inform him of a treasure which she had concealed at Ilium. When he arrived with his two sons, Hecuba murdered the children and tore out the eyes of Polymnestor.

MINYAS, son of Chryses and ancestral hero of the race of the Minyans, is said to have built the first treasury, of which ruins are said to be still extant (in Orchomenos) (Paus. 9. 38.2).

TROPHONIUS, a son of Erginus, king of Orchomenos, or of Apollo, with his brother,

Agamedes, built the temple at Delphi and the treasury of King Hyrieus in Boeotia (Hom. *Hymn.in Apoll.* 296; Paus. 9. 37, 39; Strab. 9. 421). (See also AGAMEDES)

Tree

DIONYSUS was regarded as the protector of trees in general. (See also PENTHEUS)

DRYADS (See NYMPHS)

ERYSICHTHON, son of Triopas, cut down trees in a grove sacred to Demeter, for which he was punished by the goddess with fearful hunger (Callim. *Hymn.in Cer.* 34; Ov. *Met.* 8. 738).

HAMADRYADS (See NYMPHS)

HELEN DENDRITIS, "the goddess of the tree," was a surname of Helen at Rhodes. When Helen fled to Rhodes, she sought the protection of her friend, Polyxo, who secretly bore her a grudge, since her own husband, Tlepolemus, had been killed in the Trojan War. Once while Helen was bathing, Polyxo sent out her servants in the disguise of the Erinyes with the command to hang Helen on a tree. For this reason the Rhodians afterwards built a sanctuary to Helen Dendritis (Paus. 3. 19.10).

MELIDES (See NYMPHS)

NYMPHS. They were believed to die with the trees they inhabited. They were called Dryads or Hamadryads. Nymphs of fruit trees were called Melides.

ORPHEUS. He enchanted with his music not only the wild beasts but the trees and rocks from Olympus, so that they moved from their places to follow the sound of his golden harp (lyre).

PENTHEUS, king of Thebes, was said to have climbed a tree for the purpose of witnessing in secret the revelry of the Bacchic women, but on being discovered by them he was torn to pieces (Eurip. *Bacch.* 816, 954, 1061; Theocrit. 26. 10). According to a Corinthian tradition, the women were afterwards commanded by an oracle to find that tree and to worship it like Dionysus himself, and out of the tree two carved images of the god were accordingly made (Paus. 2. 2.6).

PHILEMON was an aged Phrygian and husband of Baucis, who kindly received Zeus and Hermes, who traveled in the guise of ordinary mortals. For this favor, Zeus rescued them from a flood and appointed them guardians of one of his temples. He granted them the favor of letting them die at the same moment and metamorphosed them into trees (Ov. *Met.* 8. 621).

PHYLLIS, daughter of a Thracian king, loved Demophon, who promised to marry her, but when he failed to return when expected, she put an end to her life and was metamorphosed into a tree. When Demophon returned and saw what had happened, he embraced the tree and pressed it to his bosom, whereupon buds and leaves immediately came forth (Ov. *Ars Am.* 3. 38).

SAGARITIES was a nymph in whose embraces Atys became faithless to Cybele. The goddess avenged the wrong done to her by causing the tree with which the nymph's life was connected to be cut down (Ov. *Fast.* 4. 229).

SILVANUS was a Latin divinity of the fields and the forests. He especially presided over plantations and delighted in trees growing wild (Tibull. 2. 5.30; Lucan 3. 402; Plin. *H.N.* 12. 2; Ov. *Met.* 1. 193).

SMYRNA (MYRRHA). When she was pursued by her father to avenge an act of incest, she was changed into a tree (smyrna). When the tree burst into bloom, Adonis was born.

See also: Names of individual trees

Trident

AJAX (the Lesser). When he was rescued by Poseidon from a shipwreck, he defied the gods, and Poseidon split with his trident the rock on which Ajax stood, thereby drowning him.

AMYMONE. Upon being pursued by a satyr, she invoked Poseidon, who cast a trident at the satyr, but the trident stuck in a rock. After

Poseidon had ravished the maiden, he bade her draw the trident from the rock, from which a threefold spring gushed out. This was named the Well of Amymone (Lucian *Dei Marin.* 6; Paus. 2. 37.1).

CYCLOPES. For his part in assisting in their release from Tartarus, they provided Poseidon with a trident (Apollod. 1.1; Hes. *Theog.* 503).

NEREUS was the old man of the sea. Virgil mentions the trident as his attribute.

POSEIDON. The symbol of his power was the trident, or a spear with three points, with which he used to shatter rocks, to call forth or subdue storms, and to shake the earth. In order to take possession of Attica, he thrust his trident into the ground on the acropolis, where a well of seawater was thereby called forth, but Attica was assigned to Athena. (See also AMYMONE and AJAX)

TELCHINES were a mysterious order of artisans who worked in brass and iron and made the trident of Poseidon.

Tripod

AMPHITRYON. After successfully conquering the Taphians, he dedicated a tripod to Apollo Ismenius (Apollod. 2. 4.6, 7; Paus. 9. 10.4; Herod. 5. 9).

XENOCLEIA was a Delphian priestess, who refused to give an oracular response to Heracles before he was purified for the murder of Iphitus; but she was compelled by him, for he threatened to take away her tripod (Paus. 10. 13.4).

Trophy

NIKE (NICE), goddess of victory, in her appearance resembles Athena and is engaged in raising a trophy.

Trumpet

ATHENA invented the trumpet.

MALEUS, son of Heracles and Omphale, is said to have been the inventor of the trumpet (Stat. *Theb.* 4. 224).

PAN. Cnossus in Crete is said to have originally been inhabited by Titans, who were hostile to Zeus but were driven away by Pan with the fearful sounds of his shell trumpet (Hom. *Hymn.in Apoll.* 336; Diod. 3. 57, 5. 66).

TRITON was a son of Poseidon and Amphitrite. He was described as riding over the sea on horses or sea monsters, and is often referred to in the plural. The chief characteristic of Tritons in poetry as well as in art is a trumpet consisting of a shell (*concha*), which they blew at the command of Poseidon to soothe the restless waves of the sea (Ov. *Met.* 1. 333), and in the fight of the giants, this trumpet served to frighten the enemies (Paus. 8. 2.3; Mosch. 2. 20; Virg. *Aen.* 10. 209; Ov. *Met.* 2. 8; Plin. *H.N.* 9. 5).

Turtledove

EUMENIDES. White turtledoves were sacred to them.

Twine

THESEUS. When he volunteered to be one of the sacrifices to the Cretan Minotaur, Ariadne, the daughter of Minos, king of Crete, fell in love with him and provided him with a sword with which to kill the creature. She also provided him with a length of thread by which he found his way out of the labyrinth which housed the Minotaur.

Ugliness

BROTEAS, son of Vulcan and Minerva, burnt himself so that he would not be taunted for his ugliness (Ov. *Ib.* 517).

HEPHAESTUS, the god of fire, was ugly and slow, and owing to the weakness of his legs, he was held up, when he walked, by artificial supports, which were skillfully made of gold (Hom. *Il.* 18. 410; Hom. *Od.* 8. 311, 330).

PRIAPUS was the son of Dionysus and Aphrodite. Hera, unhappy with Aphrodite's conduct with Adonis while Dionysus was in India, caused her to give birth to a child of extreme ugliness and with unusually large genitals.

THERSITES, a son of Agrius, was the most ugly and most impudent talker among the Greeks at Troy.

Underworld

ACHILLES was regarded by some as a judge of the underworld after his death.

AEACUS was said to have been a judge in Hades.

ASCLEPIUS was thought by some to have been killed by Zeus at the insistence of Hades for depriving the underworld of population by bringing people back to life after their death.

CERBERUS was the many-headed dog which guarded the entrance of Hades. The den of Cerberus is usually placed on the further side of the Styx, at the spot where Charon landed the shades of the departed.

CHARON, son of Erebus, conveyed in his boat the shades of the dead across the rivers of the lower world. For this service he was paid with an obolus or danace, which coin was placed in the mouth of every corpse previous to its burial. He is represented as an aged man with a dirty beard and a mean dress.

CIRCE prevailed on Odysseus to descend into the lower world to consult the seer, Tiresias.

FEBRUUS, the ancient Italian divinity, was regarded as the god of the lower world. The festival of the dead (Feralia) was celebrated in February (Ov. *Fast.* 2. 535). He was identified with Pluto.

FERONIA was regarded in Italy by some as a goddess of the earth or the lower world, because she is said to have given to her son three souls, so that Evander had to kill him thrice before he was dead (Virg. *Aen.* 3. 564).

GAEA at Rome was worshipped under the name of Tellus or Terra and was regarded as an infernal deity.

HADES was god of the lower regions and king of the shades of the departed. (See also PERSEPHONE)

HECATE. When Persephone was found, Hecate remained with her as an attendant and companion and thus came to be regarded as a deity of the lower world.

HERCYNA, daughter of Trophonius, was worshipped as a divinity of the lower world.

HERMES. Zeus made him herald of the gods of the lower world.

HERMES AGETOR was a surname from his office of conducting the shades of the dead to the underworld.

HERMES CATAEBATES. As HERMES AGETOR.

HERMES NECROPOMPOS. As HERMES AGETOR.

HERMES PSYCHOGOGOS. As HERMES AGETOR.

HERMES PSYCHOPOMPOS. As HERMES AGETOR.

INFERI signifies the gods of the lower world in contradistinction from those of heaven or from the Olympian gods. The Inferi also could mean the souls of departed mortals.

MANIA, an ancient and formidable Italian, probably Etruscan, divinity of the lower world, is called the mother of the Manes or Lares (Varr. *De Ling.Lat.* 9. 61).

MINOS, king of Crete, became one of the judges of the underworld.

ODYSSEUS. Before he could leave the island of Circe, she begged him to descend into the underworld to consult Tiresias, the famous seer (Hom. *Od.* 10. 135).

ORPHEUS. When his wife, Eurydice (or Agriope) died from the bite of a serpent and went to the underworld, Orpheus followed his lost wife to the abode of Hades, where the charms of his lyre suspended the torments of the

Orpheus

damned and won back his wife from the most inexorable of all deities. But his prayer was only granted upon the condition that he not look back upon his restored wife until they had arrived in the upper world. At the very moment they were about to pass the fatal bounds, anxiety overcame the poet: he looked around to see that Eurydice was following him, only to behold her caught back into the infernal region.

PERSEPHONE was the daughter of Zeus and Demeter and the infernal goddess of death and the dead. As a young girl, she was abducted by Hades and carried to the underworld. Demeter wandered endlessly to find her. When she eventually did, it was discovered that Persephone had consumed part of a pomegranate in Hades and was thus obliged to remain there for a part of every year.

PLUTO was another name for Hades, king of the underworld.

RHADAMANTHYS was one of the judges of the lower world.

SARPEDON became one of the judges of the lower world.

SATURN, like many other mythical kings, suddenly disappeared, being removed from earth to the abodes of the gods. It is further related that Latium received its name (from *lateo*) from this disappearance of Saturn, who for the same reason was regarded by some as a divinity of the nether world (Plut. *Quaest.Rom.* 24).

SCYLLA. Virgil (*Aen.* 6. 286) speaks of several Scyllae and places them in the lower world (comp. Lucret. 5. 893).

SISYPHUS. For various sins he was condemned to an unusually severe punishment in the lower world. He had to roll a large stone to the top of a hill, and the stone would then roll to the bottom again, so that he was compelled to roll the stone endlessly.

SORANUS was a Sabine divinity of the lower world.

SUMMANUS was an ancient Roman or Etruscan divinity often regarded as a deity of the lower world.

TANTALUS. For revealing divine counsels to men or for other impieties, he was condemned to an especially severe punishment in Hades. He stood in the middle of a lake, which retreated when he stooped to drink; boughs of fruit hung over his head but withdrew when he reached for them to satisfy his hunger. A huge stone was suspended over his head, ever ready to fall.

TELLUS (See GAEA)

TERRA (See GAEA)

TIRESIAS (TEIRESIAS), the famous soothsayer, was said to have retained his powers of divination and prophecy, even after he had died and descended into Hades. He was visited there by Odysseus, who had been sent to consult him by Circe.

Unification

APHRODITE PANDEMOS was a surname of Aphrodite meaning "common to all people" (she was thought to unite all the inhabitants of a country into one social or political body). The worship of Aphrodite Pandemos occurs at Athens, Megalopolis, and at Thebes.

Urn

DIONYSUS. Fleeing from the unkind reception by Lycurgus of Thrace, he leapt into the sea to seek refuge with Thetis, whom he rewarded afterwards with a golden urn wrought by Hephaestus (Hom. *Il.* 6. 135; Hom. *Od.* 24. 74).

EUNEUS, son of Jason, purchased Lycaon, a Trojan prisoner, from Patroclus for a silver urn (Hom. *Il.* 23. 741; Strab. 1. 41).

PATROCLUS. His ashes were collected in a golden urn, which Dionysus had once given to Thetis and were deposited under a mound, where subsequently the remains of Achilles also were buried (Hom. *Il.* 23. 83, 92, 126, 240; Hom. *Od.* 24. 74).

Uxoricide, see Murder (of Wife)

Valor, see Bravery

Vampire

LAMIA. Her namesakes, the Lamiae, were conceived as handsome ghostly women, who by voluptuous artifices, attracted young men in order to enjoy their fresh, youthful, and pure flesh and blood. They were thus in ancient times what the vampires are in modern legends (Philostr. *Vit.Apoll.* 4. 25; Hor. *Ars Poet.* 340; Apul. 1. 57). They were often identified with the Empusae and the Mormotyceiae.

Vegetation

PERSEPHONE. The story according to which Persephone spent one part of the year in the lower world and the other with the gods above made her the symbol of vegetation which shoots forth in spring, the power of which withdraws into the earth at other seasons of the year.

Veil

ANNA PERENNA. When Mars was in love with Minerva, he applied to the aged Anna, a Roman divinity, for assistance. She appeared before him, herself in disguise of Minerva, and when the god took hold of her veil and wanted to kiss her, she laughed him to scorn (Ov. *Fast.* 3. 657).

HERA was often represented with a veil hanging down the back of her head, to characterize her as the bride of Zeus.

HESIONE, daughter of Laomedon, ransomed her brother, Podarces (Priam) with her veil, when Heracles was about to kill him along with his brothers and Laomedon (Hom. *Il.* 5. 265, 640, 23. 348; Apollod. 2. 5.9, 6.4; Diod. 4. 32, 49).

RHEA, mother of the gods, in works of art is usually represented sitting on a throne adorned with the mural crown, from which a veil hangs down.

SELENE was the moon goddess. In works of art, her veil forms an arch above her head, and above it there is the crescent.

Veneration

PIETAS was a personification of faithful attachment, love, and veneration among the Romans. At first she had a small sanctuary in Rome, but in B.C. 191, a larger one was built (Plin. *H.N.* 7. 36; Liv. 40. 34).

Vengeance

ATE was avenger of evil deeds and inflicter of just punishment upon the offenders and their posterity (Aeschyl. *Choeph.* 381).

ATHENA AXIOPOENOS was a surname of Athena meaning avenger. Heracles built a temple to her at Sparta, after he had chastised Hippocoon and his sons for the murder of Oeonus (Paus. 3. 15.4).

EUMENIDES were considered by the tragedians as the avengers of crimes.

MARS ULTOR was a surname of Mars meaning the avenger, to whom Augustus built a temple at Rome in the forum, after taking vengeance upon the murderers of his great-uncle, Julius Caesar (Suet. *Div.Aug.* 21, 29; Suet. *Calig.* 24; Ov. *Fast.* 5. 577).

NEMESIS was a divinity who was a check upon extravagant favors conferred upon man by Tyche or Fortune, and from this idea arose that of her being an avenging and punishing power of fate who sooner or later overtakes the reckless sinner (Apollon.Rhod. 4. 1043; Soph. *Phil.* 518; Eurip. *Orest.* 1362; Catull. 50).

ZEUS avenged those who were wronged and punished those who had committed a crime.

ZEUS ALASTOR was a surname of Zeus as avenger of evil deeds.

Vessel

PANDORA. Later writers speak of a vessel of Pandora, containing all the blessings of the gods, which would have been preserved for the human race, had not Pandora opened the vessel, so that the winged blessings escaped irrecoverably.

Veterinary

PROMETHEUS brought the knowledge of veterinary to men.

Victory

APHRODITE. When she was represented as the victorious goddess, she had the attributes of Ares—a helmet, a shield, a sword or lance, and an image of Victory.

APHRODITE NICEPHORUS was a surname describing Aphrodite as bringing victory (Paus. 2. 19.6).

ATHENA NIKE (NICE) was a surname, meaning victorious, under which Athena had a sanctuary on the acropolis at Megara (Paus. 1. 42.4; Eurip. *Ion* 1529).

HECATE was a mysterious divinity who bestowed victory on individuals or withheld it, according to their deserts.

NEMESIS. The Rhamnusian statue of Nemesis wore on its head a crown adorned with stags and an image of Victory.

NIKE (NICE) was the goddess of victory and a sister of Zelus (zeal), Cratos (strength), and Bia (force). She and her sisters, all daughters of Pallas and Styx, assisted Zeus against the Titans, and he was so pleased with their readiness that he caused them ever after to live with him on Olympus (Hes. *Theog.* 382; Apollod. 1. 2.2).

NIKE APTEROS, "the wingless," was a surname of Nike at Athens to signify that victory, usually depicted as winged, could never fly away from the city.

VACUNA was a Sabine divinity identified with Victoria.

VICTORIA was the personification of victory among the Romans, as Nike was among the Greeks.

ZEUS was often represented holding in his hand a statue of Victory.

Vigor

JUVENTUS was the Roman goddess of youth and vigor, corresponding to the Greek Hebe.

Vine

ALCATHOE (ALCITHOE). When she and her sisters, Arsippe and Leucippe, sat at home doing their everyday chores instead of joining in the Bacchic revels newly introduced into Boeotia, Dionysus changed them into bats and their needlework into vines.

GANYMEDE. Some writers state that the compensation Zeus gave Ganymede's father for his loss was a golden vine.

MELPOMENE, the Muse of tragedy, is often represented with her head surrounded by vine leaves.

MEMNON. According to some, Memnon was sent to Troy as an ally by his father, Tithonus, because Priam had once made Tithonus a present of a golden vine.

ORESTHEUS was a son of Deucalion and king of the Ozolian Locrians in Aetolia. His dog is said to have given birth to a piece of wood, which Orestheus concealed in the earth. In the spring, a vine grew forth from it, from the sprouts of which he derived the name of his people (Paus. 10. 38.1).

SATYRS were dressed with the skins of animals and wore wreaths of vine, ivy, or fir.

See also: GRAPEVINE

Violet

IAMUS, son of Apollo, was exposed as an infant and was found lying amid violets and was thus called Iamus by his mother, Evadne.

Virginity

ABROTA, as a monument to her chastity, ordered all the women of Megara to wear garments modeled from hers.

ARTEMIS never married and always remained a virgin. The priests and priestesses who were devoted to her service were bound to live pure and chaste.

ARTEMIS PARTHENIA, i.e., Artemis the maiden, was a surname bespeaking the goddess' virginity (Callim. *Hymn.in Dian.* 110).

ATALANTA (ATALANTE). After she grew up, she lived in pure maidenhood. She vowed to be chaste all her life, but eventually was forced to wed any man who could beat her in a footrace.

ATHENA. Some accounts of her birth say her father was Pallas, the winged giant, whom she afterwards killed because he attempted to violate her chastity. She was forever a virgin divinity.

ATHENA PALLAS (PALLAS ATHENA). The most likely derivation of the surname is from *pallax,* "a virgin or maiden."

ATYS. Cybele made him her priest on condition that he preserved his chastity inviolate (Ov. *Fast.* 4. 221).

BONA DEA, a Roman divinity, was worshipped from earliest times as a chaste and prophetic divinity. She was also called Fauna, Fatua, or Oma.

BRITOMARTIS, the Cretan goddess, was fond of solitude and vowed to live in perpetual maidenhood.

CAMILLA. Her father, Metabus, brought her up in pure maidenhood, and she became one of the servants of Diana.

DIANA was the Roman equivalent of Artemis. She so hated the sight of male beings that no man was allowed to enter her temple, and she herself remained forever a virgin (Hor. *Epist.* 2. 1.454).

EILEITHYIA punished lack of chastity by increasing the pains at the birth of a child, and was therefore feared by maidens (Theocrit. 27. 28).

FATUA (See BONA DEA)

FAUNA (FAULA) (See BONA DEA)

HESTIA, Olympian goddess of the hearth, was, like Artemis and Athena, a maiden.

IPHINOE, daughter of Alcathous, died a virgin. The women of Megara, previous to their marriage, offered to her a funeral sacrifice and dedicated a lock of hair to her (Paus. 1. 43.4).

NEMESIS was usually represented as a virgin divinity.

OMA (See BONA DEA)

PALLAS ATHENA (See ATHENA PALLAS)

SIRENS. Later poets represent them as provided with wings, which they are said to have received from Aphrodite because they wished to remain virgins (Apollon. Rhod. 4. 896).

VESTA, one of the great Roman divinities, was identical with the Greek Hestia. The goddess was not represented in her temple by a statue, but the eternal fire burning on the hearth or altar was her living symbol, and was kept up and attended by the vestals, her virgin priestesses. The goddess herself was regarded as chaste and pure like her symbol, the fire.

Virtue

JUPITER was regarded as protector of virtue.

Vital Organs

CARNA. The heart, lungs, and liver were entrusted to the protection of this Roman divinity.

Volcano

CYCLOPES. Later traditions regard them as assistants of Hephaestus. Volcanoes were the workshops of the god.

GIANTS were killed one after the other by the gods and Heracles, and some of them were buried under volcanic islands.

HEPHAESTUS was regarded as the god of fire, especially insofar as it manifests itself as a power of physical nature in volcanic districts. Volcanic islands such as Lipara, Hiera, Imbros, and Sicily are called his abodes or workshops.

VULCAN was the Roman equivalent of Hephaestus.

Vomitive

METIS, daughter of Oceanus and Tethys, at the instigation of Zeus, gave Cronus a vomitive, whereupon he brought back his children whom he had devoured (Apollod. 1. 2.1; Hes *Theog.* 471).

Voracity

CHARYBDIS was a daughter of Poseidon and Gaea and a voracious woman, who stole oxen from Heracles and was hurled by the thunderbolts of Zeus into the sea, where she retained her voracious nature.

HERACLES BUPHAGUS was a surname of the hero from his having eaten a whole bull at once (Apollod. 2. 5.11, 7.7).

IDAS, son of Aphareus and brother of Lynceus, had an enormous appetite. Once the Aphareidae and Dioscuri carried off some herds from Arcadia, and Idas was requested to divide the booty into equal parts. He thereupon divided a bull into four parts, declaring that he who ate his quarter first would have half the booty, and the one who could finish his next would have the other half. Idas himself not only devoured his own quarter, but also that of his brother, and then drove the whole herd into Messenia. This act led to the fatal feud between the Aphareidae and the Dioscuri (Apollod. 2. 11.2).

IRUS was the well-known beggar of Ithaca, who was celebrated for his voracity.

LEPREUS, son of Caucon, Glaucon, or Pyrgeus and grandson of Poseidon, was said to be a rival both in strength and powers of eating of Heracles, who conquered and slew him (Athen. 10. 411).

Vulture

ARES. Vultures were sacrificed to him.

EURYNOMUS, the cannibalistic demon of the lower world, was represented as sitting on the skin of a vulture (Paus. 10. 28.4).

HERACLES. On his eleventh labor he killed the vulture which consumed the liver of Prometheus.

MELAMPUS. Iphiclus, in order to cure his sterility, was advised by Melampus, the soothsayer, to do certain things to restore his capacity for fathering children. Melampus, who could speak the language of birds, got this information from a vulture.

PHYLLIUS. Cycnus imposed on his persistent admirer, Phyllius, three tasks, one of which was to catch alive some monstrous vultures which devoured men.

PROMETHEUS was punished by Zeus for a variety of sins against heaven by being chained to a rock and having his liver devoured daily by an eagle or vulture. The liver was restored during the night, so the process continued every day until the sufferer was delivered by Heracles.

ROMULUS. When he and Remus were arguing over where to build the city of Rome, it was agreed that the question should be decided by augury; and each brother took his station on the top of the hill he had chosen for the site. At dawn, Remus saw six vultures, but at sunrise when this was told to Romulus, twelve vultures flew by him, and Remus was obliged to yield.

SPHINX. Sometimes the monster appears with the forepart of the body as a lion and the lower part that of a man with the claws of a vulture and the wings of an eagle.

TITYUS was a giant in Euboea, a son of Gaea. For assaulting Leto (or Artemis), he was cast into Tartarus, where he lay outstretched on the ground. Two vultures or snakes devoured his liver (Hom. *Od.* 11. 576).

Wages

APOLLO. Because he had revolted against Zeus, he was forced to serve Laomedon, king of Troy, for wages. When he had finished his work, Laomedon refused to pay what he had promised him and expelled him from his kingdom (Hom. *Il.* 21. 441; Hor. *Carm.* 3. 3.21).

HERACLES. An oracle told him that his illness would disappear if he would work for three years for wages and surrender his wages to Eurytus (Apollod. 2. 6.1, 2; Diod. 4. 31). He thus entered the employ of queen Omphale.

POSEIDON (See APOLLO for identical story)

Wall

AEACUS assisted Poseidon in building the walls of Troy for Laomedon. The portion of the walls he built was the weakest (Pind. *Ol.* 8. 41). When a dragon appeared and forced through the part he had built, it was prophesied that the Aeacids would be responsible for the fall of Troy.

ALCATHOUS restored the walls of Megara, which had been destroyed by the Cretans. He was assisted in this work by Apollo.

AMPHION. By playing his lyre, he moved stones and caused them to fit together to form the walls of Thebes (Apollon. Rhod. 1. 740, 775).

APOLLO. By playing his lyre, he caused stones to move into place to build the walls of Troy (Ov. *Her.* 16. 180). (See also POSEIDON)

ASTYANAX was the son of Hector and Andromache. After the taking of Troy, the Greeks hurled him from the walls of the city to prevent the fulfillment of a decree of fate, according to which he was to restore the kingdom of Troy (Hom. *Il.* 6. 400; Ov. *Met.* 13. 415).

ATHENA was defender of walls of cities.

CAPANEUS, son of Hipponous and one of the Seven against Thebes, during the siege said that even the fire of Zeus could not prevent his scaling the walls of the city, but when he was ascending the ladder, Zeus struck him with a flash of lightning (Eurip. *Phoen.* 1172; comp. Soph. *Antig.* 133; Apollod. 3. 6.7; Ov. *Met.* 9. 404).

CYCLOPES. The walls of Argos, Tiryns, and Mycenae were in later times regarded as their works and referred to as Cyclopean (Apollod. 2. 1.2; Strab. 8. 373; Paus. 2. 16.4).

HECTOR. When he and Achilles finally confronted each other, Hector took to flight and was chased thrice around the walls of Troy (Hom. *Il.* 22. 90). When he took his stand finally against Achilles, he was conquered and pierced by the spear of Achilles (Hom. *Il.* 22. 182–330). Achilles tied his body to his own chariot and thus dragged him into the camp of the Greeks; but later traditions relate that he first dragged the body thrice around the walls of Ilium (Virg. *Aen.* 1. 483).

HYPERBIUS was a mythical artist of Corinth, said to be, in conjunction with Agrolas or Euryalus, the inventor of brick walls.

POSEIDON in conjunction with Apollo is said to have built the walls of Troy for Laomedon (Hom. *Il.* 7. 452; Eurip. *Androm.* 1014). In the Trojan War, though otherwise well disposed towards the Greeks, he was jealous of the wall which the Greeks built around their own ships, and he lamented the inglorious manner in which the walls erected by himself fell by the hands of the Greeks (Hom. *Il.* 12. 17, 28).

ROMULUS. When he was raising the walls of Rome, Remus, his twin brother, resenting having been defeated in the choice of the city's site, leapt over the wall in scorn, whereupon Romulus slew him.

Wantonness

EROS. After the time of Alexander the Great, Eros was often represented as a wanton and mischievous boy, from whose tricks neither men nor gods were safe.

War

ALALA was the Roman goddess of war, sister of Mars.

APHRODITE AREIA, "the warlike," was a name by which Aphrodite was called when she was represented in armor like Ares (Paus. 3. 17.5).

ARES was the Olympian god of war.

ARES ALLOPROSALLOS was a surname describing Ares as war god, who assisted one and sometimes the other side in battle (Hom. *Il.* 5. 889).

ARES ENYALIUS, "the warlike," was used either as an epithet of Ares or as a proper name instead of Ares (Hom. *Il.* 17. 211; 2. 651; 8. 166; Pind. *Ol.* 13. 102; Pind. *Nem.* 9. 37).

ARES STRATIUS was a surname describing Ares as warlike (Strab. 14. 659; Herod. 5. 119).

ATHENA was the prudent goddess of war. Unlike Ares, she did not love war for its own sake, but for the advantage it could bring to the state.

BELLONA was a goddess of war among the Romans.

ENYALIUS was in later times a god of war separate from Ares, who was regarded as his father (Aristoph. *Pax* 457; Dionys. 3. 48). (See also ARES ENYALIUS)

ENYO, the goddess of war, delighted in bloodshed and the destruction of towns and accompanied Ares in battles (Hom. *Il.* 5. 333, 592).

ERIS was the goddess who called for war and discord.

MAMERS was the Oscan name of the god Mars.

MARS was an ancient Roman god who was early identified with the Greek Ares and thus considered the god of war.

MARS GRADIVUS was a surname among the Romans for the warlike Mars.

MINERVA guided men in the dangers of war, where victory is gained by cunning, prudence, courage, and perseverance.

ZEUS AREIUS was a surname of Zeus pertaining to his warlike nature.

ZEUS STRATIUS. As ARES STRATIUS.

War Dance

DIOSCURI, Castor and Polydeuces, were believed to have invented the war dance and warlike music.

War Shout, see Battle Cry

Water

DANAUS was said to have provided water at the site of the acropolis at Argos by digging wells (Strab. 1. 23, 8. 371).

HESTIA. Water was sacred to her.

POSEIDON originally might have been a personification of the fertilizing power of water.

Water Bearer

EPEIUS. Later traditions of Troy called him a water bearer of the Atreidae (Athen. 10. 457).

Wax

ICARUS was the son of Daedalus, who on their flight from Crete attached to his and Icarus' body wings made partially of wax. As they flew, Icarus flew too near the sun, and the wings melted so that he fell to his death into the sea (Ov. *Met.* 8. 195).

ODYSSEUS was able to escape the fatal attraction of the voices of the Sirens by filling the ears of his companions with wax and lashing himself to the mast of his ship (Hom. *Od.* 12. 39, 166).

PTERAS of Delphi was a mythical artist who was said to have built the second temple of Apollo at Delphi. The tradition was that the first temple was made of branches of the wild laurel from Tempe, and that the second was made of wax and bees' wings.

Weakness

HEPHAESTUS. From his birth he was delicate and weak, and his mother, Hera, because of this, dropped him from the heights of Olympus.

Wealth

EIRENE (IRENE). Her statue at Athens carried in its arms Plutus, the god of wealth (Paus. 1. 8.3).

ERICHTHONIUS, son of Dardanus, was declared to be the wealthiest of mortals, for three thousand mares grazed in his fields, which were so beautiful that Boreas, the north wind, fell in love with them.

FORTUNA was the Roman goddess of riches and was often represented with the cornucopia.

HADES PLUTON, "the giver of wealth," was a surname later used as the real name of the god (Eurip. *Herc.Fur.* 1104).

HECATE was a mysterious divinity who bestowed wealth on individuals or withheld it according to their deserts.

HERMES. Since commerce is a source of wealth, Hermes, as god of commerce, was also god of gain and riches, especially of sudden and unexpected riches.

MIDAS was a wealthy king of Phrygia. When he was a child, ants carried grains of wheat into his mouth to indicate that one day he would be the richest of all mortals.

PLUTON (See HADES and PLUTUS)

PLUTUS, sometimes called Pluton (Aristoph. *Plut.* 727), the personification of wealth, is described as a son of Iasion and Demeter (Hes. *Theog.* 969; Hom. *Hymn. in Cer.* 491; Hom. *Od.* 5. 125). Zeus is said to have blinded him in order that he not bestow his favors on righteous men exclusively but so that he would distribute them blindly and without regard to merit (Aristoph. *Plut.* 90). At Thebes, there was a statue of Tyche, at Athens one of Eirene, and at Thespiae one of Athena Ergane. In each of these cases, Plutus was represented as the child of those divinities, symbolically expressing the sources of wealth (Paus. 9. 16.1, 26.5).

Weasel

GALINTHIAS (GALANTHIS). When she deluded the goddesses of childbirth so that Alcmena, her friend, was able to give birth to Heracles, she was punished by being metamorphosed by them into a weasel or cat.

Weather

HORAE were the Olympian divinities of weather.

Weaving

ARACHNE, greatly skilled in the art of weaving, challenged Athena to a competition. Athena, unable to find fault with the work, tore the cloth to pieces, whereupon Arachne hanged herself. Athena saved her, only to change the rope to a spider web and Arachne to a spider.

ARCAS. After succeeding to the government of Arcadia, he taught his subjects the art of weaving (Paus. 8. 4.1).

LAODAMEIA, daughter of Bellerophon and mother of Sarpedon, was killed by Artemis while she was engaged in weaving (Hom. *Il.* 6. 197–205).

MENIPPE and her sister, Metioche, after the death of their father, Orion, were taught the art of weaving by Athena. To avert a plague in Aonia, where they lived, they offered themselves as a sacrifice (in response to an oracle) and killed themselves with their shuttles. Hades and Persephone metamorphosed them into comets (Ov. *Met.* 13. 685).

Web

ARACHNE. When she hanged herself after challenging Athena to a weaving contest and thereby incurring the goddess' wrath, Athena changed her into a spider and the rope into a spider web.

Wedding, see Marriage

Wedge

DAEDALUS was credited with the invention of the wedge.

Weed

OPS RUNCINA. By this surname she was invoked by the people of Italy to prevent the growth of weeds among the wheat and promote the harvest (August. 4. 8).

Weights

HERMES was said to have invented weights.

Well

ACIS, beloved of Galatea, was changed by her into a fountain when he was killed by a rival Cyclops.

AGNO was a nymph who was changed into a fountain on Mt. Lycaeus.

ALOPE was changed into a fountain by Poseidon after she had delivered Hippothoon, her son by the god, and exposed him to hide her shame.

AMPHITRITE threw magic herbs into a well where Scylla bathed, causing her to be changed into a monster.

AMYMONE. When Poseidon rescued her from a pursuing satyr, he appropriated her for himself and showed her the wells at Lerna (Apollod. 2. 1.4). She was changed into a fountain near Argos.

ARETHUSA. When pursued by Alpheius, the river god, she was changed into a well (Ov. *Met.* 5. 572).

ATALANTA (ATALANTE). A spring is supposed to have gushed from a rock near the ruins of Cyphanta, when she struck it with her spear (Paus. 3. 24.2).

BORMUS, son of Upius, was a youth distinguished for his extraordinary beauty. While drawing water for the reapers, he was pulled into a well by nymphs and never appeared again.

BUTES. For having abducted Coronis, he was struck mad by Dionysus and threw himself into a well (Diod. 5. 50).

BYBLIS, a daughter of Miletus and Cyane, loved her brother, who fled from her advances. She was changed into a fountain from her tears at not finding him.

CADMUS. On the site of Thebes he sent some men to the well of Ares to fetch water. The well was guarded by a dragon, which killed the men.

CYANE was a nymph who was changed into the fountain now called Pisme near Syracuse.

DANAUS was said to have provided water at the site of the acropolis at Argos by digging wells (Strab. 1. 23, 8. 371).

DAPHNIS. When he was raised up to heaven by his father Hermes, a well gushed forth on the spot from which he ascended.

DRYOPE was a daughter of Dryops. When she was carried off by the Hamadryads, they left in her stead in the temple of Apollo in Oeta a well and a poplar (Ov. *Met.* 9. 325).

EGERIA was a nymph who melted away at the death of her beloved Numa and became a fountain.

HYLAS. When the Argonauts landed on the coast of Mysia, Hylas went to fetch water for Heracles, but when he came to the well, his beauty so excited the love of the Naiads that they drew him down into the water and he was never seen again (Val.Flacc. 3. 545; Theocrit.

13. 45). When Heracles went searching for him and came to the well where Hylas disappeared, the voice of Hylas was heard from the bottom of the well like a faint echo, whence some say he was actually metamorphosed into an echo.

ICARIUS. For his hospitality to Dionysus, he was taught by the god the cultivation of the vine. He was given bags filled with wine. When he distributed these to his neighbors, some of them became intoxicated, and their friends, thinking he had poisoned them, slew him and threw his body into the well Anygrus, or buried it under a tree.

MANTO was a prophetess who was changed into a fountain by grief over the misfortunes of Thebes.

MIDAS. Once a satyr played jokes on him and ridiculed him for his satyr's ears. Midas, who had learned from his mother how satyrs might be caught and brought to reason, mixed wine in a well, and when the satyr had drunk of it, he fell asleep and was caught (Philostr. *Vit.Apoll.* 6. 27).

MUSES presided over sacred wells, which were believed to inspire those who drank from them. Hippocrene was the most famous of these.

NAIADS were nymphs who presided over fountains, springs, and rivers.

PEGASUS, the winged horse, with his hoof called forth the inspiring well Hippocrene.

PEIRENE was the nymph of the well Peirene near Corinth, which was believed by some to have arisen out of the tears which she shed in her grief at the death of her son, Cenchrias (Paus. 2. 3.5).

PERSEPHONE. On the spot near Enna in Sicily at which she was abducted by Hades and carried to the lower world, the well Cyane arose (Diod. 5. 3; Ov. *Fast.* 4. 422).

PHARMACEIA was the nymph of a well with poisonous powers near the river Ilissus in Attica.

POSEIDON. In order to take possession of Attica, he thrust his trident into the ground on the acropolis, where a well of seawater was thereby called forth, but Attica was assigned to Athena.

SCYLLA. One tradition relates that she was originally a beautiful maiden, who was beloved by the marine god, Glaucus. He applied to Circe for means to make Scylla return his love; but Circe, jealous of the fair maiden, threw magic herbs into the well where Scylla bathed and by these herbs she was metamorphosed into a sea monster, half fish, half woman. (See also AMPHITRITE)

SISYPHUS. When Zeus carried away the daughter of Asopus, Sisyphus betrayed the abduction to Asopus and was rewarded by him with a well on Acrocorinthus, but Zeus punished him in the lower world (Apollod. 1. 9.3, 3. 12.6).

TIRESIAS (TEIRESIAS), the soothsayer, while fleeing with the defeated Thebans in the war with the Epigoni, drank from the well of Tilphossa and died (Apollod. 3. 7.3; Paus. 9, 33.1; Diod. 4. 66).

Wheat, see Grain

Wheel

IXION. As punishment for his lust for Hera, he was chained by Hermes to a wheel, which is described as winged or fiery and is said to have rolled perpetually in the air or in the lower world.

NEMESIS was the goddess of retribution. Sometimes she appears in a pensive mood, holding in her right hand a wheel with a sword or a scourge.

Whining

ACHILLES was originally called Ligyron, the whiner. His name was changed by Cheiron, the centaur (Apollod. 3. 13.6).

Whirlpool

CHARYBDIS. On the rock where this monster dwelt on the Sicilian coast opposite Italy grew an immense fig tree. She lived under the tree and thrice a day swallowed down the waters of the sea and thrice threw them up again. She and the rock opposite on the Italian coast, where the monster Scylla dwelt, were formidable to the ships which had to pass between them (Hom. *Od.* 12. 73, 235).

White

JUPITER. The color white was sacred to Jupiter as the prince of light, and white animals were sacred to him. His chariot was thought to be drawn by four white horses. His priests wore white caps, and his consuls were attired in white.

Whiteness

CHLORIS, daughter of Amphion and Niobe, was originally called Meliboea. She and her brother, Amyclas, were the only children of Niobe not killed by Apollo and Artemis, but she was so terrified by the deaths of her brothers and sisters that she turned perfectly white and was therefore called Chloris.

Whoop, see Hoopoe

Widowhood

GORGOPHONE. After the death of her husband, Perieres, she is said to have married Oebalus and to have been the first widow in Greece who married a second husband (Paus. 2. 21.8, comp. 3. 1.4).

HERA CHERA was a name believed to have been given to her by Temenus, son of Pelasgus. At Stymphalus he had built three sanctuaries to her: *pais* (maidenhood), *teleia* (as wife of Zeus), and *chera* (the widow, alluding to her separation from Zeus) (Paus. 8. 22.2).

Willow

ARTEMIS LYGODESMA. Her statue was found by the brothers, Astrabacus and Alopecus, under a bush of willows, by which it was surrounded in such a manner that it stood upright (Paus. 3. 16.7).

Wind

ACHILLES. When the funeral pyre of Patroclus could not be made to burn, Achilles promised to offer sacrifices to the winds, and Iris, hastening to them, found them feasting in the palace of Zephyrus in Thrace. Boreas and Zephyrus, at the invitation of Iris, sped across the Thracian Sea into Asia to cause the fire to blaze (Hom. *Il.* 23. 185, comp. 2. 145, 5. 534, 9. 5; Hom. *Od.* 5. 295).

AEOLUS was the ruler of the winds. (See also ODYSSEUS)

ARGESTES was mentioned by Hesiod (*Theog.* 378, 869) as a beneficial wind and a son of Astraeus and Eos.

ASTRAEUS, a Titan, became by Eos the father of the winds, Zephyrus, Boreas, Notus, and Eosphorus (the morning star), and all the stars of heaven (Hes. *Theog.* 376).

ATHENA ANEMOTIS was a surname describing Athena as subduer of the winds, under which name she was worshipped and had a temple at Mothone in Messenia.

AUSTER was a personification of the south wind, or the southwest wind, by the Romans.

BOREAS was a personification of the north wind. (See also ACHILLES)

EURUS was a personification of the east wind.

HARPIES, in Homeric poems, are personified storm winds (Hom. *Od.* 20. 66, 77).

ICARIUS. His murderers fled from Athens to Cos, where a drought promptly descended. The inhabitants were enjoined to propitiate Icarius with many sacrifices and to beg Zeus to send winds called Etesiae, which Zeus, in consequence, made blow at the rising of the dog star for forty days (Apollod. 3. 14.7; Paus. 1. 2.4).

IRIS. In the Trojan War, she served Achilles by calling the winds to his assistance (Hom. *Il.* 23. 199). (See also ACHILLES)

JUPITER URIUS was a surname of Jupiter as sender of favorable wind (Cic. *In Verr.* 4. 57).

LAELAPS. The storm wind is personified by the legend of the dog of Procris, which bore this name.

NOTUS was a personification of the south wind.

ODYSSEUS. After spending a month on the island of Aeolus, he departed with a bag of winds, a gift of Aeolus, which were to carry him home, but his companions, without Odysseus' knowledge, opened the bag and let the winds escape (Hom. *Od.* 10. 1).

TYPHON was mentioned by Hesiod (*Theog.* 378, 869) as a destructive wind and as a son of Typhoeus.

VENILIA was a Roman divinity connected with the winds and the sea (Virg. *Aen.* 10. 75; Ov. *Met.* 14. 334).

VENTI. The winds are usually represented as beings with wings at their heads and shoulders (Ov. *Met.* 1. 264; Philostr. *Imag.* 1. 24).

ZEPHYRUS was the personification of the west wind, a son of Astraeus and Eos (Hes. *Theog.* 579). (See also ACHILLES)

ZEUS EVENEMUS, "the giver of favorable winds," was a surname of Zeus under which he had a sanctuary at Sparta (Paus. 3. 13.5).

Wine

ACRATOPOTES, "a drinker of unmixed wine," was a hero companion of Dionysus. He was also called Acratus.

ACRATUS (See ACRATOPOTES)

AGATHODAEMON. The Greeks drank a cup of unmixed wine in honor of this divinity (probably an epithet of Zeus) at the end of every repast.

AMPHICTYON was credited with introducing the custom of mixing wine with water.

ANCAEUS was a vinegrower whom a seer warned that he would not live to taste the wine of his vineyard. As he lifted a cup to his lips, he scorned the seer, and the seer remarked: "There is many a slip between the cup and the lip." A tumult arose outside, and Ancaeus went out in time to be killed by a wild boar.

BONA DEA was said to have intoxicated herself by emptying a large vessel of wine, whereupon Faunus killed her, but later raised her to a goddess. At her festivals, wine was present, and the women drank of it and performed Bacchic dances, but the name of wine was avoided, and it was called milk instead.

CABEIRI were mystic divinities who presided over vineyards. They offered the Argonauts plenty of Lemnian wine (Plut. *Quaest. Conviv.* 2. 1).

CALCHAS. According to one account, a soothsayer foretold upon seeing him plant vines that he would not live to drink any of the wine produced by them. When the vines were grown and the wine was made, Calchas invited the soothsayer among his other guests. Even as Calchas held the cup of wine in his hand, the soothsayer repeated his prophecy. This excited Calchas to such a fit of laughter that he dropped the cup and choked to death. (For a similar story, see ANCAEUS)

CHARITES moderated the exciting influence of wine (Hor. *Carm.* 3. 19.15; Pind. *Ol.* 13. 18).

CRONUS. Because of the hospitality of a Roman country man, father of Entoria, he taught the father the cultivation of the vine and the preparation of wine, enjoining him to teach his neighbors the same. This was done accordingly, but the country people, who became intoxicated with their new drink, thought it to be poison and stoned their neighbor to death, whereupon his grandsons hanged themselves in grief. Other versions of this account name

Dionysus as the one who taught Entoria's father the cultivation of the vine.

DIONYSUS, the youthful, beautiful, but effeminate god of wine, was described as the god who teaches men the preparation of wine, hence he is called the "drunken god." In his wanderings and travels, the god rewarded those who received him kindly and adopted his worship; he gave them vines and wine. (See also CRONUS)

DIONYSUS ACRATOPHORUS was a surname of the god at Phigaleia in Arcadia, describing him as a giver of unmixed wine.

DIONYSUS BASSAREUS was a surname taken, perhaps, from the Hebrew word meaning the precursor of the vintage.

DIONYSUS LENAEUS was a surname derived from *lenas,* the winepress or the vintage (Virg. *Georg.* 2. 4.529).

ELEUTHER, son of Apollo, was said to have erected the first statue of Dionysus and spread the worship of the god.

ELPENOR, a companion of Odysseus, one day fell asleep intoxicated on the roof of Circe's residence, fell off and broke his neck (Hom. *Od.* 10. 550).

EUMOLPUS was sometimes described as having invented the cultivation of the vine (Hom. *Hymn.in Cer.* 476).

EUNEUS was a son of Jason by Hypsipyle, queen of Lemnos. During the Trojan War, he supplied the Greeks with Lemnian wine (Hom. *Il.* 7. 468).

GENIUS. Every man at Rome had his own genius, whom he worshipped as *sanctus sanctissimus deus,* especially on his birthday, with libations of wine and garlands of flowers (Tibull. 2. 2.5; Ov. *Trist.* 3. 13.18, 5. 5, 11; Senec. *Epist.* 114; Hor. *Carm.* 4. 11.7).

HERACLES. While in pursuit of the Erymanthian boar, he became involved with the centaurs through Pholus, a centaur who had received from Dionysus a sack of excellent wine. Heracles opened it, and the delicious fragrance attracted the other centaurs, who besieged the grotto of Pholus. Heracles drove them away, and they fled to the house of Cheiron, who was mortally wounded in the resulting fracas.

HESTIA. Wine was sacred to her.

ICARIUS. For his hospitality to Dionysus, he was taught by the god the cultivation of the vine. He was given bags filled with wine. When he distributed these to his neighbors, some of them became intoxicated, and their friends, thinking he had poisoned them, slew him and threw his body into the well Anygrus or buried it under a tree.

JANUS. Wine was sacred to him.

MARON was a son of Evanthes (or of Oenopion, Silenus, or Bacchus) and a grandson of Dionysus and Ariadne. He was the hero of sweet wine and is mentioned among the companions of Dionysus (Hom. *Od.* 9. 197; Athen. 1. 33; Diod. 1. 18).

MELAMPUS, son of Amythaon, was looked upon by the ancients as the person who established the worship of Dionysus in Greece (Apollod. 2. 2.2). He taught the Greeks how to mix wine with water (Athen. 2. 45). (See also PROETUS)

MIDAS. Once a satyr played jokes on him and ridiculed him for his satyr's ears. Midas, who had learned from his mother how satyrs could be caught and brought to reason, mixed wine in a well, and when the satyr had drunk of it, he fell asleep and was caught (Philostr. *Vit.Apoll.* 6. 27).

OENOTROPAE, "the changers of or into wine," was the name of the three or four daughters of king Anius in Delos, because they had received from Dionysus the power of changing water into wine, and anything else they chose into grain and olives.

POLYPHEMUS. In order to escape his cave, Odysseus contrived to make the Cyclops drunk with wine, and then with a burning pole put out his one eye.

PRIAPUS was the son of Dionysus and Aphrodite and god of the fructifying powers and manifestations of nature. Sacrifices to him included the first fruits of the vineyards.

PROETUS. His daughters, Iphinoe, Lysippe, and Iphianassa, were seized with madness because they opposed the worship of Dionysus (Diod. 4. 68; Apollod. 1. 9.12). They were cured by Melampus, the soothsayer.

SATYRS are always described as fond of wine, whence they often appear either with a cup or thyrsus in their hands (Athen. 11. 484). (See also MIDAS)

SILENUS (SEILENUS) was one of the satyrs, the son of Hermes or Pan. He was described as a jovial old man with a bald head, a pug nose, fat and round like his wine bag, which he always carried with him, and generally intoxicated. He had a temple at Elis, where Methe (Drunkenness) stood by his side handing him a cup of wine.

SILVANUS was a Latin divinity of the fields and forests. Sacrifices to him included wine.

STAPHYLUS was a son of Dionysus (or Theseus) and Ariadne. His daughters, Molpadia and Parthenos, were to guard their father's wine, but they fell asleep and swine overturned and spoiled the wine. The sisters, on discovering the mischief, threw themselves from a rock.

THYIA, a daughter of Castalius or Cephisseus, was said to have been the first to have sacrificed to Dionysus and to have celebrated orgies in his honor.

ZEUS AGATHODAEMON (See AGATHODAEMON)

See also: GRAPEVINE, INTOXICATION

Wings

ACHILLES. Thetis affixed the wings formerly belonging to Arce to Achilles' feet, and he was thereafter called Podarces.

ARCE, daughter of Thaumas and sister of Iris, was deprived of her wings for siding with the Titans in their war with the gods.

ATHENA. When she killed the winged giant, Pallas, she fastened his wings to her own feet.

CERAMBUS. Ovid (*Met.* 7. 455) mentions a certain Cerambus on Mt. Othrys, who escaped from the Deucalonian flood by means of wings which he had received from the nymphs.

COMUS, a Roman divinity, was represented as a winged youth.

DAEDALUS was imprisoned by Minos, but with his son, Icarus, escaped by making wings of wood and sealing them with wax.

EOS, goddess of the dawn, is sometimes represented in works of art as winged.

EROS was often represented with golden wings.

EUMENIDES were represented as winged beings (Eurip. *Orest.* 317; Eurip. *Iphig. Taur.* 290; Virg. *Aen.* 12. 848).

FORTUNA. When she entered Rome, she put off her wings and shoes and threw away the globe, as she intended to make her permanent abode among the Romans.

GENIUS, or guardian spirit of people and places, was usually represented in works of art as a winged being.

GORGONS were described as having wings (Aeschyl. *Prom.* 794; Aeschyl. *Choeph.* 1050).

HARPIES were represented by Hesiod (*Theog.* 267) as fairhaired and winged maidens. Later writers described them as ugly and repulsive monsters with wings.

HERMES was represented in a traveling hat with a broad brim, which was later adorned with two little wings. Sometimes these wings were seen to be arising from his locks, his head not being covered by a hat. His staff was later represented as winged. His sandals were also later represented as winged. (See also IXION)

HERMES ALIPES was a surname from his having wings at his ankles (Ov. *Met.* 11. 312).

HERMES PTEROPEDILOS. As HERMES ALIPES.

ICARUS was the son of Daedalus, who on their flight from Crete attached to his and Icarus' bodies wings made partially of wax. As they flew, Icarus flew too near the sun, and the wings were melted so that he fell to his death in the sea (Ov. *Met.* 8. 195).

IRIS, the goddess of the rainbow, was represented with wings attached to her shoulders and sometimes to her sandals.

IXION. As punishment for his lust for Hera, he was chained by Hermes to a wheel, which is described as winged or fiery, and is said to have rolled perpetually in the air or in the lower world.

NIKE (NICE) was goddess of victory. In her appearance she resembles Athena but has wings.

NIKE APTEROS, "the wingless," was a surname of Nike at Athens to signify that victory, usually depicted as winged, could never fly away from the city.

NYX. In later accounts she is described as winged.

ONEIRATA. Dreams were often conceived as genii with black wings.

PEGASUS. Whether Hesiod considered Pegasus as a winged horse cannot be inferred with certainty from the word *apoptamenos*; but Pindar, Euripides, and the other writers expressly mention his wings.

SELENE, the moon goddess, is represented with long wings.

SIRENS. Late poets represent them as provided with wings, which they are said to have received at their own request, in order to be able to search for Persephone (Ov. *Met.* 5. 552), or as a punishment from Demeter for not having assisted Persephone or from Aphrodite because they wished to remain virgins (Aelian. *De Nat.Anim.* 17. 23; Apollon.Rhod. 4. 896). Once, however, they allowed themselves to be prevailed upon by Hera to enter into a contest with the Muses, and, being defeated, they were deprived of their wings (Paus. 9. 34.2).

SPHINX. The common idea of a Greek (as opposed to Egyptian or Ethiopian) Sphinx is of the winged body of a lion, having the breast and upper part of a woman (Aelian. *De Nat.Anim.* 12. 7; Apollod. 3. 5.8). Or the forepart of the body is that of a lion and the lower part that of a man with the claws of a vulture and the wings of an eagle.

THETIS received the wings taken from Arce at her marriage to Peleus.

VENTI, the winds, are usually represented as beings with wings at their heads and shoulders (Ov. *Met.* 1. 264; Philostr. *Imag.* 1. 24).

ZETES was a son of Boreas and Oreithyia and a brother of Calais. The brothers are generally described as winged beings. Some say that they had wings at their heads and feet and others that they had them only at their feet (Apollon.Rhod. 1. 219) or at their shoulders (Pind. *Pyth.* 4. 325).

Wisdom

ARRIBAS was a descendant of Achilles. When he came to the throne of the Molossians in Epeirus at a young age, he displayed so much wisdom that he won the admiration and affection of his subjects.

ATHENA was the Olympian goddess of wisdom.

HECATE was a mysterious divinity who bestowed wisdom on individuals or withheld it according to their deserts.

MINERVA was thinking, calculating, and investigative power personified by the Romans.

NESTOR was regarded by the Greeks at Troy as eminently wise, just, brave, knowledgeable about war, and eloquent.

PALAMEDES, son of Nauplius, was described as a sage among the Greeks.

SILENUS (SEILENUS), one of the satyrs, a son of Hermes or Pan by a nymph, was viewed as a sage who despised all the gifts of fortune (Cic. *Tusc.* 1. 48), so that he becomes the representative of that wisdom which conceals itself behind a rough and uncouth external appearance, whence he is likened to Socrates (Plat. *Sympos.* 32; Xenoph. *Sympos.* 5.7).

TAGES, a mysterious Etruscan being, is described as a boy with the wisdom of an old man. He is said to have instructed the Etruscans in the art of haruspicy.

Witchcraft

CARDEA was a Roman divinity who protected little children in their cradles from witches.

FASCINUS was an early Latin divinity who was worshipped as the protector from sorcery, witchcraft, and evil daemons.

See also: SORCERY

Woe

HYACINTHUS. When Apollo accidentally killed him with a thrown discus, he caused a flower known as the hyacinth to spring forth from the blood of the slain youth. On the leaves of the flower there appeared an exclamation of woe.

Wolf

APOLLO was said to have assumed the shape of a wolf and to have destroyed the mysterious tribe called Telchines, descendants of Thalassa or Poseidon. The wolf was one of the chief sacrifices offered to Apollo, since the wolf was the enemy of the sheepfold, and Apollo was god of shepherds.

APOLLO LYCEIUS was a surname of Apollo meaning, perhaps, "the wolf slayer." In nearly all cases where the god appears with this name, we find traditions concerning wolves. Thus, the descendants of Deucalion, who founded Lycoreia, followed a wolf's howl; Latona came to Delos as a she-wolf, and she was conducted by wolves to the river Xanthus; wolves protected the treasuries of Apollo; and near the great altar at Delphi there stood an iron wolf with inscriptions (Paus. 10. 14.4). The attack of a wolf upon a herd of cattle occasioned the worship of Apollo Lyceius at Argos (Plut. *Pyrrh.* 32); the Sicyons are said to have been taught by Apollo how to get rid of wolves (Paus. 2. 19.3). By the name of Lyceius he is generally characterized as the destroyer.

APOLLO LYCIUS. This surname is often used in the sense of Lyceius. (See also APOLLO LYCEIUS)

APOLLO LYCOREUS was a surname used perhaps in the same sense as Lyceius (wolf killer) but also in reference to Lycoreia on Mt. Parnassus (Apollon. Rhod. 4. 1490; Callim. *Hymn. in Apoll.* 19). (See also APOLLO LYCEIUS)

ATHAMAS. An oracle stated that he should settle wherever he found hospitality from animals. He came upon wolves devouring a sheep, and they ran away. He founded the town of Athamania at that place.

DANAUS. At Argos, a dispute arose between him and Gelanor about the government. While a settlement was being reached, a wolf rushed among the cattle and killed one of the oxen. This occurrence symbolized to the Argives how the dispute should terminate, and Danaus was made king (Paus. 2. 19.3).

LUPERCA (LUPA) was an ancient Italian divinity, the wife of Lupercus. In the shape of a she-wolf she suckled Romulus and Remus.

LUPERCUS was an ancient Italian divinity who was worshipped by shepherds as the protector of their flocks against wolves.

LYCAON sacrificed a child on the altar to Zeus and during the sacrifice he was changed into a wolf (Paus. 8. 2.1; Ov. *Met.* 1. 237). (See also ZEUS LYCAEUS)

LYCASTUS and his twin brother, Parrhasius, sons of Ares, were thrown into the river Erymanthus by their mother, Philonome, from fear of her father. The river god carried them into a hollow oak tree, where they were suckled by a she-wolf until the shepherd Tyliphus found them and carried them home.

MARS. The wolf was sacred to him and was, with the horse, his favorite sacrifice.

MILETUS was a son of Acacallis and Apollo, who was exposed in the forest but was suckled by wolves.

PELEUS. The flocks which had been given by Peleus to Acastus as an indemnification for the murder of his son, Actor, were destroyed by a wolf, who was changed by Thetis into a stone. Another account says that Peleus, being abandoned during the chase by Acastus, was kindly received by Cheiron, and, having acquired the possession of flocks, he took them to Irus as an atonement for his son, Eurytion, whom he had killed. But as Irus refused to accept them, Peleus allowed them to wander about without shepherds, until they were attacked by a wolf. This wolf was sent by Psamathe to avenge the murder of Phocus, but she herself afterwards, on the request of Thetis, changed him into a stone.

POSEIDON. Theophane, a daughter of Bisaltes, because of her extraordinary beauty, was beleaguered by lovers, but was carried off by Poseidon to the isle of Crinissa. As the lovers followed her even there, Poseidon metamorphosed the maiden into a sheep and himself into a ram, and all the inhabitants into animals. As the lovers began to slaughter these animals, he changed them into wolves.

ROMULUS. When he and his twin, Remus, were set adrift and left to die as infants, they eventually floated in their cradle into the Tiber. The cradle lodged finally in the root of a wild fig tree, and a she-wolf, coming to the river to drink, found them and suckled them. (See also LUPERCA)

SILVANUS was a Latin divinity of the fields and the forests. He was described as the divinity protecting the flocks of cattle, warding off wolves, and promoting the fertility of flocks (Virg. *Aen.* 8. 601; Tibull. 1. 5.27; Cato 83; Nonn. 2. 324).

SILVIA, the mother of Romulus and Remus, while still a vestal virgin, went one day to draw water and was frightened by a wolf. She ran into a cave and there Mars overpowered her and became by her the father of the twins.

SORANUS was a Sabine divinity of the lower world. It is related that during a sacrifice to him, wolves snatched away the entrails of the victims from the altar and that shepherds pursuing them came to a cave, the poisonous vapors of which caused a pestilence among them. An oracle ordered them to live, like wolves, on prey, and hence these people are called Hirpini, from the Sabine word *hirpus,* a wolf, which was joined to that of Soranus, so that their full name was *hirpini Sorani.*

ZEUS LYCAEUS was named by Lycaon, a son of Pelasgus, who built the first and most ancient town of Lycosura. He erected a temple there and instituted the festival of the Lyceia in honor of him. He further offered to him bloody sacrifices and, among others, his own son, in consequence of which he was metamorphosed into a wolf (Paus. 8. 2.1, 38.1; Callim. *Hymn.in Jov.* 4; Ov. *Met.* 1. 218).

Women

ARES was worshipped in Argos as a patron deity of women.

ARES GYNAECOTHOENAS, "the god feasted by women," was a surname of Ares at Tegea, where the women singlehandedly won a battle by surprising the enemy from ambush.

MENA was goddess of women at Rome.

MINERVA. Among the Romans, she was the patroness of females.

VESTA was the Roman goddess of the hearth. On the 9th of June, the Vestalia was celebrated in honor of the goddess, on which occasion none but women walked to the temple, and then with bare feet.

Wood

CALLIPOLIS. When hastening to tell his father Alcathous of his brother's death, he found his father sacrificing to Apollo and, thinking it unfit to be sacrificing at such a moment, he snatched the wood away. Alcathous, seeing this as sacrilege, killed his son on the spot with a piece of wood.

MELEAGER. When he was seven days old, the Moirae appeared, declaring that the boy would die as soon as a piece of wood burning on the hearth was consumed. His mother, Althaea, immediately extinguished the firebrand and concealed it in a chest. He therefore became invulnerable as long as the wood remained unburned, but when he killed his mother's brothers, she lighted the piece of wood and Meleager died.

ORESTHEUS was a son of Deucalion and king of the Ozolian Locrians in Aetolia. His dog is said to have given birth to a piece of wood, which Orestheus concealed in the earth. In the spring, a vine grew forth from it, from the sprouts of which he derived the name of his people (Paus. 10. 38.1).

Wooden Horse of Troy

ACAMAS was one of the Greeks concealed in the wooden horse.

CAPYS was a Trojan who is mentioned among those who were of the opinion that the wooden horse should be thrown into the water (Virg. *Aen.* 2. 35).

DIOMEDES was one of the Greeks concealed in the wooden horse.

EPEIUS, son of Panopeus, was called the artist, and he built the wooden horse (Hom. *Od.* 8. 492, 11. 532).

LAOCOON. When the Greeks left behind the wooden horse and pretended to sail home, Laocoon cautioned the Trojans against the danger of pulling the horse into Troy. While thus warning them, he thrust his lance into the side of the horse (Virg. *Aen.* 2. 40).

MACHAON, son of Asclepius by Epeione, was mentioned by later writers as one of the Greek heroes who were concealed in the wooden horse (Virg. *Aen.* 2. 263).

MENELAUS was one of the heroes concealed in the wooden horse (Hom. *Od.* 4. 280; comp. Virg. *Aen.* 2. 264).

NEOPTOLEMUS was one of the heroes who were concealed in the wooden horse (Hom. *Od.* 11. 508, 521).

ODYSSEUS was said by some to have devised the strategem of the wooden horse and he was one of the heroes concealed in its belly (Hom. *Od.* 4. 280, 8. 494, 11. 525).

SINON, the Greek spy who infiltrated the ranks of the Trojans, pretending ill treatment by the Greeks, was asked the purpose of the wooden horse. He told them that it had been constructed as an atonement for the Palladium, which had been carried off, and that if the Trojans ventured to destroy it, their kingdom would fall, but that if they would draw it with their own hands into their own city, Asia would gain supremacy over Greece (Virg. *Aen.* 2. 57). The Trojans took his advice, and when the horse was drawn into the city, Sinon gave the prearranged signal, opened the door of the horse, and the Greeks, rushing out, took possession of Troy (Virg. *Aen.* 2. 259).

STHENELUS was a son of Capaneus and Evadne and commander of the Argives under Diomedes in the Trojan War. He was one of the Greeks concealed in the wooden horse.

THERSANDER was a son of Polyneices and Argeia. Virgil (*Aen.* 2. 261) enumerates Thersander among the Greeks concealed in the wooden horse.

THYMOETES was one of the elders of Troy (Hom. *Il.* 3. 146). A soothsayer had predicted that on a certain day a boy should be born by whom Troy would be destroyed. On that day, Paris was born to Priam, and Munippus to Thymoetes. Priam ordered Munippus and his mother, Cylla, to be killed. Hence, Aeneas, in Virgil (*Aen.* 2. 31) says that it was possible that

Trojan Horse

Thymoetes, in order to revenge himself, advised that the wooden horse be drawn into the city.

Woodpecker

MARS. In the neighborhood of Reate there had been a very ancient oracle of the god (Dionys. 1. 41), in which the future was revealed through a woodpecker (*picus*), which was sacred to him.

PICUS, the famous Latin soothsayer, made use of a *picus* (a woodpecker) in his augury. He was represented in a rude and primitive manner as a wooden pillar with a woodpecker on the top of it, but afterwards as a young man with a woodpecker on his head (Dionys. 1. 14; Ov. *Met.* 14. 314; Virg. *Aen.* 7. 187). The whole legend of Picus is founded on the notion that the woodpecker is a prophetic bird, sacred to Mars. Pomona, it is said, was beloved of him, and when Circe's love for him was not requited, she changed him into a woodpecker, who, however, retained the prophetic powers which he had formerly possessed as a man (Virg. *Aen.* 7. 190; Ov. *Met.* 14. 346; Plut. *Quaest.Rom.* 21; Ov. *Fast.* 3. 37).

ROMULUS and his twin, Remus, having been adopted and suckled by a she-wolf when they were set adrift in the river to perish, were also fed by a woodpecker, a bird sacred to Mars, their father (Ov. *Fast.* 3. 54).

Wool

MELUS, son of Melus and Peleia, after his parents' death was ordered by Aphrodite to return with a colony to Delos, where he founded the town of Delos. He first taught the inhabitants to shear sheep and make cloth out of their wool.

Worm

MELAMPUS. For attempting to steal the cattle of Iphiclus for his brother to give to Neleus in exchange for the hand of Pero, he was thrown in prison, but was released when he demonstrated his prophetic powers. From the woodworms in the walls of the prison, he knew the building would collapse and demanded to be let out (Apollod. 1. 9.12).

PHOENIX. When this fabulous bird died, a worm crept forth from his body and was developed into a new Phoenix by the heat of the sun (Plin. *H.N.* 10. 2; Ov. *Met.* 15. 392).

Wound

PHILOCTETES, son of Poeas, on his way to the Trojan War, was either bitten by a snake or wounded by his own poisoned arrows. The wound is said to have become ulcerated and to have produced such an intolerable smell and such intolerable pains that the moanings of the hero alarmed his companions. He was left on the coast of Lemnos at the advice of Odysseus and the Atreides (Ov. *Met.* 13. 315). According to some, he was left behind because the priests of Hephaestus in Lemnos knew how to heal the wound, and Pylius, a son of Hephaestus, is said to have actually cured him; while, according to others, he was believed to have died from the wound (Paus. 1. 22.6). According to the common tradition, he remained on Lemnos for the duration of the Trojan War. The tradition that he was cured has him proceeding to Troy, where he was cured by Machaon (or Podalirius or even Asclepius himself).

TELEPHUS was a king of Mysia at the time of the Trojan War. When the Greeks invaded Mysia, he repelled them. He was, however, wounded by Achilles. The wound could not be healed, and when he consulted the oracle, he received the answer that only he could cure him who had wounded him. The Greeks had received an oracle that without the aid of Telephus they could not reach Troy. A reconciliation was brought about, and Achilles cured Telephus by means of the rust of the spear by which the wound had been inflicted; Telephus in return pointed out to the Greeks the road which they had to take (Ov. *Met.* 12. 112; Ov. *Trist.* 5. 2, 15; Ov. *Rem.Am.* 47; Ov. *Ep.ex Pont.* 2. 26; Philostr. *Vit.Apoll.* 2. 14).

Wrestling

ANDROGEUS, son of Minos and Pasiphae,

was famous for his skill in wrestling. He was assassinated by Aegeus, for which reason Attica had to pay tribute to Crete by sending youths and maidens to be sacrificed to the Minotaur.

ANTAEUS, the giant, invincible as long as he remained in contact with his mother earth, compelled strangers to wrestle with him. He invariably won and slew his victims, till Heracles discovered his secret, held him in the air and crushed him (Apollod. 2. 5.11; Diod. 4. 17).

AUTOLYCUS was mentioned as the teacher of Heracles in the art of wrestling.

CERCYON, son of Poseidon, challenged all strangers to Eleusis to wrestle with him, whereupon he killed them. He challenged Theseus and was killed by him.

HERACLES PALAEMON was a surname of Heracles meaning the wrestler (Lycoph. 663). Heracles was instructed in wrestling by Autolycus.

ILUS won the prize as a wrestler in the games which the king of Phrygia celebrated. The prize consisted of fifty youths and fifty maidens and also a cow of different colors.

LAODAMAS, son of Alcinous, offered to wrestle Odysseus, but Odysseus refused the offer because of the hospitality of Alcinous.

ODYSSEUS. On the voyage to Troy, he wrestled in Lesbos with Philomeleides, the king of the island, and conquered him (Hom. *Od.* 4. 342). (See also LAODAMAS)

PELEUS. At the funeral games of Pelias, he gained the prize in wrestling.

PHILOMELEIDES was a king in Lesbos who compelled his guests to engage with him in a contest of wrestling and was conquered by Odysseus (Hom. *Od.* 4. 343, 17. 134).

TELEGONUS was a son of Proteus and a brother of Polygonus. He was killed, together with his brother, by Heracles, whom they had challenged to a contest in wrestling (Apollod. 2. 5.9).

Writing

CALAMITES was regarded as the patron of the art of writing and of writing masters.

EVANDER. In Italy he was said to have taught his neighbors the art of writing, with which he himself had been made acquainted by Heracles (Plut. *Quaest.Rom.* 56).

PROMETHEUS brought the knowledge of writing to men.

Wryneck

APHRODITE. The iynx, or wryneck, was sacred to her.

IYNX was a daughter of Peitho (or Echo) and Pan. She endeavored to charm Zeus or make him fall in love with Io by magic means. As a result Hera metamorphosed her into the bird called iynx (*Iynx torquilla*). According to another story, she was the daughter of Pierus, and as she and her sisters had presumed to enter into a musical contest with the Muses, she was changed into the bird iynx. This bird, the symbol of passionate and restless love, was given by Aphrodite to Jason, who, by turning it round and pronouncing certain magic words, excited the love of Medea (Pind. *Pyth.* 4. 380).

Yew

DIONYSUS. The yew was sacred to him.

Youth

APOLLO INTONSUS, "the unshorn," was a surname of Apollo, alluding to the eternal youth of the god, as the Greek youths allowed their hair to grow until they attained the age of manhood.

ARTEMIS. She was the protectress of the young.

BACCHUS INTONSUS. As APOLLO INTONSUS.

ENDYMION. According to some legends,

Zeus granted him a request, and Endymion begged for immortality, eternal sleep, and everlasting youth (Apollod. 1. 7.5).

HEBE, daughter of Zeus and Hera, was the personification of youth.

HECATE was a mysterious divinity who bestowed prosperity on youth.

HERMES was regarded as the protector of young males, particularly those who entered into gymnastic exercises and contests (Pind. *Nem.* 10. 53).

HORAE appear as protectresses of youth and newly-born gods (Paus. 2. 13.3; Pind. *Pyth.* 9. 62; Philostr. *Imag.* 1. 26; Nonn. 11. 50).

JUVENTUS was the Roman goddess of youth, corresponding to the Greek Hebe.

ODYSSEUS. When he floated to the island of Calypso after his ship had been destroyed, she received him with kindness and wanted him to marry her, promising immortality and eternal youth if he would consent and forget Ithaca.

PHAON was a boatman at Mitylene and already of an advanced age and of ugly appearance; but on one occasion he very willingly and without accepting payment, carried Aphrodite across the sea, for which she gave him youth and beauty. After this, Sappho is said to have fallen in love with him (Lucian *Dial.Mort.* 9).

THALLO was one of the Horae and was mentioned by Athenian youths on being admitted among the *epheboi* in the oath they took in the temple of Agraulos.

TITHONUS. When Eos, goddess of the dawn, prayed to Zeus to grant her beloved Tithonus immortality, she forgot to ask for eternal youth. So he lived, growing older and weaker, until he eventually dried up and was metamorphosed by Eos into a cricket (Hom. *Hymn.in Ven.* 218; Hor. *Carm.* 1. 22.8, 2. 16.30; Apollod. 3. 12.4).

Zeal

ZELUS, the personification of zeal or strife, is described as the son of Pallas and Styx and a brother of Nike (Hes. *Theog.* 384; Apollod. 1. 2.4).

Surnames, Epithets, and Patronymics

Absyrtus

PHAETHON was a nickname given to Absyrtus, son of Aeetes, by the young Colchians because he outshone them all (Apollod. Rhod. 3. 245).

Achilles

AEACIDES. A patronymic from his grandfather, Aeacus.

LIGYRON. His original name, which meant "whining."

PELIADES (PELEIDES or PELIDES). A patronymic from his father, Peleus (Hom. *Il.* 1. 146, 188, 197, 277; Ov. *Met.* 12. 605).

PYRRHA. His name when he was disguised as a maiden to escape service in the Trojan War. It refers to his golden locks.

Actis

HELIADES. A patronymic with his brothers, Cercaphus, Macareus, Tanages, and Triopas, from their father, Helios.

Admetus

PHERETIAS (PHERAEUS). A patronymic from Pheres, his father.

Adrastus

PHORONIDES. A patronymic from his Argive ancestor, Phoroneus (Paus. 7. 17.3; Theocrit. 25. 200).

TALIONIDES. A patronymic from his father, Talaus, son of Bias and Pero (Hom. *Il.* 2. 566; Pind. *Ol.* 6. 24).

Aeetes

PERSEIDES (PERSEIUS). A patronymic as a descendant of Perse (Val. Flacc 5. 582, 6. 495).

Aegeus

PANDIONIDES. A patronymic from his father, Pandion.

Aeneas

ANCHISIADES. A patronymic from his father, Anchises (Hom. *Il.* 17. 754).

Aeolus

HIPPOTADES. A patronymic from his father, Hippotes (Hom. *Od.* 10. 2; Ov. *Met.* 14. 224).

Aesa

PANDORUS. A surname of Fate as the giver of all.

Aethra

PITTHEIS. A patronymic from Pittheus, her father (Ov. *Her.* 10. 31).

Agamemnon

ATREIDES. A patronymic from his father, Atreus. In the plural, the patronymic referred to Agamemnon and Menelaus (Hom. *Il.* 1. 12; Hor. *Carm.* 2. 4.7).

Alcimede

PHYLACEIS. A patronymic from her father, Phylacus (Apollon. Rhod. 1. 47).

Alcmaon

AMPHIARAIDES. A patronymic from his father, Amphiaraus (Ov. *Fast.* 2. 43).

Alcmene

ELECTRYONE. A patronymic from her father, Electryon (Hes. *Scut.Herc.* 16).

MIDEATIS. A name derived from the town of Midea in Argolis, where her father, Electryon, ruled as king (Paus. 2. 25.8; Theocrit. 13. 20, 24. 1).

Althaea

THESTIA. A patronymic from her father, Thestius (Eurip. *Iphig.Aul.* 49; Aeschyl. *Choeph.* 606).

Amphiaraus

PHORONEIDES. A patronymic from his Argive ancestor, Phoroneus (Paus. 7. 17.3; Theocrit. 25. 200).

Amphitrite

HALSODYNE. A surname meaning "the sea-fed" or "the sea-born" goddess (Hom. *Od.* 4. 404).

Amyntor

ORMENIDES. A patronymic from his father, Ormenus.

Antigone

LABDACIDEIS. A patronymic from her great-grandfather, Labdacus.

Antilochus

NELEIDES (NELEIADES or NELEIUS). A patronymic from his grandfather, Neleus.

NESTORIDES. A patronymic from his father, Nestor (Hom. *Il.* 6. 33, 15. 589, 23. 353).

Antiope

NYCTEIS. A patronymic from her father, Nycteus (Apollod. 3. 5.5).

Aphrodite (Venus)

ACIDALIA. A surname derived from the well Acidalius near Orchomenos, in which Aphrodite bathed with the Graces. The name may be connected with the Greek *akides,* without care or sorrow.

ALITTA (ALILAT). The name by which the Arabs called Aphrodite Urania (Herod. 1. 1313, 3. 8).

ALMA. A surname of Venus by which she was known at late dates.

AMATHUSIA (AMATHUNTIA). A surname derived from the town of Amathus in Cyprus, one of the most ancient seats of her worship (Tacit. *Ann.* 3. 62; Ov. *Amor.* 3. 15.15).

AMBOLOGERA. A surname designating the goddess as delaying old age. There was a statue at Sparta under this name (Paus. 3. 18.1).

ANADYOMENE. A surname pertaining to the story of her being born from the foam of the sea.

ANTHEIA. A name meaning the blooming or the friend of flowers, under which she was worshipped at Cnossus.

APATURIA. "The deceitful," a name under which she was worshipped at Phanagoria and other places in the Chersonesus. By deceit she lured giants who had attacked her to a cave where Heracles killed them (Strab. 11. 495).

APHACITIS. A surname derived from the town of Aphace in Coele-Syria, where she had a temple with an oracle.

APOTROPHIA. "The expeller," under which name she was worshipped at Thebes and which described her as the goddess who expelled from the hearts of men desires for sinful pleasure and lust (Paus. 9. 16.2).

ARACYNTHIAS. A surname derived from Mt. Aracynthus, on which she had a temple.

ARCHITIS. A surname under which she was worshipped on Mt. Libanus.

AREIA. "The warlike," a name under which she was worshipped when she was represented in armor like Ares, as at Sparta (Paus. 3. 17.5).

ARGENNIS. A surname derived from Argennus, a favorite of Agamemnon, who, after his friend's death, built a sanctuary to Aphrodite on the river Cephissus (Athen. 13. 608).

AUTOMATE. When Aphrodite assisted Meliboea and Alexis, Ephesian lovers, they dedicated a sanctuary to her under this name.

BARBATA. "The bearded," a surname of Venus among the Romans. One writer mentions a statue of Venus in Cyprus, representing the goddess with a beard in female attire, but resembling in her whole figure a man.

BYBLIA. A surname of Aphrodite.

CALLIPYGOS. A surname of Aphrodite meaning "beautiful buttocks" (Athen. 12. 554).

CALVA. A surname of Venus at Rome, under which she had two temples in the neighborhood of the Capitoline Hill. Some believed that one of them had been built by Ancus Marcius, because his wife was in danger of losing her hair; others thought that it was a monument of a patriotic act of the Roman women, who, during the siege of the Gauls, cut off their hair and gave it to the men to make strings for their bows; others connected it to the fancies and caprices of lovers, *calvere* meaning "to tease." But it probably refers to the fact that on her wedding day the bride, either actually or symbolically cut off a lock of hair to sacrifice to Venus.

CLOACINA (CLUACINA). A surname of Venus, under which she is mentioned in Rome from very early times (Liv. 3. 48). The name is probably best explained by the purification rites the forces of Tatius and Romulus undertook when the Sabine women prevented them from bloodshed. They purified themselves with myrtle branches, and the spot was afterwards the site of a temple of Venus Cloacina. According to some, the name was derived from the fact that an image of the goddess was found in the great sewer (*cloaca*) and was set up by the Sabine king, T. Tatius, in a temple near the forum (comp. Liv. 3. 48; Plaut. *Curcul.* 4. 1.10). She was considered also as presiding over and purifying sexual intercourse in marriage.

CNIDIA. A surname derived from the town of Cnidus in Caria, for which Praxiteles made his celebrated statue of Aphrodite (Paus. 1. 1.3).

COLIAS. A name derived from having a statue on the Attic promontory of Colias (Paus. 1. 1.4). Strabo (9. 398) places a sanctuary of Aphrodite Colias in the neighborhood of Anaphlystus.

CTESYLLA. Aphrodite was worshipped under this name at Ceos, where she was believed to have had a love affair with a mortal.

CYPRIA (CYPRIS, CYPRIGENEIA, or CYPROGENES). A surname from her having been born in Cyprus, one of the principal seats of her worship.

CYTHERA (CYTHERAEA, CYTHEREIA, or CYTHERIAS). A surname from the town of Cythera in Crete or from the island of Cythera, where the goddess was said to have first landed and where she had a celebrated temple (Hom. *Od.* 8. 288; Herod. 1. 105; Paus. 3. 23.1; Anacr. 5. 9; Hor. *Carm.* 1. 45).

DELIA. A surname from her being worshipped on Delos.

DESPOENA. A surname designating her as the ruling goddess or the mistress (Theocrit. 15. 100).

DIONAEA. A name derived from her mother, Dione (Virg. *Aen.* 3. 19).

EPIDAETIA. When she assisted Meliboea and Alexis, Ephesian lovers, they dedicated a sanctuary to her under this name.

EQUESTER (EQUESTRIS). A surname of Venus of unknown derivation.

ERYCINA (ERUCINA). A surname of Aphrodite derived from Mt. Eryx in Sicily, where she had a famous temple, which was said to have been built by Eryx, king of the Elymi, son of Aphrodite and the Sicilian king, Butes (Diod. 4. 83). At the beginning of the second Punic War, the worship of Aphrodite Erycina was carried from Sicily to Rome, and a temple was dedicated to Venus Erucina on the Capitoline Hill, to which subsequently another was added outside the Colline gate (Liv. 22. 9, 10).

GENETRIX. "The mother," a surname of Venus, under which her worship was established under Scipio Africanus. Julius Caesar dedicated a temple to her at Rome as the mother of the Julia gens.

GENETYLLIS. A surname designating Aphrodite as protectress of births (Aristoph. *Nub.* 52).

HECAERGE. "Hitting at a distance," a surname of Aphrodite at Iulis in Cos.

HIPPIA. A surname of Venus at Rome.

IDALIA. A surname of Aphrodite derived from the town of Idalion in Cyprus (Virg. *Aen.* 1. 680, 692, 5. 760, 10. 86; Ov. *Ars Am.* 3. 106).

LIBENTINA (LUBENTIA or LUBENTINA). A surname of Venus among the Romans, by which she was described as the goddess of sexual pleasure (*dea libidinis*) (Var. *De Ling.Lat.* 5. 6; Cic. *De Nat.Deor.* 2. 23; August. 4. 8). There was a temple of Venus Libentina at Rome, where young women dedicated their childhood toys.

LIMENIA (LIMENITES, LIMENITIS, or LIMENOSCOPUS). A surname designating Aphrodite as the protector or superintendent of the harbor (Paus. 2. 34.11).

LUCRINA. A surname of Venus, who had a temple at Baiae near the Lucrine lake (Mart. 11. 81).

MECHANITIS. A surname designating the goddess as skilled in inventing. She was worshipped under this name at Megalopolis.

MELAENIS. "The dark," a surname of Aphrodite at Corinth (Paus. 2. 2.4).

MELINAEA. A surname of Aphrodite derived from the Argive town of Meline (Lycoph. 403).

MIGONITIS. A surname of Aphrodite derived from Migonium, a place in or near the island of Cranne in Laconia, where the goddess had a temple (Paus. 3. 22.1).

MILITARIS. A surname of Venus at Rome, of which the derivation is unknown but which is probably similar to AREIA.

MORPHO. "The fair-shaped," a surname under which Aphrodite was worshipped at Sparta. She was represented in a sitting position with her head covered and her feet fettered (Paus. 3. 15.8; Lycoph. 449).

MURCIA (MURTEA or MURTIA). A surname of Venus at Rome, where she had a chapel in the circus with a statue (Apul. 6. 395; Tertull. *De Spect.* 8; Varr. *De Ling.Lat.* 5. 154; August. 4. 16; Liv. 1. 33). This surname, which is said to be the same as Myrtea (from *myrtus,* a myrtle), was believed to indicate the fondness of the goddess for the myrtle tree, and in ancient times there is said to have been a myrtle grove in the front of her chapel at the foot of the Aventine (Plin. *H.N.* 15. 36; Plut. *Quaest.Rom.* 20). Some of the ecclesiastical writers preferred the derivation from *murcus,* i.e., stupid or awkward (August. 4. 16). Others derived the name from a Syracusan word meaning tender.

NICEPHORUS. "Bringing victory," a surname of Aphrodite (Paus. 2. 19.6).

OBSEQUENS. A surname of Venus, under which her worship was founded by Fabius Gurges at the close of the Samnite war.

PANDEMOS. A surname of Aphrodite meaning "common to all the people," and the name was used in a twofold sense, first describing her as the goddess of low sensual pleasures as *Venus vulgivaga* or *popularis,* in opposition to Venus (Aphrodite) Urania, or the heavenly Aphrodite (Plat. *Sympos.* 180; Lucret. 4. 1067). She was represented at Elis by Scopas riding on a ram (Paus. 6. 25.2). The second sense is that of Aphrodite uniting all the inhabitants of a country into one social or political body. The worship of Aphrodite Pandemos occurs at Athens, Megalopolis, and Thebes. The sacrifice offered to her consisted of white goats (Lucian *Dial. Meret.* 7).

PAPHIA. A surname of Aphrodite derived from the celebrated temple of the goddess at Paphos in Cyprus. A statue of Aphrodite also stood in the sanctuary of Ino between Oetylus and Thalamae in Laconia (Tacit. *Hist.* 2. 2; Hom. *Hymn.in Ven.* 59; Apollod. 3. 14.2; Strab. 14. 683).

PEITHO. A surname of Aphrodite, whose worship was said to have been introduced at Athens by Theseus, when he united the country communities into towns (Paus. 1. 22.3).

PLACIDA. A surname of Venus by which she was known at late dates.

POSTVORTA. A surname of Venus, under which her worship was founded by Fabius Gurges at the close of the Samnite war.

PRAXIS. A surname of Aphrodite at Megara, where, in a temple near that of Dionysus, she had a beautiful statue of ivory.

RHAMNUSIA. A surname of Venus, by which she was known at late dates.

SALACIA. A surname of Venus, possibly derived from her having risen from the sea.

TELEUTE. A surname of Venus among the Egyptians.

URANIA. A surname of Aphrodite, describing her as "the heavenly" or "spiritual" to distinguish her from Aphrodite Pandemos.

VERTICORDIA. A surname of Venus, describing her as the goddess who turns the hearts of men. In the year B.C. 114, a vestal virgin was killed by lightning and her body was found naked; as the general moral corruption, especially among the vestals, was believed to be the cause of this disaster, the Sibylline books were consulted, which contained the order to build a temple of Venus Verticordia on the Via Salaria (Ov. *Fast.* 4. 160).

VICTRIX. A surname of Venus, under which her worship was established by Julius Caesar.

ZEPHYRITIS. A surname of Aphrodite derived from the promontory of Zephyrium in Egypt (Athen. 7. 318).

ZERYNTHIA. A surname of Aphrodite derived from the town of Zerinthus in Thrace, where she had a sanctuary said to have been built by Phaedra.

Apollo

ABAEUS. A surname from Abae in Phocis, where the god had a rich temple.

ABELLIO. In Crete, Apollo was called Abelios, and in Italy, Apello (cf. Belis, Belenus, Bela, Belus, and Baal).

ACERSECOMES. A surname of the god because of his beautiful hair, which was never cut or shorn.

ACESIUS. A surname of the god in Elis, meaning averter of evil. He had a temple there.

ACESTOR. A surname as god of the healing art, or, in general, as averter of evil.

ACRAEPHEUS. A surname derived from a town where he was worshipped.

ACTIACUS. A surname from Actium, a principal place of his worship.

AEGLETES. A surname meaning the radiant. He was known by this name on the island of Anaphe (Apollon. Rhod. 4. 1730).

AGETOR. A surname of Apollo as leader of men.

AGONIUS. A surname as helper in struggles and contests.

AGRAEUS. A surname as hunter.

AGYIEUS. A surname of Apollo from *agyia,* a street, because sacrifices were offered to him in the public streets of Athens. He was also worshipped under this name at Acharne, Mycenae, and Tegea as protector of streets and public places.

ALEXICACUS. A surname as averter of evil, so called, particularly by the Athenians, who believed he had stopped a plague which raged during the Peloponnesian War.

AMAZONIUS. A surname at Pyrrichus in Laconia, where he had a temple. Perhaps the Amazons had penetrated as far as Pyrrichus, where they might have founded a temple (Paus. 3. 25.2).

AMYCLAEUS. A surname from the town of Amyclae in Laconia, where he had a sanctuary.

APELLO (See ABELLIO)

ARCHEGETES. A surname under which he was worshipped at several places, as at Naxos in Sicily (Thuc. 6. 3; Pind. *Pyth.* 5. 80) and at Megara (Paus. 1. 42.5). The name has reference either to protector of colonies or as founder of towns in general.

BOEDROMIUS. A surname at Athens, because the god had assisted the Athenians in the war with the Amazons, who were defeated on the seventh of Boëdromion (Plut. *Thes.* 27). According to others, the name arose because in the war of Erechtheus and Ion against Eumolpus, Apollo had advised the Athenians to rush upon the enemy with a war shout (*boe*) if they wanted to conquer (Callim. *Hymn.in Apoll.* 69).

BRANCHIADES. A surname of Apollo.

CARNEIUS. A surname under which he was worshipped in various parts of Greece, especially in the Peloponnesus (Sparta, Sicyon) and also in Thera, Cyrene, and Magna Graecia (Paus. 3. 13.2; Pind. *Pyth.* 5. 106). The name was connected either with Carnus, an Acarnanian soothsayer, whose murder by Hippotes provoked Apollo to send a plague on the army of Hippotes, or from Carnus (or Carneius), son of Zeus and Europa, who was a favorite of Apollo (Paus. 3. 13.3).

CATAEBATES. The god was invoked under this name to grant a happy return home to those who were traveling abroad (Eurip. *Bacch.* 1358).

CHRYSAOR. A surname meaning the god with the golden sword or arms (Hom. *Il.* 15. 256).

CLARIUS. A name derived from his celebrated temple at Claros in Asia Minor.

CORYDUS. A name under which he had a temple eighty stadia from Corone on the coast (Paus. 4. 34.4).

CYNTHIUS. A name derived from Mt. Cynthus on the island of Delos, his birthplace (Callim. *Hymn.in Del.* 10; Hor. *Carm.* 1. 21.2, 3. 28.12; Lucan 1. 218).

DAPHNAEUS. A surname derived from laurel, which was sacred to him.

DECATEPHORUS. "The god to whom the tenth part of the booty is dedicated," a surname at Megara (Paus. 1. 42.5).

DELIUS. A surname derived from Delos, his

birthplace (Virg. *Aen.* 6. 12; Virg. *Ecl.* 7. 29; Val.Flacc. 1. 446).

DELPHICUS. A surname of Apollo from the worship paid to him at Delphi.

DELPHINIUS. A surname of Apollo, because he guided, by means of a dolphin, a Cretan colony, which at last arrived at Delphi, and built in gratitude an altar to the god under that name. Some said that he led the colonists to Delphi by metamorphosing himself into a dolphin. Under this name he had temples at Athens, Cnossus, Didyma, and Massilia.

DIDYMAEUS. A surname of Apollo.

DROMAEUS. A surname of Apollo in Crete and at Lacedaemon.

EMBASIOUS. A surname meaning the god who conducts men on board a ship, in the same sense as EPIBATERIUS (Apollon.Rhod. 1. 404).

EPACTAEUS (EPACTIUS). A surname describing the god as worshipped on the coast (Apollon.Rhod. 1. 404).

EPIBATERIUS. "The god who conducts men on board a ship." To the god under this name, Diomedes on his return from Troy built a temple at Troezen (Paus. 2. 32.1).

EPICURUS. The helper, under which name he was worshipped at Bassae in Arcadia. Every year a wild boar was sacrificed to him in his temple on Mt. Lycaeus. He received the surname because he had at one time delivered the country from a pestilence (Paus. 8. 38.6, 41.5).

EPOPSIUS. A surname meaning the superintendent (Soph. *Phil.* 1040).

EUTRESITES. A surname derived from Eutresis, a place between Plataea and Thespiae, where he had an ancient oracle.

GALAXIUS. A surname in Boeotia, from the stream Galaxius.

GRYNEUS. Under this name he had a temple, an ancient oracle, and a beautiful grove near the town of Grynion, Gryna, or Grynus in Aeolis in Asia Minor (Paus. 1. 21.9; Athen. 4. 149). He was also worshipped under this name in the Hecatonnesi (Strab. 13. 618).

HEBDOMAGETES. A name derived from the fact of sacrifices being offered to him on the seventh of every month, the seventh of some month being looked upon as the god's birthday. Others connect the name with the fact that at the festival of Apollo, the procession was led by seven boys and seven maidens (Aeschyl. *Sept.* 804; Herod. 6. 57).

HECAERGES. "Hitting at a distance," a surname of Apollo (Hom. *Il.* 1. 147).

HYLATUS. A name derived from the town of Hyle in Crete, which was sacred to him (Lycoph. 448).

INTONSUS. A surname meaning the unshorn, alluding to the eternal youth of the god, as the Greek youths allowed their hair to grow until they attained the age of manhood (Hom. *Il.* 20. 39; Hom. *Hymn.in Apoll.* 134; Hor. *Epod.* 15. 9; Ov. *Met.* 3. 421; Ov. *Amor.* 1. 14.31; Mart. 4. 45).

ISMENIUS. A surname at Thebes, where he had a temple on the river Ismenius (Paus. 2. 10.4, 4. 27.4, 9. 10.2, 5).

ISODETES. "The god who binds all equally," was a surname of Apollo used to express his impartiality.

IXIUS. A surname of Apollo from a district of the island of Rhodes, which was called Ixiae or Ixia (Strab. 14. 655).

LAPHRAEUS. A surname at Calydon (Strab. 10. 459).

LEUCADIUS. A surname from a temple to him in Leucas (Ov. *Trist.* 3. 1.42; Propert. 3. 11.69; comp. Thuc. 3. 94).

LIBYSTINUS. "The Libyan," a surname under which Apollo was worshipped by the Sicilians, because he was believed to have destroyed by a pestilence a Libyan fleet which sailed against Sicily.

LOEMIUS. A surname meaning deliverer from plague, in Lindus on Rhodes.

LOXIAS. This surname is derived by some from his intricate and ambiguous oracles (*loxa*), but it is unquestionably connected with the verb *legein* and describes the god as the prophet or interpreter of Zeus (Herod. 1. 91, 8. 136; Aeschyl. *Eum.* 19; Aristoph. *Plut.* 8).

LYCAEUS (See LYCEIUS, LYCIUS, LYCOCTONUS, and LYCOREUS)

LYCEGENUS. A surname describing him as either the god born in Lycia or as the god of light (Hom. *Il.* 4. 101, 119).

LYCEIUS. This surname is derived, perhaps, from *lykos,* a wolf, so that it would mean "the wolf-slayer." Others derive it from *lyce,* light, according to which it would mean "giver of light." Still others derive it from the country of Lycia, where he was worshipped at Mt. Cragus and Ida. In nearly all cases where the god appears with this name, we find traditions concerning wolves. Thus, the descendants of Deucalion, who founded Lycoreia, followed a wolf's howl; Leto came to Delos as a she-wolf, and she was conducted by wolves to the river Xanthus; wolves protected the treasuries of Apollo; and near the great altar at Delphi there stood an iron wolf with inscriptions (Paus. 10. 14.4). The attack of a wolf upon a herd of cattle occasioned the worship of Apollo Lyceius at Argos (Plut. *Pyrrh.* 32); and the Sicyonians are said to have been taught by Apollo how they should get rid of wolves (Paus. 2. 19.3). By the name of Lyceius he is generally characterized as the destroyer. (See also LYCEGENUS, LYCIUS, LYCOCTONUS, and LYCOREUS).

LYCIUS. "The Lycian," a surname of Apollo, who was worshipped in several places of Lycia and had a sanctuary and oracle at Patara in Lycia (Pind. *Pyth.* 1. 39; Propert. 3. 1.38; Virg. *Aen.* 4. 143, 346, 377). Lycius is often used in the sense of Lyceius and in allusion to his being the slayer of wolves (Paus. 2. 9.7, 19.3).

LYCOCTONUS. A surname by which Apollo was sometimes called (cf. LYCEIUS) (Soph. *Elect.* 7; Paus. 2. 9.7).

LYCOREUS. This surname is used in the same sense as Lyceius but also in reference to Lycoreia on Mt. Parnassus (Apollon. Rhod. 4. 1490; Callim. *Hymn. in Apoll.* 19).

MALEATES. A surname derived from Cape Malea in the south of Laconia. Under this name Apollo had sanctuaries at Sparta and on Mt. Cynortium (Paus. 3. 12.7, 2. 27).

MALLOEIS. A surname at Lesbos. The sanctuary here to Apollo Malloeis derived its name from Melus, son of Manto.

MOIRAGETES. A surname as leader or guide of fate, at Delphi (Paus. 10. 24.4).

MUSAGETES. A surname as leader of the choir of the Muses (Diod. 1. 18).

NOMIUS. A surname as divinity who protects the pastures and shepherds.

OETOSYRUS. The name of a Scythian divinity whom Herodotus (4. 59) identifies with the Greek Apollo.

ONCAEUS. A surname derived from Onceium on the river Ladon in Arcadia, where he had a temple (Paus. 8. 25.5).

PAGASAEUS. "The Pagasaean," from Pagasus, or Pagasae, a town in Thessaly, where the god had a sanctuary said to have been built by Trophonius (Hes. *Scut. Herc.* 70).

PALATINUS. A surname at Rome, where Augustus, in commemoration of the battle of Actium, dedicated a temple to the god on the Palatine Hill, in which subsequently a library was established (Dio Cass. 53. 1; Hor. *Carm.* 1. 31; Hor. *Epist.* 1. 317; Propert. 4. 6.11; Ov. *Ars Am.* 3. 389).

PARNOPIUS. "The expeller of locusts," under which name the god had a statue on the acropolis at Athens (Paus. 1. 24.8).

PARRHASIUS. A surname of Apollo, who had a sanctuary on Mt. Lyceius, where an annual festival was celebrated to him as the *epicurius,* or helper (Paus. 8. 38.2, 6).

PATAREUS. A surname derived from the Lycian town of Pataras, where the god had an oracle and where, according to some, he used to spend the six winter months in every year (Hor. *Carm.* 3. 4.64; Lycoph. 920; Herod. 1. 162; Strab. 14. 665; Paus. 9. 41.1).

PHILESIUS. A surname at Didyma, where Branchus was said to have founded a sanctuary of the god and to have introduced his worship (Plin. *H.N.* 34. 8).

PHOEBUS. "The shining, pure, or bright," occurs both as an epithet and a name of Apollo in his capacity as god of the sun (Hom. *Il.* 1. 43, 443; Virg. *Aen.* 3. 251; Hor. *Carm.* 3. 21, 24). Some ancients derived the name from Apollo's grandmother, Phoebe (Aeschyl. *Eum.* 8).

PHYXIUS. A surname as the god who protects fugitives.

PYTHIUS. A surname meaning the Pythian, from Pytho, the ancient name of Delphi, where the god's most famous oracle was located (Hom. *Hymn.in Apoll.* 373; Aeschyl. *Agam.* 521; Hor. *Carm.* 1. 16.6; Tacit. *Hist.* 4. 83).

SALGANEUS. A surname derived from the town of Salganeus in Boeotia (Strab. 9. 403).

SARPEDONIUS. A surname in Cilicia, as brother of Artemis Sarpedonia.

SMINTHEUS. A surname which is derived by some from *sminthos,* a mouse, and by others from the town of Sminthe in Troas (Hom. *Il.* 1. 39; Ov. *Fast.* 6. 425; Ov. *Met.* 12. 585). The mouse was regarded by the ancients as inspired by the vapors arising from the earth and as the symbol of prophetic power. In the temple of Apollo at Chryse there was a statue of the god by Scopas with a mouse under its foot (Strab. 13. 604), and on coins Apollo is represented carrying a mouse in his hands.

SOSIANUS. A surname at Rome derived from the quaestor C. Sosius' bringing Apollo's statue from Seleucia to Rome (Cic. *Ep.ad. Att.* 8. 6; Plin. *H.N.* 13. 5, 36. 4).

SPODIUS. A surname at Thebes derived from *spodos,* ashes, because his altar consisted of the ashes of the victims which had been sacrificed to him (Paus. 9. 11.5).

TEGYREIUS. A surname derived from the town of Tegyra in Boeotia, where, according to some traditions, the god was born (Plut. *Pelop.* 8).

TELCHINOS. A surname in Lycia, when Lycus, one of the mysterious tribe of the Telchines migrated from Rhodes and built the temple of the Lycian Apollo. This god had been worshipped by them at Lindus.

TELMISSIUS. A surname from the Lycian town of Telmissus, or Telmessus (Cic. *De Div.* 1. 41; Strab. 14. 665).

TEMENITES. A surname derived from the god's sacred temenus, or sanctuary, in the neighborhood of Syracuse (Suet. *Tib.* 74; Thuc. 6. 75, 100).

THEORIUS. A surname of Apollo at Troezen, where he had a very ancient temple. The word signifies clearsighted.

THEOXENIUS. A surname of Apollo (Paus. 7. 27.2).

THYMBRAEUS. A surname derived from a place in Troas called Thymbria, where he had a temple in which Achilles was wounded, or from a neighboring hill of the same name (Strab. 13. 598; Eurip. *Rhes.* 224; Hom. *Il.* 10. 430).

ZOSTERIUS. A surname in Attica on the strip of land stretching into the sea between Phaleron and Sunium.

Arachne

MAEONIA (MAEONIDES). A surname from her origins in Lydia, the ancient name of which was Maeonia (Ov. *Met.* 6. 103).

Ares (Mars)

ALLOPROSALLOS. A surname as war god, who assisted one and sometimes the other side in battle (Hom. *Il.* 5. 889).

APHNEIUS. A surname as giver of food or plenty, under which he had a temple on Mt. Cnesius, near Tegea, in Arcadia. When Aerope became by him the mother of Aeropus, she died at childbirth, and Ares caused the child to suckle from the breast of its dead mother.

ENYALIUS. "The warlike," used either as an epithet of Ares or as a proper name instead of Ares (Hom. *Il.* 2. 651, 7. 166, 17. 211; Pind. *Ol.* 13. 102; Pind. *Nem.* 9. 37).

EQUESTER. A surname of Mars (Paus. 5. 15.4).

GRADIVUS. "The striding or marching," a surname of Mars in Rome (Liv. 1. 20, 7.23; Ov. *Fast.* 6. 191).

GYNAECOTHOENAS. "The god feasted by women," a surname at Tegea, where the women singlehandedly won a battle by surprising the enemy from ambush.

HIPPIUS. A surname of Ares(Paus. 5. 15.4).

MAMERTUS. An ancient surname of Mars, which must have arisen after the identification of the Italian Mamers with the Greek Ares (Lycoph. 938, 1410).

QUIRINUS. A surname of Mars at Rome from an ancient sanctuary to him on the Quirinal Hill (Varr. *De Ling.Lat.* 5. 52). According to Dionysius of Halicarnassus (2. 48), the name was derived from a Sabine word, *quiris,* a lance or spear.

SILVANUS. A surname of Mars as protector of fields and flocks.

STRATIUS. A surname of Ares, referring to his warlike nature (Strab. 14. 659; Herod. 5. 119).

THEREITAS. A surname from his nurse, Thero, although Pausanias thinks that this name arose from the fierceness of the god (Paus. 3. 19.8).

ULTOR. A surname of Mars as the avenger, to whom Augustus built a temple at Rome in the forum after taking vengeance upon the murderers of his great-uncle, Julius Caesar (Suet. *Div.Aug.* 29; Suet. *Calig.* 24; Ov. *Fast.* 5. 577).

Arethusa

ALPHEIA. A surname of the nymph, Arethusa, because she was loved and pursued by the river god Alpheius (Ov. *Met.* 5. 487).

Argus

ARESTORIDES. A patronymic of Argus Panoptes from his father, Arestor (Apollod. 2. 1.3).

PANOPTES. "The all-seeing," a surname of Argus because he had a hundred eyes.

Aristaeus

AGREUS. A surname from his love of hunting (Pind. *Pyth.* 9. 115; Apollon.Rhod. 3. 507; Diod. 4. 81).

NOMIUS. Under this name he was worshipped as the divinity who protects the pastures and shepherds.

Artemis (Diana)

ACRAEA. A surname from a temple built to her by Melampus.

AEGINAEA. A surname at Sparta meaning either a huntress of chamois or wielder of the javelin.

AETOLE. A surname at Naupactus, where in her temple was a statue of white marble of the goddess throwing a javelin.

AGRAEA. A surname as huntress (cf. Apollo Agraeus).

AGROTERA. At Agrae and Aegeira, a surname as huntress.

ALPHAEA (ALPHEAEA, ALPHEIA, or ALPHEIUSA). A surname from the river god, Alpheius, who loved her, and under which name she was worshipped at Letrini in Elis (Paus. 6. 22.5; Strab. 8. 343) and in Ortygia.

AMARYNTHIA. A surname from the town of Amarynthus or from the hunter by the same name.

AMARYSIA. As AMARYNTHIA. She was worshipped by both names in Attica (Paus. 1. 31.3).

AMPHIPYROS. A surname of Artemis because she is represented carrying a torch in both hands.

ANAITIS. A surname of Artemis in Lydia.

ANGELOS. A surname under which she was worshipped at Syracuse. According to some accounts, this was the original name of Hecate.

APANCHOMENE. A surname meaning "the strangled (goddess)" from an incident which took place at Caphyae in Arcadia. Some boys in their play put a string on the statue of Artemis Condyleatis in a sacred grove and said they were strangling her. When discovered at this, they were stoned to death. After this, all the women in Caphyae had stillbirths until the boys were honorably buried. An annual sacrifice to their *manes* was commanded by an oracle (Paus. 8. 23.5). The surname Condyleatis was changed to Apanchomene.

ARICINA. A surname from the town of Aricia in Latium, where she was worshipped. Hippolytus, upon being restored to life, came to Italy and dedicated a grove to Artemis in Aricia.

ARISTO. "The best," a surname at Athens (Paus. 1. 20.2).

ARISTOBULE. "The best advisor," to whom Themistocles built a temple at Athens and in it dedicated his own statue (Plut. *Them.* 22).

ASTRATEIA. A surname under which she had a temple near Pyrrhichus in Laconia, because she was believed there to have stopped the progress of the Amazons (Paus. 3. 25.2).

BRAURONIA. A surname from the demos of Brauron in Attica. Under this name she had a sanctuary on the acropolis of Athens.

CALLISTE. A surname by which she was worshipped at Athens and Tegea (Paus. 1. 29.2, 8. 35.7).

CARYATIS. A surname derived from the town of Caryae in Laconia. Here the statue of the goddess stood in the open air, and maidens celebrated a festival to her every year with dances (Paus. 3. 10.8, 4. 16.5).

CEDREATIS. A surname in Orchomenos because her images were hung on lofty cedars.

CHITONE. A surname describing her with her chiton girt up. Others derived the name from the Attic village of Chitone, or from the circumstance of the clothes in which newly-born children were dressed being sacred to her (Callim. *Hymn. in Dian.* 225).

CHRYSAOR. A surname describing her as the goddess with the golden sword or arms (Herod. 8. 77).

CNAGIA. A surname derived from Cnageus, a Laconian, who accompanied the Dioscuri in their war against Aphidna and was made prisoner. He was sold as a slave and carried to Crete, where he served in the temple of Artemis. But he escaped with a priestess of the goddess and carried Artemis' statue to Sparta (Paus. 3. 18.3).

COLAENIS. A surname in the Attic demos of Myrrhinus from the mythical king, Colaenus, who was believed to have reigned even before the time of Cecrops (Paus. 1. 31.3).

CONDYLEATIS (See APANCHOMENE)

CORDACA. A surname in Elis, derived from an indecent dance which the companions of Pelops are said to have performed in honor of the goddess after a victory (Paus. 6. 22.1).

CORYPHAEA. "The goddess who inhabits the summit of mountains," under which name she had a temple on Mt. Coryphaeon near Epidaurus (Paus. 2. 28.2).

CORYTHALLIA. A surname of Artemis at Sparta, at whose festival of the Tithenidia the Spartan boys were carried into her sanctuary (Athen. 4. 139).

CYNTHIA. A surname from Mt. Cynthus on the island of Delos, her birthplace (Callim. *Hymn.in Del.* 10; Hor. *Carm.* 1. 21.2, 3. 28.12; Lucan 1. 218).

DAPHNAEA. A surname which was probably an allusion to her statue being made of laurel wood (Paus. 3. 24.6).

DELIA. A surname derived from Delos, her birthplace (Virg. *Aen.* 6. 12; Virg. *Ecl.* 7. 29; Val.Flacc. 1. 446). (Cf. Apollo Delius)

DELPHINIA. A surname at Athens, as the feminine form of Delphinius, which was applied to Apollo.

DERRHIATIS. A surname derived from the town of Derrhion on the road from Sparta to Arcadia (Paus. 3. 20.7).

DICTYNNIA. A surname from Dictynna, one of her attendants and inventor of the hunting net.

ELAPHIAEA. A surname at Elis.

EUCLEIA. A surname at Athens, where she had a sanctuary (Plut. *Aristid.* 20). Artemis Eucleia also had a temple at Thebes (Paus. 9. 17.1).

EURYNOME. A surname at Phigalea in Arcadia. Here she was represented as half woman, half fish (Paus. 8. 41.4).

FASCELIS. A surname of Diana in Italy, believed to have been received from the circumstance of Orestes having brought her image from Tauris in a bundle of sticks (Sil.Ital. 14. 260). The original name was probably Facelis or Facelina (from *fax*), as the goddess was generally represented with a torch in her hand.

GAEEOCHUS. "Holder of the earth," a surname describing her as a protector of Thebes (Soph. *Oed.Tyr.* 160).

GENETYLLIS. A surname as protectress of births. Under this name women sacrificed dogs to her (Aristoph. *Lys.* 2).

HECAERGE. "Hitting at a distance," a surname of Artemis referring to marksmanship.

HEGEMONE. Leader or ruler, a surname at Sparta and in Arcadia (Paus. 3. 14.6, 8. 36.7, 47.4; Callim. *Hymn.in Dian.* 227).

HEMERESIA. "The soothing goddess," a name under which she was worshipped at the well Lusi in Arcadia (Paus. 8. 18.3; Callim. *Hymn.in Dian.* 236).

HEURIPPE. "The finder of horses," a surname of Artemis under which Odysseus was said to have built a temple at Pheneus in common with Poseidon Hippius, when at length he there found his lost horses (Paus. 8. 14.4).

HYMNIA. A surname under which she was worshipped throughout Arcadia.

IMBRASIA. A surname of Artemis (Callim. *Hymn.in Dian.* 228).

IPHIGENEIA. Artemis had a temple at Hermione under this surname (Paus. 2. 35.2).

ISSORIA. A surname in Laconia, derived from Mt. Issorion, on which she had a sanctuary (Paus. 3. 14.2, 25.3; Plut. *Ages.* 32).

LAPHRIA. A surname among the Calydonians, from whom the worship of the goddess was introduced at Naupactus and Patrae, in Achaia. The name Laphria was traced back to a hero Laphrius, son of Castalius, who was said to have instituted her worship at Calydon.

LEUCOPHRYNE. A surname from the town of Leucophrys in Phrygia, where she had a splendid temple (Xenoph. *Hellen.* 3. 2.19; Strab. 14. 647; Tacit. *Ann.* 3. 62; Athen. 15. 683).

LIMENIA (LIMENITES, LIMENITIS, or LIMENOSCOPUS). "The protector or superintendent of the harbor" (Callim. *Hymn.in Dian.* 259).

LIMNAEA (LIMNETES or LIMNEGENES). A surname as inhabiting or born in a lake or marsh or having a temple near a lake. Artemis was so addressed at Sicyon, near Epidaurus (Paus. 2. 7.6), on the frontiers between Laconia and Messenia (Paus. 3. 2.6, 7.4; Tacit. *Ann.* 4. 43), near Calamae (Paus. 4. 31.32), at Tegea (Paus. 3. 14.2, 8. 53.11), and Patrae (Paus. 7. 20.7).

LOCHEIA. A surname as protectress in childbed (Plut.*Quaest.Conviv.* 3. 10).

LOXO. A surname from Loxo, daughter of Boreas and one of the Hyperborean maidens who brought the worship of Artemis to Delos (Callim. *Hymn.in Del.* 292).

LUCINA. "Goddess of light," or rather "the goddess who brings the light," and hence the goddess who presides over the birth of children, a surname of Diana (Varr. *De Ling.Lat.* 5. 69; Catull. 34. 13; Hor. *Carm.Saec.* 14; Ov. *Fast.* 2. 441, 6. 39; Tibull. 3. 4.13).

LYCEIA. A surname under which she had a temple at Troezen, built by Hippolytus (Paus. 2. 3.6).

LYCOATIS. A surname from her temple at Lycoa in Arcadia (Paus. 8. 36.5).

LYGODESMA. A statue of Artemis had been found by the brothers, Astrabacus and Alopecus, under a bush of willows, by which it was surrounded in such a manner that it stood upright (Paus. 3. 16.7).

LYSIZONA. "The goddess who loosens the girdle," a surname at Athens (Theocrit. 17. 60).

MELISSA. A surname as goddess of the moon, in which capacity she alleviated the suffering of women in childbed.

MUNYCHIA. A surname derived from the Attic port town of Munychia, where she had a temple. Her festival at Athens was celebrated in the month of Munychion (Paus. 1. 1.4; Strab. 14. 639).

MYSIA. A surname under which she was worshipped in a sanctuary near Sparta (Paus. 3. 20.9).

NOCTILUCA. A surname of Diana. She had a temple at Rome on Mt. Palatine, where torches were generally lighted in the night.

OENOATIS. A surname at Oenoe in Argolis (Eurip. *Herc.Fur.* 376).

ORTHIA. A surname as goddess of the moon. At the Limnaeon in Sparta her image was worshipped, the one reputedly brought by Iphigeneia and Orestes from Tauris (Paus. 3. 16). It was at the altar of Artemis Orthia that Spartan boys had to undergo the ritual flogging (Herod. 4. 87). She had temples also at Brauron, in the Cerameicus at Athens, in Elis, and on the coast of Byzantium. The ancients derived her surname from Mt. Orthosium or Orthium in Arcadia.

ORTYGIA. A surname derived from the island of Ortygia, the ancient name for Delos, or an island off Syracuse (Ov. *Met.* 1. 694). The goddess bore this name in various places but always with reference to the island in which she was born (Strab. 10. 486).

PAEONIA. "The healing goddess," under which name she had a statue at Athens and an altar in the temple of Amphiaraus at Oropus (Paus. 1. 2.4, 34.2).

PARTHENIA. A surname meaning "the maiden" (Callim. *Hymn.in Dian.* 110).

PEITHO. A surname of Artemis (Paus. 2. 21.1).

PHERAEA. A surname at Pherae in Thessaly, at Argos and Sicyon, where she had temples (Callim. *Hymn.in Dian.* 259; Paus. 2. 10.6, 23.5).

PHOEBE. A surname in her capacity as the goddess of the moon (Luna), the moon being regarded as the female Phoebus, or sun (Virg. *Georg.* 1. 431; Virg. *Aen.* 10. 215; Ov. *Her.* 20. 229).

PITANATIS. A surname derived from the little town of Pitana in Laconia, where she had a temple (Callim. *Hymn.in Dian.* 172; Paus. 3. 16.9; Eurip. *Troad.* 1101).

PROPYLEA. A surname at Eleusis, where she had a temple.

SARPEDONIA. A surname from Cape Sarpedon in Cilicia, where she had a temple with an oracle (Strab. 14. 676).

SOTEIRA. "The saving goddess," a name by which she was known at Pegae in Megaris (Paus. 1 40.2, 44.7), at Troezen (2. 31.1), at

Boeae in Laconia (3. 22.9), and near Pellene (7. 27.1).

TAURIONE (TAURO, TAUROPOLOS, or TAUROPOS). Under this surname she was identified with the Taurian goddess. The name is explained either by the idea of the goddess protecting the country of Tauris or the goddess to whom bulls are sacrificed. Others explain it to mean the goddess riding on bulls, drawn by bulls, or killing bulls. All ideas seem to indicate that the bull was probably the ancient symbol of the savage worship of the Taurian divinity (Eurip. *Iphig. Taur.* 1457).

THOANTEA. A surname of the Taurian Artemis, derived from Thoas, king of Tauris (Val. Flacc. 8. 208; Ov. *Ib.* 386).

TITANIA. A patronymic of Diana as a descendant of Titan.

TRIVIA. A surname given to Artemis, because she presided over all places where three roads met, where her image was placed with three faces, one looking towards each way. At the new moon, the Athenians offered her sacrifices and a sumptuous entertainment, which was generally distributed among the poor.

UPIS. A surname of Artemis as assisting women in childbirth (Callim. *Hymn. in Dian.* 240).

Asclepius (Aesculapius)

AULONIUS. A surname derived from a temple he had in Aulon, a valley in Messenia (Paus. 4. 36.5).

CAUSIUS. A surname derived from Caus in Arcadia, where he was worshipped (Paus. 8. 25.1).

COTYLAEUS. A surname of Asclepius, under which appellation he was worshipped on the borders of the Eurotas. His temple was raised by Heracles.

DEMAENETUS. A surname derived from the name of a temple of his on the Alpheius (Paus. 6. 21.4).

PHILOLAUS. "A friend of the people," under which name he had a temple in Laconia (Paus. 3. 22.7).

Asius

HYRTACIDES. A patronymic from his father, Hyrtacus (Hom. *Il.* 2. 837; Apollod. 3. 12.5).

Astydameia

ORMENIS. A patronymic from her grandfather, Ormenus.

Astynome

CHRYSEIS. A patronymic from her father, Chryses, priest of Apollo.

Athena (Minerva)

ACHAEA. A surname at Luceria in Apulia, where the *donaria* and arms of Diomedes were preserved in her temple.

AETHYIA. A surname at Megara, in reference to the goddess teaching the art of shipbuilding or navigation.

AGELEIA. A surname as leader or protectress of the people.

AGORAEA. A surname, especially at Sparta, as protector of assemblies of the people in the agora.

ALALCOMENEIS. A surname from the hero, Alalcomenes, or from the Boeotian village of Alalcomenae, where she was believed to have been born. The name might have come from the verb *alalkein* signifying the "powerful defender" (Hom. *Il.* 4. 8).

ALCIS (ALCIDES). A surname meaning "the strong"; she was worshipped by this name in Macedonia.

ALEA. A name under which she was worshipped at Alea, Mantineia, and Tegea. The temple at Tegea was said to have been erected by Aleus, son of Apheidas. The statue of the goddess, made of ivory, was removed by Augustus to Rome.

AMBULIA. A surname at Sparta, meaning, perhaps, "delayer of death" (Paus. 3. 13.4).

ANEMOTIS. A surname as subduer of the winds, under which she was worshipped and had a temple at Mothone in Messenia.

APATURIA. "The deceitful," a name given to her by Aethra (Paus. 2. 33.1). In a temple to Athena Apaturia in Troezen, maidens were required to dedicate their girdles before marriage.

AREIA. A surname at Athens. Her worship under this name was instituted by Orestes after he had been acquitted by the Areiopagus for matricide (Paus. 1. 28.5). Athena cast a deciding vote in case of a tie. The surname could therefore be derived from the word meaning to propitiate or atone for. Orestes in gratitude dedicated an altar to Athena Areia.

ASIA. A surname in Colchis. Her worship was believed to have been brought from there by Castor and Polydeuces to Laconia (Paus. 3. 24.5).

ASSESIA. A surname derived from the town of Assesus in Ionia, where she had a temple (Herod. 1. 19).

AXIOPOENOS. A surname meaning the avenger. Under this name Heracles built a temple to her at Sparta, after he had chastised Hippocoon and his sons for the murder of Oeonus (Paus. 3. 15.4).

BELISAMA. The name of Minerva among the Gauls. The word signified queen of heaven. She was represented with a helmet on her head but without either her aegis or her spear in her hand (Caes. 6).

CAPTA (CAPITA). A surname of Minerva as worshipped on the Caelian Hill at Rome. Its origin was not known.

CHALCIOECUS. "The goddess of the brazen house," so called at Sparta, derived from the brazen temple which the goddess had in that city (Paus. 3. 17.3; 10. 5.5).

CHALINITIS. "The tamer of horses by means of the bridle," a name under which she had a temple at Corinth. She was said to have so tamed Pegasus before she gave him to Bellerophon (Paus. 2. 4.1).

CORIA. A surname of Athena in Arcadia.

CORYPHAGENES. A surname of Athena from having been born from the brain of Zeus.

CORYPHASIA. A surname derived from the promontory of Coryphasion on which Athena had a sanctuary (Paus. 4. 36.2).

CYDONIA. A surname under which she had a temple at Phrixia in Elis, which was said to have been built by Clymenus of Cydonia (Paus. 6. 21.5).

ERGANE. A surname meaning the worker, who was believed to preside over and instruct man in all kinds of arts (Paus. 5. 14.5; 1. 24.3).

EQUESTER. A surname of Athena (Minerva) (Paus. 1. 30.4, 31.3).

GLAUCOPIS. A surname frequently given to Athena from the blueness of her eyes.

GORGONIA. A surname of Athena because Perseus, armed with her shield, had conquered the Gorgon, Medusa.

HELLOTIA (HELLOTIS). A surname at Corinth, derived, according to some from the fertile marsh near Marathon, where Athena had a sanctuary; or from Hellotia, one of the daughters of Timander, who fled into the temple of Athena when Corinth was burned down by the Dorians and was destroyed in the temple with her sister, Eurytione. Soon after, a plague broke out at Corinth, and the oracle declared that it would not cease until the souls of the maidens were propitiated and a sanctuary was erected to Athena Hellotis.

HIPPIA. A surname at Athens, Tegea, and Olympia (Paus. 1. 30.4, 31.3; 5. 15.4; 8. 47.1).

HIPPOLAITIS. A surname at Hippola in Laconia (Paus. 3. 25.6).

HYGIEIA. A surname as giver or protectress of (mental) health (Paus. 1. 23.5).

IASONIA. A surname at Cyzicus (Apollon. Rhod. 1. 960).

ITONIA (ITONIAS or ITONIS). A surname derived from the town of Iton in the south of Phthiotis (Paus. 1. 13.2; Plut. *Pyrrh.* 26; Polyb. 4. 25). She had there a celebrated sanctuary. According to another tradition, she received the surname from Itonus, a king or priest (Paus. 9. 34.1).

LAPHRIA. A surname of Athena (Lycoph. 356).

LARISSAEA. A surname derived from the river Larissus between Elis and Achaia, where the goddess had a sanctuary (Paus. 7. 17.3).

LINDIA. A surname from Lindus on the island of Rhodes, where she had a celebrated temple (Diod. 5. 58; Herod. 2. 182; Strab. 14. 655).

LONGATUS. A surname which she derived from being worshipped in a Boeotian district called Longas (unknown today).

MAGARSIA. A surname from Magarsos, a Cilician town near the mouth of the river Pyramus, where the goddess had a sanctuary (Arrian 2. 5).

MECHANITIS. A surname describing the goddess as skilled in inventing, at Megalopolis (Paus. 8. 31.3, 36.3).

NARCAEA. A surname in Elis from her temple there which was erected by Narcaeus, son of Dionysus and Physcoa.

NAUTIA. When an oracle demanded that Diomedes restore the Palladium to the Trojans, Diomedes attempted to deliver the statue to Aeneas but left it with Nautes when unable to give it to Aeneas. Minerva bestowed many favors on Nautes and his family after him. The image was preserved in the most secret part of the temple of Vesta and was regarded as one of the safeguards of the state (Virg. *Aen.* 5. 704; Lucan 1. 598).

NEDUSIA. A surname under which she had a sanctuary on the river Nedon and another at Poieessa on the island of Cos.

NIKE (NICE). A surname meaning victorious, under which she had a sanctuary on the acropolis at Megara (Paus. 1. 42.4; Eurip. *Ion* 1529).

ONCA. A surname from the town of Oncae in Boeotia, where she had a sanctuary (Aeschyl. *Sept.* 166, 489; Paus. 9. 12.2).

PALLANTIAS. A variation of Pallas, the surname of Athena.

PALLAS. Plato (*Cratyl.* 406) derives the surname from *pallein,* to brandish, in reference to the goddess brandishing the spear or aegis, whereas Apollodorus (1. 6.2) derives it from the giant Pallas, who was slain by Athena. But it is probable that Pallas is the same word as *pallax,* i.e., a virgin or maiden.

PALLENIS. A surname under which she had a temple between Athens and Marathon (Herod. 1. 62).

PANACHAEA. "The goddess of all the Achaeans," a surname in Laphiria (Paus. 7. 20.2).

PAREIA. A surname under which she had a statue in Laconia, perhaps so called only from its being made of Parian marble (Paus. 3. 20.8).

PARTHENOS. "The virgin," a surname at Athens where the famous Parthenon was dedicated to her (Paus. 8. 41.5).

PHRYGIA. A surname referring to the Palladium, which was brought from Phrygia (Ov. *Met.* 13. 337).

POLIAS. "The goddess protecting the city," a surname at Athens, where she was especially worshipped as the protecting divinity of the acropolis (Paus. 1. 27.1).

POLIUCHOS. "Protecting the city," occurs as a surname of several divinities, such as Athena Chalcioecus at Sparta (Paus. 3. 17.2), and Athena at Athens.

PROMACHORMA. "The protectress of the bay," a surname under which she had a sanctuary on Mt. Buporthmos near Hermione (Paus. 2. 34.9).

PRONAEA. A surname under which she had a chapel at Delphi in front of the temple of Apollo (Herod. 1. 92; Aeschyl. *Eum.* 21; Paus. 9. 10.2).

SAITIS. A surname under which she had a sanctuary on Mt. Pontinus near Lerna in Argolis (Paus. 2. 36; comp. Herod. 2. 175). The name was traced by the Greeks to the Egyptians, among whom Athena was said to have been called Saïs.

SOTEIRA. "The saving goddess," a surname of Athena (Aristot. *Rhet.* 3. 18).

STRATEA. A surname of Minerva, referring to her martial character.

TAURIONE (TAURO, TAUROPOLOS, or TAUROPOS). A surname identifying her with the Taurian goddess. The name is explained either by the idea of the goddess protecting the country of Tauris or the goddess to whom bulls were sacrificed (Eurip. *Iphig. Taur.* 1457).

TELCHINIA. A surname at Teumessus in Boeotia, to which one of the tribes of the mysterious Telchines migrated from Rhodes.

TRITOGENEIA (TRITO). A surname either from Lake Tritonis in Libya, near which she is said to have been born (Eurip. *Ion* 872; Apollod. 1. 3.6; comp. Herod. 4. 150, 179), or from the stream Triton near Alalcomenae in Boeotia, where she was worshipped and where, according to some statements, she was born (Paus 9. 33.4; comp. Hom. *Il.* 4. 8); or from *trito,* which, in the dialect of the Athamanians, is said to signify "head," so that it would be the goddess born out of the head of her father (Hes. *Theog.* 924).

TRITONIS (See TRITOGENEIA). Any of these names could signify her being born on the third day of the month.

UNCA. A surname of Athena among the Phoenicians and the Thebans. The goddess was first known in Egypt by that name, and Aeschylus is the first Greek writer who gives her that appellation, which probably had been introduced into Boeotia by Cadmus. (See also ONCA)

UNIGENA. A surname of Minerva as having sprung from Jupiter alone.

XENIA. A surname as presiding over the laws of hospitality and protecting strangers (Paus. 3. 11; Hom. *Od.* 14. 389; Cic. *Ep. ad Q. Frat.* 2. 12).

ZOSTERIA. A surname among the Epicemidian Locrians (Herod. 8. 107).

Atlas

IAPETIDES. A patronymic from his father, Iapetus, the Titan (Hes. *Theog.* 528; Ov. *Met.* 4. 631; Pind. *Ol.* 9. 59).

TELAMON. A surname describing him as the sufferer or bearer of heaven.

Attis

PAPAEUS (PAPAS). A surname meaning "father" (Diod. 3. 58).

Aurora

PALLANTIAS. A patronymic from her father, the giant Pallas (Ov. *Met.* 4. 373, 6. 567, 9. 420).

Bormus

MARIANDYNUS. A surname from his being one of the Mariandynian people of Bithynia (Aeschyl. *Pers.* 938).

Britomartis

DICTYMNA (DICTYNNA). A surname from the word for net (Diod. 5. 76).

Calais

BOREADES. A patronymic from his father, Boreas.

Canaus

MAENDRIUS. A patronymic from his father, Maeandrus, the river god (Hes. *Theog.* 339; Ov. *Met.* 9. 450, 473).

Carmenata

POSTVERTA (POSTVORTA). A surname describing her as turning backward and looking at the past, which she revealed to poets and other mortals. In like manner, the prophetic power with which she looked into the future is indicated by Antevorta, Prorsa (Proversa), and Porrima. Poets, however, have personified these attributes of Carmenata, and describe them as companions of the goddess (Ov. *Met.* 1. 638; Gell. 16. 16).

Castor

OEBALIDES. A patronymic from Oebalus, whose name was applied not only to his descendants but to the Spartans generally (Ov. *Ib.* 590; Ov. *Fast.* 5. 705; Ov. *Her.* 16. 126). (See also DIOSCURI)

Cercaphus

HELIADES. A patronymic from his father, Helios.

Clymenus

PRESBONIADES. A patronymic from his father, Presbon, a son of Phrixus by a daughter of Aeetes, king of Colchis (Paus. 9. 35. 5, 37. 2).

Clytoneus

NAUBOLIDES. A patronymic from Naubolus, son of Ornytus (Hom. *Il.* 2. 518).

Cteatus

ACTORIDES. A patronymic from his father, Actor (Hom. *Il.* 2. 621, 11. 750, 13. 185, 23. 638).

MOLIONES. A matronymic from Molione, his mother.

Cybele

ANTAEA. A surname as a goddess man may approach in prayers.

BERECYNTHIA. A surname derived either from Mt. Berecynthus, or from a fortified place of that name in Phrygia, where she was particularly worshipped.

BRIMO. A surname which means the angry or terrifying.

DAMIA. A surname of Cybele.

DINDYMENE. A surname derived either from Mt. Dindymus in Phrygia, where a temple was believed to have been built to her by the Argonauts (Apollon. Rhod. 1. 985; Strab. 12. 575; Callim. *Epigr.* 42) or from Dindymene, the wife of Maeon and mother of Cybele (Diod. 3. 58).

GENETRIX. A surname meaning "the mother" (Ov. *Met.* 14. 536).

IDAEA. A surname of Cybele (Virg. *Aen.* 5. 252).

Cyclopes

ACMONIDES. Another name for Phracmon or Arges, one of the Cyclopes.

AETNAEUS. A surname from their assistance to Hephaestus in his workshop under Mt. Aetna.

GERAESTUS. Hyacinthus, a Lacedaemonian, in compliance with an oracle, went to Athens and caused his daughters to be sacrificed on the tomb of Cyclops Geraestus for the purpose of delivering his city from famine and plague.

Daphne

LADOGENES (LADONIS). A patronymic from her father Ladon.

Demeter (Ceres)

ACHAEA. A surname at Athens by the Gephyraeans, who had immigrated there from Boeotia.

AMPHICTYONIS. A surname at Antheia, where she was worshipped under this name because it was the place of meeting for the amphictyons of Thermopylae and because sacrifices were offered to her at the opening of every meeting (Herod. 7. 200; Strab. 9. 429).

ANESIDORA. A surname as sender of gifts; there was a temple under this name at Phlius in Attica (Paus. 1. 31.2).

ANTAEA. A surname as a goddess man may approach in prayers.

AZESIA. A surname having to do with the verb *azo,* to pine away with grief, applied in connection with Demeter's search for Persephone.

BRIMO. A surname which means the angry or terrifying.

CABEIRIA. A surname of Demeter, probably after the mysteries of the Cabeiri were incorporated into her worship at Eleusis.

CALLIGENEIA. A surname of Demeter or of her nurse and companion (Aristoph. *Thes.* 300).

CARPOPHORI. "The fruitbearers," a surname of Demeter and Cora, under which they were worshipped at Tegea (Paus. 8. 53.3). Demeter Carpophoros appears also to have been worshipped in Paros.

CHAMYNE. A surname in Elis, which was probably derived from one Chamynus, to whom the building of a temple of Demeter at Elis was ascribed (Paus. 6. 21.1).

CHLOE. "The blooming," a surname as protectress of green fields. Under this name she had a sanctuary at Athens cojointly with Gaea Curotrophos (Paus. 1. 22.3).

CHRYSAOR. A surname designating her as the goddess with the golden sword or arms (Hom. *Hymn.in Cer.* 4).

CHTHONIA. A surname meaning the subterranean, or goddess of the earth, or protectress of the fields (Herod. 2. 123; Apollon. Rhod. 4. 987). One legend says she received this name from Chthonia, daughter of Phoroneus, who with Clymenus, her brother, founded at Hermione a sanctuary of Demeter. Another legend says she was ill received in her wanderings by Colontas of Argolis and was defended by Chthonia, the daughter, who was rescued by Demeter when she burned Colontas and his house. She carried Chthonia to Hermione, where Chthonia built a sanctuary to Demeter and instituted the festival of Chthonia in her honor (Paus. 2. 35.3).

CIDARIA. Surname of the Eleusinian Demeter at Pheneus in Arcadia, derived either from an Arcadian dance or from a royal headdress of the same name (Paus. 8. 15.1).

DELIA. A surname from being worshipped on Delos.

DESPOENA. A surname meaning the ruling goddess or the mistress (Aristoph. *Thes.* 286).

ELEUSINA (ELEUSINIA). A surname from Eleusis in Attica, the principal seat of her worship (Virg. *Georg.* 1. 163).

EPIPOLE. A surname at Lacedaemon.

ERINYS. A surname of Demeter, on account of her *amour* with Poseidon in the form of a horse mating with her in the disguise of a mare. She had a temple under this name on the banks of the Ladon in Arcadia, with a statue which represented her holding a basket in the left hand

and a flambeau in the right. At Phigalia her statue represented her dressed in black, with a horse's head, having a dove in one hand and a dolphin in the other (Apollod. 3. 6.8; Paus. 8. 25.4 – 10). The surname refers to her Fury-like wrath toward Poseidon.

EUROPA. A surname of Demeter (Paus. 9. 39.4).

EURYSTERNOS. A surname describing her as the goddess with a broad chest (Hes. *Theog.* 117), under which she had a sanctuary on the Crathis near Aegae in Achaia, with a very ancient statue (Paus. 5. 14.8, 7. 25.8).

HERCYNA. A surname of Demeter, since Hercyna, daughter of Trophonius, founded the worship of Demeter at Lebadeia (Lycoph. 153).

MALLOPHORA. A surname under which Demeter had a temple at Megara, because she had taught the inhabitants the utility of wool and the means of tending sheep. This temple was represented as so old in the age of Pausanias that it was falling to decay.

MYCALESSIA. A surname derived from Mycalessus in Boeotia, where the goddess had a sanctuary (Paus. 9. 19.4).

MYSIA. A surname from an Argive, Mysius, who received her kindly during her wanderings and built a sanctuary to her (Paus. 2. 18.3).

PANACHAEA. "The goddess of all the Achaeans," a surname at Aegae in Achaia (Paus. 7. 24.2).

PELASGA (PELASGIS). Under this surname she had a temple at Argos. The name was believed to have been derived from Pelasgus, the son of Triopas, who had founded her sanctuary (Paus. 2. 22.2).

RHARIAS. A surname which she derived from the Rharian plain in the neighborhood of Eleusis, the principal seat of her worship (Paus. 1. 38.6).

SITO. A surname describing her as the giver of food or grain (Athen. 3. 109, 10. 416).

TELPHUSSAEA (TILPHUSSAEA). A surname of Demeter Erinys, derived from a town, Telphussion.

THESMIA (THESMOPHOROS). "The lawgiver," in whose honor the Thesmophoria were celebrated at Athens in the month of Pyanepsion (Herod. 2. 171, 6. 16; Aristoph. *Thes.* 303).

Dionysus (Bacchus)

ACRATOPHORUS. A surname at Phigalia in Arcadia as the giver of unmixed wine.

ACROREITES. A surname at Sicyon, which is synonymous with Eriphius, under which name he was worshipped at Metapontum in southern Italy.

ADONEUS. A surname signifying the ruler.

AEGOBOLUS. A surname at Potniae in Boeotia, meaning the goat-killer.

AESYMNETES (See ASYMNETES)

AGRIONIUS. A surname at Orchomenos in Boeotia, from which his festival, Agrionia, there derived its name.

AMPHIETES (AMPHIETERUS). It is believed that at Athens, where the Dionysiac festivals were held annually, the name signified yearly, while at Thebes, where they were celebrated every third year, it was interpreted to be synonymous with *trietes*.

ANTHEUS (ANTHIUS). "The blooming," a surname at Athens (Paus. 7. 21.2).

ASYMNETES (AESYMNETES). In Troy there was an ancient image of Dionysus Asymnetes kept in a chest. When Troy fell, Cassandra left the chest, knowing that it would bring harm to the one possessing the image. The chest fell to Eurypylus, who went mad when opening it. He was restored to health by surrendering the chest to the town of Aroe to remove an ancient curse from its inhabitants, who later worshipped him under this name. The name signified the lord or ruler.

BACCHUS. "The noisy or riotous god," originally a Roman surname of Dionysus, but it does not occur till after the time of Herodotus.

BASSAREUS. A surname either from the long robe worn by the god and the Maenads, the word fox (the skin of which originally was used in making these robes) or the Hebrew word meaning the precursor of the vintage.

BIFORMIS. A surname of Bacchus. He received it because he changed himself into an old woman, to fly from the persecution of Juno; or, perhaps, because he was represented sometimes as a young, and sometimes as an old man; or because wine, over which he presided altered the feelings and the character of men, and, from sedate, sober, and grave, rendered them furious, intemperate, and disorderly.

BIMATER. A surname of Bacchus, which signifies that he had two mothers, because when he was taken from his mother's womb, he was placed, till his second birth, in the thigh of his father, Jupiter.

BRISAEUS. A surname derived from Mt. Brisa in Lesbos or from a nymph, Brisa, who was said to have brought up the god.

BROMIUS. A surname explained by some from his having been born during a storm of thunder and lightning (Diod. 4. 5; Dio Chrys. 27). Others derive it from the nymph Brome, who helped bring him up; others from the noise of the Bacchantic processions (Apollod. 2. 1.5).

CALYDONIUS. A surname of Dionysus.

CORYMBIFER. A surname of Bacchus, from his wearing a crown of *corymbi,* berries that grow on the ivy (Ov. *Fast.* 5. 393; Virg. *Ecl.* 3. 5.39).

CRESIUS. A surname at Argos, where he had a temple in which Ariadne was said to be buried (Paus. 2. 23.7).

DITHYRAMBUS. A surname of Dionysus (Bacchus), given to him either because he was twice born, or because Demeter collected and restored to life his limbs, which had been cut to pieces in the wars of the giants, or because the cave in which be was brought up had two entrances. The hymns sung in his honor were called Dithyrambics, and expressed in irregular numbers an enthusiastic poetical fury, similar to that caused by intoxication.

EBON. A name given to Bacchus by the people of Neapolis.

ELELEUS. A surname of Dionysus, from the word which the Bacchanals loudly repeated during his festivals. His priestesses were in consequence called Eleleides (Ov. *Met.* 4. 5.15).

ELEUTHEREUS. A surname derived either from Eleuther or the Boeotian town of Eleutherae, or referring to the god as the deliverer of man from care and sorrow (Paus. 1. 20.2, 38.8; Plut. *Quaest.Rom.* 101).

ENORCHES. A surname either from Enorchus, son of Thyestes, who built a temple to him, or from descriptions of the god as a dancer.

ENYALIUS. A surname sometimes applied to Dionysus.

ERIPHIUS. A surname at Metapontum, where he was worshipped; synonymous with Acroreites.

EUBULEUS. A surname used for a god of good counsel.

EVAN. A surname of Dionysus, which he received from the wild shout used by his priestesses; or, according to a less accurate source, from a temple or a mountain of the same name in Messenia.

EVIUS. A surname of Dionysus, which he received from the exclamation of his father, Zeus, in the war against the giants: "*Evie!* courage, my son." Thence originated the *evoe! evoe!* so loudly and frequently repeated at the celebration of his festivals.

HYES. A mystic surname of Dionysus.

IACCHUS. A surname of Dionysus, from the noise and shouts of the Bacchanals raised at the festivals of this deity (Claud. *Rapt.Proserp.* 1). Some suppose that he was a son of Demeter, who accompanied his mother in her travels through the world, and assuaged her grief for the loss of Persephone. In consequence of this, it is said that in the celebration of the Eleusinian mysteries, the word Iacchus was frequently repeated.

INTONSUS. "The unshorn," a surname of Bacchus, alluding to the eternal youth of the god, as the Greek youths allowed their hair to grow until they attained the age of manhood.

ISODAETES. "The god who distributes his gifts equally to all," a surname of Dionysus Zagreus (Plut. *De E ap.Delph.* 9).

LAMPTER. "The shining or torchbearer," under which surname he was worshipped at Pellene in Achaia, where a festival was celebrated in his honor (Paus. 7. 27.2).

LAPHYSTIUS. A surname from the Boeotian mountain Laphystius, whence the female Bacchantes were called in the Macedonian dialect Laphystiae.

LENAEUS. A surname derived from the winepress or the vintage (Virg. *Georg.* 2. 4.529).

LIBER. A surname of Bacchus, which signifies free. He received this name from his delivering some cities of Boeotia from slavery, or, according to others, because wine, of which he was the patron, delivered mankind from their cares. The word is often used for wine itself.

LIMNAEUS (LIMNETES or LIMNEGENES). "Inhabiting or born in a lake or marsh or having a temple near a lake." Dionysus was thus addressed at Athens (Thus. 2. 15; Aristoph. *Ran.* 216; Athen. 10. 437, 11. 465).

LYAEUS. The god who frees men from care and anxiety (Virg. *Georg.* 2.229).

LYSIUS. "The deliverer," under which name he was worshipped at Corinth (Paus. 2. 2.5). He was worshipped under this name also at Sicyon and at Thebes, where he was said to have received the surname from the fact of his once having delivered Theban prisoners from the hands of the Thracians in the vicinity of Haliartus (Paus. 9. 16.4).

MEILICHIUS. "The god that can be propitiated, or the gracious," a surname at Naxos (Athen. 3. 78).

MELANAEGIS. "Armed or clad with a black aegis," a surname at Eleutherae (Paus. 1. 38.6) and at Athens (Paus. 2. 35.1).

MELPOMENUS. "The singer," a surname at Athens and in the Attic demos of Acharne (Paus. 1. 2.4, 31.3).

MESATEUS. A surname derived from the town of Mesatis, where, according to a tradition at Patrae, he had been educated (Paus. 7. 18.3, 21.2).

NYCTELIUS. A surname of Dionysus, because his orgies were celebrated in the night. The words *latex Nyctelius* signify wine.

NYSAEUS (NYSIUS, NYSEUS, or NYSIGENA). A surname derived from Nysa, a mountain or city either in Thrace, Arabia, or India, where he was said to have been brought up by nymphs. According to some, it was derived from Nisus, who is said to have been his father, or at least to have educated him (Apollon. Rhod. 2. 905, 4. 431; Diod. 1. 15, 3. 68; Cic. *De Nat.Deor.* 3. 23; Virg. *Aen.* 6. 806; Ov. *Met.* 4. 13).

OMADIUS. "The flesh-eater," a surname of Dionysus, to whom human sacrifices were offered in Chios and Tenedos.

PHLEON. "The giver of plenty," a surname describing the god as promoting the fertility of plants and trees.

PHLYUS. A surname perhaps connected with the Attic demos of Phlya, where there were many temples.

PSILAS. "The unbearded," a name under which he was worshipped at Amyclae (Paus. 3. 19.6).

SABAZIUS. A surname from his identification with this Phrygian agricultural divinity, a son of Rhea or Cybele (Aristoph. *Av.* 873).

SOTER. A surname meaning "the savior" (Lycoph. 206).

TAUROCEPHALUS. A surname in the Orphic mysteries.

TAURUS. A surname meaning bull (Eurip. *Bacch.* 918; Athen. 11. 476; Plut. *Quaest.Gr.* 36; Lycoph. 209).

THRIAMBUS. A surname of Bacchus.

THYONEUS. A surname from *thyo,* "to rage, to be inspired" (in the sense of Bacchic frenzy) (Ov. *Met.* 4. 13; Hor. *Carm.* 1. 17.23).

ZAGREUS. A surname of the mystic Dionysus, whom Zeus, in the form of a dragon, is said to have begotten by Persephone, before she was carried off by Hades (Ov. *Met.* 6. 114; Nonn. 6. 264). He was torn to pieces by the Titans, though he defended himself bravely and assumed various forms, and Athena carried his heart to Zeus.

Dioscuri

AMBULII (AMBULLI). A surname at Sparta, meaning, perhaps, "delayers of death" (Paus. 3. 13.4).

ANACES (ANACTES or ANACES PAIDES). A surname of the Dioscuri among the Athenians. Their festivals were called Anacea (Paus. 2. 22.7, 10. 38.3).

LAPERSAE. A surname from the Attic demos of Lapersae, or, according to some, from a mountain in Laconia.

OEBALIDAE. A patronymic from Oebalus, whose name was applied not only to his descendants but to the Spartans generally (Ov. *Ib.* 590; Ov. *Fast.* 5. 705; Ov. *Her.* 16. 126).

TYNDARIDAE. A patronymic of the Dioscuri from Tyndareus, their father (Hom. *Od.* 11. 298).

Echepolus

ANCHISIADES. A patronymic from his father, Anchises of Sicyon (Hom. *Il.* 23. 296).

Eileithyia

LYSIZONA. "The goddess who loosens the girdle," a surname at Athens (Theocrit. 17. 60).

Electryone

HELIADES. A patronymic from his father, Helios.

Epaphus

INACHIS. A patronymic from his grandfather, Inachus (Ov. *Met.* 1. 753).

Ephialtes, see Otus (and Ephialtes)

Epimetheus

IAPETIDES. A patronymic from the Titan, Iapetus, his father (Hes. *Theog.* 528; Ov. *Met.* 4. 631; Pind. *Ol.* 9. 59).

Erinys

MELANAEGIS. A surname meaning armed or clad with a black aegis (Aeschyl. *Sept.* 700).

MIXOPARTHENOS. "Half-maiden," a surname of the Erinys (Lycoph. 669; comp. Herod. 4. 9).

TILPHUSA. A surname of the Erinys, by whom Ares became the father of the dragon which was slain by Cadmus.

Eros (Cupid)

PANDEMOS. A surname meaning "common to all the people" (Plat. *Sympos.* 180).

Eteocles

LABDACIDES. A patronymic from Labdacus, his great-grandfather.

Eumelus

PHERETIADES. A patronymic as grandson of Pheres.

Eunomia

SOTEIRA. A surname meaning "the saving goddess" (Pind. *Ol.* 9. 25).

Europa

HELLOTIS. A surname at Crete, where a festival, Hellotia, was celebrated to her.

Eurytus

ACTORIDES. A patronymic from his father, Actor (Hom. *Il.* 2. 621, 13. 185, 11. 750, 23. 638).

MOLIONES. A matronymic from Molione, his mother.

Evadne

IPHIAS. A patronymic from her father, Iphis (Ov. *Ep. ex Pont.* 3. 1.111; Eurip. *Suppl.* 985).

Evander

NONACRIATES (NONACRIUS). A surname used in the general sense of Arcadian (Ov. *Fast.* 5. 97).

PALLANTIUS. A patronymic from Pallas, his grandfather (Ov. *Fast.* 5. 647).

Fauna

FATUA (FATUELLA). A surname derived from *fatum,* a divine utterance.

Faunus

AEGIPAN. A name sometimes applied because his shape resembled that of a goat.

Fortuna (Tyche)

AUTOMATIA. A surname which characterizes her as the goddess who manages things according to her own will without any regard to the merit of man.

CONSERVATRIX. A surname of Fortuna.

EQUESTER. The Roman Fortuna bore this surname, and temples were dedicated to her under this name, particularly at Antium (Tacit. *Ann.* 3. 71).

HIPPIA. A surname of Fortuna at Rome (Liv. 40. 40, 42. 3).

MEILICHIA. A surname designating her as the goddess who can be propitiated, or the gracious.

MULIEBRIS. A surname of Fortuna.

PRAENESTINA. A surname as having a temple and oracle at Praeneste (Ov. *Fast.* 6. 62; Suet. *Domit.* 15).

PRIMAGENIA (PRIMIGENIA). Under this name she had a celebrated sanctuary at Praeneste and at Rome on the Quirinal (Cic. *De Div.* 2. 41; Liv. 34. 53).

PRIVATA. A surname of Fortuna.

PUBLICA. A surname of Fortuna.

REDUX. A surname as the divinity who leads the traveler back to his home in safety (Mart. 8. 85; Claud. *De Consul.Hon.* 6. 1).

REGINA. A surname of Fortuna.

VIRGINENSIS. A surname under which Fortuna was worshipped by newly married women, who dedicated their maiden garments and girdles in her temple.

VIRILIS. A surname under which Fortuna was worshipped by women who prayed to her to preserve their charms and thus enable them to please their husbands.

Gaea

ANESIDORA. A surname as sender of gifts.

CALLIGENEIA. A surname of Gaea (Aristoph. *Thes.* 300).

CUROTROPHOS. A surname at Athens, where she had a sanctuary (Paus. 1. 22.3).

EURYSTERNOS. "The goddess with the broad chest," a surname of Gaea, under which she had a sanctuary on the Crathis near Aegae in Achaia (Paus. 5. 14.8, 7. 25.8).

PANDORA (PANDORUS). A surname as the giver of all (Philostr. *Vit.Apoll.* 6. 39).

Ganymede

DIA. A surname under which he had a temple at Sicyon (Paus. 2. 13.3).

Gorgons

PHORCYDES (PHORCIDES or PHORCYNIDES). A patronymic as the daughters of Phorcys.

Graeae

PHORCYDES (PHORCIDES of PHORCYNIDES). A patronymic as the daughters of Phorcys.

Hades (Pluto)

AGESANDER (AGESILAUS). A surname as the god who carries away all men.

CLYMENUS. A surname referring to his ultimately assembling all mortals in his kingdom and bringing them to rest and peace.

EUBULEUS (EUBULUS). "God of good counsel;" when applied to Hades, the name is a mere euphemism (Plut. *Quaest.Conviv.* 7. 9).

ISODETES. "The god who binds all equally," a surname of Pluto to express his impartiality.

PANCOITES. As CLYMENUS.

PLUTON. A surname as giver of wealth. This was later used as the real name of the god (Eurip. *Herc.Fur.* 1104).

POLYDECTES. As CLYMENUS.

POLYDEGMON. "The one who receives many," a surname of Hades (Hom. *Hymn.in Cer.* 431; Aeschyl. *Prom.* 153).

PYLARTES. A surname describing him as keeping the gates to the lower world closed.

SUMMAMUS. A surname of Pluto, as prince of the dead, *summus manium.* He had a temple at Rome, erected during the wars with Pyrrhus; and the Romans believed that the thunderbolts of Jupiter were in his power during the night.

Hebe

DIA. A surname under which she had a temple at Phlius (Strab. 8. 382).

Hecate

BRIMO. A surname meaning the angry or terrifying. Some give the derivation from *bromos,* so that it would refer to the crackling of the fire, as Hecate was represented bearing a torch.

CHTHONIA. A surname meaning the subterranean, or goddess of the earth, or protectress of the fields (Apollon.Rhod. 4. 148).

PERSEIS. A patronymic as daughter of Persaeus or Perses (Apollod. 1. 2.4; Apollon. Rhod. 3. 478).

PHERAEA. A patronymic as daughter of Zeus and Pheraea, the daughter of Aeolus, or because she had been brought up by the shepherds of Pheres, or because she was worshipped at Pherae.

Hector

EURYDAMAS. "Ruling far and wide," a surname of Hector (Ov. *Ib.* 331).

Helen

DENTRITIS. "The goddess of the tree," a surname of Helen at Rhodes. When Helen fled to Rhodes, she sought the protection of her friend, Polyxo, who secretly bore her a grudge, since her own husband, Tlepolemus, had been killed in the Trojan War. Once while Helen was bathing, Polyxo sent out her servants in the disguise of the Erinyes with the command to hang Helen on a tree. For this reason the Rhodians afterwards built a sanctuary to Helena Dendritis (Paus. 3. 19.10).

OEBALIDES. A patronymic from Oebalus, whose name was applied not only to his descendants but to the Spartans generally (Ov. *Ib.* 590; Ov. *Fast.* 5. 705; Ov. *Her.* 16. 126).

Helios

HYPERIONIDES (HYPERIONION). A patronymic from his father, the Titan Hyperion (Hom. *Od.* 1. 8, 12. 132; Hom. *Il.* 8. 480; Hes. *Theog.* 1011; Ov. *Met.* 15. 406).

PANOMPHAEUS. "The author of all signs and omens," a surname of Helios (Q.Smyrn. 5. 624).

PHAETHON. A surname of Helios (Apollon.Rhod. 4. 1236; Virg. *Aen.* 5. 105).

SOTER. "The savior," a surname of Helios (Paus. 8. 31.4).

Hephaestus (Vulcan)

AETNAEUS. A surname of Vulcan because he had his workshop in the mountain of Aetna.

AMPHIGYEEIS. A surname meaning lame or limping on both feet; Hephaestus was lamed from birth when Zeus threw him from Olympus (Hom. *Il.* 1. 599; comp. Apollod. 1. 3.5).

MULCIBER. A surname which seems to have been given to Vulcan as a euphemism and for the sake of a good omen, that he might not consume by ravaging fire the habitations and property of men, but might kindly and benevolently aid men in their pursuits (Ov. *Met.* 2. 5; Ov. *Ars Am.* 2. 562).

Hera (Juno)

ACRAEA. A surname in Corinth. Medea had left her younger children by Jason as suppliants at the altar of Hera Acraea (Apollod. 1. 9.16; Ov. *Met.* 7).

AEGOPHAGUS. A surname meaning the goat-eater, by which she was worshipped by the Lacedaemonians.

ALEXANDER. "The defender of men," a surname under which she was worshipped at Sicyon.

AMMONIA. A surname as wife of Zeus Ammon, whose oracle the inhabitants of Elis were in the habit of consulting (Paus. 5. 15.7).

ANTHEIA. "The blooming" or "the friend of flowers," a surname under which she had a temple at Argos.

ARGEIA. A surname at Argos, the principal seat of her worship (Paus. 3. 13.6).

ARGIVA. A surname of Hera, under which she was worshipped at Argos. She had also a temple at Sparta, consecrated to her by Eurydice, daughter of Lacedaemon.

BUNAEA (BUNEA). A surname derived from Bunus, son of Hermes and Alcidameia, who is said to have built a sanctuary to Hera on the road which led up to Acrocorinthus (Paus. 2. 3.8, 4.7).

CAPRATINA. A surname of Juno at Rome. When an invading army threatened to destroy

Rome unless women were sent out to them, the female slaves volunteered to pose as free women and meet the demand. Later, while the sated and drunken invaders slept, the slaves gave a signal from a wild fig tree (*caprificus*), and the Romans came forth and defeated the enemy. This event gave rise to an annual festival (Varr. *De Ling.Lat.* 6. 18; Plut. *Romul.* 29; Plut. *Camil.* 33).

CHERA. A surname believed to have been given to her by Temenus, son of Pelasgus. At Stymphalus, he had built three sanctuaries to her: *pais* (maidenhood), *teleia* (as wife of Zeus), and *chera* (the widow, alluding to her separation from Zeus) (Paus. 8. 22.2).

CINXIA. A surname of Juno, as goddess of marriage, alluding to her symbolic untying of the girdle of newly married women.

CUPRA. A surname of Juno in Etruria derived from the name of a town, but it may be connected with the Sabine word *cyprus,* which, according to Varro (*De Ling.Lat.* 5. 159), signified good.

CURIATIA. A surname of Juno as presider over public affairs.

DIRPHYA. A surname of Hera from Dirphys, a mountain of Euboea, where a temple was erected in honor of the goddess.

DOMIDUCA. A surname of Juno at Rome as the goddess of marriage who conducted the bride into the house of the bridegroom (August. 7. 3, 9. 6).

ELEUTHO. A surname of Hera Lucina from her presiding over the delivery of pregnant women (Pind. *Ol.* 6).

EMPANDA (PANDA). A possible surname of Juno at Rome as having a temple always open for asylum.

EQUESTER. A surname of Juno (Paus. 5. 15.4).

FEBRUATA (FEBRULIS, FEBRUTA, FEBRUALIS, or FEBRUTIS). A surname of Juno as the goddess of marriage, in Italy (cf. Februus, the Italian divinity).

FLUONIA. A surname of Juno.

GAMELIA. A surname of Juno, as Gamelius was applied to Jupiter, on account of their presiding over marriages.

HIPPIA. A surname of Hera (Paus. 5. 15.4).

HYPERCHEIRA. "A goddess who holds her protecting hand over a thing," a surname under which Hera had a sanctuary at Sparta, which had been erected to her at the command of an oracle when the country was inundated by the river Eurotas (Paus. 3. 13.6).

IMBRASIA. A surname from the river Imbrasus in Samos, on which the goddess was believed to have been born (Apollon.Rhod. 1. 187; Paus. 7. 4.4).

INTERDUCA. As DOMIDUCA.

JUGA (JUGALIS). "Goddess of marriage," a surname of Juno, under which she had a temple at Rome in the forum.

LACINIA. A surname of Juno, under which she was worshipped in the neighborhood of Croton, where she had a rich and famous sanctuary (Strab. 6. 261, 281; Liv. 24. 3). The name is derived from some Italian hero, Lacinius, or from the Lacinian promontory on the eastern coast of Bruttium, which Thetis was said to have given to Juno as a present. After Hercules had killed the robber, Lacinius, he built a temple to Juno, surnamed Lacinia (Diod. 4. 24).

LUCERIA (LUCETIA). "Giver of light," a surname of Juno, especially among the Oscans.

LUCINA. "Goddess of light," or rather "the goddess who brings the light," and hence the goddess who presides over the birth of children, a surname of Juno (Varr. *De Ling.Lat.* 5. 69; Catull. 34. 13; Hor. *Carm.Saec.* 14; Ov. *Fast.* 2. 441; 6. 39; Tibull. 3. 4.13).

MATRONA. A surname of Juno under which she was worshipped both at Lanuvium and Rome (Liv. 24. 10; 27. 3; 32. 30; Ov. *Fast.* 2. 56; Cic. *De Div.* 1. 2.).

MATUTA. A surname of Juno at Rome (Liv. 34. 53).

MONETA. A surname among the Romans, by which she was characterized as the protectress of money. Moneta signifies the mint. Another explanation of the name: Cicero (*De Div.* 1. 45; 2. 32) relates that during an earthquake, a voice was heard issuing from the temple of Juno on the Capitol and admonishing (*monens*) that a pregnant sow should be sacrificed. In the war with Pyrrhus and the Tarentians, the Romans, needing money, prayed to Juno and were told by the goddess that they would not lack money, so long as they fought with the arms of justice. As the Romans by experience found the truth of the words of Juno, they called her Juno Moneta. Her festival was celebrated on the first of June (Ov. *Fast.* 6. 183).

OPIGENA. As MATRONA.

PANDA (See EMPANDA)

PARTHENIA. A surname derived from the river Parthenius.

PELASGA (PELASGIS). "The Pelasgian (woman or goddess)" occurs as a surname of the Thessalian Hera (Apollon. Rhod. 1. 14; Propert. 2. 28.11).

PERTUNDA. A surname of Juno as goddess of marriage, from *pertundo,* to perforate.

PHARYGAEA. A surname from the town of Pharugae in Locris, where she had a temple (Strab. 9. 426).

POPULONIA. A surname of Juno among the Romans, as the protectress of the whole Roman people. In her temples there was a small table, the symbol of political union.

PREMA. A surname of Juno as goddess of marriage, from *premo,* to press (together).

PRONUBA. A surname of Juno among the Romans, describing her as the deity presiding over marriage (Virg. *Aen.* 4. 166, 7. 319; Ov. *Her.* 6. 43).

REGINA. A surname of Juno in Rome as queen of the gods.

SAMIA. A surname derived from her temple and worship in the island of Samos (Herod. 3. 60; Paus. 7. 4.4; Tacit. *Ann.* 4. 14).

SATURNIA. "A daughter of Saturnus," a patronymic of Juno in Rome (Virg. *Aen.* 1. 23, 12. 156; Ov. *Fast.* 1. 265, 6. 383).

SORORIA. A surname of Juno under which an altar is said to have been erected in common with Janus Curiatius, when Horatius, on his return home, had slain his sister and had been purified of the murder (Liv. 1. 26).

SOSPITA (SISPITA). "The saving goddess," a surname at Lanuvium and at Rome, in both of which she had a temple. The ancient Romans called her Sispita.

TELCHINIA. A surname of Hera at Ialysos and Cameiros. This name is connected with the mysterious tribe of the Telchines, who migrated to various places from Rhodes.

UNXIA. A surname of Juno derived from *ungere,* to anoint, because it was usual among the Romans for the bride to anoint the threshold of her husband, and from this necessary ceremony wives were called *unxores,* and afterwards *uxores,* from Unxia, who presided over them.

VIRGINALIS. As MATRONA.

VIRIPLACE. "The goddess who soothes the anger of man," a surname of Juno, describing her as the restorer of peace between married people.

ZYGIA. A surname of Hera as presiding over marriage. Zygia is derived from the verb meaning to yoke.

Heracles (Hercules)

ALCIDES (ALCEIDES). A name of Heracles from his strength, or from his grandfather, Alcaeus. According to some, Alcaeus (Alceides) was the original name of the hero.

ALEXICACUS. "Averter of evil," a surname of Heracles.

AMPHITRYONIADES (AMPHITRYONIDES). A patronymic from Amphitryon, whom his mother, Alcmene, married (Ov. *Met.* 9. 140, 15. 49; Pind. *Ol.* 3. 26; Pind. *Isth.* 6. 56).

BUPHAGUS. A surname from his having eaten a whole bull at once (Apollod. 2. 7.7, 5.11).

BURAICUS. A surname from the Achaean town of Bura, near which he had a statue on the river Buraicus.

CHAROPS. "Bright-eyed or joyful-looking," a surname under which he had a statue near Mt. Laphystion on the spot where he was believed to have brought Cerberus from the underworld (Paus. 9. 34.4).

CLAVIGER. A surname of Hercules as being armed with a club.

INDEX. "The indicator or denouncer," a surname of Heracles. Once a golden vessel was stolen from the temple of Heracles at Athens, and Heracles appeared repeatedly in a dream to Sophocles, until the latter informed the Areiopagus of it, the thief was arrested and confessed his crime. Thereafter, the temple was called the temple of Heracles Menytes, or Index (Cic. *De Div.* 1. 25).

MACISTUS. A surname from his having a temple in the neighborhood of the town of Macistus in Triphylia (Strab. 8. 348).

MECISTEUS. A surname of Heracles (Lycoph. 651).

MELAMPYGES. A surname of Heracles from the black and hairy appearance of his backside.

MENYTES (See INDEX)

MONOECUS. A surname signifying the god who lives solitary, perhaps because he alone was worshipped in the temples dedicated to him (Strab. 4. 202; Virg. *Aen.* 6. 831; Plut. *Quaest.Rom.* 87).

MUSAGETES. A surname of Hercules in Rome, from his association with the Musae, or Muses.

OGMIUS. A name of Hercules among the Gauls. He was considered by this nation as the god of eloquence and of persuasion, and since reason and the oratorical powers were associated with age, he was represented under the form of an old man, bald and wrinkled. The god wore the lion's skin and a quiver, while he held a bow in one hand and his club in the other.

OLYMPIUS. A surname of Heracles after his apotheosis (Herod. 2. 44).

PALAEMON. A surname of Heracles as the wrestler (Lycoph. 663).

PROMACHUS. "The champion," a surname at Thebes (Paus. 9. 11.2).

Hermaphroditus

ATLANTIADES (ATLANTIUS). A patronymic from Atlas, his great-grandfather.

Hermes (Mercury)

ACACESIUS. A surname possibly from the Arcadian town of Acacesium, where he was believed to have been brought up by king Acacus. It is possibly from the Greek *kakos,* suggesting the god who cannot be hurt, or who does not hurt (Callim. *Hymn.in Dian.* 143).

AGETOR. A surname as conductor of souls to the underworld. Under this name he had a statue at Megalopolis (Paus. 8. 31.4).

AGONIUS. A surname as presider over solemn contests (Paus. 5. 14.7; Pind. *Ol.* 6. 133).

AGORAEUS (AGORAEIOS). A surname as god of commerce; the name refers to the agora, or marketplace, over which he presided.

ALIPES. A surname from having wings at his ankles (Ov. *Met.* 11. 312).

ARCAS. A surname of Hermes (Lucan 9. 661; Mart. 9. 34.6).

ARGEIPHONTES (ARGIPHONTES). A surname by which he is designated as the murderer of Argus Panoptes (Hom. *Il.* 2. 103; 24. 182).

ATLANTIADES. A patronymic from Atlas, his grandfather.

CATAEBATES. A surname given because he conducted the shades into Hades.

CERDEMPOROS. A surname from his being god of commerce.

CTESIUS. A surname from his being protector of property (Paus. 1. 31.2).

CYLLENIUS. A surname from Mt. Cyllene in Arcadia, where he had a temple (Paus. 8. 17.1) or from the circumstance of Maia having given birth to him on that mountain (Virg. *Aen.* 8. 139; Hom. *Od.* 8. 335; Hom. *Hymn. in Merc.* 1; Ov. *Met.* 1. 682, 14. 291).

DEMPOROS. A surname from his being god of commerce.

ERIUNIUS (ERINNES). A surname as giver of good fortune (Hom. *Il.* 24. 440, 457; Hom. *Od.* 8. 322; Aristoph. *Ran.* 1143).

EURYMEDON. "A being far and wide," a surname of Hermes.

HEGEMONIUS. Under this name Hermes was invoked by Athenian generals setting out on expeditions.

IMBRAMUS (IMBRASUS). This name had been identified with the Pelasgian Hermes, who went from Attica to Lemnos, Imbros, and Samothrace.

MALEVOLUS. "The ill-willed," a surname of Mercury, under which name he had a statue in what was called the *vicus sobrius,* or the sober street, in which no shops were allowed to be kept, and milk was offered to him there instead of wine. This statue had a purse in its hand to indicate his function (commerce). His festival was celebrated on the 25th of May.

NECROPOMPOS. A surname from his office of conducting the shades of the dead to the underworld.

NOMIUS. A surname designating him as a divinity who protects the pastures and shepherds.

NONACRIATES (NONACRIUS). A surname in the general sense of Arcadian (Ov. *Fast.* 5. 97).

PALENCAPELOS. A surname from his being god of commerce.

PROMACHUS. "The champion," a surname at Tanagra (Paus. 9. 22.2).

PRONAUS. "In front of the temple," occurs as a surname of Hermes (Paus. 9. 10.2).

PSYCHOGOGOS. A surname from his office of conducting the shades of the dead to the underworld.

PSYCHOPOMPOS. As PSYCHOGOGOS.

PTEROPEDILOS. A surname from having wings at his ankles (Ov. *Met.* 11. 312).

QUADRATUS. A surname given to Mercury because some of his statues were square. The number four, according to Plutarch, was sacred to Mercury, because he was born on the fourth day of the month (Plut. *Quaest. Conviv.* 9).

TEUTAS (TEUTATES). A name of Mercury among the Gauls, probably the same as the Thoth of the Egyptians. The people offered human victims to this deity.

THEOXENIUS. A surname of Hermes (Paus. 7. 27.2).

Hestia (Vesta)

PENETRALIA. A surname of Vesta in Rome, from being worshipped in the Penetrale, or central part of the house.

SATURNIA. A patronymic as a daughter of Saturn (Virg. *Aen.* 1. 23, 12. 156; Ov. *Fast.* 1. 265, 6. 383).

Hippodameia

BRISEIS. A patronymic from her father Briseus. She was the subject of the quarrel between Achilles and Agamemnon (Hom. *Il.* 1. 184).

Hyacinthus

AMYCLIDES. A patronymic from his father, Amyclas (Ov. *Met.* 10. 162).

OEBALIDES. A patronymic from Oebalus, whose name was applied not only to his descendants but to the Spartans generally (Ov. *Ib.* 590; Ov. *Fast.* 5. 705; Ov. *Her.* 16. 126).

Idas

APHARETIDES. A patronymic from his father, Aphareus.

Ilus

DARDANIDES. A patronymic from his great grandfather, Dardanus (Hom. *Il.* 11. 372).

Io

INACHIA. A patronynmic from her father, Inachus (Virg. *Georg.* 3. 153; Ov. *Fast.* 3. 658; Ov. *Met.* 9. 686; Aeschyl. *Prom.* 591; Callim. *Hymn.in Dian.* 254).

PHORONIS. A name from being either a descendant or a sister of Phoroneus (Ov. *Met.* 1. 668).

Iphiclus

PHYLACIDES. A patronymic from his ancestor, Phylacus (Hom. *Il.* 2. 705; Propert. 1. 19).

THESTIADES. A patronymic from his father, Thestius (Apollon. Rhod. 1. 261).

Iphitus

NAUBOLIDES. A patronymic from his father, Naubolus, son of Ornytus (Hom. *Il.* 2. 518).

Iris

AELLOPUS. A surname meaning swift-footed (Hom. *Il.* 8. 409).

THAUMANTIAS (THAUMANTIS). A name given to Iris, the messenger of Hera, because she was the daughter of Thaumas, the son of Oceanus, by one of the Oceanides.

Itymoneus

HYPEIROCHIDES. A patronymic from his father, Hypeirochus (Hom. *Il.* 11. 672).

Janus

BIFORMIS. A surname sometimes applied to Janus.

BIFRONS. A surname of Janus, because he was represented by the Romans with two faces, as acquainted with the past and future.

CLAVIGER. A surname given to Janus, from his being represented with a key.

CLUSIUS (CLUSAVIUS). A surname pertaining to his power over the entrance of heaven (Ov. *Fast.* 1. 129).

CONSIVIUS. A surname as god of beginning.

CURIATIUS. Under this name an altar was erected to him in common with Juno Sororia, when Horatius, on his return home, had slain his sister and had been purified of the murder (Liv. 1. 26).

EANUS. The name of Janus among the ancient Latins.

JUNONIUS. A surname of Janus from Juno, to whom the first part of every month was sacred.

MATUTINUS. A surname from his presiding over the beginning of every day.

PATULCIUS (PATULCUS). A surname of Janus, which he received from *patulus,* because the doors of his temple were always open in time of war. Some suppose that he received it because he presided over gates, or because the year began with the celebration of his festivals.

QUADRIFRONS. It is said that after the conquest of the Faliscans, an image of Janus was found with four foreheads. The fact of the god being represented with four heads was considered by the ancients to be an indication of his being the divinity presiding over the year with its four seasons (August. 7. 4).

QUIRINUS. According to Dionysus of Halicarnassus (2. 48), the name was derived from a Sabine word and perhaps meant a lance or spear, *quiris*.

Jason

AESONIDES. A patronymic from his father, Aeson.

PAGASAEUS. "The Pagasaean," from Pagasus, a town in Thessaly, because the ship Argo was said to have been built at Pagasus (Ov. *Met.* 7. 1; Ov. *Her.* 16. 345).

PHERAEUS. A surname of Jason, as being a native of Pherae.

Laertes

ARCEISIADES. A patronymic from his father, Arceisius.

Leda

THESTIA. A patronymic from her father, Thestius (Eurip. *Iphig.Aul.* 49; Aeschyl. *Choeph.* 606).

Leto (Latona)

PHYTA. "The creator," a surname for her having changed the daughter of Galateia into a male in order to prevent her being killed by her father who desired a son.

Lycus

PANDIONIDES. A patronymic from his father, Pandion.

Lynceus

APHARETIDES. A patronymic from his father, Aphareus.

Macareus

HELIADES. A patronymic from his father, Helios.

Maia

ATLANTES. A patronymic from her father, Atlas.

PLEIAS. A matronymic from her mother, Pleione.

Mecisteus

TALIONIDES. A patronymic from his father, Talaus, son of Bias and Pero (Hom. *Il.* 2. 566; Pind. *Ol.* 6. 24).

Meges

PHYLEIDES. A patronymic from his father, Phyleus (Paus. 5. 3.4; Apollod. 2. 5.5; Strab. 10. 459).

Melampus

AMYTHAONIUS. A patronymic from his father, Amythaon (Virg. *Georg.* 3. 550).

Meleager

OENEIDES. A patronymic from Oeneus, his father.

Melicertes (Palaemon)

INOUS. A matronymic from Ino, his mother (Virg. *Aen.* 5. 823; Virg. *Georg.* 1. 437).

Melinoe

CHTHONIA. "The subterranean," or "goddess of the earth," or "protectress of the fields."

Menelaus

ATREIDES. A patronymic from his father, Atreus.

Menoetius

IAPETIDES. A patronymic from his father, Iapetus the Titan (Hes. *Theog.* 528; Ov. *Met.* 4. 631; Pind. *Ol.* 9. 59).

Mestra

TRIOPEIS. A patronymic from her grandfather, Triopas (Ov. *Met.* 8. 872).

Mopsus

AMPYCIDES. A patronymic from Ampycus, or Ampyx, his father (Ov. *Met.* 8. 316, 350, 12. 456, 524; Apollon.Rhod. 1. 1083).

TITARESIUS. A surname from the river Titaresius in Thessaly, near which he was born (Hom. *Il.* 2. 751).

Morpheus

EPIDOTES. "The liberal giver," a surname applied to the god of sleep at Sicyon, where he had a statue in the temple of Asclepius, which represented him in the act of sending a lion to sleep (Paus. 2. 10.3).

Muses

ARDALIDES (ARDALIOTIDES). A surname from Ardalus, who built a sanctuary to them at Troezen (Paus. 2. 31.3).

ILISSIADES. A surname from having an altar on the Ilissus in Attica (Paus. 1. 19.6).

LIBETHRIDES (NYMPHAE LIBETHRIDES). A surname which they derived from the well Libethra in Thrace; or, according to others, from the Thracian mountain Libethrus, where they had a grotto sacred to them (Virg. *Ecl.* 7. 21; Strab. 9. 410, 10. 471). Pausanias (9. 34.4) connects it with Mt. Libethrius in Boeotia (comp. Lycoph. 275; Varr. *De Ling.Lat.* 7. 2).

OLYMPIADES. A surname designating them as Olympian goddesses (Hom. *Il.* 2. 491).

PEGASIDES. A surname from their association with the Hippocrene well, which Pegasus called forth with his hoof (Mosch. 3. 78; Ov. *Trist.* 3. 7.15).

PIERIDES. A surname derived from Pieria near Mt. Olympus, where they were first worshipped among the Thracians (Hes. *Theog.* 53; Hor. *Carm.* 4. 3.18; Pind. *Pyth.* 6. 49). Some derived the name from an ancient king, Pierus, who is said to have emigrated from Thrace into Boeotia and established their worship at Thespiae (Eurip. *Med.* 831; Pind. *Ol.* 11. 100; Ov. *Trist.* 5. 3.10; Cic. *De Nat.Deor.* 3. 21).

PIMPLEIS (PIMPLEIA). A surname derived from Mt. Pimplias in Pieria, which was sacred to them.

THESPIADES. They were probably so called because their worship was brought to Thespiae in Boeotia from Thrace by Pierus (Ov. *Met.* 5. 310).

Mutunus

TUTUNUS (TUTINUS). A surname probably connected with the verb *tueri* (to guard).

Narcissus

CEPHISIUS. A patronymic from his father, Cephissus (Apollod. 3. 5.1; Ov. *Met.* 3. 343).

Nemesis

ADRASTEIA. A surname either from Adrastus, who is said to have built the first sanctuary of Nemesis on the river Asopus, or from the verb *didrasko,* signifying the goddess from which no one can escape.

ICHNAEA. "The tracing goddess," a surname of Nemesis.

RHAMNUSIA (RHAMNUSIS). A surname from the town of Rhamnusis in Attica, where she had a celebrated sanctuary and temple (Paus. 1. 33.2, 7. 53; Strab. 9. 396).

Neoptolemus (Pyrrhus)

ACHILLIDES. A patronymic from his father, Achilles (Ov. *Her.* 8. 3).

AEACIDES. A patronymic from his great-grandfather, Aeacus.

PELIDES. A patronymic from his grandfather, Peleus.

Nereides

NEREIS (NERINE). Another name from their father, Nereus (Virg. *Ecl.* 7. 37).

Nestor

NELEIDES (NELEIADES or NELEIUS). A patronymic from his father, Neleus.

Nike (Nice)

APTEROS. "The wingless," a surname at Athens to signify that victory, usually depicted as winged, could never fly away from the city.

Nyx (Nox)

CHTHONIA. A surname meaning the subterranean, or goddess of the earth, or protectress of the fields.

Ochimus

HELIADES. A patronymic from his father, Helios.

Odysseus

AEOLIDES. A patronymic from his grandfather, Aeolus (according to some accounts, Odysseus was the son of Sisyphus, son of Aeolus) (Virg. *Aen.* 6. 529).

ARCEISIADES. A patronymic from his grandfather, Arceisius (Hom. *Od.* 4. 755, 24. 270).

ITHACUS. As king of Ithaca, Odysseus is sometimes simply called Ithacus (Ov. *Ep.ex Pont.* 1. 3.33; Virg. *Aen.* 2. 104).

Oedipus

LABDACIDES. A patronymic from Labdacus, his grandfather.

Oenone

PEGASIS. A name given to Oenone by Ovid (*Her.* 5) because she was daughter of a river *(pega).*

Omphale

MAEONIS (MAEONIDES). A surname from her origins in Lydia, the ancient name of which was Maeonia (Ov. *Fast.* 2. 310).

Ops

CONSIVA. A surname from the verb *serere,* to sow.

RUNCINA. A surname by which she was invoked by the people of Italy to prevent the growth of weeds among the grain and to promote the harvest (August. 4. 8).

Otus (and Ephialtes)

ALOEIDAE (ALOIADAE or ALOADAE). A patronymic from Aloeus, whose wife, Iphimedeia, bore these giant sons to Poseidon.

Palaemon, see Melicertes

Pallas

PANDIONIDES. A patronymic from his father, Pandion.

Pan

AEGIPAN. A name of Pan because he had goats' feet.

AEGOCERUS. A name of Pan, describing him with the horns of a goat.

AGREUS. A surname as hunter (Pind. *Pyth.* 9. 115; Apollon.Rhod. 3. 507; Diod. 4. 81).

LIMENIA (LIMENITES, LIMINITIS, or LIMENOSCOPUS). A surname as protector or superintendent of the harbor.

LYCAEUS. A surname from having been born and having a sanctuary on Mt. Lycaeus (Paus. 8. 38.4; Strab. 8. 388; Virg. *Aen.* 8. 344).

LYTERIUS. "The deliverer," under which surname he had a sanctuary at Troezen, because he was believed during a plague to have revealed in dreams the proper remedy against the disease (Paus. 2. 35.5).

MAENALIUS (MAENALIDES). A surname from Mt. Maenalus in Arcadia, which was sacred to the god (Paus. 8. 26.2, 36.5; Ov. *Fast.* 4. 650).

NOMIUS. A surname as a divinity who protects pastures and shepherds.

SINOEIS. A surname from Sinoe, an Arcadian nymph who brought him up (Paus. 8. 30.2).

Patroclus

ACTORIDES. A patronymic from Actor, his grandfather (Ov. *Met.* 5. 79, 13. 273; Ov. *Trist.* 1. 9).

Peirithous

IXIONIDES. A patronymic from Ixion, his father (Ov. *Met.* 8. 566).

Peisistratus

NESTORIDES. A patronymic from his father, Nestor (Hom. *Od.* 3. 36, 482).

Periphas

EPYTIDES. Periphas was a companion of Iulus and is called by the patronymic Epytides from his father, Epytus (Virg. *Aen.* 2. 340, 5. 547, 579; Hom. *Il.* 17. 323).

Periphetes

CORYNETES. Periphetes, son of Hephaestus, was surnamed Corynetes, that is, club-bearer, and was a robber at Epidaurus, who slew travelers he met with an iron club. Theseus at last slew him and took his club for his own use (Apollod. 3. 16.1; Plut. *Thes.* 8; Paus. 2. 1.4; Ov. *Met.* 7. 437).

Persephone (Proserpina)

AUXESIA. A surname as the goddess who grants growth and prosperity to fields.

AZESIA. A surname in common with Demeter, referring to her loss and grieving and neglect of crops while Persephone was being sought.

BRIMO. A surname meaning the angry or terrifying. Some give the derivation from *bromos,* so that it would refer to the crackling of the fire.

CARPOPHORI. "The fruitbearers," a surname of Demeter and Cora (Persephone), under which they were worshipped at Tegea (Paus. 8. 53.3).

CORE (CORA). "The maiden," a surname of Persephone.

DEIONE (DEIOIS). A matronymic as daughter of Deo, or Demeter.

DESPOENA. A surname as the ruling goddess or the mistress (Paus. 8. 37.6).

ELEUSINA (ELEUSINIA). A surname from Eleusis in Attica, the principal seat of her worship (Virg. *Georg.* 1. 163).

EPAINE. A surname meaning the fearful (Hom. *Il.* 9. 457). Plutarch (*De Aud.Poet.* 23) derives the name from *ainos,* which suggests that it might also be understood in a euphemistic sense as the praised goddess.

MELIBOEA. A surname of Persephone.

MELITODES. "Sweet as honey," occurs as a euphemistic surname of Persephone (Theocrit. 15. 94).

PHEREPHATE (PHEREPHATTA). A surname of Persephone, from the production of grain.

PRAXIDICE. With the Orphic poets, Praxidice seems to be a surname of Persephone meaning the goddess who carries out justice.

SOTEIRA. "The saving goddess," a surname in Laconia (Paus. 3. 13.2) and in Arcadia (7. 27.1).

THESMIA (THESMOPHOROS). "The lawgiver," a surname of Persephone in honor of whom the Thesmophoria were celebrated at Athens in the month of Pyanepsion (Herod. 2. 171, 6. 16; Aristoph. *Thes.* 303).

Perseus

ACRISIONIADES. A patronymic from his grandfather, Acrisius (Ov. *Met.* 5. 70).

AGENORIDES. A patronymic from his ancestor, Agenor (Ov. *Met.* 4. 771).

EURYMEDON. "A being far and wide," a surname of Perseus (Apollon.Rhod. 4. 1514).

INACHIS. A surname of Perseus because he was born at Argos, the city of Inachus (Ov. *Met.* 4. 719).

Phaethon

HELIADES. A patronymic from his father, Helios.

Philoctetes

POEANTIADES. A patronymic from his father Poeas (Ov. *Met.* 13. 313).

Phocus

AEACIDES. A patronymic from Aeacus, his father.

NEREIUS. A patronymic from Nereus, his ancestor (Ov. *Met.* 7. 685, 13. 162; Virg. *Aen.* 9. 102).

Phoebe

LEUCIPPIDA. A patronymic from Leucippus, her father.

Phylacus

PHYLACIDES. A patronymic from his ancestor, Phylacus (Hom. *Il.* 2. 705; Propert. 1. 19).

Polyneices

LABDACIDES. A patronymic from Labdacus, his great-grandfather.

Poseidon (Neptune)

AEGAEUS. A surname from Aegae in Euboea, near which town a temple to him was located on a hill.

ASPHALIUS (ASPHALEIUS). A surname under which he was worshipped in various towns of Greece. It describes him as the god who grants safety to ports and to navigation in general (Strab. 1. 57; Paus. 7. 21.3).

DOMATITES. "The domestic," a surname at Sparta. It is probably synonymous with *epichorios,* belonging to the country.

ENNOSIGAEUS. "Earth-shaker," a surname of Neptune.

EPACTAEUS (EPACTIUS). "The god worshipped on the coast," a surname in Samos.

EPOPSIUS. "The superintendent," a surname at Megalopolis (Paus. 8. 30.1).

EQUESTER. A surname of Neptune, who had created the horse and in whose honor horse races were held (Liv. 1.9; Paus. 5. 15.4).

EURYMEDON. "A being far and wide," a surname of Poseidon (Pind. *Ol.* 8. 31).

GAEEOCHUS. "Holder of the earth" (Hom. *Od.* 11. 240), a surname near Therapne in Laconia, where he had a temple (Paus. 3. 20.2).

GENESIUS. The father, under which surname he had a sanctuary near Lerna, on the seacoast (Paus. 2. 38.4).

GENETHLIUS. A surname with much the same meaning as GENESIUS. Under this name the god had a sanctuary at Sparta (Paus. 3. 15.7).

HIPPIUS. A surname of Poseidon (Paus. 6. 20.8, 1. 30.4; Liv. 1. 9).

ISTHMIUS. A surname meaning the god worshipped on the Isthmus of Corinth, in honor of whom the Isthmian games were celebrated (Paus. 2. 9.6).

MELANTHUS. A surname of Poseidon (Lycoph. 767).

PROSCLYSTIUS. A surname of Poseidon among the Greeks, because he was prevailed upon by the entreaties of Hera not to oblige the rivers of Argolis to inundate the country, as he threatened to do since they had judged the goddess superior to himself. A temple was raised to the god, on the spot where the waters had retired to their bed, by the name of Prosclystius, expressive of the subsiding of streams (Paus. 2. 22).

SAMIUS. A surname derived from his temples in Samos and Samicon in Elis (Strab. 14. 637, comp. 8. 343, 347; Paus. 6. 25.5).

SATURNIUS. A patronymic of Neptune as a son of Saturn (Virg. *Aen.* 4. 372, 5. 799).

TARAXIPPUS. A surname of Poseidon Hippius, according to Pausanias (6. 20.8). Taraxippus was the name of a particular spot in the racecourse at Olympia, where horses often became shy and frightened, and superstition had assigned several reasons for this phenomenon.

TAUREUS. A surname because bulls were sacrificed to him, or because he was the divinity that gave green pasture to bulls on the seacoast (Hes. *Scut.Herc.* 104; Hom. *Od.* 3. 6).

Priapus

LIMENIA (LIMENITES, LIMINITIS, or LIMENOSCOPUS). A surname as the protector or superintendent of the harbor.

Prometheus

ACACESIUS. "The god who cannot be hurt or who does not hurt." Hesiod (*Theog.* 614) assigns this name to Prometheus, and it may be inferred that its meaning is that of benefactor or deliverer from evil.

IAPETIONIDES. A patronymic from his father, Iapetus (Hes. *Theog.* 528; Apollon. Rhod. 3. 1087).

Protesilaus

PHYLACIDES. A patronymic from his ancestor, Phylacus (Hom. *Il.* 2. 705; Propert. 1. 19).

Pyrrha

TITANIA. A patronymic applied to Pyrrha as granddaughter of a Titan.

Pyrrhus, see Neoptolemus

Rhea

ANTAEA. A surname as a goddess man may approach in prayers.

Romulus

QUIRINUS. After his sudden disappearance and deification, he reappeared to let the Romans know that they would be lords of the world and that he would watch over them as their guardian god Quirinus. The festival of the Quirinalia was celebrated in his honor on the 17th of February (Virg. *Aen.* 1. 292; Cic. *De Nat.Deor.* 2. 24; Ov. *Amor.* 3. 8.51; Ov. *Fast.* 4. 56, 808, 6. 375; Ov. *Met.* 15. 862). According to Dionysus of Halicarnassus (2. 48), the name was derived from a Sabine word, *quiris,* and probably meant lance or spear.

Selene

HILAEIRA. A surname of Selene.

Semele

THYONE. This was the name under which Dionysus fetched Semele from Hades and introduced her among the immortals (Apollod. 3. 5.3; Cic. *De Nat.Deor.* 3. 23; Pind. *Pyth.* 3. 99; Diod. 4. 25; Apollon.Rhod. 1. 636).

Sirens

ACHELOIDES. A patronymic from Achelous, their father (Apollod. 1. 7.10).

Sisyphus

AEOLIDES. A patronymic from his father, Aeolus (Hom. *Il.* 6. 154; Hor. *Carm.* 2. 14.20).

Talaus

CRETHEIADES. A patronymic from his great grandfather, Cretheus (Paus. 8. 25.9, from a fragment by Antimachus).

Tanages

HELIADES. A patronymic from his father, Helios.

Themis

ICHNAEA. "The tracing goddess," a surname of Themis. Or the name could have been derived from the town of Ichnae, where she was worshipped (Hom. *Hymn.in Apoll.* 94; Lycoph. 129; Strab. 9. 435).

Thetis

HALSODYNE. "The sea-fed" or the "sea-born goddess," a surname of Thetis (Hom. *Il.* 20. 207).

Thoas

ANDRAEMONIDES. A patronymic from his father, Andraemon (Hom. *Il.* 2. 638, 7. 168).

Titans

URANIDAE. A patronymic from their father, Uranus.

Triopas

HELIADES. A patronymic from his father, Helios.

Zetes

BOREADES. A patronymic from his father, Boreas.

Zeus (Jupiter)

ABRETTENUS. A surname of Zeus in Mysia.

ACRAEUS. A surname of Zeus for his having temples situated on hills.

AEGIDUCHOS (AEGIOCHOS). A surname of Zeus as the bearer of the aegis, or an allusion to his being suckled by a goat.

AENEIUS (AENESIUS). A surname on the

island of Cephallenia, where he had a temple on Mt. Aenos.

AETHIOPS. "The glowing" or "the black," a surname under which he was worshipped on the island of Chios.

AETNAEUS. A surname because of a statue of him on Mt. Aetna and also a festival celebrated there.

AGATHODAEMON. Pausanias conjectures that this name (meaning "good god") was probably an epithet of Zeus (8. 36.3). The Greeks drank a cup of unmixed wine to him at the end of every repast. A temple dedicated to him was situated on the road from Megalopolis to Maenalus in Arcadia.

AGETOR. A surname as ruler and leader of men.

AGONIUS. A surname as helper in struggles and contests.

AGORAEUS. A surname as protector of assemblies of the people in the agora.

ALASTOR. A surname as avenger of evil deeds.

ALEXICACUS. A surname as averter of evil.

AMBULIUS. A surname at Sparta, meaning, perhaps, delayer of death (Paus. 3. 13.4).

AMMON. A surname in Egypt, where his principal seats of worship were Meroe (Herod. 2. 29), Thebes (2. 42), oasis of Ammonium (Siwah), and Cyrenaica (Paus. 10. 13.3).

ANCHESMIUS. A surname derived from the hill of Anchesmus in Attica, where there was a statue of the god (Paus. 1. 32.2).

APEMIUS. Under this surname he had an altar on Mt. Parnes in Attica, on which sacrifices were offered to him (Paus. 1. 32.2).

APESANTIUS. A surname from Mt. Apesas near Nemea, where he had a temple and where Perseus first offered sacrifices to him (Paus. 2. 15.3).

APOMYSIUS. "Driving away the flies," a surname from Heracles' having offered a sacrifice to Zeus to get rid of flies at Olympia. Thereafter, the Eleans sacrificed to Zeus under this name (Paus. 5. 14.2).

ARBIUS. A surname from Mt. Arbius in Crete, where he was worshipped.

AREIUS. A surname meaning either warlike or the propitiating and atoning god.

ASBAMAEUS. A surname as the protector of the sanctity of oaths.

ASIUS. A surname from the town of Asos or Oasos in Crete (Virg. *Aen.* 10. 123).

ATABYRIUS. A surname derived from Mt. Atabyris or Atabyrion in Rhodes, where the Cretan Althemenes was said to have built a temple to him (Apollod. 3. 2.1). Upon this mountain there were, it is said, brazen bulls which roared when anything extraordinary was going to happen.

ATHOUS. A surname from Mt. Athos, on which there was a temple to him (Aeschyl. *Agam.* 270).

CAPITOLINUS. A surname of Jupiter from his temple on the Capitoline Hill, which was considered by the Romans as the center of the destinies of their empire. The name also pertains to the god's position at the top of heights from which he regarded the forum and the city of Rome and the whole of Latium. The Roman games and the Feriae Latinae were celebrated under this name.

CARIUS. "The Carian," a surname under which Zeus had a temple at Mylassa in Caria (Herod. 1. 171). He was also worshipped under this name in Thessaly and Boeotia.

CASIUS. A surname derived from Mt. Casion not far from Pelusium, on which the god had a temple (Strab. 16. 760; Plin. *H.N.* 4. 20, 5. 14).

CATAEBATES. A surname as the god who descends in thunder and lightning. Under this name he had an altar at Olympia (Paus. 5. 14.8; Lycoph. 1370). Places which had been struck by lightning were sacred to him.

CATHARSIUS. "The purifier or atoner," under which surname he, in conjunction with Nike, had a temple at Olympia (Paus. 5. 14.6).

CENAEUS. A surname derived from Cape Cenaeum in Euboea, on which the god had a temple (Apollod. 2. 7.7; Ov. *Met.* 9. 136).

CHRYSAOREUS. "The god with the golden sword or arms," under which surname Zeus had a temple in Caria (Strab. 14. 660).

CLARIUS. A surname as the god who distributes things by lot (Aeschyl. *Suppl.* 360). A hill near Tegea was sacred to him under this name.

CONIUS. "The god who excites or makes dust," a surname from an unearthed temple in the arx of Megara (Paus. 1. 40.5).

CORYPHAEUS. A surname to designate the highest or supreme god (Paus. 2. 4.5).

CROCEATAS. A surname derived from Croceae near Gythium in Laconia (Paus. 3. 21.4).

CRONIDES (CRONION). A patronymic from Cronus, his father (Hom. *Il.* 1. 526, 2. 111).

CTESIUS. "The protector of property," a surname at Phlyus (Athen. 11. 473).

DICTAEUS. A surname derived from Mt. Dicte in the eastern part of Crete.

DIESPITER. A surname of Jupiter as being the father of light.

DODONAIS. A surname from Dodona in Epeirus near Mt. Tomarus. At Dodona, Zeus was mainly a prophetic god, and the oak tree was sacred to him.

DOMIDUCUS. A surname of Jupiter at Rome as the god of marriage, who conducted the bride into the house of the bridegroom.

ELEUTHERIUS. A name meaning the deliverer (Plut. *Quaest.Conviv.* 7; Pind. *Ol.* 12. 1; Strab. 9. 412; Tacit. *Ann.* 15. 64).

ELICIUS. A surname of Jupiter at Rome having to do with the Etruscan prayers and sacrifices which called forth (*eliciebant*) lightning or invited Jupiter to send lightning.

EPIDOTES. "The liberal giver," a surname at Mantineia and Sparta (Paus. 8. 9.1).

EPOPSIUS. A surname meaning superintendent (Apollon.Rhod. 2. 1124).

EUXEINOS (See GENETAEUS)

EVANEMUS. "The giver of favorable wind," a surname at Sparta, where he had a sanctuary (Paus. 3. 13.5).

FERETRIUS. A surname of Jupiter, which is probably derived from *ferire,* to strike. Persons who took an oath called upon Jupiter to strike them, as they struck the victim they sacrificed to him, if they swore falsely. Others derived it from *ferre,* because he was the giver of peace, or because people dedicated (*ferebant*) to him *spolia omnia* (Liv. 1. 10; Propert. 4. 10.46).

FULGURIUS (FULGURATOR). A surname of Jupiter as presider over changes in the heavens. He had a temple erected to him under the name of Jupiter Fulgurius at Rome.

FULMINATOR. A surname of Jupiter as presider over changes in the heavens.

GAMELIUS. A surname of Jupiter as presiding over marriages.

GENETAEUS. A surname derived from Cape Genetus on the Black Sea, where he was worshipped as Euxeinos, the hospitable, and where he had a sanctuary (Apollon.Rhod. 2. 378, 1009; Val. Flacc. 5. 148; Strab. 12. 548).

HECALUS (HECALEIUS). A surname from Hecale, a poor old woman who extended hospitality to Theseus and agreed to offer up sacrifices for his safe return from his encounter with the Marathonian bull. She died before he returned, and he ordered the inhabitants of Attica to sacrifice to her and to Zeus (Plut. *Thes.* 14; Ov. *Rem.Am.* 747).

HECATOMBAEUS. A surname in Gortyn in Crete.

HERCIUS. A surname of Jupiter at Rome as

the protector of property (from *herctum,* inheritance).

HETAEREIUS. "The protector of companies or associations of friends," a surname of Zeus, to whom Jason was believed to have offered the first sacrifices, when the Argonauts were assembled for their expedition (Athen. 13. 572).

HOMAGYRIUS. "The god of the assembly or league," a surname of Zeus, under which he was worshipped at Aegium on the northwestern coast of Peloponnesus, where Agamemnon was believed to have assembled the Greek chiefs to deliberate on the war against Troy. Under this name Zeus was also worshipped as the protector of the Achaean League (Paus. 7. 24.1).

HOMOLOIUS. A surname from Homolois, a priestess of Enyo.

HOSPITALIS. A surname given to Jupiter among the Romans, the same as the Xenios of the Greeks. The god was so called because he presided over hospitality and punished every violation of its most sacred laws (Cic. *Ep.ad Q.Frat.* 2. 12).

HYES. "The moist or fertilizing god," a surname of Zeus as the sender of rain.

HYETIUS. As HYES. Under this name he had an altar at Argos and a statue in the grove of Trophonius near Lebadeia (Paus. 2. 19.7, 9. 39.3).

HYPATUS. A surname meaning the most high. An altar of Zeus Hypatus existed at Athens in front of the Erechtheum, and only cakes could be offered to him at the altar (Paus. 1. 26.6, 8. 2.1). Zeus Hypatus was also worshipped at Sparta (3. 17.3) and at Glisas near Sparta (9. 19.3).

ICMAEUS. A surname at Cos. Aristaeus delivered the inhabitants of Cos from a destructive drought by erecting an altar to Zeus Icmaeus.

IDAEUS. A surname of Zeus, probably from Mt. Ida, his birthplace (Hom. *Il.* 16. 605).

IMPERATOR. A surname of Jupiter, under which name victorious generals celebrated their triumphs. He was worshipped especially under this name at Praeneste.

INVICTUS. As IMPERATOR.

ITHOMATAS. A surname derived from the Messenian hill of Ithome, where the god had a sanctuary and where an annual festival, the Ithomaea, was celebrated in his honor (Paus. 4. 33.2).

LABRADEUS. A surname of Zeus in Caria. The word is derived from *labrys,* a hatchet, which Zeus' statue held in its hand. The hatchet originally belonged to the queen of the Amazons, and from her conqueror, Heracles, passed into the hands of Omphale, queen of Lydia, and of her descendants on the throne till the age of Candaules, when it was given to the Carians and exchanged for the sceptre in the hand of Zeus' statue. Some, however, suppose that Zeus is called Labradeus because rain proceeded from him.

LABRANDEUS. A surname of Zeus Stratius, which he derived from a temple he had at Labranda (Herod. 5. 119; Strab. 14. 659; Plut. *Quaest.Gr.* 46).

LAPERSIUS. A surname derived from the Attic demos of Lapersae (Lycoph. 1369).

LAPHYSTIUS. A surname derived from Mt. Laphystius in Boeotia, where he had an altar, or from the verb *laphyssein,* signifying "the voracious," in reference to the human sacrifices which were offered to him in early times (Paus. 1. 24.2, 9. 34.4).

LAPIS. "The stone," a surname of Jupiter at Rome. It was formerly believed that Jupiter Lapis was a stone statue of the god, or originally a rude stone serving as a symbol, around which people assembled for the purpose of worshipping Jupiter. But it is now generally acknowledged that the pebble or flint stone was the symbol of lightning, and that, therefore, in some representations of Jupiter, he held a stone in his hand instead of a thunderbolt.

LARISSAEUS. A surname derived from the arx Larissa at Argos (Paus. 2. 24.4; Strab. 9. 440, 14. 649).

LATIALIS (LATIARIS). A surname of Jupiter

as the protecting divinity of Latium (Liv. 21. 63, 22. 1).

LECHEATES. "Protector of childbed," a surname of Zeus, who, as father of Athena, was worshipped under this name at Aliphera (Paus. 8. 26.4).

LEUCAEUS. A surname under which he was worshipped at Lepreus in Elis (Paus. 5. 5.4).

LIBERATOR. A surname of Jupiter, answering to the Greek Eleutherius, to whom Augustus built a temple on the Aventine (Tacit. *Ann.* 15. 64, 16. 35).

LIMENIA (LIMENITES, LIMINITIS, or LIMENOSCOPUS). A surname as protector of the harbor.

LUCERIUS (LUCETIUS). "Giver of light," a surname of Jupiter, found especially among the Oscans.

LYCAEUS (LYCEUS). A surname given to him by Lycaon, a son of Pelasgus, who built the first and most ancient town of Lycosura. He erected a temple there and instituted the festival of the Lyceia in honor of him. He further offered to him bloody sacrifices and, among others, his own son, in consequence of which he was metamorphosed into a wolf (Paus. 8. 2.1, 38.1; Callim. *Hymn.in Jov.* 4; Ov. *Met.* 1. 218). No one was allowed to enter the temple, and if anyone forced his way in, he was believed to stay inside for one year and to lose his shadow (Paus. 8. 2.1, 38.4; Pind. *Ol.* 13. 154). According to others, those who entered were stoned to death by the Arcadians or were called stags and obliged to take flight to save their lives (Plut. *Quaest.Gr.* 39).

MAEMACTES. "The stormy," a surname of Zeus, from which the name of the Attic month Maemacterion was derived (Plut. *De Ir. Cohib.* 9).

MARIANUS. A surname given to Jupiter, from a temple built to his honor by Marius at Rome. It was in this temple that the Roman senate assembled to recall Cicero, a circumstance said to have been communicated to him in a dream.

MECHANEUS. A surname as skilled in inventing, at Argos (Paus. 2. 22.3).

MEILICHIUS. A surname meaning the god that can be propitiated, or the gracious. The name was applied to Zeus as the protector of those who honored him with propitiatory sacrifices. At Athens, cakes were offered to him every year at the festival of the Diasia (Thuc. 1. 126; Xenoph. *Anab.* 7. 7.4). Altars were erected to Zeus Meilichius on the Cephissus (Paus. 1. 37.3), at Sicyon (2. 9.6), and at Argos (2. 20.1; Plut. *De Ir.Cohib.* 9).

MESSAPEUS. Under this name he had a sanctuary between Amyclae and Mt. Taygetus. It was said to have been derived from a priest of the name of Messapeus (Paus. 3. 20.3).

MOIRAGETES. "The guide or leader of fate," a surname at Delphi (Paus. 10. 24.4).

MORIUS. "The protector of the sacred olive trees," a surname of Zeus (Soph. *Oed.Col.* 705).

NEMEIUS. "The Nemeian," under which surname he had a sanctuary at Argos with a bronze statue, the work of Lysippus, where games were celebrated in his honor (Paus. 2. 20.3, 24.2).

OGOA. The Carian name of Zeus at Mysala, in whose temple a sea wave was seen from time to time (Paus. 8. 10.3). Strabo (14. 659) calls the god of Mysala, in the Carian dialect, Osogo.

OLYMPIUS. A surname meaning the Olympian (Hom. *Il.* 1. 353).

OMBRIUS. "The rain giver," under which surname Zeus had an altar on Mt. Hymettus in Attica (Paus. 1. 32.3; comp. Hes. *Op.et D.* 587, 620).

OPITULUS. A surname of Jupiter because he extended his assistance to mankind.

OSOGO (See OGOA)

PANHELLENIUS. "The god common to, or worshipped by, all the Hellenes or Greeks," a surname of the Dodonean Zeus, whose worship had been transplanted by the Hellenes in the emigration from Thessaly to Aegina. Subsequently, when the name Hellenes was applied to all the Greeks, the meaning of the god's surname likewise became more extensive, and it was derived from the propitiatory sacrifices which Aeacus was said to have offered on behalf of all the Greeks, and by the command of the Delphic oracle, for the purpose of averting a famine (Paus. 1. 44.13).

PANOMPHAEUS. "The author of all signs and omens," a surname under which he had a sanctuary on the Hellespont between capes Rhoeteum and Sigeum (Hom. *Il.* 8. 250; Ov. *Met.* 11. 198).

PAPAEUS (PAPAS). "The father," a surname among the Scythians (Herod. 4. 59).

PARNETHIUS. A surname derived from Mt. Parnes in Attica, on which there was a bronze statue of the god (Paus. 1. 32.2).

PECUNIA. A surname of Jupiter in Rome by which he was characterized as the protector of money.

PENETRALIS. A surname of Jupiter at Rome from being worshipped in the Penetrale, or central part of the house.

PHYXIUS. "The god who protects fugitives," a surname in Thessaly (Paus. 2. 21.3, 3. 17.8).

PISTIUS. "The god of faith and fidelity," a surname of Zeus (Dionys. 2. 49; Eurip. *Med.* 170).

PISTOR. "The baker," a surname at Rome, where its origin was thus related: when the Gauls were besieging Rome, the god suggested to the besieged the idea of throwing loaves of bread among the enemies to make them believe that the Romans had plenty of provisions and thus cause them to give up the siege (Ov. *Fast.* 6. 359, 394).

PLUVIUS. "The sender of rain," a surname of Jupiter among the Romans, to whom sacrifices were offered during protracted droughts.

POLIEUS. "The protector of the city," under which surname he had an altar on the acropolis at Athens. Upon this altar barley and wheat were strewn, which were consumed by the bull about to be sacrificed to the god. The priest who killed the victim threw away the ax as soon as he had struck the fatal blow, and the ax then was brought before a court of justice (Paus. 1. 24.4, 28.11).

PRAEDATOR. A surname of Jupiter, under which victorious generals celebrated their triumphs.

PRODIGIALIS. A surname of Jupiter as the sender of prodigies (Plaut. *Amphitr.* 2. 10.107).

SABAZIUS. A surname from his identification with this Phrygian agricultural divinity, a son of Rhea or Cybele (Aristoph. *Av.* 873).

SATURNUS. "A son of Saturn," a patronymic of Jupiter (Virg. *Aen.* 4. 372, 5. 799).

SERENATOR. A surname of Jupiter as presider over one or another of changes in the heavens.

SOSPES (SISPES). "The saving god," which surname sometimes appears in inscriptions as Sispes.

SOTER. "The savior," a surname in Argos (Paus. 2. 20.5), at Troezen (2. 31.14), in Laconia (3. 23.6), at Messene (4. 31.5), at Mantineia (8. 9.1), at Megalopolis (8. 30.5; comp. Aristoph. *Ran.* 1433; Plin. *H.N.* 34. 8).

STATOR. A surname of Jupiter at Rome, describing him as staying the Romans in their flight from an enemy, and generally in preserving the existing order of things (Liv. 1. 12, 10. 37; Cic. *Cat.* 1. 13; Senec. *De Benef.* 4. 7; Plin. *H.N.* 2. 53; August. 3. 13). When the Sabines drove the Romans before them and all seemed lost, Romulus prayed to Jupiter Stator, whereupon the Romans took courage and returned again to combat.

STHENIUS. "The powerful or the strengthening," under which surname he had an altar in a rock near Hermione, where Aegeus concealed the sword and shoes, which were found there by Theseus after he had lifted up the rock (Paus. 2. 32.7, 34.6).

STRATIUS. "The warlike," a surname of Zeus (Strab. 14. 659; Herod. 5. 119).

TARANIS. A name of Jupiter among the Gauls, to whom human sacrifices were offered.

TARPEIUS. A surname of Jupiter from his position at the top of heights from which he regarded the forum, the city of Rome, and the whole of Latium.

TERMINALIS (TERMINUS). A surname of Jupiter at Rome, as protector of boundaries, not only of personal property but also of the state. His worship preceded that of the god Terminus, but some, particularly Dionysus, suppose that Jupiter and Terminus are the same divinity (Dionys. 2).

TONANS. A surname of Jupiter as presider over changes of the heavens.

TONITRUALIS. As TONANS.

TRIUMPHATOR. A surname of Jupiter, under which victorious generals celebrated their triumphs.

URIUS. "Sender of favorable wind," a surname of Jupiter (Cic. *In Verr.* 4. 57).

VICTOR. As TRIUMPHATOR.

XENIOS. "Presider over hospitality and protector of strangers," a surname of Zeus in Greece (cf. HOSPITALIS in Rome) (Hom. *Od.* 14. 389; Cic. *Ep.ad Q.Frat.* 2. 12; Paus. 3. 11).

ZYGIUS. A surname of Zeus as presiding over marriage.

Heroic Expeditions

ARGONAUTS

Argo—Passenger List

ACASTUS, son of Pelias and Anaxibia, from Iolcus (Apollon. Rhod. 1. 224; Apollod. 1. 9.10).

ADMETUS, son of Pheres and Clymene, from Pherae in Thessaly (Apollon. Rhod. 1. 47; Apollod. 1. 9.16).

AETHALIDES, son of Hermes and Eupolemeia, from near the river Amphryaus, was the herald of the Argonauts (Apollon. Rhod. 1. 51).

AMPHIDAMAS, son of Aleus, from Arcadia (Apollon. Rhod. 1. 162).

AMPHION, son of Hyperasius, from Pellene (Apollon. Rhod. 1. 176).

AMPHISTRATUS and his brother, Rhecas, charioteers of the Dioscuri, were believed to have taken part in the expedition of Jason to Colchis, and to have occupied a part of that country which was called, after them, Heniochia, which signifies a charioteer (Strab. 11. 495). Pliny (*H.N.* 6. 5) calls them Amphitus and Thelchius.

AMPHITUS (See AMPHISTRATUS)

ANCAEUS (1), son of Lycurgus, from Maenalus in Arcadia (Apollon. Rhod. 1. 164).

ANCAEUS (2), son of Poseidon, from Samos (Apollon. Rhod. 1. 187).

AREIUS, son of Bias, from Argos (Apollon. Rhod. 1. 121).

ARGUS, son of Arestor, was builder of the Argo under the direction of Athena (Apollon. Rhod. 1. 112, 226).

ARMENIUS was one of the Argonauts, who was believed to have been a native of Rhodes, or of Armenion, in Thessaly, and to have settled in the country which was called, after him, Armenia (Strab. 11. 530).

ASCALAPHUS, son of Ares and Astyoche, from Orchomenos (Apollod. 1. 9.16).

ASTERION, son of Cometes, Pyremus, or Priscus, from Peiresiae (Apollon. Rhod. 1. 35).

ASTERIUS, son of Hyperasius, from Pellene (Apollon. Rhod. 1. 177).

AUGEAS, son of Helios and lord of the Eleans (Apollon. Rhod. 1. 173).

AUTOLYCUS (1), son of Deimachus or Tricca in Thessaly, joined the Argonauts at Sinope after having gone astray in the expedition with Heracles against the Amazons (Apollon. Rhod. 2. 955). His brothers, Deileon and Phlogius, also joined the expedition.

AUTOLYCUS (2), son of Hermes, a resident on Mt. Parnassus (Apollod. 2. 4.9).

AZORUS was helmsman of the Argo and is said to have built the Pelagonian town of Azoros.

BUTES, son of Teleon of Attica (Apollon. Rhod. 1. 90).

CAENEUS, son of Elatus and Hippeia, from Larissa in Thessaly (Ov. *Met.* 12. 497).

CALAIS (See ZETES)

CANTHUS, son of Canethus and grandson of Abas, from Cerinthus in Euboea (Apollon. Rhod. 1. 75; Apollod. 3. 8.1).

CASTOR (See DIOSCURI)

CEPHEUS, son of Aleus and Neaera, from Tegea in Arcadia, of which he was king (Apollon. Rhod. 1. 162).

CLYTIUS, son of Eurytus of Oechalia, was one of the Argonauts and was killed either by Heracles or Aeetes during the expedition (Apollon. Rhod. 1. 86).

CORONUS, son of Caeneus, from Gyrton (Apollon. Rhod. 1. 56).

DEILEON (See AUTOLYCUS [1])

DEUCALION, son of Minos and Pasiphae, from Crete (Apollod. 3. 1.2, 3.1; Diod. 4. 60).

DIOSCURI (Castor and Polydeuces) from Sparta (Apollon. Rhod. 1. 149).

ECHION, son of Hermes and Antianeira, from Alope, with his twin brother, Erytus (or Eurytus) took part in the expedition of the Argonauts (Apollon. Rhod. 1. 49; Apollod. 1. 9.16; Val. Flacc. 1. 439).

ERGINUS, son of Poseidon, from Miletus (Apollon. Rhod. 1.186).

ERIBOTES (See EURYBATES)

EUPHEMUS, son of Poseidon, from Taenarum, was helmsman of the Argo and by a power which his father granted him he could walk on the sea just as on firm ground (Apollon. Rhod. 1. 182).

EURYALUS, son of Mecisteus, of Thebes (Apollod. 1. 9.16).

EURYBATES (ERIBOTES), son of Teleon, was skilled in medical art and dressed the wound which Oileus received from one of the Stymphalian birds (Apollon. Rhod. 1. 73, 2. 1040; Val. Flacc. 1. 402).

EURYDAMAS, son of Ctimenus, from Ctimene near the lake of Xynia (Apollon. Rhod. 1. 67). He has also been called a son of Irus and Demonassa.

EURYTION, son of Irus and Demonassa (Apollon. Rhod. 1. 71).

EURYTUS (ERYTUS) (See ECHION)

GLAUCUS, son of Copeus (or of Polybus, Anthedon, or Poseidon), from Anthedon in Boeotia accompanied the Argonauts as their steersman. He is also said to have built the Argo. In the sea fight of Jason against the Tyrrhenians, Glaucus alone remained unhurt; he sank to the bottom of the sea, where he became a marine deity and was of service to the Argonauts thereafter.

HERACLES, son of Zeus and Alcmene, undertook an expedition to Colchis, which brought him in connection with the Argonauts (Apollon. Rhod. 1. 126; Apollod. 1. 9.16; Herod. 7. 193).

HIPPALCMUS was one of the Argonauts.

HYLAS, son of Theiodamas, king of the Dryopes was a favorite of Heracles, who took the boy with him when he joined the expedition of the Argonauts (Apollon. Rhod. 1. 131).

IALMENUS, son of Lycus and Pernis is mentioned among the Argonauts (Apollod. 3. 10.8; Paus. 9. 37).

IDAS, son of Aphareus, from Arene (Apollon. Rhod. 1. 155).

IDMON, son of Apollo and Asteria, from Argos, was one of the soothsayers who accompanied the Argonauts (Apollon. Rhod. 1. 140).

IPHICLUS (1) (IPHICLES), son of Phylacus (or of Cephalus) and uncle of Jason, from Phylace (Apollon. Rhod. 1. 43).

IPHICLUS (2) (IPHICLES), son of Thestius, from Calydon (Apollon. Rhod. 1. 201).

IPHIS, son of Sthenelaus and one of the Argonauts who fell in the battle with Aeetes (Val. Flacc. 1. 441; Diod. 4. 48).

IPHITUS (1), son of Eurytus of Oechalia (Apollon. Rhod. 1. 86; Hom. *Od.* 21. 14; Apollod. 2. 6.1; Paus. 3. 15.2).

IPHITUS (2), son of Naubolus, from Phocis (Pytho) (Apollon. Rhod. 1. 207; Hom. *Il.* 2. 518, 17. 306; Paus. 10. 4.1; Apollod. 1. 9.16).

JASON, son of Aeson, was the leader of the Argonauts in the quest for the Golden Fleece (Apollon. Rhod. 1. 1–18).

LAERTES, son of Arceisius and father of Odysseus, took part in the expedition of the Argonauts (Apollod. 1. 9.16).

LAOCOON, brother of Oeneus, from Calydon (Apollon. Rhod. 1. 192).

LAODOCUS (LEODOCUS), son of Bias and Pero, from Argos (Apollon. Rhod. 1. 199).

LEITUS, son of Alector or Alectryon, from Boeotia (Apollod. 1. 9.16).

LYNCEUS, son of Aphareus and brother of Idas, from Arene, was one of the Argonauts, famous for his keen sight (Apollon. Rhod. 1. 54; Apollod. 1. 8.2, 4.17, 3. 10.3).

MELEAGER, son of Oeneus, of Calydon (Apollon. Rhod. 1. 191).

MENOETIUS, son of Actor and Aegina and father of Patroclus, resided at Opus (Apollon. Rhod. 1. 69; Hom. *Il.* 11. 785, 16. 14, 18. 326).

MOPSUS, son of Ampyx, or Ampycus, of Titaresia, was the famous prophet of the Argonauts (Apollon. Rhod. 1. 65).

NAUPLIUS, son of Clytoneus, was a descendant of Nauplius, son of Poseidon (Apollon. Rhod. 1. 134).

NELEUS. Some called him the son of Hippocoon and mentioned him among the Argonauts.

NESTOR, son of Neleus and Chloris, of Pylos (Ov. *Met.* 8. 313; Val. Flacc. 1. 380).

OILEUS, son of Hodoedocus, was king of the Locrians and the father of Ajax (Apollon. Rhod. 1. 74; Apollod. 5. 10.8).

ORPHEUS, son of Oeagrus and Calliope, from Pieria (Apollon. Rhod. 1. 24). Pindar describes him among the Argonauts as the celebrated harp player, father of songs, sent forth by Apollo (*Pyth.* 4. 315).

PALAEMON (PALAEMONIUS), a son of Hephaestus, or Aetolus, or Lernus (Apollon. Rhod. 1. 202; Apollod. 1. 9.16).

PELEUS, son of Aeacus, from Phthia (Apollon. Rhod. 1. 90).

PENELEOS, son of Hippalcmus, from Boeotia (Apollod. 1. 9.16, 3. 108).

PERICLYMENUS, son of Neleus and Chloris, from Pylos (Apollon. Rhod. 1. 156).

PHALERUS, son of Alcon, from Attica, was founder of Gyrton (Apollon. Rhod. 1. 97).

PHILAMMON, son of Apollo and Chione. According to some, it was Philammon, not Orpheus, who accompanied the Argonauts.

PHLIAS, a son of Dionysus and Chthonophyle, also called Phlius, was a native of Araithyrea in Argolis (Apollon. Rhod. 1. 115; Paus 2. 12.6; Val. Flacc. 1. 411).

PHLOGIUS (See AUTOLYCUS [1])

Jason

POEAS, a son of Phylacus or Thaumacus, was said to have killed Talaus in Crete with an arrow (Apollod. 1. 9.26).

POLYDEUCES (See DIOSCURI)

POLYPHEMUS, son of Elatus (or Eilatus) or Poseidon and Hippia, from Larissa, was one of the Argonauts but was left behind by them in Mysia, where he founded Cios (Apollod. 1. 9.16, 19; Hom. *Il.* 1. 264; Val.Flacc. 1. 457).

RHECAS (See AMPHISTRATUS)

STAPHYLUS, a son of Dionysus and Ariadne or of Theseus and Ariadne (Plut. *Thes.* 20), was one of the Argonauts (Apollod. 1. 9.16).

TALAUS, son of Bias and Pero and king of Argos (Apollon.Rhod. 1. 118).

TELAMON, a son of Aeacus and Endeis, from Salamis (Apollod. 1. 8.2, 9.16, 3. 12.7; Paus. 1. 42.4).

THELCHIUS (See AMPHISTRATUS)

THESEUS, son of Aegeus, king of Athens, and Aethra. He was, by some, named as one of the Argonauts (the anachronism of the attempt of Medea to poison him at Aegeus' court notwithstanding). Apollonius Rhodius says: "Meanwhile Theseus, finest of Attic line, who had gone with Peirithous into the underworld, was kept a prisoner in unseen bonds below the earth at Taenarum. Had this pair been with them, the Argonauts would indeed have had a lighter task" (Apollon.Rhod. 1. 101–5, trans. E. V. Rieu [Harmondsworth, Middlesex, Eng.: Penguin, 1975]).

TIPHYS, a son of Phorbas, or of Agnius and Hyrmine, of Siphae (Tiphae), was helmsman of the ship Argo (Apollon.Rhod. 1. 105; Paus. 9. 32.3; Apollod. 1. 9.22).

ZETES, a son of Boreas and Oreithyia and a brother of Calais, from Thrace, is mentioned with his brother among the Argonauts (Apollon.Rhod. 1. 212; Apollod. 1. 9.16).

THE CALYDONIAN BOAR HUNT

The Hunting Party

ACASTUS, son of Pelius, king of Iolcus and Anaxibia (Ov. *Met.* 8. 305).

ADMETUS, son of Pheres, king of Pherae in Thessaly (Apollod. 1. 8.2).

AMPHIARAUS, son of Oicles, from Argos (Apollod. 1. 8.2).

AMYNTOR, son of Ormenus of Eleon in Thessaly (Ov. *Met.* 8. 307, 12. 364).

ANCAEUS, son of Lycurgus, from Arcadia (Apollod. 1. 8.2).

ATALANTA, daughter of Schoeneus, from Arcadia, the only woman to take part in the hunt (Apollod. 1. 8.2).

CASTOR (See DIOSCURI)

CEPHEUS, son of Lycurgus, from Arcadia (Apollod. 1. 8.2).

CTEATUS, son of Actor and Molione (Ov. *Met.* 8. 308; Hom. *Il.* 23. 638).

DEUCALION, son of Minos, from Crete (Apollod. 3. 1.2, 3.1).

DIOSCURI, Castor and Polydeuces, sons of Zeus and Leda, from Lacedaemon (Apollod. 1. 8.2).

DRYAS, son of Ares, from Calydon (Apollod. 1. 8.2).

ECHION, son of Hermes, from Alope (Apollod. 1. 8.2).

EUPHEMUS, a son of Poseidon, from Taenarum.

EURYTION, son of Irus and Demonassa.

EURYTUS (1), son of Actor and Molione (Ov. *Met.* 8. 308; Hom. *Il.* 23. 638).

EURYTUS (2), son of Hermes, from Alope (Apollod. 1. 8.2).

HERACLES, son of Zeus and Alcmena.

HIPPASUS, son of Eurytus (Ov. *Met.* 8. 313).

HIPPOCOON. Ovid (*Met.* 8. 314) mentions three sons—no names given—among the Calydonian hunters. Apollodorus calls his sons: Alcinus, Alcon, Bucolus, Doryclus, Enarophorus, Eurytus, Eutiches, Hippocorystes, Hippothous, Lycaethus, Scaeus, and Tebrus.

HYLEUS was a hunter who was killed by the Calydonian boar (Apollod. 1. 8.2; Ov. *Met.* 8. 312).

IDAS, son of Aphareus, from Messene (Apollod. 1. 8.2; Ov. *Met.* 8. 305).

IPHICLES (IPHICLUS) (1), son of Amphitryon, from Thebes (Apollod. 1. 8.2).

IPHICLES (IPHICLUS) (2), son of Thestius, from Calydon (Apollod. 1. 8.2).

JASON, son of Aeson, from Iolcus (Apollod. 1. 8.2).

LAERTES, son of Arceisius and father of Odysseus.

LELEX was one of the Calydonian hunters (Ov. *Met.* 8. 312).

LEUCIPPUS, son of Perieres and Gorgophone (Ov. *Met.* 8. 306).

LYNCEUS, son of Aphareus, from Messene (Apollod. 1. 8.2; Ov. *Met.* 8. 305).

MELEAGER, son of Oeneus, from Calydon, slew the Calydonian boar and dedicated the spear which made the kill in the temple of Apollo at Sicyon (Apollod. 1. 8.2; Paus. 2. 7.8).

MOPSUS, son of Ampyx, or Ampycus, from Titaresia (Ov. *Met.* 8. 316).

NESTOR, son of Neleus and Chloris, from Pylos (Ov. *Met.* 8. 313).

PANOPEUS, son of Phocus (Ov. *Met.* 8. 312).

PELAGON, from Lycia (Hom. *Il.* 5. 695; Ov. *Met.* 8. 300).

PELEUS, son of Aeacus and Endeis, from Phthia in Thessaly (Apollod. 1. 8.2).

PHOENIX, son of Amyntor, king of the Dolopes (Ov. *Met.* 8. 307).

PEIRITHOUS, son of Ixion, from Larissa (Apollod. 1. 8.2).

POLYDEUCES (See DIOSCURI)

TELAMON, son of Aeacus and Endeis, from Salamis (Apollod. 1. 8.2).

THESEUS, son of Aegeus, king of Athens, and Aethra (Apollod. 1. 8.2).

THE TROJAN WAR

Greek Forces and Allies

ACHILLES was leader, with fifty ships, of the Myrmidons in the war with Troy (Hom. *Il.* 2. 685).

AGAMEMNON, son of Atreus and Aerope, was commander-in-chief of the Greek forces in the war with Troy. He led the forces of Mycenae, Corinth, and neighboring cities in one hundred ships (Hom. *Il.* 2. 575).

AGAPENOR led the Arcadians to Troy in sixty ships (Hom. *Il.* 2. 609).

AJAX (1), son of Oileus, was captain of the Locrian fleet of forty ships (Hom. *Il.* 2. 528).

AJAX (2), son of Telamon, led twelve ships from Salamis (Hom. *Il.* 2. 558).

AMPHIMACHUS, son of Cteatus, sailed with ten ships to Troy, with part of the Epeian forces (Hom. *Il.* 2. 620).

ANTIPHUS (See PHEIDIPPUS)

ARCESILAUS was leader of the Boeotians in the Trojan War with ten ships (Hom. *Il.* 2. 495).

ASCALAPHUS, with Ialmenus, his brother, led the Minyans of Orchomenos against Troy in thirty ships (Hom. *Il.* 2. 511).

AUTOMEDON sailed with ten ships against Troy.

CLONIUS was one of the leaders of the Boeotians; he was captain of ten ships (Hom. *Il.* 2. 495).

DEMOPHON, son of Theseus, accompanied the Greeks against Troy and there liberated his grandmother, Aethra, who was with Helen as a slave (Paus. 10. 25.2).

DIOMEDES, king of Argos, led a fleet of eighty ships to the Trojan War (Hom. *Il.* 2. 570).

DIORES, son of Amarynces and one of the leaders of the Epeians, sailed to Troy with ten ships (Hom. *Il.* 2. 622).

ELEPHENOR, son of Chalcodon and prince of the Abantes in Euboea, sailed against Troy in fifty ships (Hom. *Il.* 2. 540).

EPEIUS went with thirty ships from the Cyclades to Troy.

EPISTROPHUS (See SCHEDIUS)

EUMELUS, son of Admetus, went with eleven ships from Pherae, Boebe, Glaphyrae, and Iolcus to Troy. He was distinguished for his excellent horses, which had once been under the care of Apollo, and with which Eumelus would have gained the prize at the funeral games of Patroclus, if his chariot had not been broken (Hom. *Il.* 2. 711, 764, 23. 375, 536; Hom. *Od.* 4. 798; Strab. 9. 436).

EURYALUS, son of Mecisteus, with Diomedes and Sthenelus, led the Argives against Troy (Hom. *Il.* 2. 565).

EURYPYLUS, son of Eusemon and Ops, led the men of Ormenion to Troy with forty ships. He slew many Trojans, was wounded by Paris, but was nursed and cured by Patroclus (Hom. *Il.* 2. 841, 15. 390).

GUNEUS from Cyphos led twenty-two ships, manned by the Enienes and Peraibians, to Troy (Hom. *Il.* 2. 748).

HELORUS was a son of the Scythian, Istrus. Later traditions state that he accompanied Telephus in the war against Troy.

IALMENUS (See ASCALAPHUS)

IDOMENEUS, with Meriones, led the Cretans in eighty ships against Troy (Hom. *Il.* 2. 651, 4. 254).

LEITUS, son of Alector or Alectryon, was one of the commanders of the Boeotians in the war against Troy (Hom. *Il.* 2. 494; 17. 602; Paus. 9. 4.3).

LEONTEUS, son of Coronus and prince of the Lapithae, in conjunction with Polypoetes, led the Lapithae in forty ships against Troy (Hom. *Il.* 2. 745).

MACHAON, son of Asclepius by Epeione, with his brother, Podaleirius, went to Troy with thirty ships, commanding the men who came from Tricca, Ithome, and Oechalia (Hom. *Il.* 2. 728).

MEDON, son of Oileus, took over the command of the fleet from Methone, Thaumacia, Meliboea, and Olizon when Philoctetes was left on Lemnos as a result of a snake bite (Hom. *Il.* 2. 722).

MEGES, son of Phyleus, in forty ships led his bands from Dulichium and the Echinades against Troy (Hom. *Il.* 2. 625; Paus. 10. 25.2).

MENELAUS, brother of Agamemnon, in sixty ships led the inhabitants of Lacedaemon, Pharis, Sparta, Messe, Bryseiae, Amyclae, Helos, Laas, and Oetylus against Troy (Hom. *Il.* 2. 581).

MENESTHEUS, son of Peteus, was an Athenian king who led the Athenians in fifty ships against Troy and surpassed all other mortals in arranging the war steeds and the men for battle (Hom. *Il.* 2. 552).

MENESTHIUS, son of the river god Spercheius, was one of the commanders of the hosts of Achilles (Hom. *Il.* 16. 173).

MERIONES (See IDOMENEUS). Meriones was a son of Molus, half-brother of Idomeneus.

NESTOR sailed with his Pylians in ninety ships to Troy (Hom. *Il.* 2. 591).

NIREUS, from the island of Syme (between Rhodes and Cnidus), commanded three ships and a small number of men against Troy. According to Diodorus (5. 53), he also ruled over Cnidus.

ODYSSEUS joined the Greeks with twelve ships and men from Cephallene, Ithaca, Neriton, Crocyleia, Zacynthus, Samos, and the coast of Epeirus (Hom. *Il.* 2. 303).

PENELEUS was one of the leaders of the Boeotians in the war against Troy (Hom. *Il.* 2. 494).

PHEIDIPPUS, son of Thessalus, the Heracleid, and his brother, Antiphus, led the warriors of the Sporades in thirty ships against Troy (Hom. *Il.* 2. 678).

PHILOCTETES, son of Poeas and Demonassa, led the warriors from Methone, Thaumacia, Meliboea, and Olizon against Troy in seven ships (Hom. *Il.* 2. 720). He did not complete the journey, however, since on the island of Lemnos he was bitten by a snake and was unable to recover from the wound.

PODALEIRIUS (See MACHAON)

PODARCES, a son of Iphiclus and a grandson of Phylacus, was a younger brother of Protesilaus and led the Thessalians of Phylace against Troy (Hom. *Il.* 2. 695; Apollod. 1. 9.12).

POLYPOETES, a son of Peirithous and Hippodameia, was one of the Lapithae, who joined the Greeks in the Trojan War, commanding the men of Argissa, Gyrtone, Orthe, Elone, and Oloosson in forty ships (Hom. *Il.* 2. 738).

POLYXENUS, a son of Agasthenes, was one of the commanders of the Epeians in the war against Troy. He sailed with ten ships (Hom. *Il.* 2. 623).

PROTESILAUS, son of Iphiclus and Astyoche, led the warriors of several Thessalian places against Troy in forty ships (Hom. *Il.* 2. 699).

PROTHOENOR, a son of Areilycus, was one of the leaders of the Boeotians against Troy, sailing in ten ships (Hom. *Il.* 2. 495).

PROTHOUS, a son of Tenthredon, was commander of the forty ships of the Magnetes, who dwelt on Mt. Pelion and near the river Peneius (Hom. *Il.* 2. 758).

SCHEDIUS, son of Iphitus by Hippolyte, was commander of the Phocians in forty ships, and his command was shared by his brother, Epistrophus (Hom. *Il.* 2. 517). Apollodorus (3. 10.8) calls Epistrophus the father of Schedius.

STHENELUS, a son of Capaneus and Evadne, commanded the Argives under Diomedes in the Trojan War (Hom. *Il.* 2. 564).

THALPIUS, a son of Eurytus, was one of the leaders of the Epeians in the Trojan War. He sailed with ten ships (Hom. *Il.* 2. 620; Paus. 5. 3.4).

THOAS, a son of Andraemon and Gorge, was king of Calydon and Pleuron in Aetolia and went with forty ships against Troy (Hom. *Il.* 2. 638).

TLEPOLEMUS, a son of Heracles, joined the Greeks against Troy with nine ships (Hom. *Il.* 2. 653; Apollod. 2. 8.2).

Trojan Allies

ACAMAS was one of the commanders of the Thracians against the Greeks (Hom. *Il.* 2. 845).

ADRASTUS, son of Merops of Percote, with his brother Amphius, led the warriors of Adrastea and Apaesus against the Greeks (Hom. *Il.* 2. 830).

AMPHIMACHUS, son of Nomion, led a host of Carians to the assistance of the Trojans (Hom. *Il.* 2. 870).

AMPHIUS (See ADRASTUS)

ANTIPHUS, son of Talaemenes, was one of the leaders of the Maeonians (Hom. *Il.* 2. 865).

ASCANIUS was one of the leaders of the Phrygians from Ascania (Hom. *Il.* 2. 862).

ASIUS, son of Hyrtacus, ruled several towns near Troy and brought auxiliary forces to aid the Trojans (Hom. *Il.* 2. 835).

ASTEROPAEUS, son of Pelegon, was commander of the Paeonians and an ally of the Trojans (Hom. *Il.* 21. 139).

CHROMIS was one of the leaders of the Mysians (Hom. *Il.* 2. 858).

ENNOMUS, the seer, was one of the leaders of the Mysians (Hom. *Il.* 2. 858).

EPISTROPHUS, one of the chiefs of the Halizoni, assisted the Trojans (Hom. *Il.* 2. 856).

EUPHEMUS, son of Troezenus, was captain of the Ciconian spearmen (Hom. *Il.* 2. 847).

GLAUCUS, son of Hippolochus, led his Lycians from the vicinity of the Xanthus river to the assistance of Priam (Hom. *Il.* 2. 875).

HAEMUS was a son of Ares and an ally of the Trojans.

HIERA was the wife of Telephus and in the Trojan War commanded the Mysian women on horseback.

HIPPOTHOUS, son of Letheus, with his brother Pylaeus led a band of Pelasgian auxiliaries from Larissa to the assistance of the Trojans (Hom. *Il.* 2. 840).

MEMNON, son of Tithonus and Eos, was described as a handsome prince, who with his subject Ethiopians assisted Priam against the Greeks (Hes. *Theog.* 984; Hom. *Od.* 4. 188, 11. 522; Apollod. 3. 12.4).

MENTES was leader of the Cicones in the Trojan War. It was his appearance which Apollo assumed when he went to encourage Hector (Hom. *Il.* 17. 73).

MENTOR, the father of Imbrius and son of Imbrus at Pedaseus, was an ally of the Trojans (Hom. *Il.* 13. 171).

MESTHLES, son of Talaemenes, was one of the leaders of the Maeonians (Hom. *Il.* 2. 865).

NASTES, son of Nomion, led the Carians against the Greeks (Hom. *Il.* 2. 871).

ODIUS, one of the captains of the Halizoni, assisted the Trojans against the Greeks (Hom. *Il.* 2. 856).

OTHRYONEUS was an ally of king Priam from Cabesus. He sued for the hand of Cassandra and promised in return to drive the Greeks from Troy (Hom. *Il.* 13. 363).

PANDARUS, son of Lycaon, a Lycian, commanded the inhabitants of Zeleia on Mt. Ida (Hom. *Il.* 2. 844).

PEIRUS, son of Imbrasus of Aenus, was one of the commanders of the Thracians who were allied with Priam during the Trojan War (Hom. *Il.* 2. 844).

PENTHESILEIA, queen of the Amazons, assisted the Trojans and offered gallant resistance to the Greeks (Ov. *Her.* 21. 118).

PHORCYS, a son of Phaenops, was commander of the Phrygians of Ascania and assisted Priam in the Trojan War (Hom. *Il.* 2. 862).

PYLAEMENES was a king of the Paphlagonians and an ally of Priam in the Trojan War (Hom. *Il.* 2. 850).

PYLAEUS (See HIPPOTHOUS)

PYRAECHMES was an ally of the Trojans and commander of the Paeonian archers from Amydon (Hom. *Il.* 2. 848).

RHESUS was a son of king Eioneus in Thrace and an ally of the Trojans. He possessed horses white as snow and swift as the wind, which were carried off at night by Odysseus and Diomedes, the latter of whom murdered Rhesus in his sleep (Hom. *Il.* 10. 435, 495; Virg. *Aen.* 1. 469).

SARPEDON, a son of Zeus and Laodameia, was an ally of the Trojans from Lycia, where he was a prince (Hom. *Il.* 2. 876).

CASUALTIES

Greeks

ACHILLES, according to the usual story, was slain by Paris by an arrow wound in his vulnerable heel. His death is foretold in the *Iliad* (22. 359–60), where his slayers are named as Paris and Apollo.

AESYMNUS was slain by Hector (Hom. *Il.* 11. 303).

AGELAUS was slain by Hector (Hom. *Il.* 11. 303).

ALCMAON, son of Thestor, was killed by Sarpedon (Hom. *Il.* 12. 398).

AMPHIMACHUS, son of Cteatus, was killed by Hector (Hom. *Il.* 13. 190).

ANCHIALUS was slain by Hector (Hom. *Il.* 5. 610).

ANTILOCHUS, son of Nestor, was slain by Memnon (Pind. *Pyth.* 6. 30).

APHAREUS, son of Caletor, was killed by Aeneas (Hom. *Il.* 13. 540).

ARCESILAUS, friend and comrade of Menestheus and leader of the Boeotians, was slain by Hector (Hom. *Il.* 15. 329).

ASAEUS was slain by Hector (Hom. *Il.* 11. 302).

ASCALAPHUS, son of Ares and leader of the Minyans, was slain by Deiphobus (Hom. *Il.* 13. 321).

AUTONOUS was slain by Hector (Hom. *Il.* 11. 302).

BATHYCLES, son of Chalcon, the richest man among the Myrmidons, was killed by Glaucus, captain of the Lycians (Hom. *Il.* 16. 595).

CLEODORUS, son of Lernus, was killed by Paris (Q.Smyrn. 10. 213).

CLONIUS was killed by Agenor (Hom. *Il.* 15. 337).

COERANUS, a follower and charioteer of Meriones, from Lyctus, was killed by Hector (Hom. *Il.* 17. 611).

CRETHON, son of Diocles of Pherae, was slain by Aeneas (Hom. *Il.* 5. 542; Paus. 4. 30.2).

DEIOCHUS was killed by Paris (Hom. *Il.* 15. 338).

DEIPYRUS was slain by Helenus (Hom. *Il.* 13. 580).

DEMOLEON, son of Hippasus, was slain by Paris (Q.Smyrn. 10. 119).

DEMOLEUS was slain by Aeneas, who offered Demoleus' coat of mail as a prize in the games which he celebrated in Sicily (Virg. *Aen.* 5. 258).

DIORES, captain of the Epeians, son of Amarynceus, was slain by Peirous (Hom. *Il.* 4. 520).

DOLOPS, son of Clytius, was slain by Hector (Hom. *Il.* 11. 302).

ECHIUS, father of Mecisteus, was slain by Polites (Hom. *Il.* 15. 335).

EIONEUS was slain by Hector (Hom. *Il.* 7. 10).

ELEPHENOR, son of Chalcodon, was slain by Agenor (Hom. *Il.* 4. 463).

EPEIGEUS, son of Agacles and a prominent warrior among the Myrmidons, was slain by Hector (Hom. *Il.* 16. 573).

EPIPOLE, daughter of Trachion of Carystus in Euboea, went in the disguise of a man with the Greeks against Troy, but when Palamedes discovered her sex, she was stoned to death by the Greek army.

EUCHENOR, son of Polyidus, the Corinthian prophet, was slain by Paris (Hom. *Il.* 13. 673).

Polyidus revealed to his son that he would either stay home and die from a terrible disease or go to Troy and perish in battle.

EUDORUS, son of Hermes and one of the five leaders of the Myrmidons under Achilles, was sent to accompany Patroclus but was killed by Pyraechmes.

EUENOR of Dulichium was slain by Paris (Q.Smyrn. 1. 275).

HELENUS, son of Oenops, was killed by Hector with the assistance of Ares (Hom. *Il.* 5. 706–7).

HIPPONOUS was killed by Hector (Hom. *Il.* 11. 303).

HYPSENOR, son of Hippasus, was killed by Deiphobus (Hom. *Il.* 13. 407).

IASUS, son of Sphelus and a leader of the Athenians, was killed by Aeneas (Hom. *Il.* 15. 330).

IPHINOUS, son of Dexius, was killed by Glaucus (Hom. *Il.* 7. 17).

LEIOCRITUS, son of Arisbas and follower of Lycomedes was slain by Aeneas (Hom. *Il.* 17. 341).

LEUCAS, comrade of Odysseus, was slain by Antiphus (Hom. *Il.* 4. 490).

LYCOPHRON, son of Mastor, accompanied the Telamonian Ajax against Troy, where he was slain by Hector (Hom. *Il.* 15. 430).

MACHAON, son of Asclepius, was killed by Eurypylus, son of Telephus, and his remains were carried to Messenia by Nestor (Q.Smyrn. 6. 400).

MECISTEUS, son of Echius, was killed by Polydamas (Hom. *Il.* 15. 335).

MEDON, bastard son of Oileus and brother to Ajax, from Phylace, was slain by Aeneas (Hom. *Il.* 15. 330).

MEGES, son of Phyleus, was killed in the Trojan War.

MENESTHES was killed by Hector (Hom. *Il.* 5. 610).

MENESTHIUS, son of Areithous, from Arne, was killed by Paris (Hom. *Il.* 7. 8).

MENIPPUS, who accompanied Protesilaus from Phylace, was killed by the Amazon Clonia (Q.Smyrn. 1. 230).

MOLION was killed by the Amazon Penthesileia (Q.Smyrn. 1. 227).

NIREUS, from the island of Syme, was slain by Eurypylus or Aeneas.

OENOMAUS was killed by Hector with the assistance of Ares (Hom. *Il.* 5. 706–7).

OPHELTIUS was slain by Hector (Hom. *Il.* 11. 303).

OPITES was slain by Hector (Hom. *Il.* 11. 302).

ORESBIUS, from the neighborhood of the Cephissian lake in Boeotia, was slain by Hector with the assistance of Ares (Hom. *Il.* 5. 706–7).

ORESTES, the renowned charioteer, was slain by Hector with the assistance of Ares (Hom. *Il.* 5. 706–7).

ORSILOCHUS, son of Diocles, was slain by Aeneas (Hom. *Il.* 5. 550).

ORUS was slain by Hector (Hom. *Il.* 11. 303).

OTUS of Cyllene, a companion of Meges and chief of the Epeians, was slain by Polydamas (Hom. *Il.* 15. 513).

PALAMEDES, son of Nauplius, was killed by Paris with an arrow. The usual story is that Odysseus falsely accused him of treason, and the Greeks stoned him to death.

PATROCLUS, son of Menoetius and friend of Achilles, was slain in the armor of Achilles by Hector (Hom. *Il.* 16. 857).

PENELEUS, son of Hippalcmus, was slain by Eurypylus (Paus. 9. 5.8).

PERIPHAS, son of Ochesius, was left to die by Ares, when he was attacked by Athena and Diomedes (Hom. *Il.* 5. 853).

PERIPHETES of Mycenae, son of Copreus, was killed by Hector (Hom. *Il.* 15. 638).

PODARCES, son of Iphiclus, was killed by the Amazon Penthesileia (Q.Smyrn. 1. 240).

PROMACHUS, son of Alegenor of Boeotia, was killed by Acamas (Hom. *Il.* 14. 480).

PROTESILAUS, son of Iphiclus and Astyoche, was the first of all the Greeks that was killed by the Trojans, for he was the first who leaped from the ships upon the Trojan coast (Hom. *Il.* 2. 695). According to the common tradition, he was slain by Hector (Lucian *Dial.Mort.* 23.1; Ov. *Met.* 12. 67), but, according to others, he fell by the hand of Achates, of Aeneas, or of Euphorbus.

PROTHOENOR, son of Areilycus, was slain by Polydamas (Hom. *Il.* 14. 450).

SCHEDIUS(1), son of Iphitus and commander of the Phocians at Troy, was slain by Hector (Hom. *Il.* 17. 306; Paus. 10. 4).

SCHEDIUS (2), son of Perimedes, a Phocian, was killed by Hector (Hom. *Il.* 15. 515).

STICHIUS, a leader of the Boeotians, was slain by Hector (Hom. *Il.* 15. 326).

TEUTHRAS, a Greek of Magnesia, was slain by Hector (Hom. *Il.* 5. 705).

THERSANDER was a son of Polyneices and Argeia and one of the Epigoni. After being made king of Thebes, he went with Agamemnon to Troy and was slain in that expedition by Telephus.

THERSITES, son of Agrius, mutilated the body of the Amazon Penthesileia and also insulted Achilles, who slew him.

TLEPOLEMUS, a son of Heracles, was slain by Sarpedon (Hom. *Il.* 5. 660).

TOXAECHMES, a friend of Philoctetes, was killed by Aeneas (Q.Smyrn. 11. 488).

Trojans

ABAS, son of Eurydamas, was slain by Diomedes (Hom. *Il.* 5. 150).

ABLERUS was slain by Antilochus (Hom. *Il.* 6. 35).

ACAMAS(1), son of Eussorus, was killed by Ajax (Hom. *Il.* 6. 8).

ACAMAS(2) was slain by Meriones (Hom. *Il.* 16. 341).

ADAMAS was killed by Meriones (Hom. *Il.* 13. 573).

ADRASTUS (1) was slain by Agamemnon (Hom. *Il.* 6. 65).

ADRASTUS (2) was slain by Patroclus (Hom. *Il.* 16. 694).

AENIUS, a Paeonian, was killed by Achilles (Hom. *Il.* 21. 212).

AESEPUS, son of Bucolion, was killed by Euryalus (Hom. *Il.* 6. 27).

AGASTROPHUS, son of Paeon, was killed by Diomedes (Hom. *Il.* 11. 338).

AGELAUS (1), son of Phradmon, was slain by Diomedes (Hom. *Il.* 8. 258).

AGELAUS (2), son of Hippasus, was slain by Meges (Q.Smyrn. 1. 279).

ALASTOR was slain by Odysseus (Hom. *Il.* 5. 675).

ALCANDRUS was slain by Odysseus (Hom. *Il.* 5. 675).

ALCATHOUS, son of Aesyetes and one of the Trojan leaders, was slain by Idomeneus with the help of Poseidon, who struck Alcathous with blindness and paralysis so that he could not flee (Hom. *Il.* 13. 430).

ALCIBIA, the Amazon, was killed by Diomedes (Q.Smyrn. 1. 260).

AMOPAON, son of Polyaemon, was slain by Teucer (Hom. *Il.* 8. 274).

AMPHICLUS was killed by Meges (Hom. *Il.* 16. 313).

AMPHIMACHUS, son of Nomion, led a host of Carians to the assistance of the Trojans but was thrown into the Scamander by Achilles (Hom. *Il.* 2. 870).

AMPHIUS, son of Selagus, was killed by Ajax (Hom. *Il.* 5. 612).

AMPHOTERUS was killed by Patroclus (Hom. *Il.* 16. 417).

ANTIPHATES was killed by Leonteus (Hom. *Il.* 12. 188).

ANTIPHUS, son of Priam and Hecuba, was killed by Agamemnon (Hom. *Il.* 11. 102).

APISAON (1), son of Phausius, was killed by Eurypylus (Hom. *Il.* 11. 578).

APISAON (2), son of Hippasus from Paeonia, was killed by Lycomedes (Hom. *Il.* 17. 343).

ARCHELOCHUS, son of Antenor, was killed by Ajax (Hom. *Il.* 14. 462).

ARCHEPTOLEMUS, charioteer of Hector, was killed by Teucer (Hom. *Il.* 8. 312).

AREILYCUS was killed by Patroclus (Hom. *Il.* 16. 308).

AREITHOUS, squire to Rhigmus, was killed by Achilles (Hom. *Il.* 20. 488).

ARETAON was slain by Teucer (Hom. *Il.* 6. 34).

ARETUS was killed by Automedon (Hom. *Il.* 17. 522).

ASIUS (1) was a son of Dymas and brother of Hecuba. Apollo assumed the appearance of this Asius when he wanted to stimulate Hector to fight against Patroclus (Hom. *Il.* 16. 715). According to others, he was slain by Ajax.

ASIUS (2), son of Hyrtacus, was killed by Idomeneus (Hom. *Il.* 13. 394).

ASTEROPAEUS, son of Pelegon, was killed by Achilles (Hom. *Il.* 21. 180).

ASTYALUS was killed by Polypoetes (Hom. *Il.* 6. 32).

ASTYNOUS (1) was killed by Diomedes (Hom. *Il.* 5. 142).

ASTYNOUS (2), son of Protiaon, was slain by Neoptolemus.

ASTYPYLUS was killed by Achilles (Hom. *Il.* 21. 211).

ATYMNIUS, son of Amisodorus and comrade of Sarpedon, was killed by Antilochus (Hom. *Il.* 16. 318).

AUTONOUS was slain by Patroclus (Hom. *Il.* 16. 695).

AXION, son of Priam, was slain by Eurypylus, son of Euaemon (Paus. 10. 27).

AXYLUS, son of Teuthras, from Arisbe, was killed by Diomedes (Hom. *Il.* 6. 14–20).

BIENOR was killed by Agamemnon (Hom. *Il.* 11. 93).

CALESIUS, squire and charioteer of Axylus, was slain by Diomedes (Hom. *Il.* 6. 14–20).

CALETOR, son of Clytius, was killed by the Telamonian Ajax (Hom. *Il.* 15. 419).

CEBRIONES, charioteer to Hector and a bastard son of Priam, was killed by a stone thrown by Patroclus (Hom. *Il.* 16. 738).

CHALCON of Cyparissus was in love with the Amazon, Penthesileia, but on hastening to her assistance was killed by Achilles. The Greeks nailed his body to a cross.

CHERSIDAMAS was killed by Odysseus (Hom. *Il.* 11. 425).

CHROMIUS (1), son of Priam, was killed with his brother, Echemmon, by Diomedes (Hom. *Il.* 5. 160).

CHROMIUS (2) was slain by Odysseus (Hom. *Il.* 5. 675).

CHROMIUS (3) was slain by Teucer (Hom. *Il.* 8. 274).

CLEITUS, son of Pisenor and comrade of Polydamas, was killed by Teucer (Hom. *Il.* 15. 444).

CLEOBULUS was killed by Ajax the Lesser (Hom. *Il.* 16. 330).

COERANUS was slain by Odysseus (Hom. *Il.* 5. 675).

COON, son of Antenor, wounded Agamemnon but was later slain by him (Hom. *Il.* 11. 256, 19. 53; Paus. 5. 19.1).

COROEBUS, a Phrygian, son of Mygdon, was one of the suitors of Cassandra and later one of the Trojan allies. He was slain by Neoptolemus or Diomedes (Paus. 9. 27.1; Virg. *Aen.* 2. 341).

CROESMUS was killed by Meges (Hom. *Il.* 15. 521).

CYCNUS, son of Poseidon, was one of the Trojan allies. Poseidon had made him invulnerable to weapons, but Achilles finally strangled him with his own helmet thongs.

DAETOR was slain by Teucer (Hom. *Il.* 8. 274).

DAMASUS was killed by Polypoetes (Hom. *Il.* 12. 181).

DARDANUS, son of Bias, was killed by Achilles (Hom. *Il.* 20. 460).

DEICOON, son of Pergasus, was slain by Agamemnon (Hom. *Il.* 5. 535).

DEIOPITES, son of Priam, was mortally wounded by Odysseus (Hom. *Il.* 11. 420; Apollod. 3. 12.5).

DEMOCOON, son of Priam, came from Abydos to assist his father in the Trojan War but was slain by Odysseus (Hom. *Il.* 4. 500).

DEMOLEON, son of Antenor and Theano, was slain by Achilles (Hom. *Il.* 20. 394).

DEMUCHUS, son of Philetor, was slain by Achilles (Hom. *Il.* 20. 457).

DERIMACHEIA, an Amazon, was slain by Diomedes (Q. Smyrn. 1. 260).

DERINOE, an Amazon, was slain by Ajax the Lesser (Q. Smyrn. 1. 230).

DEUCALION was slain by Achilles (Hom. *Il.* 20. 477).

DOLON, a Cretan, was a son of Eumedes and famous for his swiftness. He went as a spy to the Greek ships but was caught and betrayed information about the Trojan placements. He was beheaded by Diomedes (Hom. *Il.* 10. 457).

DOLOPS, son of Lampus, was slain by Menelaus (Hom. *Il.* 15. 543).

DORYCLUS, son of Priam, was killed by Ajax (Hom. *Il.* 11. 489).

DRESUS was killed by Euryalus (Hom. *Il.* 6. 27).

DRYOPS was slain by Achilles (Hom. *Il.* 20. 455).

ECHECLUS (1) was slain by Patroclus (Hom. *Il.* 16. 695).

ECHECLUS (2), son of Agenor, was killed by Achilles (Hom. *Il.* 20. 477).

ECHEMMON, son of Priam, was killed by Diomedes (Hom. *Il.* 5. 160; Apollod. 3. 12.5).

ECHEPOLUS, son of Thalysius, was slain by Antilochus (Hom. *Il.* 4. 455).

ECHIUS was slain by Patroclus (Hom. *Il.* 16. 418).

EETION, king of the Placian Thebe in Cilicia, with his seven sons, was killed by Achilles (Hom. *Il.* 6. 415).

ELASUS was slain by Patroclus (Hom. *Il.* 16. 696).

ELATUS of Pedasus was slain by Agamemnon (Hom. *Il.* 6. 36).

ENIOPEUS, son of Thebaeus, charioteer of Hector, was slain by Diomedes (Hom. *Il.* 7. 124).

ENNOMUS (1) was killed by Odysseus (Hom. *Il.* 11. 425).

ENNOMUS (2), a Mysian ally of the Trojans, was killed by Achilles (Hom. *Il.* 2. 858).

EPALTES was slain by Patroclus (Hom. *Il.* 16. 418).

EPICLES, a comrade of Sarpedon, was killed by Ajax (Hom. *Il.* 12. 379).

EPISTOR was slain by Patroclus (Hom. *Il.* 16. 695).

ERYLAUS was slain by Patroclus (Hom. *Il.* 16. 412).

ERYMAS (1) was slain by Patroclus (Hom. *Il.* 16. 412).

ERYMAS (2) was slain by Idomeneus (Hom. *Il.* 16. 345).

EUANDRA, an Amazon, was slain by Meriones (Q.Smyrn. 1. 255).

EUIPPUS was slain by Patroclus (Hom. *Il.* 16. 419).

EUPHORBUS, son of Panthous, was wounded by Patroclus but was afterwards slain by Menelaus (Hom. *Il.* 17. 47). Menelaus subsequently dedicated the shield of Euphorbus in the temple of Hera near Mycenae (Paus. 2. 17.3).

EURYPYLUS, son of Telephus and king of Mysia or Cilicia, assisted the Trojans against the Greeks. He killed Machaon but was slain by Neoptolemus (Strab. 13. 584; Paus. 3. 26.7).

GLAUCUS (1), son of Hippolochus, was slain by Ajax and his body was carried back to Lycia (Q.Smyrn. 4. 1).

GLAUCUS (2), son of Antenor, was slain by the Telamonian Ajax (Paus. 10. 27).

GORGYTHION, son of Priam and Castianeira, was killed by Teucer (Hom. *Il.* 8. 304).

HALIUS was killed by Odysseus (Hom. *Il.* 5. 675).

HARPALION, son of king Pylaemenes, was killed by Menelaus (Hom. *Il.* 13. 643).

HECTOR, son of Priam and Hecuba and greatest of the Trojan heroes, was killed by the spear of Achilles (Hom. *Il.* 22. 182–330).

HIERA, wife of Telephus and commander of the Mysian women on horseback, fell by the hand of Nireus.

HIPPODAMAS (1) was killed by Odysseus (Hom. *Il.* 11. 332).

HIPPODAMAS (2) was killed by Achilles (Hom. *Il.* 20. 398).

HIPPOLOCHUS, son of Antimachus, was slain by Agamemnon (Hom. *Il.* 11. 145).

HIPPOMACHUS, son of Antimachus, was slain by Leonteus (Hom. *Il.* 12. 186).

HIPPONOUS was slain by Achilles (Q.Smyrn. 3. 155).

HIPPOTHOUS, son of the Pelasgian Lethus, while dragging away the body of Patroclus, was slain by the Telamonian Ajax (Hom. *Il.* 17. 298).

HIPPOTION, a Phrygian ally of the Trojans, was slain by Meriones (Hom. *Il.* 14. 513).

HYPEIROCHUS, son of Priam, was killed by Odysseus (Hom. *Il.* 11. 335; Apollod. 3. 12.5).

HYPERENOR was slain by Agamemnon (Hom. *Il.* 14. 516).

HYPERION was slain by Diomedes (Hom. *Il.* 5. 142).

HYPSENOR, son of the Trojan priest Dolopion, was killed by Eurypylus (Hom. *Il.* 5. 76).

HYRTIUS, son of Grytius and a captain of the Mysians, was slain by Ajax (Hom. *Il.* 14. 510).

IAMENUS was slain by Leonteus during the

attack of the Trojans on the camp of the Greeks (Hom. *Il.* 12. 193).

ILIONEUS (1), son of Phorbas, the wealthy Trojan sheep owner, was killed by Peneleus (Hom. *Il.* 14. 490).

ILIONEUS (2), a Trojan, was slain by Diomedes (Q.Smyrn. 18. 180).

IMBRIUS, son of Mentor, was slain by Teucer (Hom. *Il.* 13. 171; Paus. 10. 25.2).

IPHEUS was killed by Patroclus (Hom. *Il.* 16. 418).

IPHIDAMAS, son of Antenor and Theano, was killed by Agamemnon (Hom. *Il.* 11. 240; Paus. 4. 36.2).

IPHITION, son of Otrynteus, from Hyle, was killed by Achilles (Hom. *Il.* 20. 380).

ISUS, son of Priam, was killed by Agamemnon (Hom. *Il.* 11. 102).

ITYMONEUS, a Milesian, was slain by Meges (Q.Smyrn. 1. 279).

LAODAMAS, son of Antenor and captain of the Trojan foot soldiers, was slain by Ajax (Hom. *Il.* 15. 516).

LAOGONUS (1), son of Bias, was slain by Achilles (Hom. *Il.* 20. 460).

LAOGONUS (2), son of Onetor who was a priest on Mt. Ida, was killed by Meriones (Hom. *Il.* 16. 604).

LYCAON, son of Priam and Laothoe, originally was sold by Achilles as a slave in the island of Lemnos but was ransomed and returned to battle. After Patroclus' death, Achilles encountered him again and killed him (Hom. *Il.* 21. 120).

LYCON was slain by Peneleus (Hom. *Il.* 16. 338).

LYCOPHONTES was slain by Teucer (Hom. *Il.* 8. 275).

MARIS, son of Amisodorus and comrade of Sarpedon, was killed by Thrasymedes (Hom. *Il.* 16. 319).

MEDON was killed by Philoctetes (Q.Smyrn. 11. 481).

MELANIPPUS (1), son of Hicetaon, was slain by Antilochus (Hom. *Il.* 15. 575).

MELANIPPUS (2) was slain by Teucer (Hom. *Il.* 8. 275).

MELANIPPUS (3) was slain by Patroclus (Hom. *Il.* 16. 695).

MELANTHUS was killed by Eurypylus (Hom. *Il.* 6. 38).

MEMNON, son of Eos and Tithonus, was slain by Achilles.

MENON was killed by Leonteus (Hom. *Il.* 12. 190).

MERMERUS was slain by Antilochus (Hom. *Il.* 14. 512).

MNESUS was slain by Achilles (Hom. *Il.* 21. 211).

MOLION, squire to Thymbraeus, was slain by Odysseus (Hom. *Il.* 11. 320).

MORYS was slain by Meriones (Hom. *Il.* 14. 514).

MULIUS (1) was slain by Patroclus (Hom. *Il.* 16. 695).

MULIUS (2) was slain by Achilles (Hom. *Il.* 20. 475).

MYDON (1) was killed by Achilles (Hom. *Il.* 21. 211).

MYDON (2), son of Atymnius, charioteer to Pylaemenes, was killed by Antilochus (Hom. *Il.* 5. 580).

MYNES, son of Evenus of Lyrnessus and husband of Briseis (Hippodameia), was slain by

Achilles at the taking of Lyrnessus (Hom. *Il.* 2. 692, 19. 296).

NOEMON was slain by Odysseus (Hom. *Il.* 5. 675).

ODIUS, captain of the Halizoni, was killed by Agamemnon (Hom. *Il.* 5. 41).

OENOMAUS was slain by Idomeneus (Hom. *Il.* 13. 507).

OILEUS, charioteer of Bianor, was slain by Agamemnon (Hom. *Il.* 11. 93).

OPHELESTES (1) was slain by Teucer (Hom. *Il.* 8. 274).

OPHELESTES (2), a Paeonian, was slain by Achilles (Hom. *Il.* 21. 212).

OPHELTIUS was killed by Diomedes (Hom. *Il.* 6. 21).

ORESTES was slain by Leonteus (Hom. *Il.* 12. 186).

ORMENUS (1) was slain by Teucer (Hom. *Il.* 8. 274).

ORMENUS (2) was slain by Polypoetes (Hom. *Il.* 12. 185).

ORSILOCHUS was slain by Teucer (Hom. *Il.* 8. 274).

ORYTHAON was slain by Achilles (Q.Smyrn. 3. 150).

OTHRYONEUS from Cabesus was a suitor of Cassandra, and he agreed to help dispel the Greeks in exchange for Priam's daughter. He was killed by Idomeneus (Hom. *Il.* 13. 366).

PAMMON, son of Priam, was killed by Achilles (Q.Smyrn. 13. 214).

PANDARUS, son of Lycaon, a Lycian, was slain by Diomedes, or, according to others, by Sthenelus (Hom. *Il.* 2. 824, 5. 290; Strab. 14. 665).

PARIS, son of Priam and Hecuba, was said to have been slain with a poisoned arrow by Philoctetes (Soph. *Phil.* 1426; Apollod. 3. 12.6).

PEDAEUS, son of Antenor, was killed by Meges (Hom. *Il.* 5. 70).

PEDASUS, son of Bucolion, was slain by Euryalus (Hom. *Il.* 6. 27).

PEIROUS, son of Amarynceus and a captain of the Thracians, was killed by Thoas (Hom. *Il.* 4. 530).

PENTHESILEIA, the queen of the Amazons, fell by the hand of Achilles (Paus. 5. 11.2, 10. 31; Q.Smyrn. 1. 40).

PERIMUS, son of Megas, was slain by Patroclus (Hom. *Il.* 16. 695).

PERIPHETES was slain by Teucer (Hom. *Il.* 14. 513).

PHAESTUS, son of Borus of Maeonia, was slain by Idomeneus (Hom. *Il.* 5. 45).

PHALCES was slain by Antilochus (Hom. *Il.* 14. 512).

PHEGEUS, son of Dares, priest of Hephaestus at Troy, was slain by Diomedes (Hom. *Il.* 5. 9).

PHERECLUS, son of Tecton, was slain by Meriones (Hom. *Il.* 5. 59).

PHORCYS, son of Phaenops, commander of the Phrygians of Ascania, was slain by Ajax (Hom. *Il.* 17. 312; Paus. 10. 26.2).

PHYLACUS was slain by Leitus (Hom. *Il.* 6. 37).

PIDYTES of Percote was slain by Odysseus (Hom. *Il.* 6. 33).

PISANDER (1), a son of Antimachus, was slain by Agamemnon (Hom. *Il.* 11. 142).

PISANDER (2) was killed by Menelaus (Hom. *Il.* 13. 613).

PODES, son of Eetion and a companion of Hector, was slain by Menelaus (Hom. *Il.* 17. 579).

POLITES, a son of Priam and Hecuba, was slain by Neoptolemus (Virg. *Aen.* 2. 526, 5. 564).

POLYDORUS, the youngest son of Priam and Laotoe (or of Hecuba), was stoned to death by the Greeks at the instigation of Achilles (Hom. *Il.* 20. 406).

POLYIDUS, a son of the Trojan Eurydamas and a brother of Abas, was slain by Diomedes (Hom. *Il.* 5. 148).

POLYMELUS, son of Argeas, was slain by Patroclus (Hom. *Il.* 16. 419).

PRIAM. When the Greeks entered Troy, he put on his armor and started to rush among them, but Hecuba prevailed on him to take refuge with her and their daughters in the temple of Zeus Herceius. His son, Polites, pursued by Pyrrhus (Neoptolemus), rushed into the temple, and Priam took aim at Pyrrhus but was killed by him (Virg. *Aen.* 2. 512; Eurip. *Troad.* 17; Paus. 2. 24.5, 4. 17.3).

PRONOUS was slain by Patroclus (Hom. *Il.* 16. 398).

PROTHOON was killed by Teucer (Hom. *Il.* 14. 513).

PRYTANIS was killed by Odysseus (Hom. *Il.* 5. 675).

PYLAEMENES, a leader of the Paphlagonian warriors, was killed by Menelaus (Hom. *Il.* 5. 576).

PYLARTES was killed by Patroclus (Hom. *Il.* 16. 695).

PYLON was killed by Polypoetes (Hom. *Il.* 12. 185).

PYRAECHMES, commander of the Paeonian horsemen from the vicinity of Amydon and the Axius river, was slain by Patroclus (Hom. *Il.* 16. 287).

PYRIS was slain by Patroclus (Hom. *Il.* 16. 418).

RHESUS, a son of king Eioneus in Thrace and an ally of the Trojans, was slain in his sleep by Diomedes (Hom. *Il.* 10. 495).

RHIGMUS, son of Peires, from Thrace, was killed by Achilles (Hom. *Il.* 20. 484).

SARPEDON, son of Zeus by Laodameia, was slain by Patroclus (Hom. *Il.* 16. 480).

SATNIUS, son of Enops, was killed by Ajax the Lesser (Hom. *Il.* 14. 446).

SCAMANDRIUS, son of Strophius, was killed by Menelaus (Hom. *Il.* 5. 51).

SIMOEISIUS, son of Anthemion, was killed by Ajax (Hom. *Il.* 4. 470).

SOCUS, son of Hippasus, was killed by Odysseus (Hom. *Il.* 11. 455).

STHENELAUS, son of Ithaemenes, was killed by Patroclus (Hom. *Il.* 16. 584).

TENES, son of Cycnus, was slain by Achilles.

TEUTHANTIUS was killed by Ajax.

THERMODOSA, an Amazon, was killed by Meriones (Q.Smyrn. 1. 254).

THERSILOCHUS was killed by Achilles (Hom. *Il.* 21. 180).

THESTOR, son of Enops, was slain by Patroclus (Hom. *Il.* 16. 409).

THOAS was slain by Menelaus (Hom. *Il.* 16. 311).

THOON (1) was killed by Antilochus (Hom. *Il.* 13. 549).

THOON (2) was killed by Odysseus (Hom. *Il.* 11. 425).

THOON (3), son of Phaenops, was slain by Diomedes (Hom. *Il.* 5. 153).

THRASIUS was killed by Achilles (Hom. *Il.* 21. 212).

THRASYMELUS, squire of Sarpedon, was killed by Patroclus (Hom. *Il.* 16. 465).

THYMBRAEUS was slain by Diomedes (Hom. *Il.* 11. 320).

TLEPOLEMUS, a son of Damastor, was slain by Patroclus (Hom. *Il.* 16. 416).

TROILUS, a son of Priam and Hecuba, fell by the hand of Achilles (Virg. *Aen.* 1. 474; Hor. *Carm.* 2. 9.16; Cic. *Tusc.* 1. 39).

TROS, son of Alastor, was slain by Achilles (Hom. *Il.* 20. 473).

XANTHUS, son of Phaenops, was slain by Diomedes (Hom. *Il.* 5. 153).

Guide to Persona

NOTE: Parentheses around topic headings denote indirect references to the person indicated.

AMPHISSUS
(Lotus)
Strength
AMPHISTRATUS
Charioteer
AMPHITRITE
Hair
Herb
(Human Sacrifice)
Net
Sea
Well
AMPHITRITE HALSODYNE
Sea
AMPHITRYON
(Cattle)
Dog
Fox
Hair
Ox
Purification
Stone
Tripod
AMPHOTERUS
Necklace
AMYCUS
Boxing
Laurel
Quarrel
Ship
AMYMONE
Stag
Trident
Well
AMYNTOR
(Blindness)
Helmet
AMYTHAON
Games
ANAXARETE
Statue
Stone
ANAXO
Abduction
ANCAEUS
Boar
Cup
Grapevine
Helmsman
Wine
ANCHIALUS
(Arrow)
(Poison)
ANCHISES
Beauty (Male)
Blindness
Lameness
Lightning
Prophecy
(Shoulder)
ANCHURUS
Earthquake
Engulfment
Gold
Patriotism
Suicide
ANDROCLEA
Patriotism
Suicide
ANDROGEUS
Agriculture
Bull
Games
Plow
Resurrection
Wrestling
ANDROMEDA
Beauty (Female)
Chain
Flood
Rock
Stars and Constellations
ANGERONA (ANGERONIA)
Anguish
Disease
Fear
Mouth
Silence
ANGITIA (ANGUITIA)
Serpent
ANIGRIDES
Cave
Disease
ANIUS
(Chest)
Prophecy
ANNA PERENNA
Abundance
Disguise
Drowning
Health
Hunger
Spring (Season)
Suicide
Veil
ANTAEUS
Hill
Rain
Skeleton
Skull
Wrestling
ANTEIA
Seduction
ANTENOR
Ambassador
(Beauty [Male])
Panther
Treason
ANTEVORTA
Childbirth
Prophecy
ANTHEIS
(Human Sacrifice)
ANTHELII
Sun
ANTHROPOPHAGI
Cannibalism
ANTHUS
Bird
Horse
ANTIGONE
(Blindness)
Burial
Cave
Entombment
Hair
Hanging
Stork
Suicide
ANTILOCHUS
Beauty (Male)
(Chariot)
Dog
Friendship
Infant Exposure
Suitor (under HELEN)
ANTIMACHUS
Ambassador
ANTINOE (AUTONOE)
Serpent
ANTINOUS
Footstool
Suitor (under PENELOPE)
ANTIOPE
Abduction
Insanity
Prison
ANTIPHATES
Cannibalism
ANTIPHUS
Ransom
Shepherd
AOEDE
Song
APHRODITE
(Abduction)
(Ambrosia)
(Anemone)
Apple
April
Arrow
(Bath)
Beauty (Female)
(Blindness)
(Blood)
(Boar)
(Boatman)
(Chest)
(Cloud)
Disguise
Dove
Fish
Flower
Foam
Girdle
Hand
Helmet
Lance
Lotus
Love
Marriage
Myrtle
Poppy
(Rejuvenation)

  - Rose
  - Sea
  - Shield
  - Sparrow
  - Swallow
  - Swan
  - Sword
  - Victory
  - Wryneck
- APHRODITE AMBOLOGERA
  - Old Age
- APHRODITE ANADYOMENE
  - Foam
  - Sea
- APHRODITE ANTHEIA
  - Flower
- APHRODITE APATURIA
  - Deception
- APHRODITE APOTROPHIA
  - Lust
  - Sensuality
- APHRODITE AREIA
  - Armor
  - War
- APHRODITE CALLIPYGAS
  - Buttocks
- APHRODITE GENTYLLIS
  - Childbirth
- APHRODITE HECAERGE
  - Marksmanship
- APHRODITE LIMENIA (LIMENITES, LIMENITIS, or LIMENOSCOPUS)
  - Harbor
- APHRODITE MECHANITIS
  - Invention
- APHRODITE NICEPHORUS
  - Victory
- APHRODITE PANDEMOS
  - Goat
  - Ram
  - Sensuality
  - Unification
- APOLLO
  - (Abduction)
  - Ambrosia
  - (Archer)
  - Arrow
  - Beauty (Male)
  - (Blood)
  - Boar
  - (Booty)
  - Bow
  - Cattle
  - Childbirth
  - (Cloud)
  - Cock
  - Cowherd
  - Crow
  - Death
  - (Discus)
  - Disguise
  - (Dolphin)
  - Dragon
  - (Ear)
  - Evil
  - Flock
  - Flute
  - Goat
  - Grasshopper
  - Griffin
  - Hawk
  - Heifer
  - (Homosexuality)
  - Horse
  - Laurel
  - Lion
  - Lotus
  - Lyre
  - Music
  - Nectar
  - Nurse
  - (Ox)
  - Phorminx
  - Plague
  - Poetry
  - Prophecy
  - (Purification)
  - Serpent
  - Seven
  - Sheep
  - Shepherd
  - Staff
  - Statue
  - Stone
  - Swan
  - Wages
  - Wall
  - Wolf
- APOLLO ACERSECOMES
  - Hair
- APOLLO ACESIUS
  - Evil
- APOLLO ACESTOR
  - Healing
  - Medicine
- APOLLO AEGLETES
  - Radiance
- APOLLO AGETOR
  - Leadership
- APOLLO AGONIUS
  - Contest
- APOLLO AGRAEUS
  - Hunting
- APOLLO AGYIEUS
  - Street
- APOLLO ALEXICACUS
  - Evil
  - Plague
- APOLLO ARCHEGETES
  - Colonization
- APOLLO BOEDROMIUS
  - Battle Cry
- APOLLO CARNEIUS
  - Homosexuality
  - Plague
- APOLLO CATAEBATES
  - Traveler
- APOLLO CHRYSAOR
  - Armor
  - Sword
- APOLLO DAPHNAEUS
  - Laurel
- APOLLO DECATEPHORUS
  - Booty
  - Ten
- APOLLO DELPHINIUS
  - Dolphin
  - Dragon
- APOLLO EMBASIOUS
  - Ship
- APOLLO EPACTAEUS (EPACTIUS)
  - Coast
- APOLLO EPIBATERIUS
  - Ship
- APOLLO EPICURUS
  - Boar
  - Plague
- APOLLO HEBDOMAGETES
  - Seven
- APOLLO HECAERGES
  - Marksmanship
- APOLLO INTONSUS
  - Hair
  - Youth
- APOLLO ISODETES
  - Impartiality
- APOLLO LIBYSTINUS
  - Plague
- APOLLO LOEMIUS
  - Plague
- APOLLO LOXIAS
  - Prophecy
- APOLLO LYCEGENES
  - Light
- APOLLO LYCEIUS
  - Light
  - Wolf
- APOLLO LYCIUS
  - Wolf
- APOLLO LYCOREUS
  - Wolf
- APOLLO MOIRAGETES
  - Fate
- APOLLO NOMIUS
  - Field
  - Shepherd
- APOLLO PALATINUS
  - Library
- APOLLO PARNOPIUS
  - Locust
- APOLLO PHOEBUS (PHOEBUS APOLLO)
  - Sun
- APOLLO PHYXIUS
  - Fugitive
- APOLLO PYTHIUS
  - Dragon
- APOLLO SMINTHEUS
  - Mouse
- APOLLO SPODIUS
  - Ashes
- APOTROPAEI
  - Evil

Nurse
Nymph
Plague
Poppy
Prosperity
(Purification)
Quiver
Stag
Statue
Street
Town
Virginity
Youth
ARTEMIS AEGINAEA
Chamois
Goat
Javelin
ARTEMIS AETOLE
Javelin
ARTEMIS AGRAEA
Hunting
ARTEMIS AGROTERA
Bow
Hunting
ARTEMIS AMPHIPYROS
Torch
ARTEMIS APANCHOMENE
Childbirth
Stoning
Strangulation
ARTEMIS ARISTOBULE
Counsel
ARTEMIS CEDREATIS
Cedar
ARTEMIS CHITONE
Garment
ARTEMIS CHRYSAOR
Armor
Sword
ARTEMIS CONDYLEATIS
Childbirth
Stoning
Strangulation
ARTEMIS CORDACA
Dance
ARTEMIS CORYPHAEA
Mountain
ARTEMIS DAPHNAEA
Laurel
ARTEMIS DELPHINIA
Dragon
ARTEMIS EURYNOME
Fish
ARTEMIS GENETYLLIS
Childbirth
Dog
ARTEMIS HECAERGE
Marksmanship
ARTEMIS HEGEMONE
Leadership
ARTEMIS HEURIPPE
Horse
ARTEMIS LIMENIA
(LIMENITES, LIMENITIS, or
LIMENOSCOPUS)
Harbor
ARTEMIS LIMNAEA (LIMNETES
or LIMNEGENES)
Lake
ARTEMIS LOCHEIA
Childbirth
ARTEMIS LYGODESMA
Statue
Willow
ARTEMIS LYSIZONA
Girdle
ARTEMIS MELISSA
Childbirth
Moon
ARTEMIS ORTHIA
Moon
Scourging
Statue
ARTEMIS PAEONIA
Healing
Medicine
ARTEMIS PARTHENIA
Virginity
ARTEMIS PHOEBE
Moon
ARTEMIS TAURIONE (TAURO,
TAUROPOLOS, or
TAUROPOS)
Bull
ARTEMIS TRIVIA
Crossroads
Road
ARTEMIS UPIS
Childbirth
ASBOLUS
Bird
Crucifixion
Prophecy
ASCABULUS
Lizard
ASCALAPHUS
Owl
Pomegranate
Stone
Suitor (under HELEN)
ASCANIUS
(Nurse)
Stag
ASCLEPIUS
Blood
Cock
Dog
Dragon
Fire
Goat
Healing
Infant Exposure
Lightning
Medicine
Plague
Resurrection
Serpent
Staff
Stars and Constellations
Statue
Underworld
ASCUS
Bag
Flaying
Skin
ASOPUS
Charcoal
Lightning
ASSAON
(Incest)
ASTERIA
Bird
(Eagle)
Quail
Rock
ASTERION
(Drought)
ASTERIUS
Stature
ASTEROPAEUS
Stature
ASTEROPEIA
Murder (of Father)
ASTRABACUS
Justice
Stars and Constellations
ASTRAEUS
Incest
Stars and Constellations
Suicide
Wind
ASTYANAX
Wall
ASTYDAMEIA
Dismemberment
(Seduction)
ASTYLUS
Seer
ASTYNOME
Abduction
Booty
(Ransom)
ATALANTA (ATALANTE)
Apple
(Arrow)
Bear
Chariot
Desecration
Games
Hind
Hunting
Infant Exposure
Lion
Race
Rock
Suitor
Swiftness
Virginity
Well
ATE
Evil
Punishment

AUTOMEDON
Charioteer
AUTONOE
(Dismemberment)
AUXESIA
Famine
Insanity
Knee
Lightning
Olive
Rope
Statue
Stoning
Thunder
AZAN
Games
AZORUS
Helmsman

BACCHE
Nurse (under DIONYSUS)
BACCHUS INTONSUS
Hair
Youth
BACCHUS LYAEUS
Anxiety
BAETYLUS
Stone
BAEUS
Helmsman
BALIUS
Horse
BARGYLUS
Horse
BASSARAE
Nurse (under DIONYSUS)
BATON
Charioteer
Engulfment
BATTUS
Bribery
Cattle
Pumice
Shepherd
Stone
BAUBO
Hospitality
Nurse (under DEMETER)
BAUCIS
(Flood)
(Hospitality)
(Tree)
BELLEROPHON
Ambush
Arrow
Blindness
Bridle
(Girdle)
(Horse)
Lameness
Lead
Murder (of Brother)
(Seduction)
BELLONA
Blood
Scourging
War
BENDIS
Lance
Moon
BEROE
Nurse (under Semele)
BIA
Force
BIADICE (DEMODICE)
Seduction
BIAS
Insanity
Ox
Suitor (under PERO)
BITON
Chariot
Death
BLIAS
(Incest)
BONA DEA
Apotheosis
Chamois
Healing
Hen
Intoxication
Milk
Misandry
Myrtle
Prophecy
Serpent
Virginity
Wine
BOOTES
(Chariot)
BOREAS
(Abduction)
(Discus)
(Homosexuality)
(Mare)
Serpent
Wind
BORMUS
Beauty (Male)
Flute
Harvest
Well
BRANCHUS
Beauty (Male)
Prophecy
Sun
BRISEIS
Abduction
Booty
(Friendship)
BRISEUS
Hanging
BRITOMARTIS
Apotheosis
Fisherman
Harbor
Homosexuality
Hunting
Moon
Navigation
Net
Sailor
Virginity
BRITOMARTIS DICTYMNA
(DICTYNNA)
Net
BRIZO
Dream
Prophecy
Ship
Sleep
BROMIA (BROMIE)
Nurse (under DIONYSUS)
BRONTES
Eye
BROTEAS
Disfigurement
Statue
Ugliness
BROTHEUS
Immolation
BUBONA
Stable
BUPHAGUS
Hospitality
BUSIRIS
Famine
Human Sacrifice
BUTES
(Abduction)
Drowning
Insanity
Pirate
Plow
Shepherd
Well
BYBLIS
Girdle
Hanging
Incest
Rock
Tears
Well

CAANTHUS
Arrow
Fire
CABEIRI
Agriculture
Fidelity
Wine
CACA
Cattle
Fire
CACUS
Cattle
Cave
(Ox)
Robber
Shepherd
CADMUS
(Abduction)
Alphabet
(Boat)
(Chest)

DEMOLEUS
Armor
DEMOPHON
(Almond)
Fire
Immolation
Immortality
Nurse
(Tree)
DEMOPTOLEMUS
Suitor (under PENELOPE)
DERCYNUS
(Ox)
DEUCALION
Bone
Flood
Ship
Stone
DEVERRA
Childbirth
DIA
(Incest)
DIANA
Misandry
Slave
Virginity
DIANA FASCELIS
Statue
Stick
Torch
DIANA LUCINA
Childbirth
Light
DIANA NOCTILUCA
Torch
DICTYMNA (DICTYNNA)
Net
DICTYS
Fisherman
DIDO
Abandonment
Abduction
Bull
Horse
Immolation
Sword
DIOMEDE
Abduction
DIOMEDEA
Friendship
DIOMEDES
Bravery
Chariot
Games
(Letter)
Lion
Mare
Statue
(Stoning)
Storm
Suitor (under HELEN)
(Sword)
Wooden Horse of Troy
DION
Prophecy

DIONYSUS
(Abduction)
(Apotheosis)
Asphodel
Ass
(Bag)
(Bat)
(Boat)
Bridge
Bull
Cannibalism
Cauldron
Cave
Chest
Civilization
Disease
Dismemberment
Dolphin
Famine
Fig
Fir
(Fire)
Flute
Goat
Grapevine
Healing
(Honey)
Human Sacrifice
Insanity
Ivy
Lake
Laurel
Law
Lion
Lynx
Magpie
Nurse
Owl
Panther
Peace
Pirate
Prophecy
Ram
Resurrection
Serpent
Ship
Stars and Constellations
Statue
Theatre
Thigh
Tiger
Tragedy
Transvestism
Tree
Urn
Wine
Yew
DIONYSUS ACRATOPHORUS
Wine
DIONYSUS AEGOBOLUS
Goat
DIONYSUS ASYMNETES
Chest
DIONYSUS BACCHUS
Boisterousness

DIONYSUS BASSAREUS
Fox
Garment
Wine
DIONYSUS BROMIUS
Revelry
Storm
DIONYSUS ELEUTHEREUS
Sorrow
DIONYSUS ENORCHES
Dance
DIONYSUS EUBULEUS
Counsel
DIONYSUS ISODAETES
Impartiality
DIONYSUS LAMPTER
Torch
DIONYSUS LENAEUS
Wine
DIONYSUS LIMNAEA
(LIMNETES or
LIMNEGENES)
Lake
DIONYSUS MEILICHIUS
Atonement
DIONYSUS MELANAEGIS
Shield
DIONYSUS MELPOMENUS
Song
DIONYSUS OMADIUS
Human Sacrifice
DIONYSUS PHLEON
Fertility
DIONYSUS PSILAS
Beard
DIONYSUS SABAZIUS
Agriculture
DIONYSUS TAUROCEPHALUS
Bull
DIONYSUS TAURUS
Bull
DIONYSUS THYONEUS
Inspiration
DIONYSUS ZAGREUS
Dismemberment
Heart
Metamorphosis
DIORES
(Incest)
DIOSCURI
(Abduction)
(Ambush)
(Egg)
Games
Hat
Helmet
Horse
Hospitality
Music
Ox
Resurrection
Sailor
Sea
Shipwreck
Spear

GEILISSA
Nurse (under ORESTES)
GENETYLLIDES (GENNAIDES, GENNEIDES, GENETYLLIS)
Childbirth
Generation
GENIUS
Cornucopia
Cup
Flower
Generation
Guardian
Serpent
Wine
Wings
GERANA
Beauty (Female)
Crane
Tortoise
GERYON
Head
Ox
GIANTS
Blood
Dragon
Herb
Invulnerability
Volcano
GLAUCE
(Crown)
(Fire)
(Garment)
Immolation
(Poison)
Sea
GLAUCUS
(Abduction)
Ball
Dismemberment
Fish
Fisherman
Herb
Honey
Horse
Immortality
Mare
Mouse
Pirate
Prophecy
Resurrection
Sailor
Sea
Seaweed
Serpent
Shipbuilding
Steersman
GORGASUS
Healing
GORGE
(Bird)
(Incest)
GORGO
(Blood)
GORGONS
Claws
Hair
Serpent
Teeth
Wings
GORGOPHONE
Widowhood
GRAEAE
Eye
Foam
Hair
Sea
Swan
Teeth
GRIFFIN
Eagle
Gold
Lion
GRYPS (GRYPHUS)
Eagle
Gold
Horse
Lion
GYGES
Arm

HADES
(Abduction)
Chariot
Gate
Helmet
Horse
Invisibility
(Lyre)
Metal
Ox
Sheep
Staff
Underworld
HADES EUBULEUS (EUBULUS)
Counsel
HADES ISODETES
Impartiality
HADES PLUTON
Wealth
HADES PYLARTES
Gate
HAEMON
Suicide
HAEMUS
Mountain
HAGNO
Cup
(Nurse [under ZEUS])
Pitcher
HALIA
Sea
HALITHERSES
Seer
HAMADRYADS
(Abduction)
(Forest)
Tree
HARCALO
Poison
HARMONIA
Abduction
Chariot
(Dragon)
Garment
(Necklace)
HARPALYCE
Bird
(Cannibalism)
Grief
(Incest)
Milk
Robber
Snare
Swiftness
HARPIES
(Abduction)
Bird
Disappearance
(Food)
(Hunger)
Storm
Swiftness
Wind
Wings
HARPOCRATES
Silence
HEBE
Chariot
Cupbearer
Horse
Rejuvenation
Youth
HECATE
(Ass)
Atonement
Blood
(Brass)
Cattle
Crossroads
Dog
Head
Honey
Horse
Hunting
Lamb
Lion
Luck
Magic
Moon
Prosperity
Purification
Road
Sailor
Sorcery
Tomb
Torch
Underworld
Victory
Wealth
Wisdom
Youth
HECATE BRIMO
Anger
Fire

Prophecy
Serpent
Violet
IAPIS
Healing
IASION
Horse
Lightning
Mysteries
Statue
IASO
Recovery
IASUS
Horse
ICADIUS
Dolphin
ICARIUS
Bag
Drought
Grapevine
Hospitality
Intoxication
Ram
Stars and Constellations
Well
Wind
Wine
ICARUS
Wax
Wings
ICELUS
Dream
ICHTHYOCENTAURI
Fish
Horse
IDA
(Nurse [under ZEUS])
IDAEUS
Herald
Mysteries
IDAS
(Abduction)
(Ambush)
Bird
Boar
Chariot
Lightning
(Ox)
Stone
Voracity
IDMON
Boar
Seer
Serpent
IDOMENEUS
Beauty (Male)
Bravery
Cock
Human Sacrifice
Murder (of Son)
Plague
Shield
Storm
Suitor (under HELEN)
ILIONA
Murder (of Husband)
ILIONEUS
Arrow
ILITHYIA
Childbirth
ILUS
Blindness
Cow
Fire
(Homosexuality)
Poison
Statue
Wrestling
INACHUS
(Drought)
INFERI
Underworld
INO
Apotheosis
Bribery
Disguise
(Dismemberment)
Dolphin
Famine
(Games)
Insanity
Murder (of Son)
(Sea)
INTERCIDONA
(Childbirth)
INVIDIA
Envy
IO
Cow
Gadfly
Heifer
Moon
Olive
IOBATES
(Ambush)
IODAMEIA
Fire
Stone
IOLAUS
Charioteer
(Friendship)
ION
Blood
Cave
Dragon
Infant Exposure
Pigeon
Poison
IONIDES
Healing
IPHIANASSA
(Beauty [Female])
(Gold)
(Insanity)
(Wine)
IPHICLES
Ox
Swiftness
IPHICLUS
Dog
Knife
Rust
Sterility
IPHIGENEIA
Apotheosis
Bear
Bull
Childbirth
Crone
Human Sacrifice
Immortality
(Stag)
(Statue)
Thunder
IPHIMEDIA (IPHIMEDEIA)
(Abduction)
Pirate
Sea
IPHINOE
(Beauty [Female])
(Gold)
Hair
Hospitality
Insanity
Virginity
(Wine)
IPHIS
Hanging
Necklace
Suicide
Transexualism
Transvestism
IPHITUS
Bow
(Friendship)
Games
IPPOTEUS
Human Sacrifice
IPSOSTRATUS
Human Sacrifice
IRIS
Cake
(Cup)
Disguise
Fig
Fire
Grain
Honey
(Immolation)
Messenger
Pitcher
Rainbow
Ship
Staff
Wind
Wings
IRUS
Beggar
(Flock)
Messenger
Sheep
Suitor (under PENELOPE)
Voracity

LOTIS
Lotus
LOTOPHAGI
Lotus
LUA
Armor
Purification
LUCTUS
Grief
Mourning
LUNA
Moon
LUNUS
Months
LUPERCA (LUPA)
Wolf
LUPERCUS
Sheep
Wolf
LYCAON
(Cannibalism)
Human Sacrifice
Incest
Lightning
Wolf
LYCASTUS
Oak
Wolf
LYCO
(Insanity)
(Prophecy)
(Rock)
LYCOMEDES
Rock
LYCURGUS
(Armor)
Blindness
Chain
Dismemberment
Grapevine
Horse
Insanity
Intoxication
Murder (of Son)
Murder (of Wife)
Resurrection
Rock
Suicide
Suitor (under HIPPODAMEIA)
LYCUS
Hospitality
Mysteries
LYDAE
Nurse (under DIONYSUS)
LYNCEUS
(Abduction)
Ambush
Murder (of Father-In-Law)
Murder (of Sister-In-Law)
Oak
(Ox)
Sharpsightedness
Shield
Spear
Torch
LYNCUS (LYNCAEUS)
Lynx
LYSIPPE
(Beauty [Female])
(Gold)
(Insanity)
(Wine)
LYTAEA
(Human Sacrifice)

MA
Bull
Nurse (under DIONYSUS)
MACAREUS (MACAR)
Homosexuality
(Incest)
Seer
Suicide
MACARIA
Suicide
MACETAE
Nurse (under DIONYSUS)
MACHAEREUS
Sword
MACHAON
Disease
Medicine
Surgery
Wooden Horse of Troy
MACRIS
Honey
Nurse (under DIONYSUS)
MAENALUS
(Cannibalism)
MAERA (MERA)
Dog
Stars and Constellations
MAGNES
Magnet
MAIA
May
Nurse (under ARCA)
MALEUS
Trumpet
MALIADES
Flock
Fruit
MAMERS
War
MANA (MANA GENITA)
Good
MANES
Burial
Death
Good
MANIA
Children
Garlic
Head
Human Sacrifice
Poppy
Spectre
Underworld
MANTO
Prophecy
Well
MARON
Wine
MARPESSA
Abduction
MARS
Agriculture
(Chariot)
Horse
Lance
Misogyny
Prophecy
War
Wolf
Woodpecker
MARS GRADIVUS
War
MARS QUIRINUS
Lance
Spear
MARS SILVANUS
(Agriculture)
Field
Flock
MARS ULTOR
Vengeance
MARSYAS
Blood
Flaying
Flute
Skin
MASTUSIUS
(Blood)
(Cup)
MATUTA
Children
Dawn
Sea
MECON
Poppy
MEDEA
(Brass)
Cauldron
Chariot
Crown
Dismemberment
Dragon
Enchantment
Fire
(Fleece)
Garment
Lamb
Murder (of Brother)
Murder (of Children)
Murder (of Son)
Poison
Ram
Rejuvenation
Serpent
Sorcery
MEDITRINA
Medicine
MEDON
Herald

Night
Wings
NYX CHTHONIA
Earth
Field

OCEANIDS
(Sea)
OCHNE
Rock
(Seduction)
Suicide
ODIUS
Herald
ODYSSEUS
Ambassador
Armor
Arrow
Ass
Bag
Beggar
Boar
Bow
Cap
Cloud
Dog
Friendship
Immortality
Insanity
Knee
(Letter)
Lightning
Lotus
Mast
Navigation
Nurse
Ox
Plank
Plow
Poison
Race
Raft
Salt
Scar
Sheep
Shipwreck
(Stoning)
Storm
Suitor (under HELEN)
Suitor (under PENELOPE)
Underworld
Wax
Wind
(Wine)
Wooden Horse of Troy
Wrestling
Youth
OEDIPUS
Blindness
(Charioteer)
Chest
Feet
Incest
Infant Exposure
Murder (of Father)
Plague
Riddle
OENEUS
Boar
(Cup)
Girdle
Incest
Murder (of Son)
OENO
(Oil)
OENOE
Nurse (under Zeus)
OENOMAUS
Chariot
Incest
Lightning
Ram
Suicide
OENONE
Abandonment
(Arrow)
Hanging
Healing
Immolation
Prophecy
Tower
OENOPION
(Blindness)
OENOTROPAE
Abduction
Abundance
Dove
Grain
Oil
Olive
Wine
OEONUS
Race
OILEUS
Charioteer
OLEN
Flute
Poetry
Prophecy
OLENUS
Stone
OLYMPUS
Flute
Teacher
OLYNTHUS
Lion
OMA
Prophecy
Virginity
OMPHALE
Spinning
ONEIROS (pl. ONEIRATA)
Dream
Gate
Horns
Sleep
Wings
OPHELTES
Dolphin
Pirate
Serpent
OPHIUCHUS
Serpent
Stars and Constellations
OPS
Abundance
Agriculture
Children
Earth
Fertility
OPS CONSIVA
Sowing
OPS RUNCINA
Grain
Weed
ORBONA
Children
Disease
OREIADES
Cave
(Mountain)
OREILOCHIA
Apotheosis
Immortality
OREITHYIA
Abduction
ORESTES
(Abduction)
Ashes
(Atonement)
Disguise
Friendship
Hair
Human Sacrifice
Insanity
Messenger
Murder (of Mother)
Murder (of Uncle)
Nurse
Serpent
Statue
Stoning
ORESTHEUS
Dog
Vine
Wood
ORION
Abduction
Arrow
Beauty (Male)
Blindness
Club
Hammer
Hunting
Intoxication
Lion
Rain
Scorpion
Sleep
Stars and Constellations
Storm
Sun
Sword
ORPHE
(Insanity)

PERSEPHONE EPAINE
Fear
PERSEPHONE MELITODES
Honey
PERSEPHONE PRAXIDICE
Justice
PERSEPHONE THESMIA (THESMOPHOROS)
Law
PERSEUS
Bag
Chest
(Decapitation)
Discus
(Eye)
(Head)
Helmet
Infant Exposure
Invisibility
Mirror
Murder (of Grandfather)
Sandal
(Shield)
Sickle
(Stone)
(Teeth)
PHAEA
(Sow)
PHAEDRA
(Bull)
(Seduction)
Suicide
PHAENON
Beauty (Male)
PHAETHON
Abduction
(Amber)
Chariot
Horse
Lightning
Sun
Tears
PHAETHUSA (PHAETUSA)
Flock
(Ox)
(Sheep)
PHANES
Creation
Egg
PHANOTHEA
Poetry
PHANTASUS
Dream
(Sleep)
PHAON
Beauty (Male)
Boatman
Rejuvenation
Youth
PHARMACEIA
Poison
Well
PHARMACIDES
Childbirth
Sorcery
PHARUS
Helmsman
PHAYLLUS
Necklace
PHEMIUS
Bard
Suitor (under HELEN)
PHEMONOE
Poetry
PHERECLUS
Shipbuilding
PHILAMMON
Choral Music
Cithara
PHILEMON
Flood
Hospitality
Tree
PHILIA
Nurse (under DIONYSUS)
PHILOCTETES
Archer
Armor-Bearer
Arrow
Bow
(Friendship)
Immolation
Serpent
Suitor (under HELEN)
Wound
PHILOETIUS
Cowherd
PHILOMELA
(Ax)
Garment
(Grief)
Nightingale
(Swallow)
Tongue
PHILOMELEIDES
Wrestling
PHILOMELUS
Chariot
PHILONOE
Immortality
PHILONOME
(Seduction)
PHILLOTUS
Dismemberment
PHINEUS
Abduction
Blindness
Food
Hunger
Scourging
Seer
Stone
PHLEGON
Horse
PHLEGYAS
Arrow
Incest
PHOBETOR
Dream
(Sleep)
PHOBUS (METUS)
Fear
Lion
PHOCUS
(Discus)
PHOEBE
Abduction
PHOEBUS APOLLO
Sun
PHOENIX
Alphabet
Bird
Blindness
Egg
Fire
Myrrh
Regeneration
Sun
Worm
PHOENODAMAS
Human Sacrifice
PHOLUS
(Wine)
PHORBAS
Boxing
Serpent
Stars and Constellations
PHORCUS (PHORCYS or PHORCYN)
Sea
PHOSPHORUS
Stars and Constellations
PHRASIUS
Famine
Human Sacrifice
Seer
PHRIXUS
(Famine)
Fleece
Human Sacrifice
Ram
(Seduction)
PHRONTIS
Helmsman
Steersman
PHYLLIS
Almond
Hanging
Suicide
Tree
PHYLLIUS
(Bull)
(Homosexuality)
Vulture
PHYTALUS
Fig
Hospitality
Purification
PICUMNUS
Children
(Couch)

Manure
Marriage
PICUS
Prophecy
Seer
Woodpecker
PIERIDES
Magpie
PIERUS
Bird
PIETAS
Altar
Children
Fidelity
Incense
Love
Stork
Veneration
PILUMNUS
(Childbirth)
Children
Couch
Grain
(Marriage)
PIPO
(Bird)
PISTAS
Breast
PITTHEUS
Rhetoric
PITYOCAMPTES
Robber
PITYS
Fir
PLEIADES
Dove
Grief
Stars and Constellations
Suicide
PLEIONE
(Dove)
PLUTO
(Abduction)
Underworld
PLUTON
Wealth
PLUTUS
Blindness
Cornucopia
Wealth
PODALEIRIUS
Medicine
PODARCES
Swiftness
POEAS
Arrow
(Immolation)
POEMANDER
Murder (of Son)
Purification
POENA
Retaliation
POENE
Serpent
POLEMOCRATES
Medicine
POLITES
Human Sacrifice
POLYDECTES
Stone
POLYDEUCES (POLLUX)
(Abduction)
(Ambush)
Boxing
(Egg)
Immortality
Stars and Constellations
(Stone)
POLYDORA
Grief
Suicide
POLYDORUS
Blood
Stoning
POLYGONUS
(Wrestling)
POLYHYMNIA
Nurse (under NYSEIDES)
POLYIDES
Purification
POLYIDUS
Bee
Cow
Entombment
Mulberry
Owl
Riddle
Seer
(Serpent)
POLYMELA
Incest
POLYMESTOR (POLYMNESTOR)
Blindness
(Blood)
Murder (of Son)
Prophecy
POLYMNIA (POLYHYMNIA)
Hymn
POLYNEICES
Lion
(Necklace)
POLYPEMON
Bed
POLYPHEMUS
Blindness
Cannibalism
Cave
Eye
Intoxication
Pole
Wine
POLYPHONTES (POLYPHETES or POLYPOETES)
Charioteer
POLYPOETES
Ball
POLYTECHNUS
Cannibalism
Pelican
POLYXENA
Human Sacrifice
Suicide
POLYXENUS
Suitor (under HELEN)
POLYXO
Nurse (under HYPSIPYLE)
Prophecy
POMONA
Fruit
PONTUS
Sea
PORPHYRION
Arrow
Lightning
PORTUNUS (PORTUMNUS)
Harbor
Key
POSEIDON
(Abduction)
(Beauty [Female])
(Beauty [Male])
(Blindness)
Boar
Bridle
Bull
Chariot
Charioteer
(Chest)
Disguise
Dolphin
Drought
Flood
Homosexuality
Horse
Lamb
(Metamorphosis)
Nurse
Old Age
Ram
Sea
Storm
Trident
(Trumpet)
Wages
Wall
Water
Well
Wolf
POSEIDON ASPHALIUS (ASPHALEIUS)
Harbor
Navigation
POSEIDON GAEEOCHUS
Earth
POSEIDON ISTHMIUS
Games
POSEIDON TAUREUS
Bull
POSTVORTA
(Childbirth)
Past
Prophecy

- Dog
- Goose
- Judge
- Ram
- Underworld

RHEA
- Bull
- Chariot
- Crown
- Earth
- Lion
- Oak
- Statue
- Stone
- Throne
- Veil

RHEA ANTAEA
- Prayer

RHECAS
- Charioteer

RHESUS
- Horse

RHOECUS
- Arrow

RHOEO
- Chest

ROBIGUS
- Grain

ROMA
- Ship

ROMULUS
- Abduction
- Apotheosis
- (Armor)
- Chariot
- Cradle
- Eclipse
- Fig
- Infant Exposure
- (Lotus)
- Murder
- Murder (of Brother)
- Nurse
- Plow
- (Shepherd)
- Slave
- Vulture
- Wall
- Wolf
- Woodpecker

ROMULUS QUIRINUS
- Lance
- Spear

RUMINA
- (Children)
- (Cradle)
- (Milk)

RUSOR
- Agriculture
- Earth

SABAZIUS
- Agriculture
- Horns
- Ox
- Plow
- Serpent

SAGARITIES
- Tree

SAGITTARIUS
- (Archer)

SALACIA
- Sea

SALAMACIS (SALMACIS)
- (Hermaphroditism)
- (Transexualism)

SALMONEUS
- Lightning

SALUS
- Cup
- Globe
- Health
- Prosperity
- Public Welfare
- Recovery
- Rudder
- Serpent

SAON
- Law

SAPPHO
- (Beauty [Male])
- (Youth)

SARPEDON
- Arrow
- (Beauty [Male])
- (Homosexuality)
- Ring
- Underworld

SATURN
- Agriculture
- Oil
- Olive
- Pruning Knife
- Ribbon
- Underworld

SATYRS
- Cup
- Ear
- Fir
- Flute
- Fur
- Horns
- Ivy
- Staff
- Syrinx
- Tail
- Thyrsus
- Vine
- Wine

SCEPHRUS
- Famine

SCIRON
- Robber
- Rock
- Tortoise

SCIRUS
- Seer

SCYLLA
- Beauty (Female)
- Bird
- Cannibalism
- Dog
- Drowning
- Feet
- Fish
- (Hair)
- Head
- Herb
- Lark
- Mouth
- Murder (of Father)
- Neck
- Ox
- Resurrection
- Rock
- Serpent
- Teeth
- Treason
- Underworld
- Well

SCYTHEA
- Girdle

SCYTHES
- Bow

SEGESTA
- Abduction
- (Bear)
- (Dog)

SEGETIA
- Seed

SEJA
- (Seed)

SELEMNUS
- Beauty (Male)
- Grief

SELENE
- Chariot
- Cow
- Crescent
- Crown
- Horns
- Horse
- (Light)
- Moon
- Mule
- (Sleep)
- Veil
- Wings

SEMELE
- Boat
- (Chest)
- Fire
- Immortality
- Lightning
- Nurse
- Thunder

SEMELE THYONE
- Apotheosis

SEMONIA
- (Seed)

SETIA
- (Seed)

SIBYLLA
- Book
- Prophecy

TARCHETIUS
Genitals
TARPEIA
Rock
Shield
Treason
TAURICA (DEA)
Human Sacrifice
TAYGETE
Cow
Hind
TECMESSA
Abduction
TELAMON
(Discus)
Stone
TELCHINES
Agriculture
Dog
Fin
Flood
Hail
Metamorphosis
Rain
Sea
Sickle
Snow
Sorcery
Sulphur
Trident
TELEGONUS
Murder (of Father)
Wrestling
TELEMACHUS
(Arrow)
(Friendship)
Nurse
TELEMUS
Seer
TELEPHUS
Dragon
Hind
Incest
Infant Exposure
Rust
Spear
Stag
Wound
TELESPHORUS
Medicine
Recovery
TELLUMO
Earth
TELLUS (TERRA)
Agriculture
Cow
Earth
Harvest
Seed
Underworld
TEMENUS
Teacher
TENERUS
Seer
TENES (TENNES)
Anchor
Chest
(Flute)
Rope
Seduction
TERAMBUS
Lyre
Syrinx
TEREUS
Ax
Cannibalism
Hawk
Hoopoe
Murder (of Brother)
TERMINUS
Boundaries
Cake
Fruit
Meal
Stone
TERPSICHORE
Dance
Lyre
Plectrum
Song
TERRA
Underworld
TETHYS
Sea
Teacher
TEUCER
Archer
TEUTARUS
Bow
THALASSA
Sea
THALEIA
Engulfment
THALIA
Comedy
Ivy
Mask
Poetry
Staff
THALLO
Agriculture
Oath
Spring (Season)
Youth
THAMYRIS
Bard
(Beauty [Male])
Blindness
(Homosexuality)
Lyre
Song
THANATOS
Death
Sleep
Torch
THEIA
Light
THEIAS
(Incest)
THEISOA
Nurse (under ZEUS)
THELXINOE
Delight
THELXINOEA
Head
Justice
Oath
THEMIS
Cornucopia
Law
Nurse (under APOLLO)
Order
Prophecy
Scales
THEMISTO
Hanging
Murder (of Children)
THEOCLYMENUS
Seer
THEONOE
Pirate
THEOPE
(Famine)
(Human Sacrifice)
(Patriotism)
(Plague)
THEOPHANE
Abduction
Beauty (Female)
Fleece
Sheep
THERO
Nurse (under ARES)
THERSANDER
Wooden Horse of Troy
THERSITES
Dice
Eye
Impudence
Ugliness
THESEUS
(Abandonment)
(Abduction)
(Bull)
(Dismemberment)
(Fir)
Friendship
Games
Labyrinth
(Ox)
(Poison)
(Purification)
Sail
Sandal
Sow
Sword
Twine
THETIS
(Armor)
(Cave)
Dolphin
Hospitality
Metamorphosis
Sea

(Urn)
Wings
THETIS HALSODYNE
Sea
THISBE
(Hole)
Lion
(Mulberry)
(Suicide)
THRASIUS
Seer
THYESTES
Cannibalism
(Incest)
(Murder [of Brother])
(Sword)
THYIA
Wine
THYMOETES
Wooden Horse of Troy
THYONE
Immortality
THYRIA
(Swan)
Tears
TIBERINUS
Drowning
TILPHUSA
Dragon
TIMAGORAS
(Homosexuality)
(Rock)
TIPHYS
Helmsman
Pilot
TIRESIAS (TEIRESIAS)
Bath
(Beauty [Female])
Bird
Blindness
Crone
Hair
Longevity
Plague
Prophecy
Seer
Serpent
Staff
Transexualism
Underworld
Well
TISIPHONE
Beauty (Female)
Murder
Slave
TITHONUS
Abduction
Beauty (Male)
Cricket
Grasshopper
Immortality
Old Age
Youth
TITYS (TITYUS)
Arrow
Lightning
Liver
Serpent
Vulture
TLEPOLEMUS
Murder (of Uncle)
TRICOLONUS
Suitor (under HIPPODAMEIA)
TRIPTOLEMUS
Agriculture
Chariot
Civilization
Dragon
Grain
Hat
Plow
Sceptre
TRITON
Dolphin
Fish
Hair
Horse
Scales (Fish)
Sea
Shell
Trumpet
TRITONIS
Shield
TROILUS
Strangulation
TROPHONIUS
(Architecture)
(Death)
Engulfment
Treasury
TROS
Horse
TUCCIA
Incest
Sieve
TUTANUS
Guardian
TUTELINA
Agriculture
Harvest
TYCHE
Abundance
Ball
Cornucopia
Luck
Rudder
TYCHE AUTOMATIA
Fate
TYCHIUS
Shield
TYCHON
Fertility
Luck
TYDEUS
Boar
Brain
Cannibalism
Decapitation
Immortality
Murder (of Brother)
Murder (of Uncle)
Purification
TYNDAREUS
Suitor (under PENELOPE)
TYPHON
Wind
TYPHON (TYPHOEUS)
Hurricane
Lightning
TYRRHEUS
(Stag)

UPIS
Nurse (under ARTEMIS)
URANIA
Astronomy
Globe
Staff
URANUS
(Blood)
(Emasculation)
(Foam)
Heaven
(Sickle)
(Stone)

VACUNA
Leisure
Victory
VALERIA
Incest
VALERIUS
(Incest)
VEIOVIS
Arrow
Deafness
Destruction
Lightning
VENILIA
Sea
Wind
VENTI
Lamb
Wind
Wings
VENUS
April
Beauty (Female)
Garden
Love
Prostitute
VENUS BARBATA
Beard
VENUS CALVA
Bow
Bride
Hair
Marriage
VENUS CLOACINA (CLUACINA)
Marriage
Purification
Sewer
Sexual Intercourse
VENUS LIBENTINA
(LUBENTINA or LUBENTIA)

ZEUS LIMENIA (LIMENITES, LIMINITIS, or LIMENOSCOPUS)
    Harbor
ZEUS LYCAEUS (LYCEUS)
    Human Sacrifice
    Shadow
    Stag
    Stoning
    Wolf
ZEUS MAEMACTES
    Storm
ZEUS MECHANEUS
    Invention
ZEUS MOIRAGETES
    Fate
ZEUS MORIUS
    Olive
ZEUS OGOA
    Sea
ZEUS OMBRIUS
    Rain
ZEUS PANOMPHAEUS
    Omen
ZEUS PHYXIUS
    (Fleece)
    Fugitive
ZEUS PISTIUS
    Faith
    Fidelity
ZEUS POLEIUS
    Ax
    Grain
ZEUS SABAZIUS
    Agriculture
ZEUS STHENIUS
    Rock
    Sandal
    Sword
ZEUS STRATIUS
    War
ZEUS XENIOS
    Hospitality
    Traveler
ZEUS ZYGIUS
    Marriage